Services Working Group
January 22–23, 1994

Services Working Group
January 22–23, 1994

Edited by
Eric Golo Stone

Folio Series: F

Fillip, Vancouver

Contents

Fillip's interest in the consequential economic conditions of artistic production provides a through-line to many of the projects and publications we have helped produce over the past fifteen years. This self-reflexivity on the contradictions, complexities, and conflicts of "art work" is perhaps most evident in the two volumes of *Institutions by Artists* (2012, 2021), but it also plays a significant role in the *Intangible Economies* Folio (2012), and our Means of Production (2018–) workshop series. The present volume continues this investigation, revisiting key debates on the role and place of labour in the arts as initiated and embodied in the exhibition *Services: The Conditions and Relations of Service Provision in Contemporary Project Oriented Artistic Practice*, organized by Helmut Draxler and Andrea Fraser. Reflecting on and responding to a continued history of labour practices that actively generate, promote, and legitimize relations and conditions of exploitation, deprivation, and discrimination, *Services* offers a particular case study to rethink the organization of labour within art institutions.

For its debut in 1994 at the Kunstraum of the University of Lüneburg, a noncollecting university art gallery in Lüneburg, Germany, and for subsequent iterations of the project at different art institutions in Europe and the US,[1] *Services* established a situationally specific Working Group as a central operative structure by which the exhibition was produced. The *Services* Working Group provided a social structure for the project's "producers"—invited practitioners and representatives of the hosting institution—to collectively define the project's means and materials of production. Through a form and structure that recalls earlier experimental modes of art discourse, such as that of the Halifax Conference, organized by curator Seth Siegelaub in 1970 at the Nova Scotia College of Art and Design, the two-day working group created a space for artists, curators, writers, and educators to candidly discuss their past work-related experiences and the immediate working conditions of the *Services* project. In doing so, the participants engaged in reflexive analysis, experiential research, collaborative governance, shared questioning, and direct address. Draxler and Fraser first organized the Working Group at the invitation of the Kunstraum's codirectors, Beatrice von Bismarck, Diethelm Stoller, and Ulf Wuggenig. A number of arts practitioners joined the organizers and codirectors in contributing to the Working Group discussions at the Kunstraum, invited by Draxler and Fraser: Judith Barry, Ute Meta Bauer, Jochen Becker, Ulrich Bischoff, Iwona Blazwick, Susan Cahan, Michael Clegg, Stephan Dillemuth, Renée Green, Martin Guttmann, Renate Lorenz, Christian Philipp Müller, Fritz Rahmann, and Fred Wilson. The Working Group discussions were recorded on videotape, and this compelling video document was then shown as part of the *Services* exhibition.

The *Services* Working Group sessions remain painfully relevant today as we continue to have discussions about what must be done in the face of the devastating socioeconomic realities of the art sector. This book is largely made up of transcripts of the Working Group discussions that took place at the Kunstraum in 1994, which present a history of individual and collective dilemmas facing workers in the field of art. In underscoring the structure of the *Services* Working Group, this book seeks to actualize the project's history—proposing to readers a model of psychosocial analysis and collective organizing that can be applied to the current historical moment of labour relations within and beyond the field of artistic production. Indeed, it was imperative to Fillip in producing this book that the history of *Services* was not solely reflected on but also made operational for today's context.

As part of this process, Fillip worked with colleagues from the cultural field to reconsider the legal-economic structural conditions under which this book was produced. With crucial input from legal counsel and Fillip's Editorial and Governance Boards, the writer's contract used by Fillip was completely overhauled to set a standard of mutual exchange and collaborative process while advocating for the rights and remuneration of writers in the art field. This contract template will serve as the starting point for all future writer negotiations and will be made available on the Fillip website in an effort to make our own legal-economic conditions more transparent. We are grateful to our fellow Editorial Board members (Jaclyn Arndt, Jaleh Mansoor, Sohrab Mohebbi, Jenifer Papararo, and Antonia Pinter) for their invaluable efforts in drafting this new contract.

Early in the process of developing this publication, it became clear that, to fully grapple with the legacy of the *Services* project, it would be necessary to take into consideration the English-language bias of the Working Group discussions at the Kunstraum of the University of Lüneburg. These initial conversations were conducted entirely in English, yet a majority of the Working Group members identified German as their first language and found it challenging at times to translate certain points of discussion and inquiry. After reaching out to members of the original Working Group, we made the decision to publish bilingual transcripts of the Kunstraum discussions, commissioning the translation of the newly produced English-language version into German. This translation project was executed by Fiona Bryson and coproduced by the Künstlerhaus Stuttgart and the Kunstraum of Leuphana University of Lüneburg (formerly the Kunstraum of the University of Lüneburg). We extend our gratitude to Fiona for her careful and persistent work on the translation. The translation process was aided enormously by the crucial efforts of Johanna Schindler, who copyedited the German language transcript and worked closely with Fiona in responding to translation-related questions. Additionally, we thank Romy Range for copyediting support on the translation. Susanne Leeb and Ulf Wuggenig, current codirectors of the Kunstraum, were also vital to the process of realizing the translation for this book; we are indebted to them not only for their support with the translation but also for their suggestions and feedback. We are grateful to Clemens Krümmel for his insights on the copyediting of the translation, as well as for his indispensable role in managing and providing access to the *Services* archive at the Kunstraum.

Central to this book project was the development of the methodology and processes used to produce the *Services* transcripts. While transcribed sections of the *Services* Working Group discussions were previously published in the journal *October*,[2] we felt it imperative to bring forth renewed attention to the entire project by producing a complete transcript. Both a "full verbatim" transcript and a "clean verbatim" transcript were produced from the video recordings.[3] The comprehensive work on the English-language full verbatim transcripts was completed by Robert Dayton and Nevin Kallepalli, who worked with astonishingly patient precision. We then assembled the final transcript by cross-checking these two versions and making editorial decisions for clarity. This final transcript was then reviewed against the video recording. Copyediting was done to both the English and German language transcripts for clarity, cleaning up verbal patterns for print, and to ensure reader comprehension in both languages.

By maintaining the complications of translation and eschewing the presumption of the primacy of the English language, our hope is that this bilingual transcript of the Working Group discussion at the Kunstraum will underscore the extent to which *Services* articulated distinct methods of interpretation by a specific but diverse group of transatlantic arts practitioners and that these practitioners frequently referred to their differing experiences working in the US and German art contexts.

We are extremely grateful to each of the invited practitioners who contributed to the *Services* Working Group at the Kunstraum of the University of Lüneburg in 1994. They repeatedly informed the process of bringing these bilingual transcripts to publication, with many providing direct feedback and guidance in our editing of the final versions published here. We must also acknowledge that any revisiting of the *Services* Working Group discussions or reconsideration of the history of artist-directed projects in Germany in the early 1990s is significantly limited by Fritz Rahmann's death in 2006.

We wish to thank Beatrice von Bismarck for her radical care and exceptional thought in guiding this book project to realization. Our thanks to Diethelm Stoller for taking the time to sit with us in Lüneburg and recount his experience in 1994 of organizing financial and logistical resources from the university's computer lab, which he managed at the time, for the *Services* project, as well as for the time he took looking through the receipts and invoices that detailed the economic conditions of the initial exhibition and Working Group. Substantial editorial support for this publication was provided through the tireless efforts of Fillip Editorial Board member Jaclyn Arndt, who helped prepare the manuscripts for publication, and Kate Woolf, Editorial Supervisor at Fillip, who contributed significant oversight and planning support in addition to compiling the biographies and reviewing final proofs.

Finally, and most significantly, this book emerges from, and in acknowledgement of, the great importance of Helmut Draxler and Andrea Fraser's continuing collaborative work. This Folio was nurtured by their consistent engagement—from the process of transcription to the conceptualization of the complete publication you hold in your hands. They have also provided a thoughtful "Postscript" that collects their thoughts on the *Services* project nearly three decades on, while underscoring just how active the culture sector has been these past decades in creating and authorizing exploitative working conditions. We are deeply grateful to Helmut and Andrea for their prophetic practices, which today must be fully recognized as providing indispensable examples of how to respond to the political economy of the art field and its social-psychological relations.

—Eric Golo Stone and Jeff Khonsary
Fillip

1. After its debut project at the Kunstraum, which ran from January 22 to February 20, 1994, the *Services* project travelled to the Künstlerhaus Stuttgart (1994), Kunstverein München (1994), Depot in Vienna (1995), Sous-sol in Geneva (1995), and Provincial Museum in Hasselt, Belgium (1995), and in the framework of the artist initiative *Parasite* at Clocktower P.S. 1, New York (1997). It was later installed in the exhibition *Antagonisms* at MACBA – Museu D'Art Contemporani de Barcelona (2001).

2. Andrea Fraser, "Services: Working-Group Discussions," *October*, no. 80 (Spring 1997): 117–48.

3. A "full verbatim" does not make any omissions, while a "clean verbatim" omits certain utterances, filler speech, and nonspeech sounds.

Eric Golo Stone

Reconsidering the Services Working Group

Decisions must take place somehow in the presence of those who will bear their consequences.

—Donna J. Haraway[1]

Individual and collective efforts to establish standards, regulations, and protections governing labour conditions in the art field have a long, if fragmentary, history.[2] As in the broader political economy, labour practices in the art sector demonstrate a continued historical tension between the struggles for individual rights and the struggles for collective rights. Arts practitioners, including artists, curators, writers, and educators, must today contend with a hyperindividualistic labour field dominated by precarious freelance and part-time positions. The means by which art institutions hire labour—whether commissioning artists or employing staff—is increasingly overdetermined by privately governed patronage. And arts practitioners often enter the job market with insuperable debt obligations that are enforced by privately held contracts.[3] Consequently, these working conditions in the art field atomize socio-economic struggles, reducing them to personal grievances and remediations that are isolated from collective processes capable of raising individual struggles to the realm of shared policy. Connecting individual work rights with collective bargaining efforts for the structural transformation of working conditions is also challenged by the very ideals of art itself. The pernicious narratives of art history and expectations of artistic practice most often affirm the individualistic, the monologic, and the self-sufficient. Artistic freedoms are consistently asserted as notions of independence and autonomy that transcend the dependent conditions and labour relations actually producing art.

Shared Labour Struggles

In the autumn of 1993, the artists Michael Clegg, Mark Dion, Andrea Fraser, and Julia Scher began meeting informally in New York to discuss challenges they had encountered contributing to a number of high-profile exhibitions that year, including *Project Unité* in Firminy, France; *Kontext Kunst* at the Neue Galerie im Künstlerhaus, Graz, Austria; *Sonsbeek 93* in Arnhem, the Netherlands; *On Taking a Normal Situation and Retranslating It into Overlapping and Multiple Readings of Conditions Past and Present* at MuHKA, Museum of Contemporary Art, Antwerp; *Culture in Action* in Chicago; *Viennese Story* at the Secession, Vienna; the Whitney Biennial in New York; and the 45th edition of the Venice Biennale. Initially their discussions identified the common project-based methodologies of these exhibitions, recognizing how their artistic works were made in situ—contingent on and specific to the site of exhibition—and that these site-responsive processual works were often nontransferable.[4] While identifying shared artistic methods, the discussions between Clegg, Dion, Fraser, and Scher in 1993 also addressed practical concerns over remuneration, the implications of unpaid or underpaid labour on their artistic output, and the broader socioeconomic consequences of precarious working conditions. Fraser recalls these particular challenges: *In addition to being expected to undertake site-specific projects for little or no fee, artists were routinely expected to design invitations, posters, advertisements and catalogues, write catalogue texts or prepare sections of catalogues without compensation. Artists with policies not to undertake projects without receiving a fee were treated as "difficult" and set against other artists in exhibitions. Sometimes artists were promised fees, only to be told after the exhibition opened that those fees were considered part of the project budgets and had already been used up in production. Artists' budgets were suspended when their process-oriented projects took longer to complete than the duration of the temporary exhibitions they were commissioned for.*[5]

Fraser's memory of how artists are socially and professionally alienated when they insist on receiving fair compensation for their work is consistent with the history of labour struggles. Anti-labour practices have always pitted workers against each other. Isolating workers who challenge the status quo by labelling them "difficult" and situating them in opposition to their coworkers is an age-old union-busting strategy. Artists are treated as difficult—subtly undermined, blatantly discredited, and repeatedly dismissed—when they unsettle expectations of how artists should behave. Challenging the transactional order for their work also means challenging the expected role of the artist as devoted to creating purely content-related, transferable property for acquisition. Fraser recognizes that artists are treated as difficult when they resist this expected role and make specific demands on the socially legitimated labour conditions in which their artistic works operate. By specifying how fees are frequently reallocated to cover production expenses, Fraser reminds us again of a fundamental problem with how artists are expected to produce a livelihood.[6] In the dominant economic model of the art field, the artist's fee is not a viable source of guaranteed income for living costs that is considered as separate from, and in excess of, production expenses. It is widely assumed that artists need not receive a fee separate from production expenses because, as long as funding is allocated to the production of artistic works, they are eventually paid through exposure and access to the market. This foundational problem—this exploiting of artists through the perilous assumption of back-end rewards—is also, as Fraser suggests, evidenced by commissions that make payment contingent on delivering content. Art institutions do not maintain earmarked budgets for basic necessities, such as unconditional research stipends and entrenched entitlements, in part because representatives of these institutions frequently conflate the artist fee with the production of consumable content.[7]

Clegg, Dion, Fraser, and Scher's discussions of the material conditions and social relations governing their artistic work—specifically, their attendant labour within exhibition contexts—evidenced a particularly responsive circuit. For these artists, there could not be any dissociation between an artwork and the structural conditions for its production, distribution, and reception. Artistic activity and the socio-economic conditions of labour were responsively interrelated, as intersubjective dimensions and interdependent operations. Articulating this responsibility became vital for this group of artists, and, significantly, through their discussions they sought to develop means for artists to engage with equal commitment in the different social, economic, and legal structures that constitute artistic work.

From the informal group discussions in New York, two research endeavours emerged. Clegg, Dion, Fraser, and Scher wrote a questionnaire about working conditions and sent it to some thirty artists who they felt engaged in project-based work.[8] They intended to use the responses to draft a contract for standards of professional practice.[9] The process of circulating the questionnaire and assembling a database of the responses was the first effort by Clegg, Dion, Fraser, and Scher to expand their initial discussions, gathering a wider range of individual labour-related experiences, and to organize those individual accounts within a shared legal mechanism.[10] Ultimately, however, their questionnaire and ensuing database did not produce an artists' contract. This outcome evidences the difficulties of reaching consensus within a group, as well as the complexities of applying standards of governance to address diverse practitioners' artistic activities and corresponding needs.

The impediments to realizing a broadly applicable yet individualized contract are inherent to the law of contracts and contractarian relations. Stemming from the legal fields of labour law, critical race theory, and feminist legal theory, debates continue over how contract doctrines too often codify, legitimize, and enforce individual rights at the expense of collective struggles to achieve systemic change. Contracts often reduce efforts against structural oppression to isolated individual grievances and remediations. For instance, nondisclosure stipulations foreclose a process whereby individual grievances and remediations could be openly organized and implemented as shared, transparent policy. As the American legal scholar Patricia J. Williams writes in her seminal essay "Regrouping in Singular Times": *One device by which courts have traditionally limited challenges to the social status quo is the consideration of cases and controversies constrained within a paradigm of private contract law. This insistence amounts to considering all litigation from within a contractarian paradigm that fragments the social contract into a series of little contracts.*[11]

Rather than pitting the individual against the collective, it is crucial, then, that any consideration of the case-by-case rights that are asserted for the individual in a situationally specific context also encompass the intersubjectivities, and the structural intersections and divergences, within collective societal concerns and regarding institutional implications. In response to these complex problems both affecting artists and inherent to contract law, Clegg, Dion, Fraser, and Scher directed their discussions to envisioning a broad economic framework that could be applied toward establishing governing provisions for artists' work on a case-by-case basis. That is, these artists began to think about socioeconomic policy and its application in the highly individualized art field.

Service Provision

At the time the questionnaire was being developed, Fraser began collaborating with the art historian, critic, and curator Helmut Draxler to formulate a concept of "artistic service provision." Draxler and Fraser's collaborative research endeavour aimed at identifying, in economic terms, what they considered a shared condition of art practices that, in the early 1990s, consistently resulted in ephemeral displays and activities that were not transferred into the art market as objects for sale. Draxler and Fraser considered to what extent economic theories of service provision could further an understanding of the fee structures necessary to remunerate artists exhibiting non-transferrable works for exhibiting institutions. Draxler and Fraser describe the motivation for better recognizing this economic condition: *It appears to us that, related variously to institutional critique, productivist, activist and political documentary traditions as well as post-studio, site-specific and public art activities, the practices currently characterised as "project work" do not necessarily share a thematic, ideological or procedural basis. What they do seem to share is the fact that they involve the expense of an amount of labour that is either in excess of, or independent of, any specific material production and which cannot be transacted as or along with such a production. This labour in economic terms would be called service provision (as opposed to goods production).... Whatever the sources or appropriate definitions of project-oriented practice, there seems to be a growing consensus among both artists and curators that the new set of relations they involve needs clarification.*[12]

Draxler and Fraser thus requested of the art field a re-evaluation of the economic conditions and relations under which artistic practices were being carried out. By introducing the term "service provision" to identify certain labour in the art field, they drew from a long history of legal-economic analysis of service work. Draxler and Fraser investigated how the fields of sociology, economics, and labour law have presented ongoing debates concerning service work relations, and began tracking the increasing centrality of services in the political economy.[13]

One of the key determinants of service work is that it is a form of labour that incorporates both production and consumption, interacting between these two realms and operating within ever adaptable working time requirements.[14] The temporal flexibility—the adjustable disciplining of time—required to produce in direct and immediate response to the consumer's demands places service work in the legal categories of subcontracted and freelance-contracted labour, which do not qualify for the legally sanctioned benefits and protections of temporally fixed employment.[15] Within service provision, employers and consumers increasingly share employing functions. The producer's proximity to the inclinations of consumers is significant to considering abuses, and the variable working time condition has created deeply asymmetrical relations between employers and employees. The gendered and racialized dimension of service work, and the socially structured identities and bodies of those hired to perform services, is crucial to understanding continued abuses facing service workers. The exploitation, dispossession, and deprivation exacted upon hired service workers must also be considered with relation to the foundational and continuous histories of slavery, peonage, and human trafficking. As a form of commodified labour that is contracted out entirely on demand, the provision of work services has transformed businesses and organizations into contracting agencies that shift the costs of health benefits, legal protections, and tax contributions onto the worker.[16] These legally ratified exemptions for employers have made the hiring of work services increasingly pervasive within the global economy.

Service provision studies identifies an extensive labour sector and a widely reproduced model for how labour is managed, which has yet to be fully integrated into labour law and organized labour, much less legislated policy. The obstacles to regulating service work are numerous. There are the legislative complexities to applying shared governance arrangements to distinct services that are procured through individual, privately governed contracts—written or verbal contracts that are often merely one-sided offers with no input or negotiation on terms and conditions that benefit the service worker. Moreover, there are ideological impediments to realizing labour standards for service work. The responsiveness between production and consumption and the variable working time condition that characterize service work are often held up as ideal conditions, where the service worker has seemingly greater individual autonomy. Service work, and freelance labour broadly, is promoted for its independence, allowing greater control over when, where, and for whom individuals work. But it is well known that the title of "independent curator," for instance, is a euphemism for an occupation that, through its repeated claims of being independent, disavows the actual dependencies at work. We very rarely learn who is actually being depended on, and by what means they are being depended on, when affirming independence.

Labour relations are concealed in the dominant model of artistic production in part because asserting the artist's autonomy from governing institutions, supply chains, and production systems too often also repudiates the labour relations that constitute these sites. Persistent claims of artistic autonomy foreclose a process of collectively organizing the specific conditions by which we work, and by which we could together assess the burdens of our labouring subjectivities. Ultimately, by maintaining the declarative politics of creative autonomy, artists, curators, and other cultural producers do not just compartmentalize, negate, contradict, and omit the material politics of their working conditions—they also usurp shared struggles.

In a 2004 interview reflecting on the *Services* project, Fraser underscored how instructive the economic realities of service provision are in revealing the false separation proposed by artistic autonomy: *From the "autonomous" space of the studio, we may be able to deny the functions that our work serves, but it's a denial in bad faith because we serve the same functions at cocktail parties and dinners, openings, press conferences, lectures, and interviews. We're there with our bodies and our voices serving. The distance between the moment of production and consumption, from the studio to the gallery, for instance, is eliminated with service provision. On the one hand, there's an implicit critique here because that distance is illusory anyway. The separation of the physical spaces and moments of production and consumption doesn't erase the linkages that exist between cultural producers and cultural consumers, between artists and their audiences or collectors. Eliminating that illusory separation is the first step toward taking an active and critical position in relationship to the functions that we serve and the uses to which our work is put.*[17]

Some intermediaries and linkages—those reinforcing asymmetrical labour relations—remain in place within neoliberal economics. The process of disintermediation is selective. That is, service-oriented neoliberalism does not involve the outright removal of all intermediaries and links between producers and consumers; rather, it pursues a privately mediated and legally ratified process of eliminating select regulatory bodies. The field of artistic production is indicative of this neoliberal economic reality, whereby we trade intermediary economic protections for a false sense of freedom from all economic constraints. Criticism that artists have become overly professionalized often invokes this exploitative trade-off. The problem, of course, is not that artists are becoming professionalized but rather that the professionalization of the art field does not include the development of standards and protections for artists' working relations and conditions.[18] Redeploying research findings on service provision within an art context is therefore an effort against the neutral feathering and outright depoliticization of artistic production—recognizing the extent to which labour relations in the art field are consistent with, and even exemplary of, social struggles in the broader political economy. While studying this interface between the problem field of service provision and the problem field of artistic production in the early 1990s, Draxler and Fraser emphasized actual lived relations that produce, distribute, receive, circulate, and consume art. They reached out to fellow practitioners to further discuss how the provision of work services has impacted labour relations, employment functions, and governance arrangements within art institutions, as well as other sites where arts practitioners produce a livelihood.

The Working Group

The informal meetings in New York, the questionnaire, and the concept of artistic service provision became a critical framework for the exhibition *Services: The Conditions and Relations of Service Provision in Contemporary Project Oriented Artistic Practice*.[19] Draxler and Fraser organized *Services* at the invitation of the art historian and curator Beatrice von Bismarck, mathematician Diethelm Stoller, and sociologist Ulf Wuggenig, who, in 1993, together founded and codirected the Kunstraum at the University of Lüneburg, a noncollecting university art gallery in Lüneburg, Germany. The distinct practices of the founding codirectors, and the emphasis on cultural studies, economics, and sociology within the Department of Art at the University of Lüneburg, further supported the exhibition's interdisciplinary critical framework. *Services* commenced with two days of closed-door working group discussions, which took place in the gallery of the Kunstraum on January 22 and 23, 1994. The Working Group was made up of Draxler, Fraser, and the Kunstraum's codirectors along with a number of invited practitioners, including Judith Barry, Ute Meta Bauer, Jochen Becker, Ulrich Bischoff, Iwona Blazwick, Susan Cahan, Michael Clegg, Stephan Dillemuth, Renée Green, Martin Guttmann, Renate Lorenz, Christian Philipp Müller, Fritz Rahmann, and Fred Wilson.[20]

Over the two days, they attended an introductory session, four thematic sessions titled "Serving Institutions," "Serving Audiences," "Serving Communities," and "Serving Art and Artists," and a concluding session. Draxler and Fraser's program included a short descriptive text for each thematic session that also articulated a set of related questions. Each of the fourteen invited practitioners were asked to select one session during which to give a presentation, with some presentations responding specifically to the prompted session theme and others not.[21]

The invited practitioners brought materials to support their respective Working Group presentations, which included photocopies, photographs, slides, videotapes, audio tapes, and other material documenting artist organizations, collective actions, experimental exhibition spaces, museum education department initiatives, artist proposals, prospectuses, contracts, exhibition budgets, and institutional guidelines.[22] While considering the prompted session themes—"Serving Institutions," "Serving Audiences," "Serving Communities," "Serving Art and Artists"—the practitioners often reflected on their own personal work experiences. Fred Wilson's presentation detailed the close conversations and long-term engagement he had with administrative staff working at the Maryland Historical Society in realizing his exhibition project *Mining the Museum* in 1992–93, at the society's museum in Baltimore.[23] Renée Green discussed her grant-writing obligations when working first as a curator for the Drawing Center in New York and again as an artist invited to exhibit at that same institution. Judith Barry outlined collaborative design work she had done for the New Museum in New York, reflecting on the terms and conditions of a contract she used that came from the commercial design industry and the extent to which it provided standards and protections not offered when Barry had worked with the museum as an exhibiting artist.[24]

In addition to the invited practitioners' presentations, Draxler and Fraser shared a collection of mostly photocopied documents from their research in organizing *Services*, which demonstrated how distinct artists sought to redefine their economic conditions of production. These photocopies included artists' contracts, statements, and project descriptions by Michael Asher, Daniel Buren, Louise Lawler, Group Material, and Mierle Laderman Ukeles, among others. Draxler and Fraser also presented a history of closely interrelated individual and collective labour struggles specific to the New York art context of the 1970s: statements by the Art Workers' Coalition, active in New York from 1969 to 1971, and institutional responses to these statements; documents from the Artists Meeting for Cultural Change, which convened in New York from 1975 to 1977; documents generated by the Museum of Modern Art in New York in response to its employees' formation of a labour union in 1971; and copies of archival material relating to the cancellation in 1971 of Hans Haacke's exhibition at the Guggenheim Museum in New York.[25]

The Working Group presentations and discussions at the Kunstraum were recorded on videotape, and during the exhibition component of *Services*, which opened on January 24, 1994, with a public discussion, this video documentation was presented on multiple monitors with headphones, along with the materials used to support the presentations.[26] Beyond reflecting on historical conditions and lived experiences of exhibition making, during their presentations Draxler and Fraser also spoke about why they chose the working group as the central operative structure by which the *Services* exhibition was produced. While different types of working groups exist, organized by different means and adhering to different parameters, a working group is broadly defined as a group of practitioners who coordinate to investigate and report on a particular subject and to make specific recommendations based on their findings.[27] This format is used in various fields where group work can be purposefully directed toward specific research goals. Whether appointed by institutional representatives or co-organized by individuals with shared interests, working groups typically have formal agreements with hosting institutions, consortiums, or associations that establish an operative structure and the economic conditions for the group work.[28] As group relations theory and collaborative governance theory have increasingly informed organizational methodologies applied to working groups, reflexivity has become another defining characteristic of the working group model. The coordinated social structure and immediate interrelational group dynamics of the working group itself are often considered by its organizers and contributors during the process of its formation and during its implementation.

For Draxler and Fraser, the working group as a discursive format specifically directed toward reflexive considerations of practical issues and outcomes was important.[29] They were vocal about wanting the *Services* project to be something useful for practitioners in the art field. *Services*, often referred to by Draxler and Fraser as a "working-group exhibition," realized a model of exhibition making that authorizes the exhibition's "producers"—the invited practitioners and representatives of the hosting institution—to collectively define the exhibition's means and materials of production. The idea that an exhibition would be constituted by, and comprised of, a group analyzing, debating, and actualizing the relations and conditions of the exhibition itself challenges conventional methods of exhibition making. Typically, the process of producing an exhibition is not structurally organized around critical reflection on, and enactment of, the immediate social conditions that produce the exhibition. Exhibitions are front-loaded with fundraising and production endeavours, but these socio-economic realities of funding and labour are too often compartmentalized as mere logistics or externalized as purely content-related material. The overwhelming majority of exhibitions negate, or foreclose outright, the freighted and damaging realities that directly produce them. For artists and institutional representatives alike, it is settled expectation that exhibition making is a process entirely devoted to externalization. Rarely are the immediate structural conditions that produce exhibitions substantively embodied, enacted, and altered in recognition that they are integral to the exhibition itself.[30] *Services*, on the other hand, made numerous attempts to actualize this process of integration.

It is perhaps in part because the working group format is a social structure intended to support reflexive analysis that the *Services* project was approached as something fraught and contestable.[31] Over the course of the two-day discussions, the participants repeatedly called into question the organizational structure of the Working Group. One recurring criticism centred around the role of students from the University of Lüneburg in the *Services* project. Why, asked both the invited practitioners and the students, had the Working Group been organized within a university context when students from the university were permitted to attend only the introductory and concluding sessions? Draxler and Fraser responded by emphasizing the distinct structure and purpose of the Working Group they had organized. They reiterated that the Working Group was not, in fact, organized as a seminar or public event. Rather, it was conceived as a series of working sessions by which a group of practitioners would produce an exhibition. That is to say, the Working Group emphasized specific constituents in its consideration of audience. As long as artists, curators, educators, and other exhibition makers invoke the needs of a general public as something beyond their own, they adhere to the security of speaking in generalities and remain intellectually apart from the difficult task of articulating immediate challenges facing the art field. The closed-door format of the *Services* Working Group thus countered the institutional impulse to address general audiences, which, as Fraser has pointed out, ultimately obscures the specific needs and concerns of art professionals as a primary constituency of exhibitions: *The misrecognition of specialised audiences inherent in programmes conceived as purveyors of information to a "general public," effectively limits those programmes to functioning as sites of symbolic struggles among producers. To the extent that programming is not determined by immediate concerns for particular audiences, that "general public" is reduced to no more than adherents, subscribers and investors that art professionals compete for in struggles for legitimacy and prestige.*[32]

In emphasizing the Working Group at the Kunstraum as a site of exhibition production, Draxler and Fraser also noted during the Working Group sessions that many of the invited practitioners had been working together and alongside each other under difficult conditions for various exhibitions in the years preceding *Services*. The closed-door format was meant to facilitate direct and candid exchange between the Working Group members, within an art field where explicit and confrontational discussions about the conditions of production are rarely integrated into the process of producing an exhibition. Organizing the Working Group was a structural response to the apparent lack of art world sites for producers to address each other and collaboratively reflect on their shared and yet alienated relationships with the divisions of labour, means of production, and mediating functions of the immediate exhibitionary context, and thereby the art field broadly.[33] In doing so, *Services* reaffirms the significance of analysis as a process of self-problematization—a process whereby we address a social problem by recognizing and articulating the ways we are directly implicated in its production. A significant point of potential implication and self-problematization that was not, however, directly addressed within the Working Group discussions was the fact that fees were not provided by the Kunstraum to the Working Group contributors. That this conflict was not widely discussed during the Working Group sessions is of course particularly dismaying with respect to the political position taking and socioeconomic imperatives of the project.[34]

Draxler and Fraser were encouraged by contributors to the Working Group at the Kunstraum to think about how *Services* might travel to other venues, where different practitioners and representatives of the hosting institutions could reproduce the model of the "working group exhibition" and further pursue the imperatives of the project. At one point in the Kunstraum discussions, Fraser suggested that *Services* could be a reproducible framework for exhibition makers to openly reflect on their shared and distinct struggles while also formulating coherent policy for practical application in the field. Ultimately, by proposing an operative governing structure, *Services* was a kind of policy-making effort.[35] The video documentation of the Working Group sessions and the document collection that supported the session presentations demonstrate the extent to which the governing structure of the working group was adhered to during the project. As with all policies that strive to be beneficially inclusive, the *Services* project is a course of action that must be adopted and sustained collectively by institutions and practitioners if it is to exceed the limitations of individual policy. Practitioners in the field of art should be wary of the depoliticizing of individual rights as separate from the question of collective needs and shared interests. While the operative structure of *Services* was not formally adopted as a long-term set of procedures within any one institution, it persists as an example against the politics of individual access being neutralized as separate from structural social conditions. The durability of the *Services* project as a momentary intervention into the conventional procedures of exhibition making is also notable. Working Groups with different newly invited contributors and representatives from the hosting venue were organized when the project travelled after its first manifestation in Lüneburg to the Künstlerhaus Stuttgart (1994), the Kunstverein München (1994), Depot in Vienna (1995), Sous-sol in Geneva (1995), the Provincial Museum in Hasselt, Belgium (1995), Clocktower P.S. 1 in New York (1997), and MACBA—Museu d'Art Contemporani de Barcelona (2001).[36]

Services raises fundamental questions about the operative structures of exhibiting art institutions. Perhaps most pressingly, how specifically can art institutions function as a context for the exhibiting of artistic activities, as well as a context equally committed to reconsidering the relations and conditions by which those artistic activities are exhibited? To what extent *Services* and its working group structure are being applied to the present moment of exhibition-making practices is still unclear. There is a hyperawareness today that artists and their institutions have to engage in a substantive reconsideration of the governance arrangements that define the operative structures and labour relations that produce, distribute, and receive works of art. And there are efforts being made to actualize standards of institutional conduct that extend from the demands made by individual practitioners. What are the structural restrictions and other impediments to this process of realization— from asserting individual rights to the ratification of social policy? Certainly, we have already seen the consequences of how this path toward greater collective inclusivity in governance has been obstructed by the discriminatory history and present reality of institutional bylaws, policies, and contractual relations in the field of art. *Services* shows how we must begin to appreciate the extent to which art institutions actually deal in and perpetuate not merely individual interests but also interests that govern, silence, authorize, and deauthorize constituent groups. It is this heightened awareness of the complex psycho-dynamic social relations of group work that *Services* demands of institutional governance. *Services* reaffirms how reflexive analysis is a collective governing process founded on self-critical reflection that aims to examine its own immediate assumptions and presuppositions. It is a process of self-examination that is never done alone, completed by self-sufficient means; rather it is accomplished interrelationally through active group dynamics. Drawing from long, intersubjective traditions of artistic introspection, art institutions would do well to apply reflexive governance to their operations—to become institutions where rules and procedures are actualized through reflexive adaptation, and where the governed have a capacity to transform the construction of the means and mechanisms of governance.

1. Donna J. Haraway, *When Species Meet* (Minneapolis: University of Minnesota Press, 2008), 87.

2. In the US, this history includes the American Artists' Congress (1936–42), Artists Equity Association (1947–), Art Workers' Coalition (1969–71), Professional and Administrative Staff Association of the Museum of Modern Art, New York (1971–), Artists Meeting for Cultural Change (1975–77), Black Emergency Cultural Coalition (1971–84), Working Artists and the Greater Economy (2008–), and Gulf Labor Artist Coalition (2011–). Labour unions continue to organize workers in museums and art schools, including UAW-TOP Local 2110, the American Federation of State, County and Municipal Employees, and UAW Local 2865.

3. I am referring here to the student borrower's promissory note, which in the US is serviced by for-profit financial institutions; interest on the loan is collected by private banking institutions. Student loan packages in the US include private student loans with terms and conditions that are entirely governed by private banking

institutions, with interest rates as high as nine percent in 2019. While particularly egregious in the US context, debt related to student loans for tuition and basic living expenses is an increasing problem globally. See, for example, Organization for Economic Cooperation and Development, "Student Debt Rising Worldwide," in *Education at a Glance 2018* (Paris: OECD Publishing, 2018), https://fillip.ca/inz9.

4. Additionally, these artists were, at the time, being invited to "do a project for" a particular exhibition, and so the term "project work" also simply referred to the artistic activity generated in response to such invitations. However, achieving a taxonomic understanding of project work is really beside the point. See Andrea Fraser, "Services: A Working-Group Exhibition," in *Games, Fights, Collaborations: The Game of Boundary Transgression; Art and Cultural Studies in the 90's*, ed. Beatrice von Bismarck, Dieter Stoller, and Ulf Wuggenig (Ostfildern-Ruit, Germany: Hatje Cantz, 1996), 210.

5. Fraser, "Services: A Working-Group Exhibition," 210–11.

6. Fraser has also written about the political and artistic imperatives of artist fees in the work of Michael Asher. See Andrea Fraser, "Procedural Matters: The Art of Michael Asher," *Artforum*, Summer 2008, 374–81.

7. It is worth reconsidering Fraser's emphasis on artist fees today amid the devastating global socioeconomic fallout of the 2008 financial crisis and the 2020 public health crisis. An artist fee agreement that makes liveable income noncontingent on producing transferrable property offers a model for how artists may be paid a guaranteed basic income.

8. The artists sent the questionnaire were: Vito Acconci, Dennis Adams, Fareed Armaly, Michael Asher, Judith Barry, Tom Burr, Mel Chin, Critical Art Ensemble, Stephen Dillemuth, Dan Graham, Renée Green, Group Material, Martin Guttmann, Hans Haacke, Amy Hauft, Louis Hock, John Knight, Silvia Kolbowski, Renée Kool, Joseph Kosuth, Louise Lawler, Simon Leung, Christian Philipp Müller, Dan Peterman, Gerwald Rockenschaub, Lincoln Tobier, Lawrence Weiner, Fred Wilson, Krzysztof Wodiczko, and Heimo Zobernig. A handful of these artists—Dillemuth, Green, Müller, and Wilson—would also later take part in the Working Group at the Kunstraum at the University of Lüneburg.

9. Fraser, "Services: A Working-Group Exhibition," 211.

10. The proposed contract connects Clegg, Dion, Fraser, and Scher's discussions to earlier efforts to establish contractual agreements standardizing protections for artists' interests, such as Robert Projansky and Seth Siegelaub's "The Artist's Reserved Rights Transfer and Sale Agreement" (1970). Siegelaub's research was also a reaction to a collective demand, as it resulted from the Art Workers' Coalition hearings in New York in 1969. The open hearings were the culmination of months spent negotiating with executive administrators at the Museum of Modern Art to implement various reforms, such as equal representation of artists on museum boards, royalties paid to artists, and free museum admission. Representation of women artists and artists of colour was a principal issue of contention. Siegelaub spoke with artists to gauge the particular interests they sought for their artistic work once it entered the exhibition and market context. See Maria Eichhorn, "Seth Siegelaub," in *The Artist's Contract*,

ed. Gerti Fietzek (Cologne: Buchhandlung Walther König, 2009), 39.

11. Patricia J. Williams, "Metro Broadcasting, Inc. v. FCC: Regrouping in Singular Times," *Harvard Law Review* 104, no. 2 (December 1990), 534.

12. Helmut Draxler and Andrea Fraser, "Services: A Proposal for an Exhibition and a Topic of Discussion," in Bismarck, Stoller, and Wuggenig, *Games, Fights, Collaborations*, 196.

13. The economic theory on service provision at that time had a lack of agreement concerning the terms, quantification of values ascribed to labour activities, and the benefits gained by those activities. See Andrea Fraser, "What's Intangible, Transitory, Mediating, Participatory, and Rendered in the Public Sphere," in *Museum Highlights: The Writings of Andrea Fraser*, ed. Alexander Alberro (Cambridge, MA: MIT Press, 2005), 50, 53, 54. The bibliography discussed by Fraser includes Daniel Bell, *The Coming of the Post-industrial Society: A Venture in Social Forecasting* (New York: Basic Books, 1973); Harry Braverman, *Labor and Monopoly Capital: The Degradation of Work in the Twentieth Century* (New York: Monthly Review Press, 1974); H. L. Browing and J. Singelmann, *The Emergence of a Service Society: Demographic and Sociological Aspects of the Sectoral Transformation of the Labour Force in the U.S.A.* (Springfield, VA: National Technical Information Service, 1975); Ernest Mandel, *Late Capitalism*, trans. Joris De Bres (London: Verso, 1978); Jonathan Gershuny and Ian Miles, *The New Service Economy: The Transformation of Employment in Industrial Societies* (New York: Praeger, 1983); and Jean-Claude Delaunay and Jean Gadrey, *Services in Economic Thought: Three Centuries of Debate*, trans. Aart Heesterman (Boston: Kluwer Academic Publishers, 1992). Draxler and Fraser would have benefited from the legal-economic theory that came well after the time of their research, including J. R. Bryson, P. N. Daniels, and B. Warf, *Service Worlds: People, Organizations, Technologies* (London: Routledge, 2004) and Einat Albin, "Law in a Service World," *Modern Law Review* 73, no. 6 (November 2010), 959–84.

14. Service theory is a growing field of specialized study within the law and economics. These identifying features of service work are discussed in numerous texts, including those mentioned in the previous footnote.

15. This is consistently true in various jurisdictionally specific employment sectors. "Flexibility" is an oft used euphemism to describe service work. Flexibility of course often just means the worker must produce, or at least be prepared to produce, at all times.

16. For an updated account of this dynamic, see G. Cavallini and M. Avogaro, "'Digital Work' in the 'Platform Economy': The Last (But Not Least) Stage of Precariousness in Labour Relationships," in *Precarious Work. The Challenge for Labour Law in Europe*, ed. J. Kenner, I. Florczak, and M. Otto (Cheltenham, UK: Edward Elgar, 2019), 176–96. Artists, curators, and writers, as exemplary of the neoliberal economy, are often compared to high paid "creatives" in the advertising, media, and technology industries, but for the vast majority of individuals labouring in the art field, a more apt comparison would be the low-paid and extremely precarious gig workers of the digital-platform economy.

17. Andrea Fraser and Miwon Kwon, "What Do I, as an Artist, Provide?: A Conversation," in *Andrea Fraser:*

Collected Interviews, 1990–2018, ed. Rhea Anastas, Alejandro Cesarco, and Andrea Fraser (London: Koenig Books, 2018), 204.

18. Professionalization should not be understood as a purely negative condition; it has a long, complex history that also of course includes efforts to establish standards of professional practice and protections for workers. See, for example, Merle Jacobs and Stephen E. Bosanac, *The Professionalization of Work* (Whitby, ON: de Sitter, 2006); Lori Kenschaft, *Professions and Professionalization* (Oxford: Oxford University Press, 2008); Linda Reeser, Linda Cherrey, and Irwin Epstein, *Professionalization and Activism in Social Work* (New York: Columbia University Press, 1990); and Anne Witz, *Professions and Patriarchy* (London: Routledge, 1992).

19. The exhibition ran January 22–February 20, 1994, and subsequently travelled in Europe for two years. The travel schedule was developed after the opening at the Kunstraum rather than in advance.

20. These contributors were artists, curators, and educators who were primarily working in the German, US, and UK contexts. Many were also directly involved in activism in their regions. Within and beyond the *Services* project, the artists Jochen Becker and Renate Lorenz worked together as BüroBert, and the artists Michael Clegg and Martin Guttmann worked together as Clegg & Guttmann. See Fraser, "Services: A Working-Group Exhibition," 197.

21. See Andrea Fraser, "Services: Working-Group Discussions," *October*, no. 80 (Spring 1997), 117.

22. See Fraser, "Services: Working-Group Discussions," 117.

23. For his seminal *Mining the Museum* exhibition, Wilson worked with Maryland Historical Society staff to redeploy artworks and artifacts from the society's collection, including some that had been permanently consigned to storage because they drew attention to local violent histories of enslaved and dispossessed African Americans and Indigenous Peoples. In doing so, Wilson effectively countered the society's depoliticized presentation of a white, aristocratic, museological narrative and revealed the society itself as a narrow ideological project that upheld systemic racism.

24. See J. Barry et al., "Serving Institutions," *October*, no. 80 (Spring 1997), 120–27.

25. In 1971, the director of the Guggenheim Museum in New York, Thomas Messer, refused to include Haacke's work *Shapolsky et al. Manhattan Real Estate Holdings, a Real-Time Social System, as of May 1, 1971* (1971) in the artist's exhibition, which was cancelled as a result and its curator, Edward Fry, fired.

26. Olaf Krafft, who worked for the University of Lüneburg's audiovisual media department, was the videographer, and he led the production of the video document with a technical crew: camera: Michael Coester and Olaf Krafft; live video mix: Marco Piechocki; video editing: Michael Coester and Marco Piechoki; sound: Marion Bartelt, Olaf Krafft, and Marco Piechocki.

27. E. Sundstrom, K. P. De Meuse, and D. Futrell, "Work Teams: Applications and Effectiveness," *American Psychologist* 25, no. 2 (1990), 120–21. Organizational psychology is just one of many fields that define the structures and methodologies of working groups. While mired in entrepreneurialism and managerialism,

endless literature defines the working group model within collectivity and collaborative governance.

28. Manfred Schulte-Zurhausen, *Organization*, 3rd ed. (Munich: Franz Vahlen Verlag, 2002), 64–67.

29. Throughout the *Services* Working Group, Draxler and Fraser made attempts to steer the discussions toward considering specific "useful" and "practical" issues and outcomes. In some instances, they requested that the invited practitioners' presentations avoid overviews of multiple projects and instead emphasize specific questions, problems, or proposals for discussion by the group.

30. How incapable it seems we are in the art field of substantive critical reflection on our actual immediate relations and conditions. Our sophisticated techniques of creating symbolic, sensorial, and affective systems become detrimental when they are reduced to distancing mechanisms and render lived circumstances into mere content.

31. Artists in the Working Group frequently challenged the underlying critical idea that service provision could be applicable to their own practices. Fraser has repeatedly had to clarify that the concept of service

provision did not recognize a form of artistic activity; rather, it defined the economic conditions and relations of artistic production. See I. Blazwick et al., "Serving Audiences" and "Serving Communities," *October*, no. 80 (Spring 1997), 128–48.

32. Fraser, "Services: A Working-Group Exhibition," 212–13.

33. There was also an opportunity for public address. During the opening of the exhibition component, Draxler, Fraser, Beatrice von Bismarck, and Ulf Wuggenig spoke about the project in public remarks and took questions from the audience.

34. This was verified to me by Diethelm Stoller, who reviewed the receipts and budget for the project.

35. Again looking to legal scholar Patricia J. Williams's seminal essay, she defines "policy" as "the contemporaneous society of those similarly situated." Williams, "Metro Broadcasting, Inc. v. FCC," 543.

36. No video documentation exists of the Working Group discussions at these different venues. In fact, any documentation at all that may have been made has not been well recorded or archived—a fact that leaves the research and bibliography for this book incomplete.

Transcripts

The following two sections present the bilingual transcripts of the *Services* Working Group. Please note that the short descriptive texts, which include theme titles and dates, at the outset of every Working Group session are reproduced directly from the intertitles that appear in the video recordings of the two-day Working Group discussions. These intertitle texts were written by Helmut Draxler and Andrea Fraser in 1994.

Organizers
Helmut Draxler
Andrea Fraser

Codirectors
Kunstraum of the
University of Lüneburg
Beatrice von Bismarck
Diethelm Stoller
Ulf Wuggenig

Contributors
Judith Barry
Ute Meta Bauer
Jochen Becker
Ulrich Bischoff
Iwona Blazwick
Susan Cahan
Michael Clegg
Stephan Dillemuth
Renée Green
Martin Guttmann
Renate Lorenz
Christian Philipp Müller
Fritz Rahmann
Fred Wilson

Working Group
Session One

Introductions
Saturday, January 22, 1994

Presentations:
Helmut Draxler
Andrea Fraser

The organizers restate the premises of the event and present the material collected for the exhibition.

Andrea Fraser: So Helmut Draxler and I would like to welcome all of you to the Kunstraum of the University of Lüneburg. And I think that probably most of you have met each other by now. But we'll go around and have introductions in a few minutes. We've prepared this exhibition, which is the opening exhibition of the space, in response to an invitation from Beatrice von Bismarck, Ulf Wuggenig, and Diethelm Stoller (who is not here, he is picking up another participant) and the faculty members here at the University of Lüneburg. We'd like to invite them to make a few comments about their concept for the space.

Beatrice von Bismarck: You'd like to do that before the introduction?

Fraser: Yes.

Von Bismarck: Yeah, maybe very briefly. The Kunstraum is a project that has actually come to life with the exhibition *Services*, it's something that we've planned for the last year, and for those of you who have not heard of the existence of the University of Lüneburg, it's a university which tries to have an interdisciplinary teaching program, with a certain bias on strong relations to the practical fields. So, basically, that means it positions itself outside the traditional teaching system at the university and, by this, offers the chance to integrate the practical field much more into teaching and vice versa. So the idea of a *Kunstraum* was not to constitute yet another exhibition space somewhere in the provinces, but rather to create something like a forum of exchange between the fields of scientists and artists. And this sort of forum— where I think *Services* couldn't be a better project to start in a way—this one, we think, should be constituted by activities that include not only contemporary art exhibitions but also a program of accompanying lectures, artist visits, workshops, panel discussions. So a range of activities on that side, which would also be followed up by a research program and a publication series corresponding to the nature of the Kunstraum in its form and content of those. I think you have all found an outline of the Kunstraum in your folder. It's a sort of brief statement about it. And I'm sure we're going to come back to its structure probably at some point.

Maybe just another word concerning the idea of how we try to integrate that into the university: the idea is basically that you have the chance to not only integrate it into the teaching, which we integrated into the research, but to understand that as a continuously proceeding discourse between the different fields. So the students in this case have a preparatory and integrative role in what happens concerning the events that the Kunstraum is producing. And, of course, an integration into the subsequent research, in as much as that is possible.

Fraser: Will three students be attending this session? How is that organized?

Von Bismarck: Yes, the idea was that the students who participate in the seminar preparing this exhibition, that a small group of them can attend each section. That is the arrangement so far. And that starts with the first section that is after lunch.

Fraser: Oh, see, I thought there would be—

Von Bismarck: No, they thought they shouldn't be here for the introductions.

Fraser: So after lunch there'll be three students from the university joining us.

Helmut Draxler: I mean that sounds a little bit weird. We had this discussion very extensively this week, and I think it was a very important point to make a decision between a nonpublic and a public event, because we are more than twenty, more or less, and so we would have had immediately this kind of situation. So, nevertheless, I would like to thank all of them, already, for being a great help to do this project. And, of course, we will try to invest as much as possible in creating the didactic working relationship with them in this event, and also after this event, and this is more or less the goal.

And I have another point. There is always this language problem we have. And it's very usual, you know: everything is in English. But it's still…we are usually learning with language when we are five years old. And most of you know that. But, still, it is kind of a problem at

certain points, and I think this point is mostly speed. So, we will do our best, if there are any problems for us, or to help each other to bring that up to this point. I think, to a certain degree, it's an important point, because we are used to giving up, in a very ritualized form, this point in a lot of discussions in Germany. I know that there's no way to really go around this, but I also know out of different experiences we've had in the last couple of years, it's not a very…Yeah, it's not exactly an advantage for German-speaking people here. OK.

Fraser: So this project, this exhibition, this working group exhibition *Services*, developed, really, I think, from two sides. One was the concept of the space and the fact that there really aren't—unlike in the United States and, perhaps, England—many universities that have exhibition spaces. In Germany, that's really not so common. We spoke with Ulf and Beatrice and Diethelm about the concept for this space, and felt that it would be a very important contribution to the German art scene to have a context where, perhaps, instead of trying to address a general audience, artists and academics and scientists might be able to address each other on practical issues relevant to their experiences. The other thing that this project came out of were specific discussions among a group of artists doing project work about the need to collectively establish some guidelines for working with institutions. So that's a very different side. I think that those discussions came out of their experiences over the last few years with a lot of exhibitions and a suddenly much greater demand by curators or institutions, or for particular programs for artists, or a greater interest in artists—or more invitations, at any rate, to artists to undertake work in response to specific situations and sites. Whether or not those sites were understood to be sites that the artists were already interested in working with, or whether those sites were being somehow newly defined by curators or by institutions that were in particular programs. Within this increased demand—and I think there are more and more artists who are interested in working that way—but there seemed to be a kind of lag between the demand and the invitations, and the structures of the institutions where those works were to be executed. It seemed like, in many cases, these necessary or adequate support structures didn't exist. It has to do, at least in my mind, to some extent with the development of an idea of professional practice around new kinds of activities. So that was the other motive.

Draxler: Yeah, I mean, we could already go into a kind of interpretation of that demand, of what that meant, and the experience of, especially in the last year, having shown in many shows like this, getting into this competition of curators more or less over the participation of artists. This is also a very specific point, I think, for the definition of the curatorial world, which has changed very much, in my opinion. Yet still in Germany between the different, let's say, *Kunstverein* and museum structures, this role is absolutely not clearly defined and has a totally different kind of practical aspect. It's my opinion that it started in the middle of the '80s, that this argument came out that artists participated in the show. So my predecessor in Munich

[at the Kunstverein München] never invited artists. He just got the work and installed it by himself, and artists were more or less disruptive for this kind of process. He made exhibitions as a curatorial projector, which was totally based on his ego, very concentrated, in the patriarchal model of a curator who is making the selections and in a very traditional sense. I think this model is changing a lot. It's not so easy to say in what way it will be changing and what's coming out of it. And I think this should be from a curatorial point of view—also one of the points of discussion for today and tomorrow.

Fraser: In having decided to try to develop a forum for artists and curators to talk about these kinds of practical issues, it first seemed necessary to try to develop some sort of understanding of how artists—working with different sorts of stylistic backgrounds, different sorts of procedures within different sorts of ideological and intellectual frameworks—are being grouped together, and what the meaning of this term "project" might be. "Project," I think, is a term which has been used very generically for a long time. To say, "I'm doing a project," instead of saying, "I'm doing a work" or "I'm doing a performance"—almost to describe a medium more than anything else. While backgrounds are diverse, we tried to think about what that common basis might be, and that's when we came up with this concept of "services." It emerged out of that, and I just wanted to read the introduction to the proposal that all of you received: "It appears to us that related variously to institutional critique, productivist, activist, and political documentary traditions, as well as post-studio, site-specific, and/or public art activities, the practices currently characterized as project work do not necessarily share a thematic, ideological, or procedural basis. What they do seem to share is the fact that they all involve expending an amount of labour which is either in excess of or independent of any specific material production and which cannot be transacted along with such production. This labour, which in economic terms would be called service provision, as opposed to goods production, may include the work of interpretation or analysis of sites—both in- and outside of cultural institutions, the work of presentation installation, the work of public education, and advocacy and other community-based work including organizing, education, documentary production, and the creation of alternative structures in communities, within the art community, as well as within nonart urban communities."

Draxler: I mean, this term "services" has a certain kind of history, as you know, and we were thinking about, when we were preparing this talk, kind of going into this more theoretical part of it, coming out of theories about postindustrial society and things like that. But we decided to leave this more open to academic discourse and to concentrate much more on what it would mean in a more specific, practical sense. It's important to stress that "services" is not at all thought to be a new catchword for the '90s, a "new hot art term," or whatever. Both of us [Andrea and I] think that it does not imply necessarily a progressive development. So, it is first of all a, let's say, analytical term to describe this new and partly unclear relationship between artists' projects and new curatorial worlds within certain institutions. This very specific term "services" does not describe a new autonomous sphere, a new genre of project work, but it rather describes a certain set of different practices, always in a certain relationship of artists to curators, to institutions, to audiences, to communities. And also of curators to art. I think the very specificity of the term "services" lies exactly in this total relational concept.

Fraser: But we are also very interested in—or at least *I'm* really interested in—what the relationship has been and could be between artists who have strategically or thematically taken up sort of service functions, or appropriated service functions within institutions, and the real material relationships to those institutions that that appropriation implies and how the latter has been, or has not been, formalized by the artists in contracts, letters of agreements, etc.

There's different strands that the historical materials that we gathered follow. One of the of points is the development of artist-curators, or artists taking on or executing curatorial functions within sites of cultural presentation, within galleries as well as museums. For example, I mean, what's the difference if an artist is doing that as a symbolic appropriation of that function? And what does that mean? Does that mean something different than if an artist is doing that under contract with an institution? Or in a certain way—that it's to function on a permanent basis or on a long-term basis? Those to me seem to be pretty important issues, where an artist like Louise Lawler has never had a contract or worked with a contract. For example, when she would arrange work of the artists at Metro Pictures [in New York], it was in the position of a kind of art consultant, where she was supposed to get 10 percent—but she has not wanted to, if any of the works were sold, to formalize that.

In my interpretation of that lies the next issue, which is very important to me: questions of professionalization around these kinds of activities. I see, on the one hand, through service provision, and within these relationships between artists and institutions that it implies, two different strands which seem to have… well, I'm not clear what the relationship between them might be. One, perhaps, is appropriating curatorial functions and institutional roles in a way that explicitly involves this as a critique of those roles and functions. Versus doing a very similar thing, but in a way that implies an "expert-client relationship" and certain professional models that go along with that kind of relationship. That wasn't as clear as I wanted it to be. But let me see if I can get back to a clearer point. For me personally, one of the things that I am probably most interested in achieving through this kind of forum—and if it takes place again, which I hope it does—is to try to see if it's possible to develop a kind of radical professional model, a model of radical professionalism or something like that, that might provide a material basis for progressive development of a certain kind of critical project practice. That's what I'm interested in. I hope that was clearer (laughs).

I mean, it's a kind of a New Left idea, actually: radicals and professions, and radical…

Martin Guttmann: Dress for success as a radical?

Fraser: No, no. I mean, we're talking about, well, the New Left model was, you know, social workers who go in and organize their welfare recipients against the welfare system and things like that. Which is, in a certain way, what one of the things that institutional critique has been, or, I don't know. There are other models, too. But that's a historical…

Judith Barry: It's such a paradoxical structure. I think that on a philosophical level, it's the crux of all these issues, as always: the question of institutional critique, wanting to make that critique, and then also wanting to participate at the institution. And this isn't a criticism of your statement. It's just a paradoxical divide.

Fraser: It is. But that's, I think, the source of a lot of the confusion around this kind of work. Particularly for artists who are working in an institutional critique vein. I mean, I started to be invited to institutional critique shows in the late '80s, and it's one of the most bizarre things that I can possibly imagine. But the issue for me is not only that there are a lot of ethical issues that go along with that on my side. On the other side, [the issues] have to do with relations *within* institutions, between artists and curators and between curators and their boards of trustees and their governing bodies. I think that those relationships have changed radically. And it's one of the things also that we hope we've documented a little bit in the historical material. But I think there are a lot of ethical issues that get raised also, because if we're doing institutional critique, are we working with curators? Who is the institution there? How are we identifying the institution? What is the relationship to the curator in that? Or is it just the trustees? Or is it the institution as a kind of impersonal entity, kind of just a social fact? But, where do you draw that line? I've had a lot of complicated experiences around that. And I think that many of us have.

Draxler: I think it has also to do with the desire to change the term "institutional critique," or to historicize it to a certain degree. I think it could even be seen on this wall [of materials in the Kunstraum]. Certainly not explicitly, this term was not there in the early '70s when these practices were evolved. It comes somewhere later, but we don't know yet. It would be very interesting if someone has an idea of when it came up. Who used this term for the first time?

Guttmann: Probably Bürger. Peter Bürger. No?

Draxler: No. Hmmm.

Guttmann: So anyway, it goes—

Draxler: It comes from this kind of discussion, but this—

Guttmann: But he used the term in '73.

Draxler: No. Not as—He introduced this "institutional" reference for avant-garde practice, but he didn't use it as this kind of term. And what he had in mind was clearly super Dada and surrealist concepts, and not a contemporary practice.

Guttmann: He talks about neo-pop, neo-Dadaism.

Draxler: Yes, but in very, very—you know, he doesn't like it at all. I mean, he's hating contemporary art and

holding early modernism, early avant-garde, very high. So I think it's really not so easy.

Fraser: Hans Haacke, who I spoke to—a lot of this material came from Hans Haacke—I asked him whether he describes what he does as "institutional critique." It's something I always assumed, and he said, no, he does not, that he never really used that term. As far as he knows, it was introduced in the early '80s by the *October* crowd. But, I mean, it seems a little late to me (laughs).

Guttmann: In *Theory of the Avant-Garde* that term appears, I know it.

Fraser: Yeah, but I don't think—

Guttmann: He talks about institutional critique and it's presented vis-à-vis the European reading of pop art, which makes it a little bit distant. But not that distant.

Fraser: But I think it only came to be applied to these kinds of practices later, I think that was the point. Bürger wasn't translated until the early '80s—'82 I think it came out in England. In any case…so that's what we prepared by way of an introduction. We would also like to try to briefly run through some of this material. But first, we wanted to go around and have everyone introduce themselves and say also a little bit about their background, institutional affiliation, if appropriate. And if you'd like to also say something about what you think we might try to achieve here.

Ulrich Bischoff: *Hallo. Es ist alles so heilig hier da kann ich nicht stören.* [Hello. Everything is so sacred here, I don't want to disturb.]

Draxler: *Nein, nein.* [No, no.]

(Laughter)

Fraser: I mean, I can start. I'm Andrea Fraser—I know it seems silly, but it's about creating a kind of group.

Draxler: No. It's absolutely necessary.

Von Bismarck: I'm Beatrice von Bismarck and my particular interest in this discussion is that I've been working as a curator before and I'm now teaching. And virtually any point mentioned here is one that we discover every day in the curatorial practice. So I'm very curious to see whether there's any option to come to any conclusions.

Susan Cahan: I'm Susan Cahan, and I'm the curator of education at the New Museum of Contemporary Art in New York City. And I've been there for about six years. Prior to that, I worked at the Museum of Modern Art [MoMA], also in New York City, and also in the area of education. And I'll mention this, although I didn't think it was relevant until we were talking last night and I saw this stuff on the bulletin board: when I was at MoMA, I was very active in the union, PASTA [Professional and Administrative Staff Association]. I was a board member. There's a lot of material that relates to PASTA as a result—that experience may be relevant to our discussion. My work has involved developing new models of educational practice in museums and looking at the relationship between curatorial education and the role of visitors or viewers in museums, and looking at audiences, artists, and museum professionals in terms of the relational issues that Helmut alluded to earlier.

Fred Wilson: I'm Fred Wilson and I'm an artist living in New York. For most of my career, I've been working in museums, art galleries, running art galleries, to support myself as an artist in the last…since '87. Those two practices kind of have been dovetailing and becoming one. Where now I'm not at all making exhibitions of other people's work, as I was prior to that point. I was working in museums and in the education departments in New York City, all of New York, as a preparator, as a museum guard, in all different aspects of the museum, which really began to inform my work directly. And I ran galleries in Tribeca and SoHo, but mostly my experience is in the South Bronx in New York City, and running a gallery there for artists, from all over New York, including the South Bronx. So from that point, I've been working primarily on creating exhibitions with other people's collections and other museums' collections, which initially was about how display affects your perception of the art and the artist. But—and what I hope to talk about a little more—this has become a real critique of the inner functions of the museum and its staff, and its relationships between staff, and how things get exhibited and their systems of display, behind the actual display itself. I don't have a notion of a goal or an outcome for this [Working Group] yet. As the day goes on, I'm sure I can think of something.

Fraser: Hopefully.

Ulf Wuggenig: I'm Ulf Wuggenig. I'm a member of the Faculty of Economics and Social Sciences at this university. I'm also teaching sociology of the arts in the Cultural Studies program. I'm also doing research referring to contemporary arts. For instance, a project together with Martin Guttmann and Michael Clegg. I've also studied in Vienna and in Hamburg, referring to the visitors of museums, galleries, and other exhibiting institutions.

Ute Meta Bauer: I'm Ute Meta Bauer and I'm responsible for the program of the Künstlerhaus Stuttgart, which is a place for artists with workshops and with an exhibition space. It's written down that I'm here as a curator, but I'm not really a curator. I first worked with an artist group for nine years; we were seven people. And, finally, I was left alone, so I have to decide how can I continue the same work, and the only possibility was to go into a kind of institution work, where I could continue to work with other people and to work together with other artists. The big difference to my position before is that I'm now paid for the same work—which is really a big difference. Usually, if you work in curating or in an organizational field as an artist, the people don't understand that you have to be paid. And I think these are things I'd like also to discuss, how things are held in that way. The big difference maybe for me compared to the other curators here is that [at the Künstlerhaus Stuttgart] our main audience, our main public, are other artists. I think this is the big difference. And so the program structure is also, I think, completely different than in other institutions.

Bischoff: My name is Ulrich Bischoff and I work in a museum, and this museum is a container of artworks, and I'm there since four days (laughs). What can I say?

Cahan: Which museum?

Bischoff: It is in Dresden, the museum for nineteenth- and twentieth-century painting [Gemäldegalerie Alte Meister].

(Laughter)

Fritz Rahmann: I'm Fritz Rahmann. I'm an artist. I've worked in, I think, quite divergent forms, and my experience with museums is not very rich. Most of my projects have been kind of anarchic things, and maybe the most well-known periods of the work has been in Berlin at the beginning of the '80s, or that is the best known. And that was just the experience to work without any institutional background or basis. What can be established in a single-handed way of action in the city that was Berlin. What was interesting in that time was it was not so intensely an administered space. So, there was a lot of material trends to the work, and out of this period of my work have come single projects in collaboration with institutions. But it is not an ideologically well formulated relation; it is incidental. My relation to institutions is incidental. There were actually very different experiences last year: one conflict, and one, I think, fruitful thing that is in the work. Helmut knows from Munich, maybe I could describe it afterwards. Thank you.

Iwona Blazwick : My name is Iwona Blazwick, and I'm based in London. I've worked both with institutions, primarily the Institute of Contemporary Arts, and I also run a space called the AIR Gallery [both in London]. I'm also working independently on exhibitions and projects, and also working with educational institutes, in particular, a cultural studies course in London, and also with a publisher. And so my interest really is in all aspects of, in a sense, communication, distribution, and those issues around the artist, the institution, the so-called mediators, and publics.

Renate Lorenz: I'm Renate Lorenz and I'm working with BüroBert together with Jochen Becker. And we decided for our work not to need to be paid, for the work in any case. So we don't want to be dependent on the possibility to be paid. And I've just started curating in Zurich at the Shedhalle, and I'm working there together with another woman, Sylvia Kafehsy. We try to work with thematic exhibition projects, and the first thing I'm doing there is called *Gamegirl*. This will be a project about the critique of technology. I'm not working together just with artists, but also with groups, which are doing political work. Feminist groups.

Cahan: Nonpaid?

Lorenz: I didn't say that we don't want to be paid for our work, this is not the position.

Jochen Becker: My name is Jochen Becker. I am working with Büro-Bert. I am earning my money as a critic. And we made a book called *Copyshop*. One interest in that book is to gather different projects which are not only artists', but political or social, projects. There are several groups coming together now, or forming and organizing, in the German-speaking area. The interest is to form a network—which, in Germany, it's very hard to organize very, very strictly, but to keep in contact and to organize that network. One of these, at the borderline, there is an organization of musicians

and autonomous working political groups and artists. That is, I think, a very interesting thing. And maybe we can talk about that. We work in a self-organized context and an institutional context.

Christian Philipp Müller: My name is Christian Philipp Müller, I'm Swiss, and I studied at Düsseldorf Art Academy in the early '80s, where I met Kasper König, or he met me (laughs). He asked me to become his assistant, in a way, because he had a job there that was called like "public sculpture," something like that, that was in his time, and he prepared the Münster sculpture show [Skulptur Projekte Münster] in '87. Before I studied art, I was trained as a graphic designer. And he hired me as an assistant to kind of invite a lot of artists to come to teach the students. I had to organize money, and that was my first contact in the real art world and real money and real, you know, backstage scenes. So, by using my skills as a graphic designer, Kasper König hired me as the main graphic designer for this show Skulptur Projekte Münster. I was there as a graphic designer, not as an artist. But by doing this, I was invited at the same time by a group of Belgian filmmakers from public TV to become like an artist-guide, an actor, to kind of criticize the show for them, which I was also part of— that was very tricky for me, but that was maybe an example of how you can be inside and want to be outside of the critique of something. After that, I was invited to do similar projects, for instance, in Amsterdam for an artist society which was founded in 1839. Similar to the structure of a *Kunstverein*, but I will talk about that tomorrow. I was hired as an artist, but they thought of me to curate a group show of the new members. Why I am here is to bring more clarity in what we're doing, each of us, either being a curator or an artist. I also like to have several functions. But after having the experience of last summer's group show and the failure of…um (laughs).

Fraser: We'll talk about it later.

Müller: Sorry, I'll go on for a little while longer, just for one more thing. I was researching several forms of cultural politics; for instance, I made works on André Malraux's function as cultural minister from '59 to '69 in France. We'll talk about that later, sorry.

Michael Clegg: I'm Michael Clegg, and I work with Martin Guttmann (laughs). So for the last couple of years, we've been doing work which attempted to sort of enlarge the context of the site of our exhibitions. We tried to consider work which would address a different audience, that would be in different places, besides the museum or gallery spaces, and at the same time, maintaining a link to the more traditional exhibition spaces and trying to position the work as something to mediate between these two pillars. So between a community where we'd often centre a project, to the museum that was affiliated with that community. I'm hoping in this symposium, these discussions, we will be able to…I mean, realizing that there is a great divergence between our practices, and therefore we will maybe resort generally, as a very loose term, to "services," as just a loose term that defines a set of, maybe, procedures, if not the typical shared concerns. But at the same time, it seems that possibly we could all benefit from

a simple exchange of information about how we proceed to present our work, what our relationship is to particular institutions. One feels that there is always a great benefit in the possibility of exchanging information. And it seems like a strange thing to say, because it's something that is readily available, but actually the opportunities that are possible between artists to discuss in detail what they do, and also the practical and material arrangements of how they go about producing the work, this is something that is not so common. Recently, we attempted some discussions like that in New York, and found that there's tremendous information that was very valuable and interesting for us. So I am hoping that there will be more of that here.

Stephan Dillemuth: My name is Stephan Dillemuth. I run a space in Cologne that's called Friesenwall 120. I've run this for four years; it's about to be closed down now. I started actually looking for a studio space and I found this storefront very close to the old gallery district. And then I decided to use it as a space for shows and tried to define, "How can a space like that function in a neighbourhood like that?" That means experiments with shows coming out of different sources, some from an art context, others from a more social context or neighbourhood context. I'm looking forward to what happens here. I think we should talk.

Barry: My name is Judith Barry, and I was trained as an architect and spent a long time in various schools studying lots of different things. Sometimes I collaborate with an architect, Ken Saylor, on exhibition designs, and I also work commercially in between music, television, and various other kinds of commercial video endeavours. My art practice tends toward installation, based on a research methodology, which leads to different kinds of productions. I don't know what I'm going to get out of this conference. I'm curious to see what happens.

Martin Guttmann: My name is Martin Guttmann. Michael Clegg is my partner. He mentioned a few themes that we are working with now: the idea of trying to find alternative sites for art, the idea of trying to look a little bit closer into the dynamics between various publics and the artists and institutions. We started working in 1980. The first body of work we did for quite a long time was centred around the gallery space. We looked at the gallery space as a context and we tried to ask ourselves what really defines the activities in the gallery space. We came up with this equation that artists basically produce objects that function as portraits of the people by them. And using this very basic formula, we identified portraiture as the most quintessential aspect of gallery-style pieces. We proceeded doing a lot of portraiture that used this kind of literalization strategy, actually photographing collectors as the work that was shown in the gallery. Towards the end of the '80s, we became a little bit disenchanted with our own formula. And we began to feel that it was no longer just a question of the development of our own work, but a lot of changes happened globally, and the world that we were working in was no longer the same. We felt that there was a need to really expand our own horizons and to try to really think about the place of art in the post–Cold War world, where the basic parameters are: a lot of poverty, and the existence of certain institutions cannot be taken for granted. And artists are called to justify their own practices in ways that were not absolutely needed. In earlier periods, there was a lot of…the economy was doing better, etc. So the projects that we're working on now are a way of really re-evaluating the place that art can have in the world of today. It seems that conferences like this could really be extremely useful for exchanging information, for various people who in their own practices try to expand along the horizon.

Renée Green: My name is Renée Green, and, well, I guess I'm the last person to talk. I'm an artist and I'm based in New York, but I'm living in Berlin this year on a DAAD Fellowship. I've been working in a diverse number of ways—my background is diverse. I guess that's why I'm currently—official statistics—I'm currently working as an artist with the Whitney [Museum of American Art's] Independent Study Program [in New York]. I work in ways involving various aspects of pedagogy, as well as writing criticism, and I also make work in various locations. I came [to this Working Group] partly because I'm in the process of working on a symposium, which I'm trying to figure out many things for. And I wanted to mention that I've worked with a number of the people in this room on various ways of trying to communicate about issues that I hope are going to come up during the course of the weekend in discussion.

Draxler: I'm Helmut Draxler and I'm actually an art historian. Since two years, I'm the director of the

Kunstverein München. A small institution that has no spread between its curators and its directors. So what I tried to do from the beginning is to invest strongly in projects which involve artists and what we described before: curatorial functions. So I worked with Christian for a while, and with Andrea. I also worked with Christopher Williams last fall. It's very hard for me to find guidelines for the organizational basis of these projects. And the situations are very complex, between a straightforward basis and how you are supposed to pay a fee. When you have a project—in Christian's case, for example, at the same time objects were produced by the Kunstverein, and I'm not blaming you, but objects were sold with [your] gallery and the gallery never gave us more money. But you always have this kind of problem. And with Christopher Williams, for example, it was even more complex, because we're kind of even misunderstanding what exactly the term "project" means or whatever. I mean, it was really a misunderstanding from his side. He completely understood this [show at the Kunstverein] as a situation providing him the possibility of producing new sets of objects for New York–based galleries and their never needing to pay us back. And never even intending to help us to finance things like that. Not worried about paying back any kind of material investment. So I think, for me, it was very clear that we had to take a kind of change of policy in this direction, and we're not going to work on this basis anymore. I feel that there is a very strong need to come clear about this subject. And so we need to find guidelines, in my opinion, from this symposium. This Working Group should also be about that.

Fraser: Well, maybe I'll make one or two more remarks. I've trained as an artist, I went to art school. I'm actually an art school dropout. I started writing art criticism and, in the process, became involved in questions about institutions, and particularly museums and museum education. I started doing performances in the form of gallery tours, which I initially thought of as a kind of art criticism in action and, in the process, became engaged in working with education departments, perhaps more than curatorial departments and institutions. And I always thought about taking up different kinds of institutional functions and not working in galleries. I started working in galleries in 1990, I think. In the past year I have, in particular, felt a kind of conflict between what my initial goals as an artist were—they would still represent, I think, my basic beliefs about what I want art making to be—and the kinds of demands that not only galleries but also, I suppose, exhibition spaces within museums make on artists who don't necessarily want to engage in production, which I don't. Not that I'm against production, but my interests are essentially in social relations within institutions and between institutions and audiences. And I want to work where those relations are enacted most directly. So my interest in doing this [*Services* project], and my particular interest, I suppose, in the idea of "service," is to try to develop not only a material basis but also a kind of intellectual basis for thinking about an art practice that's really not just "anti-production" or "anti-market," which I think is how this sort of line that I'm more or less in has been articulated. But more in a positive sense, as something else, and asking, "What is that going to be?" And that's what I'm interested in here for myself as an artist.

Draxler: Shall we have a brief look at the materials?

Fraser: I think that we should speak a moment about the schedule, because we were supposed to start with the second session at 2:30 pm. It's now 1:45 pm. The other thing Helmut and I wanted to do was run through some of this material. Quickly. It's an enormous amount of material. I don't know how quick we could do it. But I guess even whether we do that or not, we probably won't be able to start the second session at 2:30 pm. So, maybe we could make a presentation of this material tomorrow morning? Or we could push everything back a little bit today? Maybe have lunch, come back, have a quick presentation, and then try to start the second session at 3:00 pm instead and go a half-hour later? Are there any suggestions? Comments? Impulses?

Becker: All the people will be there on Monday, so maybe we have it at the beginning of Monday, too?

Fraser: Many people are leaving Monday morning. Yeah.

Becker: OK. But also it could be good to see the material pretty soon.

Green: I think it would be good to give all the material after lunch.

Fraser: After lunch?

Draxler: Yeah, so let's do it in a reduced form, but just to make some layers clear.

Fraser: So let's say this is a short lunch then. Can we have lunch in forty minutes, do you think? Let's plan, then, to meet back here at 2:30 pm. And we'll run through the material and maybe talk a little bit about the format for the discussions. And then let's try to start the second session at 3:00 pm. Could we synchronize our watches?

Guttmann: That would give me time to eat a Big Mac but not a large fries.

(Laughter)

Fraser: We could always get takeout and bring it in.

(Laughter)

Von Bismarck: There is a place that's apparently OK, up the road.

Fraser: That [place] is quite slow.

Draxler: Pretty good but quite slow.

Fraser: On your maps, there's a place for pizza I think? Called Vesuvio's?

(Laughter)

Fraser: And there's also a sandwich place across the street, where you can get a salad, you can get a sandwich. And there's coffee and juice and water and tea here.

Draxler: Cookies.

Fraser: And cookies.

Von Bismarck: Two other things which might be useful: If you want to collect your money, maybe the breaks will be a good idea to do that. The other thing is, those of you who need a computer, Diethelm Stoller is over at the Writing Center, which is on that map, I think. Number three. And he can supply you with the option to use the computer if you want to prepare something. It might get more difficult if you delay that, just because the centre is usually closed on the weekend.

Wuggenig: Go there and speak with him, or another time. We should arrange a time.

Draxler: We should make it probably on the second break or so.

Von Bismarck: Who needs a computer? And what do you need?

Guttmann: A printer.

Fraser: Apple?

Guttmann: Yes.

Von Bismarck: So why don't we just—I mean, I can ring him and say a time that is likely to be more convenient?

Bauer: But we can't work with four people on the same printer at the same time.

Wuggenig: There's many computers.

Working Group
Session Two

Serving Institutions
Saturday, January 22, 1994

Presentations:
Judith Barry
Renée Green
Fred Wilson

Much project work implies an expert-client relation between artist and institution. When the institution becomes the artist's client, how does this affect artistic autonomy and the possibility of critique?

What are the implications of the professional model implied? What is the nature of the institution's interest in the artist's services?

Andrea Fraser: In the process of planning this event, it grew from a weekend working group and an exhibition to an ongoing project focused on the changing relations between artists and institutions from 1969 to the present. That's extremely ambitious, and I don't know how far we will actually go, but this material [Helmut and I have collected] I think of as a sort of beginning of that project. A first effort at collecting documents relating to those changing relationships. There's a lot missing. There is little on actual artist projects before the contemporary material. There are a number of reasons for that, which I can go into later.

The material starts in 1969 with the Art Workers' Coalition. And the date, 1969—it has to do with the Art Workers' Coalition and another fact that was drawn to my attention in conversation with Michael Asher, which was that in this show, the *Spaces* exhibition, which was 1969 to '70, it was the first time that the Museum of Modern Art [in New York] provided an artist fee. It was also the first time that he received an artist fee. And it wasn't at his request; it may have been at the request of Dan Flavin, it wasn't clear… Beatrice actually tried to speak with Dan, but he didn't remember anything. It could have been Robert Morris. We don't know from looking at the files. But, for me, the idea of "service," and the relationship between a service and a fee—the minute you start talking about an artist fee, you are talking about a service; a fee is for a service. So, I'm interested in that whole history. And this is the prehistory in a way. I see that as being a culmination of a year of changing relationships between artists and the professional staff at the Museum of Modern Art. And this in a certain way is a case study of that going up to this material about the unionization of the Museum of Modern Art, which began in 1971. It came to a head during a strike in 1973, and then continued on. So, where it starts in 1969, where the Art Workers' Coalition began, it started with a group of kinetic sculptures. There was an exhibition at the Museum of Modern Art and Takis, an artist who had exhibited in that show, had a number of works in the collection of the Museum of Modern Art, and one of those works was selected for the show by the curator of the show. And Takis did not want that work to be shown. It was shown anyway, so he, and a few other artists, went in and removed that piece from the museum during a press conference. They moved it to the sculpture garden. Included in that group of artists was Hans Haacke, who was showing at the same gallery as Takis, strangely, and was doing primarily kinetic sculpture and environmental sculpture at that time. And this quickly developed within the first month to a list of demands.

Martin Guttmann: Why did he have his piece pulled out?

Fraser: Well, it's unclear. What's interesting to me is that it would be this kind of sculpture that would motivate this kind of action. My thinking is that this was a work that was demanding a different kind of treatment than other work demanded. At that point, perhaps, the installation work, the minimalist work, did not have the kind of authority that that sculpture did at that time. So those artists didn't feel comfortable making new demands on institutions around it. But this work [by Takis] did. The other artists who went with him also had complaints about the way that they were presented. I think it had to do with the way it [Takis's work] was separated or not separated from the audience, it had to do with how it was placed, it had to do with the aesthetic but also technical issues of the installation.

Helmut Draxler: It was one of these group shows where they never ask artists, they just have a thematic— a show about the machine for instance—and just put, I don't know how many artists, but with one piece next to the other, so it was very clear how the space was devised. And then this was really an original demand. We should get to the demands.

Fraser: Well, if we look at the first set of demands—and this month is the twenty-fifth anniversary—the first demand is that the museum shall hold a public hearing on the topic of the museum's relationship to artists and society. That's demand number one. Demand number twelve is that the museum should include among its staff persons qualified to handle the installation, maintenance, and technological work. So you can see the range, and perhaps why this work was instigating this kind of activity. This was in early '69, January '69, the way that the Art Workers' Coalition grew partly as the vehicle through which artists were trying to connect themselves to the movements in the United States at the time—the student movements, anti-war movements, the women's movement, and Black Power, and the school riots. And how it developed…Helmut, do you want to—

Draxler: Yeah, it developed with this original group. By March 10 it was already eighteen to twenty people, and they were requesting the public hearing, and all of those demands made formally were all related to certain items of control, and that artists should constitute a certain part of the board of trustees, and other requests like this. From March 10 to April 10 there was a massive change that took place where the number of members of the Art Workers' Coalition really exploded, but they didn't get the public hearing there at the museum, so they decided to make their own public hearing. It had a title that came from one of the committees of, well, it wasn't the Art Workers' Coalition yet, but just in its beginning: "An open public hearing on the subject: What should be the program of the art workers regarding museum reform, and to establish the program of an open art workers coalition."

So, in this hearing, the Art Workers' Coalition took a new form, and all these people invited and listed here [in the provided document] made different kinds of statements with different requests. There is "museum reform" in the title here, but this is only one part of the politicization that took place. Many different items were discussed. I quote from the statement by Lucy Lippard: "The reason for continuing from Takis's action was the fact of such a transaesthetic solidarity, the fact that there was support for further discussion despite basic disagreement with much of the first group's program." So, there was this need for broad solidarity and unity beyond the competitive structure of artistic individualism. We have it here so everyone can look through it, and it really is an amazing series of statements from different kinds of artists, if not very famous artists. Carl Andre, Hans Haacke, and Lucy Lippard, who was also a critic. But more so other people, for instance, David Lee, who I didn't know, and he wrote a really great statement where the whole program of institutional critique is formulated, and which has not been recognized in this history. There are artist statements about the critique of galleries, critique of art schools, a proposal for the establishment of a Black wing at the Museum of Modern Art in memory of Dr. Martin Luther King Jr., a statement for Black and Puerto Rican artists, and you had more anarchist statements from a Stephen Phillips, who asked for another wing in the Museum of Modern Art where artists could live and occasionally hang their work. There is such a wide variety, between very personal statements and very depressed statements about the conditions, and on the other hand you have statements like the one from Jean Toche of Guerrilla Art Action Group, which had this more anarchist position, where he says: "The actions should be directed against all museums, and all art institutions… not a reform of the museum, but wanting effective participation…not a new union of blue-collar or white-collar workers, but a real commune of artists."

Fraser: This is a great piece here, a great graphic: "Department of Cultural Affairs…No." Direct and to the point.

Ulrich Bischoff: Can you say some words about the name, Art Workers' Coalition? Where does it come from?

Fraser: It emerged around the hearing. Helmut, do you know? There was always this reference to "art workers." It was a massive group, upwards of 250 people. But I also wanted to talk about this section here, in the beginning the demands. The artists are addressing the institution as an undifferentiated entity, and what started as a dispute over curatorial practice was perhaps even more addressed to the professional staff of the Museum of Modern Art. At this point you see there is this demonstration in response to an exhibition of the collection of Nelson A. Rockefeller, who had just finished his campaign for governorship of New York. It says here: "The Art Workers Coalition is here to save artists the embarrassment of being identified with the political ambitions of Nelson Rockefeller." But at this point there is a kind of differentiation that is introduced in the institution: it's no longer seen as just a single entity but is seen within a structure, in the sense of the board of trustees and professional staff. So one of the things that's very interesting to me, and why I think this is very pertinent to our discussions, is to see the sympathy and identification that develops between the Art Workers' Coalition and the staff of the Museum of Modern Art.

Susan Cahan: But weren't there a lot of people on staff who were artists?

Fraser: Yes. I mean, I don't know how many were active at this point.

Cahan: It would be something to research, because, particularly on the security staff, there were some artists who subsequently became very well known.

Fraser: There were also artists who were not taking art world jobs, just addressing this institution as an institution, but then realizing that there are complex conflicts and sympathies of interest that emerge and develop. Artists who were working within the institution and members of the professional staff who are in conflict with the trustees themselves, and who are advocating for their own unionization and conditions. It struck me as a very important development for these kinds of relations. What the Museum of Modern Art did, instead of sponsoring this hearing that the Art Workers' Coalition demanded, they set up an artist relations committee. Here you have a report where the members of that committee are going into different places where the Art Workers' Coalition and other artists' groups are having meetings. Jennifer Licht [associate curator at the museum] reported from a meeting on the Lower East Side: "There is a suggestion by Barnett Newman that the artists demonstrate in David Rockefeller's office." And Jennifer Licht was the curator of the *Spaces* show. So, although I don't know, I would imagine there might be a connection between her response to artists' demands for a fee and her own position within the institution. I can't say anything definitive about that, because they [the Museum of Modern Art] wouldn't let me look at the files.

Draxler: I think this is very important, this next step of the collaboration between staff at the Modern and the Art Workers' Coalition. Above here [in the presented document] is an image from perhaps the most famous action of the Art Workers' Coalition, the demonstration at the Museum of Modern Art in response to the My Lai massacre, and these letters make clear the idea was to do it together between museum staff and artists. There were museum staff members who strongly supported the Art Workers' Coalition and helped produce this poster, which appropriates a photo of the My Lai massacre showing piles of bodies on a dirt road, and adds the text: "Q: And babies? A: And babies." But when the board of trustees at the museum [namely, businessmen Nelson Rockefeller and William S. Paley] saw the proofs of this poster, they pulled the museum's support for producing and distributing the poster. So, we see this kind of critical relationship between board and staff within the process of professionalization.

Fraser: The first paragraph says here: "A poster protesting the My Lai massacre was proposed during a discussion about ways artists participate in formulating the museum's program. Irving Petlin was then asked by Arthur Drexler"—who I think was assistant director at that time—"if he would be interested in attending a staff meeting at the department of painting and sculpture in which the program would be discussed. He answered: 'Can I answer your question with a question, which might confuse the issue or it might not—could you see me coming to a meeting in which the policy-making function of the museum is being discussed and I come up with a proposal that today there was a massacre at Son My, and I feel the museum should issue a vast distribution of a poster so violently outraged from this act, that it will place absolutely in print and in public this feeling that the museum's staff and all the artists who have contributed to its greatness are outraged by the massacre at Son My?' And then it notes, 'Applause.'" This is a memo from the museum.

Ute Meta Bauer: I think the big difference is that the structures of museums in America are so different from the structures here. Because here you have these board members and trustees only in the *Kunstvereins* or private organizations, which are supported governmentally but are still independent in a way. But the museums here are a completely different structure, and I think it's important to recognize, because there are a lot of people from abroad here, and maybe we should explain the structures in America and the structures here?

Draxler: I think we should come to this point a little bit later.

Fraser: I mean in 1968 there were demonstrations in Venice [at the Venice Biennale] and there were demonstrations at documenta [4].

Christian Philipp Müller: In the 1968 documenta, and there is documentation, the French artists refused and the American artists participated. There was a big discussion at the press conference in front of documenta of why after May '68 artists couldn't participate anymore in this.

Draxler: There were more specific demonstrations also, against the killing of activists. And there was activism for political art at documenta. Because documenta '68 represented almost exactly the same kind of art from documenta [III in] '64. This standard with pop art and minimalist art. So there were conflicts between participants of different aesthetic fields. But I don't know exactly why certain forms of art and self-representation were not included, and this would be something to research.

Fraser: I just want to go back to the acknowledgements from the *Spaces* show: "An exhibition in which the installation becomes the actual realization of the work of art in rooms, and must be planned and built according to the artist's needs, challenges the usual role of the museum and makes unaccustomed demands on staff and resources. A museum traditionally houses and conserves objects of art, but now it has become responsible for the execution of the artist's idea. It calls for collaboration of people and flexible adjustment in roles and responsibilities." So, I thought that was very interesting in this context.

Martin Guttmann: I wanted to ask: Was there a sense that what necessitated the Art Workers' Coalition was something about the art, or was it a question of organizing solidarity? It could be both, but looking at the composition of the people here [in the provided documentation], I find that very few of them produce... I think that the only minimalist in the group, Carl Andre...I mean, with stuff on the floor, you don't really need flexibility.

(Laughter)

Fraser: There are questions there. And questions of distribution and maintenance. When is that an art object and when is it not an art object.

Guttmann: But so there was a discussion about the art. Because it seems that the kinds of people that could benefit the most on these issues are not [listed as participating in the Art Workers' Coalition].

Fraser: Who are you thinking of who could benefit the most?

Guttmann: I don't know, like Bruce Nauman. Flavin is not here.

Fraser: It's surprising that Barnett Newman is there.

Draxler: One of the first items discussed was a show at the Museum of Modern Art of abstract expressionism in which the museum requested work from the artists, not as a loan, but as a gift to the museum. When the institution was attacked by the Art Workers' Coalition, people like Barnett Newman and some of the classicalists of the '50s had to defend themselves from the Art

Workers' Coalition, but some of them also later joined the coalition. It's also important to see that in the beginning they were all European artists, and then there were artists from the Caribbean and Black communities, so it's clear that the coalition membership goes beyond aesthetic standard parameters.

Fraser: I mean, when the meetings were 250 people…The art world is not that big. ACT UP meetings were 300 people. I think that there are more people who are participating but who are not speaking in the public hearing for instance, and that some of the people in the public hearing were not active participants. The hearing was open, anyone could go up and talk for three minutes. So I think it's difficult to answer.

What we have here is…There was an organization called Women Artists in Revolution. This is a copy of the publication, which also contains material on actions against the Whitney Museum [of American Art in New York] and other museums, specific demands that were being made by women at that time, and the emerging women's movement. Here we have a proposal for community cultural centres.

Draxler: This is also maybe an important point, because that's also in Hans Haacke's statement at the public hearing. There was a plan to build a new museum of modern art in Midtown Manhattan, and Haacke's argument was that this is totally wrong, because you have to decentralize. And this question about community cultural centres came up.

Fraser: There was a debate at that time about what it meant for the Museum of Modern Art to work in different urban communities. And whether that was a form of urban cultural imperialism or not. But I think we should move on.

This is the draft of the contract that the Art Workers' Coalition put together for galleries. This is a first draft of the contract that was drawn up by a lawyer [Robert Projansky] working with Seth Siegelaub, which was published in the catalogue for documenta 5 in 1972. And this was sent around New York with a questionnaire in 1971. These are the actual final contracts which Hans Haacke continues to use, and he gave these to us. Over here is material about the cancellation of Hans Haacke's Guggenheim [Museum] exhibition [in New York]. If you are looking at the development of the relationship between artists and museum professionals, in this case the exhibition was cancelled by the board of trustees. In this instance, the curator of the exhibition, Edward Fry, wrote a statement in support of Hans Haacke and condemning the cancellation. He was fired four days later and never worked in a museum again. And Hans Haacke never had a show with an institution in the United States again until '68 at the New Museum [in New York]—

Cahan: 1986.

Fraser: Yes, of course, '86, not '68! But, so, there were some very serious consequences for individuals in these shifting allegiances which artists and museum professionals were coming up against. I want to move into the strike at the Modern, there are a couple of quotes from this that I want to read.

This is a discussion between Lawrence Alloway and John Copeland from a strike committee of PASTA [Professional and Administrative Staff Association], the staff union of the Museum of Modern Art. This is actually a question from one of the interviewers: "I was wondering if it would be useful to say that you are in the midst of a role-searching activity, it seems to me that when the museum began it was in the hands of a few trustees who were very wealthy and put out the money, I'm talking about the Rockefellers, the Guggenheims, etc. However, there has been a continuous quarrel between their own appointees and the nature of the trustee function. It's gone on since its foundation. Nowadays there is more and more of an awareness that the professionals are not just hired functionaries but intelligent and well-trained people of their particular discipline."

[Alloway and Copeland's conversation also covers how] there is a proposal that museums which are chartered educational institutions actually function like educational institutions. And there being a model among university professors of a kind of unionization and professional association. And a professional autonomous standing which did not exist really for museum professionals at this time. There was another point also in reference to the model of university professors, in a discussion about the professional association of university professors: "Their existing in universities at the turn of the century, and the problems that university faculties then articulated, such as subsidizing institutions by their own impoverishment."

That phrase, "subsidizing institutions by their own impoverishment," this has again to do with the American museum structure. Which I think artists and museum professionals are coming up against. That is the essential situation: of people working with private nonprofit institutions, where you are living a privilege or an obligation, and to give up oneself to that institution outside of professional practices that would [not] be accepted in other kinds of contexts.

Draxler: In Germany in the 1970s, founded in '75, there was an organization called Internationales Künstlergremium, the International Artists Council. And I think we have to bring that together with this other institution, the Artists Meeting for Cultural Change, also from '75, but in New York. It indicates a shift of interests that are no longer in direct connection with the 1960s phase. I mean, the Künstlergremium, they made a list of possible members, and all these possible members are well-known artists of the time, and it wasn't an artist association but an elitist club. The program was very clearly defined away from social questions to spiritual ones, which is emphasized several times here [in] some material from the conference they had. It's interesting as a kind of symptom. From the European context, particularly the German context—here you have the cover of a German art magazine—it says: "Culture is not produced in the cultural ministries. Artists speak about what they are most interested in." So, you know, you have this state cultural politics, on a very official level, and then this opposition.

Fraser: What we have from the European context, we don't have prepared here [for the Working Group]…

Draxler: Yeah, we don't have so much here. Stressing this superiority of the spiritual element, I think this is a very symptomatic formulation of this professionalization. That's what I see. Tending away from the social concerns. It's not about self-representation but raising the level of the discussion about art. Maintaining artists' freedoms. A whole set of these kinds of more or less very conservative questions.

Bischoff: May I interrupt? I think that some of the members of the Internationales Künstlergremium became a bit corrupt. It was founded to bring artists from East Europe to West Europe. This was one of the ideas of Robert Filliou, [George] Brecht, and [Josef] Beuys: they wanted to have a council to bring artists from East Europe to come to West Europe, and also to come to the other side. So you know, it was a bridge over the wall.

Audience member (Gislind Nabakowski): Yes, this was the origin, which is why they got money. But in the end it was perverted. Already by the 1980s.

Draxler: This was not said in any of the initial statements.

Fraser: There's a lot from this point that is not included. I mean, just from the United States, one would have to include artists' organizations, the work of people like Gordon Matta-Clark, exhibitions like *Rooms* at P.S. 1 [Contemporary Art Center in New York], I mean there are all sorts of things that are not dealt with at all here.

Draxler: There's a very loose end!

Fraser: A very loose end. So, I think we will just wrap up.

Draxler: But I think from this material here that it's very clear you have this activist early history of self-representation, then you have the relationship to the professional staff of institutions, and then you also have some elements like this of very specific individual artistic practices which later become concerned with institutional critique. That's why we have within this context protests, then contracts, ironic relationships to what Seth Siegelaub is doing, and Hans Haacke's "visitors' poll" piece [*MoMA Poll*, 1970]. So, we just tried to integrate and show that these kinds of practices related directly to these beginnings—but there's always gaps—and this all continues in the '80s.

Judith Barry: I just wanted to add two points. It's important to talk about the interdisciplinary approach of minimal art. I think more than any other art practice, it actually introduced ideas from outside the art arena into art practice in an overt way. It's fairly well documented in the work of Robert Smithson in particular; even Rosalind Krauss has written about this. Also going back a bit earlier to the 1930s and '40s, if you look at the decline of the social realism movement in the US and the Marshall Plan, Serge Guilbaut's book discusses this. And also Barnett Newman's writings are really informative about that period.

Draxler: The Rockefeller case that we put up here is similar to that. It's kind of a prehistory of institutional critique.

Barry: Also the WPA movement [the Works Progress Administration's Federal Art Project] in the US is interesting to look at. Even though it didn't overtly talk about these issues, there was an implied institutional critique in the ways that artists were representing certain social issues. Unfortunately, the scholarship, to my knowledge, hasn't been done around that. Someone here might know more about that. But there was a lot of work done in that time period, mentioned in correspondence between the participants, that did, through the agency of representation, call attention to these issues.

Draxler: I mean, there are some texts about this history from the Art Workers' Coalition. I can't remember right now who exactly is stressing this point about some of the work being continued from the '30s and '40s, these very special unionizations of artists and different artist groups.

Fraser: This is not so focused, but the relationship between artists and institutions, and particularly around the development of artists taking up institutions, and through these shifting sympathies, curatorial functions within their work, and also curators developing an interest in a collaborative relationship with artists as opposed to just borrowing the work—this is sort of what we were trying to pull out of what was in fact a very broad set of struggles, and a very complex set of struggles.

The other things that were going on in terms of artistic practice at this time that we have no documentation of are, for instance Christian Boltanksi's shows where he produces museological installations from the contents of people's homes, and there is Claes Oldenburg's *The Store* [1961], which is another whole kind of trajectory. Daniel Buren we

have no material from. I had kind of a difficult situation with John Knight, about finding a way to present material documenting how he developed certain policies that he has—certain fee structures, and certain contractual relations that he works within. And with Michael Asher it's also complex. And Daniel Buren. These are three people who developed fee structures for their work in the early '70s. In terms of service, that is a notion we were trying to look at.

In terms of curatorial activity and things like that, we pick that up here with Group Material, formed in 1980, coming out of organizations, like Artists Meeting for Cultural Change, that came out of the second half of the 1970s. These were organizations of artists organized towards nonart issues. Group Material came out of that more than some of these institutional critique trajectories. In doing so, they were taking up a kind of alternative gallerist position— organizing shows, inviting people in the neighbourhood to bring work by, staging shows in the subway, and things like that. So we are looking at that here. We mostly focused on Group Material and Louise Lawler, who from the late '70s started to work within the publicity materials that galleries sent out, to work within invitation cards, press releases, to take up different kinds of institutional positions and to use gallery functions as part of her work. This here is the first instance that I know of an artist making an installation from a museum collection, and that was Louise Lawler's exhibition *Home/Museum* at the Wadsworth Atheneum [Museum of Art in Hartford, Connecticut] in 1984. So, that's where we pick up, in the '80s, to look at some of the current practices and collaborative relationships between artists and institutions. Although there are many other examples and trajectories to look at. But that's what we got.

Fred Wilson: I just wanted to mention one other example, that was going on in the late 1960s and early 1970s, concurrent with the Art Workers' Coalition, and that was the Spiral group. It was a Black art group in New York that I'm sure was also involved in the Art Workers' Coalition, but they came together primarily around issues of exclusion. What made people know about them was the Metropolitan Museum show *Harlem on My Mind* [in New York], which was [Met director] Thomas Hoving's effort to bring Harlem into the Met, but was almost an ethnographic effort, and included no African American artists. So there was this big strike, and these meetings organized by Spiral around that exhibition. Do you know when *Harlem on My Mind* was? I think it was 1969.

Bauer: There is an enormous hole for Germany. I think you must know there could be much more presented here from Germany.

Fraser: Yeah. As I said before, we were not trying to show something more comprehensive. I suppose it could be possible.

Audience member (Gislind Nabakowski): So are you going to do more of a European research as the project develops?

Fraser: I was looking into the American context to begin with. I mean, don't look at me, I was…

(Laughter)

Draxler: The European situation is decentralized so much more, so you have very different developments and very different places. It's not that you have one museum of modern art. So you have a very different situation. I mean, this problem is wherever we are. There are these kinds of European institutions which are supporting the American art scene at a very high degree and they are public institutions. Also universities. Christian can tell you how hard it is to get a job at Cooper Union [in New York], and how easy it is for an American artist to get a teaching job here.

Müller: In America, they are not used to having someone in art school teach who is not American. And Hans Haacke told me that you have to do the dirty laundry. You have to pay a lawyer a lot of money to do that…

Draxler: It's just too easy to describe European development as a kind of deficit. And it's very complex. But you just don't have that mainstream discourse.

Guttmann: At least in France, the situation of this critique of aspects of the museum is very strong. Of course in their case this critique did not take the artists towards the direction of service; on the contrary, it took them more into the direction of asking for more money. Really, in my mind, this discussion should be taken back to the late 1950s, in terms of France. What marks the difference to a certain extent is that '69 came after a whole decade where America presented itself to the world via art. And that's why '69, at the height of the Vietnam War, a lot of political activism, artists could take a position in New York vis-à-vis art and feel that they were doing something viable. This is something that is a little bit difficult to understand, because here it is one of the most eventful periods in recent history, and all these artists are doing is criticizing the Museum of Modern Art—and you can see the importance of what they were doing. But at the same time, I think art had such a central place in the self-representation of the United States to the world, so that when people were doing art-politics, they actually felt that they were doing something extremely important.

Fraser: Yes, but it was also about cleaning house. It's not just about "what in the world is the most important thing" at any given moment. I think very few of us are living our lives that way.

Guttmann: That's too easy. I think that's too easy.

Fraser: Part of it is strategic, and this is the Hans Haacke example: get Mr. Rockefeller to where he wants to look as clean as he can.

Guttmann: Yeah, but at the same time, there are the Columbia [University] riots, 1968 and '69 [in New York], so you can imagine it's the same city, very similar culturally. You have the students trying to clean house, but they really managed to mobilize all the population. They got the Harlem community activists to— You know, they really…

Fraser: But there were also people in the art world who were working in communities, who were part of the movement, again, who were involved in the anti-war movement.

Wilson: Yeah. It's all the same thing, it's all the same thing.

Draxler: There was Paris and there was Düsseldorf, and there were many other places. The same protest movement, more or less, was here [in Germany] and produced a lot of radical stuff. But it's not possible to reconstruct these histories. You just get these figures like Jörg Immendorff, or Beuys. Beuys is the biggest symptom of how that history here in Germany was historicized. So, how do we construct histories like this? Is it possible?

Fraser: Whether it's possible—and there are so many different histories you could talk about—but the question for me is where are we and what is our history.

Guttmann: I don't think they weren't doing something interesting because they weren't getting involved in riots. On the contrary, they were doing something important and they knew they were doing something important. And that's what I take to be the real difference between the European and American situations: that art was extremely important in the United States in the late 1960s, and it just didn't have the same importance in Europe. Because the whole postwar American culture was sold to Europe, in big shows like the Venice Biennale and documenta. That's how America presented itself.

Fraser: That would relate to activity in Europe more than in the United States. I don't know how many of these artists worked that much in Europe. When there were demonstrations in Venice, it was definitely about American imperialism and its relationship to the exploitation of culture, and the Museum of Modern Art is behind that, but you don't find that in any of these documents [collected for the Working Group]. They are not about the international council, they are not about programs in Latin America, or the programs in Europe. They're not about that. They are about something else.

Guttmann: Yeah, but that was given.

Fraser: Was it?

Guttmann: I think so, yeah. I mean, there are massacres in Vietnam, and you are cutting a few blocks and putting them on the floor like Carl Andre.

Fraser: A lot of people would ask the same question about what you are doing in New York in 1988 with hundreds of thousands of people dying of AIDS. So it's a question of where you are and what kind of history is your history, or which you identify with. For me, what this is about is looking at where we are in our practices, what kinds of relations we are involved in, and asking what are the social and political possibilities of those situations and relations. Some of us are working in institutions and some of us are working in communities in different kinds of ways. And there are different kinds of practices represented in this room. But to me it's very problematic to construct a hierarchy and use that as a basis for a discussion of what we are doing here now.

Bauer: There was a very strong movement throughout Europe and there are some very proud moments in friendship. I mean, you can't have all of it represented, that's clear. You can't make a comparison between American history and European, because, as you said [Helmut], it is decentralized. But there were a lot of movements, a lot of projects.

Fraser: Well, I think of this as a case study of New York and what was going on. It's not exactly what I would like to have, but it is what it is.

Audience member (Gislind Nabakowski): So are you going to further collect material? What are you looking for now?

Fraser: Well, I was interested in collecting more material about the concrete relationships of art workers, in their work and behind the work. That's what I spent a lot of time trying to get in touch with particular artists about: not wanting, or not being able, to share material.

Bischoff: I don't think we should try and get a whole history. It's good to have some aspects to continue the discussion, and if certain aspects are wrong, then we stop. But we shouldn't try to fulfill it because it's too much.

Fraser: I was invited here, but as an American, I don't feel it's appropriate for me to take on German cultural production and political activity in the last twenty-five years. I can't do that. I really want to know about that, but that can also function as a kind of appropriation.

Bauer: Then I think it just has to be clear then, the context, for this selection of material. The country of this research.

Renée Green: But if it's considered as an ongoing project, then we could see what the students want to do.

Fraser: Yes, because as this [*Services* project] goes places, for me, it's not appropriate for general audience institutions, but rather the institutions that are engaged in educational programs in one form or another. And that this [Kunstraum iteration] is the beginning, and that it would be added to by people doing their own research. My hope is that this is a catalyst.

(The Working Group concludes discussion of the research materials pinned to the wall and walk back to the table for further discussion.)

Guttmann: So, the question is: How could they bring themselves to think it was important? Did people doing art at the time think that what they were doing was really important? The answer is not so clear; some did and some didn't. But the Art Workers' Coalition did, and for good reason. The question is—

Fraser: What is the reason?

Guttmann: Yeah, and what I want to suggest is that it had something to do with their using art to present the stakes of the world.

Fraser: What I was suggesting is that it had to do with an ongoing investigation by artists of their own conditions and relations of their own practice, and that's what I'm focusing on. And the expansion of that from formal and institutional conditions starts to talk about politics in a much broader sense.

Cahan: What do you see as being the relationship between the stuff that you presented from the '60s and the '70s and what's going on now?

Fraser: What I was most interested in bringing out has to do with the collaborative relationships between artists and museum professionals that seemed to emerge at that moment around agitation for what were, to some extent, professional interests, but which were contingent upon an identification of a set of social conflicts, of class conflicts. The interests of artists and professionals were in conflict with the interests of the trustees. The function and history of those institutions were defined by those interest. I think that relates absolutely to what this is about: it's about emerging forms of collaboration and conflict between artists and curators, and artists and institutions, but particularly museum professionals.

Draxler: We should start with the presentations.

Fraser: Does everyone already feel exhausted? Judith, Renée, and Fred wanted to make presentations today on the subject of "Serving Institutions," and I guess the three of you can decide what order you would like to go in.

Barry: Who wants to go first?

Green: You've got more visual aids, [Fred].

Wilson: Yeah, this is going to be quick, so we might as well get it over with. I just thought I would go over three projects really briefly and then talk about the issues that came up around those projects in a kind of open-ended way. As I mentioned before, I was working in museums [in New York]—the American Museum of Natural History, the Metropolitan, and the American Craft Museum—all in their education departments, simultaneously, in the mid '70s. That experience really made me question not only the artist's relationship to the museum, but how museums present cultural information from various cultures and how different they are in the variety of contexts that they present them in. Even though they are all essentially the cultural production of various peoples, they get presented in different ways. So after that experience, I began working in galleries running programs for artists and eventually ran a gallery [Longwood Art Gallery] in the South Bronx for artists and had a local community audience as well as the art community that ventured up to the South Bronx.

One of the first shows I did [at Longwood] was called *Rooms with a View: The Struggle between Culture, Content, and the Context of Art*. That was not the first show, but maybe the third or fourth show. And that was in 1987. This is the first row of images, these here, and basically it was in a former public school in the South Bronx, and there were other spaces in the building, a literacy program for adults, a housing rehab program—[the artist and activist] Tim Rollins and K.O.S. were in that building—and a city agency for housing. So it was like P.S. 1 sort of, but it was much more involved with the community; we had a lot of community people coming through the building for other reasons besides the art program. The entire second floor of the building, which had studio spaces, was another important aspect of the gallery program, because there were constantly artists around, getting involved with the local community on various levels, whether hiring them to do things for them, or working for local community people. There was a constant interaction that went beyond whatever I did in the gallery space, and that inherently helped that gallery.

The show I did involved three different rooms, and I had the spaces redesigned. One room looked like a turn-of-the-century salon space, sort of; one room looked like an ethnographic museum, sort of; and one room was the white cube, exactly. And I had thirty artists participate in this. I told them I was going to experiment with their work, that it wouldn't be a regular exhibition. Each artist had two works in the exhibition, one in the white cube and one in one of the other spaces. Initially the idea for the show was to have it in three different museums: the Natural History Museum, the Met, and the Frick [Collection in Manhattan]. Of course that didn't happen, so I just did it in this one gallery space. The art really shifted meaning in [the three rooms]. In the ethnographic space, for instance, the labels may have said something like "Ceramic objects found in Williamsburg-area Brooklyn, late 20th c.," but no artists' names or anything were in that room. Whereas all artists had their names in the white cube space, and so just the environment changed the meaning of those artworks, and that really started my interest in reassessing the environment that art is placed in.

From that point, I did some other exhibitions with my own objects, and then I was invited by various museums to do that. The next grouping of photographs [in my presentation] is from the Maryland Historical Society, a very stodgy museum in Baltimore, Maryland, all deep Americana, historical objects, silver and chairs and that sort of thing, older paintings and nineteenth-century objects. Basically, I chose from that collection and reinstalled their third floor with their own objects—many things they had in their storage that they never knew they had, or that they were never planning to show. I brought them out and put them on view. As you see with the classical silver there, I placed, with a label of "Metalwork, 1700–1870," some slave shackles, which also were in the collection but never were exhibited. So the whole exhibition, besides showing things in their collection that had never been shown, it also gave a history of the museum and the community that they wouldn't talk about, and perhaps the history of the exclusion or the abuse that African American people experienced in that area of the United States, as well as the museum's viewpoint on that. That was largely what I was looking at—how the museum saw itself through its collecting patterns since it started collecting in 1840. So it really showed where they are at by what they collected, and what they didn't collect. I could go on and on, but I won't.

In order to do that exhibition, since I'm not from Baltimore, I basically interviewed all the staff people at the institution—the executive director, all the way to the woman who cleaned the silver, and the guards, and the maintenance staff. Just to get their sense of the museum, how they felt about the museum, how they felt about their city, how they felt about their jobs, and just to learn a little more about the institution and its hierarchies and relationships. What ended up happening also, which now I exploit, but at the time it was just by happenstance, is that in my being there—because I'm not a curator,

and I'm not within the permanent museum structure—I was able to solicit information from the staff people on various levels. Information that they had nobody to tell because they can't talk to people outside of the institution, because they don't want their peers to know if there are any problems inside the institution. And then they don't talk to each other, because generally they don't talk to each other—which is another issue I like to deal with when working with museums. So I became the sounding board for a lot of their problems and became very much a part of the institution. Realizing that I had to collaborate in order to do what I wanted to do, I had to give up some things, which means that I don't go around saying everything that I learned about the institution, because the next institution would probably not allow me to do what I want to do. So I still do what I want to do, I just don't blab about it when I've left the institution. That allows me a certain amount of autonomy when I go into institutions.

In addition to what happened in that situation [at the Maryland Historical Society], by involving various levels of staff in the project, it changed the relationship between various staff people. Some of the people in the under-staff were also involved in the project physically. I videotaped some of the staff who became part of the imagery in the exhibition because I used video-tapes and sound, etc. So the maintenance staff knew more about what the piece was about than the curatorial staff. When someone came in to see the show, whoever they talked to knew a lot about the project. And the other staff knew this. Since it was dealing with African American history, the maintenance staff could explain what it was about much better than the curatorial staff, who was not African American and really had no contact with African Americans outside of dealing with the maintenance staff. So, in a way, it shifted their relationship during my exhibition.

Since that particular exhibition, another aspect that makes a big difference is that the project was well received in the museum community and in the Baltimore community. Because issues of race were never brought up in Baltimore. They were just beneath the surface, always. No one would talk about it, because everyone was afraid of what would happen once you brought it up, and since I brought it up, it was sort of this great relief that *they* didn't have to bring it up. So it allowed a dialogue to happen among communities. Because, in order to do this project, I spoke with not only the museum community but also with other communities in the Baltimore area. I went to local Black historians and people who just knew a lot about their families' histories. They came to the museum because of [this collaboration], and it created some avenues of collaboration that didn't exist before I went there. Now with that institution, it's been a year, and they have invited me back to do a permanent installation of this particular piece, because it was well received. And because it was well received, it enabled them to get behind the issues I depicted in it without fear. What museums don't always want to acknowledge is the critique implicit in it. Because this particular project dealt with race, they were able to mask for themselves the critique of their institution. Because they saw it as doing good by dealing with racial issues.

But in actual fact, it was a critique of their institution. It's totally understandable to anyone who would go and see it, but to the museum itself, that's the aspect they would not discuss when giving lectures about that particular show. But what it does is when people come to see the show, it makes them ask these questions as they walk around the rest of the institution where other things are, and they ask why certain things aren't there.

Now, because [the museum is] dealing with this issue, it has brought up other cultural issues in their exhibition practices with communities other than the African American community. This is an institution that was pretty much private, that didn't have to deal with anyone because they had big money coming in to fund this place. And my exhibition was actually called by one of the board members: "Oh, that coloured installation." So they really were outside of what even their fellow museum people are engaged with. I find that my practice enables those individuals within institutions who have more of a vision than some other people, it empowers them to do something with their vision because what I've done doesn't destroy their…They see that what I've done does not make the building fall down. So that enables them to try something that they wouldn't have tried before. I view it, depending on the institution, as how much they will improve, how much they will change. With this institution in Maryland, they take very small steps, but I do see it as making small steps [in the right direction], because now the local communities are asking the institution: "Well, now, why don't you do this?" One of the things that I enjoy about these projects is that they empower local communities to ask the institution, "Well why don't you do this? Why don't you have this kind of exhibition?" It puts their feet to the fire a bit just by example, and because of the fact that I'm talking to the communities, which museums generally don't do.

I think this exhibition [at the Maryland Historical Society] really affected history museums the most, as opposed to curators, because of the way I used the material. Obviously, many people have made installations in history museums before, but history museums in the US are not as familiar with this. It was speaking directly to them about what they do with their materials and how to engage the public. In this past year, I've been asked by many people to come to their museums and do the same thing. I don't do the same thing when I go there, but it has become a way to get inside the door of some museums. Because of their naive notions of what I'm going to do: they think I'm going to make all the African Americans in their neighbourhood come to the museum. Which is never what I'm trying to do. But it is, in their naive or racist way, a reason for bringing me in. Then I just exploit that and take it in whatever direction it seems to go when I'm in that institution.

Another situation I'm finding is that when people invite me, realizing that I'm this outsider within their institution, I become this museum therapist. The staff just want to tell me about all the problems that they're having with the variety of people in their museums. I'm a little uncomfortable with that, because it's not what I plan to do every time I go to an institution, but it seems to be something that happens more and more, because institutions realize that they need to change but they don't have a clue about what to do.

The third installation [in my presentation] is at the Seattle Art Museum, a general art museum, and the installation was all over the museum. I basically looked at their collection and placed things in the wrong places—which were for me the right places. But I placed them in the wrong places for the museum, which forced the various curators to talk to one another, which in general in museums they don't really do—the decorative arts curator never talks to the Native American arts curator, the Native American arts curator never talks to the contemporary art curator, and on and on. When, of course, all of the objects have a great deal in relation with one another. So I basically forced them to talk to each other, as well as to talk with other staff people who were more engaged with the public, be it the café staff or the guards. To get feedback on what their response was to their exhibitions, and to my exhibition. The most recent outgrowth of that which i have noticed is the catalogue that they're organizing. I had no real involvement in it, but it seems that, in the spirit of my exhibition all the staff people have put in their two cents, in terms of what the catalogue should be and how the catalogue should look. So the curator who brought me in to show is not providing a master narrative of the project. Several curators and staff told the chief curator, who is on the project, that his overview of the exhibition was not appropriate to this project. So, everyone has been discussing what the process was. I don't know if this breakdown of hierarchy will manifest itself beyond my being there, but certainly in this instance I noticed it.

So I think I'll leave it right there, and come back to it later.

Fraser: Thank you, Fred. Judith?

Barry: So, do I show slides? I can't do this in ten minutes if I show slides.

Draxler: I think it's absolutely necessary to see them.

Fraser: Can you show some of them?

Barry: Yes, I can show one project.

Fraser: Right, that is what I have in mind, because you have four projects. So perhaps you can focus on one.

Barry: Well, I can talk about the others, but just show slides from one. And another question is where?

Fraser: On the projector behind you.

Barry: And should I show a video project?

Fraser: Which video project were you going to show? What we want is to use the projects as a sort of jumping-off point to talk about issues that were raised when you were doing it. Instead of a complete presentation of the projects. In the show [the *Services* exhibition], it should be possible to really see the projects, but we don't have time now to go through everything.

(Long pause)

Fraser: Renée, can you present instead?

Green: Yeah, I think I can do ten minutes.

Fraser: So, Renée will be making the next presentation.

Green: I want to focus on one project that I'm currently working on, so it's really an ongoing thing. And I also wanted to give a little background information because I really didn't say much before. To give a historical context to the way that I'm working should help a little bit. Some of the people here are people that I've actually worked with and that have had something to do with shaping a way of working. Fred is one, for example, because I worked a lot in alternative spaces during the 1980s, and I worked in a space that he was basically running in Tribeca called Just Above Midtown, or JAM. And working in these different spaces sort of allowed me to see other kinds of possibilities, or different ways of working from the commercial gallery spaces. And how to do shows completely on a shoestring, as well as various improvisational methods of working in different kinds of communities. It was an interesting time. The things that occurred in these spaces were not known about in a broader sense, but they were known about by a certain community of people who were working in these spaces. But in terms of the broader commercial art world, these things were not acknowledged, they were not even known about. The spaces were in the Bronx and in Tribeca, and that was an interesting thing about them. Because they were pockets of activity that also affected different communities, like the Longwood space that Fred used to run.

I also used to work with Susan Cahan at the New Museum when I was working in the education department as an artist. I was working with a high school art criticism program meant to develop criticality amongst high school students in public schools. We worked with teachers in the schools who were maybe in the English department, or the history department, and we worked out a kind of curriculum with them usually based on a theme that we, the artists, suggested and tried to see if the teacher would agree to. Throughout this time I worked in different ways with other organizations, for example doing a certain kind of media critique with these high school students, as well as with homeless students in a completely different situation, as well as with twelve- or thirteen-year-old kids at Bank Street College [of Education], which is connected to Columbia and Barnard universities. Susan has a sample video of one of the projects done at the New Museum with them.

Anyway, this is leading up to say that I also worked as a curator at the Drawing Center [in Manhattan], and the project I want to talk about is a project which the Drawing Center invited me to participate in as an artist after I finished working for them. They were interested in applying for a grant with the Wallace Foundation, the Lila Wallace–Reader's Digest Fund, and the grant was called Arts International. With this grant, artists are invited to work with different institutions, and the artists usually go abroad to a particular country. Certain countries are suggested because they already have connections with these countries. In a way, it's a kind of a "United Nations project" to create friendly relations between different countries. The year that I was invited to do it some changes had occurred—people on the selection committee and on the board were trying to move away from the usual people invited who were doing more craft-related work. So I was selected to do it; Mark Dion was also selected.

What I have here for documentation is broken up—it's not everything that occurred within the correspondence; it's material that began about two years ago. The invitation was extended to me at the end of 1991, and the project is still pending. After I was invited, I was asked to write a proposal about what I might do and what country I might choose to go to. I decided I wanted to focus on Portugal because of other works I had made that involved the sea and had to do with the slave trade. I was interested in a place that in contemporary times had the mark of the African diaspora. Lisbon was a location to look at that, and also to trace historical roots to Africa via the sea. That was one of the other things that I proposed and I did.

I wanted to present material that describes that back-and-forth process that exists when an artist is invited to work with an institution, and accepts the invitation to work with an institution. Trying to figure out some sort of a balance between what the artist is trying to do and what the institution is trying to do. The project was an artist project as far as I was concerned, but that of course wasn't completely possible, because there were all kinds of extenuating circumstances. For example, the agenda of the Drawing Center and the board of directors have to be appeased, and different sorts of things that are common to the structure of various institutions. So, the correspondence charts the process of the proposal—how that was arranged, and how my proposal was adapted to the institutional language to be able to fit into the way in which the Drawing Center wanted it to be presented. How I was put into their agenda so that we could get the grant together. The correspondence between us when I was away, the different roles I was taking on when I was there.

My initial proposal in the beginning stage was to do an exhibition with the Drawing Center, which I would curate, of maps from a collection in Lisbon. This changed over the course of time to became what it now is, which is a symposium—there will be no exhibition—which is entitled at present "Negotiations in the Contact Zone." That term, "contact zone," is adapted from something that was written by Mary Louise Pratt, a comparative literature professor who is speaking about it as a linguistic term, but that could be interpreted in a broader sense to refer to interactions which occur between people and places coming from disparate locations, but who wind up in the same location and have to negotiate the terms of how they are going to live. The project has continued to change and to shift, and I've documented the invitations I've sent to different people I want to invite. It's been focused on a combination of scholars, cultural producers, writers, visual artists. One of the concentrations has to do with a reassessment of certain theoretical ideas that were prominent in the mid '80s. And I was thinking about books like *Art after Modernism*, and other publications, Dia Art Foundation publications. I wanted to invite people who had participated in events there, as well as certain artists who were aware and formulating their ideas and their practices around that reassessment. I think this meeting here has something to do with that reassessment.

That's the material that I brought and maybe we can talk about some of the issues that occurred in this kind of interaction.

Barry: I brought several different types of work with which I engage, sometimes with the architect Ken Saylor, which is in exhibition design, and then some of the work I do as an artist in installation, as well as commercial projects that both Ken Saylor and I do. So four kinds of documents to possibly discuss.

There are two issues that come to mind immediately vis-à-vis this notion of a site-specific practice in terms of an institutional frame. One way to look at this might be to frame it as a philosophical approach, which is how I frame my approach. That has to do with questioning the actual content that the institution is bringing to bear on its subject, versus some very practical questions such as who is the audience, how does one get paid, and so forth. In today's discussion, it occurs to me that much of the discussion has been about the problem of getting paid or practical matter-of-fact issues. As you can see from the documentation I brought, in the art world for instance, I tend to write very thorough contracts that are much more detailed than the contracts I write in my commercial practice. The reason being that, in the art world, because business practices are so vague and loose, you need to spell things out in a more direct way than you often do for a commercial project. I think this has a lot to do with the way the art world has evolved over the years, and you can see that in the documents we brought.

Another issue that I'd like to raise parenthetically is the question of political efficacy, and that's the question of how culture produces a politic. I'll show one exhibition design. We start axiomatically with the notion that all space is ideological, so that within the exhibition design work that Ken and I have done, we assume this as a kind of given, and we expect that we're all relatively well versed in these conventions from our prior history, so we usually don't make that point overtly. Rather, what we tend to do is to isolate the curatorial practice by utilizing our own methodology. To give an example, I'll show one project I did with Brian Wallis at the Clocktower [in New York] in 1987 [called *This Is Tomorrow Today*, based on the original exhibition from 1956 *This Is Tomorrow* at Whitechapel Art Gallery, London]. It was about the work of the Independent Group, a collaborative group of artists, architects, writers, and designers who eschewed the production of singular objects and instead produced exhibition designs for new forms of art spaces. In 1990, there was a travelling show about the Independent Group. It began in London and travelled to MoCA [the Museum of Contemporary Art, Los Angeles]. In 1987, prior to this touring exhibition, Brian and I decided we would represent two of the works of this group at the Clocktower: Richard Hamilton's group and Alison and Peter Smithson's group. I'm trying to use this example as a way to show how, as exhibition designers, Ken and I try to augment the curatorial approach by fleshing out ideas in the actual work. One of the most compelling ideas in the work of the Independent Group is that this was one of the first moments in recent art history where questions about mass culture were introduced into the art world.

We were especially interested in reproducing Richard Hamilton's work in collaboration with John Voelcker and John McHale. We got the plans from him and tried to re-represent the work—which is a structure you could walk through—and inside the structure were many touchy-feely objects. There was also music in the gallery.

This image is from 1956 at Whitechapel Gallery in London. We showed clip art [magazine tear sheets] that all the members of Independent Group collected. When students visited, they could tell that someone had arranged these tear sheets in the 1980s and not the 1950s. This subtle ideological issue was noticed by students. This material was collected by the Independent Group because consumer culture after World War II was not readily available in Britain. They would go to the US and come back with trunks full of magazines and records and other consumer goods. Upstairs we re-presented the work of Alison and Peter Smithson, who collaborated with Eduardo Paolozzi and Nigel Henderson, and they built *Patio and Pavilion*, which was a British notion of the minimum one might need to survive in a city: a garden and a shed.

What I wanted to talk about in addition to the above is my approach to installation. I use a methodology that's research based. I brought one proposal from a recent project in Corsica. You'll see the contract for this proposal is more spelled out than other contracts in my other documentation. The project has more specific deliverables than any of the other contracts here, and the reason is, again, in addition to the notion of trying to make my methodology clear, it also stems from the desire to create a space in which the institution and the artist can collectively agree and, as Renée was saying, around certain issues. I think that both in the exhibition design work I do and in my own art practice, there is a particular kind of relationship that develops between an artist and a curator. I find when I'm doing projects, I do them in relationship to the institutional frame as well as the curatorial frame which we develop. Those relationships are, I think, very difficult to describe and very ambiguous. But nonetheless, they form the basis for my individual practices. I don't know how other people feel about this, but for me it's a major issue. I think that's all I wanted to say.

Wilson: I have a question. Do you find a difference in how the institution treats you when you're going in as an artist doing an installation, or as an artist creating an installation design for someone else's work?

Barry: Not initially. One project I didn't show was a project I did as an exhibition designer for *Damaged Goods* [at the New Museum in 1986]. I did that project as an artist exhibiting in the exhibition—and I should say parenthetically that I don't really distinguish between my different practices. Whereas Ken, the architect who I collaborate with, has billable hours, which is a notion that we do not have in the art world. If you look at his contracts, you'll see that everything is rated hourly, as is most work for hire in professional fields. Artists' work is not billed by the hour, so that's a major difference. What happens over time usually depends on the institution, and I find that I need different ways of working with different institutions.

Bischoff: May I ask a question? Did you participate in an exhibition which was in 1988 in Los Angeles, at the Temporary Contemporary [Museum of Contemporary Art, Los Angeles]?

Barry: Yes.

Bischoff: So, we were discussing this exhibition earlier and we were thinking about the way you concretize the curatorial frame. What is the first step for you in how you identify the curatorial frame?

Barry: We use a traditional architecture methodology that I find workable, which includes identifying the program. When Ken and I work with a curator, we try to read all the material he or she has prepared, to discern the major aims of the exhibition. What often happens is that we then end up performing primary research and analysis, so that we can address these aims more specifically. One of the issues in the project that I just showed, which is different than in a normal art exhibition, is that we, as exhibition designers, reproduce the works in the exhibition in addition to installing and displaying them. For the Independent Group show, we produced all the work. Normally in a museum, an artist comes in with the work and you install it. For two other exhibitions we did for the New Museum, we also made all the work, which, again, transforms the work issues. It's specific for each exhibition, and we follow a conventional architectural approach of identifying the program, and from there we go through different design phases.

Bischoff: Should we discuss that now, or later?

Draxler: It would be very good to see the *Damaged Goods* slides, because there—as an artist and as a designer—you also have this curatorial commitment, to a certain degree, to the artists in the show. I think that's a very important work that we shouldn't miss.

Fraser: I think we can talk about those issues. I think there are already a lot of questions.

Müller: One question I have is, if you build these pieces for the shows, who owns these pieces when the show comes down?

Barry: Usually, because we're hired, we don't. Usually the museum does.

Müller: But like the New Museum or the Clocktower, they don't have collections.

Barry: We sold part of the Clocktower show to the ICA, London. We didn't personally receive any money, but the show was expensive for the Clocktower to produce, so that was good…

Müller: You didn't get an extra fee…

Barry: No. For that show, I was paid $1,000.

Fraser: You said that your approach to exhibition design was predicated on the idea that all space is ideological, and I would assume then that you think of your installation design as ideology critique in some sense.

Barry: Not necessarily critique, but that it's presumed that there is an ideological, or several ideological, positions that one can take up vis-à-vis the work in the space.

Fraser: Because you used the word "augment," and "augment the curatorial approach," and "identify" or "make concrete" the curatorial frame and working with curators…

Barry: That's the psychological aspect that Fred was discussing. You try to sit down with them and find out what they want to do, and what they want the spectator to look at, because it's not neutral. Design is a particular way of framing ideas.

Fraser: But my question is: Does the curatorial concept itself ever become the object of ideological critique? You're saying that it is not ideology critique, but what would the object be, and where would that object be located? Would it be the curatorial concept, would it be the institution? You said that in the meetings that there is content the institution brings to bear, but if there is content "the institution" brings to bear, where exactly is that content coming from within the institution?

Barry: I think it's more collaborative than that. I can't reduce it to one answer. For instance, the television show [*From Receiver to Remote Control: The TV Set*, New Museum, 1990] was an artist-curated exhibition by Matthew Geller. He had many TV sets, but he didn't have a clear sense of what they meant, so our job was to try to define the social spaces that television produces. That show was difficult because we didn't have complete control of the television programming, which would have allowed us to detail each space more fully. Hence, a few of these social spaces remained under-enunciated.

Fraser: I wanted to cross reference between you and Fred and the different positions you seem to be taking to curators and to the kinds of invitations that you get. Judith, you're talking about working with curators to make concrete a curatorial frame, and, Fred, you're talking about a very different kind of relationship it seems to me.

Green: I want to interject something. I was also thinking about the kind of relationship I was trying to develop with the Drawing Center around the project I originally wanted to do, which involved designing the show. I was trying to reconsider the requirements of the Drawing Center on Portuguese artists to make drawings. I was trying to negotiate this position of being the artist but also of wanting to do some sort of a critique of the situation. But, at the same time, to stay within the situation so that it was possible to do a critique. That's one of the things that I was really curious about. Like, Fred asked you [Judith] about the difference between how you were perceived as a design professional versus an artist. I found that there was a difference when the idea of an art project was proposed that incorporated the use of design—that this was missed in some sort of way. Whereas I think that going in as a design consultant, or a design professional, that might add another kind of authority. At the Drawing Center, I wanted to be involved in all aspects of design relating to the project—design of the space, poster design—but usually what happened is that I was consulted after the fact, that they were going to use their own designer. I had certain ideas about what the type should be and how things should be presented, and what the press release should say. And I have experience on that,

having worked in publishing. But something about the term "artist"… the idea of what you're capable of doing—whether you're capable of writing, for example, theorizing something—seems to be in question. That's what I've encountered. I was curious if that's what's happened to others.

Wilson: When I go into an institution to do an exhibition, it's more along the lines of making an installation than as a designer, because I'm not working with a curator to realize ideas that they have. Often what I'm doing is trying to reveal what their ideas have been about a particular culture, artwork, or their view of the world from the structure they already have, from their exhibition concept. And often, as it turns out, it's such a closely held ideology that they pretend not to be aware of it. And the deeper that I go, it becomes clear that they are aware of it, and I'm sort of hitting the wall of who they are. That's what I'm really trying to break through, also for the public: that their view, which is supposedly open and objective, is in actual fact very narrow and very specific.

Guttmann: I think the use of the term "ideology" can be misleading. There is a difference between working with a person who has an idea, and trying to make that more concrete, and working to try to flesh out some of the basic premises of institutions. I think that's an important difference.

Barry: There's a big difference.

Wilson: Judith is saying—you are saying that you do both.

Barry: I don't make my institutional critique overtly, necessarily. Sometimes I do, but not always, and the reason is, I'm not as interested in that because it can be so overt. I'm much more interested in some of the deeper, more psychoanalytical, social, or political connections that one might uncover in the preliminary, investigative, research-based phase of each project. That's why I like to interview the curator and find out what they're most interested in exploring.

Guttmann: Would you work with any curator?

Barry: If the issues are interesting, then I'm interested. I'm personally interested in the relationship between "high art" and "mass culture." And how we as artists are going to negotiate the big paradigmatic shifts that we are living through. Such as the transformations that information technology is producing. I thought Renée's point about how some artists and ideas from the mid 1980s have been papered over by the recent past was insightful. She was talking about re-examining some of the ideas from *Art after Modernism* and some of the Dia conversations, because that moment in history had a much more complex view of how all these things fit together, instead of collapsing everything into short sound bites. And that is very disturbing if you have lived through that history as I have. But in terms of asking which curators I would or would not work with, I don't have a preconceived idea. It's much more about the person, the curator, and their ideas.

Guttmann: But do you care about their politics?

Barry: I do care about their politics, but it's very difficult to know what anybody's politics really are, unless you get to know them quite well. I wouldn't want to work with an overt fascist. I've never been asked to work with the KKK, nor would I.

Wilson: It's an interesting question, because working with curators who you don't really know, or curators who don't really get it, or don't even have even a similar ideological perspective, or don't understand the direction your work seems to be going…I've had that experience, and it is a difficult thing because you want to respond to things that you think are important and to things that are important to the community, but then the person whom you are directly working with is a hundred years behind. But they want you there because they see you as something trendy. So the question becomes: Do you ignore this person and do something that really has to do with what the community needs, and what you need? Or is that not helpful when the institution, or an individual representing that institution, needs to be made aware that there are big gaps in understanding? Can you do that, or are you being used by the situation if you don't directly deal with the person who has brought you there?

Barry: I used to produce exhibition designs for corporations as a young designer. For instance, I worked with Coca-Cola, which is not the most caring corporation. I would try to call them out on their commercials. Nothing that tried to do that in an overt way was ever approved, because they're not stupid, but humour sometimes worked. The art world is a benign, racist, homophobic cultural institution in which you can operate as a kind of bad conscience, in a way that corporations will not permit. You cannot be their bad conscience, as you have no power.

Beatrice von Bismarck: I have a question. From what you're saying, it sounds as if curators have a tendency to be particularly stupid. Because it seems to take them a very long time to realize exactly what you're doing. And with what you said, Fred, I can imagine that is the case. But there must be a reaction from the curators after they realize something has happened.

Wilson: During and after. Three of the museums I've worked with lost their executive directors either right before I came or right after I finished my project. I'd like to say I had something to do with it, but not really. I find that even when you're in a contentious situation, they can twist around to make themselves look good, because it's a temporary situation. Generally, along the way, they realize what you're really doing and they try to stop you.

Von Bismarck: But what does it lead to? Does it lead to the idea that the curator is made the object of a discussion? How does that alter the whole relationship between a curator and an artist?

Fraser: That's what the whole discussion here is about.

Barry: I wasn't meaning to imply that curators are stupid because they hire exhibition designers—because that's not true. I think that design is an unnamed term in how it is that an audience takes in information. A good exhibition design can make certain issues crystal clear, whereas a bad exhibition design can obfuscate everything. It's not that curators are stupid or that they are not doing their job well; it's that designers have a different way of organizing the material and restating it in a frame that provides ways for the audience to understand the exhibition. This is different than primary or academic research. Similarly, if you read an academic journal, it's often full of jargon that you can't understand unless you have an advanced degree in that field.

Wilson: The difference that I see is that curators pretend that the system they use to design is at worst a bit elitist or not communicative, but the deeper I dig, it seems that they have a very personal reason for controlling information in the way that they do. In one museum I worked in, a white curator who is curating Native American art objects, he was allowing me to do something in his gallery, which was a new gallery beloved by museum staff because the design was very elaborate. He didn't give me a lot of input, but it was fine that he was going to work with me.

I gave video cameras to young Native American artists from the region and asked them make videotapes of whatever they wanted to make videotapes of. Short videotapes that I was to install in the gallery space. I had asked the curator if he could put me in contact with any Native American artists in the community to work with, which he never got together for me, so I went out and found Native American artists. I put these tapes in the space on ten monitors, and they were showing the artists' own work or other artists' work, a Native American rock band, poetry readings. The curator thought there was only going to be one monitor in the gallery space. By having the ten monitors all stacked together showing the images, like in a store where they sell televisions, well that really competed with the design of the gallery space. The gallery space had been presented in this "dead Indian" mode, with theatrical lighting and artifacts placed in dramatic positions, in a way that denies the fact that there are any living Native American cultures. So, again, my installation competed with his design, and the problem was not the information or content so much as the effect of how my design competed with his design. It wasn't so much the information we were presenting: it was the effect of the competing design, which he knew was much more powerful for the viewer than the information presented in one corner of the room. At that point, he wanted the whole show to close. The chief curator's tack was not to say that he didn't like it. Instead, he said, "My Native American advisors wouldn't like this"—advisors he never told me he had. These particular advisors were traditional Native American artists who usually would not challenge his perspective. Many ethnographic museums in the US that show Native American art hire these advisors to come in only when the curator needs them to promote his vision. The artists I was working with would not be in that kind of dialogue with him; they had one foot in tradition and the other in the contemporary. And he saw that the artists represented in the videos were prominent, important members of the regional Native American community. So he backed down. Totally crazy. They [my collaborators] were ready to picket the building, which

I was prepared to let it get to, also because it was a real collaboration. But it never got that far.

Fraser: I wanted to introduce into this discussion the distinction that was made in the [Working Group] program between serving institutions and serving audiences. I think that distinction might be useful in this discussion in terms of what the basis of the relationship between the artist and the curator is in these instances, and whether the artist sees him- or herself to be serving the curator, serving the institution, or serving the audience. And, if serving the audience, whether serving the audience in collaboration with the institution or serving the audience by engaging in a critique of the institution. What you're talking about I think, Fred, is about serving the audience by engaging in a critique of the institution, although one could also make the argument that that is also serving the institution to the extent that the institution is an institution that was established in the public interest, supposedly, in one way or another. And, Judith, you're going at it from perhaps a somewhat different direction: working with curators to help serve the audience by helping them articulate their curatorial program in a more convincing manner.

Barry: Also illuminating certain questions that might go unacknowledged or unasked, but not in an as overt way. Because a lot of these issues, like race for instance, are so primary right now, Fred gets invited to specifically address these issues, and you [Andrea] get invited to manifest institutional critique.

Fraser: One question I would like to ask Fred is: If you're trying to serve the audience by engaging in a critique of the institution, to what extent is the condition of the success of that the collaboration with the institution, and the enlistment of the representatives of the institution in that project according to their own interests as defined by the institutional mission? This is also an ethical question for me, because I've done a lot of disclosure in certain places that have made people very uncomfortable, and in ways that I'm not comfortable with either, because I want to be working with them, and because after I'm gone, they're [still] there, you know? And so, if I come in and do something that just produces conflict or embarrassment, then when I go, it's going to be worse than when I got there.

Wilson: Yeah, I agree. The situation with the Native American arts curator was very particular because he was hiding his true feelings about having a very specific way he wanted to present Native American culture, and he didn't want anyone to mess with his view, including Native Americans. Because he masked that right up to the point that the exhibition opened, I was not able to deal with that along the way.

Green: One thing I wanted to inject into the discussion is the question of communities and what a community might be and what does that mean. I don't think we can talk about a unified single community that we can definitely identify. I mean, there are certain aspects of a community that you can't identify. I think that the whole notion of community is a fragmented one. I'm thinking about this in relation to what you [Andrea] were saying in terms of audiences. What happens in the case when you're not certain what kind of community is out there?

I'll speak of a specific project that I did with a museum in Massachusetts, in Worcester [the Worcester Art Museum, in 1991], which was called *Bequest*. It was a project also working with the museum, and with a curator, and with an idea of audience. One of the aspects of the project was to figure out who they were. I was thinking about this when Fred was talking about functioning as a kind of tension valve for this museum in Baltimore, or the function of assuaging guilt or responsibility—this therapeutic function. I was wondering about that, I was wondering about what happens when the reception is not a positive reception. Through the media reception and through the mixed information that audiences have gathered from that media reception. In that *Bequest* project, I really wanted to question who the audience is, and, in different locations, who do they become, and how do they respond to certain information.

Fraser: I think of a dynamic model for what the audience is. The audience is in a certain way being produced by the discourse of the institution. You have urban populations, then you have particular constituencies, like the constituency a museum represents as a public institution. And, so, an audience is a population being turned into a constituency. That's how I understand audience. You can only understand an audience in terms of the difference between who the museum represents itself to and what it represents.

Green: What I was trying to identify was a situation in which the audience is fighting with itself about being an audience. The audience in the case of the *Bequest* project encompassed the museum guards, the museum curators—everyone was making comments and arguing with each other about how to perceive this work.

Guttmann: Can you describe it?

Green: I will briefly try and describe it. This was another invitation by a museum to do a work, and they didn't specify what kind of work. This is a museum that has only had one contemporary artwork presented in the past ten years, but they were trying to make it into a lively contemporary space. It's in an economically depressed area in Worcester, Massachusetts, near Boston. They were trying to get people to go to the museum and were not sure who might go besides the board members, and supporters of the garden committee, or whatever. That was the situation.

What I wanted to do was to deal with my own history with New England. And not in a way that would be identified as a "Black perspective," or in a way that they would identify in that way. I wanted to deal with with more psychological aspects, and ideas of puritanism, with the notion of the "unhomely" in the area, and with the history of the museum itself. It was called *Bequest* because it dealt with all the objects that had been given to the museum by the founder. I wanted to trace the genealogy of the museum. There were large text works on the outside of the building that I made as one of the pieces of the show, with texts from W. E. B. Du Bois, Edgar Allen

Poe, and different people, focusing on Blackness and whiteness as ideas. There was a really wide range of reactions recorded in a book that was part of the exhibition project, which made the audience seem incredibly fractured.

Wilson: This is a very typical situation, where the institution is trying to make some sort of radical change, but they don't want to do it personally themselves, so they bring you in to do it. This is something we all can relate to: it doesn't have to be about race, it can be about anything. It's really about their particular denial of their predicament, and their place in their own community, and trying to put a Band-Aid on it. So, in a sense, whatever you do, if it doesn't redefine their way of reaching that audience, it's going to produce a similar reaction in that audience, because they're not reading your work—they're reading the institution that they've known for X number of years. And that gets reflected on you, but it's not really you. So, you find out the extent of how much they [the institutions] want to change by you engaging them in changing their model, their modus operandi.

Fraser: There are so many issues here. We could talk about this point alone for three days.

Michael Clegg: They only consider it to be a temporary change. They don't commit to it structurally after the exhibition space passes to someone else.

Wilson: They don't want to see it as a fundamental change they have to make. They want to see it as a moment, and then they can go back to whatever they feel comfortable with.

Fraser: I had an experience with the Wadsworth Atheneum, in Hartford, Connecticut, which is an extremely problematic city. I would say that it's more segregated than most parts of the South. It has the most active chapter of the Ku Klux Klan in the North, and the grand wizard of the Ku Klux Klan is from Connecticut. But the Wadsworth Atheneum museum is in some ways one of the most progressive institutions in the country, with an extremely liberal program and one of the most progressive contemporary art curators in the country [Andrea Miller-Keller], who organized Louise Lawler's first museum exhibition, and a lot of other people's.

What I was trying to do there was to come to grips with these two different things, and try and figure out what my function was within that economy. Assuming there was an economy there between the institution, its progressive curatorial program, and the extreme segregation in the area. It was very difficult—probably one of the most difficult projects I have ever done—because it meant challenging someone I deeply respected as a very progressive curator with an amazing track record. My analysis was: here in this town you have three-hundred-year-old liberalism that's based in colonial Yankee identity, and that serves the function of maintaining itself with this fictional autonomy of a preindustrial community. And this liberal tradition is the agency through which the segregation is effected, in a certain way. It supports this fiction that there are no conflicts of interest. The other comment I have is that, with respect to audiences, I've always assumed that there was a conflict. And that the institution was founded in order to address itself to social conflict. To recognize a kind of social alterity. If the institution is there for educational purposes for instance, then to educate someone implies already that there is a recognition that there is someone else out there who does not already share the culture of the institution. But the Wadsworth Atheneum was not recognizing that there was anyone else out there. I've never experienced direct redemption from an audience, except there with that project. And I know why...

Clegg: How did it manifest?

Fraser: The redemption of the audience?

Clegg: Yeah.

Fraser: Well, I was invited to give a performance at the annual dinner of the docent council. I told them it probably was not a good idea, but they insisted that they would love to have me. And then no one said a word to me after the performance. Not a word. They responded by saying that they "loved Hartford," without acknowledging that there was any critique, and not responding to the performance at all. Just pure repression. It's exactly what was going on in every cultural institution in the city. That's what was expressed back to me, and it was a horrifying experience.

Wilson: I've gotten to the extent that I don't want to work with education departments at museums, because I really feel that the education departments—well, not your education department at the New Museum, Susan (laughter among group)—are put in place so that the museum does not have to do what it really should do, what it is supposed to do. So, it doesn't matter how good the education department is, or how forward-thinking people are in the education department. The education department is there because the museum doesn't want to do what it has to do to really engage the public. So, this mandated effort—

Cahan: I call it "the art museum's alibi."

Wilson: Right, the alibi. So, for me, I want to talk about institutions, instead of audiences, because I'm dealing with the institution, which if it's doing what it should be doing, audiences wouldn't be such an issue. I don't address myself to audiences. The museum does this by saying, "We want them, they're out there. We want them to come in here." But if you really address who you are, and what you are really about, if you really address that, then audiences will respond in kind.

Barry: I think it is possible to work directly with communities. One of the contracts I brought pertains to an ongoing oral history project. As a white woman, occasionally the question has come up as to why I am calling attention to different, often unequal, cultural conditions in underrepresented communities. One way I navigate this is to make sure the project accurately reflects the community I am working with, by working directly with the communities I am trying to "represent." The first time I worked like this was for a project called *First and Third* for the Whitney Museum in 1987. It was an oral history project. While I had the explicit consent of the people whose stories I used, I collected them in an ad hoc manner. When I reflected on that project, I decided to adopt a much more collaborative methodology. For the next oral history project at the Riverside Studios in London [in 1990], I collaborated with five community groups, each of whom collected lost or forgotten histories they deemed important and wanted told. I was much more of a facilitator than an artist. The project became a community-based project, with the groups' names listed on all the literature, illustrating the collaborative nature of the project and underscoring that the community groups were equal participants in the project. Thus making it clear that I wasn't speaking for them.

Another project in Brussels was about the colonial relationship of the Belgian Congo to Belgium and the development of art nouveau as a style [*The Work of the Forest*, Fondation pour l'Architecture, 1992]. For that project, I chose several different groups representing competing ideological positions. There was the museum position: an anthropology museum that had thousands of mostly stolen artifacts that [King] Leopold II had collected. Hence, the museum had its own version of that history. And there was the art history community, which claimed another version of this history, as well as other artist and architecture communities. What I did was collide their points of view within the form of a panorama with the aim of producing as much friction as possible. This became controversial in the press and raised issues that had not been addressed in Brussels for a long time. For me, producing an agreement in the form of a classical narrative is not as interesting as revealing hidden histories.

Fraser: What do you do when the conflict is so repressed? Where you can't get to it, in a certain way.

Wilson: I found, at least in the Baltimore project [*Mining the Museum*, 1994], you find out who these various constituencies are, and you work with them on whatever level works best for them. It varies. Docents I found it easier to engage in a kind of lecture thing. For certain Black communities in Baltimore, it made more sense to go visit them in their homes. And for another Black community, it made more sense to have a very formal setting. So it depended also on the various economic structures of the various different Black communities in Baltimore. I don't address audiences directly, but audiences as constituencies are certainly implicit in that process. Because the museum community is not going to tell you what the issues are.

Guttmann: I don't think it should be taken as axiomatic that art institutions have an audience. They have visitors. Visitors are not an audience, let alone a public. Let alone a community. The definitions are necessary. But it also seems to me that museums don't need to sell entrance tickets to survive. A lot of them don't, albeit each museum is an entirely different case. Many art institutions really don't need any rigorous definition of their audience to generate their self-identity. That's a crucial point to remember. They have visitors, but the visitors don't make an audience.

Bischoff: I have a question for all the artists here: What would you say if people from the art museum made you the primary audience, or

visitors? So that we are looking for you? Because the institution where I come from is a container with artworks and materials from communities and society everywhere. And we are happy when someone works with these materials. The only people who really work with these materials are artists. So for some people working in the museum, this is the only chance they have to work with artists.

Fraser: Before we respond to that—Susan, you wanted to say something?

Cahan: If you look at the rhetoric in the United States, the mandate is for museums to serve "the public." Which is intentionally left undefined so that museums can position themselves as democratic institutions. When you look at actual audience demographic surveys and statistics, what you find is that the audience in American museums is very specific and very clear—it's mostly white, mostly middle-aged, slightly more women than men, the income of people who visit museums is higher than the national average, and college education is sort of the median. I think the reason why museums don't articulate who their audiences are is because they feel it would be an indictment of institutional stature. It's assumed that museums represent a broad cross-section of the populace, and by obfuscating that point, you can indulge that notion.

Guttmann: When I said that visitors are not an audience, while there may be some statistical regularities that differentiate these groups of visitors from the rest of the population, they still don't make an audience because there are not very many art institutions that create an atmosphere where people have the feeling that they are experiencing the art as an audience. You know, when someone goes to a rock concert for instance, part of the experience is the interaction with the audience itself. At certain concerts, the performer becomes the facilitator and tries to create a communal feeling, or at least that seems to be a mandate in that context. So, that's a contrast. It's very different than what you have at art museums, which is just a bunch of individuals who go in and go out.

Fraser: Very little of the art that has been collected by institutions was made for a collective experience. So I would call your analogy into question. But the other thing I wanted to say is, again, that I would make a difference between an audience and a constituency. How you are defining an audience, Martin, I would call a constituency. Not to say that it's necessarily participatory, but there are a certain set of shared interests. I would call "an audience" what you call "visitors"—and I would say that going in and out of doors, as you say, is actually a very complicated thing. It is not such a simple thing. Going in and out of the museum has a whole history and set of mechanisms and rules.

Guttmann: The salon in France, for example, was a very important place for the creation of a democratic atmosphere. The people who were standing in the salon together came from different classes, and it was the first time that they met each other, and they could converse with each other through the medium of art criticism.

Fraser: But I would say that the history in the United States is very different. Institutions in the United States were constructed to discourage certain people from coming in. The Philadelphia Museum [of Art] is hard to get to: it's a big traffic island with no stop signs. There are a lot of museums that are hard to get into, and not just in terms of urban planning and architecture.

Draxler: We are already into [the time for] our third section, and I would propose we take a break now, and come back in twenty minutes to try and go on with this. With some other participants. And Fritz and I spoke, and [we think that] we should try and have a more European-based discussion around these issues.

Working Group
Session Three

Serving Audiences
Saturday, January 22, 1994

Presentations:
Susan Cahan
Iwona Blazwick
Andrea Fraser

*As most cultural institutions are
founded in the public interest, many
project artists propose to serve
not the institution so much as its
audience.*

*Curators and other museum profes-
sionals are increasingly interested
in inviting artists to collaborate with
them in fulfilling the public service
mission they or the institutions
define.*

*What happens when the interests
of artist, institution, and audience
are found to be in conflict? Can this
model function to ends other than
that of institutional reform?*

Susan Cahan: There are a couple
of points I want to make that are
issue oriented. I'm going to present
for fifteen minutes, because I have
a short videotape. I will keep my
presentation as short as possible,
but the video is about five minutes,
and it will come in the middle of my
presentation. What I want to focus
on is the position of audiences in
museums, and probably what I say
will be more pertinent to museums
in the US than in Europe.

 I would like to begin by presenting
my simple analysis of the historical
position that museum education has
taken, and that is that curators are
the people who develop knowledge
and educators are the people who
are supposed to transmit this knowledge, usually in simplified form,
to the broadest group of people.
Historically this formulation has
entailed a division that many people
have referred to as "the curator's
interest in art" and "the educator's
interest in people." This is a dichotomy most popularly expressed
by people writing about museum
practice in the 1970s, which is really kind of interesting because in
the 1970s many artists were doing
things that specifically contradicted
this dichotomy, and instead used
the museum as a site in which social
relationships between various constituencies and various players were
totally interdependent. Where you
couldn't make this simple division
between art and people.

 What I became interested in doing
was developing new ideas about
museum education that drew on
literary criticism, specifically reader
response theory and reception
theory. I was interested in looking at
the changing relationship between
cultural production and cultural
reception, specifically looking at
reception as a form of cultural production, which is something that has
been done quite a lot with literature
but, oddly enough, not so much with
visual art. This was the mid to late
'80s and I was very influenced by
the work of Group Material. Some of
their stuff is also included in this exhibition [*Services* at the Kunstraum
of the University of Lüneburg]. I was
also influenced by a demonstration
staged by ACT UP at MoMA [the Museum of Modern Art in New York] in
1988 around an exhibition of photographs by Nicholas Nixon of people
with AIDS. I was also looking at
programs for employees developed
by the First Bank in Minneapolis. In
each of these cases what was going

on was reception as a form of cultural criticism. Or reception theory and cultural criticism coming to play in relation to each other. So the kind of work that I began doing at the New Museum involved concretizing the process of reception, trying to give what happens to people when they look at art some kind of visible form, making what is generally invisible, visible, and doing that through collaborations with artists. I was also explicitly interested in encouraging critical reception.

The first project that I did [at the New Museum of Contemporary Art, New York] was in 1989, and it was a videotape in a retrospective exhibition of work by Nancy Spero [*Nancy Spero: Works since 1950*], in which a colleague of mine and I interviewed visitors to the exhibition about which works spoke most powerfully to them and why. In effect, the visitors began to give short gallery talks in the museum, and we documented it on videotape. This all took place the first week that the show was open. We shot about thirty-five hours of video and edited it into a ten-minute orientation tape that was presented at the entrance to the exhibition and played for the duration of the show.

The next project I did was in 1990 in collaboration with an artist named Branda Miller, and it was conducted in a show called *From Receiver to Remote Control: The TV Set*, which Judith mentioned earlier [in the previous session], and which was conceived and organized by Matthew Geller and designed by Judith Barry and Ken Saylor. The show was about the role that television has played in the American home and for the American family. What Judith and Ken did was design the installation so that each of the galleries replicated a room in the home at a different point in time since the invention of the TV, so the time frame ranged from the late 1920s to the late 1980s. The project that I was involved with enabled people to make their own videotapes within the exhibition about their own experiences with TV in their own lives, or they could make tapes that critiqued the exhibition. The tapes that were produced were collected in an archive that was continuously incorporated within the exhibition so that it amplified the themes of the show. And Branda was on site every weekend to do editing sessions with people who wanted to do more work on the footage they shot. Everyone was given a copy of the tape they made. People could come back to the exhibition to edit their footage. And about two thousand people participated in that project over a period of ten weeks. It was a huge project. The videotape I am going to show you is from that project.

Another example that I just want to briefly mention—and if you want to find out more about this project, the information is up here on the bulletin board—is a collaborative project I created with Julie Ault.

Andrea Fraser: Julie Ault is also a member of Group Material.

Cahan: The exhibition that this was done in conjunction with was called *Rhetorical Image*, and it was organized by Milena Kalinovska [in 1990–91]. The theme of the exhibition was to look at ways in which various modes of communication embody power relations and the ways artists have intervened in the representation of power relations in public spaces or in architecture. Most of the work was conceptually based. What Julie and I wanted to do was to create an education project that would intervene in the museum, and make visitors more aware about the way museums embody power relations. So, visitors were asked a series of questions and were invited to respond to these questions on a postcard that people could then put up on the wall. This little booklet includes about fifty responses.

What you'll see in the photographs is that during the course of the installation, the entire room became completely papered with these responses. We really hadn't anticipated the volume of the response we would get, and what happened is that the visitors' voices really took over the space. But it was really a very nice metaphor for what we were trying to accomplish, that is, to turn the space over to people who usually don't have their own voices articulated in concrete form in museum spaces. I want to mention that the only people who had a problem with that project were art critics, and I think that's very interesting and indicative of the way in which it perhaps impinged somewhat on the territory art critics usually occupy.

The last project included in this presentation is a project that Laurie Parsons did in which she removed all the signage from a group exhibition on view called *The Spatial Drive* [in 1991–92], which had been organized by Laura Trippi. Rather than have traditional education texts, Parsons organized training sessions for all of our security and admissions staff so that they could meet with every artist in the exhibition and learn about their work. So that all the factual and interpretive information about the exhibition was conveyed through informal conversations between the visitors and the museum staff. It had a very normalizing effect on the museum space: you could walk in and touch everything and talk to everyone, and there wasn't the same kind of formal protocol and distance that one generally experiences in a museum.

There is a certain consistency to those projects, although Laurie's is somewhat different because it didn't focus on audiences per se.

I also want to show a video that was produced in the home-made TV project, and then talk to you about the question that Andrea has asked us to focus on, which is the question of what happens when conflicts arise between artists, institutions, and audiences.

This was one of the most challenging of the videotapes made during the course of the exhibition— most challenging in the most direct and explicit way.

(Video plays)

(Art Jones, speaker on video:…it's packed with so much stuff but at the same time it's really limited. I'm walking through these rooms and it's all like something out of a car commercial, just something you would see on TV. But the thing is, my house don't look like this, it never did. This is white people's houses. I've never seen anything in my neighbourhood that looks like this. Is this about the impact of video on America? Then whose America…?

So I wonder if you, the museum-going viewer, can appreciate the sense of alienation that's produced by this exhibition. I mean, what you do is interesting. But I don't know; it's hard to relate to. So this isn't so much a critique as pointing out what I think every intelligent person knows about the limitations of the museum in its context and its concept when it comes to expressing anything other than a white middle-class perspective. The whole idea of a museum is inherently alienating to someone like myself, because I feel the need to redefine the very terms that make a place like this possible, and attractive, or interesting to the people who put it together. And this whole idea of multiculturalism, 'Oh, we want to include people.' The fact is that cultures other than the one that this exhibition represents exist, and have existed for years, and this idea that you're going to include something now is kind of ass-backwards. It's something you should have realized hundreds of years ago. You're a little late, folks. Maybe try taking this show uptown to the Studio Museum [in Harlem] and see what people say. You might get a new perspective on it.")

Cahan: The next video here is with a class that Renée Green taught, when she was at Bank Street College [in New York].

(Next video plays)

(Title of video: "Tape #593 by Renée Green's Jr. High School Class Bank Street College")

(Two unidentified speakers, both junior high school aged, conduct an interview on video. Interviewer: "What is your name?" Interviewee: "My name is Alonzo Lewis." Interviewer: "What do you think about this museum?" Interviewee: "Well, I can't say much, because I haven't looked around, but it looks OK." Interviewer: "Are you mad that you can't look around?" Interviewee: "Yes, I was hoping that I would have a chance to explore things but I understand the situation." Interviewer: "What is the problem at the museum?" Interviewee: "Well, there is a leak and they don't let you go back there, you know the situation.")

Cahan: I have to explain: there was a water leak that day at the New Museum, so we had to figure out how to stop the leak before the student group got there. Renée brought her class and the kids had to wait in the lobby for a very long time—these were thirteen-year-olds. So we just gave them the camera and let them play and film themselves while they were waiting. The thing about this segment is that he has devised this ingenious way of how to get him and other students into the galleries by pretending to go to the bathrooms and then delivering this news format of "exclusive interviews on the leak." But they are also just hanging out in the lobby interviewing each other. And at one point they focus on the lobby placard that lists the board of trustees of the New Museum.

(Cahan shows a clip of one of the students reading the names of the board members. Green, speaking over the video, says that another student was discussing how these are not names of people who work at the museum, and that they are the names of the very rich.)

Cahan: I just wanted to show these clips because they point out some of the things that people who work at museums take for granted are not taken for granted by the people who visit museums. The idea behind these projects is to make the process of education one that is reciprocal, and to redefine the way knowledge is constructed in the museum. To turn the museum into a site in which knowledge is not just transmitted but produced. To forefront that by giving the practice of knowledge production some kind of physical, visible, concrete form. And to focus on the idea of dissidence, and an important value which gets to the issues we're supposed to address, which has to do with what happens when conflicts occur. Frankly, one of the main things these projects aimed to do was to acknowledge that those conflicts are there, and if they can be discussed, then that's a productive process. One of the problems that I encountered is the way in which these techniques and this information was being generated by these projects—which, I mean you see in the first tape I showed of the young man, Art Jones: that his critique was quite confrontational. I was astounded by the degree to which the museum was able to absorb this information and to absorb what was being generated through this methodology. I had envisioned that it might spur some institutional transformation. But what actually happened was that the museum just got excited about what was going on and said, "Well, we should just do this for every show, then." "Well, if you do this for every show, then we don't necessarily need to address the specific critiques that are being made through the projects themselves." And this became a source of frustration for me, and I no longer do this sort of thing. I'm now involved in a different sort of practice. The last project that I was involved in of this nature was in 1992.

I'm concerned about the degree to which audience participation is being conceived as some sort of democratic act by museums in the US. We see it in the proliferation of "audience response" books, which for me have very little to do with real issues of cultural democracy and cultural participation. So the work that I'm involved with right now is more oriented toward collaborations with people who are situated both within institutions and outside of institutions. I'm working on a project now that involves a consortium of artists, activists, and graduate students in cultural studies at the City University of New York. We've tried to come up with new structures for establishing collaborative relationships with people so that they can work with our museum and hopefully not get thoroughly co-opted by it, so that mutual interests are served.

Iwona Blazwick: I want to talk about a project that some of you were involved with last year. It was an invitation that was made to myself and two other curators, Eva Patita and Carolyn Christov-Bakargiev, to organize a project for a festival which sought to celebrate European unity. It was located in Antwerp, which was designated the European Capital of Culture in 1993, and naturally the paradoxes abound. We were, in a sense, kind of *Gastarbeiter* [guest workers] in that we were parachuted into this particular situation which was located in the Museum of Contemporary Art in Antwerp, and we were faced with a number of interesting but difficult problems. We were really creating an interface between a number of different groups and agendas. One was the [European Commission] itself, which clearly has an economic imperative in promoting ideas about European unity through culture. The other was the city of Antwerp itself, and within the city of Antwerp, the Flemish community, which has a very specific identity and its own language and which is quite separate from the French community in Belgium. The other part of this package was the knowledge that this city which is known for its liberal values and its history, for example, of publishing and the free distribution of ideas, has at present 25 percent of its city council occupied by the Vlaams Belang, which is in many ways a protofascist organization. It's essentially racist, and that was the situation in which we were working. Another part of the package was the organizers of Antwerp 93 itself, none of whom came from Antwerp, and all of whom were different cultural producers and intellectuals representing different disciplines—they were all male, and all of the assistants were female. None of these different cultural and intellectual "departments" had any representation from the communities within Antwerp itself, either from the Flemish community or from the many other people who live in Antwerp, which is one of the biggest ports in Europe. It has for example a very substantial Moroccan population, and a Turkish population, Greek, and Spanish. All of these different populations have their own histories and reasons for being there but none of them were invited to participate in any way in the decision-making around this festival. When we questioned the organizers about this, they said that they didn't feel that these groups were professional enough to understand how to engage with such an event. So that was the very particular situation that we found ourselves in.

On the other side, we were located within a museum which itself proposed another kind of agenda. It was in a way a kind of caricature of the white box; it was what someone called "marvellously misconceived," in that it was a converted warehouse in the great tradition of converted industrial spaces, in the '60s tradition of the art space as a laboratory space. But in its conversion, it had displaced a whole community, which had previously worked in this area where the museum had been developed. The museum itself really came into being in a tangential way through the work of Gordon Matta-Clark—his penultimate work was made in Antwerp. In an effort to save that work by Matta-Clark, a number of artists donated artworks. And while that didn't save Matta-Clark's building, it became the foundation of the museum, and ironically the museum then became a force for the gentrification of an area of Antwerp which had previously been an industrial harbour area.

So, we were given this set of coordinates to work with, and into that we invited a number of artists, some of whom are here, to work in that situation. I wanted to focus, however, on another aspect of the project which has to do with audiences of the project, whereby we were attempting to get a sense of how to reflect what was happening in the museum to a number of different publics. One was clearly an art world—an art world which tends to move from one disembodied space to another, and which more or less is oblivious to the fact that they're in Venice, or in Kassel, or in New York. But actually, they go from one white space to another and talk among themselves and share a set of experiences. So, our attempt was to try to disrupt that by having them make another connection to this context in which they were experiencing this body of work. And so that was one kind of audience. We tried to do that by first of all explaining to them a local history, which was the history of Antwerp and its relation to the avant-garde, and to a point between 1958 and 1969 when various artistic communities were coming into contact with each other, and what happened as a result of that. That kind of local-international activity is happening all the time everywhere, and the idea is that there isn't a centre or a margin, but constant points of interaction. So that was one attempt.

The second was really to reflect the multiple communities which coexist in some way in Antwerp, and to try and represent them in the museum but also to engage them in what we were doing. We decided that the most sensible way of going to them was through community leaders and so-called public networks. We invited three different bodies. One was the university, and they had been involved in a project that looked at the relationship between urban renewal and decay, between gentrification and all the different aspects of urban development, and the social fabric of the city. We also went to a neighbourhood group who were trying to deal with urban decay and the way that different communities form their cultural identities. And, thirdly, we worked with a pirate radio station. The way that these things represented themselves is that we had some avant-garde map-making represented in the exhibition, and we had some rather extraordinary, I think, exhibitions, which were made by two local communities. Our point really was to look at the form of the exhibition and consider what

power or meaning it can have for audiences. One of the exhibitions that we had was a very kind of tacky thing, and our point partly was that you don't need these mega budgets, these enormous spaces, these kinds of displays—that actually there is another form that is as powerful, if not more so, which has been devised through expediency but which is incredibly effective. These exhibitions had folding cardboard stands, which one neighbourhood community put together, and they made these because, as a community group, the presence of this museum that we were working in had made all the prices of the housing rise all around the museum. So it was the usual pattern of gentrification, where people can't afford to pay the rents because of the galleries and boutiques coming in. Two hundred people living in two blocks of flats were going to be evicted by the city, who owned the buildings and who was going to sell them to developers. In response to that, these groups documented all of the housing problems, but, moreover, actually gave it a visual form which was very sophisticated and very accessible and we included that in the exhibition.

We also asked the local newspaper, which was given away free, if they would have people from the community, children for example, act as reporters who would then come in and investigate the procedures of what was happening in this place.

And then, finally, we invited Radio Central, which for me was one of the most important aspects of this and relates really to my other experience with audiences at the Institute of Contemporary Arts [ICA] in London. It seems that one of the key things that made that space important for me and important for London was the presence of the talks program. This is a platform in which there is a regular series of debates, so rather than having this fragmented individual experience of coming to exhibitions, there was a constituency which was developed through a particular discourse, a constituency that would keep coming back and that could talk to each other. There was a forum for literature in which South African writers from townships were coming together in a way that they couldn't actually meet in South Africa and also speaking to a broader public in London. And similarly, there is a forum of psychoanalysts who keep meeting there, a forum of philosophers who keep meeting there, and all of these different groups who use the ICA as a meeting place. So that seemed to me to provide a useful institutional model, something where you create the platform and people can feed into it. The bookshop I felt had a similar function, bringing in different publications, from fanzines to pamphlets, for example. So trying to transpose this to Antwerp was very difficult, because in London there was a development of debate discourse and you could name the individuals who were taking part in it. But when we were parachuted into Antwerp, we just didn't know who was doing what, where the writers were, where the activists were; so that was one problem.

One form we found was this radio station, which was a fantastic organization. It has no public money and no private sponsorship, and it works from a squat essentially, and in it they've set up a program which has a daily schedule, and every hour of the day there's a program which is put together by different people, and each program has a name, so for example at 6:00 p.m. Monday, there's something called "The African Bureau." None of the DJs are paid; they volunteer. And in the ten years it has been transmitting, everyone has always shown up, never ever has a program been missed, which is pretty amazing. The way it works is that 6:00 p.m. Monday night, some three DJs bring records. The night I was there, a band from Kinshasa [in DR Congo] was playing somewhere in Holland, they knew about that slot, so they came by, and there was a DJ visiting from Zaire, and he came by. So, it's a flexible structure where there are no names attached to particular slots: the slot just exists and you can just come by and participate in it.

I went by there one day and there was a Berber slot, and there were three Moroccan kids broadcasting—they were sensational. The structure was there, and what we did was invite that structure into the museum. Once it had been circulated that people could come in and broadcast, we felt that, while this could have become a spectacle, it worked, because the radio also moves around and broadcasts from different situations depending on the group broadcasting. And they enjoyed being there [at the museum], partly because they had lots of space; they could get to the people who were coming to the exhibition and they could interview them. That became a kind of forum: broadcasting out from the museum different programming. For example, new hybrid forms of local techno music—Belgium is known for techno, so you could hear that. But at the same time there was a program called "Women Trading," dealing with prostitution in Antwerp, where a lot of women are brought in from Third World countries and their passports are taken away and they are trapped there. Through the course of the exhibition, there was one slot where those women were invited and anonymously broadcast their stories. To me, that was a kind of virtual architecture, where through the institution we were able to bring in a kind of audience which not only was coming to participate in what was going on there but also was broadcasting out.

So that is my presentation of a way of working which I felt was successful. The downside of it was—and we were talking about this as well—that the museum felt intruded upon, and it was trying to do a lot of work in a condensed time. I mean, Renée, when you sent in your statement for the exhibition, that made us have to think again. Because you actually said, "Some cultural forms have agency, and by this I mean the ability to enable people to act…Agency for whom, and where is that agency found?" So we had to think again about how we approached this project. There was a bookshop there and I tried to make the bookshop open to having publications and bringing in stuff like, for example, *Third Text*, which is a magazine that is extremely developed in terms of creating a forum for debate. I tried to get the bookshop to take all of these publications, and magazines, and fanzines. But it was impossible. We ordered it all and they never opened the boxes. It was this kind of problem where you had to be there and maintain it daily. So as kind of outsiders, we were both in the situation of having a lot of freedom but at the same time it was very difficult to maintain any of this. And actually it's

not enough to just parachute into a situation: you've got to have a really long-term working relationship to develop a dialogue and some kind of faith in a project.

Helmut Draxler: What is your material about?

Blazwick: This material is a demography of Antwerp. A text by Gordon Matta-Clark about using structures as methods of communications. And the different public networks, the neighbourhood exhibitions, and the radio program.

Fraser: What I have to say might have been more appropriate for the last session, as it has a different tone that what has been discussed so far. But I'm going to play a few minutes, less than five minutes, of a tape. The introduction explains what it is, but you probably won't get much of an idea of what it goes on to be.

(Fraser plays audio tape of a recording from her contribution to the 1993 Whitney Biennial in New York.)

Andrea Fraser: "Hello, welcome to a 1993 biennial exhibition of the Whitney Museum of American Art. My name is Andrea Fraser, I'm an artist-participant in this year's biennial exhibition."

David Ross: "My name is David Ross and I'm the director of the Whitney Museum of American Art. How does that sound?"

Elisabeth Sussman: "I'm Elisabeth Sussman, I'm curator of the Whitney Museum. And yes, I'm the person who has been the designated leader of the 1993 Whitney Biennial."

Thelma Golden: "My name is Thelma Golden, I'm associate

curator at the Whitney and one of the four curators of the 1993 Whitney Biennial at the Whitney Museum of American Art."

Fraser: "As my contribution to the exhibition, I interviewed the curators of the 1993 biennial, as well as the curator of education and the director of the museum. And I combined the material to produce the audio-tape tour you are about to hear."

John Hanhardt: "My name is John Hanhardt, I'm curator of film and video and head of the film and video department, and was one of the co-curators of the 1993 biennial."

Connie Wolf: "I'm Connie Wolf, I'm curator of education at the Whitney Museum."

Lisa Phillips: "I'm Lisa Phillips, a member of the 1993 biennial team."

Ross: "Welcome to the Whitney Museum, hope you enjoy your visit. Welcome to the Whitney Museum, look forward to your responses. I would define the biennial's purpose as an art exhibition which allows us the opportunity to understand, or at least present, the zeitgeist. And to demonstrate once again the institutional support for American artists pushing forward. It has a special place in American culture, the biennial. To assess two years of activity in this extraordinarily large and complicated nation."

Wolf: "We have to convey that complexity, and allow our public to understand that complexity."

Ross: "To reflect on contemporary American art."

Wolf: "To see what was emerging in the last two years in the 1990s."

Ross: "I'm very proud of the biennial. And I'm particularly proud of the American art world. So it's a chance for people who aren't that engaged in it to walk away from it thinking, 'My god, this extraordinary thing is happening.' Men and women of great vision, commitment, and passion and have a way of communicating those ideas and that vision and those images to us in ways that I've never before considered. It's a project, it's an exhibition, it's a program that I've learned a great deal from over the years as a loyal attendee. That's a primary source of the mission for me too."

Fraser: "Now, let's view the exhibition together. Please take the elevator or the stairs to the fourth floor. When you reach the fourth floor, go to the wall text on your right as you exit the elevator. Turn off your acoustic-guide player when you hear the beep. Turn it on again when you reach the wall text on the fourth floor."

Ross: "Buckle your seatbelts, it's going to be a rough ride."

(Fraser stops the recording.)

(Laughter)

Fraser: Oh god, I haven't listened to that for almost a year.

Renée Green: I never even heard it.

Cahan: I did. You know what the guy at the front desk said? He said: "You know, it's not really an 'acoustic guide.'"

Fraser:…I'm sort of shocked by it, and my response to it, and I don't know if it's because of the experience of making it, or some other form of stress. It was an extremely difficult experience making this audio tape. And I think of it as the most disastrous project I have ever made. It was disastrous because of the kind of conflicts it created, conflicts that I didn't anticipate. And I failed to recognize my own ambivalence, and the way that my own ambivalence contributed to those conflicts.

So, what I just want to do is to explain the circumstances of the piece and describe the chronology and maybe some of this will be relevant to the discussion.

I thought to talk about it here because I was invited by Elisabeth Sussman and Connie Wolf at a rather early date in the process of creating the list for the Whitney Biennial, and I was invited at that early date primarily on the basis of a show I had done at the Berkeley university art museum [Berkeley Art Museum and Pacific Film Archive], which was an installation of the permanent collection in which I dealt with one bequest and looked at the struggles that took place over that bequest—I don't think that that's what they saw in it, but, in any case, these individuals, and the director of the museum, who was a new director, he brought the chief curator, Elisabeth Sussman, on the biennial with him, and Connie Wolf came a little bit later. They represented a new administration at the museum and this was their first biennial exhibition, an exhibition which has come under a lot of fire for most of its existence, but particularly in the last ten years. It was attacked every year. So they were quite anxious about the exhibition in the beginning, but they were also interested in making a statement with the exhibition about the new administration at the museum, and how the museum was changing. I think they were also interested not only in making a statement about the new Whitney Museum but also in making a statement about the old Whitney Museum. My sense was that that's what they wanted me to do. They wanted me to do something with the permanent collection, or to do something about the history of the museum and perhaps with the permanent collection. My feeling was that was not appropriate for an exhibition which would take over the entire museum, where the permanent collection would be in storage during an exhibition devoted entirely to contemporary art of the past two years was on view.

So I proceeded to make a series of proposals, the first three of which were rejected without a whole lot of explanation. Their first suggestion was that I use the lobby gallery on the ground floor to make a kind of orientation room. I liked that idea, but when I began proposing possibilities, I found they took that option off the table for some reason, again without explanation. I suggested doing a performance there without an installation of objects, and this was considered inadequate use of prime real estate, or prime exhibition space. Because the live performance was not going to be on view continuously, they felt the space was not being put to good use. I didn't want to do a tour myself, because I didn't want to be producing commentary on the work of the other artists in the show, and I also didn't want to have to be there for the duration of the show. The next proposal was to produce the wall texts you read when you enter into the galleries, and most Whitney Biennials have big curatorial statements at the beginning of the floors. So I spent a few weeks' research on that and discussed it with the curators, but then was told that would not be a good idea because, in this biennial, the curators wanted to take responsibility for their decisions and for the decision-making process, and those wall texts were one of the primary sites in which they could address their audience. And they had a responsibility to address that audience and to account for the choices and the curatorial decisions that were made. That was a very strong point that was also made by the director of the museum—that instead of it being curated by committee as usual, there would be one individual with primary responsibility.

So then finally I made this proposal: I proposed to interview the curators, the director, and the education director, and edit their voices together to produce an audio-tape tour. It was actually one of my first ideas but I thought they'd never do it. But it was accepted, and it may have been accepted partly because my earlier proposals were rejected and things were getting a bit tense. I'm not sure. Then when I proceeded to do the interviews, it was clear that there was a lot of anxiety. It was clear to me that there was a lot of anxiety around the exhibition from the very beginning, but, somehow, I didn't expect that to be such a limit in their discussions with me, and in proceeding with this project, this anxiety intensified. Even though there was some tension that resulted from the rejection of my first proposals, my interest was to collaborate with the curator—that's what I wanted to do. Before that I actually made a visit to the education department, made a presentation to the docents there, and had a number of discussions with the education director. I had a number of discussions with the curator of education, I supported their ambition to change the direction of the museum, and while I may have had some questions, I basically supported the direction they were

taking. I wanted to collaborate with them on addressing the audience, and I felt that the premise was that they wanted me to collaborate with them. Also, that it was going to be a kind of collaboration. But the piece as a kind of process of collaboration completely disintegrated into threats of postponement and demands that I re-edit the piece. I was very torn in this project. Because on the one hand, I entered into it as an artist-participant in the exhibition, and, as an artist, I'm accustomed to a certain kind of autonomy and a certain kind of control. There's an assumption that any form of direct interference amounts to censorship. But on the other hand, a premise of collaboration calls some of those things into question perhaps, and if I'm collaborating and I'm asking them to speak to me, and the premise is to use their voices directly, then perhaps I can't hold on to all of those rights without there being a danger of violating the trust implied by that participation. It wasn't clear, and I'm still not clear.

Although I was limited to what they said and what I could actually do in the tape, what I was trying to do in the tape was a couple of things. One, I was asking them to speak to me to describe who they felt their audience was. The questions I asked were: Who is your audience? What do you think a particular piece can provide that audience? What do you think that audience needs to know in order to gain access to this piece? And, what do you want your audience to get out of their experience with a particular piece? So, what you hear on the tape, if you're [an audience member] listening to it, you hear the curators talking about you in the third person. Because I'm editing together different voices, you hear the conflicts in the ways that these different curators conceive of you, think of you, think of what you're getting from a particular piece, think of what the museum is there to do for you. And that's what I wanted to do, but I wanted to do that in collaboration with them [the museum staff], I wanted to try to represent the issues that they were trying to address in the biennial in terms of their own interactions and conflicts within the museum, and their own varying conceptions of audience. And to communicate that directly through the way that played out in the course of the tape. Although I sort of knew that's not the way they would want me to do it, I still felt that I did it in good faith. What was so painful about listening to that tape is how—particularly for those of us who were involved in the biennial perhaps, and know these people— you know, there is this intense response and the sort of intensity of laughter. The way that the piece was heard by people who liked it, as well as by people who didn't like it, was as a really vicious exposure of these people. Maybe they didn't like it because of that, and maybe they *did* like it because of that, but that was never what I intended to do. It's absolutely not what I wanted to do, and I'm not sure how it ended up being perceived that way. I guess I'll stop there.

Green: My reaction to the tape was partly really mixed. It's sort of difficult to locate where the reaction is coming from, because I also found that experience to be a very traumatic one. In a way, it was one of the most traumatic exhibition experiences I've ever had in my life. So, it could have been the hysterical laughter of re-experiencing and remembering the pain. But it also made me laugh because what it reminded me of was the promotional campaign for the Olympics. Somehow it had the kind of pathos of the "Berlin 2000" signs hanging all over the place still, after Australia has won the bid for the 2000 Olympics. There are some aspects of loss, of hope and ambitions, but also the total fallibility; it's just kind of depressing. But I didn't think of it as a vicious thing. It's actually quite interesting, the overlap of the voices.

Fraser: My interpretation partly of the way that it was perceived—and it's also very much a part of what I wanted to do—is that you don't hear people representing institutions speaking in this kind of unprepared way. You don't hear them speak in ways that are not necessarily in complete sentences, not necessarily in intellectually up-to-the-minute ways. It's real speech. But, also, what you hear because of the situation of the interview, and because it was clear that this material would be made public from the beginning, you hear how they are trying to represent themselves, you hear the effort at self-presentation, and you hear the anxiety behind that. And I knew about that, and I thought this could be liberating for the audience—to hear how even the representatives of the institution cannot so thoroughly identify with the institution. But of course, one never experiences anxiety in that way.

Judith Barry: I just wondered what upset them. Was it the fact that you used things out of context? I was just wondering what their rationale was for wanting you to re-edit it.

Fraser: By the time they asked me to do that, I had stopped talking to them, I had ended the discussions. If there had been a real collaborative process, and a real support, and a real dialogue, I wouldn't have been as averse to thinking about re-editing. But because that had broken down so entirely, it just seemed completely outrageous. So I never really spoke to them about it.

Barry: Have you spoken to them or anyone about it since?

Fraser: No.

Michael Clegg: But they didn't try to suppress it.

Cahan: In subtle ways they did. I knew of Andrea's project, and when I went to the Whitney Museum to see the biennial, I wanted to make sure to hear the audio guide, and simply by virtue of the audio-guide dispenser informing me that it wasn't a "real audio guide," that it was "an artist project," and asking if I still wanted it—

Fraser: He asked you if you still wanted it?

Cahan: Yes. So for one thing, he was limiting the distribution, and, secondly, he was undercutting the subversive aspect of it, and the element of surprise.

Fraser: I made it clear what it was in the introduction and in the signage, that I was an artist-participant in the exhibition and I had done this piece as my contribution, and that it contained the voices of so on and so forth. I mean, I didn't manipulate it…I edited it.

(Laughter)

Martin Guttmann: Are you seriously saying that when you listened to it for the first time after you finished editing it, that you didn't think it was funny?

Fraser: You don't know what kind of state I was in when I finished it.

Guttmann: Some people think that if it is something funny and it has people involved, then it has to be vicious. I don't know. But it is really funny.

Ulrich Bischoff: I think that if I were to work in this institution, I would understand directly what is the danger of this piece—that it is very authentic. If an institution like the Whitney Museum is really itself in danger, and you put that in the open, they would be anxious about that. But that is because it is very authentic.

Clegg: There is something real in this audio tape that is different compared to the piece in Munich.

Fraser: In Munich it wasn't the actual tapes from the interviews—the interviewees went back into a studio and reread what they had said directly from the interviews.

Bischoff: But in Munich some people were also upset.

Fraser: Munich was a dream compared to this. Munich really worked.

Bischoff: That is because the board members in Munich aren't living in this kind of art world society. But the people at the Whitney really have to identify completely with the

Whitney. In Munich, they like to have a distance.

Draxler: In Munich, it was a board and they are executives. So it was not so easy.

Guttmann: I think that one of the things that happened is that they probably had a basic ambivalence about being highlighted, because on the one hand they wanted the Whitney to change direction, but on the other hand, their candidacy was advanced for the wrong reason—they were really chosen for the wrong reasons, for political reasons. So they were sitting ducks. They knew that there was a lot going against them.

Fraser: I would like to talk about how this might function as a way of addressing an audience. There's a premise here that "it's my right to do something like that," and that these are representatives of a public institution, so there is a certain kind of disclosure that they're obliged to. But at the same time, they are individuals and have all the rights to privacy that anyone else does. In that sense, it's an ethical question, and for me that's the biggest question about that piece. Why I wanted to present it here is to discuss: When an institution invites me to collaborate in addressing their audience, and the way that I choose to do that draws attention to contradictions in their discourse in a public manner, is that a possible or recommended approach?

Ute Meta Bauer: I wanted to ask Renée why she felt that the Whitney Biennial was her most difficult exhibition experience. Why?

Green: For various reasons. Partly because of my own doubts about the way it was being situated before the exhibition happened. And how it was being approached. For example, it was being identified as the "multicultural biennial." And I was thinking: Why would I want to be part of that when I've been vocally critical of the term "multiculturalism" for a while? I was anticipating a really simplistic approach. If it was already being defined that way before it was even presented, I knew that there were problems ahead.

Then also the anxiety that I observed among the curators, which was also problematic, because I felt that, with this anxiety, they wouldn't be able to really represent their points of views strongly enough to defend their choices and the reasons for why they selected the people that they did. I don't think that they ever did that, and that was the saddest aspect of the entire thing for me. They wanted to perceive themselves as going out on a limb, which was already a problem for me, because that is a marginalization of the work and a marginalization of the people making the work. And then their reactions to the public were very disturbing to me. For example, at one point, when we were installing upstairs, the floors below were already open, and David Ross told us that a woman, who came in not knowing he was the director of the museum, spoke very critically of the exhibition and then told him that he should take his daughter, who was standing with him there at the time, to the Metropolitan Museum of Art so that she could "get a dose of real culture," or something like that. But he didn't defend that in any strong way when he described that encounter to me and another artist there.

The responses to the exhibition I observed from curators I also found incredibly disturbing. For example, there was an avoidance thing— I mean a literal avoidance—of the curators from the artists, of the curators facing up to the artists. This was my experience anyway. I mean, Fred was there too. I was not present in New York so much at the time, after the show went up. But it was a strange situation. The piece for the show was not done to my satisfaction for one thing, it was not specified in the way I wanted, and I argued it all the way, but it was never done in the right way, and so I was disappointed in that. I wasn't around so much for the reception, but I heard everything from a distance and that was even more disturbing. I was not able to be in discussion with people about the reception, and so my view of it got distorted, I think.

Fred Wilson: I have different feelings about it. I think that the exhibition is not set up for people to do installations, but the majority of people did installations—they wanted to do something special for their show— and they did that with no time and no money. I think a lot of people were very disappointed because of that aspect of it.

Fraser: I think we should go back to this point tomorrow, in the last session perhaps.

Draxler: To get back to audiences, just to take what you did, Andrea, before, and to consider the symbolic artistic appropriation of a service within an institution—a practice that comes out of an institution itself, like curatorial activity. Can we try to analyze the differences in the results, and what are the possibilities?

Fraser: I'm interested because the kind of educational strategies that Susan was talking about are all coming from the outside in a certain way. This was about trying to express the contradictions in the centre of the institution—how do we express the contradictions in the centre of the institution itself. I think there are a lot of educational programs now— and we can talk about this in terms of your project, Iwona, in Antwerp too—of bringing things in that either deal with contradictions that are considered more external, or that try to surpass the contradictions of the institution by opening it up or changing constituencies.

Cahan: The thing that I alluded to at the end of my presentation, which has been very challenging for me, is: How do you execute the kinds of projects I discussed without turning them into symbolic gestures—without having them turn into symbolic representations? Of course, they are representation, but they are not forms of discourse that are analogous to what you're doing, Andrea, when you're working with montage or re-editing recorded material. I think that accounts for the ease with which the institution I work with has been able to absorb very confrontational statements into its ongoing program, and to not have it really function as a disruption.

Fraser: In a certain way, if my tape exposed anything, it exposed the good intentions of the curators, and the good intentions which are the means of that kind of absorption.

Wilson: I think there would have been a different response if the individuals had been really comfortable, and if it had not been the Whitney Biennial, and if they had not been so worried about that particular exhibition. The issue is really representation. I know that when I'm interviewed, I tend to be more or less worried depending on the distribution and audience, so I think that it boils down to that. In my show [in Maryland], *Mining the Museum*, they could have just closed off the floor if they didn't like it, and so there were moments when I didn't know [if they would do that]. So you're pushing them to the edge, but in the end, they have control over their own voice.

Guttmann: Thinking about the tape, and why you, Susan, were thinking it was absorbed so easily: my own reaction to that—and I'm saying this in a very tentative way because it's an interesting, complex question that should not be responded to so quickly—but my feeling is that maybe it tells us that there is something faulty in the logic of disruption. You're not functioning as an artist, but I suppose that it was a form of art…

Cahan: Well, it was someone's art. All the projects I discussed are sort of weird in that they don't really fall into any pre-existing category, and, in fact, even though they have been some of the most exciting projects that I've ever been involved with in my years of museum work, none of them have gotten any grants, because when we apply in individual artist categories, we're told, "These aren't artists' project, these are education projects." And when we apply for museum education grants, we're told, "These aren't education projects, these are artist projects." All of them were either done in

collaboration with artists or, in the case of the video project, the idea was conceived by Matthew Geller, who is an artist, and the project was designed by Branda Miller, who also oversaw it. But my role is sort of weird—my role is that I work within the institution and it's my job to see that the project happens, and hopefully with integrity and in the way the artists want to see it realized. Does that make sense?

Guttmann: Yeah, it makes sense. But beyond this discussion about "qualification," my thought is that perhaps what it really tells us is that there is something faulty in the logic of disruption. In other words, to do a project where the primary concern is to create a discontinuity in a seamless texture is something that has some inherent problems because, firstly, things are not as seamless as they seem to be, and, second, because it is a very temporary gesture, which simply doesn't work for a long time. When you have an expectation that art works slightly longer over time, then maybe things like that can happen—maybe there was a disruption for five minutes, but then other things happen that took the original moment and turned it around. My thought about it is that some of the same ideas can be reformulated and transformed into other sets of concerns which are more about creating counterhegemonic practices, which are simply about leaving certain unwanted anger behind and doing other things instead of insisting on proving the imperfections of the things that you want to change.

Cahan: That's exactly the kind of transformation that I've gone through in my own work.

Blazwick: I'd like to agree with that, because I think the whole idea about "subversion" is impossible —it's naive, and it's not something that's possible. I don't even think it's worth considering as a strategy, because you're dealing with an entire society—the whole twentieth century is what one is dealing with. I agree with you: you either work within its terms and try to expose it—which I'm uncomfortable with, because exposing it is a given—or I think you develop a parallel practice. You work within it or you exploit it in some way, and that's the only possibility. But the idea about subversion in a way seems like shooting yourself in the foot.

Fraser: What are the options? A parallel practice, working within it, or…

Blazwick: Developing something outside of it, or alongside it, or using whatever structures exist within it. But to think that you can permanently disrupt or create some kind of rupture in this is…I'm not saying that it's hopeless, but that one has to take a certain number of givens, and that you work within those givens.

Cahan: I've never primarily thought about the work I show as "subversive." I've primarily thought about it as providing possibilities for a multiplication of narratives.

Wilson: It seems pretty clear to me why the New Museum was able to absorb those tapes [of museum visitors' opinions]: it's because of the authority of the people in the tapes. The powers that be do not give any authority to the people on the tapes, they don't feel the pinch of power telling them what to do. If

it was Vera List or Charles Luce or one of the donors saying the same exact thing—I mean that would be pretty funny—but anyway, if they were saying the same exact thing, it would actually affect the people at the museum.

Barry: Also implicit in that show was the notion of broadcast television as representing white middle-class America. If you analyze that show, US politics and television never mix. There is only a brief moment between 1968 and 1970 when television is political. The show was very clear about representing white middle America in an overt way. That's a reason why his [museum visitor Art Jones's] critique was part of the exhibition, and he got it.

Wilson: I think his critique was extremely cogent, but it was out of an expression of powerlessness that he was having a voice, and so that voice is not going to go any further because it was understood.

Guttmann: But it was quite threatening, very specific. He said that "it's no longer postmodernism, it's now the '90s." He really meant business.

Wilson: What *kind* of business, that's what I am trying to ask.

Green: That was Art Jones, he's a video producer himself. A film-maker and multimedia artist. He was working with the video group, really interesting.

Wilson: You can't expect that to affect the power structure, because obviously there have been voices like his speaking directly to the museum structure for a while. It's because they are coming from a place that does not affect the power structure—it's not a board member, it's not going to produce a fundamental change. It can be absorbed because he's not standing over anyone with a stick which is a threat. You know?

Fraser: I want to contrast what Susan and Iwona were talking about, and different strategies. Susan said that when people in the New Museum saw these things, they said, "Oh, let's do this permanently," so that, as you [Susan] interpreted, "we don't have to change anything." That way we can have a permanent, self-reflexive, pseudocritical, supplementary program that goes on, and even if there is an apparent participation, it's not real participation. I was thinking it's not "real" participation, because the subject is always the museum and that doesn't allow for…And then I was thinking about what you, Iwona, were doing in Antwerp, where the subject was not the museum, and I was wondering if that's one of the differences between a participatory practice or democratic process and an administered one, where you make a platform. But then what are the issues that are possible to articulate?

Blazwick: There's also an interesting model that has been developed in Britain, called Anefa, in which money has been taken from the public purse through the arts council to set up a loose network which has to do with exhibition making and publishing. So, for example, money was given to a publishing program, part of that was *Third Text* but other publishing initiatives too; for instance, they just published all of Jimmie Durham's writings. But the point is: they have given money for printing

and distribution and that, to me, is essential. It's about communication. Then they have also given money to set up exhibitions—an artist, Sunil Gupta, has been working to set up exhibitions which are then offered to different venues. And Gupta, as a [South] Asian photographer who also happens to be gay, is looking at constituencies who have not been represented in the management structure. You create your own structure, and then you create your own way of communicating and distributing that, rather than constantly slamming your head against this granite wall. Incrementally of course things do change: the very fact that there are women in those structures, that there are different constituencies who are slowly and incrementally making their way through those structures. But I think there are also other ways of doing it.

Bauer: But don't you think a big difference between Anefa and for example the Whitney is that the artists themselves are founding that situation? We know for ourselves what we want. I think it has a lot to do with serving audiences. If the Whitney Museum says they want to do a multicultural biennial, they don't want to do it for themselves; they want to hide the political problems they can't change, and they do that by putting it into an art context.

Green: That was my point. A lot of the projects that were brought into that exhibition were much more effective in other situations. And people like Art Jones were distributing their work themselves, using technology to intervene, and constantly readdressing the issue of absorption. These are people who are always aware of the possibility of being absorbed into the hegemonic structure.

Bauer: If you do a big show at the moment, you're always told that it has to be multicultural and social, because they want to support these issues now in the art field for the audience, but they don't change anything outside of that. The art world is such a small thing. You can be very open and very social, but it's a limited audience. It's a special field where you cannot change anything in the society. It's like a big trap.

Guttmann: Oppressive tolerance.

Fraser: But don't you think that there is a substantial dimension of social experience that one could say is, properly speaking, cultural? And that some of that takes place within museums? I abandoned, at least consciously, the subversive model a while ago, but I don't want to give up on doing something within museums, and I also don't want a parallel practice, because museums are a site where there is a certain social experience that takes place, which has all of these dynamics and histories of the site that are worth addressing. I think that the experiences that people have in museums is worthwhile to address.

Draxler: But do you have an idea of how to address the audience? Because how you described the Whitney piece is that it happened by accident that you hit upon this confrontational model. What you wanted was a collaboration. So if a collaboration had worked, what kind of address would it have been?

Fraser: I think it would have been the same. I just didn't want it to

be so problematic for the people who were participating. I wanted to represent them. I didn't want to hurt them. I didn't want to misrepresent them, but I wanted to represent things that were not necessarily consistent with maintaining an authoritative, legitimate representation of that kind of institution. I thought that was consistent with their own intentions: to engage in a critique of the institution and its history, a critique of the legitimacy of the culture which that institution had traditionally represented. I thought that was consistent with what they wanted to do.

Wilson: On a theoretical level, it was. But it boiled down to their need, in this particular instance, to be shored up by heroic images.

Fraser: Or that all that social contradiction is just a little too much for an individual to represent personally to an audience of thousands of people.

Clegg: What's interesting to me is that the Whitney as an institution is so much stronger than its curators. The change in the policies have been so minimal because of all these constraints that the curators have and impose on artists. The problems that you're talking about with the 1993 biennial are different versions of what we experienced four years earlier, where you were basically led to be very happy at the idea that you were allowed to be in the show. They looked very carefully at work, and they had their own idea, and their own selection. One of the things we did at one point was to do portraits of the curators, and they certainly didn't want that to be in the show, and it was not even terribly clear why, except that they didn't

want to have that kind of representation of themselves in the show.
So these Whitney Biennials are
always about change, but without
any specific representational change
themselves, not allowing really site-
specific projects.

Barry: I want to say something about
a catalogue that Andrea is showing [on the projection screen]. *The
Desire of the Museum* was a project
done by Whitney students in the curatorial program where I was teaching. I was working with the students
on that exhibition, aiding them in
the conceptualization and design of
the exhibition *The Desire of the Museum* in 1989. The students, mostly
postgraduate students in the Whitney Independent Study Program,
wanted to examine the Whitney
Museum and expose, from a psy-
choanalytic perspective, its history.
The Whitney completely censored
everything. We weren't allowed to
show any documents; we weren't
even allowed to show a chronology of the Whitney's history as a
museum. Instead of the show being
about the desire of the students for
another kind of institutional frame,
it became a show about artists'
desire for another type of institutional representation. The Whitney
censored itself and removed itself
from this context. And this is not unusual Whitney behaviour, in fact—it's
systemic there, and in many other
museums.

Renate Lorenz: I wanted to say that I
don't share your opinion, [Ute,] that
it's not important what's happening in the art field. I think it's very
important for society how decisions
are made in the art field. Because a
lot of people are looking at that, and
I think it's too easy to say, "Oh, it's

not important, because the whole
society is much bigger." In an exhibition like at the Whitney, they don't
change the structures because they
have the same kind of decision-
making structures and problems
and issues as in society. And even
if there are a lot of artists who were
not visible before, that's only a representational change.

Green: Yeah, and I also wanted to
readdress something that you said,
Ute. Because I've been harshly
against what happened at the
Whitney, but there is another aspect
to it. Despite the difficulty of breaking out of the existing framework
of the museum, there is the fact
that the audience of that biennial
was larger than previous audiences,
and it did give people something to
talk about. I was surprised by the
responses from audiences—not the
critics, because that's a whole other
thing. But, so, despite the restrictions placed by that structure on the
work, something else did happen,
and I think there were some hopeful
aspects there.

Bauer: I don't think that what goes
on in the art field is not important. I
wouldn't put so much of my energy
into it if I did think that, or if it was
just about having fun. But, for
example, the city of Stuttgart on the
one hand can't solve the problems
of people seeking asylum, while
on the other hand they're asking
an institution like ours to do more
social-cultural work. This is a trap.
They're trying to solve political
problems culturally, saying we have
a multicultural society, and while it's
important for people so see that, it
can't be that alone—they also have
to change the political policies.

Lorenz: I think that with these big exhibitions, you can't change the structures. You have to put your energy into another field where you can more direct the positions and directions of the whole social field.

Jochen Becker: The Whitney Biennial was, I think, a centralization of decentralized projects based in very different areas. But these projects were not in Midtown [Manhattan], so the Whitney centralized them there, and in doing so, they broke the institutional critique work and these other practices.

Guttmann: Yeah, in a big way. Nobody could have done more damage to this kind of work than the Whitney. The work was also displayed so badly that you couldn't relate to any thought or any idea. It was all bad form. It was all thrown together.

Wilson: It's very typical of Americans to do that, to go 180 degrees to solve something and then snap all the way back.

Becker: The question is: Why did it happen like that? If you had some pain in the stomach or so many misgivings in advance, and you knew that this was obviously a problem for more community-based projects… I mean, the Whitney Biennial is now discussed here in Germany as the big exhibition, and the turning point, and…

Draxler: That's important to say—that the critical reception in Germany of this show was really incredible. In this very basic way, it was presented as this kind of new art gossip, and it was discussed in magazines through a very conservative perspective, even in publications like *Der Spiegel*. The show that Peter Weibel made about this trajectory of institutional critique, *Kontext Kunst* [at Neue Galerie Graz am Landesmuseum in 1993], was exactly the same, just that it was not in Manhattan.

Becker: Was there any change with regard to the interest in community-based projects after the show?

Green: I want to say something about "pain in the stomach." I felt very removed. When a curator chooses a piece, you can either say, "I don't want to be in the show" or "I want to be in the show but I want it to be done in this way," and they say yes or no.

Fraser: I wouldn't think of what was in the Whitney Biennial as community-based work. A lot of the work was exhibited in places other than SoHo, but that doesn't mean that it had a participatory relationship to the communities in which it was first shown. Most of it was pretty much studio practice. It was just people with studios outside of Lower Manhattan.

Cahan: One of the problems with it was that it focused on things that are political in a topical way, so it had this weird thematic overlay.

Fraser: Nancy Spero was in the Whitney Biennial, and she had never been in a biennial before.

Cahan: Oh, OK, so this was a redressing of that omission.

Clegg: It was very strange. It was a way of showing how out of sync New York is with the rest of the country politically. Because all of these questions about the installation and display—they don't explain why there was such a backlash to the show. To me it proved that New York is really anchored in the '80s.

Wilson: The show had more attendance than any biennial ever. The press was really this reactionary press, this kind of knee-jerk press. Aren't the problems of the Whitney Biennial, and any Whitney Biennial, the same problems as the Venice Biennale and documenta? These big shows that try to culminate and sum up a particular period of years, or represent cultures of certain places. So, for the people who organize and invest in this huge symbolic gesture, that becomes personalized, and then you have a problem with the curators, because they are so tied to the show being a representation of a culmination of their idea.

Fraser: The Whitney Biennial has always been trashed. I read ten years of press, and it really has always been trashed. The New York press has a tendency to trash international shows like this. I'm surprised to hear that documenta was celebrated in the press.

Blazwick: The Whitney shouldn't dominate; it's just one little institution.

(Laughter)

Blazwick: No, really—we never talk about any of these other events or exhibitions. It's imperialism, I'm afraid.

Fraser: Yeah. I don't want to talk about Venice or documenta either.

Blazwick: Havana, Istanbul—there are other really important events and exhibitions to talk about.

Draxler: I think it would be good to talk about some of these other specific contexts, and discuss the structural conditions, or how practices were adopted there, or the culture mayor of Stuttgart—I don't know of any other city that has one, but the city of Stuttgart does. And that is a very influential position which has a lot to do with audiences and addressing audiences.

I also want to say that I have a kind of sympathy for the subversive. What the guy in the [New Museum] video, Art Jones, did was very subversive in a certain way. But what you, Susan, did was not.

Cahan: What do you mean? I wouldn't necessarily disagree with you, but I'm curious what you mean, Helmut.

Draxler: What you're doing I would describe more as creating an address to an audience.

Cahan: Well, I don't know if this is what you intended to say, but one distinction that I've started to make is between changing certain institutional practices and other activities that I would consider political, because I don't think that changing institutional practices or relationships is necessarily political. It depends on the politics of the people who are involved. Giving artists more freedom or more autonomy in museums isn't necessarily a politically progressive thing to do; it depends on the artist. If it's Helen Frankenthaler, it's not necessarily progressive.

Renée, you asked me earlier what I'm working on now. Well, what I'm working on now is a long-term collaboration with artist-activists and adult students in three predominately Latino neighbourhoods in New York to develop an installation that looks at the recent history of Latino immigration to New York through individual life histories and personal testimony. It was just installed at the New Museum, and now it's going to go to sites in those neighbourhoods. It's been very interesting from an educational standpoint, because it includes aspects of the history of New York that are not included in textbooks, so we have gotten a lot of school groups coming to learn about that history. It is a more productive practice than a deconstructive practice in terms of the art institutional relationships. One of the things we have done is, within this consortium of fifteen people, we have agreed to collectively make all the administrative decisions for the project in terms of what kinds of funding we're going after, how money is being spent, how it's represented to the press. At this point, it's an experiment that is working. There are conflicts in this kind of group work all the time, but because so many people in this consortium have activist backgrounds, they really know how to manage these collaborative situations.

Blazwick: I would like to ask about what people's experiences were in Arnhem for Sonsbeek 93. I'm interested in the question of audience in that kind of situation, when you're outside of institutions and in this city. I'm wondering what kind of possible relationships were developed.

Draxler: Stephan, you were there.

Stephan Dillemuth: I was there. It was a day trip to Arnhem and people had to look for the Easter eggs, that was it. For some people, that's fun.

Blazwick: There was a lot of tension too, it seems. I gathered from the organizers that there was a lot of aggression against the art, and people destroying the work.

Dillemuth: That may be true, but this I didn't realize. I made a film about the show and then I disappeared. I heard there were a lot of complaints about damage, but I think that if you do a show like that, you have to be aware of that possibility. I think that the damage shows something which I think may not be so bad at all. But maybe the way they dealt with the damage was problematic. For instance, I know Andreas Siekmann told the organizers to please leave it damaged like it is, because that shows something. But then they started to clean up and paint over the spray-painted slogans and build it back as it was before. They did that a couple of times and then asked Siekmann to come hold a public discussion and open the valve that way. I think it's good that art puts a pressure on a certain audience which usually stays anonymous. And if art can show that, maybe it's good.

Blazwick: There was a project in Newcastle last year which raised so much anger and complaints that I think it was a shock for everyone involved in it. The works were not only vandalized but people lost their jobs. It was really a very violent response. The curator was again in the position of being parachuted in and failed, I think, to co-opt the local politicians and the museum service, who felt that their role was being usurped, and so they tried to control the project and the expenditure on each artist's project by insisting that the head of the museum personally sign every single order. So, if you can imagine: if you wanted a packet of screws, the man at the very top of this huge bureaucratic pyramid has got to sign that piece of paper. So eventually he stopped the project, and that was quite clearly the intention.

One of the curators, who was an intermediary working in the museum, signed the orders so that artists could continue to work and receive their per diems, and he lost his job and was accused of embezzlement. It's really serious, and also various figures were leaked to the public as to the cost of the project, and inevitably there was that sort of backlash about all these other problems about housing and urban decay. The whole exhibition project acted as a flashpoint for all of those different issues. I was wondering what people felt about artists being put into these different situations where you're having to deal with a foreign community that is very complex.

Bischoff: I'm sorry to come back to the Whitney, but this reminds me of when they had Andy Warhol's painting *Before and After* (1961) above the membership desk at the Whitney Museum. And when the new director came, he immediately took it down. So it is not possible to make art politics. A big institution has to arrange things like product management.

The exhibition Sonsbeek was very good in '69, it was not as good the next time, and this time they want to arrange the new art so that it was not really made by artistic ideas but by art politics. This is typical of big exhibitions. But it was astonishing that this aggression happened in the Netherlands.

Dillemuth: But maybe people are fed up with public art in the Netherlands because they have so much.

Clegg: Often the problem is with the work itself, with cultural politics in which art is brought from the top down. Like in many places in France, where you have to wonder why it is necessary to have these museums, which obviously have no audience and don't really make any attempt to develop one, other than to present art as something that is just good for people. That art raises them up. So I think that it's interesting to think about the failure of artists in the kind of work they are doing, and how they interact with the places in which they place the works.

Barry: The issue of how people relate to art in the public realm and how the discourse around art is developed—artists try to control it, as do curators, often from different perspectives. But they don't try to control what goes out to the public directly via the press, because they cannot. In the United States, with the NEA [National Endowment for the Arts] censorship and the loss of funding around questions of art and free speech, and the right's targeting of sexuality and the representation of homosexuality, this became clear. Art was an easy target.

Guttmann: But there's an important point here, because if you go to a city where people are really poor, where there are chronic problems, then artists need to take the process of justification really seriously. It's not just that the right wing picked an easy target. The way that the New Right targets art is a cheap trick, but what we're talking about here is something that I think every person who wants to have to do with art needs to deal with.

Barry: But this is about audience and constructing a discourse that can handle that level of cultural critique when it filters into the popular press.

Guttmann: I think that in many of the cases, people don't even take the most minimal steps of addressing the people who live in the immediate vicinity where the art is. They don't make even the most benign attempt to see who lives there, what they might want, what kind of uses they made of these sites. These kinds of questions are really just the ABCs of dealing with a situation. There are so many art projects that fail on this elementary level that anything beyond that is really a matter of speculation because there's a real lack of awareness of the most elementary aspect of the ethics of working in public spaces.

Fraser: I have to make a very important point, which is that if we don't stop in the next five minutes, we won't eat.

Cahan: I want to respond to what Judith said—I think that what you're talking about reflects the really undeveloped nature of understanding reception. Which is what my work has really been centred on. It also reflects the traditional notion of art as being an object, rather than the notion of art's reception as a process.

Barry: What Martin was talking about has to do with a different set of issues.

Guttmann: The way I understood the problems in Newcastle was because

it is such a problematic area. And people freaked out, yes, but I think that they have the right to freak out. There should be new standards of accountability for how money is spent on art. I really do think this. There's just no place for frivolous adventure; there's just no point anymore, if there ever was.

Fraser: Renée could talk about adventures with public art agencies in New York City, and how if you try to do something other than put tiles on the walls in school buildings, you don't have a chance. If you try to do something community based, if you try to involve school kids in doing a project in schools, you won't get anywhere. It's a whole different ball game. The kinds of things we would like to see public art do run into all sorts of limits, which are not necessarily only the limits of artists.

Wilson: In the South Bronx, which is known for its vandalism and graffiti, we have lots of public art that's always pristine and very well kept and very well respected. People just live with it. Work by John Ahearn and Rigoberto Torres never gets touched; it's part of the neighbourhood.

Blazwick: Can artists take on this enormous responsibility of navigating the complexities of a local situation, number one. I think it's extremely difficult and it takes a huge amount of time and energy and resources to try to deal with that complexity in a satisfactory way. Secondly, it [Newcastle] was an object lesson in how not to organize something. There was a kind of patrician disregard for the powers that be. I think that one had to really work very carefully with them, because as soon as you get into the situation where you say "they're idiot politicians," or "they are stupid hierarchies," or that "we don't want to deal with them"—then it's just not possible to work.

Guttmann: But this is frivolous; this is precisely the point. You want to go from A to B and there is a C in the middle. So you say, "Well, let's just pretend that C doesn't exist."

Blazwick: I think the artists really tried very hard, and I think that they got caught up in a hierarchical structure.

Bischoff: I think this question of the extent of the responsibility of the artists and curator should be taken up tomorrow.

Draxler: Thank you, Uli!

(Laughter)

Green: Let's have dinner.

Working Group
Session Four

Serving Communities
Sunday, January 23, 1994

Presentations:
Stephan Dillemuth
BüroBert
Clegg & Guttmann

Critiques of art institutions and the art market have led some artists to form alternative art organizations and/or to undertake projects within communities not traditionally served by artists.

Can the anarchist and radical democratic basis of many alternative organizations be reconciled with the professionalization implied by expert-client models?

Can nonart communities be served through art institutions? What happens when the interests of artists and the nonart communities they attempt to serve are found to be in conflict?

Helmut Draxler: Good morning. There were some complaints raised that yesterday's presentations were not being specific enough about conditions, so I just wanted to address this and hopefully we can come back to this point during our discussions today.

Andrea Fraser: And for those of you presenting today, perhaps think about that. The comments had to do with the ratio between a narration of the project and an introduction of the issues that the project raised. That latter part is what we would like to focus on a little bit more than we were able to yesterday.

Draxler: Stephan, is it OK for you to begin?

Stephan Dillemuth: First of all, to start with a joke: I lost my manuscript on the train, so I had to rewrite it. You know the story.

(Laughter)

Dillemuth: All right. First part: practice.

A: Friesenwall 120; started January 1990 searching for a studio space; finding this space in the area of Cologne where the galleries are. Group work, with Josef Strau, Nils Norman, Merlin Carpenter, and Kiron Khosla. Experiments for a different definition of exhibitions; all the exhibitions question what an exhibition can be.

B: Space as a part of an artists' community, a hang out, a video/information exchange, and delivery of archive extension.

C: Acceptance of this. And being labelled as an "alternative space." Therefore, also fulfilling the function of a gallery and showing artists sometimes.

D: Invitation to other places, to other institutions such as Pat Hearn [Gallery in New York] and Forum Stadtpark [in Graz]; the problem of translation from one current situation to others. My participation in Sonsbeek 93, 5,000 DM honorarium; Firminy [for Project Unité in 1993], no honorarium. I tried to make a film about both of these shows, to try to see the whole show from outside.

E: Others who take distribution into their own hands. That happened at the Unfair [in Cologne in 1992].

Second part: theory. I'm not dealing with this much actually, but my friend, Kiron Khosla, when I told him about this discussion happening here, he gave me an article by Gilles Deleuze called "Postscript on the Societies of Control." Also, referring to what we discussed so much yesterday, which is the question of what is an institution that is being criticized in general. So, to make a short overview, Michel Foucault introduces the recognition of disciplinary societies of the eighteenth and nineteenth centuries, which consist of the organization of spaces of enclosure— that in life you have to transgress from the organization of family, to school, to barracks, to factory, to hospital, to prison, and I add now: to the museum. This is a structure of capitalism in the old definition. The crisis came at the turn of the century. The reform of all of these organizations meant that new forces and new technologies emerged.

So this developed more and more into societies of control in which enclosures open up and incorporate other strategies of authority and power to re-establish the old strength. The corporation replaced the factory. The system of bonuses is realized through challenges, contests, group sessions, and built-in critique. Even unions fulfill a healthy form of integration. Perpetual training replaces schooling. Codes, not words, mark access to information or reject it. Surfing replaced other sports. Machines changed from levers and clocks to computers. Capitalism changed from the concentration of production and specialization and colonization to selling services and buying stocks. And even art has left spaces of enclosure in order to enter open circuits. Man is no longer man enclosed, but man in debt.

That's all coming from this article, that's not mine.

Control is not only the erosion of ruptures, it is also substituting the sites of enclosure. Museums, *Kunst-vereins*, cultural institutions, other shanty towns or ghettos—whatever crisis is proclaimed. Substitution instead of penalties, perpetual training instead of research, new ways of handling money and profits. The crisis of institutions will also concern the ineptitude of the unions, which is tied to their history of struggle against the discipline.

So it all ends with my question: What are the new forms of resistance against societies of control? If we apply this to what happened here, I don't think we ever talked about institutions of art as power positions in the differentiated complex of the society of control. To choose artworks and exhibit them seems like a society of enclosure. And while this is also a service—a service for whom? To incorporate artists within curatorial functions or critical functions. To incorporate audience participation and critique. To incorporate marginal positions like ethnic issues, pirate radio, and discos are also still strategies of the aforementioned corporation practice within the society of control. I think these strategies can mean a good service—but again, for whom? There is a question of authenticity.

For the institutions of art, it seems there is a new strategy to keep the power structure alive—to incorporate the workers, give criticality a chance, care about the margins, and work with the unions. But this is what Martin yesterday called "oppressive tolerance." On the other hand, as Susan said yesterday, to build in audience participation is to question whether education is not again there to stabilize the system. Or, as I think Iwona said, a pirate radio on the rooftop of the museum still takes more power away from

the people who use it, and ultimately puts the corporation in a stronger position. Also, no wonder the curators of the Whitney Biennial agreed to Andrea's third proposal—the guilt of their own authority and their wish for transparency was, in this case, I think, a pseudotransparency of self-representation and self-legitimation. Only, that was complicated by the editing of the tape.

Now a short conclusion. From my perspective, there are only a few possibilities for how to proceed from this vicious circle. My comments on the schedule of this event: we made a lot of introductions but we are right in the middle of the topic. Serving institutions in general, I think, means breaking them down. For artists I think the best thing is to use institutions to the full extent possible. We haven't yet talked specifically about financial problems, fees, honorariums, blah blah blah. Be aware they use you, so you use them. For curators and educators, I would say take the institution you are working in apart, or build fractions into it. Or if this is not possible, show art as art, and serve the mainstream, use the institution as a middle-class shell…What was that I wrote…

(Laughter)

Dillemuth: Oh yes, serve the mainstream, but have a split personality in doing so—build up another second personality that is truly based in hardcore politics, sexual extremes, terrorism, and suicide.

Serving audiences—for me that means the more we like them, the harder they come. Serving communities—actually, they serve you, so never forget this. Serving art and artists: it's like a good relationship or marriage, something you arrange yourself, something where you fight and love each other. And I'm looking forward to the concluding discussion.

The postscript, my material—well, it's not really mine alone—is on the table. There is a file about Friesenwall 120, some slides, and there is a new catalogue we just put out. There is a copy of the Deleuze text that Kiron Khosla gave me. And there is material about alternative spaces in the US, from *Paper Tiger*. And you can find information about the Sonsbeek and Firminy exhibitions. Thank you.

Draxler: Thank you for your presentation.

Renate Lorenz: I have some notes about the discussions yesterday, and perhaps for the concluding discussions. With relation to the program text, I don't think that the "expert-client model" is appropriate to projects that I am interested in. I don't feel like an expert, and therefore I try to realize coalitions to gather knowledge, critique, experience, and ideas. In my next project, which is a critique of technology, I even attack, for example, experts like gene technologists. The self-proclaimed experts transform others into non-experts. For me it seems important to describe, for example, the model of the human body from different points of view, to use text analysis or feminist critique or natural science. I want to refer to a text of Pierre Bourdieu in *Die Tageszeitung* where he tried to propose a model of coming together for art, science, politics, and philosophy. I think that's something we could discuss, because he says that the splitting of all these parts is very unpolitical. In this same

way, I don't want to call myself an artist, because I am and I do other things which are not well described by this category, or categories like woman, writer, and so on. Because I don't identify as an expert, I didn't like the situation yesterday where the students were hidden behind the monitors. I would have preferred it if the students who worked on the event and the exhibition were here, not as an audience but as participants. It is also their money which is used for this event. I personally don't think that a greater number of participants would have changed the situation, certainly not any more than the cameras and the microphones, which may have an effect on what will be discussed and how.

How the term "art" is made, what it means—we all have to deal with this. Art is not independent from academic work, from exhibitions like this, and from students working on things. The Art Workers' Coalition, for example, maybe changed something about how we define art. My second point is that yesterday I realized that it is not the best idea that every presenter talks about his or her project, because some of us saw the projects while others did not, and therefore the discussion has to stay on a very general level. When I first worked on *Copyshop* [*Copyshop—Kunstpraxis und Politische Öffentlichkeit* (Practices of art and counterpublic), 1993], I had to write a common text about all the projects described in the publication, for example, how they are non-institutional, self-organized, and so on. But then I realized that every two projects are so different in how they are realized that it simplifies them to treat them that way.

For me, "institution" is a very unclear term. What makes a situation something we call an institution? The question of what an institution is has to do with very concrete things like people, space, and how much money there is and where that money comes from. Therefore, I think that the decision of whether one would work with a space or people is a question of whether it is possible to realize a coalition which supports the planned issues and projects. To be more concrete, I propose that we talk about this exhibition here, which opens tomorrow. Let's discuss how visitors to this exhibition can get access to the material presented here, about the Art Workers' Coalition, organizations, and additional information. How can we deal with the language and translation problem that we have even here? Is it possible to address a special audience which is not only an art audience? How can we here connect to theory? How can it be used on an academic level, and how can students work with it? Just to offer a few questions.

Michael Clegg: We're really racing ahead today here toward lunch. We [Martin Guttmann and I] want to start with a very short description of a project. But I think it's necessary to speak about this particular project we have in mind and to anchor the discussion in something concrete, which is perhaps related to what you are suggesting, Renate. I'll just describe it very briefly.

The research material we are presenting pertains to social stratification in Hamburg, which helped us make choices about where to position the particular libraries that constituted the project. This is material we got from the city, but all the advice we got about what to do with this information was from Ulf and the course he was teaching. What we did was establish three small lending libraries in three parts of the city of Hamburg—south, middle, north, which are actually very diverse parts of the city economically and socially. And we collected books in those different neighbourhoods after an elaborate procedure of announcing the project locally, receiving feedback from the area residents, and also interviews were conducted prior to the establishment of the libraries. Then the libraries were open for three months. People were encouraged to bring in books.

Martin Guttmann: The books were placed in these unlocked open bookcases without guardians or librarians. Bookcases we made from repurposing city utility power closets [outdoor cabinets that house electrical switches]. Power closets we recycled for use as open libraries.

Clegg: These power closets are a very common object. We can speak later if anyone is interested in the different results and the differences between the neighbourhoods, but I think what's important in connection to the discussion today is to stress the other element of this project, which was that we were also exhibiting an installation at the Kunstverein in Hamburg. It was part of a show with Stephan Schmidt-Wulffen, called *Backstage* [in 1993]. That area of our installation functioned as a documentation centre where materials about the current state of the lending libraries were being brought in by the students who researched the project. Questionnaires were displayed there. There was also a questionnaire presented to the visitors of the Kunstverein in order to establish a relationship between the institute here at the University [of Lüneburg] and the communities. So this is a very broad sketch of the project in the interest of getting to issues.

Guttmann: On a more theoretical level, what we want to propose is to expand the model of portraiture, and suggest the idea of portraying a community. To think about this project as portraits of community. And this idea is heuristic—it's taking something from its proper context and expanding it, but it also allows one to set some guidelines, especially ethical guidelines, that can be transferred from the realm of portraiture to work with a community. The model can of course be criticized, but at least for us it was a very important model, first of all because the body of work that we did prior to that had a lot to do with portraiture, so this was something we knew and could follow up with. But also hopefully it is something that has some value in its own right.

The definition of the portrait, in a very abstract way, is that a portrait is a device to elicit a reaction. The device is placed in a particular location, reactions are elicited, recorded, and made available to the group of persons who reacted. The last aspect is optional, because not every portrait is actually given back to or displayed for the benefit of the person or group portrait. But at the same time, the whole idea of portraiture is that, by providing a representation, you give something which has a cognitive value. Because a portrait can become a centre for organizing thought about identity. This is basically the idea: that by concentrating on some kind of material representation, you can organize thoughts about

subjectivity, and this is especially necessary for bodies that do not have such representation because they are marginal, or because they just don't present themselves as entities. So the whole mechanism of portraying can really benefit from the portrayed.

Of course, we have to talk about good portraits and bad portraits. Only good portraits are valuable; bad portraits just don't give enough back to the people portrayed. So we are not saying that a portrait in itself has a value. The idea is to give a good portrait so that it is something that can actually be used.

The other point about portraiture is that the presentation of the artist is not as a social worker or as someone who has an expert knowledge about the portrait. The artist presents a device and that's the job of the artist. The device is the work of art, but only as it is completed by the person represented in the portrait. So there is an element of symbiosis between the artist portraying and the portrait—it is not a question of doing favours for anybody, but more about really understanding the symbiosis between the person working in the context and the context itself. Especially for people who come out of the tradition of conceptual art, they should appreciate the fact that the insistence on working on particular contexts is not a luxury but necessary for art that is not escapist. This is a point worth emphasizing. And the self-presentation of artists as the helpers of community has a lot of false consciousness; it should be really clear that artists get something out of it, and it's not just for the communities.

Clegg: To use the same analogy of the portrait, the community has a means of rejecting that portraiture, in the sense that they can interrupt that process. They don't have to co-operate in using the libraries. It happened in one particular location that all the books were gone after the first day. So an important part of the project is to provide, from the very beginning, a description of what could be done, how people might react to it. There is a press conference where people can just come up and say, "We do not want this project in our community." I think that a very important feature of this is to say that we are making an intervention in the community, and there's a variety of interests that emanate from that; there are different uses that this intervention can be put to. We have a certain stake, we get certain things, the community can use it in a certain way, it can become a focal point. The communities address the question of how to treat that foreign object, the libraries, which are there for a period of three months. Also, in this particular case, this project was conceived as a research work by the university, and so there are various aspects of that relation. We are happy to have very different interests involved, and the project being multilayered, and that people can use it in different ways.

Guttmann: Another thing that is more biographical about our own work, but which is maybe of some use for the discussion here, is that there has been a transformation in our own work from gallery- or museum-based pieces, to extra-gallery/museum-based pieces, or at least pieces which do not rely solely on exhibiting institutions like galleries or museums. I think that this point may have some relevance to the general discussion.

At a certain point, I think that we all should really ask ourselves a very simple question about the structure of the art institution: suppose the recession continues for ten years and there is a lot less money; most of the corporate support would stop and the budget of state funding for the arts would be extremely low—does that mean that art would stop? It's a simple question, but it's a fairly cardinal question. Many people who really bite the bullet would say, "Yes, art is basically a service for the bourgeois class—we cannot speak about art without the bourgeoisie, because art is the way the bourgeois class articulates itself to itself." So, what could be an art form that would not be subsumed under the paradigm of the bourgeoisie, of this paradigm of their presenting themselves to themselves?

One of the responses to this question is the search for alternative ways of showing art that is conducted through an analysis of what constitutes an art context or an art institution. In other words, the question is really to reflexively identify some aspects of the presentation of art that are really necessary, and to try to distinguish between them and some of the epiphenomena of art for the bourgeoisie, about the bourgeoisie. Our project falls short of that. It is just a very broad theoretical level where we are working right now. But I think that something along these lines should really be presented as one of the most basic questions about the relation to institutions, simply because we can no longer take the existence of such institutions for granted, and we shouldn't.

So, one of the questions should be: How can we translate the practices coming from institutional critique to a world where the existence of institutions cannot be taken for granted?

Fraser: I just want to say that your point is well taken about art serving the bourgeoisie and having to formulate other possibilities, but that's what all the categories of this event are about: institutions, audiences, communities, and artists. I think this is about trying to focus on strategies that have emerged and practices that have tried to remove themselves from that model in a way that might provide them with greater possibilities for effect. From these three presentations, there were some important points to focus on. Your point, Renate, about the community here—for us to look at this event here, and recognize how effectively, or in what way, it's serving a community, and what community it's proposing to serve. And then to make a connection between that and your project, Clegg & Guttmann, where you made a distinction between the university institute here and the community. But why don't we say that there are two communities, in fact: the communities in Hamburg in which the libraries were installed, and the community here. And you're serving both communities and in different ways. I wanted to put that on the table as something that could be focused on for the discussion.

Lorenz: Maybe, Ulf, you can give us some information about this exhibition project here. I would be very interested to know how this project is being provided for from your side, and what the plans are going forward with this—what are the connections planned between the University of Lüneburg and the exhibition space in this special case?

Ulf Wuggenig: Our general concept is to integrate this project—these discussions—very much with the teaching here. There was a problem in doing this initially, due to the lack of time, but we have seminars organized around this project and we will pick up from what we see here, from what happens here. We also didn't know exactly what would happen in these discussions, what they would be about. So we will look at this event very carefully, meet with students, and work with them to understand what the exhibition is about. We also have the possibility of course to put it in a more theoretical framework. For example, the problem of services here is relevant—we have an economic faculty here at the university who also work in the services economy, or the economy of nonprofit organizations, and things like that. So, this would be one possibility. Another possibility would be to put these discussions within a theoretical framework of exchange theories, which have a long tradition in sociology from the nineteenth century up to now. Because what we are discussing is: What is equity of exchange between artists and institutions? I think there are many different theories which are apt to deal with these questions and problems.

Draxler: I have to say that when we agreed to do this, I also offered to do more service provision for the student community, but that didn't happen for various reasons. The Kunstraum is funded mostly by the Foundation of Lower Saxony, not the university, and so it has a certain kind of independence. And this project is also going to other spaces, so it can be connected to different kinds of communities and different kinds of discussions. I also see it as an interesting opportunity to further consider the partly theoretical question of service provision, and on the other hand to consider what this project is about.

I think how to address the community here is a very important question; I mean, we have discussed this explicitly. But I also don't think that there is one total identity between what this work in the Kunstraum is and the university seminars. This kind of difference between the programs is also, in a certain way, constituting this event. This doesn't exclude that the Kunstraum is using these other projects, like Clegg & Guttmann's, in a very direct relationship with the student community here. And that was also our advice: that the Kunstraum should be used for these different kinds of possibilities.

Fraser: For me, there is also a question that I would like to put to the group, actually: How and who can this [project] serve? And how do we think it should be used, by a university community for example. I think that in organizing this Working Group, I conceived of it primarily as an event that would serve a practicing community, and a community of people involved in practical work, and not to be serving a general audience in the sense that many art-presenting organizations propose to serve a general audience. And also not to be serving as material for theoretical study, but to be more directly related to present and future practical work. That was the premise for me. But this is something I think it would be worthwhile to discuss, because when this moves on, it will also move to some organizations that have artistic constituencies and some organizations that have student constituencies.

Susan Cahan: I would like to respond to the question Martin raised in his presentation. I think that it's important to think about how this material will be used, but I feel like that's a metadiscourse that we could discuss during the concluding session. I think it's a very interesting question: What would we do if there were no museums or nonprofit arts organizations? I think that clearly there are many forms of cultural production that exist outside of the contexts of museums and art institutions, which may or may not be identified as fine art practices. We can all talk about what "it" is, but it seems to me that one thing that museums do that other kinds of institutions don't do is that they collect it, and save it, and hold on to it. And I think that the kind of work we're talking about here is the kind of work that most lends itself to being developed and nurtured outside the context of traditional collecting museums and can exist, like this, in school contexts and other businesses. Publishing is a venue, video—I mean, the possibilities are really quite extensive. And one of the things I'm quite interested in is whether or not the idea of collecting needs to be rethought, and how. US museums are struggling to keep up with other organizations that are doing more service-oriented art, and really questioning whether or not their permanent collection should be the primary focus anymore.

Guttmann: I think documenting, nurturing, keeping the residues—that's clearly something that needs to be done. But the question is more what constitutes a frame or a pedestal or something that makes an activity into art. And this question really comes out of a basic twentieth-century avant-garde tradition. What does it mean to take an object and put it on a pedestal and call it "art." If it's an object, it's a bit easier; if it's an activity, it's a bit more difficult. But the question has been posed as a theoretical issue for a long time. In the background, behind this question, there has always been a strong sense of security with respect to the basic premises of the art institutions, these buildings that house the works, that collect and protect them. And the idea that there can be a radical shift in the objective conditions also necessitates that we pose the question in different terms—not as an abstract philosophical issue, but as a very concrete issue about what will happen to the spirit of the avant-garde under conditions in which institutional support cannot be taken for granted.

Fraser: I just want to say, it seems to me that this is the topic of the next session: serving art and artists and how institutions were founded to collect. So I just wanted to see if we could get back to communities in some way.

Dillemuth: About the community here, I think the students might be able to say something about how they receive this. It would be good to hear from this community. So maybe the students should come, and we should hear from them.

Fraser: I think that's a good suggestion, but, Uli, did you have something to say?

Ulrich Bischoff: Yeah. I will try to make it very short, because this may be for the next session.

Dillemuth: So now we are back to this—I don't know if this is a good strategy for a talk…

Fraser: I interrupted Uli; I should have made that clear.

Bischoff: The question is about framework, and I think one point in the participation here is that artists are building a framework for art that operates outside of the museum and a framework for art that works with museums. I just wanted to say this.

Guttmann: I don't think we should implement such a rigid distinction between the various categories. Our presentation had to do with the fact that our work with communities is precisely a response to a change in objective conditions. There is a real connection, in our opinion, between the two topics, and it is possible to divide them, provided the connection is made visible. The idea of working with a community is not a separate topic, but a question of how to expand the frame of twentieth-century art to other areas, and not really primarily a question of addressing the community. Because we are artists; we are not social workers.

Fraser: That's a question, and I think it should be presented as such.

Guttmann: I just don't think it's that now we talk about "community work" and then "museum work."

Fraser: I think it's appropriate that you are relating the topic of community to that topic, but I think Christian had something to say.

Christian Philipp Müller: Who might be the link between the communities and the artists, if it is not the institution? Who actually commissions you to do a work? Who represents the community?

Clegg: There are a variety of solutions. There are many people working not through museums but through local organizations.

Müller: Who is the link between the communities and us?

Lorenz: But I'm not outside of the community. As I said, I don't see myself just as an artist—I am also part of different communities, and the question is if there are possibilities between them and links there.

Fred Wilson: I'm feeling very much outside of this conversation, because for the majority of my art-making life, I was outside of the art community. Most African Americans were outside of the art community, and not by design. So our art practice inherently had nothing to do with the art community and had everything to do with local communities. And it was only recently that the art community was forced to accept artwork by others in the United States. So, to my mind, the basis for connecting communities is to resist, or hold suspect, the hierarchical market and star system that is so insidious in the art community. There have been a lot of artists who came to the art world from other communities.

Renée Green: I think that's a useful point. I want to address the use of terms here. Like the idea of an "artist." We're all coming from different backgrounds, and I don't think we should get caught up in the idea of "'artist" as being something necessarily isolated from other activities. You could say "cultural producer," although that term is getting so overused. So, terms themselves are a kind of problem; it's a problem of language—how we use language and translation. Artists have always been connected to various backgrounds and areas of study. But that's something I think we should be conscious of in this discussion, so that we don't get stuck. What Fred mentioned is really important in terms of the contexts people are working within, or coming out of, and thinking about how to approach a practice.

The idea of an institution as an "in-between" space is interesting. I think if we look at other models, we can see that there are other ways that people are able to function in terms of communicating. The whole history of cultural production by African Americans has been one of having to subvert that situation, because they were excluded. So it was necessary to create other channels, or work with other institutions that existed in other communities, and that came out of social structures. There are so many different possibilities for the way people communicate: it depends on what your goals are, it depends on what your agendas are, and how you're trying to be represented, and if you're trying to be part of a kind of hierarchical model. That's one way to think. But the possibilities are really vast, if you think of all of the other ways that people have communicated cultural ideas.

Lorenz: I want to say again that I'm not just an artist. One must include more differences in that term of "artist." Like in feminist groups, I don't want to say anymore that we are just "women"—we are other things, women who are mothers, women who are not. The problem is identification. You don't want to identify yourself with just one community, one label, and so on.

Fraser: I think that's what institutions do to you. I think that was part of Christian's point.

Müller: Right, for example, I'm gay, and I have no voice in the gay community. I don't know how to raise my voice for instance within the New York gay community. As an artist, my practice is completely outside of those communities.

Draxler: How I understood you, Fred, is that for a certain community, it could be interesting to be an "artist" because you are so excluded traditionally from a certain art context. It's a very specific situation where one can say, "Oh, I don't want to be identified as *just* an artist." Whereas from another point of view, it could be interesting to go into institutions as an artist where you were excluded for the past three hundred years.

Green: I want to get away from, and really question, a certain rigidity of isolating the various kinds of practices that people work with. I think it's much more fluid. At least the desire is; whether or not the results are visible that way is maybe another matter.

Audience member (Vera Kockot, a student): It's very interesting to see how both sides, institutions and communities, can be addressed. Maybe the institution has a special role and you're defined by it, but on the other hand you are free to address different communities, or not. And in this project now, for instance, I am trying to represent the student community. With Clegg & Guttmann's project, it was very interesting because it created different values, there was an exchange value; it was a work of art, so different values were included, and different communities could use it on different levels. Some people exchanged books out in the communities, while others just looked at it in the Kunstverein as a piece of art. I think that's an interesting transgression of the borders of institutions—if you really can include communities that normally never would have any kind of contact with art institutions. The project was also connected to the university here. It was interesting that social research and sciences were such an integral part of that project. I can say that, for us students, it was a very fruitful exchange; it showed a real possibility.

Draxler: University interests and art community interests, in a very broad sense, are just not necessarily the same. This Working Group is defined by addressing each other as participants of this Working Group, and that doesn't mean that we address ourselves exclusively as artists or curators, but as participants who are working in particular situations with certain goals. And this working-group approach could be transferred to other models or modes of activity. Of course, we should talk about what kind of possibilities exist to connect the university interests to the items discussed here, but I don't think that's a major point for me.

Ute Meta Bauer: There is a difference in serving communities if there is an institution—whether a museum or university—that is asking people, artists, to do a project for a community. How is the institution initiating that? With you, Fred, you took those communities on yourself; the institution did not initiate that. I think it's very different when artists have their own interest in engaging communities and work with communities on a long-term basis beyond the institutional invitation. There is a difference there. And you have to ask how an institution wants to pay for that service, how they see the status of cultural work, and how they are dealing with things like this. It would be another field of work for artists if they didn't have to have this construction of the "artist" who is doing a genuine artwork. If they could understand themselves as cultural workers, we would have a different idea of their profession.

Bischoff: I think there is a difference between a social worker and an artist, because as an artist you first work for yourself.

Bauer: Mmmmm…I don't know about that.

Bischoff: Well, that's my opinion.

Bauer: Social workers also work for themselves.

Wilson: Yeah, that's a thing. I've worked with lots of social workers and…Well, we can talk about that.

Fraser: That's the whole point for me, and that was the catalyst for this—if I was working for myself, I probably wouldn't have so many questions about the equity of the exchange. But the fact that I'm working at the invitation of institutions and organizations, almost exclusively, in a way that my activity is contingent upon that context, it becomes a very different story.

Wilson: Social workers, and artists, and everyone, are doing what they are doing to fulfill something of their own needs.

Fraser: That is if we're not all completely confined to totally alienated labour.

Wilson: But I think that in professions that purport to be doing for others, sometimes that aspect can be lost.

Bischoff: If you are asked to make a piece for a house, there are special conditions. So you either say, "I'll do it," and you follow the conditions, or you'll do it only without following the conditions. There still is a question of what you are interested in.

Fraser: This is the situation of the independent profession essentially: you have terms that you have to negotiate, but you're not entirely free. It's a relative autonomy. A relative independence.

Jochen Becker: I have become used to using the term "project," but I would rather use the term "initiative." What you did, Andrea, at the Kunstverein München [*Eine Gesellschaft des Geschmacks* (A society of taste), 1993] was of course a project, but I wouldn't use that term for what Stephan does with Friesenwall 120.
Maybe we can differentiate between a "project," and an "initiative," and an "institutional invitation." You can get money or infrastructure from any number of different places if you work very hard, but it's very

difficult. You can decide where you want to place the work and who you want to address very specifically, and perhaps that is not possible within a museum. If you work on an initiative basis, maybe the connection is easier with initiatives in the social field.

Martin Guttmann: I want to respond to what you [Jochen] said and also draw on what Renate said. And try to draw a contrast between belonging to different contexts simultaneously, and the idea of erasing boundaries between different contexts. I think it is an important and interesting question of whether we should prefer the model of erasing boundaries and calling ourselves "cultural producers," or whether we should say we are doing various things at the same time. And because we are not unified individuals and we embody contradictions, at various moments various aspects of ourselves are given voice. Maybe to make this distinction less philosophical and more practical: what really struck me when Fred was talking about working in the particular context of the South Bronx, running a gallery for a long time—

Wilson: I was just now talking about my experience prior to running a gallery, of working in a social service agency for seven years.

Guttmann: I see. Well, at any rate, there seems to be a need to distinguish between a situation where someone is working in one particular context which necessitates a lot of various functions and where you may have a strong sense of identity but not a lot of control over what you do, as opposed to another situation, which is where your circumstances

make you go from one place in the world to another. You do not lose your sense of context—what happens is that you just become much more aware of the fact that you have to address each context on its own terms. And of course it creates a very different sense of working with context.

We are originally from Israel, we went to the United States, and now we are working in Germany. That fact in and of itself creates a framework for the activity that we engage in. We draw the material for the work from the concrete place where we are working. It's another contrast to draw between the idea of the nomadic artist who changes contexts all the time and has more means but less identity, and another model where you may have more identity but less means. Some people have both, some people have neither.

Wilson: I was responding to your question about "where would we be if there was no more funding for art production." And I was just saying that there are a whole host of communities in which this has been an issue for years, and who have been dealing with it. So perhaps those are models we could look at.

Guttmann: Absolutely. It's extremely beneficial to look at those models of work without much institutional support, no doubt about it.

Fraser: I was thinking about what you, Iwona, were talking about yesterday, the situation in Antwerp with nomadic artists [for the European Capital of Culture project]. And that situation seems to be very much an issue of serving communities, and how if not through institutions… It's like, here, we are serving our own communities and communities which have been left out of this institutionalized presentation structure, and serving other communities through institutions. Those seem to be the options which have been noted.

Bauer: I think it is very interesting what Fritz did with Büro Berlin, because in Berlin you didn't have that institutional structure before. And it is such a big city with so many artists. For the artist group that I was involved with, that project, Büro Berlin, was always the model which we found very inspiring. Because they created their own structure, they were their own commissioning organization. So, I thought that it was a pity that it wasn't discussed yesterday, because they just did their work—they didn't wait for anyone to ask them. They just did it. They financed it. They found ways of rejecting the expectation that artists don't know how to organize projects and raise money. For me, it would be interesting to hear about their project.

Fritz Rahmann: I can try to characterize what we did now, but that is what I will do anyhow in a few moments in the next session.

Dillemuth: I think we should also make a distinction in this topic of serving communities—I think there is no service for communities. I think that a community together can, to a certain extent, create something out of themselves. I don't have the feeling that I serve the community, but that the community is participating. If we take that model to a higher level, then it becomes institutionalized. Maybe I need money once, then every year, then I need more money, and then maybe I get the money, and then it becomes something like a *Kunstverein*. Then there is the question of whether that institution has a mission to serve something back. If it has a mission to serve something back, then the artists have to fulfill this need or mission of the institution to be in debt to a service-industry function.

Draxler: But what you did with Friesenwall 120 was to offer the Cologne art world a lot of services—offering them an archive of very specific videotapes, and that's a service. They came and made use of it. That is more or less what clients of institutions do. I think in your case it was very clear how this was set up by Friesenwall with relation to the galleries of Friesenplatz.

Dillemuth: It was something we tried out. And then it happened that the community took a chance, to contribute things, to exchange things.

Lorenz: This is the way I would describe our work too, like the Copyshop [in Cologne], which wouldn't have been the same project if a lot of people worked with it and participated in it. I can't say I served them. I looked for the space and the money, but it wouldn't have been the same project. And I think that it's the same with Friesenwall 120. I don't like this "service" concept either.

Iwona Blazwick: But do you think that endemic to setting up any kind of initiative is its procedure into being an institution? Setting up a kind of expertise by virtue of negotiating a site, paying the rent, paying the bills, devising some kind of platform or program schedule, and a way of communicating what's happening in that place? Do you not then set up all of the infrastructure of an institution with an expert within it?

Lorenz: I don't know if there is such a great difference between institution and non-institution. If you have no money, you still have this relationship to money, because you can't do certain projects. The question is: What are the structures? How are decisions made? Who's the person who decides? And so on.

Becker: The difference between Friesenwall 120 and a *Kunstverein* is that Friesenwall is now closing. A *Kunstverein* wouldn't close by itself. They wouldn't say, "OK, we stop tomorrow."

Guttmann: An institution exists above and beyond the individuals who run it.

Fraser: Renée has been trying to speak for some time.

Green: I want to say something that has to do with the idea of communities. What Stephan said about Friesenwall 120 and how it came together was making me think that the idea of a community is something you have to put in quotation marks. It's something we have to question. A community is something that is created—it is not necessarily pre-existing. And I think that expertise and service come into this question, along with the idea of the role of the artist. If a person has an idea, for example, and they present it and figure out how to distribute it, it's like a message in a bottle. And I think that's often what artists do, and after that seeing who responds. It's not necessarily known who will respond, but it's the reaction

to that which will come together. Friesenwall was not definite; it was flexible. I remember when I went to Friesenwall that I thought it was a different way of approaching the idea of a space.

I would like to examine the idea of how communities are formed based on something that's initiated in some way and not necessarily by a fixed institution.

Fraser: I just want to contrast that with what Martin and Michael were talking about during their presentation about representing communities. Because I thought that that's actually a different model. You were talking about a site where a community might form through its own collective agency, and on the other hand, an idea of serving a community that already exists. It seems to me that's one of the differences here.

Guttmann: It's an interesting distinction, but in our case we chose a location in which we came as portraitists, and not as commissioned ones. The whole project was like one big camera, and something comes out. If it's set up right, then it gives something back. There is an aspect of service there. The idea of "artist as portraitist" does resonate from the idea of having the capacity to contribute self-presentation. It seems to me that some people know how to do it better than others, even if they don't really know the community well. As long as people don't work in a fixed context, then there is really a big question of what we are doing at a particular location. We always find ourselves in places where we don't speak the language—what are we doing here, what is it that we want to get here, how can we justify an activity like that? And the answer doesn't really have so much to do with the question of expertise, in the sense that we had some new technology that didn't exist. It's more just having set up something that could be used and had validity on its own terms. As long as we had the right feedback—and this is part of the responsibility of working in a situation like that—because very few people can claim to really understand the communities they work with. That should be highlighted, because most artists don't work in a situation in which they really understand the community.

Wilson: The whole notion of having a problem with expertise is odd. In the communities that I've worked in, the notion of the expert or of someone having a different experience, when they bring it to the community, they actually have something to offer—and that is respected. It becomes an important aspect of your involvement in a particular community, because you have something, or a certain way of seeing the world, that is new or considered valuable in the community. Or it becomes valuable through your engaged interaction with the community. So, I don't see the problem with expertise, unless you assume you're an expert at more than you are.

Clegg: The point is that very often they [institutions] want us to come in and do something very specific. And I think there is a problem with a situation where someone invites you and says, "Well, I know that you do a certain type of work, and that is what we want you to do." It's difficult to speak about expertise when the service rendered is not specific. We can do a number of different things, but there is always a question for us:

How do we establish what is really needed there, and to what extent do we want to find ourselves thinking about that as the main motivating condition?

Cahan: I think it's important to recognize that there are multiple forms of expertise. Not just the ones an artist might bring into a geographical location with which he or she might be unfamiliar, but also the forms of expertise that are based on lived experience and the negotiation of those multiplicities.

Fraser: I think that the problem with expertise has to do with divisions of labour and knowledge within hierarchies that are set up by organizations and professional structures. The problem of that is specific, and it doesn't have so much to do with experience.

Wilson: Or with the individual. It's about the structure placed around the individual. I was struck by what you were saying about being portraitists in a particular community. I can see, just from my experiences with artists in different communities, how value can be placed on the artist by the community, even if they are not so familiar with the form of what they're doing. Sometimes just the involvement and the interaction of artists can enlarge that community's or individual's view of the world. And that alone can become a value to that community. Then whatever you produce becomes more important because that relationship has developed.

Guttmann: In one of the locations in which a library was installed, people actually started a petition and collected signatures to keep it open after its time. They produced posters, and it became very clear that they wanted to own it. It became part of something that defined their identity as a community. It became very clear when there was a moment of acceptance: the community wanted it—and rejected us.

Clegg: And it's a moment of transformation, because then it became something different: just a library there, and the connection to us was severed.

Wilson: I often feel that with some of my projects—and for me, the organization sort of becomes my community—when it takes the piece as if it's theirs and sort of shoves me out of the way, and they've decided that it's theirs because of whatever it's doing for them, then it's functioning for me. Even if it is in a funny way. It's working even though, you know, let's just not mention that I was involved.

Fraser: On the one hand, there's this problem of bringing expertise out of an institutional context and applying it within a community that may or may not exist, and you may or may not be constructing.

Blazwick: Could we use the word "skills" instead [of "expertise"]?

Fraser: Well, we could, but I wanted to make a distinction between that and trying to construct a participatory or democratic situation within an institution. So, on the one hand, there's a critique of the status of expertise or skills, specialized skills within nonspecialized communities. And on the other hand there is this question of: Can one create a participatory, democratic structure for

communities that would not itself be subject to the kinds of divisions that expertise represents? I think that's the view that Stephan and Renate were presenting, and also perhaps what Iwona was trying to do in Antwerp [for the European Capital of Culture project].

Judith Barry: This is going to throw the discussion off, but I wanted to mention activist art in the US. In particular, artists volunteering to work with other nonprofit organizations. With the Women's Action Coalition [WAC, in New York], for example, a number of artists volunteered to produce media, including a poster and slide campaign for [Bill] Clinton's election last year, and the Democratic Convention in Texas. There was tremendous mistrust of the use of visual aids to produce certain subject positions among a broad constituency of Clinton's people. We were volunteering, not charging for these services, and we were mistrusted because we were invoking spectacle, and using sophisticated visual aids to foster recognition across a wide swath of the electorate in Texas. Even though, if you look at the model of artists' involvement in ACT UP, you can see how effective their visual campaign has been. It produced an identity and provided a voice to call for AIDS research, among other things, in the US and beyond.

Fraser: I don't think that throws anything off. It introduces a third term of artistic skills: being brought to bear to influence or serve democratically organized groups or community groups.

Barry: Maybe it's a different notion of institutions.

Fraser: Well, I don't think it differs so much from the kind of interactions you, Renate, were having with Copyshop. These are politically goal-oriented organizations too.

Cahan: Did issues of spectacle go into feminist concerns?

Barry: Spectacle figures into feminist concerns and the way in which you are then positioned and potentially subsumed. I think in a number of community-based groups—and I've worked with many over the years—there is an inherent mistrust of visuals. It's deep and it's systemic. It comes from communities not having resources, or mainstream affect, so that they can't imagine or identify with themselves if they are represented in this way. I have tried to work with women's groups who insist on a simple graphic approach to visuals and reject anything more visually complex or sophisticated.

Lorenz: I know that in Berlin there is the WAC chapter with just a few women artists, and they always just thought that the overall WAC group was more organized and had more interesting artists who have this kind of ascetic approach to visuals.

(Laughter)

Barry: Some of the WAC campaigns have been more acceptable to the overall WAC organization than others. And, generally, it was simpler visuals.

Fraser: These issues about specialization, divisions of labour, have been so central to radical women's groups. There are some arguments which say that it has been battles over those kind of issues that destroyed the radical feminist groups of the late 1960s and early 1970s. They were aiming the argument at radically egalitarian group structures and refused to have spokeswomen, for example, refused to allow people who had a tendency or experience in public speaking to represent the group. They wanted to try and encourage and administer equal participation throughout a group. But there were a lot of problems as a result. So, that's maybe what happens when you refuse any kind of skills.

Guttmann: What really struck me about ACT UP was that their graphics were too dominant. Thinking of these very snappy visuals and slogans instead of thinking of people. I think the organized graphics dehumanized the group a bit.

Fraser: When I look at a lot of public art projects that use, for instance, billboards, there is a question about resources. When art uses billboards in a subversive way, but everyone knows how much it costs—billboards are supposed to be a democratic form, but they are of course very expensive, and who can get access to that? So you know that if you can access to that, it means you have certain backing from institutions, from corporations, from individuals.

Guttmann: It's also not necessarily money well spent. If you know how much these billboards cost and then the best you can get out of it is a little bit of subversion…

(Laughter)

Clegg: No, it [ACT UP's billboard work] was extremely successful in the beginning. Now it's changing.

Barry: I wanted to say something about ACT UP's visual strategy. After a certain time, the pink triangle got used up. Its iconic power dissipated. This is similar to when an artist is identified with a certain form of production, and the power of the work often dissipates.

Bauer: I just wanted to ask you in relation to what billboards cost—what *do* events like this cost?

Guttmann: A lot of people in the early '80s were talking about subverting the message. Creating breaks in the seamless texture of life. Things like that, as a main type of strategy. There is a danger in doing that, because you are really looking down at the audience. And this kind of attitude has a real paternalistic overtone. Like: we are the smart ones, we have the right politics, and the rest of the country are stupid hicks. All we need are some nice visuals to shake them up, and once we shake them up, then they will see the light.

Cahan: I think the issue that Judith puts on the table is the issue of artists sharing their graphic or design skills, but in another sense, also other kinds of skills that have to do with negotiating the interrelationships between various cultural spheres. And negotiating access to various public cultural spaces. So, I think when we are talking about something like billboards, we need to talk about it on that level and not just in terms of artists using advertising strategies.

Fraser: Because mass audiences are not communities.

Barry: I don't think artists have the naive view that just by popularizing something they are providing social solutions. For instance, Barbara Kruger recently participated in a project about battered women that was funded by [the fashion house] Liz Claiborne. Part of that project included billboards. Simultaneously, both fundraising and outreach were done for battered women's shelters in the cities where the project was located.

Lorenz: Just to go back to this point about expertise: Andrea, I would not say that there should not be skilled graphic artists or other skilled workers. But as for spokeswomen and spokesmen, for example, in the student movement in 1968—it was the media and the TV who looked for spokespeople, and they brought them into the schools, and this is one of the reasons that the movement ended.

Fraser: Well, yes. In the United States, the women's movement came out of the New Left largely because there was a very well-defined hierarchy of spokesmen within SDS [Students for a Democratic Society] that would not listen to women and would not allow women to speak.

Cahan: Group Material did a project called *Your Message Here* [1990], and they were brought in by Randolph Street Gallery as consultants to design and implement a project, for which anybody could submit a design for a billboard project. I think there were eighteen billboards produced in total. So what the artists did was to help facilitate the execution of this particular project. It wasn't that their own voices were being publicly broadcast—they instead helped facilitate the presentation of other voices, specifically voices in the communities where the billboards were located. So this idea of an artist providing a service is expansive.

Draxler: There are these questions about the meaning of the term "service," but we can also use it to understand the relationship.

Lorenz: You can always see the service from the other side.

Cahan: I can't speak for Group Material, but judging from their previous work, their interest might have been in questions of cultural access: Who is generating culture, and who is that culture being generated for?

Lorenz: But this is a political goal, that people should have cultural access. I'm just against that idea of service where there is an institution that gives you money, 20,000 DM, and then you give a service and you have no goals and you don't look for how you can realize them.

Becker: ACT UP used the infrastructure. The infrastructure of the advertising firms, of media firms, of the press, of the galleries, and so on. These are institutions too. But perhaps we can also call this infrastructure.

Blazwick: That's what I was trying to say yesterday. That you find this confluence between different means of communication. For me, my biggest service, or function, that an institution had was when I was a student going to the ICA [Institute of Contemporary Arts in] London and discovering this thing called feminism, and meeting other women

there, and hearing them speak, and looking at their art and watching their films. That was to me a radical, pivotal experience in my life. That point of exchange meant something very valuable. It was this regular platform where you could go every week where there was someone making some contribution.

Guttmann: I think the idea of creating collectivity, so that you lose this sense that you are alone, that you are this atomized individual, and then to organize structures that enhance this collectivity—this is a slightly different project than the project of "speaking to." So one of the services that artists can do is to create place for collectivity. In the 1980s, there were so many artists just putting up messages in undifferentiated spaces, whether it was Keith Haring or Jenny Holzer.

Green: I want to get back to something that Judith said about skills and distrust. I was thinking about differences between WAC and ACT UP in terms of how they came together and how they evolved. From the beginning with WAC, there was a separation between specific groups of people and communities who were working on particular projects involving legal cases. And in the very beginning—because I was only there in the very beginning—they wanted to create a media event to draw attention to the particular situation, but it was just a liberal desire to "do good." There was a separation from some of the people who were already there, doing the legal work, before the attention. And so that attention is a problem. I was just wondering about that service—what if it is distrustful?

Barry: Well, WAC had a very specific history, because it started in the art world, and it was immediately problematic—it was very white and upper middle class. There were incredible divisions from the beginning. And, as a number of the artists were also well known, this contributed to further divisions. Nonetheless, the larger issue of distrust around visual imagery is systemic among public-service groups.

Green: Right—I'm trying to get back to what you are saying is a "systemic distrust." It's a division that has been repeated a lot of times within politically active groups. And in Berlin I was talking to Beatrice about how some students invited different art-related magazines to come and have a discussion. And the discussion developed around how there were some conflicts with one of the magazines that appeared to be more sophisticated—that the production was more expensive, so then maybe the content wasn't genuine or authentic.

Fraser: Whether you are talking about a lecture series at the ICA, or graphic works, or what have you—is it introducing discourse or cultural production, or is it imposing certain standards of discourse or cultural production that are tied to particular material conditions of the individuals and groups and communities? That is an issue for me, because it took me years to free myself from the standards of discourse imposed by the forums in New York in the early 1980s.

Cahan: Not to harp on WAC, but there was a split in that group between the people who supported more of an expressionist approach to the politically oriented, and those who supported a more neoconceptual approach. And that division relates to definitions of what it means to be an artist, and what definitions, or languages, or practices are appropriate to engage in as an artist.

Fraser: Discourse is specialized, and it has to comply with internal structures and standards that are defined by competition.

Guttmann: I've been living in San Francisco for the last few years, and there is a big difference between New York–based politics and Northern California–based politics. A lot of it has to do with these kinds of issues.

(Bauer asks a mostly inaudible question in German about the Wohlfahrtsausschuss.)

Becker: So, Ute, you asked in German about the Wohlfahrtsausschuss. There are several histories. I will tell one, my own history: it was founded in Hamburg after the attack and murder of Turkish people and the burning down of immigrants' houses in Rostock [in 1992]. There was an idea to form a coalition of people from the squat houses, which is a political focus in Hamburg. Critics, musicians, club people. And there were different groups, in Düsseldorf, Cologne, and Munich, with different backgrounds. A loose coalition. I was surprised to read the description of the Art Workers' Coalition, that it was this same loose coalition of very different people. And to find an organization that did not represent one issue. This is one idea of the Wohlfahrtsausschuss. They were organizing actions against an exhibition in Düsseldorf called *Deutsch Sein,* or "To Be German," which was just before the decision to rescind certain immigration laws in Germany—a basic law in Germany that was founded after the Second World War to protect immigrants and migrants. So at this time, they [the government] eliminated, destroyed, that very basic law. So there were demonstrations around that exhibition.

Dillemuth: I think it's interesting, this loose configuration out of nothing, and it happened in every major city. These Wohlfahrts were organized by a variety of people. And people tried to define it, but it was difficult—is it a party, is it a club, what is it? People wanted to get together and talk. And these were people from totally different factions.

Draxler: Yeah, there were a lot of conflicts between these groups.

Dillemuth: Yes, and there seems to be a need for that! Also in this forum here, there seems to be a need for that with our very different positions.

Lorenz: There is a difference between practical work, or very specific discussion like this here, and a broader, more general discussion. I now know more people who I can call if something happens. This is important.

Audience member (Vera Kockot, a student): This community was constituted by a pre-existing network, and out of that there grew special groups. But it's important to mention that there were already established networks, from Cologne and from Hamburg, for instance. These were social networks that then

built up an infrastructure to make political work. And Renate makes an important point that this is the same situation here, where there is a pre-existing network that can grow from independent work to communities. From this group, and correlating to this model here.

Fraser: Yes, thank you. I should mention that it has been two hours. Beatrice is actually finding out about ordering pizza in. Does that sound like a good idea? Here she comes, maybe she can tell us.

Guttmann: Pizza from American Pizza Center?

(Laughter)

Fraser: Or we could go out for an hour—it doesn't seem to be raining this minute.

Working Group
Session Five

Serving Art and Artists
Sunday, January 23, 1994

Presentations:
Fritz Rahmann
Ulrich Bischoff
Ute Meta Bauer
Christian Philipp Müller
Helmut Draxler

Many art institutions were founded to serve art and artists first, and the public second. Many museum professionals find themselves split between these two constituencies.

Curators often find themselves limited by institutions or the artists themselves to roles of service, support, and production for artists and their gallerists.

Meanwhile, many project artists feel that they don't get the support they need. How can these conflicts be addressed?

Helmut Draxler: So, we agreed in a previous meeting to make a presentation tomorrow of the material specifically for the students here. Of course, I invite everyone who is still here to also join us for that, around 12:30 or 1:00 pm. And later we should also discuss a bit how we will organize the public presentation. OK, so, Fritz, would you please start?

Fritz Rahmann: There is one point of doubt all the time in my mind with regard to the word "service." The opportunity to talk about this was yesterday when you, Andrea, were asked whether or not your piece at the Whitney Biennial would have been different depending on the answer of the trustees, whether they accepted it or not. To me it appeared quite normal that you said it would have been the same piece, in a way serving the institution. But that it did not practically depend on the reaction of those people is proof that it is autonomous. That is the point I want to make.

We are always talking about those difficult historical concepts, which are also those of art discourse. There is always a historical factor. There is a position in time to be regarded even when we say "art," and when we here speak of "service," and quote historical instances like those of the late '60s. So much has happened, and so it is most important to focus on the position of a concept in a certain context. I wanted to mention this because it is my impression that we do not give enough attention to this point. So, it is important to recognize the purpose you have given to these meetings—to establish permanent concepts for professional practice. But that cannot succeed. That is in opposition to all the experiences that I have had with my practice. So, this is a general objection.

What I can say about Büro Berlin is that it is about time, and that is why I make this general remark. The main point of the practice was to design places—the actual material pieces were the places. It was not art; it was the place. We found, after a few experiences, that it influenced the design of the projects and works very strongly to have that be the intention of every project. I remember that intention very intensely: to make interesting pieces as places. Ideological inheritance was gone then. I was coming from Holland, and had indulged in a way in this general moral discussion about art in society, and when I came to Berlin it was absolutely out. It was only about how to do an interesting piece. And every discussion like what we are trying to have here was considered to be fussy. That was the situation. From this situation there came this awareness, a small opportunity—that the very place would give you what could be used to make a piece. And so this was the practice, which I'll try to be brief about.

I was not aware then, but now I know, that one was employing the real estate value, the social value of real estate, as a consistent part of the project. And that is a very political thing. But we were not aware of that at the time. That is also a very strong condition for work. But, so, it can only be thought of as temporary. Not permanent. Otherwise you are just this monumental artist who puts down these big monuments. Having sections of the place as consistent parts of the work was only possible temporarily. I think we observed that a place only had this power for a short while—a few days, sometimes. You couldn't contain those places. And we didn't want to. So, there was a tendency towards performance. Even though all the participants were from visual art backgrounds, they worked with theatre and performance. The meaning of those pieces, places, was about art in society. But the main point of the project was that it was restricted to small periods of time.

I have always done projects with the awareness of the time factor in the performance of the piece. I am working now on the space around the Alte Pinakothek in Munich. I think there is a connection between this project and what I tried to describe with the Büro Berlin

practice, because this building and the area around it in Munich is just this historical thing. We are talking about this historical concept of art that has become architecture there, and I think I am really interested in this task because I can practice this awareness of the validity of a structure in time. A building that is designed in order to establish the concept of art as we still have it here in Europe, and as it was exported to America. Classical pieces in a certain time. People like King Ludwig [II of Bavaria] would buy them in Italy or in Paris to deliberately establish the power of country through the collection of art. And that was the very idea of the museum. Maybe of all museums.

You can read that very clear history of the museum in the papers when Ludwig planned the building in 1810 and 1815. My work was to study the history of the building. The meaning of the building and the concept of art were identical—they were to be like the architecture: a permanent presence. So, this historical concept of the building and its art to be an eternal structure was the thing itself for me. It was in a way what caused the disastrous history of the building. It was made part of the National Socialist planning in Munich as a representative of Nazi architecture there. The building was used as a backdrop for the ideology of Nazi power. Allied bombers then later aimed at the building there in Munich. Then there came a modernist architect to reconstruct the building. The opposition between modernism and this classical idea of the eternal art. Then there was the Munich Society, and a committee was formed to restrain reconstruction work on the building. Some work was done, and some things were changed. Some things unchanged. One enters from the back now. It is such a crazy situation. They have put sculptures there to somehow make it better looking. You see those sculptures—that art—is functioning to give a destroyed place, and idea, a better look. So, that is the subject of the work I'm doing there.

Draxler: What are your proposals?

Rahmann: No, there are no proposals, I tried all the time…

Ulrich Bischoff: Thank you for the invitation to come here and to speak here. Why I was invited here I really don't know. Maybe I was invited because I was the person who invited Fritz to work there in the Alte Pinakothek in Munich when I was working at that museum. But now I work at another museum. The whole theme of "services" for me is a chance to look at what the artists I was working with in that situation had done. And to see what I have done and what I'm doing. To imagine for myself how services can change the frameworks.

I think of a work by Chris Burden, *Exposing the Foundation of the Museum*, which he made temporarily in the Temporary Contemporary [Museum of Contemporary Art, Los Angeles, in 1986]. And if you don't know, Burden made an excavation of the real foundations of the architectural structure. But exposing the [metaphorical] foundation of the museum of course is one of the main fundamental things that we should be working on.

This situation here is one for me that is otherworldly. I feel here in another world, very different than my normal everyday world. My normal world is, for example, on Friday evening, I had a meeting at the museum in Dresden where I work [the Gemäldegalerie Neue Meister at the Staatliche Kunstsammlungen Dresden]. The museums in Dresden are one of the important places where tourists go to give this old city a new life. There is a society of friends called, in Latin, Muse Saxony e Usui, and they invited 180 people from all over Germany who give money to the museums. And they had a meeting there—we had the meeting in the Zwinger, where the most important collections of seventeenth- and eighteenth-century paintings in Germany are kept today. Then we were going with torches to another place in the city, called the Albertinum. These 180 people could see, for the first time, the [Wilhelm] Lehmbruck sculpture [*Kneeling Woman*, 1911], which was taken out of the museum by the Nazis, and which was then bought in New York and brought back to Dresden. This is a normal situation for me, now. But on the other hand, there is a situation where I am working in a museum in East Germany [the Gemäldegalerie Neue Meister], where the normal frameworks are broken, and the structures of conservation are broken, and educational initiatives are broken, and half of the people were laid off. We have very few people now. And what we have to do is to rebuild the structures. So, I'm here to get help from artists in creating better structures for this museum.

When I was still in Munich—you know, there is a very strong structure in the museums in Munich. Bavarian state galleries are very, very well established. And my job was just to rearrange these art pieces on the grass in the back area of the

Pinakothek in Munich. This is like what the museum director would normally do when arranging things in his own house garden: "There in the middle you put this, and there is this, and a little bit of this." Just working in a simple aesthetic way, and doing these things without seeing the social structures—without seeing the social structures or the function of the building or institution. So, I was not able to do this. I had known Fritz for a very long time, and I had very good expectations that he would see something I could not. I don't know—we will see, and we will make a publication next year, and we will make some rearrangements. So this is my situation in the museum.

I think we should discuss, in the very short time we have, what can be done. Because first the museum needs help. And this is a service I ask from artists. My question is: Why are you interested in doing this kind of work? This is a question of what this institution is for you. Is this a kind of art? How can this kind of art be paid for, be bought? I think we both, curators and artists, have to discuss this kind of art. I think this art is what Fritz is doing, when he makes a kind of description of the Pinakothek.

I had a chance to make an exhibition with John Cage two years ago in the Neue Pinakothek, which opened in July 1991. He made the museum circle. He rearranged the museum. The idea of the museum circle was that he also feared the museum—that it was not the best format for presentation. So he asked me as a curator to speak with all my colleagues at the other museums in Munich—the historical museum, the paleontological museum, the ethnographic museum—all the museums associated with the Pinakothek, and from the various city museums. Cage asked me to ask these colleagues for loans. So, he asked for loans but he didn't say what sort of loans. The idea was that I would ask my museum colleagues to please give us ten or twelve pieces on loan from their collections, but Cage did not have a list of *which* loans. He told me, "You just ask them for a list of things, and then I will make a chance operation and randomly select from those lists." My colleagues thought this was nonsense, but the Pinakothek is an important institution, so they worked with us. Cage used chance also in selecting where the loans would be put on display at the Pinakothek. So, all of a sudden there was a very new structure within the museum, and this was very refreshing. Audiences and the people were very happy with it. It was very nice because there was a portrait of [Otto von] Bismarck next to a very old bear from twenty thousand years ago.

But this was just one experience, with John Cage. It was a simple example of how artists can make real changes to structures. I have four more pages of my presentation but I think I will stop now.

Draxler: Christian?

Christian Philipp Müller: I want to talk to you about a project I did in 1987–88, because I thought it would fit into this category of serving art and artists. I was invited in 1987 by an association in Amsterdam called Arti et Amicitiae, or Art and Friendship, to curate a show there, but it was completely unclear what they felt my specific mission was supposed to be in working there. I understood it as an opportunity for reflection and research on this institution. I did over forty interviews with new members of the organization. This organization, as far as I know, is one of the oldest artists' associations. It was founded in 1839 by artists, in a way copying the structure of the German *Kunstvereins*. The difference here is that there were no bourgeois people who were the founders. It was really done entirely by artists, because these artists were frustrated by their conditions in Amsterdam, and because at this time there were no museums for them. In the nineteenth century, a famous Rembrandt painting, *The Night Watch* [1642], was only visible in a staircase a few hours a day in the summer, so they wanted greater control over how art was shown.

They also wanted to raise their social status as artists. The only opportunity they had to show works normally was in the annual salon on overcrowded walls. So, they were not satisfied with their conditions. For me, it was very interesting because they really wanted to control their conditions. So, they put money together and bought part of a house, and then a little bit later, the whole house. And they transformed it into their vision of what a museum should be. A space where their works would be shown properly. One of the things we are talking about is control, and how much control can we as artists get. These people were really trying to gain 100 percent control by designing their own space. They made a combination of exhibition space on the upper floors, and on the ground floor they had a place where they could meet and invite people. And meet potential buyers too.

They also created a format so that they could welcome the king

of the Netherlands there. Over 150 years, these people, these artists, lost control. They lost their direction. So, I engaged in research for about a year, going every month to their archives. I tried to learn what the goal was in the beginning for those artists, and I found out that it was not just to control their architectural space and social space—they also came up with their own magazine and their own art criticism. They tried to control their own critical reception; often the artists even wrote reviews of their own work. The whole model only functioned for that generation of artists. For the next generation, the impressionists, this historical guild was no longer useful anymore.

So, my question was how a historical structure could serve a contemporary art community. The new association members were unsatisfied with the organization and voted for an artistic director who would make changes. I did more than forty visits to the new members' studios, and I asked them what they would change about the organization. I left the main exhibition spaces empty; I just designed a wallpaper with the symbol of St. Luke, which is the symbol of the association. I used that first symbol from 1839, and then also the symbol of the association from the 1980s, which is an abstract form. I used this in repetition as a wallpaper pattern, trying to underline the domestic character of the institution, because, for the members, it is like a home. The book I did is written like a travelogue—me the invited artist who comes to Amsterdam and enters the house by chance and meets people in the stairwell, and visits all the different rooms, and starts to talk with others. A fiction written out of interviews I really did with the members. The show I did caused a very strong reaction—they immediately fired the artistic director, and went back to making compromising shows, and shows that were completely tied to finding a sponsor. Like, for instance, the Dutch railway company would come up and say, "OK, we have $100,000, can you make a show about train stations?" I mean, maybe I should read just a tiny bit of what the artistic director wrote in the introduction to this book. Because for me it was strange how violent their reaction was, and their refusal of this show. I just saw myself as a mirror, to show them what they had—the incredible structure and possibilities they had. I just wanted to talk to the new members, but in a way, they couldn't stand it.

The artistic director writes in the introduction: "Arti et Amicitiae presents its new members by exhibiting their work. I have asked the Swiss artist Christian Philipp Müller to develop some new ideas for this purpose." I was invited as an artist, but they expected from me the service of a curator as someone who just arranges the art of forty new members. I decided not to show the art pieces of forty artists, but to instead show the possibilities they had.

Just to read from the interviews, one member said, "I appreciate that Arti et Amicitiae is not a gallery and sees the potential of establishing a lively forum here. I love the carefully preserved oasis in the midst of the hectic modern city, but nevertheless I see its death from suffocation because of the self-imposed isolation." And another member: "In the history of art the good ideas always came from individuals. Each one has to advance in his own work. To make art one has to retire into oneself."

Another member stated, "Art should present the newest developments in art to the Amsterdam public. It is in Arti et Amicitiae's favour to be neither museum, nor gallery—no commercial conditions should determine the exhibition program. By purchasing well-sited real estate at the right time, a healthy financial basis has been provided." I tried to find out what the members personally considered to be the difference between a small museum or *Kunstverein* and Arti et Amicitiae as an institution. I understood that, at Arti et Amicitiae, the control is still completely in the hands of the artists, so why do they need an exhibition organizer who provides ideas? But some members thought that, by being employed by the association, the artistic director was more often present in this house than anyone else, and thereby guaranteed continuity—he knew different people, and thereby had the possibility to introduce to Arti artists the work of other artists with which they were not acquainted.

Anyway, with relation to that project, I was invited to work another time in France with an artist association. In the midst of that experience, I found out that I was hired just to be the voice of the curator who was working there—to provide a critique which he couldn't provide himself. Or, he just wouldn't do it. And so, I was playing this role, criticizing [the early twentieth-century French novelist and art critic] André Malraux. But also raising the question of how one can actually show contemporary art in a '60s modernist building, where the art space was. How important is the context or the frame in viewing art and looking at art? It was always a fight to convince these people that you should pay an artist who does research over half a year. To get them to pay an artist a fee was impossible. You know, in the end, I didn't walk out with a product. At Arti et Amicitiae, they said I left the spaces empty. They said I didn't use it! Which is the same argument they had with Andrea over the lobby gallery at the Whitney Museum—you cannot leave it empty. But of course it was not empty. I also did a drag performance piece there where I dressed like the Dutch king. And I showed one of the paintings the association artists made in the 1800s to impress the king.

Draxler: Ute?

Ute Meta Bauer: I can start at the same point on which Christian just stopped, because the Künstlerhaus Stuttgart, where I'm artistic director, is also an artist-founded space. And there are a lot of these spaces, not only in Germany, from the mid to late 1970s, when artists said they wanted to have their own spaces and their own structures. But the situation in Stuttgart at the Künstlerhaus is that they have a director who is independent in their programming. My predecessor was a social worker, and the one before was an artist. The difference from other institutions is that the Künstlerhaus asks artists to be the program director, and for a number of years. It is clear that the people I have to deal with are artists, and they are a specialized audience. The Künstlerhaus does not deal with a general audience. So, the structure of the program has to be different.

But what has been a fight from the beginning is that I didn't want to show the works which are made by our members. There are about five

hundred members of our association, and most of them are artists. The space is funded by money from the city, from the cultural budget, and so the members see it as their money. The question was what can I do there besides just showing the members' works…which I found stupid. So, I thought the thing to do was to work on the structure. On the one hand, to show exhibitions on the possibilities of artistic practice—different kinds of practices that artists work with—so that the members were introduced to different kinds of work. On the other hand, I was inviting artists and asking them to come work with the space, to work with the topography of the space. For example, Maria Eichhorn was working with our children's workshop, which she transferred into the exhibition space. Or Serge Kliaving—he didn't want to show his art there to other artists, as he was more interested in public space. So we helped him to do a work outside in the public space. We try to give a kind of structure, and facilities, to the artists we invite. At the same time, we also try to give facilities to the local artists—there are workshops there, like printmaking workshops and video production workshops. And artists can come use the office space too, the fax machine and the phone. I think what is most important is to show the younger artists that they should not wait until someone is picking them up to be shown, but to learn that they can do it, force it, and enlarge the scope of what is possible.

I also realized that you have an enormous power in a position like this. Even if we don't have much money. All of a sudden, I choose who to invite—if I'm interested in an artist, I can call and say, "Come, we'll pay your flight" and so on. It's a position of luxury. You have a lot of power in those positions. We always say that artists work for themselves, and that curators also work for themselves, but actually they both invite people they want to work with. So it's always a service, back and forth. The question is how you work with the people you invite. And how you come back to this point of serving art and artists with fees. How do you pay the artists for what they do? For example, for the magazine I am making, I have an artist doing the layout, and another artist is giving a lecture. And that is clear that they should be paid for that, but artists are not always paid for that work. These are things that we can change.

With the Künstlerhaus Stuttgart, I also become part of the structure of the city. We are one part of a local art community. I'm also depending on this. I'm an audience of them, and they are our audience. So you are also very connected to the local structure. What is also important is that, if you bring people in from outside, that there is a kind of connection. But you cannot institutionalize that connection—it happens through solidarity or if there is a shared interest. The last thing is that I'm not only program director there, I'm also a member of IG Medien, which is a kind of union for artists—and this is what I am presenting up there on the wall [in the Kunstraum]. They advocate for artists to be paid, and to organize fees for their work. But one thing I am not satisfied with in IG Medien's approach is that they ask that artists be paid per individual work, which is an idea of the work as an individual object, instead of…

Jochen Becker: Yeah, a picture— they describe an artwork as "a picture." This is a very traditional view.

Bauer: In a way, I think IG Medien is a good idea, because they're saying that being an artist is a profession like other professions, and they need unions, and when they get old they need insurance. We are still human beings. Artists get old; they are not special or somehow invulnerable. So, it's a good idea that IG Medien started. But their idea of art and artists is so traditional, and it's not identifying with what is going on. This is their problem. But I think discussions like this can help them. They really want to force the issue, and they are really engaged in the political structure. But more than these qualities, what I think we have to learn is a kind of teamwork. Teamwork that is also about the conditions. If curators ask artists to do curatorial work, then they should split the money they get. I haven't done that before—but these are things we can talk about. We have to talk about money. On the abstract level, but we also need to start by talking on these specific practical points. That's it.

Draxler: There's more material [available to the Working Group] about these questions of unions, and German organizations of artists, for insurance and so on. And you are right that they are based on a very traditional idea of art. It reflects a certain kind of historical process here in Germany. When the BBK, the Professional Association of Visual Artists, was founded in 1971, it already had certain kinds of conservative bureaucratic elements built into it. That doesn't mean that in specific situations they didn't do some great work in the '70s. But they didn't build up a tradition that was open enough. They had a good idea, something elaborate, but at the same time they are totally bureaucratic and totally conservative in what they are trying to transmit. And, so, I think there are a lot of problems here that should be discussed.

The Kunstverein München, where I'm working, is a very different model from a *Künstlerhaus*. It's important for the American participants here to see these distinctions. We have institutions which are based on artist members like a *Künstlerhaus*, and then there is the institution in which I am working, these *Kunstvereins*, which are mostly based on lower-bourgeois, art-lover kind of supporters. They were constituted in the nineteenth century in Germany in opposition to the museums that were founded by the king. And in opposition to what happened in France and England, which was that the national museums there were founded by the bourgeois state. That did not happen in Germany. So, the lower bourgeoisie founded their *Kunstvereins*. They came together and made, on a lower social level, their own politics. And they had some very important moments in their history. For example, the Edvard Munch exhibition at the end of the last century was cancelled by the state administration in Berlin through direct influence of the emperor. But then the *Kunstvereins* stepped in and took up the show, and they could show this work, and it could travel through Germany, and it had a great influence on establishing modernism in this country. Of course, there was a lot of change that took place after the war. *Kunstvereins* began to get public money beginning in the early 1960s. In receiving public money, they couldn't only address their own members, and they couldn't rely entirely on jury models or on the decision-making process being dominated by lawyers and doctors from a certain town, etc.

There are more than a hundred *Kunstvereins* in Germany, each with a very complex history. In Munich, for example, in the early 1970s, people from the Communist Party of Germany took over the Kunstverein München and made very explicitly leftist programs there, but they were thrown out because the money was immediately cancelled by the state of Bavaria. Then in the '70s, what happened was that the social democrats took over the Kunstverein and they established a funding system through the city of Munich—not through the regional government of Bavaria, but through the city. In 1985, they had a kind of late-conservative revolution there, although the group doing this was not necessarily conservative—there were also social democrats involved—so it was a complex situation. What they did was move away from the 1970s idea of participation and more popular cultural history programs, which was also intended to attract people from the suburbs and bring them together in the Kunstverein around shows about political topics, like apartheid in South Africa, and shows with women artists. So, instead of this, an art-world-type model was installed. What they wanted was the figure of a curator as "a strong man, who is able to make strong-man decisions," in opposition to a very strong board— it was described in very conservative language, especially the way the functions were defined. And I think this model of the "strong-man curator" has been present in general since the late 1960s. We know these types—Harald Szeemann, and people like this.

Out of this competitive situation between institutions and free exhibition places, it's very interesting to follow the way Szeemann went from working in an institution, the Kunsthalle Bern, and then leaving that. His life really represents this complex historical process which installed this social function of the curator. So, what emerged, and what we can see with someone like Jan Hoet, is this totally crazed curator, in this total power position, which is not constituted by his special artistic knowledge but just by the history he has behind him. And through this kind of corruption, he's able to express a position in the service of certain touristic industries—this is especially true for Kassel. But I also think there was always this other idea, of a very committed curator who would open up this functioning within certain structures, and who tried to make work possible which also would establish a critical relationship within the institution. Edward Fry, for instance, didn't really have a lot of followers, and Szeemann, Hoet, and Rudi Fuchs were much more successful. And then there was Kasper König in the early 1980s, who created this model of the curator as total pragmatist—and what that means for this discussion here is that this was the beginning of a kind of curator who is just totally serving artists. Serving artists as the utmost curatorial effort. This kind of curator who makes artwork possible, and supports artists, and the belief that this should be the only goal of curatorial activity.

When I took over this job in Munich [at the Kunstverein München],

it was clear to me that it could only be an extremely ambivalent position, a position which already had a lot of projections on it. Because the board that asked me to take the position was also the same board which installed in 1985 this strong-man model. And I knew very well what they wanted from me. And that was more or less the given situation in which I tried to start my work. But what I basically tried to do is function on different levels. I couldn't see serving artists as an adequate basis for curatorial work. I think there are certain points which have to be made to describe this kind of work, and one for me was that it was important to establish a discourse about the social meaning of this institution—how it is constituted, and how it functions in a historical and specific social sense. Maybe the historical point has an importance because the location of the Kunstverein is where the *Degenerate Art* show took place [in 1937, organized by the Nazi Party]. And it also has a very specific meaning with relation to Munich institutions like the Haus der Kunst and the Pinakothek, which Fritz was describing before.

So the problem for a curator is the enormous problem of taking over certain functions, and being a representative of an institution— and how do you do that while also trying to work within this trajectory of institutional critique with certain people. I think that the results are contingent on the question of to what degree institutions can actually be changed. To a certain degree, the board accepts what I'm doing there with the help of artists, working more and more in the direction of project-oriented work. The board accepts this to a certain degree, but is not really involved anymore. I have a four-year contract, and so after four years they may try again to flnd someone who is working more for them, and fulfilling what they want in a much more direct way.

Bauer: I want to say that at the same time, now this very weekend, there is a panel discussion at the Reina Sofía museum [Museo Nacional Centro de Arte Reina Sofía in Madrid] about the ideal exhibition, and it's very interesting because it's Achille Bonito Oliva, Kasper König, and Dan Cameron [on the panel]. So there is no artist—they [these art historians and curators] decide what the ideal exhibition is and what will go on in the institutions.

Müller: There is another symposium going on right now in Bonn about the function of the museum, and amongst others, Hans Haacke is on that panel.

Andrea Fraser: And that's why he couldn't be with us here today.

Fred Wilson: Nothing is happening in the United States right now.

(Laughter)

Draxler: What I wanted to come to was the practical terms, but I got stuck in the historical material. What I think, and what is also a point of this Working Group here, is that there is on the one hand the relationship curators have with artists, and they involve them in their own discourse, and they try through curatorial work on different levels to establish a certain institution. So to raise these kinds of conflicts within the institution on the level of the board. Not how different audiences are interested in a general discourse,

but really trying to introduce this practical aspect—how can this institutional change really happen? The experience here, for me, is a very complex one. And for me it means I am tending to work less with individual artists and more directly with certain groups, like students from the academy, or through programs that are not shows. Because this process of bringing artists into curatorial situations is in many respects so difficult, and last year was occupied almost completely in unguided processes that were absolutely unproductive, because it was just unclear as to what the conditions are that we can set up for artists. The conflicts were there.

One artist, for instance, he just absolutely wanted this total support He just wanted a curator of this type who would just support his vision. But he also wanted a curator who created a certain kind of discourse. And I think these two things are quite different. I think that's why there is a real need for this discussion, because so much time and energy is spent on this expectation of what a curator does, on this basic level understanding of a what a curator does. And that's where curatorial work ends up very often, and for me it produced a really serious crisis.

Fraser: In my experience—and I don't know if Fred had this experience—but in the Whitney Biennial, the grounds for the threatened suppression, or "postponement," of my piece was the concern of the curators about how my piece would impact the work of other artists in the show. So this supposed collaboration stopped at the point where they felt obliged to serve the other artists in the show. And I had, in a way, evacuated the position of artist by doing this piece.

Bischoff: I would like to return to Stephan's remark yesterday, when he said: "They use you, so you use them." I would like to ask precisely what you mean when you say "use the institution." Because my interest is of course in the institution. There is an archive there, and there is a usual way to deal with the museum's archive, but this is not always the best way to handle the archive. So, my question is: What does the artist have in mind when they say "we want to use it," something like the institutional archive? Is there a different way of handling the material? Which way would you prefer to use the museum?

Stephan Dillemuth: When I said that, I was saying that you should be aware of the fact that you are used to re-establish the power structure of the institution. So, an awareness of what lies behind that power structure, and knowing that, may give you more self-confidence. Usually when you get the opportunity to make a show in a museum, you're glad—you think, "Now I've got it, now I've finally made it, now I'm there where I always wanted to be." But to be aware that you use that power position, and with an awareness that this whole apparatus is even bigger than you first imagined. Think of the capacity of these institutions to raise money, to get access—this is huge.

Bischoff: This is the normal way we think of artists using the museum.

Dillemuth: The museum, with the archive and the storage, it's a really super playground. But on the other

hand, I don't want what happened in Sonsbeek 93, because there seemed to be an enormous amount of money there. I had the feeling that a lot of artists thought, "Well, now my time has come, and now I can really fulfill my dreams." The artist Ann Hamilton hired a barge for three months along with a driver and seventeen thousand tulip bulbs in a pile on the barge, and a juggler hired for three months to stand on the pile of tulips. I mean, I'm sorry, but…

I can give you an example of what happened to me when I was invited to do something in a museum. I invited these art fanzine people to work with me, and we had access in the museum to the whole storage facility, which is an interesting aspect of what the museum does of course. The museum shows what it wants to show, but then there are these pieces down in the storage. So, we could pull all that out of storage and show it. And we wanted to put it together with the old artworks, and use it as material for a layout. We thought about using the walls, not as an opportunity to hang pieces there, but instead to make something like a layout or collage with all these things. We had a lot of problems with the restoration department—they did not want us to put the prints on the ground, even though they were packaged. Then the director came and said, "Please, we have to draw a line." There are certain restrictions.

Fraser: That was partly what I was talking about. I want to address this to Susan, as it is also particular to museum education, but also in curatorial interpretation. If you're talking about serving living artists but also dead artists, that often ends up meaning serving artistic intention—this obligation to the idea of artistic intention that becomes a limitation in serving an audience, a limit to the interpretive possibilities curators and educators have.

Wilson: You have to understand a little bit about the professions within the museum structure—what kind of limitations they place on themselves, and what the basis is, and then decide for yourself how much of that you want to deal with. Or how to make them aware of how much those limitations have no basis in reality—but that these are just things that they developed, such as the fact that artists titling their paintings really only came into being very recently, and prior to that titles were made up by the collector, or the dealer, or the curator. So it seems ridiculous to change the name of a painting, but that name may not have been the artist's decision in the first place. And it can be the same with the placement of things, like upside down or right side up. Curators are always making these value judgments about the placement of things, and the meaning of things, and sometimes they don't want to acknowledge their involvement with that. They place the onus on the artist—they place you in the position of doing something destructive to the work, when in fact you're only hurting their belief system about that artist. So you have to go beneath the surface and find out what is real and what has been created over time.

Fraser: A lot of the invitations from curators or museums, from older museums anyway, is like what you're saying, Uli, about museums needing help from artists. That has a lot to do with being stuck in that role of serving artists. So you ask artists to help you, because you're stuck in the role of serving those historical notions. And we are not necessarily obliged in that way, so we have a certain freedom.

Bauer: Sometimes it stops at very pragmatic and stupid things. We're talking at a theoretical level, but, for example, Katharina Fritsch in the BiNationale Biennial at the Kunsthalle Düsseldorf, she was just asking for three quiet days to install her work and they didn't give it to her, so on the last day she cancelled. In response to this, they said, "Oh, she's a very difficult artist." And it really had a negative impact on the invitations she received after that. She was just asking for three days and the work needs it. Or with *Metropolis* [*International Art Exhibition*, Martin-Gropius-Bau, Berlin, 1991]: the artists were not even paid to come to the opening. I mean, there was a big event, and they were not able to pay the artists to come to the opening.

What I ask for is for artists to take a stand and say, "No, I won't participate in that anymore." And curators should be more honest. If an artist is asking them for something, curators should say, "No, I can't do it" or "It doesn't make sense," and be clear. Mostly everything is done in a very vague way. Just say whether we can do it or not.

Wilson: Often the system of a museum is a cover up for the personal needs or preferences of the curator. They say the museum can't do something, when in actual fact it's just their personal lack of interest.

Fraser: To me it's also a question of priorities. Particularly in the United States, institutions have to raise money for every exhibition.

Draxler: Here it's the same.

Fraser: But, so, then they should say, "We just can't do that." But it's a matter of priorities, and it's a matter of institutional policy. How money is allocated, and for whom.

Susan Cahan: I think that often, for practical and financial reasons, projects end up going toward preserving the institution. Understanding that institutions exist in order to present a program. But I wanted to respond to what you [Andrea] asked earlier about projects I have done which may not put the artists' intentions in the forefront. I think that establishing trust and rapport is absolutely essential. For individuals—even if they are representatives of institutions working with other individuals—to really get a lot done, and have that trust there, one of the things that I've found is that it's important to be really clear about what the goals are of what it is that I'm trying to accomplish. People are generally reasonable if you make it clear what you want to do. It's possible to build a consensus. What has been important for me is to invoke methodologies from other fields. Ideas coming in from other disciplines has really helped make sense in the art institutional framework that might not have otherwise. If there wasn't a consensus around challenging ideas of artistic intentionality in the late '80s, there was no way I could have done those projects.

Fraser: It's a contradiction for me in my own experience, because I've done shows in which I've situated other artists' work in ways that didn't have anything to do with accepted standards of museological practice, or could easily be interpreted as being against the intention of the artist. But then with people like John Knight, for example, or Daniel Buren, who have very specific policies, I absolutely feel that those policies should be respected. That's a contradiction I'm not sure how to resolve.

Wilson: It has to do with basic respect. Curators are really across the board on this, too: they either respect what they think the artist's intention is, or not at all. But as an artist, you have a responsibility to put forth a certain amount of respect to whatever degree makes sense. That can be a limitation, but it's a limitation that can be worked with.

Draxler: At the Kunstverein München, we've only made one group show up to this point—one which had a more thematic intention—and that was the only time we used a kind of artist list. Because the artist list itself is considered to be a very dubious object, which is usually very often used within this curatorial process for prestige. So we tried to make the list very long and in very small type, and only use the first name, and absolutely not to care about who was really in or not. To make a really ridiculous artist list. And then this was behind the mistake that happened here for this group project with inviting John Knight. The only way in the end to avoid it is to just not make a list at all. On the one hand, there is an absolute respect for these kinds of policies; on the other hand, there is the really ridiculous artist list. Like Kasper König always has a list of artists in his notebook, and he is just rearranging that list from one show to the next.

Becker: I have a question for Uli: What is that artists can do that you can't do? So, you want to invite an artist to help you [change the infrastructure of the institution]—why can't you do that which you think artists can do?

Bischoff: First of all, 80 percent of my job is to take care of conservation problems, and they are very big. In Dresden, there is a big storage facility in the building, which is from the sixteenth century. And I have to take care of personnel, and other things. On the other hand—and it's a problem—it's just easier to answer your question through the arrangement of the outdoor sculptures in Munich in front of the Pinakothek. I don't want to be a person who makes a nice sitting room in an aesthetic way; I don't like to use my personal taste and just make an arrangement of works of art. Because if you see how these outdoor sculptures are placed, it's horrible, and I don't want to just change it in another horrible way. I can't do this.

Becker: But what is the difference? Why can't you throw them away, or put them away, or arrange them like Fritz might do?

Bischoff: I have no possibility to make the research Fritz, as an artist, can make, because my job in Munich was to be the person for all the artists in Bavaria. I was the person from the state who needed to look at the work of everyone who invited me. I had to travel around to all the cities and so on, and I had to make the arrangements in the Galerie Neue Meister—and this is a big difference to the United States. There are only two museums in Germany, I think maybe now three, which have a registrar. And in the US, every big museum has a whole department with three or four, ten, twelve, sixteen registrars. So the internal situation is very different. I know a lot of colleagues who make arrangements very quickly. You know, you have forty artworks and "this can go there, and this is nice, and that can go there," and after an afternoon, it's finished. This is not the real way to deal with art.

I have the experience that artists are going to a museum for years to look at one or two artworks, and they know the work better than the curator. Artists are people who are interested in art, not just their own art, but other art too. And this is what I have been asking about. The museum is a box with pieces in it, and these pieces are mostly important for the artists. This is my experience, and I would like to invite artists to work with those pieces which are of interest to them. The tourists come to a city to see the town, and the most important artworks. In Dresden, it's Raphael's *Sistine Madonna* [1512], and they see it, and then they leave. This is not the right way to deal with art, but it's the normal practice. And that is why I like to work closely with artists. In Munich, for three years I invited artists to look at one painting for half a day or so, and then I invited other people and we were sitting there and just looking together. That is one way of getting nearer to art in the museum.

Ulf Wuggenig: One problem might be that there are many different kinds of artists with many different interests, so it's not a real solution to the problem of the taste of art historians or curators, to delegate it to artists.

Bischoff: I'm changing, curators are changing, the museums are changing, we are changing. But we have to qualify this notion of "changing" with the quality that comes from the artistic view to the art, and not from the art historical view to the art.

Cahan: Some curators do employ unusual exhibition strategies, and when they do, they are often criticized in ways that artists aren't. They are criticized for imposing their ideas on the artwork. I'm curious why that is, and why you think that curators don't do this.

Beatrice von Bismarck: You used the word "trust," and I have heard a couple of times today the word "exploitation" used by both sides— the curator exploiting the artist, the artist exploiting the curator. What interests me is whether one could actually formulate that in a positive way. And what would the expectations on both sides be to do so. Because so far we have only talked really about the conflicts that can arise. So, can we talk about anything else? It seems to me, Helmut, that for you any cooperation in that sense would not be in your interest.

Dillemuth: In my last statement, I said that this is like a marriage, this is a relationship. Sometimes you have to hate the other, and then you love them again.

Michael Clegg: I don't understand why you [Helmut] put such an emphasis on the artist as the audience. I think we are talking about artists making work for others.

Draxler: I think there's a historical reason; I'm an art historian. Late nineteenth-century academics took this function over from the artists as the custodians of the museums. And now we give the job back. So, I see it more as a crisis of art history as an academic discipline.

Cahan: Now artists are academics too.

Fraser: That creates a crisis for me.

Wilson: I wanted to get back to the question of why curators are turning to artists to make exhibitions. I think it has to do with curators and their peers feeling the pressure of doing something that may be considered unscholarly, or that pushes boundaries and opens them up to being looked at by their peers. So, they bring in artists who maybe don't have that kind of pressure to recreate historical positions. But I also feel that the artists often function to spark something that pushes the curators forward, so when they go back, they [the curators] don't do what an artist would do, but their practice is expanded by that experience of what an artist did.

Fraser: I've had the experience that an artist who has taken up certain institutional forms or practices of the curator does not expand the possibilities for the curators, but actually limits them. Because those forms and practices then become identified with particular artists, and curators can't use them anymore. I had an experience with the *Desire of the Museum* show [at the Whitney Museum of American Art, New York, in 1990], where the students wanted to put up wall labels that weren't directly related to the works, and the person in charge said, "You can't do that—do you think you're Andrea Fraser?" It was the most perverse thing. And there is this division of labour. And curators being criticized for making interventions.

Bischoff: Moreover, I think that curators are much more into the hierarchy of meaning of art history. For example, in the National Gallery in London, I think in the past five years there were exhibitions where artists were invited to choose paintings they were interested in to show in new ways. But it is very important to break out of this traditional art historical meaning. The artist—and this is an answer to your question [Jochen] of how I see artists—they have the privilege to work more on art than the art historians, because the art historians who work in universities or museums are so engaged with activities which have nothing to do with art at all. So, it is a chance to come back to the art. I also understand why some artists ask curators or art historians what they are doing there in these areas of the museum or archive all the time. In reality, it is very seldom that an artist can make a trip to work in the storage facility or the archive of the museum.

Becker: I just want to give two examples. First, the Osthaus Museum [in Hagen, Germany], where Michael Fehr, who is an art historian, works. He organized the museum so that he could work with what he has there, and he invites cultural projects. He did an exhibition about streamline [machines], he brought in a zeppelin and bombs together with artworks and cultural objects that are not art, combined in a very unique kind of exhibition. The other example is: I'm thinking about doing a work with the Landesmuseum Volk und Wirtschaft, the Museum of People and Economy, in Düsseldorf. Very interesting. I'm more interested in working in that museum than an art museum.

Martin Guttmann: I think there's an issue of democratization of museums. I think it's a very serious issue. Different museums have different charters, but when museums have a mandate to present art to their constituencies, then there is some obligation and responsibility to do it right. With the mandate, there is a question of getting some input from the constituencies. And in various contexts there's a feeling among museum professionals of a real need to get input, and perhaps artists could be useful as the first stage of a democratization process. But I think it should be thought of as a first stage, not as a question of exchanging one kind of taste for another, but as getting some input from a constituency that usually doesn't have a voice. If artists can negotiate between a constituency and a bureaucratic structure, then that might be a good position for art. If it works…

Bischoff: But this only functions if the artists have an interest in the art museum. Cage was very interested in the geological department in Munich, and other departments, at the museum. I want to mention that a lot of the pieces which have to be shown in museums, they are shown there according to the terms of the contracts written by the people who donated the art to the museum. Especially in the United States, there are a lot of rules, such as that it all has to be shown together and for a certain amount of time, you can't put it in storage, etc. In some museums, 60 percent or 40 percent of the work that has to be shown all the time is under these contract agreements. So if you work with artists, it is also easier to break this rule than as a curator. This is one way to democratize the institution. Especially in the Eastern part of Germany, they really want to have new structures. The Ministry of Culture I think is the most democratic structure in a museum.

Fraser: Your example of what happens in museums in America and here is an example of what motivates curators to invite artists often. And that is to work through a conflict with their governing bodies, their board of trustees, or the Ministry of Culture. Like Christian's experience at the MCC [Maison de la Culture et de la Communication] in France, where you were brought in to articulate the curator's critique of the Ministry of Culture in France—I think that happens a lot. The other thing that hasn't been discussed is like what happened at the Museum of Applied Arts in Vienna, where they reinstalled all the galleries, having artists do the installation. And I think that kind of phenomena, like Jan Hoet installing the *David* in Kassel [for documenta IX in 1992], is about spectacle and about museums trying to compete with other kinds of—

Bischoff: But that's like Michael Asher reinstalling the statue of George Washington in Chicago [at the Art Institute of Chicago in 1979 for the 73rd American Exhibition].

Fraser: But it's totally different.

Renée Green: That's what's so funny about that project.

Fraser: But that's what this is about: about how the practices of these people—Michael Asher, and Hans Haacke, and Daniel Buren, and John Knight, and Louise Lawler—are becoming more and more common, and their meaning changes entirely.

Bauer: I want to hear from the artists about how they want to get rid of the museums, because so often museums really disturb the work. If you think of the retrospective of Marcel Broodthaers at the Jeu de Paume [in Paris in 1991–92], I think it really destroyed Broodthaers's work. Or if you see the reinstallations of Joseph Beuys's work, they really destroyed the work of the artist. How can artists save themselves from being taken over by the museums? And museums create art history, but art that is not an object—like the Situationists or activist art—that is not in museums, is left out of art history. So if we are talking about serving art and artists, what can we do about that?

Draxler: That's about the meaning of such places, and what they articulate as a social meaning. In many places, especially German museums, they always try to establish this continuous line from the '30s from [Emil] Nolde to [Georg] Baselitz [in the '60s] without any break in it, and that is a totally revisionist ideal of this country. About establishing very strict art historical categories. Of course, everything else then just remains outside. A lot needs to be done there, but as long as the social reproduction of museum staff is based on this very academic model, this won't change. So, I think that in specific situations, like the one in Dresden, I think it's absolutely necessary to do this work, because it's a more open situation there. Whereas in Vienna, with the Museum of Applied Arts, there's just a huge amount of money which is spread around, and it's not about the meaning of the museum. I think it's a question of how to distinguish these things, and define very precise ways of doing exactly that.

Judith Barry: That raises the question about different ways of collecting. For instance, how artists, especially makers of ephemeral works, might want to have their practices preserved. This also raises issues about how work is collected if it is not an object. I've been to several museum panels where I thought this might be addressed, and it was not. No one seems to discuss the preservation of ephemeral work. Will some art forms be lost to future generations? I teach the history of performance art, and you cannot show a class of nineteen-year-olds a photograph of three guys in a café and assume that this image can stand in for the history of Dada. But, that's often all you have to work with.

Fraser: This relates to the temporary model that Fritz was talking about. But to take that not as a problem of institutions being institutionalized, but as a critique of institutions and how institutions actively institutionalize. Rather than curators having to objectify models of history in installations, to instead open things up by making temporary interventions that can't be accommodated in a permanent installation.

Cahan: The way in which the discussion was framed for this session mentioned an "overidentification between curators and artists [that] can set museum professionals against their boards." Well, what you were just saying, Judith, made me think of the other identification in some cases of institutions with artists. And I think that museums in the US do perceive themselves as undergoing a shift from being primarily collecting and presenting organizations to being more service oriented. That is perhaps analogous to shifts going on in artistic practice. And I think that's a very important issue that you raise, because it's another way that museums can reconceptualize their roles as collecting institutions.

Iwona Blazwick: I just wanted to offer a clarification of terms between "temporary contemporary exhibition space" and "the museum collection," because they keep getting mixed together. But I think they're quite separate in terms of what they can and can't do. In terms of a sense of patrimony, or building up an archive, or protecting works of art, or building up histories—that's a very specific function. And the other one is more a temporary incursion. I guess the question is how the temporary *Kunsthalle* model—if it exists, and provides a platform—what kind of meaning does it have if it's temporary?

On a very practical level, a project that I was involved in, with some of the artists here, was within that kind of model—there was none of the skill or expertise in looking after things. Therefore, there was no maintenance in looking after works. Once the event, the opening, had happened, all the thinking was on to the next thing. It was over as far as they were concerned. So, all of these works languished in the space. They weren't turned on, they weren't maintained, none of the people in the space had any opportunity to discuss what the whole thing was about. And yet, they were at the frontline. They were so alienated from what they were actually sitting amongst, and so disconnected from it. It was a disaster. After the day it opened, the project was left fallow.

Guttmann: As a tentative suggestion on the question of how to preserve ephemeral art, some of the answers can come from ethnographic studies. The standards in ethnography are horrible, and maybe that problem can be a chance to rethink these standards—the problems with how we "preserve" other cultures would be directed inwards.

Green: Can you expand on that? What do you mean by the enabling aspects of ethnography?

Guttmann: Ways of recording dance, music, rituals. These were all sorts of techniques developed by ethnographers that were applied… These bad techniques could be emphasized and become useful in a reconsideration…

Green: I was thinking about what Ute had mentioned, the question she raised, and the comments that followed after that. I mean, there needs to be some sort of location, there needs to be something that allows people to have some sort of access to things that happened. If not a museum, then something else for things that are ephemeral. I'm talking about things I've worked on myself—incorporating that process used in ethnographic methodology to record information and events. Creating some archive in a different sense, rethinking the way an archive can function. And moving it into

a computer age, or knowing that space is limited, and it's not possible to have vaults. But thinking of other ways that works can be represented. And then what Iwona was saying about the difference between a space that's meant for temporary works and a space that's meant to care for works, and to follow up on the artists' intentions. I guess it just requires a re-evaluation of methods of educating the staff and sharing the information between the artists and the people working with the material, so that it's possible to have some sort of reference to ephemeral work, even if you know it's an altered form.

Fraser: I just want to say that I'm deeply ambivalent. And I think a lot of artists who do ephemeral work are deeply ambivalent about what should happen to it. Because when I do performance or when I do ephemeral work, I do it for a reason. But at the same time, I don't want it to disappear. Michael Asher makes sure everything is destroyed when he leaves, when the show is over. Other artists have other conditions as well.

Green: But you see representations of those Michael Asher works.

Fraser: Yes, but those representations do not get presented in institutions, they get presented in books. And maybe the books are in libraries, but they are completely marginalized.

Green: But books are part of that process of being able to transmit information beyond the time that something happens. We're talking about two different things.

Fraser: Yeah, we are talking about two different things. I'm saying that there are other forms of documentation which may satisfy the intentions of artists doing ephemeral work, but they will remain marginal within art-presenting structures as they are now defined.

Clegg: I think one can imagine that, in these questions of who should be the guardian of the flame, the burden is in many ways on the artist to imagine and to remember one can simply not control the life of a work. There are only so many ways that work gets decontextualized, and certainly if one produces object-based work, it moves around the world from hand to hand and shifts in meaning.

I always thought it was interesting to imagine these eventualities, and to build in a kind of safeguard that would simply take into consideration all those things that can happen to the work. And I don't think it is an appropriate request to an institution to say you should invent new ways to protect these kinds of works that are produced, because they are perishable or difficult to document. Because that is actually a lot about one's intentions.

Draxler: There's even a history of artistic strategies in exploding this.

Bauer: The museums are also very much a history. There is this tape from [dancer and choreographer] Simone Forti which is about her story, and about how most artists who work in painting and sculpture form art history, and how women artists are working in other fields, and so women are not represented by history.

Bischoff: I think we have the same problem as fifteen to twenty years ago, because artists are more interested in situations and structures, and not so much in their own products which can be sold. And the art market is not responding to this. You know, in 1982, after the *Zeitgeist* exhibition [at Martin-Gropius-Bau, Berlin], the market said, "We prefer paintings, please." And this is a repeating of the same situation. It was already happening in the beginning of the '60s when artists like Stanley Brouwn in Amsterdam were saying that we should think about the museums, we should think over the possibility of changing our archives. A museum is an archive, and Fred's work, for example—this is the only form of documentation here on this wall [of the Kunstraum exhibition space], Fred, of your work.

Wilson: Yeah, unfortunately. Well, it's not completely true—I do have some permanent installations now. What we seem to be talking about here... It's interesting how we've gone from ephemeral work to ethnographic material, to what is meant to disappear. But what we are talking about is not saving the actual work, but saving some portion of what the artist feels represents him and the work. The whole museum structure, especially in the US, of what's displayed and not displayed, is based on the monetary value of things. So, when we get into ephemeral work and reproductions, the value is really lost. But since museums are becoming more service-oriented sites of education—or that's the rhetoric, anyway—what we're talking about is structures and spaces for archives that can also provide easy access to information, be it video or computer. You have resource rooms now in many museums that serve quasi-educational functions, but what we're talking about is not an ancillary environment that's just tacked on but a "main event" environment that is placing some value on the representation of former events and ephemeral artworks. And which will go hand in hand with the dialogue of whatever is hanging on the walls of those gallery spaces.

But my experience has been that every museum documents their exhibitions. My experiences have been that they're just not familiar with, or aware of, the need for large-scale documentation of installations or ephemeral work with a little more specificity. If you're doing a catalogue, you get closer to specificity. I'm beginning to ask the museums to make architectural floor plans after the work is done, so there is an actual document of where things were. So, all the media that goes into documenting needs to be formalized more, and perhaps a group like this could come up with specific proposals for a museum.

Fraser: When I do a performance, I make video documentation part of the museum's obligations.

Wilson: Right, and if it's movement oriented, then maybe you need more than one videotape.

Wuggenig: I want to come back to this discussion of conservation and the museum, because I think it has much to do with the theoretical notion of "service," which has not really been discussed as an everyday notion of services—a notion of services which is used here at the university very often. I think that in economics, there are two ways of conceiving this notion. One way is the classical

one. In classical political economics, for example, Jean-Baptiste Say, this French economist [from the eighteenth century], says there are products whose consumption occurs at the moment of creation. The same idea can be found in the work of Karl Marx—this is my translation: "The useful effect is only consumable during the process of production." So, services are things that are consumed in the act, so to speak—they can have exchange value but no use value afterwards. I think that could also be an interesting framework for thinking about this problem of ephemeral work and conservation.

Fraser: But they have a use value for a professional community.

Wilson: It's idea value and historical value. It's something that needs to be put into place the moment you begin talking with the museum to do a project.

Fraser: Apropos that definition of "service."

Wuggenig: That is only one definition of "service." There are many.

Fraser: Right. There are fees and compensation—and thinking about this was one of the motives for organizing this group here. Michael Asher established a fee structure and had very, very strong feelings about artists getting fees for production. That fees for production does not have any integrity and is a misappropriation of what a fee is. That a fee is outside of market structures of goods production. And that is what a fee is for. So, to play a double game is incoherent. This happened at Firminy [for Project

Unité in 1993], with the curator, where it was said, "Well, you are going to go sell the thing, so why should I also give you a fee?" So I just to say that I really want to come up with a coherent policy that will protect artists and curators.

Barry: I want to go back to issues that Fritz and Christian raised about redeploying spaces, in light of what Fred said about ephemeral objects having some kind of value, even if it is not monetized. I think the point you raised about ephemeral collections not having any value, like Asher's—I am personally upset that he cannot be represented in a museum, but he cannot. This is an important question about space and how space could be reconsidered for temporal work, including installations, and if the artist gives permission.

Wilson: What we are talking about is the different kinds of museums and how they display things. There are museums that don't have the same hierarchy of value as art museums have in valuing their collections.

Bischoff: The best idea in the biggest room, huh?

Draxler: I think it's a question about political strategies that are developed. If Michael Asher developed this fee structure strategy in the early '70s, then he might have had reasons for it. His strategy has been very successful in establishing him as an authority of ethical ways to deal with art issues. So, maybe, why should we care about what is going on in museums? What the Art Workers' Coalition did was collective participation, not reform. So, I think we have to go into a very specific kind of work, develop very specific strategies.

Cahan: I'm trying to understand the distinction between "participation" and "reform." When I think about the genesis of participation strategies, or its roots, I think of certain cultural ideas coming out of Cuba, '60s revolutionary contexts, or postrevolutionary contexts, but I don't see that in the United States. Maybe there was a quasi-revolutionary climate there in the late '60s…But anyhow, I don't see a difference there between that and what might be called "reformist."

Draxler: I would not see much difference there either, but I was just referring to statements by the Art Workers' Coalition that were against reformist approaches. I mean, today, we are so far from demands like this that were made for artists to be on museum boards. Over the past twenty years, we have lost so much; we have much more to overcome.

Guttmann: Susan, you don't think artists have a problem organizing themselves in collective action?

Cahan: No, I'm not saying that at all. I was just thinking of this contrast of terms that was used in the Art Workers' Coalition material of "participation" versus "reformist." And my question is: What would constitute anything other than a reformist position at this point in history?

Guttmann: But there certainly is a way of distinguishing between topic-based demands, which can be called reformist, and participation, which is more about activities that are not guided in issues.

Cahan: But I guess I have just been listening to artists here at this table who have been discussing how their participation is so vulnerable to serving status quo institutional ends. So participation cannot be assumed to be taken to revolutionary ends.

Audience member (Bettina von Dziembowski, a student): I just wanted to call attention to the work that the students have done for this event: installing, serving coffee, cleaning the room yesterday. They have not been able to be an audience here. I don't want to blame anyone here, but just so you know that some of the students feel exploited in a certain way. I also have a practical question about this show and how it will travel. Will the results of this research become part of future research—like in Stuttgart, for example?

Fraser: There have been some discussions about the points that you are raising. And we should take that up in the conclusion [in the next session]. We have to have a break now. And these discussions were not raised earlier, which has to do with the conditions of this space, the Kunstraum here. And the fact that there is not a structure in place for it. So, it's coming into being now. From the very beginning, this event was conceived as a closed-door working group, not as a seminar, not as a public event. And the faculty here never addressed a question about that to Helmut or myself... until just last Tuesday. Then it had to be dealt with in a way that was not satisfactory. That is because it had not been dealt with prior to that point. This is a site of production of these videotapes. And it could only be a site for the kind of work that

we wanted to produce, that is, if it were a practical meeting between practitioners who shared certain experiences. We needed to be able to discuss those experiences without having to address them in a way that a public panel or symposium has to. Because we are well familiar with the problems of those public panels or symposiums.

So, this was an effort to set up a structure that could avoid those problems. Perhaps it wasn't necessary...You know, I didn't expect that the discussion would be so easy. Because the history of this particular group, or parts of this group, over the past year or two years—we have been engaged in a lot of complicated interactions and competition and conflict. Given that history, I assumed there would be complications here as well. So, I think Helmut and I can take some responsibility, but this discussion that you are raising should have taken place a lot earlier, when the concept was established. Then to the second point [about the exhibition travelling]: I always thought of this [exhibition and event at the Kunstraum of the University of Lüneburg] as a starting point. So to go on and work with what happened here. That if it goes on to Geneva, where there is a curatorial program, that there could be a dialogue between the students there and the students here. So that is my response.

Barry: Do the students have a position or opinions about how they might benefit from our interaction? New models that the students are looking at now for these types of situations?

Audience member (Bettina von Dziembowski, a student): The

students just hoped for the opportunity to listen. Not to participate.

Audience member (Vera Kockot, a student): But maybe we can invite you back to make a seminar and reflect on this, on what has happened here.

Fraser: I just want to make one more point about student labour in this event—subsidizing education with one's own impoverishment. I don't know what the exact situation is here, but in the US, it's standard procedure to force graduate students to teach undergraduate students for next to nothing. Perhaps there is a similar situation that is being reproduced here. Where making coffee and cleaning up is not an educational activity, but then it is being required of you as a payment for participation. And at the same time, we are being asked to engage in a pedagogical labour which may not be the conditions of the engagement. So, it's a real issue and it's contiguous with what we are discussing here when we talk about institutions. How to define the conditions of exchange? And I think the students need to ask this of the school, and the Kunstraum, as well as the participants.

Bischoff: It's not so nice.

Fraser: It's not so nice, but it's necessary. It's a tough job—this is serious. But can we take a break now? And we need chairs for the public presentations. We can all get chairs. I will sit on the floor!

Working Group
Session Six

Concluding Discussion
Sunday, January 23, 1994

Helmut Draxler: So, we have a kind of complicated situation at the moment. This very complex problem was raised about how this group is functioning, in the space, and how the space is in the student community, and how it is conceived. I really would say that it's an important subject that really should be discussed. On the other hand, the last section ended with some points which seemed to be interesting. And I think it's absolutely also important to finish and to have this concluding discussion now. So, what I would suggest is that we continue now with this discussion and we have the meeting we offered to have tomorrow [with the students]. I would say we should start it at 1:00 pm or so, if this is OK, and that who is here should come and we should try to focus on this problem very explicitly, because I think it's very important to discuss how the Kunstraum [of the University of Lüneburg] is going to continue this work and what kind of problematic ideas—this relationship between an academic and an artistic community—are defined. They should be addressed in a very open way, so that we can try to find a way out of this little bit of a difficult situation.

Andrea Fraser: We should also, I think, explain to the participants, because they don't know that there's this session tomorrow. We had made an arrangement to talk to the students about the show and about the group tomorrow at 1:00 pm. So that's what Helmut's referring to, and I know some of you are leaving in the morning, but it would be very nice if those of you who are not leaving could also come to that and participate in the discussion. Yeah? Is that—?

Draxler: No?

Fraser: Or—?

Susan Cahan: I want to say one thing, which is that the issues related to the students, and the relationship of this project to the ongoing program of this university and the Kunstraum, is one of the things that personally interests me the most and that I think is really important in order to make some links to the future. So, if there is other support in this room for talking about that a little bit this evening, I'd like to just sort of propose that as a possibility, especially since I'm not going to be here tomorrow because Fred and I have to leave in the middle of the day.

Fraser: Well, perhaps—yes?

Martin Guttmann: I second the suggestion, and I think that maybe one of the ways of making it a more interesting subject—although it's interesting enough (laughs)—is to just think about a slightly larger issue that wasn't really brought up in one of the sections, but actually could have been brought up. And that is the ability to have projects done in collaboration with academic contexts, which seems like a very broad topic. But at the same time, it seems like we've been talking a lot about the relation of art, audience, and museum. And so, respecting the context, you know, could be brought up also in a more direct form. It seems that there's a really

big potential for more, very fruitful collaborations with academic institutions. So that's why it seems it could actually be an interesting topic in its own right.

Fraser: Do you have a response to Susan?

Fred Wilson: I mean, one thought is that perhaps we could also try to come up with a model for a symposium of this nature, where there's a core group speaking about something that relates very personally to them, and then there's a larger group that also relates to that subject. And there should be some way that there is interaction. I mean, this is not the first symposium I've been to where situations come up like this. So it might be helpful in that way.

Fraser: Well, I guess I would also like to ask the group who have been participating in the sessions this weekend about what other issues they feel would be important to discuss, by way of conclusion, in addition to the issue of the relationship between the Working Group and the project and the schools.

Iwona Blazwick: I think, firstly, it needs to be broader in its geography, because it's very, very narrow. It's absolutely located actually on America and a slice of Europe and that axis. It seems to me that there's some very interesting models being developed and working, I swear, that are just not represented here at all. And our terminology is a bit vague as well—like this whole thing about "museums" versus "temporary spaces." It just seems to me that there's such a broad range of institutions, from ones that have no building, to publications, to technology. There's a huge array of possible terms of distribution and communication and so forth. So perhaps we need to be more specific about identifying what the models are. That would be my two comments.

Fraser: So, you would like to talk about that more during the concluding session, or is that a—?

Blazwick: Oh. It's just a general observation.

Fraser: OK.

Cahan: Well, you're going to be having more of these Working Groups in the future?

Fraser: Well...

Cahan: Because one thing that—

(Laughter)

Wilson: She's tired.

Cahan: Well, if there is the possibility of further discussion in the future, some of the points that are made in this discussion could clearly be taken up in these forums also.

Fraser: Yeah, sure.

Cahan: But it might be interesting to hear what those other issues are.

Fraser: Well, if no one has any objection, then I think that we could open the discussion to the question of the Kunstraum and the relationship to the students, if that's what seems to be of interest. I mean...

Cahan: What have you planned?

Fraser: Well, I think that often it's necessary. It's a kind of symbolic conclusion of the process that's been taking place between different people. This can be helpful, have a beneficial psychological effect, as well as some others. But in particular, I want to revisit this question that emerged at the end of the last session about whether or not this is a reform, what is reform, what is reforming institutions, and what is not. And whether all of this discussion here is based on the acceptance of certain given terms in contemporary structures—whether it accepts the structure positions or not, is how I would put it. That seems to me to be a very important discussion, but I also think that it's not a discussion that we can conclude in any way. So, that's the one thing that I would suggest, but if I'm not, you know... OK, well, let's...

Draxler: It would be good to hear, have some opinions.

(Voices talking over each other)

Guttmann: What is the question?

Fraser: The question that I just raised? Or the question now?

Guttmann: "It would be nice to hear some opinions concerning" what?

Fraser: Concerning the question of what kind of concluding discussion we should have.

(Laughter)

Renée Green: Maybe we need a blackboard or something (laughs). So we could go over it, and put everything on the table. Like what certain points are, to kind of bring up, and then they'd be visible, so we wouldn't forget them and we could refer to them.

Fraser: There was a blackboard here.

Green: Or just think in that way. Think about that—just kind of, structure. I'm just saying that maybe it would be a good idea at this point for the different people who have comments to make about how they might want to proceed with whatever was raised and wasn't, what they haven't gone into, or whatever. That maybe it could be listed, so we could keep track of what these things were and discuss them. That's all.

Fraser: It seems to me that this is actually kind of pointless because in fact…I mean, I think that with the presence of all of you and the way that the last session concluded, it's actually really not possible to imagine having a concluding discussion that does not recognize that change. So, I think that we should just then proceed to address the questions that were raised at the end of the last session about the status of this event in relationship to a student community and a professional community. So I would like to open the discussion on that point. And I would like to invite the students, of course, to participate.

Ulrich Bischoff: It was too elegant the form of presentation of this point, I think, so I didn't understand. The question of the community?

Fraser: The question that came up earlier actually about—I think you [Ulrich] brought it up first—how this event is functioning to serve or not to serve a student community, an academic community, and also a professional community of artists and curators. As I've said, or as we've said, it was conceived to, I suppose, most directly and in the first instance, to provide a forum to in fact serve a purpose. Or its use value—its initial or primary use value—was oriented toward a community of practitioners in relationship to their practice. To open up a practical discussion for practitioners, and to have a secondary function to the extent that I didn't think that discussion could take place outside of a closed forum, but that it could then function via videotape for a community of people who were not participating in that discussion— for geographical reasons and other reasons—but who would then be going into cultural administration and into a lot of other practical work in institutions and cultural institutions.

So, the question is whether the fact that the discussions did not have the opportunity for direct participation—is that a violation of perhaps our obligation to serve a student community? Or the space's obligation? Or, I mean, it could be phrased in any number of ways, I don't know. Someone else—someone else take it over.

Green: Well, did some people talk with some of the students during the break? I did. I noticed some other people were talking. Maybe we could discuss some of the things that we talked about with them.

Fraser: Yeah, I would like someone else to talk besides me.

Green: To address directly what you just said, and what Fred said about the structure of this kind of event where there's the idea of a working group that's trying to actually address certain problems that are pertinent to what they're doing and trying to figure things out: I don't really see a problem with having that existing and also having that be a kind of discussion amongst themselves, which at some point becomes…

I was discussing with one of the students about how some of the students wanted maybe to participate in the discussion, and others wanted to observe and listen to what the discussion that we had was going to be. So I think finding some sort of way of allowing that to happen—so that we can have a discussion about particular situations that we need to address or whatever, and then, at some point, allow other people to speak about it. But I think, for this particular instance, it was my understanding that the intention of why we are meeting is to hash out things and devise some sort of way of working. But if this [*Services* project] is going to continue in some sort of form, then we can take some of these things into consideration for future situations [future exhibitions and Working Groups related to the project].

Bischoff: Perhaps I can make a suggestion. My situation is, when I'm back tomorrow in Dresden, they will ask me: "What did you do there in Lüneburg?" And I will say, "They were discussing some things." For me, the experience is that way: that the artists are speaking for themselves, and have interest in changing the art world and to get in the institutions. There is one [historical] movement [that we've been looking at], it started from artists and it is from maybe thirty years ago—but this [situation of artists in relation to institutions] is changing all the time.

At this moment now, I'm interested to be here, to hear what sort of movements of getting [artists] into the institution and changing it is discussed…What sort of making… Sorry, I cannot speak in this special way. I mean: in which ways they like to get in it, and which form of interest they have.

It was, for me, a good example, your example [Fred], of how you work in these museums. And there are very different forms by artists, in which way they go into the institution. Then I look back on my own institution where I have to work, and I see, "Oh there are a lot of artists who want to do this." So that's a good idea. I could invite them to come to Dresden [to the Gemälde-galerie Neue Meister at the Staatliche Kunstsammlungen Dresden]. This is, for instance, one answer I can give when they [my colleagues] ask me, "What are you doing here?"

And it is really very interesting that there was the same question when I was in another group that prepared an exhibition which had to do with land problems in Poland, and in the Turkish republic—a project for five years where they looked at what they were doing with ecological problems. The difference is we should not be in a situation where we have to ask the artists, "Do you want to participate in these questions?" But we instead have to look at the artists who work in this way. You know what I mean? The difference. This is, I think, not very often the situation. And, on the other hand, different from this situation: artists work in their own way—have different ways to make projects and solutions to work with the situation. So they come from different backgrounds, and this special point, I think, is very fruitful, to put a finger on.

Audience member (Bettina von Dziembowski, a student): May I ask something? Do you think that you got enough information that you could know what you would like to change here? In the institution?

Fraser: Which institution?

Audience member (Bettina von Dziembowski, a student): This one, the university.

Fraser: I don't feel that it's my role to make a recommendation. I mean, originally when Helmut and I came in the summer, we wrote a set of recommendations, actually. It wasn't requested, we just decided that we would do that: write up a list of recommendations about the concept of the space. But I mean, I don't feel that—besides responding to the invitation—not being and not working within this institution, there are certain limits to what is possible for me to do, and also to what I think it'd be to anyone's advantage for me to do. Because I can make recommendations until I'm blue in the face, and they may be totally wrong or they may be totally useless. And I think it's not so much a matter of the content of the recommendation anyway, but a matter of the kind of participation within a system where there are certain responsibilities and certain kinds of exchanges.

Audience member (Bettina von Dziembowski, a student): So, you want to produce something here.

Fraser: You mean with this event? I've produced quite a lot of material at this point.

Ulf Wuggenig: Speaking about this video that you'll be showing tomorrow [Andrea and Helmut], since this is a form of communication with a larger audience. How do you think you will proceed to do that?

Draxler: Yeah, I mean, this is a question we have to discuss: how to organize the public presentation. But the point of the discussion is, more or less, how the Kunstraum wants to define its role between a more artistic community and an academic community. I think that's the point where most of the problems are coming out of. I think it's very, very much also about you [Ulf, as director of the Kunstraum]—how to make up your mind about how could this [institution] function. I mean, the problem is: Is the space only legitimate when it is a kind of seminar room? Or is it the process you were also describing: that this space, more or less, has the function of a seminar room, but could go away from this definition so that it could be a kind of art space? I'm not saying that I'm so much interested in these differences. Not at all. But I think it's very important for you—you have to make the decisions, and to provide the people you invite with this very clear set of information of what it is about, and also [to inform] the students in exactly the same way. Because in my experience what has happened is a kind of lack of communication.

Wuggenig: Yes, you're right. But you have to see that we said that you should come before and make a seminar. Both of you or one of you. And if that would have happened, many of the problems we now have, we wouldn't have had. That's a problem, because of a lack of time, this wasn't possible. So, I think one shouldn't make the problems greater than they are. They are very simple in my mind. If we would have had the seminar in December (last month), we could have discussed participation and all those things. For me, that's the only problem. We found a compromise. I don't think it's so necessary to discuss this to such an extent anymore, because we have discussed this so much in the last days. I think…

Fraser: That doesn't seem resolved. Otherwise it wouldn't have been a question half an hour ago. I'm sorry.

Audience member (Vera Kockot, a student): I have a question. So many different people out here are experiencing different kinds of institutions, and for our program, which is called Cultural Studies, we try to find the meeting points of different cultural workers. There have been many questions raised around this table, but I have not heard any answers yet. And we are looking for answers, searching for answers. How can artists and institutions work together? How far can they go? And what are the differences and the similarities of these institutional organizations, and the freedom of artistic work? Those are the subjects which interest us.

Cahan: OK, I feel like a really interesting kind of shift occurred just before, when you two [Ulf and Vera] were having your exchange, because, all of a sudden, those of us who were invited to be part of the Working Group became sort of spectators to this interaction going on amongst the people who are associated with the university, which is sort of like a transformation of what we had originally been thinking

would happen, which would be that the students would be the spectators. But I—well, I'll just let that lie.

(Laughter)

Fraser: I just want to make something clear: my assumption was that there would be five students—the students who are directly working on this Kunstraum project who would be participating as participants. Not that this would be part of a seminar with the students participating and us as seminar leaders. That was my assumption from the beginning. And that was what I communicated to all of the participants. While it would have been possible for me to certainly think about changing the structure to have all of you [students] present, I said that, if that's going to happen, then you have to contact all the participants to inform them that the structure has changed. Because I made certain commitments that I felt responsible for under what I thought were very clear premises. I just want to make that clear.

Cahan: I'm sorry that I said that actually now, because it sort of then became a flashpoint for the continuation of that discussion, which wasn't my intention at all. My intention was to suggest a way of addressing the issue of cultural studies and arts institutions from a different standpoint that perhaps could be productive.

Over the last couple of days, one of the things that we've heard a lot of is ways in which some of the people sitting around this table look at their practice in terms of a variety of cultural spheres. Judith mentioned the way in which her work engages with issues related to mass culture. Fred and Renée talked about the way in which their work engages with methodologies or critiques of methodology from ethnography. I see my work as being related to different ways of conceiving the idea of popular culture, and how popular culture, in the sense of "a people's culture," could be incorporated into arts institutions which are generally associated with high art and not people's cultural production. And maybe to do something productive with this time, it might be interesting to hear some of the people around this table talk about how their work relates to the area of cultural studies. Like: What is the relationship between cultural studies and arts institutions? And how have people approached that in terms of their practice? Again, it's just a proposal, because I feel like we have this time together and maybe we can use it.

Beatrice von Bismarck: I have another proposal. And that would be trying to combine maybe two interests. I have the feeling that it would be really useful to use this session, maybe not as a concluding discussion but rather to show all that has remained open. What you said is critical, since you [Andrea] want to continue this, since you probably want to do another Working Group.

It would be interesting to know what everybody thinks we *haven't* discussed and what might have been interesting for the work everybody's doing. And, for me at least, I think we have circled around a lot of issues. And it has become more precise today than yesterday. But still, I think everybody has their own interests, and maybe we have questions that have not been approached at all.

I think one of the questions that concerns me—and I think that has a lot to do maybe with the questions that we raised here—is precisely this way that different communities, even the members of those communities, actually shift between one another, and how that community can function. I think the scientific community or the university community is another participant, or could be another participant in that way of exchange. So I have the feeling that if we talk more about what has not been answered, we would include questions about the Kunstraum necessarily, because that's part of my interest, at least.

Wilson: For me, in addition to that, perhaps people have things that they got specifically from this discussion that they feel made some particular sense that they didn't have before they came. When I'm writing things down, I come up with things that are not exactly broad and encompassing, not to be sort of a concluding notion about what this conference is about, necessarily. But I did come up with three different ideas that I didn't come here with, that arose in the end of the last session, that I think are kind of concrete and that could be developed in other ways. In discussion with other working groups or with students, or whoever.

Those three things are: this whole notion that we could create a model for this gallery archive of ephemeral material. But the model being more central in the museum structure, I think, and sort of shifting how museums look at ephemeral material and place it within the structure of the museum. I've seen different museums try to do that a little bit, but it just hasn't been thought out enough. And now we have a great deal of material in this vein, so it seems to make sense to somehow think about that a little deeper. In addition—which would definitely go along with that—was taking documentation really seriously. As was brought up about ethnography, but ethnography is a problematic model. But at least really looking at the development of documentation of various forms of ephemeral art making. So that when this model for this gallery—an archive model or whatever—comes to be, that there's something to put in it that really is engaging for an audience that can create a dialogue between that kind of material and other kinds of art-making practices. Thirdly, of course, we discussed the model for a symposium, which, to my mind, would be an important aspect to a museum as well.

Guttmann: I have to say that I think that the discussion was really interesting at times and there were a lot of interesting points, but I kind of hesitate to try to sum up the seminar. I mean, the last few days of the conference went too quickly, because I think it really should be conceived of—or at least I conceive of it this way—as a very preliminary conversation between people from various disciplines and from various points of view. We have some shared discontent with the present relation between artists and institutions; maybe it can be expanded in some interesting exchanging of notes about each other's counterhegemonic practices. And I think that that's good enough for me, in the sense that, if there's a feeling that this discontent is not just something that applies to each of us individually, but that there are some structural reasons for why various discontents can be combined together. I think

that this, in and of itself, is quite an important step. It's very clear to me that the discontent may come from a lot of different directions. I think that it's very clear to me that various participants are interested in taking the discussions into different directions. Particularly the idea of reducing the discussion to the question of "what artists can do for the museum"—this is not exactly the first issue on my list of priorities. And I really wouldn't like to reduce the whole thing to questions of documentation.

But I think that I really identify with a basic idea of "services," because I think that it's a better formulation for a certain type of activity that is not so object oriented. So, I think that this was a good idea of defining it [the Working Group] around that. But, bearing that in mind, I think that the kinds of activities that I have experienced personally, and the kind of stuff that I hear from other people, are really very remote from really constructive issues having to do with, or what to do with, a particular thing. I think that a lot of people here have an interest in much more politicized activity and in working with real confrontational situations. And I think that it's important just to keep in mind that we come from different points of view, and there's really no need to come out of the discussion feeling that from now on we'll have the same kind of project.

I think that, bearing that in mind, taking it one step further and communicating or connecting to the issue of the participation of the students—I think that it will be much more...I mean, the condition for expanding the discussion should be that people will not just come to listen, but will voice their own discontent, and if they have an experience more with the university, they should come up with their own ideas of how to reform the university. That seems to me generally a better model for expanding discussions. In other words, the people will bring an issue rather than put themselves in the position of listeners, because there's nothing really to listen to, so much as comparing notes from different practices. That's my feeling.

Draxler: Yeah, I think the idea to invite a working group—and to invite a working group within a time schedule which was extremely tight—was more or less so there would be the chance to say, "Let's work everything out much more. Let's make everything much later." Then we wouldn't have had maybe some of these holes and the list of materials [would have been more complete] and things like that. But I think, for us, we felt that problems, especially in the last year, in extremely increased competitive situations for a lot of very big shows and things like that—so very public, very, very bad experiences in different kinds of artistic groups—to put this situation on a more collective level and to initiate this kind of collective level, on the basis of this material, on the basis of this history. To try to create a discourse—not as ours, not as Andrea's discourse, as Andrea's art or whatever, or as my curatorial discourse about whatever—but really to go a little bit beyond that.

I think the term "services" was interesting, for me at least, mostly because it offered an opportunity to integrate. I don't mean to say that there are no differences between different fields—let's say, from an alternative space or alternative interests, or geopoliticized interests on the basis of an initiative, to the

interests of a director of the Neue Galerie in Dresden—but rather that the service orientation on a schematic basis is shared by all of them. So it's a kind of attempt to—I mean, not at all to find a compromise—but to make a kind of conversation possible beyond this not-so-good situation which has been felt the last couple of years. And I think that's what it's about. I say we should probably try to go back a little bit to this level, to where we started from in a certain way. I mean, of course, there are a lot of other reasons here that have to do with different kinds of histories and trajectories which have built up, but…I mean, that's it.

Judith Barry: I think that Martin's point and your point [Helmut] are well taken, because in the presentations, it was fascinating to hear everyone's very different experiences. But I think that the concluding moments might be well spent trying to tie things together, in a sense underscoring certain questions and issues. My question to some of the curators, for those of you who've curated site-specific exhibitions, is: How do you feel about the last two years in terms of what you have produced, and the organization of these site-specific exhibitions, and the kinds of residues that they've left? And for artists, I have similar questions. It seems to me—and this wasn't really addressed—that it is in these site-specific exhibitions that artists and curators spend more time working together than in more conventional exhibitions. And that it is in these moments of working together that the institutional frames are bent a little, or transformed, or even changed. I wonder, thinking proactively—in the sense of thinking that these models could be developed and honed so that that the discussion is not always so dichotomized: artists on one side and curators and/or institutions on another side, which is often the case in these big shows.

Perhaps this would lead to a rapprochement. This is what was most interesting to me in the last session, in particular.

Bischoff: I would like to ask a question we haven't asked to the artists especially. Is there a big difference for you if you make an exhibition with questions of institutions and others in an alternative space, in a normal museum, or in a private gallery? I think we haven't spoken about private galleries, and I know, for instance, you [Andrea] remembered me actually in a gallery in Cologne. There are private-gallery contexts, and is this, for the artists, a big difference?

Fraser: Well, we have a question posed to artists and a question posed to curators. Which one of you would like to start?

Ute Meta Bauer: To your question [Judith], before I first started to work in Stuttgart [as artistic director of Künstlerhaus Stuttgart], I was working for a project in Hamburg, which was called Hamburg Project. It was art in public space. And, for example, I was working with Michael Asher, who mentioned all the people working on his project in the exhibition pamphlet made for his project. And then there were other artists. We had really hard work to do for weeks, and the people [assistants and prepators working for the artists] were really working. And they were paid little... There were artists who were so horrible to them. And sometimes, I mean,

at the end it was their [the artists'] work, but they had just sent a sketch. After this project, I was very happy to go to Stuttgart and work with one artist I could choose.

Sometimes it's really...What they [artists] expect from you, and how they treat people. I mean, you really get fed up with it. Especially if you work on site-specific projects where a lot of people are involved. With other artists who always respect your work [as a curator]—like we mentioned Dan Graham, or Michael Asher, or Lawrence Weiner, for example—you like to work with them. And it's real...Yeah, I think there's much more than we have discussed here. The expectations you get from artists in this work, and how you feel sometimes like a real "service person" who has to do all the shit for them. And finally, at the end, there's their name on the invitation card, and it's their opening, and the people who have been working hard [the prepators and assistants]— I mean, they're not even invited to the dinners. And I think artists, if they work in that way, they are also responsible. Like, if you do a movie, there's the director mentioned, but all the other people are also mentioned. I think then artists should think about authorship and which role they have in this work, and they should share it a bit more, and be a bit more transparent.

(Wilson and Müller start talking at the same time)

Wilson: I think it works both ways. I'm sorry.

Christian Philipp Müller: No...

Wilson: Because, sometimes I've been in situations where the curators don't want you to bring in all these people who worked so hard, and don't want you to list them, because they're not used to that shifting model. It's a wonderful situation when the curator is of like mind, but sometimes I've found it's the other way around: that the curator likes the old mode of curator and artists, and sort of imagines that there was nobody else involved with the project.

Fraser: I think that it has to be seen as assistance though. I just—OK, you go first [Christian].

Müller: I just wanted to thank Ute. Because I think this idea of copying the credits of a movie, this is really great, and we should try to work that out. Not just for the assistants of the artists, but also for the assistants of the curators. I mean, so many big shows are really done by the assistants who get paid nothing at all. And the credit lines should be much bigger and longer and…

Fraser: But in terms of the point that I wanted to make which is—and I guess it's the same point I made before—but it's a system where… I'm sorry, go ahead [Christian].

Müller: I just wanted to say that, on both sides, there's more people than just the star curator and the star artist. And these people should be mentioned, in a way. I mean—

Fraser: But it's not that they should only be mentioned, it's that there should be—

Müller: They should be involved!

Fraser: There should be an articulated system where the kind of labour and resources that are required to do the kinds of projects that artists want, that institutions want, that public art agencies want, that Ministries of Culture want, that boards of trustees want—that the necessary conditions and resources and labour be made clear, and an equitable system of the distribution for those things be articulated. Because otherwise we have this system where, well, if you're on top in a particular situation, then you can exploit everyone else. And otherwise, you're on the bottom. And these positions shift, whether it's the *Metropolis* show [*Metropolis: International Art Exhibition*, Martin-Gropius-Bau, Berlin, 1991] where the artists aren't invited for the opening, or whether it's the Hamburg Project, where the people working on the show aren't invited for the opening. Those positions circulate because it doesn't get—Iwona or Susan? Iwona?

Blazwick: I wanted to come back to you about this experience of working in a kind of intermediary position, of being neither the institution nor the artists, but this kind of secondary agent. In a sense, I suppose that role is a bit akin to being a film producer, in that you're kind of navigating a lot of different agendas and different bodies of interests. And it struck me that one of the reasons that the project [Antwerp 93] failed in some ways, I think, was precisely this issue of both the preamble to the whole thing of somehow being able to involve everybody who was part of it and sharing information. And it's a very long and complex process of actually sharing a discourse as well, and laying the ground for some kind of understanding as to what's going to happen. And thereafter, almost building it into the project that you keep there. Actually, because it is this syndrome of—and I think it happened in Sonsbeek 93, and I don't know if it happened in Chicago [for the 1993 exhibition *Culture in Action*]? Well, if someone, either artist or curator or the person who's involved in the project, doesn't just open it and then leave it, but actually is somewhat intrinsically involved with its life throughout the course of the project. There are all sorts of aspects of the banalities of maintenance which are absolutely key to things like the way that the work is received, and how much information you can make available about it, and what kind of access is made into it, and what kind of meaning it has. And my frustration with it—the day after the opening, bam, that was it. There was no facility for us [participants] to stay, there was no money, there was no procedure. It created huge problems for everybody involved.

Fraser: I think Susan was next.

Cahan: Thank you. But if you wanted to…

Müller: I just wanted to go with a tiny little comment on Chicago (laughs). There were two crucial differences, or ways of doing it. People to the extreme, like Mark Dion, who would stay there during the whole time and was always teaching his students. That is complete self-exploitation. Then other people are just sending in a proposal in the same show where you just have eight artists. That's it. I think both ways are an extreme—you should meet somewhere in between.

Cahan: Well, I'm neither an artist nor a curator. But being an educator, I've had the opportunity to work with artists in both an educational capacity and work with them on their contributions to exhibitions. What I've found is that, when artists work with me on education projects, they have much less of a personal investment in certain ways—or their personal investment is really different when they work with me or with the New Museum [in New York], as compared to when making an artistic contribution to a show. And what I've found is that working with artists whose project-based work is their contribution to a show—is their artwork—is that all of a sudden, the parameters or the boundaries of those projects, they become kind of like…well, they disappear. Certain boundaries and certain kinds of…

I've had the experience of finding that it becomes much harder to administer the projects, that certain things that I would ordinarily take for granted, the artist doesn't necessarily take for granted. So every point needs to be kind of renegotiated or negotiated. A lot of the projects that we've heard about over these last two days—and the one that I'm thinking of in particular is Laurie Parsons's project, which I was involved with at the New Museum [*The Spatial Drive: Security and Admissions Project*, 1991], where her intention was to really disrupt the way in which the museum ordinarily works by having the security staff function as educators. It meant that, in my role as the director of education, I had to turn over a great deal of authority to her as an artist. The role of the security staff completely changed. I mean, the whole museum was overhauled. The curator then became like the education coordinator. It was extremely complicated. And we all bought into it. But the thing was, it was really hard to then know what it was that we were even supposed to be doing in order to perform our jobs. I think that that created a lot of challenges and a lot of problems. It also created a lot of opportunity and a lot of excitement. One of the end results of that project is that now our security guards continue to participate in seminars with the artists that show at the New Museum, and they informally still function as interpreters in the gallery.

But it seems to me that there's something intrinsically disruptive about a lot of the projects that we're talking about, and so it creates new factors and new variables that that don't necessarily have codified answers at this point, and intrinsically aren't going to have codified answers.

Fraser: Renée?

Green: I wanted to just go along with, or just kind of underscore, what Susan was saying, just in terms of work experiences with museums, and thinking of that idea of disruption. But in this way that is actually quite interesting and can affect the way that the different people working in the museum function. In my experience, it's had something to do with—actually, from the point of view of having worked in the education department at the New Museum, developing other ways of trying to communicate with audiences, and then being kind of sensitive to the various people who are working in the museum. This is actually coming out of certain problems that I observed while being at the New Museum, because we had lots of meetings where everyone was supposed to be involved, and we

were trying to question the whole idea of the hierarchy of the museum and all of these sort of things.

But in terms of a specific example, I was thinking of working with MOCA [the Museum of Contemporary Art] in LA. When I was working on a project over a period of time there for my show, I visited various times and I met with people from every part of the staff. So during the course of that time, people were being informed about the project from the very beginning. I think the first people I met with were the production crew, to try to develop a rapport with them, rather than to think of them as the people who were just executing the thing without an understanding of what the work is about. Trying to actually meet with all the different groups. And this was encouraged [by MOCA] in the beginning. It was what the curator ideally wanted—officially, anyway. And that was what I tried to do. But what happened was, I think, I got really involved in making my own connections with the people in the different areas. So I was directly involved with working with the production crew, and I was directly involved with working with the education department, I was directly involved working with the publications department—all the different departments in the museum that had a part in the show. I was very concerned with having some sort of access to them. What happened during the course of the show was what you [Susan] were mentioning: this sort of disruption, so that the curator was confused about what her role was in relationship to me. It was as if I had become like this kind of director of everything, and actually we had different kinds of confrontations about this. I mean, she felt like she was a social worker. It was like she was the education person, and that was very interesting in terms of how that role was perceived. So I think that more of this would be useful to do, in terms of opening up the institutions in the ways that we seem to be talking about in some way. And it was very intense.

Bischoff: It's a private gallery, no? I ask for your experience: Is there a difference about where you would prefer to make exhibitions? Because I know that some of the artists here have worked with a [private] gallery in Cologne, for instance.

Fraser: I think for the most part—

Guttmann: The majority of artists—

(Laughter)

Green: In what way do they contextualize working in the gallery itself, do you mean?

Fraser: It's a sort of a totally different ball game, as far as I'm concerned. I mean, there are a lot of problems that I think at least the artists here— as far as I know from my discussions with them—would also like very much to deal with and to address. But I think that it's a topic for a different forum.

Guttmann: It's probably fair to say that a lot of people present here have some problem with dealing exclusively with gallery spaces.

Bischoff: But it's a different form of institution. So it is quite possible to discuss this together with—

(Multiple Voices talking over each other)

Michael Clegg: …we're talking about museums more because there are certain problems in the private sphere with galleries. There's a reason there. I mean, we can certainly go into it and speak about it, but there's a whole other set of problems that exist. But, structurally, there's a reason that it's not been mentioned really, because there's been a certain shift of possibilities—

Draxler: But projects and services are intended to produce organizational problems, which we wanted to discuss here, which we actually didn't do. And it's presently outside of the gallery, collector, and then museum systems. So the question was also to the museum: How is the museum working with certain kinds of practices?

Cahan: When artists go into institutions to do things, like some of the things we've been talking about, they often do so under the—I mean, I don't know if they often do so. But I know for instance, Fred, when you went into Baltimore [for *Mining the Museum*, 1994], right, you had certain conditions, and the freedoms that you are able to confirm for yourself are actually much greater than the freedoms that many museum employees have in their own work. The relationships with accountability are very, very different for artists. And which, Renée, you were talking about. I mean, that's, to me, one of the biggest challenges as a museum employee in working with artists in this capacity.

Wilson: I mean, their [museum workers'] limitations are self-imposed. It's imposed by this notion of "pure scholarship." I mean, it's really no more than that.

Cahan: It's also very logistical.

Wilson: What do you mean?

Cahan: Well.

Wilson: I don't believe in doing things that will harm a work, that a conservator would be against or something like that. But what I'm working within is the area that is a constructed reality that really doesn't exist—but over the history of museums, this museum structure has been created that really there's no reason for. So curators are working within the structure and are afraid to break out of it because of some kind of peer pressure.

Guttmann: I think that another point, in the way of follow up, is, at least in my mind, the discussion about the relation between arts as an institution. I think this should be generalized, really, beyond the question of how artists work with museums. And I think that a lot of us voiced this point in various individual presentations, but somehow become pulled back into it, and I think that it's really important to emphasize this point again.

I think that if I read into this idea of "services," what I read is that we should think about museums as particular environments which artists can work with, and not as something that should really define their artistic activity. In other words, it's a way of normalizing the question of museums, and saying that these institutions are a certain type of environment, are maybe even communities, and they have their own problems. Especially with Fred—when I heard you talking about your experience, it really became very evident when you were talking about how all of a sudden you [came to be included] on the list of the museums [of desireable artists to work with], and it became very evident that they are really special environments with special problems. Maybe they are communities; maybe part of the point about "services" is to look at an institution as a community, as an environment. But the precondition for doing so is that the discussion itself could be conducted on a more abstract level. In other words, not to talk about museums, really, but more about the question of "activism" that is conducted between artists operating privately more or less, unless they are grouped together, and "institutions," which have an existence that is more permanent—they have their own budget, and they will identify a set of problems. To think about activities that negotiate the issue of art within institutional environments, and in a way where the whole problem of "museums" will become really secondary. In other words, that an analogous set of issues can be applied.

For example, when an artist would—this is just an example—would be approached by a workers' union, or by a university, or by other types of institutions who will say, "Well, here's an environment. Here's a community, you have some experience in working with environments and communities. Do you think that part of your activities can be involved in this type of institution?" Personally, I think that a lot of the problems that really define the relation with museums just seem straightforward. But you know, I think that it's just that a lot of this stuff that is specifically connected to the museum can become really banal very easily. I mean, it's just one structure, just one institution. It's important, but it's really not the only topic to talk about.

Bauer: But still, from the artists' view…I mean, how do you see your work, and what are you defining as your work, and how do you take control over this work?

Guttmann: It's complicated.

Bauer: It's complicated. I mean, that's the reason why we're here.

Guttmann: Life is not an insurance company.

Bauer: I sometimes wonder how easily artists go and sell their work. And you can take it into any context—I mean, do you think it's like you can cut away the arm and then it doesn't belong to them anymore? For example: if you see this contract that you want to have, where if it [a work] sells or gets sold again, that you want to know where it goes…A lot of artists don't even care where it goes. I mean, the work for them is to do it, and then when it's gone, it's like nothing which has to do with them anymore.

Guttmann: You are referring to which contract?

Fraser: The resale contract.

Guttmann: Oh, the resale contract.

Bauer: How to handle this with words, which then, for example, it's no longer a painting, or it's something else? How do you deal with things like this?

Guttmann: This sounds like the real idea of "services," isn't it? Maybe

it's just my own interpretation. But I think the idea of services is an attempt to generalize artistic activity beyond the constraints for existing ideas. And the idea of services can be applied to the museum, but it can apply to other institutions, and the idea of services has a built-in capacity to expand the notion of art. At least that's how I—

Fraser: Yeah, from what you were just saying—I didn't hear the tail end of it, but I thought that it was unfortunate that Mark Dion couldn't be here because he's had experiences approaching conservation institutions and organizations, like zoos and ecological activist organizations. And he can tell you stories about how difficult it is just to get in the door and how completely uninterested they are in working with artists, so. It's just a comment. It's not really a response. Yeah, Vera?

Audience member (Vera Kockot, a student): On that point, I mentioned again that I think there is this possibility here that the university could help find definitions which already exist in other theories and could make an exchange. So that there was a presentation of one model of service, and that could be discussed, and it could be seen if there are some similarities or not in the system. So, you could compare the other different systems, and maybe there could be an exchange of theory to explain what is going on in the art system. You spoke about this special experience in art systems, but I think there are lots of similarities to other systems. Like you mentioned, Andrea, that Dion had experiences being in other systems, and as was already said in another context, we all are part of other communities and have experiences with maybe similar structures. So I think that could be a good exchange between these two fields: the academic and the art field. Maybe that could be something, if this forum is continued, where each side could give each other information. And I think, on the other hand, for the university, it's also very interesting how you are dealing with immaterial things. Because in the university world, there are also presentations, and they are correlated to how famous a person is, and in which university you present something, and so on. So there are similarities between these two systems. So maybe that's just a little remark to what Martin just said, from the idea of services.

Green: I think that's a really useful point. I think that's an interesting point. And I think it relates in a way to what Susan mentioned earlier about raising the issue of cultural studies, and how different people's practices intersect with the area of cultural studies. I was thinking, actually, that, at some point, some of the discussions that we have could be clarified, or we could use some sort of ideas from other areas—for example, economics, or various areas in the social sciences—to analyze some of the things that we do. To just sort of, not necessarily in a definitive way, but just to be able to look at them better in some way. I mean, Susan, you mentioned that before: about using different methodologies, and certain ones being able to help. You'd mentioned literary criticism being a model that was useful in adapting in some sort of way to a visual area. But that seemed like a concrete thing you could actually do.

Fraser: Part of the motive for me for organizing this [Working Group] is my feeling that, while there has been some use by artists within the artistic community of academic discourses, there has not been an exchange. Because there's a hierarchy between theoretical and practical knowledge, I don't think there can be a real exchange until that's addressed. My interest here was to create a forum for this sort of practical knowledge. And then the second question in response to what you [Vera] said, it's a question about use, and then use for what. And what are the conditions of use and what…I mean, that could bring us back to the question of service, to another meaning of service.

Clegg: Part of the hopes that we have in coming here, and that we spoke about in our initial round of remarks, was a sudden interest in seeing if there could be some discourse developing here that would amount to a feeling of community. To find ourselves being able to speak about our practices in a mode that is a bit different. I discussed this also during the previous break among a few people, and I think there was sort of a consensus that we felt it was really something different with this occasion, because we are really familiar with different modes of addressing each other in public. Of course it connects to why it was useful that this was a working group—we felt that there was a certain possibility to listen to each other, to not have the impulses that one often finds in discussions of these kinds, of exploring the differences, and being abrasive with each other, of distinguishing one's own practice. So, I just want to say that I think that that's another thing that has come up. It gives us a possibility for something that could connect to the continuation of this work. It will be interesting to hear from you a bit more about how you [Andrea and Helmut] are thinking of precisely doing that. But what I think is useful is to see such a possibility. I think this for me has been an experience that's been very valuable. But I just want to ask, technically, how are you thinking…

Draxler: I think, if we would like to continue this [*Services* project], we should now be able to produce some reasons for that. I mean, this was kind of an outline. But we shouldn't go and say, "OK, let's do it again," because, you know, when it never happens, that's clear. But so there should be a kind of…

I think we brought some discussions up to a point that was very interesting, because we're going into these passionate political strategies and things like that. Like how to address institutions, which is very complicated, and how to work within institutions, and to work with artists, or with whomever. But to have this kind of interest in a certain way. I think we all live in this not so clearly defined situation. There are some other models which are very clear here—what we are doing more in the political sense—but I think that most of us are not living in this way; most of us live in very contradictory situations, and we try to have them become clear. And I think that's also a very important point. I mean, we didn't even get to a practical discussion, and that's of course very important, and I am sure there are reasons why we didn't get to it. But I think these practical discussions should happen, in a certain relation to these items of political

discussion about the meaning of what we are doing. Using the term "services" tried to combine exactly this. It would have been necessary to clarify this term in a more historical sense, to say, "What does it mean especially in relation to production in the classical sense?" And what, more or less, came out of the productivist ideal of artistic production? And how these things can be related to this term "services." Or, if you come to the conclusion that it's not possible to do it in this way, then we probably should forget this term: "It's not about the term 'services.' Yeah, it's not about that." It should only be helpful to make some points clear, because we have to try to make these points clear. Otherwise, I would say, it's absolutely useless to repeat [this *Services* Working Group].

Fraser: Which point's clear?

(Laughter)

Guttmann: No, but seriously: How did you think about continuing it? You had something in mind, right?

Fraser: Oh, I had a big plan! Yeah, I thought about continuing it, not necessarily with the same participants, with some different participants. The idea of continuing it arose from a discussion that I happened to have with a woman from Geneva at the same time that Helmut and I were formulating this proposal, and it seemed that it would be a very appropriate context—a context perhaps a little bit similar to this one, as far as I understand. So, I've described this project to her, and she expressed interest, and then other people expressed interest. So it was on the basis, really, of interest expressed before the fact that the idea of continuing it [the *Services* project] was put into place. Although, I also thought it wasn't just about those different institutions being interested in sponsoring something like this, but also the idea of having a publication. Of having something that could go on—a publication that could exist as a public forum for discussions which I don't think there's a forum for now. You know, with a lot of the things that we talked about—I don't think there's a forum for the things we're talking about. I still don't think there is. I mean, whether they're important things to talk about is another question.

Green: But that's what this is about partly.

Fraser: Yeah. So that's how the idea of continuing it emerged, and the idea of doing something, another project, with this material. I mean, the Art Workers' Coalition stuff, that's sort of a separate deal, because that stuff has disappeared and someone should publish it. So that's, I think, a separate thing. But to do a book documenting the different ways that artists—at least this is how I would describe it—have formalized the concrete relations around their work. Whether those relations are in an institution, or a market, or what have you. Because I think that that's such a central aspect of what artists have been doing for the last twenty-five years, and it's something that doesn't get written about. So that was my vision.

Bauer: Would you say the show should be travelling with the material?

Draxler: Yeah, sure.

Bauer: So the people who take it [who tour the *Services* exhibition to their various institutions], do they get a box with photocopies and with videotapes? Or do they get any instructions, what they should do with it or…?

Fraser: I mean, that's a question, because I don't want this to be, you know, *our* show. It's a resource.

Bauer: Yeah.

Fraser: So, I would document how it was presented. And if you wanted to put it up the same way, then put it up the same way. If you want to put up other stuff, put up other stuff. If you feel that this material, for example, is oriented too much toward a particular New York experience, then put some of this material up and add other stuff to it.

I mean, what I hope the entire installation would convey is the fact that it's something to be used. That's just as an important premise, in a certain way, as any other that this [Working Group] was about: trying to formulate an exhibition model defined in terms of use value, as opposed to the sort of "prestige value" for artists, for curators, or for institutions. And then used for whom? Well, used for a professional community, used for an academic community. Hopefully both, you know. But I think in order for it to be used, it has to be an open structure, because otherwise it's just being transferred, or appropriated, or misappropriated.

(Long silence)

Draxler: So we still should think about how to make a kind of public presentation tomorrow.

Blazwick: What about a person for translation? Or is that too…

Fraser: Translation?

Blazwick: Well, most of this material is in English. It should be made available in other languages.

Draxler: It should.

Fraser: If you have a grant. Yeah.

Draxler: I mean, the University of Lüneburg did a lot of translation on different items [in the *Services* exhibition]. It's a very basic problem we are dealing with, with a lot of our work. But I think it's not so much what's on the wall. I mean, the problem is much more in situations like this, which are also for participants, etc., which are things from the beginning totally excluding [non-English speakers], in this kind of structure. But I also think that it's absolutely necessary to keep on going. We can't say, like we have in Vienna, after different kinds of events, which were very clearly importing American art into a certain structure, where the students came up and said, "Oh, no, we want ourselves." But it's also very typical that this kind of outside pressure on the different kinds of possibilities which are given. And so, this [need to have things translated] proceeds from inside only as a kind of total competition for these few places which constitute an institutional situation. And the reaction is, of course, totally wrong in a certain way. But it's very typical that it happens. We had that already when Ute held her symposium two years ago. That was the first I remember. From the beginning of the outline, it was very clear that this symposium is going to happen in English. So there were different kinds of attempts to change this and to try to work with different models. But all the different translations I've ever heard are just horrible.

Cahan: I think that the issue of translation is…What it says for me is the value of a lot of this material. My personal desire is to see it made more accessible to people. I hope that you continue to work on this project. And, actually, I think that a book that included the historical material as well as other research that might be generated from the students in this program, or individuals in other places that may have particular kinds of expertise, would be just an extraordinary thing. I would very much like to see the [*Services*] project take on some more fully articulated form that could then be shared with a wider audience of people.

Fraser: I actually, though, would like to return to the question of the continuation of the Working Group, because in a certain way, material can be collected. It's a separate thing, I think. We could all collect material and send it to a central place. But I mean, I think that your question—

Cahan: It's not just how much material. The framing of the issue is: What does the material lead to?

Fraser: No, right—I'm not trying to diminish that. I just wanted to return actually to this other point, because it is an issue of what…If you could all talk about…If this were to happen again, how would it happen, or what would your interest in it be?

Draxler: Yeah, I mean, I think that's the question. We should have probably used a blackboard, in the corporate style, to write down those items.

Fraser: I think there is a blackboard somewhere stored back here, I can hold it up (mimes holding up a blackboard).

(Laughter)

Barry: One approach might be to listen to the tapes [the video recordings of the Working Group sessions] and not necessarily watch them. It occurs to me, like you [Andrea] and Michael were saying earlier, that the university could be a useful resource for analyzing this material and positing some conclusions: "OK, there's agreement here, there's disagreement here," "There are some underlying philosophical issues that might be brought to bear in this section," and so forth. All of us could do this as well. I would be curious to know what we said as I didn't take copious notes.

I think through some form of analysis, something further, could be developed using this material. I don't think it can happen today.

Green: I think it's been really useful, to get back to the term of "use." In terms of what I was interested in.

Fraser: That's not the question I want to be asking. The question I want to be asking is: "Would you do it again? And if so how would you—"

Green: That's why I want to express why I would do it. I mean, what the reasons would be, what prompted the original thing. And then since we've met, and how I see it now. I think it's connected to why I would do it again—like the use value of it for particular ways of being able to think about things. I think it's important, though, the experiences of the participants—their particular experiences—because I think that they're not…

I was speaking with Christian about this earlier: there's not really a lot of people who seem to be formulating these ideas. I mean, as you [Andrea] were saying, there doesn't seem to be a forum for them. And there might be different points at which people might touch on these things, but not in a kind of in-depth way, or a way that's rigorous. And I think that, in this context, it's possible to do something more rigorous than has been done before—which I think is a real vacuum at the moment, in terms of what's around. I mean, I certainly feel it. And that's partly what prompted me to try to direct my grant money towards doing the symposium for the Drawing Center [*Negotiations in the Contact Zone*, which would take place in 1994]. This has been useful for me to be able to think about how that can go along, and to also hear what other people here have had to say which intersects with some of the ideas that I, in some kind of isolation, have been formulating and have been putting out. And seeing what the reactions were, and then reassessing from the reactions, and going back and forth.

I think that, in this situation—in working with a university—it's possible to actually amass this information in a way that's different than, for example, the way that some of the Dia [Art Foundation] symposiums took place [in New York], which I found really stimulating during the time in the mid to late '80's, when I was going to those. And which prompted me to ask other questions for the current situation. So I don't know what the form would be for it to continue. But I do really feel that there is a necessity, in a way, for a continuation.

Guttmann: I think that one of the successes of this forum is the fact that it really takes a few spheres and intersects them. And, finally, we are sitting in a university, not in a museum. I think that's really interesting. I think that some of the logistical problems—let's face it—some of the logistical problems come from the fact that there are not that many people who have enough investment in the idea of shifting things around the institution. So the few who do that end up having problems. I think that it's really important to remember that. You know, the commonplace is always much easier. And I think that when you shift things around, all sorts of problems are created.

So, I think that this has been a pretty interesting and good experience, even if some problems are created, because, to me, the problems seem like the inevitable consequence of working in nontraditional ways. I think that that aspect of it—that's something that I would like to see continue, rather than doing things like that, you know, in a very well-defined art context. Because I think that's pretty important. And what you [Andrea] were saying about doing the kind of shows that have more use value than—I don't remember the quote…

Fraser: Than prestige value.

Guttmann: Right, more use value than prestige value. I think that [this Working Group] is really predicated on something like that, because some of the ability to look at issues and to try to explore them is predicated precisely on the possibility of looking at them not from prestige value—which again, necessitates some institutional shift. That, I think, is something that should be continued, including the problems that arise, and there's really no way to avoid them, because that's really the nature of the beast.

Fraser: So, what you're saying [Martin] sounds a bit consistent with what you said earlier, Iwona? That it's about looking at other kinds of contexts and possibilities, that you would want to open the discussion up more and not focus so much on institutions. But what kind of things were you thinking about actually when you said that?

Blazwick: Well, it's partly different. For example, I was thinking about the Havana Biennial in Cuba, and a couple of people involved in it. And thinking about some very interesting methodologies that they developed. But also looking at different… Because I'm at the moment thinking very much about publishing and distribution and computer programs. It's just something which I've got very involved in, in the last six months of looking at those different forms. As well as the building, the institution as a form of communication, which isn't necessarily a museum or a *Kunstraum*.

Fraser: So you would say the function would be to try to develop those kinds of—

Blazwick: Also, presumably, over time people are in different working situations, gleaning something from this—which I certainly am—and trying to feed it back into what we're doing. And just the opportunity to report back from that process. I think it would be really valuable to see what's happening in a year's time or something. Has anything changed? What kind of things have developed out of it?

Bischoff: I would suggest if we, or someone, is doing such meetings again, I think it is good if there is practical experience there. I think this time, there were a lot of examples, and they are very important. So that you don't have to discuss structures alone, but you have examples. If the people who are invited are engaged in these examples of projects, perhaps they could be even a little bit more concrete. So that there are one, two, or three projects which are done, and they are the stimulating points for where the discussion starts. I think this would be good. That's my opinion.

Wilson: Maybe the next Working Group has to look at the tape [video documentation of this Working Group] and respond to that. I don't know who you could get to come to do that.

(Laughter)

Fraser: We could fast-forward the tape.

(Laughter)

Fraser: I was informed that we would have to be at the restaurant by 9:15 pm in order to eat, and it's presently 8:56 pm. So I'd say that gives us about four minutes to wrap up. Do we need them? The question about the presentation tomorrow: I guess we'll go ahead and we'll meet with the students from the seminar again tomorrow at 1:00 pm. And then also I hope that any of you who plan to be here at 5:00 pm will participate in some sort of presentation. I have no idea what kind of presentation it should be, but hopefully we can also talk about that tomorrow at 1:00 pm.

Draxler: I mean, hopefully there will be an idea.

Fraser: Yeah, there'll definitely be an idea.

Green: Question—what time is this space open tomorrow?

Von Bismarck: This space?

Green: Yeah.

Von Bismarck: When you want it to.

Green: OK.

Fraser: The slide projectors and the videos have to be set up and I know, Christian, you need a piece of wall.

Draxler: Yeah, yeah, we've arranged that already.

Fraser: OK, good.

Draxler: I mean, what I think could be an item of consideration for a repetition of events like this is... What was beginning a little bit with some artists who were involved in thinking about the same situation— unionization, or creating this. A decision for this event was that it could be done with only artists discussing this specific subject and then going public with combined forces. What we decided in the end was to have this situation also with curators and critics, or people whose working definition is not so clear, and to bring them together. And I think that is important. I mean, just to think about that overnight and to address that tomorrow a little bit, if it makes sense. And in front of a background of this history (pointing to the pinboard of historical documents on display as part of the *Services* exhibition), if it is reasonable to keep up the discussion on this level. Or if it wouldn't be much better if artists and curators or whatever would go back into their corners. I also feel a little bit that, with my own interests, I couldn't really articulate them. Maybe others feel the same way, and this could just be because of this structure. So this [Working Group] was so much about the kinds of relationships but maybe not really about interests in a certain way.

OK, let's go to dinner, huh?

Fraser: We can also continue talking at dinner. We don't have to eat dinner in silence!

(Laughter)

Plates 1–13
Documentation of the *Services* Working Group at the Kunstraum of the University of Lüneburg, 1994.

All photos by Michael Koch. Courtesy of the Kunstraum of the Leuphana University of Lüneburg.

Participants
(listed left to right)

Plate 1
Andrea Fraser

Plate 2
Working Group

Plate 3
Christian Philipp Müller
Iwona Blazwick

Plate 4
Fred Wilson

Plate 5
Working Group

Plate 6
Martin Guttmann
Judith Barry
Renée Green

Plate 7
Ulf Wuggenig
Ute Meta Bauer

Plate 8–9
Working Group

Plate 10
Jochen Becker
Michael Clegg

Plate 11
Beatrice von Bismarck

Plate 12
Working Group

Plate 13
Helmut Draxler

KÜNSTLER-
VERKAUFS- UND
RECHTS-
ABTRETUNGS-
V...
THE ARTIST'S
RESERVED
...HTS
...SFER
...SALE
...MENT
ART POLITICS

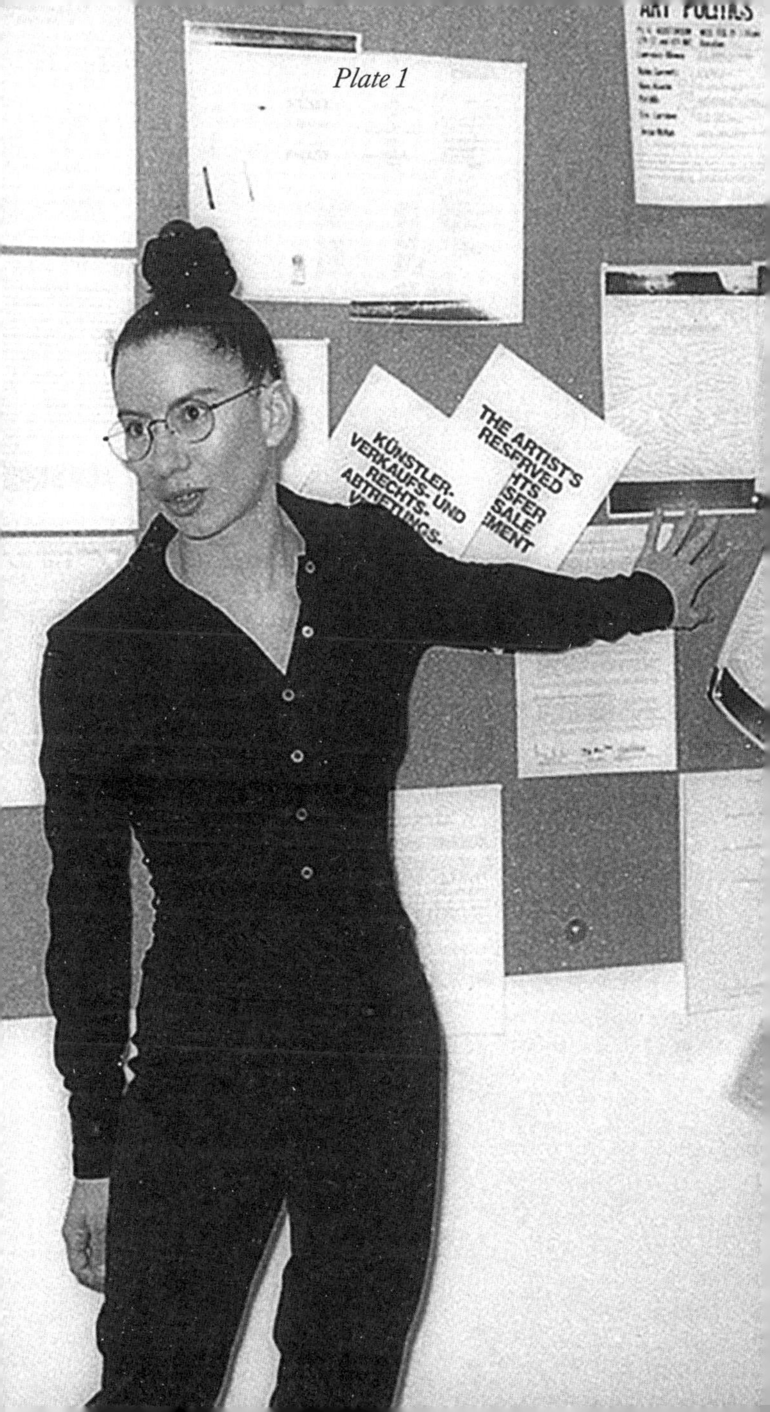

Plate 1

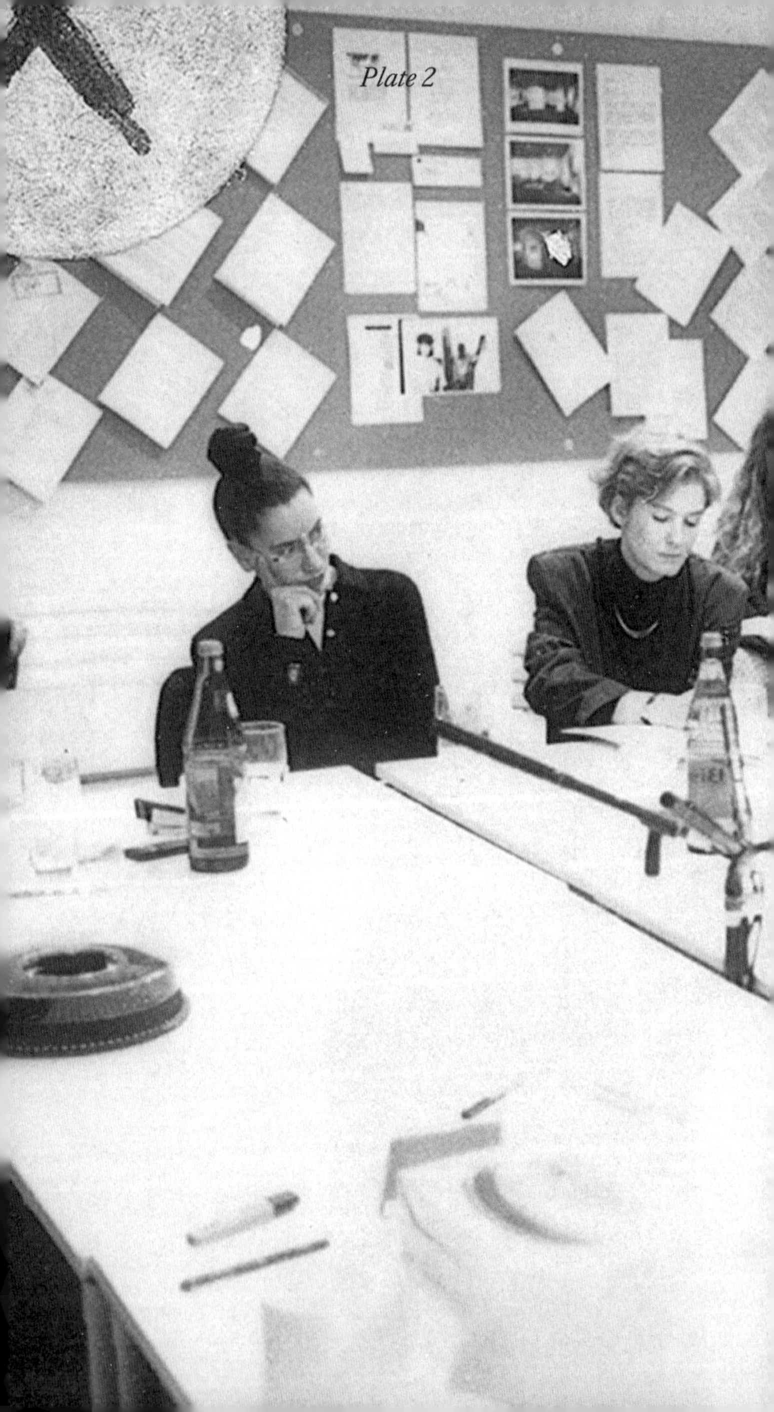
Plate 2

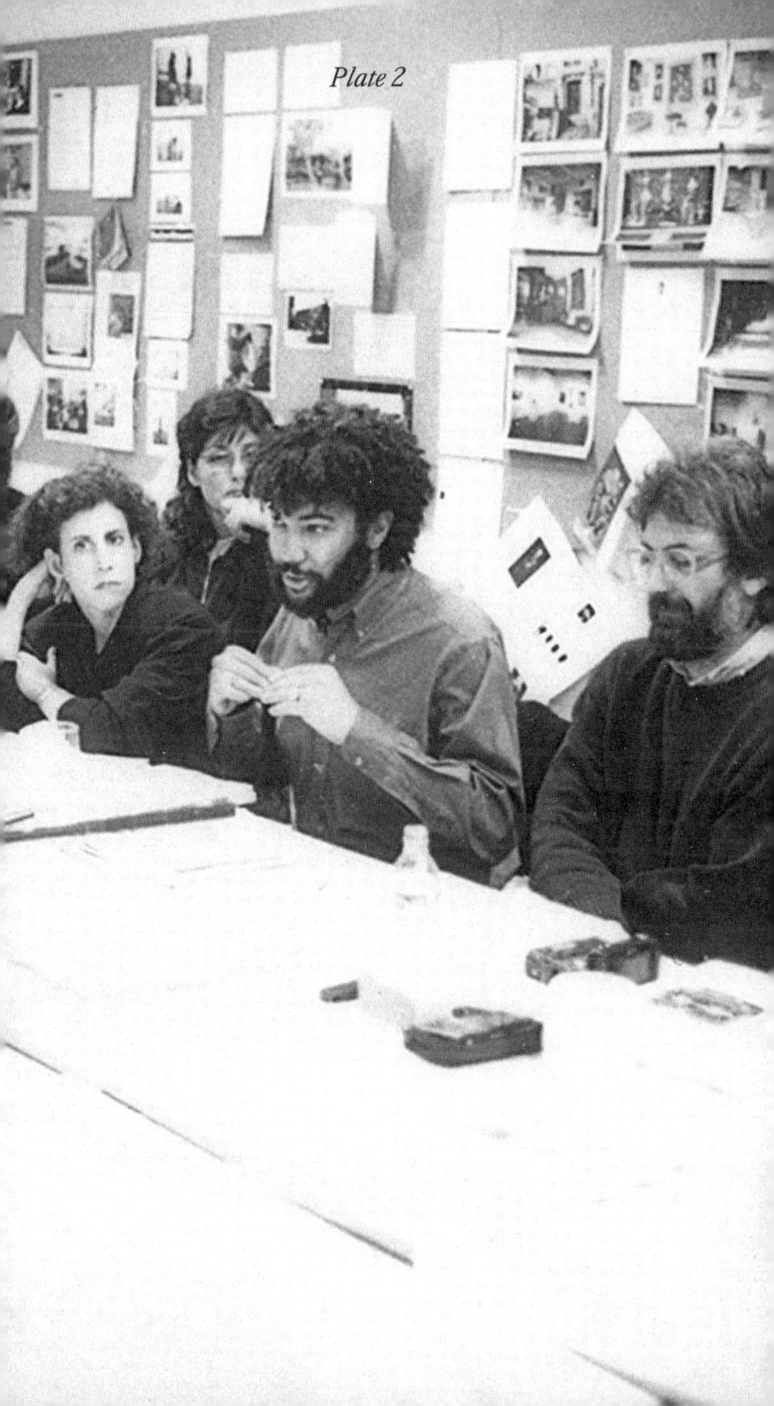

Plate 2

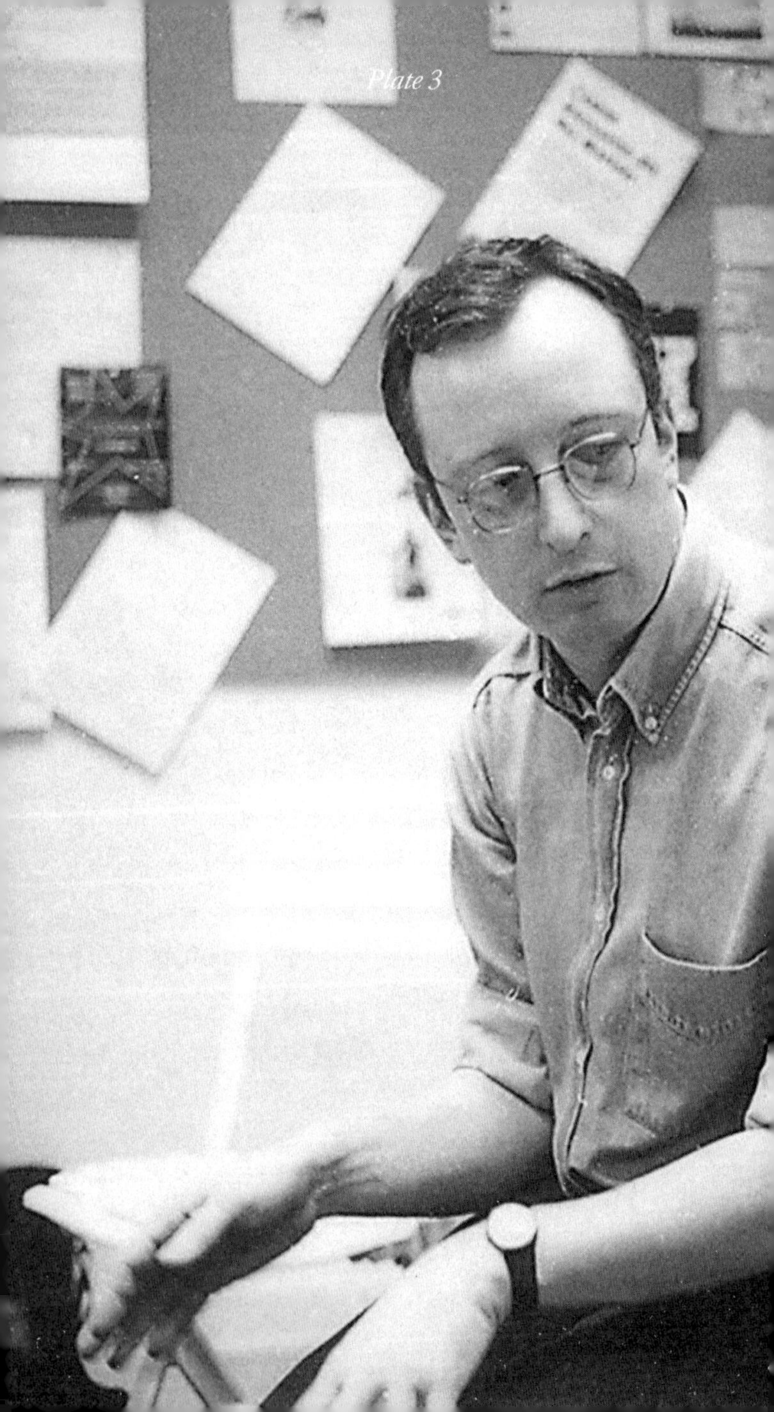
Plate 3

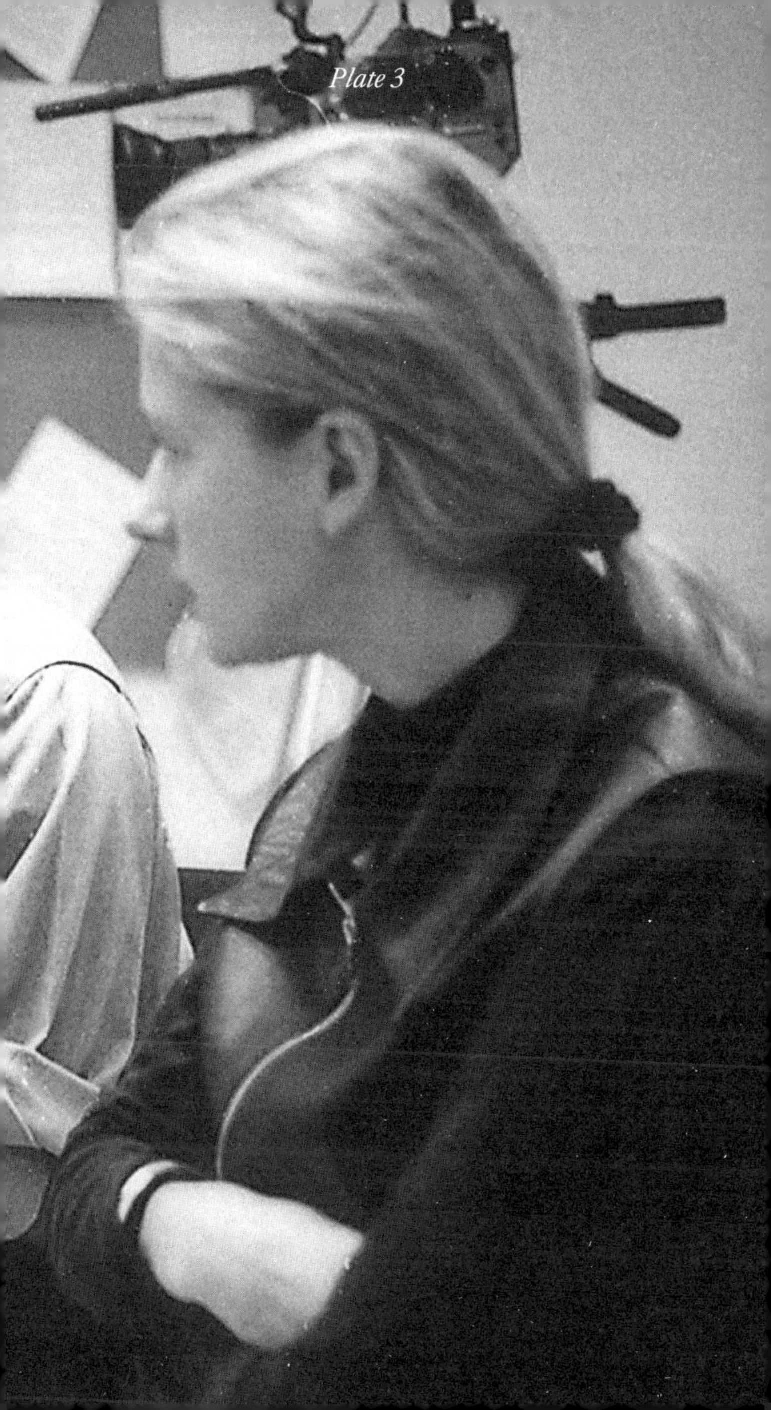

Plate 3

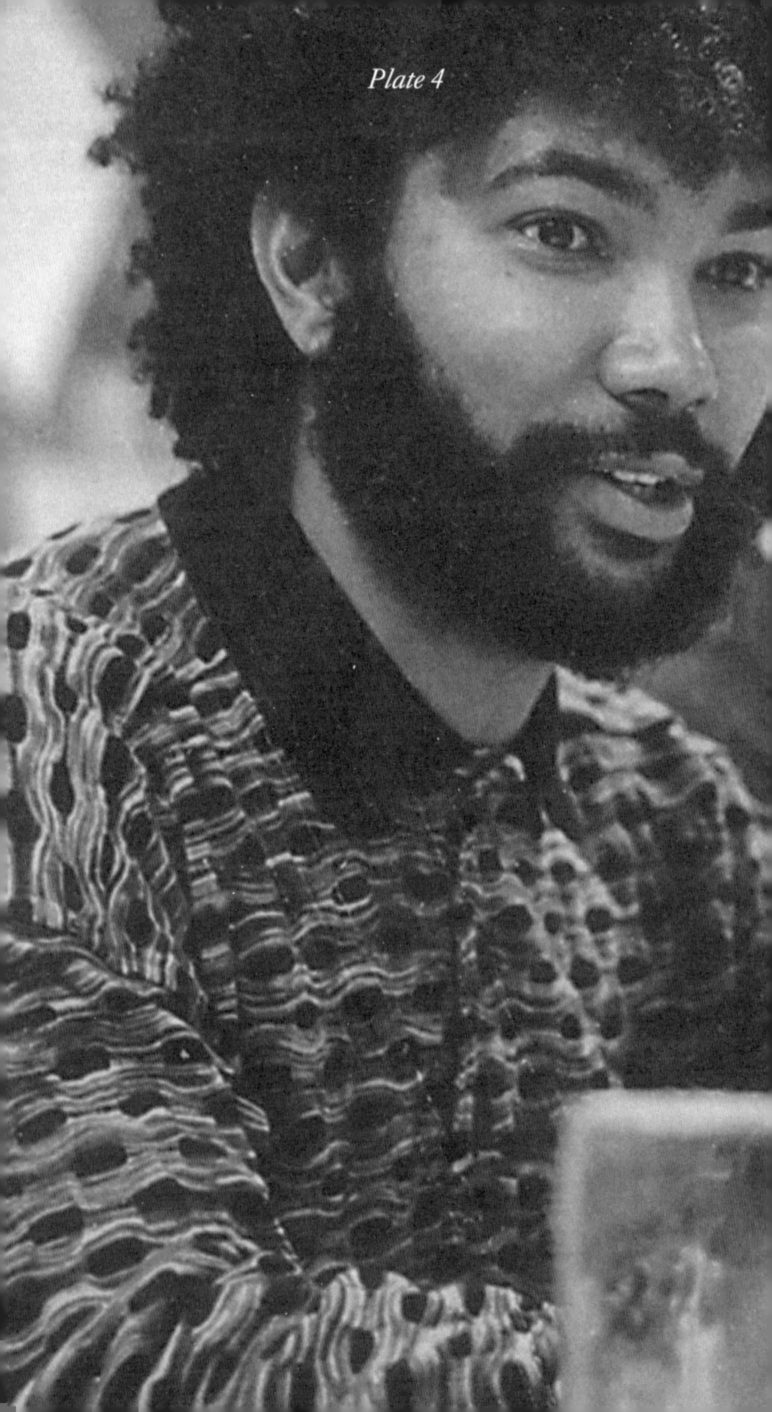

Plate 4

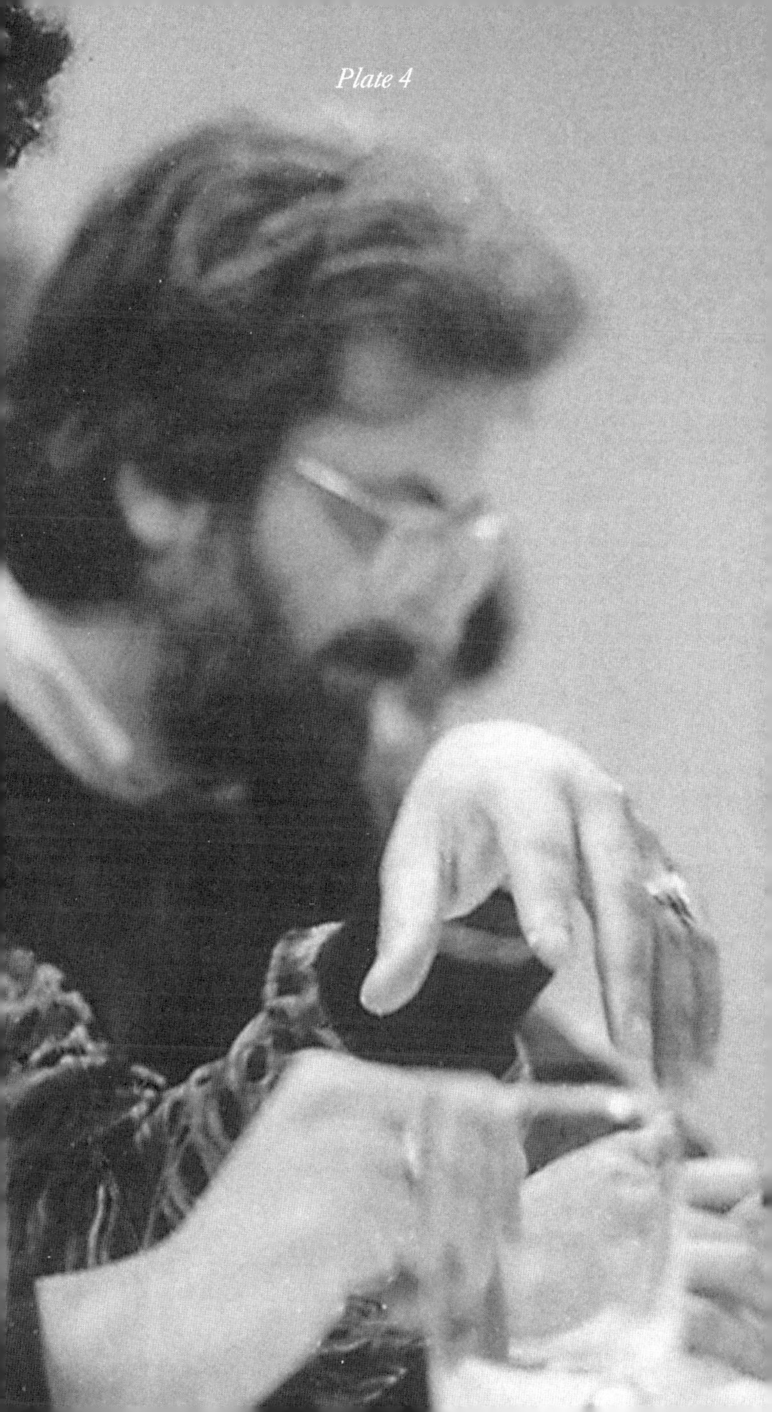

Plate 4

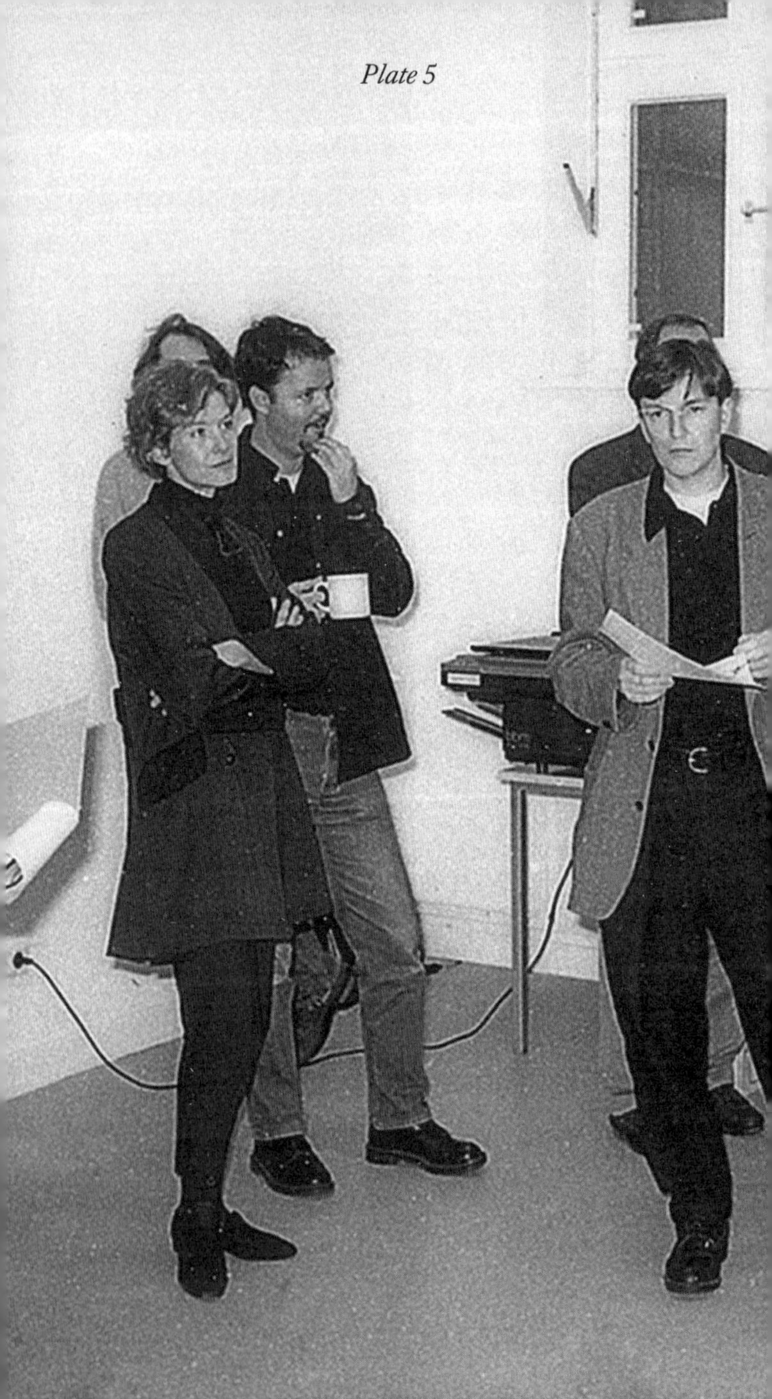

Plate 5

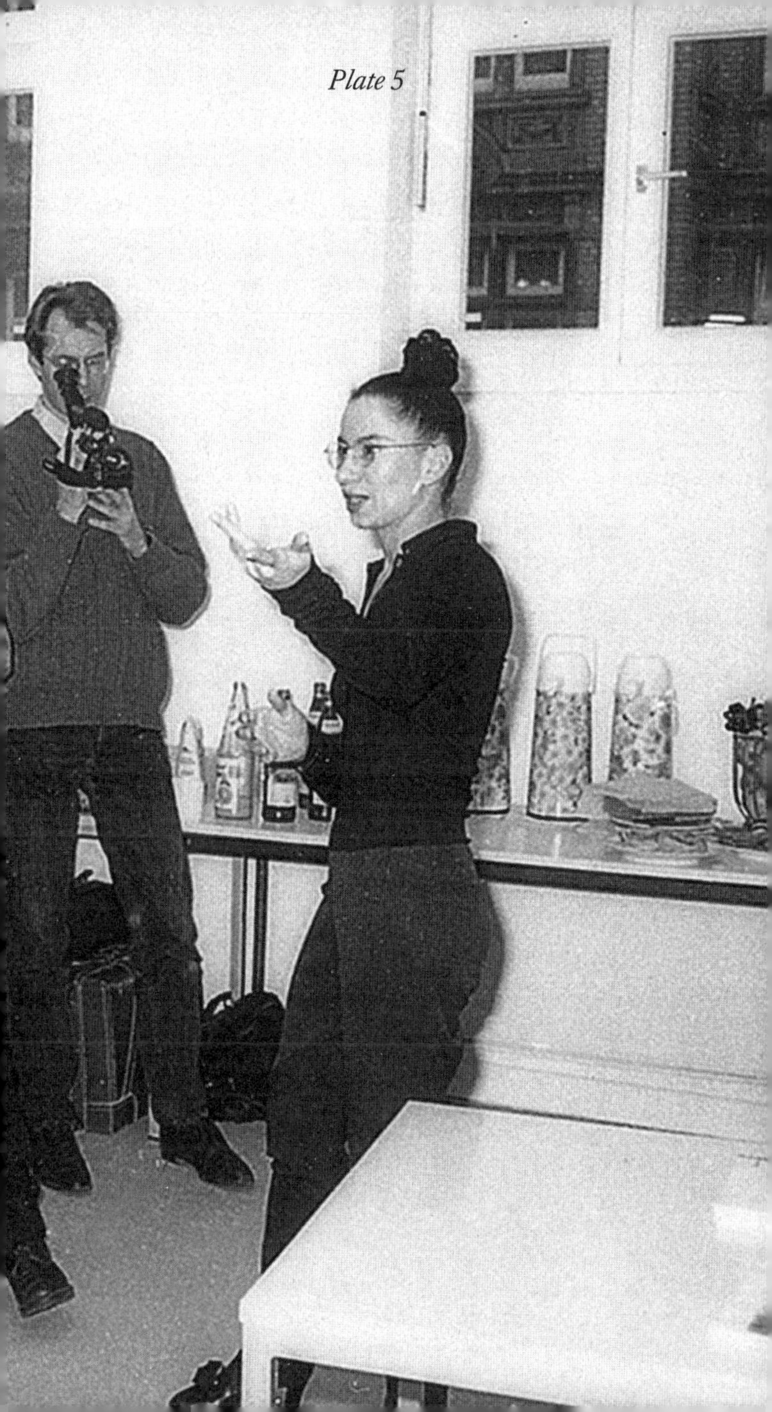

Plate 5

Plate 6

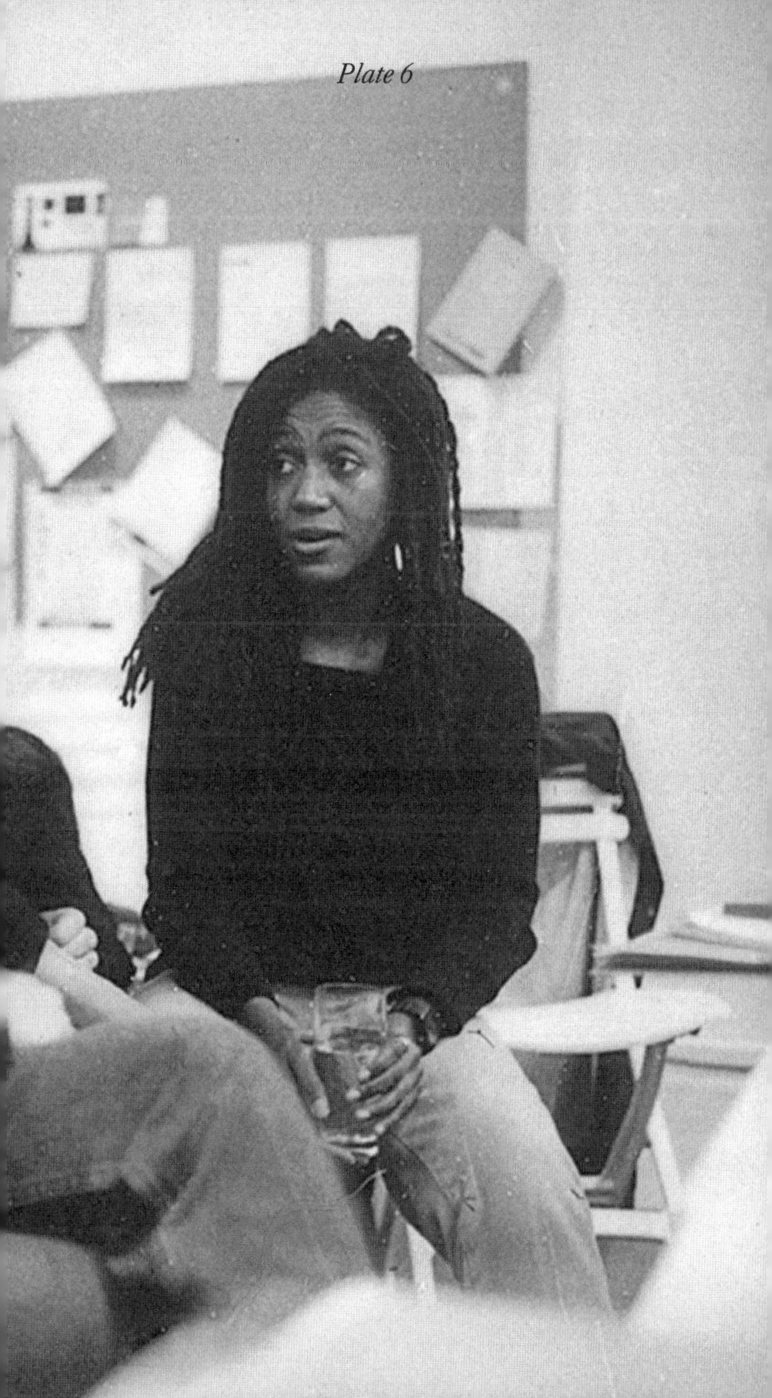

Plate 6

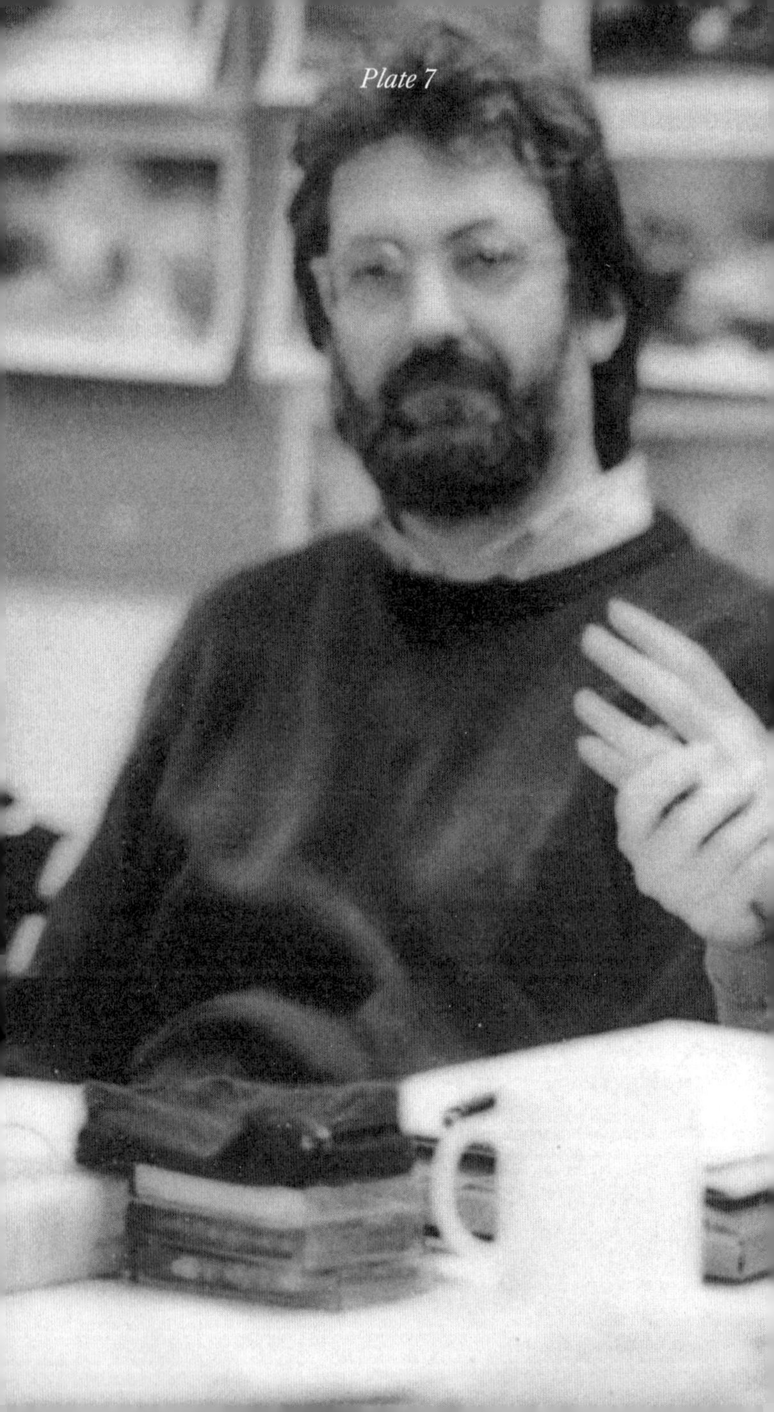

Plate 7

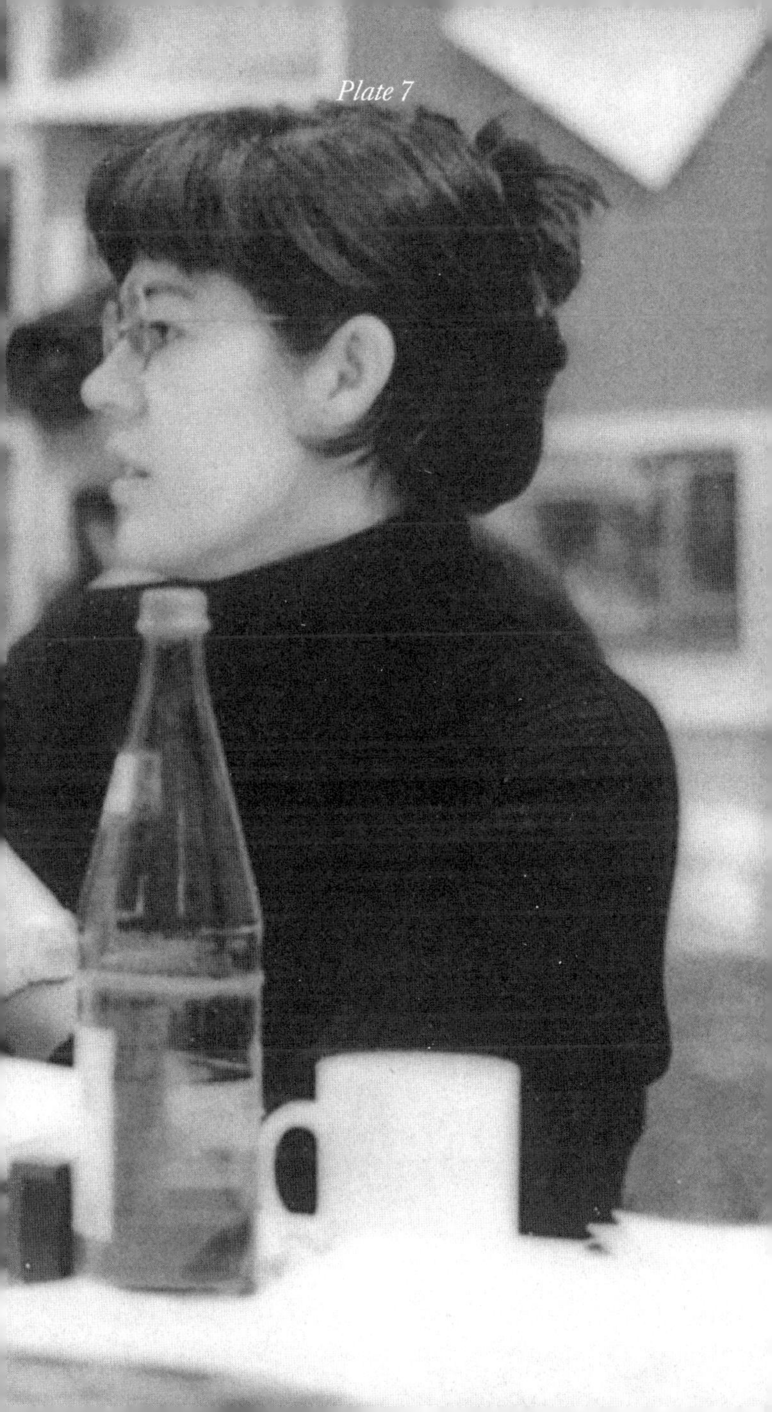

Plate 7

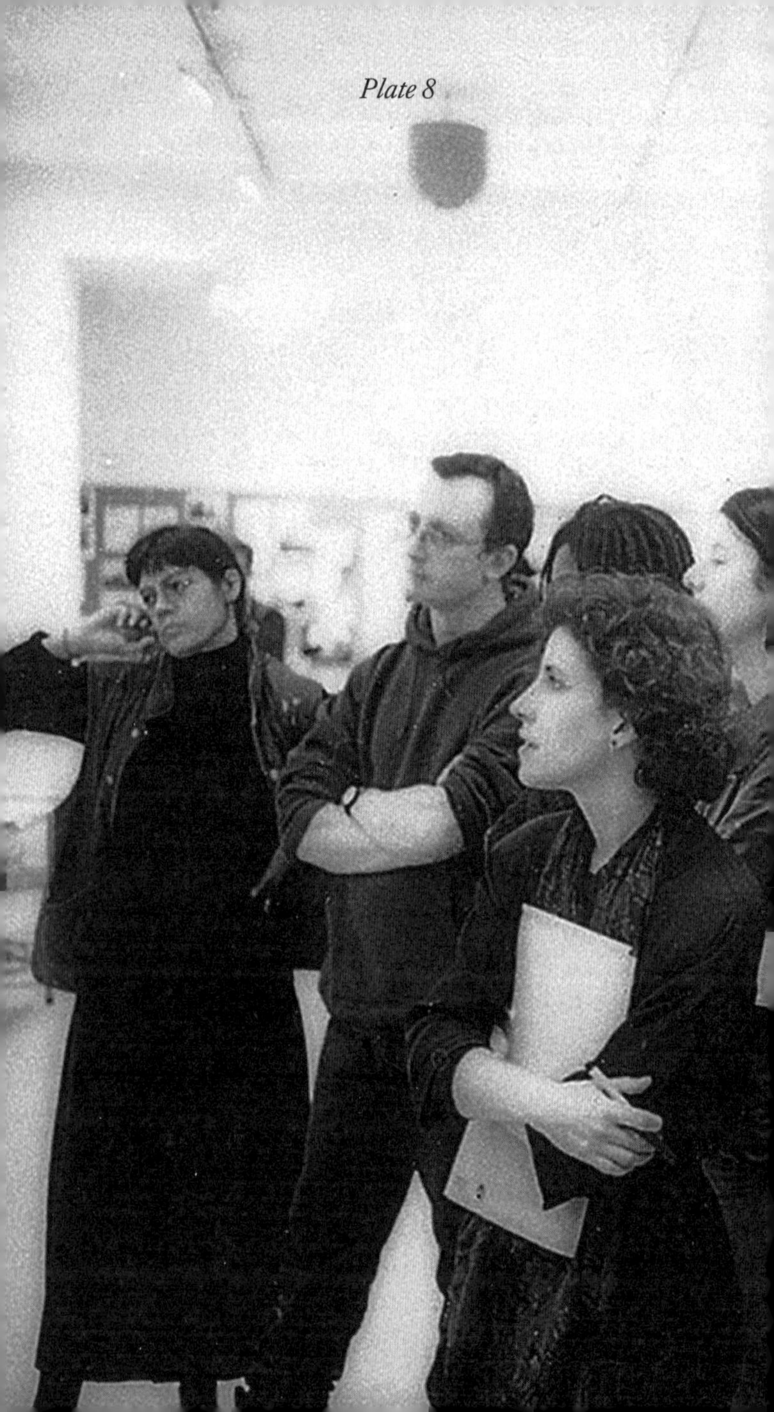

Plate 8

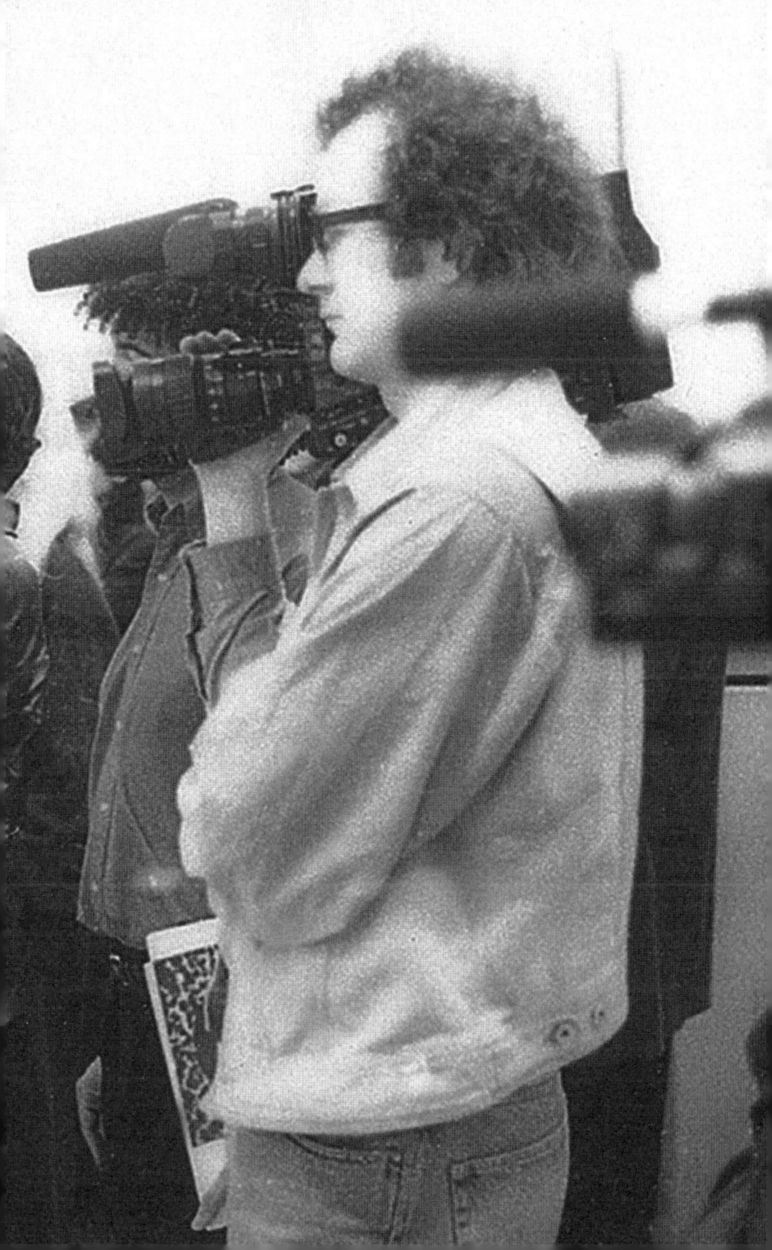

Plate 8

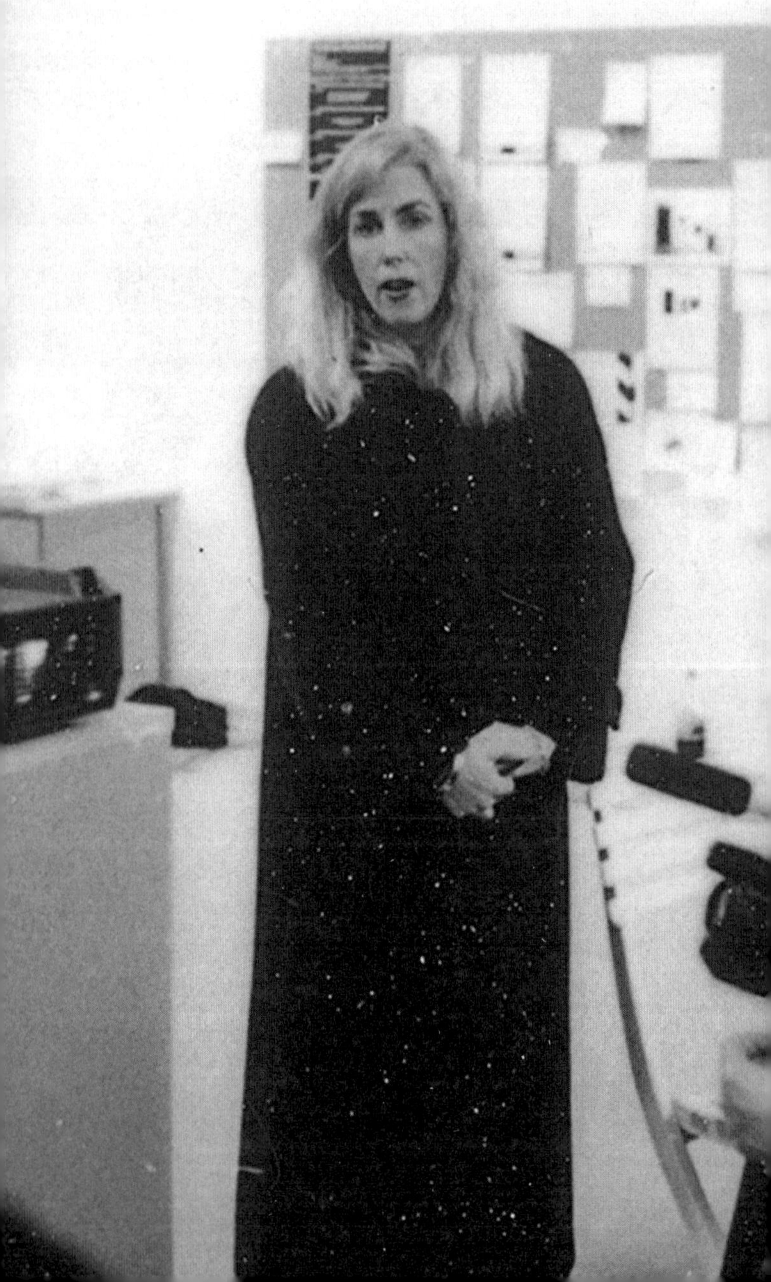

Plate 9

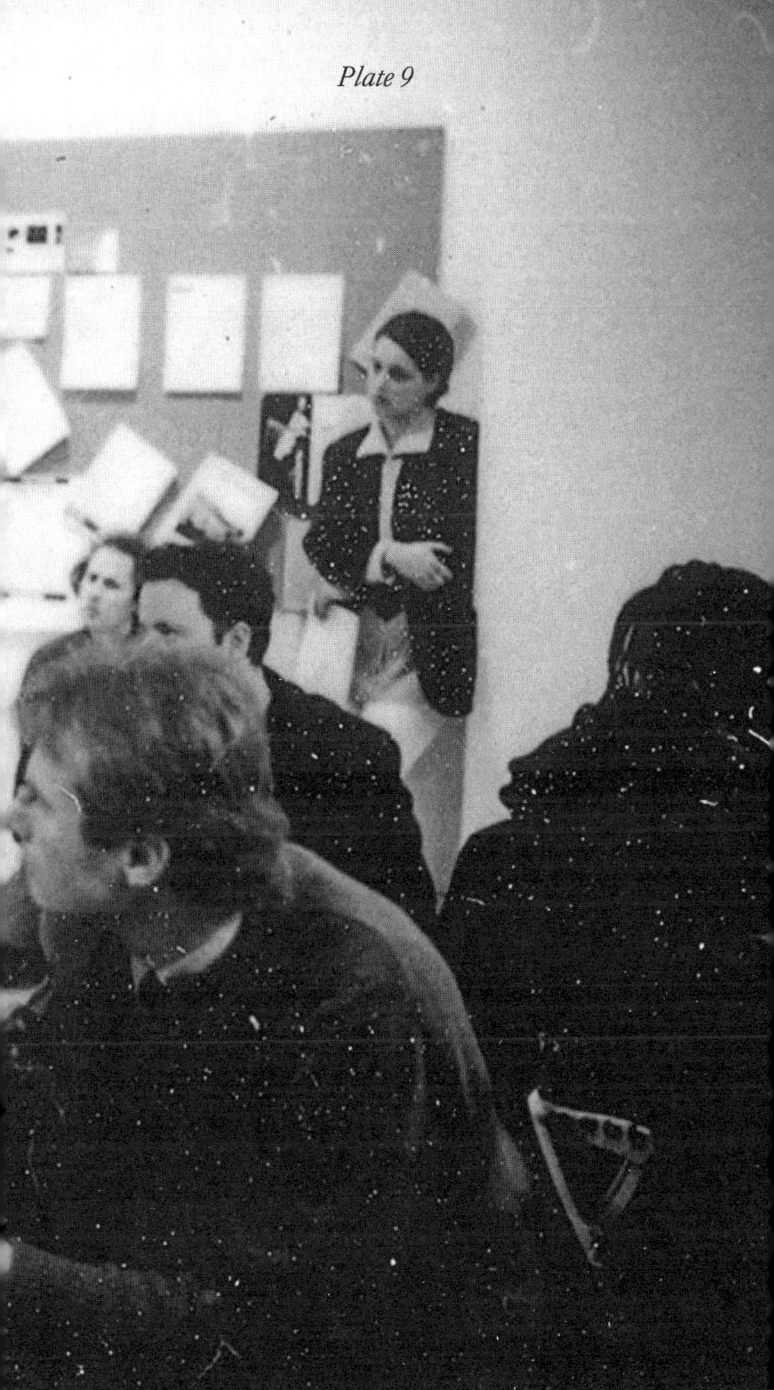

Plate 9

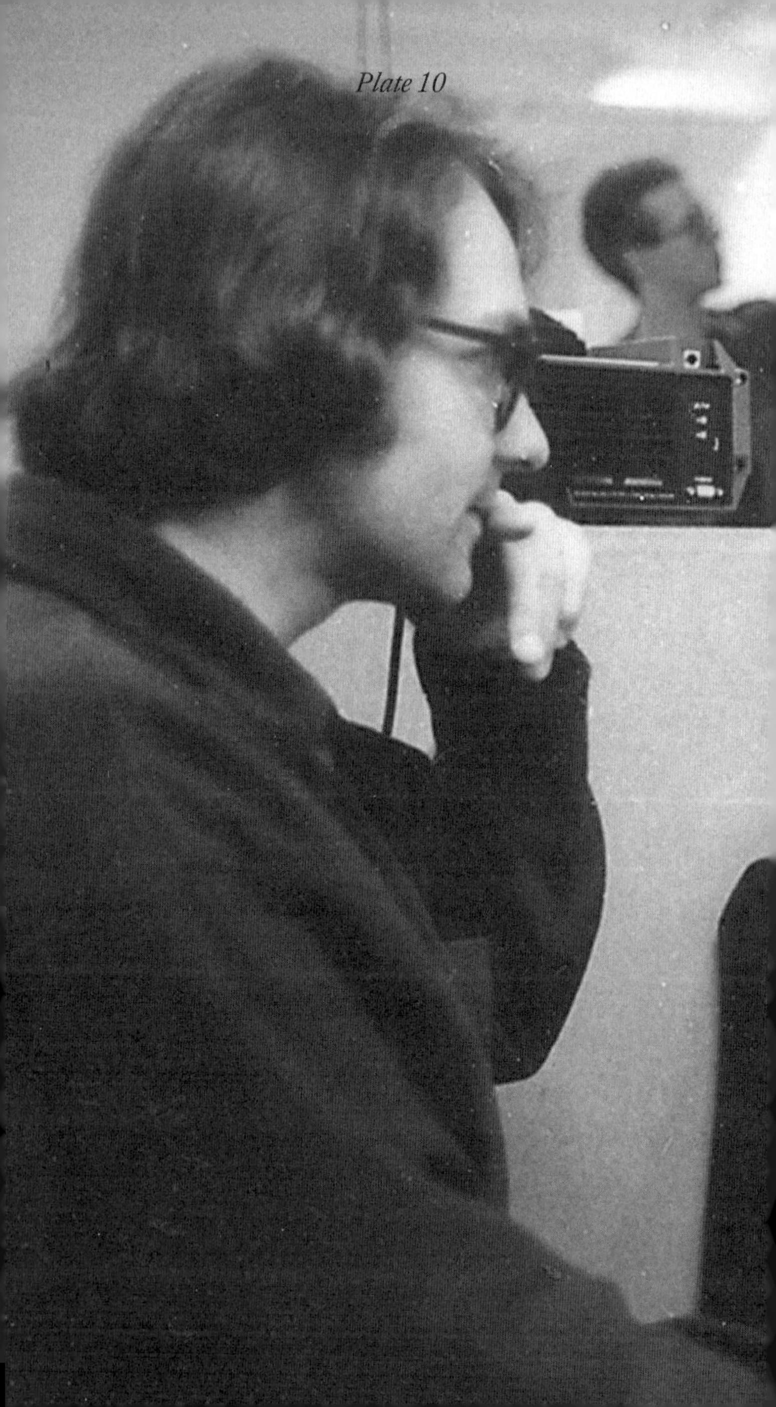

Plate 10

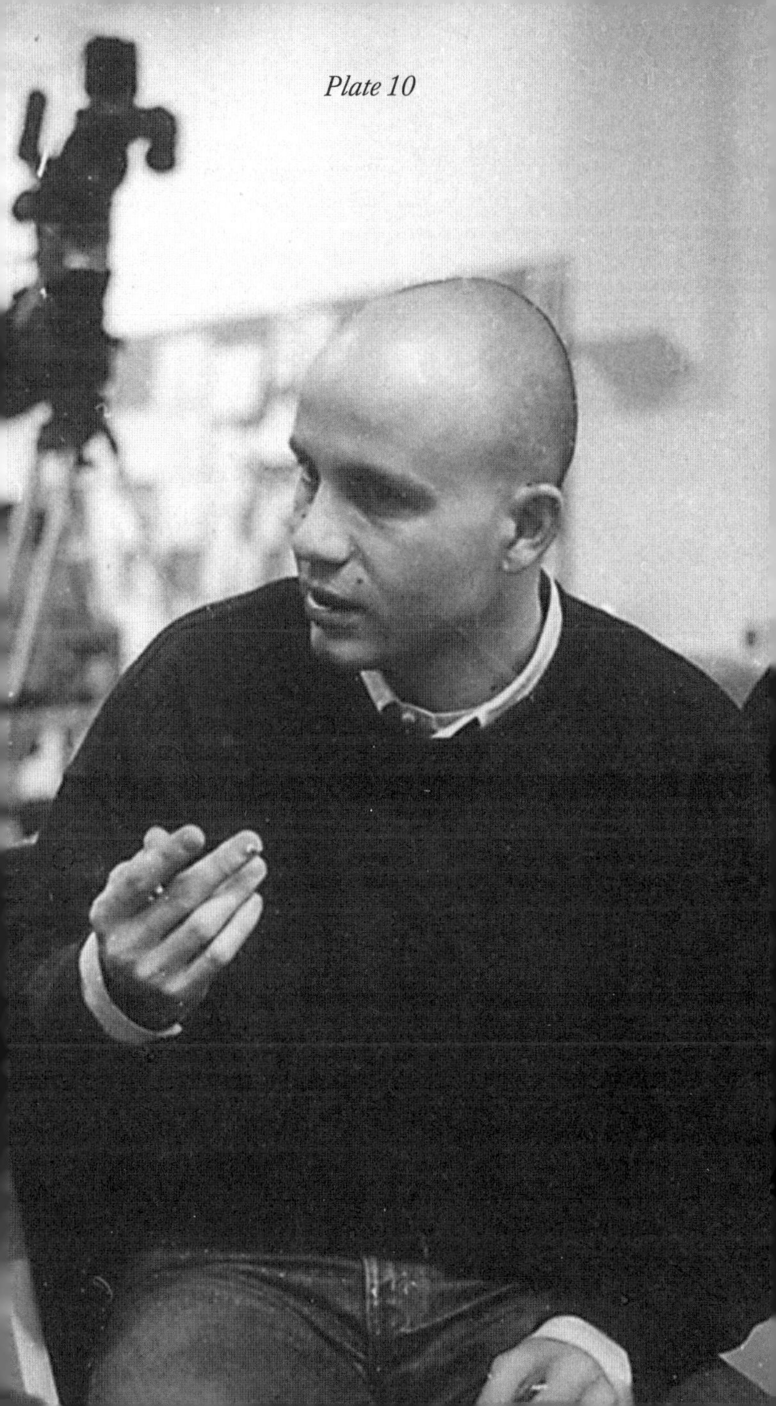

Plate 10

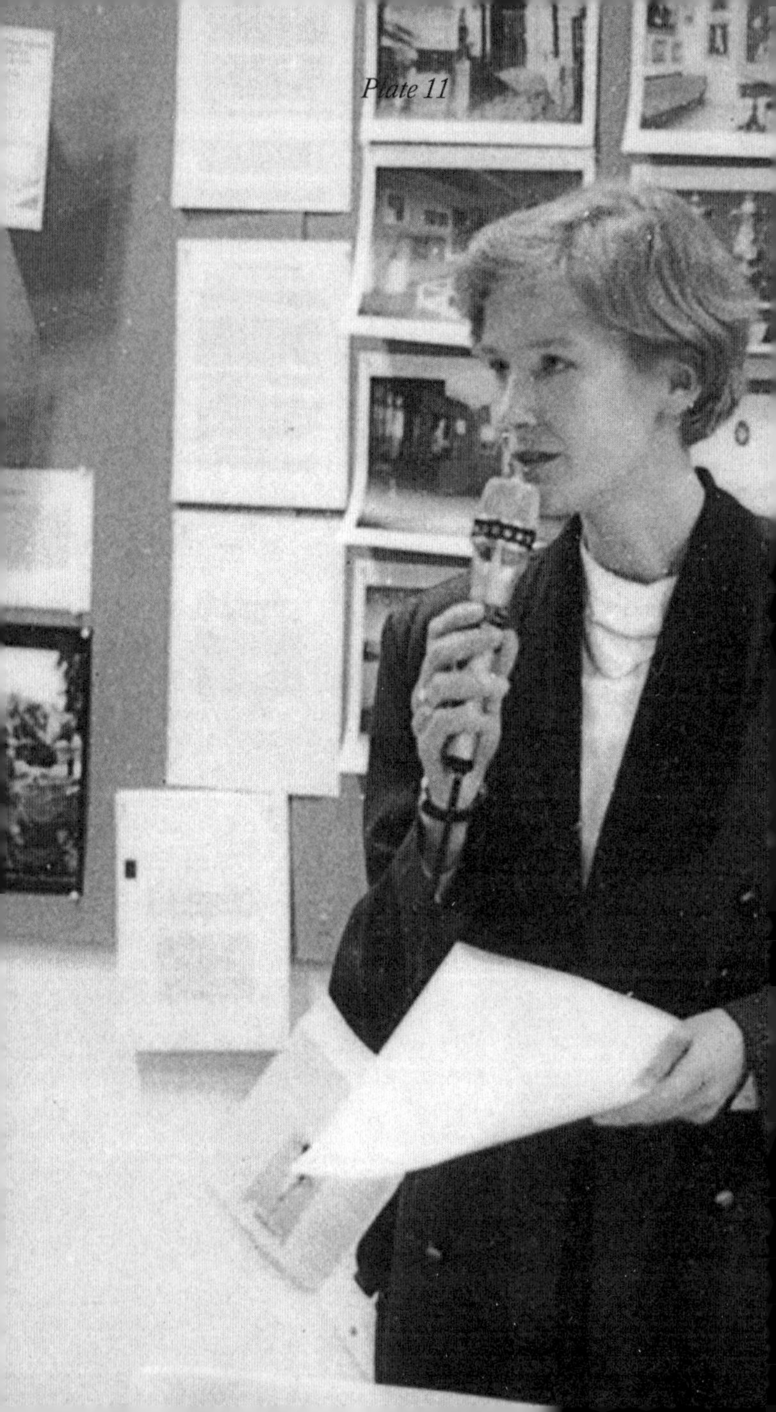

Plate 11

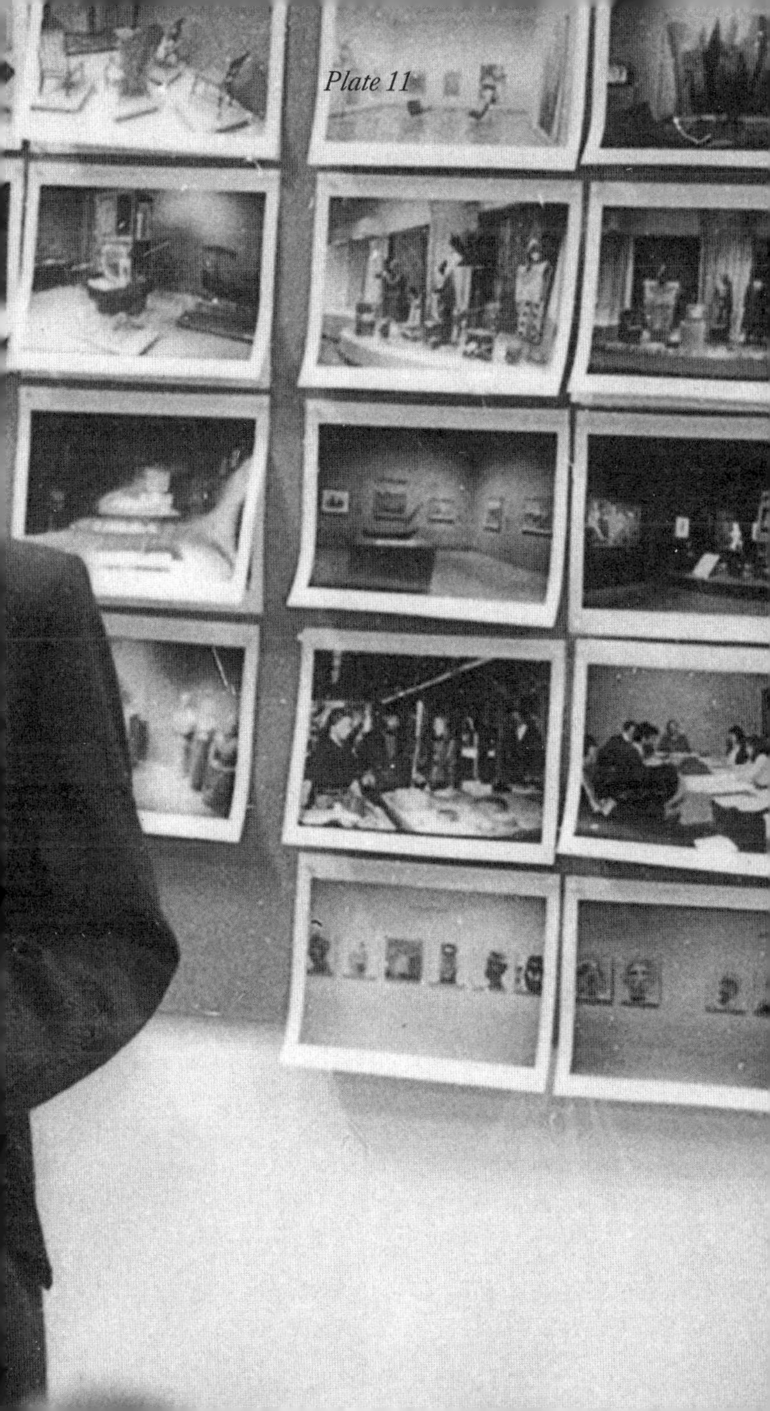
Plate 11

Plate 12

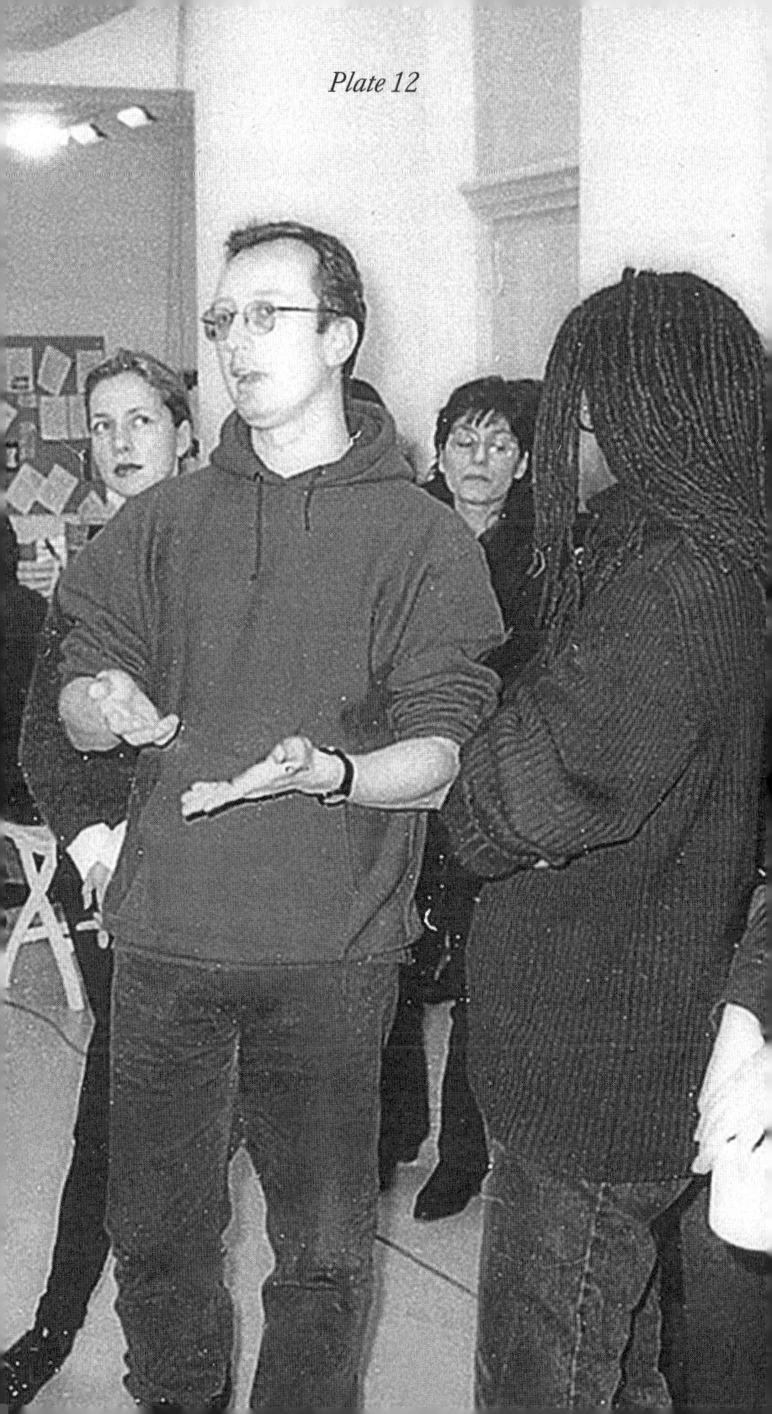

Plate 12

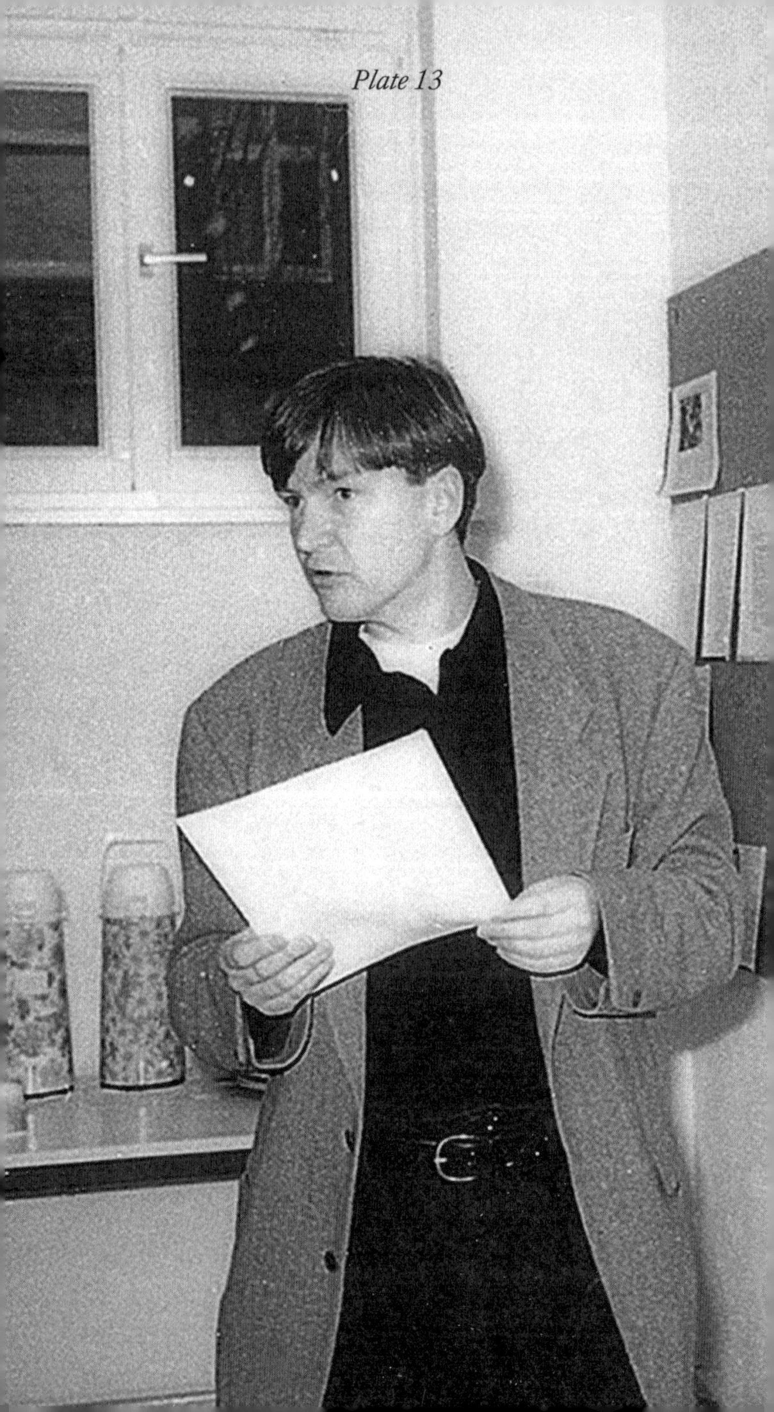

Plate 13

Arbeitsgruppe
Sitzung Eins

Einführung
Samstag, 22. Januar 1994

Vorträge:
Helmut Draxler
Andrea Fraser

*Die Organisator*innen erläutern das
Vorhaben der Veranstaltung und
präsentieren das Material, das für
die Ausstellung gesammelt wurde.*

Andrea Fraser: Helmut Draxler
und ich möchten euch also alle im
Kunstraum der Universität Lüneburg
willkommen heißen. Und ich glaube,
dass die meisten von euch sich
wahrscheinlich mittlerweile kennen-
gelernt haben. Trotzdem werden
wir in ein paar Minuten eine Vorstellungsrunde machen. Wir haben
diese Ausstellung als Eröffnungs-
ausstellung des Raums auf Einladung von Beatrice von Bismarck,
Ulf Wuggenig und Diethelm Stoller
– der nicht hier ist, er holt gerade
einen anderen Teilnehmer ab – und
den Fakultätsmitgliedern der Universität Lüneburg vorbereitet. Und
wir möchten diese Personen dazu
einladen, ein paar Worte zu ihrem
Konzept für den Raum zu sagen.

Beatrice Von Bismarck: Du möchtest
das vor der Vorstellungsrunde tun?

Fraser: Ja.

Von Bismarck: Ja, vielleicht ganz
kurz. Der Kunstraum ist ein Projekt,
das tatsächlich mit der Ausstellung
Services ins Leben gerufen wurde.
Es ist etwas, das wir schon seit
letztem Jahr planen, und diejenigen,
die noch nicht von der Universität Lüneburg gehört haben, es ist

eine Universität, die versucht, ein
interdisziplinäres Lehrprogramm
mit einem starken Bezug zur Praxis
zu gestalten. Im Grunde bedeutet
das also, dass sie sich außerhalb
des traditionellen akademischen
Lehrsystems positioniert und somit
die Chance bietet, den praktischen
Bereich viel stärker in die Lehre
zu integrieren und umgekehrt. Die
Idee eines Kunstraums war also
nicht, einen weiteren Ausstellungsraum irgendwo in der Provinz zu
eröffnen, sondern so etwas wie ein
Forum zum Austausch zwischen den
Wissenschaften und den Künsten zu
schaffen. Und dieses Forum – und
Services könnte im Grunde genommen kein besseres Auftaktprojekt
sein – dieses Forum sollte durch
Aktivitäten erzeugt werden, die nicht
nur zeitgenössische Kunstausstel-
lungen umfassen, sondern auch ein
dazugehöriges Begleitprogramm
mit Vorträgen, Studiobesuchen,
Workshops, Podiumsdiskussionen.
Also einer Reihe von Aktivitäten
in diesem Bereich, auf die auch
ein Forschungsprogramm folgen
würde, und eine Publikationsreihe,
die mit dem Wesen des Kunstraums
in Form und Inhalt einhergeht. Eine
Zusammenfassung über den Kunstraum müsstet ihr in eurem Handout
gefunden haben. Es ist eine Art
kurze Stellungnahme dazu. Und ich
glaube, dass wir zu einem späte-
ren Zeitpunkt nochmal auf seine
Struktur zurückkommen werden.
Vielleicht noch ein Wort dazu, was
die Idee betrifft, wie wir versuchen,
das Konzept in die Universität zu integrieren. Die Idee ist grundsätzlich,
dass man die Chance hat, den Raum
und sein Programm nicht nur für die
Lehre zu nutzen, die bei uns in die
Forschung eingebunden ist, sondern
das Konzept als kontinuierlich fort-
schreitenden Diskurs zwischen den

beiden Feldern Kunst und Wissenschaft zu verstehen. Die Studierenden haben also in diesem Fall eine vorbereitende und integrative Rolle in den Veranstaltungen, die der Kunstraum produziert. Und natürlich sollen die Projekte auch in die darauffolgende Forschung integriert werden, soweit dies möglich ist.

Fraser: Werden drei Studierende an dieser Sitzung teilnehmen? Wie ist das organisiert?

Von Bismarck: Ja, die Idee war, dass die Studierenden, die an dem Seminar zur Vorbereitung dieser Ausstellung teilnehmen, dass eine kleine Gruppe von ihnen an jedem Abschnitt teilnimmt. Das ist die bisherige Vereinbarung. Und es fängt mit der ersten Sitzung an, die nach dem Mittagessen beginnt.

Fraser: Ach so, ich dachte es gäbe –

Von Bismarck: – Nein, sie dachten sie sollten bei der Einführung nicht dabei sein.

Fraser: Also werden nach der Mittagspause drei Studierende von der Universität zu uns kommen.

Helmut Draxler: Ich meine, das klingt ein bisschen seltsam, aber wir hatten diese Woche eine ausgiebige Diskussion dazu, ich glaube die Entscheidung zwischen einer nicht öffentlichen und einer öffentlichen Veranstaltung zu treffen, war ein sehr wichtiger Punkt. Denn wir sind mehr oder weniger zwanzig, und so hätten wir dann sofort so eine Situation gehabt. Nichtsdestotrotz möchte ich den Studierenden schon mal im Voraus für ihre große Hilfe bei der Umsetzung dieses Projekts danken. Und natürlich werden wir so

gut wie möglich versuchen, während und auch nach dieser Veranstaltung eine didaktische Arbeitsbeziehung zu ihnen aufzubauen, das ist mehr oder weniger das Ziel. Und ich habe noch einen weiteren Punkt. Es gibt immer dieses Sprachproblem, das wir haben. Und es ist sehr geläufig, wisst ihr, dass alles auf Englisch ist. Aber es ist immer noch so, dass wir normalerweise alles lernen, was mit Sprache zu tun hat, wenn wir fünf Jahre alt sind. Und die meisten von euch wissen das. Aber trotzdem ist es an bestimmten Stellen noch ein Problem, und ich glaube, dieser Punkt ist vor allem Geschwindigkeit. Wir werden daher unser Bestes tun, falls es Probleme geben sollte, oder uns gegenseitig helfen, wenn es notwendig ist. Ich denke schon, dass das wichtig ist, da wir es gewohnt sind, diesen Punkt aufzugeben, mehr oder weniger in einer höchst ritualisierten Form – dieser Aspekt kommt in vielen Diskussionen in Deutschland vor. Ich weiß, dass es keinen wirklichen Ausweg aus dieser Situation gibt, aber ich weiß auch aus verschiedenen Erfahrungen, die wir in den letzten Jahren gemacht haben, dass es kein sehr, naja, es ist nicht gerade ein Vorteil für deutschsprachige Menschen hier. Okay.

Fraser: Also dieses Projekt, diese Ausstellung, diese Arbeitsgruppenausstellung *Services* entwickelte sich im Grunde aus zwei Seiten, glaube ich. Eine war das Konzept des Raumes und die Tatsache, dass es wirklich kaum Universitäten gibt, die Ausstellungsräume haben, im Gegensatz zu den Vereinigten Staaten und möglicherweise England. In Deutschland ist das wirklich nicht sehr üblich. Wir haben mit Ulf und Beatrice und Diethelm über das Konzept für diesen Raum gesprochen und wir waren der Meinung, dass es ein sehr wichtiger Beitrag für die deutsche Kunstszene sein würde, einen Kontext zu haben, in dem, anstatt ein allgemeines Publikum anzusprechen, Künstler*innen, Akademiker*innen und Wissenschaftler*innen eine Möglichkeit haben würden, sich über praktische Fragen auszutauschen, die für ihre Erfahrungen relevant sind. Die andere Sache, aus der dieses Projekt entstanden ist, waren Diskussionen zwischen einer Gruppe von projektbezogen arbeitenden Künstler*innen über die Notwendigkeit, gemeinsam Grundlagen für die Arbeit mit Institutionen zu erstellen. Das ist also ein vollkommen anderer Gesichtspunkt. Und ich glaube, dass diese Diskussionen aus ihren Erfahrungen mit vielen Ausstellungen, die in den letzten Jahren entstanden sind, und einer plötzlich viel größeren Nachfrage der Kurator*innen oder Institutionen, oder nach bestimmten Programmen für Künstler*innen oder einem größeren Interesse an Künstler*innen – oder zumindest allgemein mehr Einladungen an Künstler*innen, mit ihren Arbeiten auf bestimmte Situationen und Orte zu reagieren. Unabhängig davon, ob diese Orte als Orte verstanden wurden, an denen die Künstler*innen bereits für ihre Arbeiten interessiert waren, oder ob diese Orte von Kurator*innen oder von Institutionen, die Teil bestimmter Programme waren, auf eine bestimmte Weise neu definiert wurden. Und innerhalb dieser erhöhten Nachfrage, und ich glaube, dass es immer mehr Künstler*innen gibt, die daran interessiert sind, auf diese Art und Weise zu arbeiten, aber es schien eine Art Verzögerung zu geben, zwischen der Nachfrage und den Einladungen und den Strukturen der Institutionen, in denen

diese Arbeiten realisiert werden sollten. Und es schien, dass es die notwendige oder ausreichend unterstützende Struktur in vielen Fällen einfach nicht gab. Und das hatte, zumindest in meiner Wahrnehmung, zu einem gewissen Grad mit der Entwicklung des Verständnisses einer professionellen Praxis um neue Aktivitäten zu tun. Das war also das andere Motiv.

Draxler: Ja, ich meine, wir könnten uns schon in eine Art Interpretation dieser Nachfrage hineinbewegen, was dies bedeutet, und mit der Erfahrung besonders des letzten Jahres, in dem viele solcher Ausstellungen gezeigt haben, dass sich die Kurator*innen mehr oder weniger in Konkurrenz um die Teilnahme von Künstler*innen begeben. Dies ist auch ein sehr spezieller Punkt, glaube ich, für die Definition der kuratorischen Welt, die sich meiner Meinung nach sehr verändert hat. Aber in Deutschland ist diese Rolle zwischen den verschiedenen, sagen wir, Kunstvereins- und Museumsstrukturen immer noch nicht klar definiert und hat einen ganz anderen praktischen Aspekt. Meiner Meinung nach ist dieses Argument, dass Künstler*innen an der Ausstellung teilnehmen, Mitte der achtziger Jahre aufgekommen. Mein Vorgänger in München [am Kunstverein München] zum Beispiel hat nie Künstler*innen eingeladen. Er hat sich einfach die Arbeiten besorgt und sie selbst installiert, Künstler*innen haben diese Art von Vorgang mehr oder weniger gestört. Und er machte Ausstellungen als souveräner Kurator, die vollkommen auf seinem Ego basierten, sehr konzentriert, nach dem patriarchalischen Modell des Kurators, der die Auswahl in einem sehr traditionellen Sinn trifft.

Ich glaube, dieses Modell verändert sich sehr. Es ist nicht so einfach zu sagen, inwiefern es sich verändern wird und was sich daraus entwickeln wird. Meiner Meinung nach sollte dies heute und morgen von einem kuratorischen Standpunkt aus auch einer der Diskussionspunkte sein.

Fraser: Bei der Entscheidung über den Versuch, ein Forum für Künstler*innen und Kurator*innen zu entwickeln, in dem sie über praktische Probleme sprechen können, schien es zunächst wichtig, ein Verständnis dafür zu entwickeln, wie Künstler*innen mit unterschiedlichen stilistischen Hintergründen, unterschiedlichen Vorgehensweisen innerhalb verschiedener ideologischer und intellektueller Rahmenbedingungen arbeiten und auf welcher Basis diese Künstler*innen gruppiert werden und was die Bedeutung des Begriffes „Projekt" sein könnte. Und „Projekt" ist glaube ich ein Begriff, der seit einiger Zeit sehr allgemein verwendet wird. Der Ausdruck „Ich mache ein Projekt", statt zu sagen „Ich mache eine Arbeit" oder „Ich mache eine Performance" – wie, um ein Medium mehr als alles andere zu beschreiben. Obwohl die Hintergründe vielfältig sind, haben wir versucht herauszufinden, was die gemeinsame Grundlage sein könnte, und dann sind wir auf das Konzept der Dienstleistungen [Services] gekommen. Es ist daraus entstanden, und ich wollte kurz die Einleitung zu dem Entwurf vorlesen, den ihr alle bekommen habt: „Es erscheint uns, daß projektorientierte künstlerische Praktiken, die sich auf institutionelle Kritik, auf produktivistische, aktivistische und politisch-dokumentarische Traditionen sowie auf Post-Studio-Aktivitäten, auf ortsspezifische Kunst und/

oder Kunst im öffentlichen Raum beziehen, nicht notwendigerweise eine gemeinsame thematische, ideologische oder das Verfahren betreffende Basis besitzen. Ihnen tatsächlich gemeinsam ist dagegen die Tatsache, daß sie alle einen gewissen Arbeitsaufwand leisten, der entweder über eine spezifische materielle Produktion hinausgeht oder unabhängig von ihr ist und der nicht zusammen mit einer solchen Produktion gehandelt werden kann. Diese Arbeit, die im ökonomischen Bereich als Dienstleistung bezeichnet werden würde (im Gegensatz zur Warenproduktion), könnte beinhalten: die Arbeit der Interpretation oder Analyse von Orten sowohl innerhalb als auch außerhalb der kulturellen Institutionen; die Arbeit der Präsentation oder Installation (dort, wo solche Begriffe sich stärker auf die Aktivität als auf das produzierte Umfeld beziehen); die Arbeit der öffentlichen Erziehung sowohl innerhalb als auch außerhalb kultureller Institutionen; Anwaltsfunktionen oder andere gemeinschaftsbezogene Arbeit, die Organisation, Didaktik, dokumentarische Produktion und Schaffung alternativer Strukturen miteinschließt („Gemeinschaft" beinhaltet hier sowohl kunstbezogene als auch städtische Gemeinschaften)."

Draxler: Dieser Begriff „Dienstleistungen" hat natürlich eine gewisse Vorgeschichte, wie ihr wisst, und als wir diesen Vortrag vorbereitet haben, hatten wir überlegt, uns mit diesem eher theoretischen Aspekt auseinanderzusetzen, der sich aus Theorien über die postindustrielle Gesellschaft und solchen Dingen ergibt. Wir haben uns dann aber für einen offeneren akademischen Diskurs entschieden und dafür, uns viel mehr auf die konkreten praktischen Implikationen zu konzentrieren. Dabei ist es wichtig zu betonen, dass „Dienstleistungen" keineswegs als neues Schlagwort für die Neunziger gedacht ist, ein „neuer heißer Kunstbegriff", oder so etwas. Und wir beide [Andrea und ich] sind der Meinung, dass der Begriff auch nicht unbedingt eine progressive Entwicklung, einen Fortschrittsgedanken, impliziert. Es ist zuallererst, sagen wir mal, ein analytischer Begriff, um dieses neue und zum Teil unklare Verhältnis zwischen Projekten von Künstler*innen und neuen kuratorischen Welten innerhalb bestimmter Institutionen zu beschreiben. Dieser sehr spezifische Begriff „Dienstleistungen" beschreibt also nicht etwa eine neue autonome Sphäre, ein neues Genre der Projektarbeit, sondern eine Reihe unterschiedlicher Praktiken, die Künstler*innen immer in ein bestimmtes Verhältnis zu Kurator*innen, zu Institutionen, zum Publikum, zu Gemeinschaften setzen. Und Kurator*innen zu Kunst. Ich glaube, die Spezifizität des Begriffs „Dienstleistungen" liegt genau in diesem absolut relationalen Konzept.

Fraser: Aber wir sind auch sehr daran interessiert, oder zumindest bin *ich* sehr daran interessiert, wie die Beziehung zwischen Künstler*innen war und sein könnte, die Dienstleistungsfunktionen strategisch oder thematisch aufgegriffen haben oder sich innerhalb von Institutionen Dienstleistungsfunktionen angeeignet haben, und an den realen materiellen Beziehungen zu diesen Institutionen, die diese Aneignung impliziert und wie diese letztlich von Künstler*innen in Verträgen, Vereinbarungen usw. formalisiert – oder eben nicht formalisiert – wurde.

Die historischen Materialen, die wir gesammelt haben, folgen verschiedenen Strängen. Einer der Punkte ist zum Beispiel die Entwicklung von Künstler-Kurator*innen oder Künstler*innen, die kuratorische Funktionen an Orten kultureller Präsentation, in Galerien und auch Museen, ausüben. Zum Beispiel, ich meine, wo liegt der Unterschied darin, wenn ein*e Künstler*in sich diese Funktion als symbolische Geste aneignet? Und was bedeutet das? Bedeutet das etwas anderes, als wenn ein*e Künstler*in das unter Vertrag mit einer Institution macht? Oder auf eine Weise, die dauerhaft oder langfristig funktioniert? Das sind ziemlich wichtige Themen, wenn beispielsweise eine Künstlerin wie Louise Lawler noch nie einen Vertrag hatte oder mit einem Vertrag gearbeitet hat. Als sie zum Beispiel Arbeiten von Künstler*innen bei Metro Pictures [in New York] organisierte, war sie in der Position einer Art von Kunstberaterin, in der sie 10 Prozent bekommen sollte. Wenn aber eine der Arbeiten verkauft wurde, hatte sie nie vor, dies irgendwie zu formalisieren. In meiner Interpretation hiervon liegt die nächste Frage, die mir sehr wichtig ist: Fragen zur Professionalisierung dieser Art von Tätigkeiten. Einerseits deuten sich durch die Erbringung von Dienstleistungen und innerhalb dieser Beziehungen zwischen Künstler*innen und Institutionen zwei verschiedene Stränge an, die scheinbar, na ja, ich bin mir nicht sicher, was die Verbindung zwischen den beiden sein könnte. Eine ist möglicherweise die Aneignung kuratorischer Funktionen und institutioneller Rollen auf eine Art und Weise, die eine explizite Kritik dieser Rollen und Funktionen mit einbezieht. Im Gegensatz zu einem sehr ähnlichen

Vorgehen, das aber eine „sachkundige" Kund*innenbeziehung impliziert und bestimmte professionelle Modelle, die mit dieser Beziehung im Einklang stehen, hervorbringt. Das war nicht so eindeutig, wie ich es haben wollte. Aber vielleicht kann ich auf einen verständlicheren Punkt zurückkommen. Für mich persönlich ist einer der Punkte, der für mich wahrscheinlich am interessantesten ist, durch so ein Forum zu erreichen – und falls es noch einmal statt findet, was ich doch hoffe – der Versuch ob es möglich ist, ein radikales professionelles Modell zu entwickeln, ein Modell der radikalen Professionalisierung oder so etwas ähnliches, das eventuell eine materielle Grundlage für eine progressive Entwicklung einer kritischen Projektpraxis bieten könnte. Daran bin ich interessiert. Ich hoffe das war nun eindeutiger. (Lacht)

Ich meine, es ist eigenlich eine Idee der Neue Linken, Radikale und Berufe und radikale…

Martin Guttmann: Sich für den Erfolg als Radikaler kleiden [„dress for success"]?

Fraser: Nein, nein. Ich meine, wir reden hier von, nun, das Neue Linke Modell war, dass Sozialarbeiter*innen hingehen und ihre Sozialhilfeempfänger*innen gegen das Sozialhilfesystem organisieren, sowas in der Richtung. Was in gewisser Weise eines der Dinge ist, die Institutionskritik ausmachen, oder ich weiß nicht – es gibt auch andere Modelle. Aber das ist ein historisches…

Judith Barry: Es ist so eine paradoxe Struktur. Ich glaube, auf philosophischer Ebene ist die Krux all dieser Anliegen wie immer die,

dass Institutionskritik diese Kritik ausüben und dann auch an der Institution teilhaben will. Und das ist keine Kritik an deiner Erklärung – es ist einfach eine paradoxe Kluft.

Fraser: Das ist es. Aber ich glaube, das ist auch die Ursache für viele Missverständnisse über diese Art von Arbeit. Vor allem für Künstler*innen, deren Arbeiten institutionskritisch sind. Ich meine, ich wurde in den späten achtziger Jahren zu Ausstellungen eingeladen, in denen es um Institutionskritik ging, und es ist eins der seltsamsten Dinge, die ich mir überhaupt vorstellen kann. Aber die Sache ist für mich nicht nur, dass es auf meiner Seite viele ethische Fragen gibt, die damit zusammenhängen. Andererseits haben [die Probleme] mit den Beziehungen *innerhalb* der Institutionen zu tun, zwischen Künstler*innen und Kurator*innen und zwischen Kurator*innen und ihren Treuhänder*innen und den Verwaltungsinstanzen. Ich glaube, dass diese Beziehungen sich radikal verändert haben. Und es ist auch eines der Dinge, von denen wir hoffen, dass wir sie ein wenig im historischen Material dokumentiert haben. Aber ich glaube, es gibt viele ethische Fragen, die ebenfalls aufgeworfen werden, denn wenn wir Institutionskritik ausüben, arbeiten wir dann mit Kurator*innen zusammen? Wer ist da die Institution? Wie identifizieren wir die Institution? Wo liegt dabei die Beziehung zu Kurator*innen? Oder sind es nur die Treuhänder*innen? Oder ist die Institution dann so etwas wie eine unpersönliche Einheit, eine Art bloße soziale Tatsache? Wo zieht man da die Grenze? Ich habe eine Menge komplizierter Erfahrungen gemacht, was das angeht. Und ich glaube, einigen unter uns geht es ähnlich.

Draxler: Ich glaube, das hat auch mit dem Wunsch danach zu tun, den Begriff „Institutionskritik" zu verändern, oder ihn ein Stück weit zu historisieren. Das könnte sogar auf dieser Wand [mit Ausstellungsmaterialien] sichtbar werden. Sicherlich nicht explizit, den Begriff gab es in den frühen siebziger Jahren nicht, als diese Praktiken entwickelt wurden. Er kommt irgendwo später, aber wir wissen noch nicht [wann und wo]. Es wäre sehr interessant, ob jemand eine Idee hat, wann er zuerst auftauchte. Wer hat diesen Begriff zum ersten Mal benutzt?

Guttmann: Wahrscheinlich Bürger. Peter Bürger. Nicht?

Draxler: Nein. Hmmm.

Guttmann: Jedenfalls es ist so –

Draxler: Das kommt aus dieser Diskussion, aber diese –

Guttmann: Aber er hat den Begriff '73 benutzt.

Draxler: Nein. Nicht als – Er stellte diese „institutionelle" Referenz für Praktiken der Avantgarde her, aber er benutzte ihn nicht in diesem Sinn. Und was er im Kopf hatte, waren ganz klar super-dadaistische und surrealistische Konzepte, und keine zeitgenössische Praxis.

Guttmann: Er spricht von Neo-Pop, Neodadaismus.

Draxler: Ja, aber auf eine sehr, sehr – wisst ihr, er mag [diese Richtungen] überhaupt nicht. Ich meine, er hasst zeitgenössische Kunst, und hält die frühe Moderne, die frühe Avantgarde sehr hoch. Deswegen, glaube ich, ist es wirklich nicht so einfach.

Fraser: Hans Haacke, mit dem ich gesprochen habe – vieles von diesem Material stammt von Hans Haacke – ich habe ihn gefragt, ob er das, was er macht, als „Institutionskritik" beschreibt. Ich hatte das immer vermutet, und er sagte: nein, tut er nicht, dass er diesen Begriff eigentlich nie benutzt hat. Soweit er weiß, wurde er in den frühen achtziger Jahren von der *October* Truppe eingeführt. Aber ehrlich gesagt erscheint mir das ein wenig spät. (Lacht)

Guttmann: In *Theorie der Avantgarde* kommt dieser Begriff vor, das weiß ich.

Fraser: Ja, aber ich glaube nicht –

Guttmann: Er spricht von Institutionskritik, und sie wird der europäischen Interpretation der Pop Art gegenübergestellt, was sie ein wenig distanziert wirken lässt. Aber auch nicht so distanziert.

Fraser: Ich glaube aber, er wurde erst später für diese Art von Praktiken verwendet, ich glaube, darum ging es. Bürger wurde erst in den frühen achtziger Jahren übersetzt, ich glaube '82 kam es in England heraus. Naja…also das ist, was wir als Einleitung vorbereitet haben. Wir würden gerne auch kurz einen Teil des Materials durchgehen. Aber zuerst wollten wir eine Vorstellungsrunde machen, sodass alle etwas über ihre Hintergründe sagen können, ihre institutionellen Anbindungen, falls das zutrifft. Und wenn ihr vielleicht auch etwas dazu sagen möchtet, was wir hier eurer Meinung nach versuchen könnten, zu erreichen.

Ulrich Bischoff: Hallo. Es ist alles so heilig hier, da kann ich nicht stören.

Draxler: Nein, nein.

(Gelächter)

Fraser: Also ich kann gerne anfangen. Ich heiße Andrea Fraser. Ich weiß, es klingt albern, aber es geht darum, eine Art Gruppengefühl herzustellen.

Draxler: Nein. Es ist absolut notwendig.

Von Bismarck: Ich heiße Beatrice von Bismarck, und mein Interesse an dieser Diskussion ist, dass ich früher als Kuratorin gearbeitet habe und jetzt lehre. Und praktisch jeder der hier erwähnten Punkte begleitet uns in der alltäglichen kuratorischen Praxis. Daher bin ich sehr neugierig, ob irgendwelche Schlussfolgerungen möglich sind.

Susan Cahan: Ich heiße Susan Cahan und ich bin Kuratorin für Bildungsprogramme am New Museum for Contemporary Art in New York City. Ich bin seit ungefähr sechs Jahren dort. Davor habe ich im Museum of Modern Art [MoMA] gearbeitet, ebenfalls in New York City und auch im Bereich Bildung und Vermittlung. Und obwohl ich es bis zu unserem Gespräch gestern Abend und bis ich diese Dinge am schwarzen Brett gesehen habe nicht für relevant gehalten habe, würde ich gern folgendes hinzufügen: als ich am MoMA war, war ich stark in deren Gewerkschaft [für Verwaltungsmitarbeiter*innen] PASTA [Professional and Administrative Staff Association] eingebunden – ich war Vorstandsmitglied. Aus diesem Grund gibt es einiges an Material, das sich auf PASTA bezieht, und diese Erfahrung ist für unsere Diskussion möglicherweise relevant.

In meiner Arbeit habe ich neue Modelle der Museumsvermittlung entwickelt und mir die kuratorische Ausbildung im Verhältnis zur Rolle von Besucher*innen oder Betrachter*innen in Museen angeschaut, und das Publikum, Künstler*innen und Museumsfachleute in Bezug auf die relationalen Aspekte, die Helmut vorhin angesprochen hat, untersucht.

Fred Wilson: Ich heiße Fred Wilson, ich bin Künstler und lebe in New York. Den größten Teil meiner Karriere habe ich in Museen und Galerien gearbeitet, und Galerien geleitet, und so meinen Unterhalt für meine künstlerische Tätigkeit verdient, in den letzten…seit '87. Diese beiden Praktiken haben sich irgendwie zusammengefügt und sind zu einer geworden. Wobei ich jetzt im Gegenteil zu früher überhaupt keine Ausstellungen mit Arbeiten von anderen mache. Ich habe in Museen und in den Bildungs- und Vermittlungsabteilungen in New York City gearbeitet, in ganz New York, als Präparator, als Museumswächter, in ganz vielen verschiedenen Bereichen des Museums, was sich wirklich direkt auf meine Arbeit ausgewirkt hat. Und ich habe Galerien in Tribeca und SoHo geleitet, aber die meiste Erfahrung kommt aus der Zeit, als ich eine Galerie in der South Bronx in New York City geleitet habe, für Künstler*innen aus ganz New York, einschließlich der South Bronx. Von diesem Moment an habe ich hauptsächlich an Ausstellungen mit den Sammlungen anderer und anderen Museumssammlungen gearbeitet, wobei der Fokus am Anfang darauf lag, wie Ausstellungsdisplays die Wahrnehmung von Kunst und die der Künstler*innen beeinflusst. Aber – und darüber werde ich hoffentlich noch ein wenig mehr sprechen – das wurde zu einer regelrechten Kritik an den inneren Funktionsweisen von Museen und deren Mitarbeiterstrukturen, und an den Beziehungen zwischen Mitarbeiter*innen, und daran, wie Dinge ausgestellt werden und an den Systemen hinter der eigentlichen Displays. Ich habe noch keine Vorstellung von einem Ziel oder Ergebnis der Arbeitsgruppe. Aber im Laufe des Tages wird mir bestimmt etwas einfallen.

Fraser: Hoffentlich.

Ulf Wuggenig: Ich heiße Ulf Wuggenig und bin Mitglied der Fakultät für Wirtschafts- und Sozialwissenschaften an dieser Universität. Ich unterrichte unter anderem Kunstsoziologie im Studiengang Kulturwissenschaften und forsche mit Bezug zu zeitgenössischer Kunst, zum Beispiel in einem Projekt, das ich zusammen mit Martin Guttmann und Michael Clegg mache. Ich habe auch in Wien und in Hamburg studiert, wo ich mich mit Besucher*innen von Museen, Galerien und anderen ausstellenden Institutionen beschäftigt habe.

Ute Meta Bauer: Ich heiße Ute Meta Bauer, und ich bin für das Programm des Künstlerhaus Stuttgart zuständig, ein Ort für Künstler*innen mit Werkstätten und einem Ausstellungsraum. Hier steht, dass ich als Kuratorin hier bin, aber ich bin im Grunde gar keine Kuratorin. Ich habe neun Jahre mit einer Gruppe von Künstler*innen zusammengearbeitet, wir waren sieben Personen. Und zuletzt war ich alleine, also musste ich entscheiden, wie ich die gleiche Arbeit weiterführen kann. Und die einzige Möglichkeit war, in eine Art Institutionsarbeit zu gehen, wo ich weiterhin mit

anderen zusammenarbeiten kann, auch mit anderen Künstler*innen arbeiten kann. Der große Unterschied zu meiner bisherigen Position ist, dass ich jetzt für die gleiche Arbeit bezahlt werde, was wirklich ein entscheidender Unterschied ist. Normalerweise, wenn man als Künstler*in kuratorisch oder in einem organisatorischen Bereich arbeitet, verstehen die Leute nicht, dass man bezahlt werden muss. Und diese Dinge möchte ich auch diskutieren, wie diese Dinge gehandhabt werden. Für mich besteht der vielleicht größte Unterschied zu den anderen Kurator*innen hier darin, dass wir [am Künstlerhaus Stuttgart], dass unser Hauptpublikum, unsere Haupt-Öffentlichkeit andere Künstler*innen sind. Ich glaube, das ist der große Unterschied. Und daher glaube ich, dass auch die Programmstruktur ganz anders ist, als in anderen Institutionen.

Bischoff: Ich heiße Ulrich Bischoff und arbeite in einem Museum, und dieses Museum ist ein Behälter für Kunstwerke, und ich bin seit vier Tagen dort. (Lacht) Was soll ich sagen?

Cahan: Welches Museum?

Bischoff: Es ist in Dresden. Das Museum für Malerei aus dem 19. und 20. Jahrhundert [Gemäldegalerie Alte Meister].

(Gelächter)

Fritz Rahmann: Ich heiße Fritz Rahmann. Ich bin Künstler, ich habe, glaube ich, in ziemlich unterschiedlichen Formen gearbeitet und habe nicht viel Erfahrung mit Museen. Die meisten meiner Projekte waren bisher relativ anarchische Sachen, die vielleicht bekannteste Arbeitsphase war in den frühen achtziger Jahren in Berlin. Und das war einfach die Erfahrung, ohne irgendeine Form von institutionellem Hintergrund oder Basis zu arbeiten. Was kann in der Stadt, die Berlin damals war, durch eigenständige Aktionen etabliert werden. Was in dieser Zeit interessant war, war ein nicht so stark verwalteter Raum. Es gab also viele materielle Trends in den Arbeiten und aus dieser Arbeitsphase sind einzelne Projekte in Zusammenarbeit mit Institutionen entstanden. Aber es ist kein ideologisch ausformuliertes Verhältnis – es ist zufällig. Mein Verhältnis mit Institutionen ist zufällig. Und es gab tatsächlich sehr unterschiedliche Erfahrungen im letzten Jahr: einen Konflikt, und eine nützliche Sache, wie ich glaube, die sich in der Arbeit zeigt. Helmut kennt sie aus München, vielleicht kann ich sie nachher beschreiben. Vielen Dank.

Iwona Blazwick: Ich heiße Iwona Blazwick, und ich lebe in London. Ich habe sowohl mit Institutionen gearbeitet, in erster Linie mit dem Institute of Contemporary Arts, und ich leite einen Raum, der AIR Gallery heißt [beide in London]. Ich arbeite außerdem an freien Ausstellungen und Projekten und mit Bildungsinstituten, vor allem mit einem Cultural Studies Studiengang in London, und mit einem Verleger. Ich interessiere mich daher für alle Aspekte der Kommunikation, der Verbreitung und für alle Fragen, die mit den Künstler*innen, der Institution, den sogenannten Vermittler*innen und dem Publikum zu tun haben.

Renate Lorenz: Ich heiße Renate Lorenz und zusammen mit Jochen Becker arbeite ich mit BüroBert. Und wir haben uns entschieden, dass

unsere Arbeit nicht bezahlt werden muss, zumindest nicht die Arbeiten. Wir wollen also nicht von der Möglichkeit abhängig sein, bezahlt zu werden. Und ich habe gerade in der Shedhalle in Zürich angefangen zu kuratieren, und ich arbeite dort mit noch einer Frau, Sylvia Kafehsy. Wir arbeiten mit thematischen Ausstellungsprojekten, und das erste, was ich dort mache, heißt *Gamegirl*. Das wird ein Projekt über Technologiekritik. Ich arbeite nicht nur mit Künstler*innen zusammen, sondern auch mit Gruppen, die politische Arbeit leisten. Feministische Gruppen.

Cahan: Unbezahlt?

Lorenz: Ich habe nicht gesagt, dass wir für unsere Arbeit nicht bezahlt werden wollen, das ist nicht unsere Position.

Jochen Becker: Ich heiße Jochen Becker. Ich arbeite mit BüroBert zusammen. Ich verdiene mein Geld als Kritiker. Und wir haben ein Buch produziert, das *Copyshop* heißt. Ein Ziel dieses Buches ist, unterschiedliche Projekte zu versammeln, die nicht nur von Künstler*innen stammen, sondern auch politische oder soziale Projekte. Im deutschsprachigen Raum kommen gerade mehrere Gruppen zusammen, oder bilden und organisieren sich neu. Das Interesse liegt darin, ein Netzwerk zu schaffen, das – in Deutschland ist es sehr schwierig, so etwas sehr strikt zu organisieren – aber in Kontakt zu bleiben und dieses Netzwerk zu organisieren. Eine dieser Gruppen, an der Grenze, es gibt sowohl eine Organisation von Musiker*innen als auch autonom arbeitende politische Gruppen und Künstler*innen. Das ist, glaube ich, sehr interessant.

Und vielleicht können wir darüber sprechen. Wir arbeiten sowohl selbstorganisiert als auch in institutionellen Zusammenhängen.

Christian Philipp Müller: Ich heiße Christian Philipp Müller, ich bin Schweizer, und ich habe in den frühen achtziger Jahren an der Kunstakademie Düsseldorf studiert, wo ich Kasper König kennen gelernt habe, oder er mich. (Lacht) Er fragte mich gewissermaßen, ob ich sein Assistent werden will, weil er dort einen Job hatte, der so ähnlich hieß wie: „Öffentliche Skulpturen", das war zu der Zeit, als er '87 die Skulptur Projekte Münster vorbereitete. Vor meinem Kunststudium habe ich eine Ausbildung zum Grafikdesigner gemacht. Und er hat mich als Assistent eingestellt, im Grunde um viele Künstler*innen einzuladen, die die Studierenden unterrichten würden. Ich musste Geld organisieren, und das war mein erster echter Kontakt mit der echten Kunstwelt und echtem Geld, und echten, na ja, Backstage-Szenarien. Mit meinen Grafkdesign-Kenntnissen stellte Kasper König mich als Hauptgrafiker für diese Skulptur Projekte Münster-Ausstellung an. Ich war als Grafiker dort, nicht als Künstler. Aber durch diese Tätigkeit wurde ich gleichzeitig von einer Gruppe belgischer Filmemacher*innen aus dem öffentlichen Fernsehen eingeladen, eine Art Künstlerführer zu sein, ein Schauspieler, letztlich um die Ausstellung für sie zu kritisieren, in die ich ja auch involviert war – das war sehr schwierig für mich, aber das war vielleicht ein Beispiel dafür, wie man innerhalb und außerhalb der Kritik an etwas stehen kann. Danach bin ich eingeladen worden, ähnliche Projekte zu machen, zum Beispiel für eine Künstler*innenvereinigung

in Amsterdam, die 1839 gegründet wurde. Ähnlich den Strukturen eines Kunstvereins, aber darüber werde ich morgen sprechen. Ich wurde als Künstler eingestellt, aber sie wollten, dass ich eine Gruppenausstellung mit den neuen Mitgliedern kuratiere. Der Grund, warum ich hier bin ist, mehr Klarheit in das zu bringen, was wir tun, jede*r einzelne von uns, ob als Kurator*in oder Künstler*in. Ich habe auch gerne verschiedene Funktionen. Aber nach der Erfahrung mit der Gruppenausstellung letzten Sommer und dem Scheitern von… (Lacht)

Fraser: Darüber sprechen wir später.

Müller: Entschuldigung, ich mache noch kurz weiter, nur noch eine Sache. Ich habe über verschiedene Formen der Kulturpolitik geforscht, beispielsweise habe ich Arbeiten über André Malraux [französischer Schriftsteller und Kunstkritiker des frühen 20. Jahrhunderts] und seiner Funktion als Kulturminister von '59 bis '69 in Frankreich gemacht. Wir sprechen später darüber, Entschuldigung.

Michael Clegg: Ich heiße Michael Clegg und ich arbeite mit Martin Guttmann zusammen. (Lacht) In den letzten Jahren haben wir Arbeiten geschaffen, mit denen wir sozusagen versucht haben, den Kontext unserer Ausstellungsorte auszuweiten. Wir haben versucht, Arbeiten zu konzipieren, die ein anderes Publikum ansprechen, die an anderen Orten als in Museen oder Galerieräumen sind und dabei gleichzeitig eine Verbindung zu traditionelleren Ausstellungsräumen bewahren, und diese Arbeiten als etwas zu positionieren, dass zwischen diesen beiden Grundpfeilern vermittelt. Also zwischen einer Gemeinschaft, auf die sich unsere Projekte häufig fokussierten, und Museen, die mit dieser Gemeinschaft verbunden waren. Ich hoffe, dass wir in diesem Symposium, in diesen Diskussionen, dass wir es schaffen… Ich meine, man merkt, dass sich unsere Praktiken stark voneinander unterscheiden, daher greifen wir vielleicht gewissermaßen auf den Begriff „Dienstleistungen" zurück, als sehr losen Begriff, einfach als losen Begriff, der eine Reihe von Prozeduren definiert, wenn auch nicht die typischen gemeinsamen Anliegen. Gleichzeitig scheint es aber, als könnten wir alle von einem einfachen Austausch darüber profitieren, wie wir weiter vorgehen sollen, um unsere Arbeit zu präsentieren. Was unser Verhältnis zu bestimmten Institutionen ist. Es ist immer ein gutes Gefühl, wenn man die Möglichkeit hat, Informationen auszutauschen. Und es klingt seltsam, so etwas zu sagen, weil es etwas ist, das so problemlos verfügbar ist, aber eigentlich sind die Gelegenheiten für Künstler*innen, im Detail zu besprechen, was sie tun und wie die praktischen und materiellen Grundlagen ihrer Arbeitsprozesse aussehen, gar nicht so häufig. Kürzlich haben wir solche Diskussionen in New York organisiert und haben festgestellt, dass es viele Informationen gibt, die für uns enorm wertvoll und interessant sind. Ich hoffe also, dass es hier noch mehr davon geben wird.

Stephan Dillemuth: Ich heiße Stephan Dillemuth. Ich leite einen Raum in Köln, der Friesenwall 120 heißt. Ich leite ihn seit vier Jahren und nun steht er kurz vor der Schließung. Ich hatte eigentlich ein Atelier gesucht und habe diese Ladenfront ganz in der Nähe des alten Galerieviertels gefunden. Und dann habe ich beschlossen, sie als Raum für Ausstellungen zu nutzen und habe versucht, zu definieren: „Wie kann so ein Raum in so einer Gegend funktionieren?" Das heißt, der mit Ausstellungen experimentiert, die aus verschiedenen Quellen stammen, manche aus einem Kunstkontext, andere aus einem sozialeren Umfeld oder der Nachbarschaft. Ich bin gespannt darauf, was hier passieren wird. Ich glaube, wir sollten reden.

Judith Barry: Ich heiße Judith Barry und ich bin als Architektin ausgebildet und habe viel Zeit an verschiedenen Universitäten verbracht, und viele verschiedene Dinge studiert. Manchmal arbeite ich mit einem Architekten zusammen, Ken Saylor, an Ausstellungsdesigns, und ich arbeite außerdem kommerziell zwischen Musik, Fernsehen und verschiedenen anderen kommerziellen Videoprojeken. Meine künstlerische Praxis geht in Richtung Installation und beruht auf einer Forschungsmethode, die zu verschiedenen Arten von Produktionen führt. Ich weiß nicht, was ich aus dieser Konferenz mitnehmen werde. Ich bin gespannt darauf, was passiert.

Martin Guttmann: Ich heiße Martin Guttmann. Michael Clegg ist mein Partner. Er hat einige der Themen erwähnt, an denen wir jetzt arbeiten – die Idee, alternative Räume für Kunst zu finden, die Idee, uns die Dynamik zwischen verschiedenen Publika und Künstler*innen und Institutionen etwas näher anzuschauen. Wir haben 1980 angefangen, gemeinsam zu arbeiten. Die erste Werkgruppe, an der wir lange gearbeitet haben, beschäftigte sich mit dem Galerieraum.

Wir betrachteten den Galerieraum als größeren Zusammenhang und haben uns gefragt, was die Tätigkeiten im Galerieraum tatsächlich definiert. Wir haben dann die Gleichung aufgestellt, dass Künstler*innen im Grunde Gegenstände produzieren, die als Porträts derjenigen Personen fungieren, für die sie angefertigt werden. Und mit dieser einfachen Formel haben wir Porträtkunst als den zentralsten Aspekt der für Galerien typischen Arbeiten identifiziert. Dann haben wir viel mit Porträtkunst gearbeitet, die diese Art von wortwörtlicher, direkter Strategie nutzte, tatsächlich indem wir Sammler*innen als die Arbeit fotografierten, die in der Galerie gezeigt wurde. Gegen Ende der achtziger Jahre entzauberte sich unsere eigene Formel für uns etwas. Wir hatten das Gefühl, dass es nicht mehr nur um die Entwicklung unserer eigenen Arbeit ging, sondern dass auf globaler Ebene viele Veränderungen stattfanden und die Welt, in der wir arbeiteten, nicht mehr dieselbe war. Wir empfanden es als notwendig, unsere Horizonte zu erweitern und uns ernsthaft Gedanken über den Stellenwert der Kunst in der Welt nach dem Kalten Krieg und der Wende zu machen, wo die grundlegenden Parameter so aussehen: sehr viel Armut, und die Existenz bestimmter Institutionen ist nicht mehr selbstverständlich. Und Künstler*innen müssen ihre eigene Praxis auf unnötige Art und Weise rechtfertigen. Früher hatte es viel…die wirtschaftliche Lage war besser usw. Die Projekte, an denen wir aktuell arbeiten, sind also ein Weg, um den Stellenwert der Kunst in der heutigen Welt wirklich neu zu beurteilen. Konferenzen wie diese können denke ich sehr hilfreich sein, um Informationen zwischen verschiedenen Menschen auszutauschen, die in ihrer eigenen Praxis versuchen, den Horizont zu erweitern.

Renée Green: Ich heiße Renée Green, und na ja, ich schätze, ich bin die letzte Person, die spricht. Ich bin Künstlerin und wohne in New York, aber dieses Jahr lebe ich als Stipendiatin des DAAD in Berlin. Ich arbeite auf ganz unterschiedliche Art und Weise – mein Hintergrund ist vielfältig – ich schätze deswegen bin ich im Moment – offizielle Statistik – ich arbeite im Moment als Künstlerin mit dem Independent Study Program des Whitney [Museum of American Art in New York]. Ich arbeite auf eine Weise, die verschiedene pädagogische Aspekte einbezieht, schreibe auch Kritiken, und ich produziere Arbeiten an unterschiedlichen Orten. Ich bin unter anderem hierhergekommen [zu dieser Arbeitsgruppe], weil ich derzeit ein Symposium vorbereite, für das ich noch viele Dinge besser verstehen und ausarbeiten möchte. Und ich wollte erwähnen, dass ich mit einigen Personen in diesem Raum an verschiedenen Methoden gearbeitet habe, um über Themen zu kommunizieren, von denen ich hoffe, dass sie im Laufe des Wochenendes in der Diskussion auftauchen.

Draxler: Ich heiße Helmut Draxler und ich bin eigentlich Kunsthistoriker. Seit zwei Jahren bin ich der Direktor des Kunstverein München. Eine kleine Institution, die nicht zwischen Kurator*innen und ihren Direktor*innen unterscheidet. Was ich also von Anfang an versucht habe, ist stark in Projekte zu investieren, die Künstler*innen einbeziehen und, was wir vorher beschrieben haben, kuratorische

Funktionen haben. Ich habe also eine Weile mit Christian gearbeitet und mit Andrea. Ich habe letzten Herbst ebenfalls mit Christopher Williams gearbeitet. Es ist sehr schwierig für mich, Richtlinien für die Organisation dieser Projekte zu finden. Und die Situationen sind sehr komplex, zwischen einer klaren Grundlage und der Art, wie man ein Honorar bezahlen soll. Wenn man ein Projekt hat – wie im Fall von Christian, zum Beispiel – war es so, dass Objekte vom Kunstverein zeitgleich produziert wurden und – ich gebe dir keine Schuld, aber Objekte wurden über deine Galerie verkauft, und die Galerie hat uns nie mehr Geld dafür gegeben. Aber solche Probleme man hat immer. Und bei Christopher Williams zum Beispiel, war es noch komplizierter, weil wir sogar irgendwie den Begriff „Projekt" unterschiedlich verstanden haben, oder so. Es war wirklich ein Missverständnis auf seiner Seite. Er hat das Projekt [die Ausstellung im Kunstverein] ganz und gar als eine Situation verstanden, in der er neue Objekte für Galerien mit Sitz in New York anfertigen konnte, die uns kein Geld zurückzahlen müssten, und auch nie die Intention hatte, uns bei der Finanzierung solcher Dinge zu unterstützen, sich nicht darum gekümmert hat, uns Materialkosten zu erstatten. Ich glaube also, für mich war es ganz klar, dass wir eine Art politischen Richtungswechsel vornehmen mussten, und dass wir auf dieser Grundlage nicht mehr arbeiten werden. Ich glaube, dass es ein sehr starkes Bedürfnis gibt, Klarheit über dieses Thema zu bekommen. Und deswegen müssen wir Richtlinien finden. Meiner Meinung nach sollte dieses Symposium, diese Arbeitsgruppe, auch dies beinhalten.

Fraser: Nun, vielleicht mache ich noch ein oder zwei Anmerkungen. Ich bin als Künstlerin ausgebildet, ich war auf einer Kunsthochschule. Eigentlich bin ich eine Kunsthochschulabgängerin. Ich fing an, Kunstkritik zu schreiben und in diesem Zuge setzte ich mich mit Fragen über Institutionen auseinander, vor allem in Bezug zu Museen und Museumsvermittlung. Ich fing an, Performances in Form von Galerieführungen zu machen, was ich anfänglich als eine Art Kunstkritik in Aktion betrachtete, und in diesem Zusammenhang fing ich an, mit Bildungs- und Vermittlungsabteilungen zu arbeiten, vielleicht mehr als mit kuratorischen Abteilungen und Institutionen. Und ich hatte immer überlegt, verschiedene institutionelle Funktionen zu übernehmen und nicht in Galerien zu arbeiten. Ich fing 1990 an, in Galerien zu arbeiten, glaube ich. Vor allem im vergangenen Jahr empfand ich eine Art Konflikt zwischen meinen ursprünglichen Zielen als Künstlerin – sie [die Galerien] würden zwar immer noch meine grundlegende Überzeugung vertreten von dem, was ich hoffe, das Kunstschaffen bedeutet – und der Art von Anforderungen, die nicht nur Galerien, sondern ich würde sagen auch Ausstellungsräume in Museen an Künstler*innen stellen, die nicht unbedingt produzieren möchten, was ich nicht tue. Nicht, dass ich gegen Produktion bin, aber mein Interesse liegt im Wesentlichen in den sozialen Beziehungen innerhalb von Institutionen und zwischen Institutionen und dem Publikum. Und ich möchte dort arbeiten, wo diese Verhältnisse am direktesten wirken. Mein Interesse, mich hier [am *Services* Projekt] zu beteiligen, und mein spezifisches Interesse an der Idee der Dienstleistung besteht denke ich also darin, zu versuchen, nicht nur eine materielle, sondern auch eine intellektuelle Grundlage für das Nachdenken über eine Kunstpraxis zu entwickeln, die nicht nur „gegen die Produktion" oder „gegen den Markt" gerichtet ist, was die Haltung ist, mit der die Richtung, in der ich mich mehr oder weniger bewege, bisher beschrieben wurde. Und zwar in einem positiven Sinne, als etwas anderes, und zu fragen: „Was wird das sein?" Und daran bin ich – hier und für mich selbst als Künstlerin – interessiert.

Draxler: Sollen wir uns die Materialien anschauen?

Fraser: Ich glaube, wir sollten kurz über den Zeitplan sprechen, da wir eigentlich um 14:30 Uhr mit der zweiten Sitzung anfangen wollten. Es ist jetzt 13:45 Uhr. Die andere Sache, die Helmut und ich tun wollten, war, einen Teil der Materialien durchzugehen. Zügig. Es ist wirklich eine Menge Material. Ich weiß nicht, wie schnell wir das hinbekommen. Ich glaube aber, egal ob wir es schaffen oder nicht, werden wir die zweite Sitzung wahrscheinlich nicht um 14:30 Uhr beginnen können. Vielleicht könnten wir das Material also morgen früh zeigen? Oder wir könnten heute alles ein wenig nach hinten schieben? Vielleicht zu Mittag essen, zurückkommen, eine kurze Präsentation machen, und dann stattdessen versuchen, die zweite Sitzung um 15:00 Uhr anzufangen, und eine halbe Stunde dranhängen? Gibt es irgendwelche Vorschläge? Kommentare? Impulse?

Becker: Alle Teilnehmer*innen werden Montag auch da sein, vielleicht können wir es Montag gleich zu Anfang machen?

Fraser: Viele Teilnehmer*innen reisen am Montagmorgen ab. Ja.

Becker: In Ordnung. Aber es wäre auch gut, das Material bald zu sehen.

Green: Ich glaube, es wäre gut, das ganze Material nach der Mittagspause zu zeigen.

Fraser: Nach dem Mittagessen?

Draxler: Ja, also lasst es uns in reduzierter Form machen, nur um einige der Ebenen klar zu machen.

Fraser: Sagen wir also, das ist dann jetzt eine kurze Mittagspause. Glaubt ihr, wir schaffen es, in vierzig Minuten zu Mittag zu essen? Wir treffen uns also um 14:30 Uhr wieder hier. Und dann gehen wir das Material durch und sprechen vielleicht über das Format für die Diskussionen. Und dann lasst uns versuchen, die zweite Sitzung um 15:00 Uhr zu beginnen. Können wir unsere Uhren synchronisieren?

Guttmann: Damit hätte ich genug Zeit, einen Big Mac zu essen, aber keine große Pommes.

(Gelächter)

Fraser: Wir können ja auch etwas zum Mitnehmen holen und es mit hierher bringen.

(Gelächter)

Von Bismarck: Es gibt ein Lokal die Straße hoch, das angeblich in Ordnung ist.

Fraser: Das ist ziemlich langsam.

Draxler: Ganz gut, aber ziemlich langsam.

Fraser: Auf euren Karten ist eine Pizzeria, glaube ich? Die Vesuvios heißt?

(Gelächter)

Fraser: Es gibt auch einen Sandwich-Laden gegenüber, wo es Salat gibt, und Sandwiches. Und Kaffee und Saft und Wasser und Tee gibt es hier.

Draxler: Kekse.

Fraser: Und Kekse.

Von Bismarck: Zwei Sachen noch, die vielleicht nützlich sind. Wenn ihr Geld abheben möchtet, wären die Pausen vielleicht eine gute Zeit, um das zu erledigen. Die andere Sache ist, wer von euch einen Computer braucht, Diethelm Stoller ist drüben im Schreibzentrum, das auf dieser Karte ist, glaube ich. Nummer drei. Und er kann euch einen Computer zur Verfügung stellen, falls ihr etwas vorbereiten wollt. Es wird eventuell schwieriger, wenn ihr euch damit zu viel Zeit lasst, weil das Zentrum am Wochenende normalerweise geschlossen ist.

Wuggenig: Geht dorthin und sprecht mit ihm, oder ein anderes Mal. Wir sollten eine Zeit ausmachen.

Draxler: Wir sollten das wahrscheinlich in der zweiten Pause machen, oder so.

Von Bismarck: Wer braucht einen Computer? Und was braucht ihr?

Guttmann: Einen Drucker.

Fraser: Apple?

Guttmann: Ja.

Von Bismarck: Warum machen wir es nicht einfach – ich meine, ich kann ihn anrufen und eine Zeit ausmachen, die vermutlich besser passt?

Bauer: Wir können aber nicht mit vier Personen gleichzeitig an einem Drucker arbeiten.

Wuggenig: Es gibt viele Computer.

Arbeitsgruppe
Sitzung Zwei

Den Institutionen dienen
Samstag, 22. Januar 1994

Vorträge:
Judith Barry
Renée Green
Fred Wilson

*Projektarbeit impliziert häufig eine Expert*innen-Auftraggeber*innen-Beziehung zwischen Künstler*innen und Institutionen. Wenn eine Institution zum Auftraggeber von Künstler*innen wird, was bedeutet dieses Verhältnis für künstlerische Unabhängigkeit und das Ausüben von Kritik?*

*Welche Auswirkungen hat das dahinterliegende Arbeitsmodell? Worin genau liegt das Interesse von Institutionen an den Dienstleistungen von Künstler*innen?*

Andrea Fraser: Während des Planungsprozesses dieser Veranstaltung entwickelte sich die Wochenend-Arbeitsgruppe inklusive Ausstellung zu einem Langzeit-Projekt, das die sich wandelnden Verhältnisse zwischen Künstler*innen und Institutionen von 1969 bis zur Gegenwart in den Blick nimmt. Das ist extrem ambitioniert, und ich weiß nicht, wie weit wir tatsächlich damit kommen, aber ich sehe dieses [von Helmut und mir gesammelte] Material als eine Art Projektbeginn. Ein erster Versuch, Dokumente zu sammeln, die sich auf diese wandelnden Verhältnisse beziehen. Vieles fehlt. Es gibt wenig Material zu früheren Projekten von Künstler*innen. Dafür gibt es viele Gründe, auf die ich später noch eingehen kann.

Das Material fängt 1969 mit der Art Workers' Coalition an. Und das Datum – 1969 – bezieht sich auf die Art Workers' Coalition und einen weiteren Aspekt, auf den ich durch Michael Asher aufmerksam wurde – und zwar, dass in dieser Ausstellung, der *Spaces* Ausstellung, die von 1969 bis '70 lief, das Museum of Modern Art [in New York] zum ersten Mal ein Künstler*innenhonorar bezahlte. Es war ebenfalls das erste Mal, dass er ein Künstlerhonorar bekam. Und das geschah nicht auf seine Anfrage hin; möglicherweise hatte Dan Flavin das eingefordert, das ist nicht ganz klar…Beatrice hat sogar versucht, mit Dan zu sprechen, aber er konnte sich nicht erinnern. Es könnte auch Robert Morris gewesen sein, anhand der Unterlagen können wir das nicht genau feststellen. Aber für mich ist die Idee der „Dienstleistung" und das Verhältnis zwischen einer Dienstleistung und einem Honorar – in dem Moment, in dem man von einem Künstler*innenhonorar spricht, geht es um eine Dienstleistung; ein Honorar ist für eine Dienstleistung. Ich bin an der ganzen Geschichte [dieses Aspekts] interessiert. Und das hier ist sozusagen die Vorgeschichte. Ich sehe das als den Höhepunkt eines ganzen Jahres der sich wandelnden Beziehungen zwischen Künstler*innen und dem Personal des Museum of Modern Art. Und das ist eine Art Fallbeispiel dafür, bis hin zu diesem Material über die Gewerkschaftsbildung des Museum of Modern Art, die 1971 anfing. Es spitzte sich während eines Streiks 1973 zu, und ging dann weiter. Dort, wo es also 1969 anfängt, wo die Art Workers' Coalition begann, ging es um eine Reihe kinetischer Skulpturen. Es gab eine Ausstellung am Museum of Modern Art und Takis, ein Künstler, der Teil dieser Ausstellung war, hatte einige Arbeiten in der Sammlung des Museum of Modern Art, und eine dieser Arbeiten wurde vom Kurator der Ausstellung für diese Ausstellung ausgewählt. Und Takis wollte nicht, dass diese Arbeit gezeigt wird. Sie wurde trotzdem gezeigt, also gingen er und einige andere Künstler*innen während einer Pressekonferenz ins Museum und entfernten die Arbeit. Sie brachten sie in den Skulpturengarten. Zu dieser Gruppe von Künstler*innen gehörte Hans Haacke, der seltsamerweise im selben Raum wie Takis gezeigt wurde und zu der Zeit hauptsächlich kinetische Skulpturen und Land Art machte. Innerhalb des ersten Monats entwickelte sich das Ganze rasch zu einer ganzen Liste von Forderungen.

Martin Guttmann: Warum hat er seine Arbeit entfernen lassen?

Fraser: Das ist nicht ganz klar. Was ich spannend finde ist, dass genau solche Skulpturen Ausgangspunkt solcher Aktion waren. Ich denke, es war eine Arbeit, die einen anderen Umgang als andere Arbeiten erforderten. Zu diesem Zeitpunkt hatten installative Arbeiten, minimalistische Arbeiten, möglicherweise nicht dieselbe Autorität wie diese Art von Skulptur. Diese Künstler*innen fühlten sich also nicht wohl damit, neue Forderungen an Institutionen zu stellen, was das betraf. Aber diese Arbeit [von Takis] hatte sie [diese Autorität]. Die anderen Künstler*innen, die sich ihm anschlossen, waren ebenfalls unzufrieden mit der Art, wie ihre Arbeiten präsentiert wurden. Ich denke, es hatte mit der Art zu tun, wie Takis' Arbeit vom Publikum getrennt oder nicht getrennt wurde, es hatte damit zu tun, wie sie platziert wurde, es hatte mit der

Ästhetik, aber auch den technischen Bedingungen der Installation zu tun.

Helmut Draxler: Es war eine von diesen Gruppenausstellungen, bei denen sie nie die Künstler*innen fragen, sie haben einfach ein Thema – eine Ausstellung über die Maschine zum Beispiel – und einfach, ich weiß nicht wie viele Künstler*innen mit einer Arbeit neben der anderen, sodass sofort klar ist, wie der Raum gedacht wurde. Das war also tatsächlich eine einzigartige Forderung. Wir sollten mit den Forderungen weitermachen.

Fraser: Nun, wenn wir uns die ersten Forderungen anschauen, und diesen Monat ist das 25-jährige Jubiläum – die erste Forderung war, dass das Museum eine öffentliche Anhörung über sein Verhältnis zu Künstler*innen und der Gesellschaft veranstaltet. Das ist Forderung Nummer Eins. Forderung Nummer Zwölf ist, dass das Museumspersonal um Personen erweitert werden soll, die für Installations-, Instandhaltungs- und technische Arbeiten qualifiziert sind. Das war das Spektrum und vielleicht könnt ihr verstehen, warum diese Arbeiten solche Initiativen hervorgebracht haben. Das war Anfang '69, Januar '69, und die Ausweitung der Art Workers' Coalition war zum Teil ein Mittel, mit dem Künstler*innen versuchten, sich den damaligen Bewegungen in den Vereinigten Staaten anzuschließen – der Student*innenenbewegung, der Antikriegsbewegung, der Frauenbewegung und Black Power und den Schulaufständen. Und wie es sich entwickelt hat…Helmut willst du –

Draxler: Ja, es entwickelte sich aus dieser ursprünglichen Gruppe, am 10. März waren es schon achtzehn bis zwanzig Personen und sie haben die öffentliche Anhörung gefordert und all diese offiziellen Forderungen hatten mit verschiedenen Aspekten von Kontrolle zu tun, auch dass Künstler*innen Teil des Vorstands werden sollten und solche Sachen. Zwischen dem 10. März und dem 10. April gab es eine große Welle, die Anzahl der Mitglieder der Art Workers' Coalition explodierte regelrecht, aber die öffentliche Anhörung im Museum konnten sie nicht durchsetzen, also entschlossen sie sich, ihre eigene öffentliche Anhörung zu veranstalten. Der Titel kam von einem der Komitees der – damals war es noch nicht die Art Workers' Coalition, sie war noch ganz am Anfang: „Eine offene und öffentliche Anhörung zum Thema: Wie soll das Programm der Kunstarbeiter*innen in Bezug auf die Museumsreform aussehen, mit dem Ziel, das Programm einer offenen Art Workers' Coalition zu entwickeln."

So hat die Art Workers' Coalition in dieser Anhörung eine neue Form angenommen, und all diese Leute, die eingeladen waren und hier [in dem vorliegenden Dokument] aufgelistet sind, haben unterschiedliche Statements mit verschiedenen Forderungen abgegeben. In der Überschrift steht „Museumsreform", aber das ist nur ein Teil der damaligen Politisierung. Es wurden ganz verschiedene Punkte diskutiert. Ich zitiere aus der Erklärung von Lucy Lippard: „Der Grund für die Weiterführung der Aktion Takis waren eine tatsächliche, über ästhetische Dimensionen hinausgehende Solidarität und die tatsächliche Befürwortung weiterer Diskussionen, auch wenn es grundlegende Uneinigkeiten hinsichtlich des Programms der ersten Gruppe gibt." Es gab also einen großen

Bedarf nach Solidarität und Einheit, die über die Wettbewerbsstrukturen des künstlerischen Individualismus hinausgingen. Wir haben es hier, alle können es sich anschauen, es ist wirklich eine unglaubliche Reihe von Aussagen verschiedener Künstler*innen, wenn auch nicht sehr erfolgreicher Künstler*innen. Carl Andre, Hans Haacke und Lucy Lippard, die auch Kritikerin war. Aber auch noch andere Personen, wie beispielsweise David Lee, den ich nicht kannte, er schrieb eine wirklich tolle Erklärung, in der das ganze institutionskritische Programm ausformuliert wird, das in der Geschiche bisher nicht anerkannt worden ist. Es gibt Statements von Künstler*innen über die Kritik an Galerien und Kunsthochschulen, einen „Vorschlag für die Einrichtung eines Schwarzen Flügels am Museum of Modern Art in Gedenken an Dr. Martin Luther King Jr.", ein Statement für Schwarze und puerto-ricanische Künstler*innen, und es gab anarchistischere Statements von einem Stephen Phillips, der einen weiteren Flügel im Museum of Modern Art forderte, in dem Künstler*innen leben und ab und zu ihre Arbeiten ausstellen können sollten. Die Vielfalt zwischen sehr persönlichen und sehr niedergeschlagenen Aussagen über die Bedingungen ist wirklich groß, und dann hat man Statements wie die von Jean Toche von der Guerrilla Art Action Group, die eine eher anarchistische Position einnahm, wo er sagt: „Die Aktionen sollten sich gegen alle Museen und alle Kunstinstitutionen richten…wir wollen keine Museumsreform, sondern effektive Teilhabe – keine neue Arbeiter*innen- oder Angestelltengewerkschaft, sondern eine echte Künstler*innen-Kommune."

Fraser: Das hier ist eine tolle Arbeit, eine tolle Grafik: „Abteilung für kulturelle Angelegenheiten…Nein." Direkt und auf den Punkt.

Ulrich Bischoff: Kannst du etwas mehr zum Namen sagen: „Art Workers' Coalition?" Woher kommt er?

Fraser: Er entstand aus der Anhörung heraus. Helmut, weißt du das? Es gab immer diesen Bezug zu „art workers" [Kunstarbeiter*innen]. Es war eine riesige Gruppe, mehr als 250 Personen. Ich wollte aber auch über diesen Abschnitt hier sprechen, am Anfang richten sich die Forderungen, die Künstler*innen, an die Institution als undifferenzierte Einheit, und was vielleicht als Auseinandersetzung über kuratorische Praxis begonnen hat, war vielleicht sogar noch viel mehr an die Museumsfacleute des Museum of Modern Art gerichtet. An dieser Stelle wird eine Demonstration gezeigt, die auf eine Ausstellung der Sammlung von Nelson A. Rockefeller reagiert, der gerade seine Wahlkampagne für das Gouverneursamt von New York beendet hatte. Hier steht: „Die Art Workers' Coalition ist hier, um Künstler*innen die Peinlichkeit zu ersparen, mit den politischen Zielen Nelson Rockefellers in Verbindung gebracht zu werden." Aber an dieser Stelle wird die Institution zum ersten Mal auch differenzierter betrachtet: sie wird nicht mehr als eine einzelne Einheit angesehen, sondern innerhalb einer Struktur von Vorstandsmitgliedern und Museumsfachleuten betrachtet. Eine Sache, die ich wirklich spannend finde und von der ich denke, dass sie stark mit unserer Diskussionen zusammenhängt, ist die Sympathie und Identifikation, die sich zwischen der Art Workers' Coalition und den Mitarbeiter*innen des Museum of Modern Art entwickelt.

Susan Cahan: Aber waren nicht viele der Angestellten auch Künstler*innen?

Fraser: Ja. Ich meine, ich weiß nicht, wie viele zu dem Zeitpunkt aktiv waren.

Cahan: Das wäre etwas, was man recherchieren könnte, vor allem unter dem Aufsichtspersonal waren einige Künstler*innen, die im Nachhinein sehr erfolgreich wurden.

Fraser: Es gab auch Künstler*innen, die nicht in der Kunstwelt arbeiteten und sich für diese Institution einfach als Institution interessierten, aber dann feststellten, dass dort auch komplexe Interessenkonflikte aufkommen und wertvolle Sympathien entstehen können. Künstler*innen, die in der Institution arbeiteten und Museumsfachleute, die in Konflikt mit dem Vorstand stehen und sich für ihre eigene Gewerkschaft und Arbeitsbedingungen einsetzen. Das ist doch eine wirklich wichtige Entwicklung für diese Verhältnisse. Was das Museum of Modern Art gemacht hat, anstatt diese Anhörung zu fördern, die die Art Workers' Coalition verlangt hat, war ein Komitee für Künstlerbeziehungen zu schaffen. Und hier gibt es einen Bericht, in dem die Mitglieder dieses Komitees an verschiedene Orte gehen, an denen sich die Art Workers' Coalition und andere Künstler*innengruppen treffen. Jennifer Licht [Assistenzkuratorin am Museum] berichtet dort von einem Treffen auf der Lower East Side [Gegend in New York City]: „Barnett Newman schlägt vor, dass die Künstler*innen in David Rockefellers Büro demonstrieren sollen." Und Jennifer Licht hat die *Spaces* Ausstellung kuratiert. Und obwohl ich es nicht sicher weiß, könnte ich mir vorstellen, dass ihre Reaktion auf die Forderungen der Künstler*innen nach einem Honorar vielleicht mit ihrer eigenen Position innerhalb der Institution zusammenhing. Ich kann darüber nichts Genaues sagen, weil sie [das Museum of Modern Art] mich die Akten nicht haben einsehen lassen.

Draxler: Ich denke, dieser nächste Schritt der Zusammenarbeit zwischen dem Modern [MoMA]-Personal und der Art Workers' Coalition ist sehr wichtig. Das Bild hier oben [im vorliegenden Dokument] zeigt die vielleicht wichtigste Aktion der Art Workers' Coalition, die Demonstration beim Museum of Modern Art als Reaktion auf das Massaker von My Lai, und diese Briefe erläutern ganz klar, dass die Idee war, diese Aktion gemeinsam mit dem Museumspersonal und den Künstler*innen durchzuführen. Teile des Museumspersonals haben die Art Workers' Coalition vielfach unterstützt und geholfen, dieses Plakat zu produzieren. Es zeigt ein Foto des My Lai-Massakers mit auf einem Feldweg neben- und aufeinanderliegenden [Kinder-] Leichen und dem folgenden Text: „F: Und Babies? – A: Und Babies." Aber als der Museumsvorstand [namentlich die beiden Geschäftsmänner Nelson Rockefeller und William S. Paley] die Druckproben des Plakats sahen, zogen sie die Unterstützung des Museums für die Produktion und den Vertrieb des Plakats zurück. Das verdeutlicht noch einmal das kritische Verhältnis zwischen Vorstand und Fachleuten innerhalb dieses Professionalisierungsprozesses.

Fraser: Im ersten Abschnitt hier steht: „Der Vorschlag für ein Protestplakat gegen das My Lai-Massaker wurde während einer Diskussion darüber entwickelt, wie Künstler*innen sich an der Formulierung des Museumsprogramms beteiligen könnten. Irving Petlin wurde dann von Arthur Drexler" – ich glaube, der war zu dem Zeitpunkt stellvertretender Direktor – „gefragt, ob er daran interessiert wäre, an einer Mitarbeiter*innenbesprechung der Abteilung für Malerei und Skulptur teilzunehmen, bei der das Programm besprochen werden würde. Er antwortete: ‚Kann ich Ihre Frage mit einer Frage beantworten, die das Thema eventuell durcheinanderbringt, oder auch nicht – könnten Sie sich mich bei einer Besprechung vorstellen, in der die politische Funktion des Museums diskutiert wird und ich den Vorschlag mache, dass es heute ein Massaker in Son My gab und ich denke, das Museum sollte ein Plakat, das gewaltsames Entsetzen über diese Tat ausdrückt, das in gedruckter Form und in der Öffentlichkeit unmissverständlich den Eindruck vermittelt, dass das Museumspersonal und alle Künstler*innen, die zu seiner Ausdruckskraft beigetragen haben, von dem Massaker in Son My entsetzt sind, breitmöglichst verteilen?'" Und dann steht da: „Applaus." Das ist ein Vermerk vom Museum.

Ute Meta Bauer: Ich glaube, der große Unterschied ist, dass die Strukturen der Museen in den USA so anders sind, als die Strukturen hier. Denn hier gibt es Vorstandsmitglieder nur im Kunstverein oder in privaten Organisationen, die staatlich gefördert werden, aber trotzdem irgendwie unabhängig sind. Aber die Museen hier haben eine ganz andere Struktur, und ich denke, es ist wichtig, das anzumerken, weil viele der Anwesenden aus dem Ausland sind, und vielleicht sollten wir die Strukturen in den USA und die Strukturen hier erläutern?

Draxler: Ich denke, wir sollten ein wenig später auf diesen Punkt eingehen.

Fraser: Ich meine, 1968 gab es Demonstrationen in Venedig [auf der Biennale in Venedig] und es gab Demonstrationen bei der [4.] documenta.

Christian Philipp Müller: Bei der documenta 1968, und davon gibt es Unterlagen, haben die französischen Künstler*innen abgelehnt, und die amerikanischen Künstler*innen zugesagt. Es gab eine große Diskussion bei der Pressekonferenz vor der documenta darüber, warum Künstler*innen nach Mai '68 nicht mehr daran teilnehmen konnten.

Draxler: Es gab auch noch spezifischere Demonstrationen, gegen die Ermordung von Aktivist*innen. Und es gab Aktionen für politische Kunst auf der documenta. Weil auf der documenta '68 fast genau die gleiche Art von Kunst vertreten war, wie auf der documenta [III] '64. Dieser übliche Standard mit Pop Art und minimalistischer Kunst. Es gab also Konflikte zwischen Teilnehmer*innen verschiedener ästhetischer Bereiche. Aber ich weiß nicht genau, warum bestimmte Kunstformen und Modelle der Selbstrepräsentation nicht vertreten waren, das müsste man nachschauen.

Fraser: Ich möchte kurz zu den Danksagungen der *Spaces* Ausstellung zurückkehren. „Eine Ausstellung, in der die Installation zur eigentlichen Realisation des Kunstwerks in Räumen wird, und

die nach den Bedürfnissen der Künstler*innen geplant und gebaut werden muss, stellt die übliche Rolle des Museums in Frage und das Museumspersonal und die Ressourcen vor ungewohnte Herausforderungen. Ein Museum beheimatet und konserviert traditionsgemäß Kunstobjekte, aber nun ist es für die Ausführung der Ideen von Künstler*innen verantwortlich. Dies erfordert die Zusammenarbeit von Menschen und eine flexible Anpassung von Rollen und Verantwortlichkeiten." Also ich fand das in unserem Kontext sehr interessant.

Guttmann: Ich wollte fragen, hatte das Verständnis dessen, was die Art Workers' Coalition erforderlich machte, etwas mit der Kunst zu tun oder war es eine Frage von solidarischer Organisation? Es könnte beides sein, aber wenn man sich die Zusammensetzung der Personen hier [in der vorliegenden Dokumentation] anschaut, sieht man, dass sehr wenige von ihnen produzieren…Ich glaube, dass der einzige minimalistische Künstler in der Gruppe, Carl Andre…Ich meine, mit Sachen, die auf dem Boden liegen, ist Flexibilität nicht wirklich notwendig.

(Gelächter)

Fraser: Da stehen viele Fragen im Raum. Fragen der Verbreitung und Instandhaltung. Wann ist etwas ein Kunstobjekt und wann ist es kein Kunstobjekt.

Guttmann: Es gab also eine Diskussion über Kunst. Denn es sieht aus als seien die Personen, die am meisten davon profitieren würden, nicht als [an der Art Workers' Coalition] beteiligt aufgeführt.

Fraser: An wen denkst du, der am meisten davon profitieren könnte?

Guttmann: Ich weiß nicht, zum Beispiel Bruce Nauman. Flavin ist nicht dabei.

Fraser: Es ist verwunderlich, dass Barnett Newman dabei ist.

Draxler: Eines der ersten Beispiele, die diskutiert wurden, war eine Ausstellung am Museum of Modern Art über Abstrakten Expressionismus, für die das Museum Arbeiten von den Künstler*innen nicht als Leihgabe, sondern als Geschenk an das Museum anfragte. Als die Institution von der Art Workers' Coalition dafür angegriffen wurde, mussten sich Personen wie Barnett Newman und einige der Klassizisten der fünfziger Jahre gegenüber der Art Workers' Coalition verteidigen, aber einige haben sich der Coalition später dann auch angeschlossen. Es ist ebenfalls wichtig zu betonen, dass die Mitglieder am Anfang alle europäische Künstler*innen waren, und dann kamen Künstler*innen aus der Karibik und Schwarzen Gemeinden dazu, es wird also klar, dass die Mitgliedschaft in der Coalition über standardisierte ästhetische Parameter hinausgeht.

Fraser: Ich meine, Versammlungen mit 250 Personen…So groß ist die Kunstszene auch wieder nicht. Die ACT UP-Versammlungen fanden mit dreihundert Personen statt. Ich glaube, es gibt mehr Mitglieder, die aber zum Beispiel nicht bei der öffentlichen Anhörung sprechen, und dass einige der Sprecher*innen bei der öffentlichen Anhörung keine aktiven Mitglieder waren. Die Anhörung war offen, jede*r konnte hingehen und drei Minuten lang sprechen. Ich denke also, es ist schwierig, das zu beantworten.

Hier haben wir…Es gab eine Organisation: Women Artists in Revolution. Dies ist eine Ausgabe einer Publikation, die unter anderem auch Material über mehrere Aktionen gegen das Whitney Museum [of American Art in New York] und andere Museen beinhaltet, dezidierte Forderungen, die zu der Zeit von Frauen und der aufkommenden Frauenbewegung gestellt wurden. Hier haben wir einen Vorschlag für Gemeinde-Kulturzentren.

Draxler: Das ist vielleicht auch ein wichtiger Punkt, weil Hans Haacke darauf auch in seiner Erklärung bei der öffentlichen Anhörung eingeht. Es gab einen Plan für ein neues Museum für moderne Kunst in Midtown Manhattan, und Haackes Argument war, dass dies völlig falsch wäre, da man dezentralisieren müsse. Und so kam auch diese Frage nach Kulturzentren auf.

Fraser: Es gab zu der Zeit eine Diskussion darüber, was es für das Museum of Modern Art bedeutete, in verschiedenen städtischen Gemeinden zu arbeiten. Und ob das eine Form des urbanen kulturellen Imperialismus wäre oder nicht. Aber ich denke, wir sollten weitermachen. Das hier ist der Vertagsentwurf, den die Art Workers' Coalition für Galerien hergestellt hat. Das hier ist ein erster Entwurf des Vertrags, der von einem Anwalt [Robert Projansky], der mit Seth Siegelaub arbeitete, ausgearbeitet und im Katalog der documenta 5 1972 veröffentlicht wurde. Und der hier wurde 1971 in ganz New York zusammen mit einer Umfrage verschickt. Dies sind die tatsächlichen endgültigen Verträge, die Hans Haacke immer noch

benutzt und die er uns gegeben
hat. Hier drüben ist die Absage
von Hans Haackes Ausstellung im
Guggenheim [Museum in New York]
dokumentiert. Wenn man sich die
Entwicklung des Verhältnisses zwischen Künstler*innen und Museumsfachleuten anschaut, in diesem
Fall wurde die Ausstellung von den
Vorstandsmitgliedern abgesagt.
In diesem Fall schrieb der Kurator
der Ausstellung, Edward Fry, eine
Erklärung, in der er Hans Haacke
seine Unterstützung aussprach und
die Absage verurteilte. Er wurde vier
Tage später entlassen und arbeitete
nie wieder in einem Museum. Und
Hans Haacke hatte keine Ausstel-
lung mehr in einer Institution in den
Vereinigten Staaten bis '68 im New
Museum [in New York] –

Cahan: 1986.

Fraser: Ja natürlich, '86, nicht '68!
Aus diesen sich verschiebenden Ver-
trauensverhältnissen und Gefolg-
schaften, auf die Künstler*innen und
Museumsfachleute stießen, ergaben
sich also mitunter sehr ernste Kon-
sequenzen für einzelne Personen.
Ich möchte auf den Streik im Modern zu sprechen kommen, es gibt
einige Zitate dazu, die ich vorlesen
möchte. Sie stammen aus einer Diskussion zwischen Lawrence Alloway
und John Copeland während eines
Streikkomitees der PASTA [Profes-
sional and Administrative Staff Association, die Personalgewerkschaft
des Museum of Modern Art]. Das
ist jetzt eine Frage, die von einer*m
Interviewer*in gestellt wurde: „Ich
habe mich gefragt, ob es hilfreich
wäre zu sagen, dass Sie sich mitten
in einer Rollensuche befinden, es
scheint mir, dass sich das Museum
in seinen Anfängen in den Händen
einiger weniger Vorstandsmitglieder

befand, die sehr wohlhabend waren
und das Geld zur Verfügung gestellt
haben. Ich spreche von den Rockefellers, den Guggenheims und so
weiter. Allerdings gibt es einen an-
haltenden Konflikt zwischen den von
ihnen berufenen Personen und der
Struktur und Funktion des Vorstands
selbst. Er besteht schon seit seiner
Gründung. Heute ist das Bewusstsein darüber viel größer, dass die
Fachleute nicht nur Angestellte sind,
sondern intelligente und in ihrer
jeweiligen Disziplin gut ausgebil-
dete Personen." [Das Gespräch von
Alloway und Copeland handelt auch
von] dem Vorschlag, dass Museen,
die angeheuerte Bildungsinstitutio-
nen sind, wie Bildungseinrichtungen
funktionieren sollten. Und dass es
unter Universitätsprofessor*innen
eine Art der Gewerkschaftsbildung
und professionelle Vereinigung gibt.
Und von einer professionellen auto-
nomen Stellung, die für Museumsfachleute zu der Zeit nicht wirklich
existierte. Es gab einen weiteren
Punkt in Bezug auf das Modell der
Universitätsprofessor*innen, in einer
Diskussion über die Berufsvereini-
gung der Universitätsprofessor*innen: „Ihr Dasein in Universitäten
um die Jahrhundertwende, und die
Schwierigkeiten, die die Fachbe-
reiche zu dem Zeitpunkt formulierten, beispielsweise Institutionen
durch ihre eigene Verarmung zu
subventionieren."
Diese Aussage: „Institutionen
durch ihre eigene Verarmung zu
subventionieren", das hat wiederum mit der amerikanischen
Museumsstruktur zu tun. Von der
ich glaube, dass Künstler*innen und
Museumsfachleute sich stark damit
auseinandersetzen müssen. Das
ist im Wesentlichen die Situation:
Personen, die mit privaten gemeinnützigen Organisationen arbeiten,

dort ein Privileg oder eine Verpflichtung leben und sich selbst für diese Institution aufgeben, außerhalb der Berufspraxis, die in anderen Kontexten [nicht] akzeptabel wäre.

Draxler: In Deutschland gab es in den siebziger Jahren das Internationale Künstlergremium, eine Organisation, die '75 gegründet wurde. Und ich glaube, wir müssen das in einen Zusammenhang bringen mit dieser anderen Institution, dem Artists Meeting for Cultural Change, das auch '75 entstand, aber in New York. Sie deuten auf eine Verlagerung von Interessen hin, die nicht länger in direkter Verbindung mit der Phase der sechziger Jahre stehen. Das Künstlergremium hat eine Liste möglicher Mitglieder zusammengestellt, und all diese potenziellen Mitglieder sind bekannte Künstler*innen aus dieser Zeit, und es war weniger ein Künstler*innen-Verbund als vielmehr ein elitärer Club. Und das Programm wurde sehr klar definiert, es bewegte sich weg von gesellschaftlichen hin zu spirituellen Fragen, was hier mehrmals hervorgehoben wird, [in] einem Teil des Materials über eine Konferenz, die sie veranstaltet haben. Es ist interessant als eine Art Symptom. Aus dem europäischen Kontext, vor allem dem deutschen Kontext – hier ist die Titelseite eines deutschen Kunstmagazins – darauf steht: „Kultur wird nicht in Kultusministerien gemacht. Künstler sprechen über das, was sie am meisten interessiert." Man hat also die staatliche Kulturpolitik, auf einer sehr offiziellen Ebene, und dann wiederum diesen Gegensatz.

Fraser: Was wir aus dem europäischen Kontext haben, haben wir hier [für die Arbeitsgruppe] nicht vorbereitet.

Draxler: Ja, wir haben nicht so viel hier. Dass sie den Vorrang des Spirituellen so stark betonen ist, denke ich, ein sehr symptomatischer Ausdruck der Professionalisierung, so sehe ich das. Weg von gesellschaftlichen Belangen. Es geht nicht um Selbstrepräsentation, sondern darum, das Niveau der Diskussion über Kunst zu steigern. Die Freiheiten der Künstler*innen beibehalten. Eine ganze Reihe dieser mehr oder weniger sehr konservativen Fragen.

Ulrich Bischoff: Darf ich mal unterbrechen? Ich glaube, dass einige der Mitglieder des Internationalen Künstlergremiums etwas korrupt geworden sind. Es wurde gegründet, um Künstler*innen aus Osteuropa nach Westeuropa zu bringen. Das war eine der Ideen von Robert Filliou, Brecht und Beuys: sie wollten einen Rat gründen, um Künstler*innen aus Osteuropa nach Westeuropa zu bringen, und auch, um auf die andere Seite zu kommen. Es war sozusagen eine Brücke über die Mauer.

Publikum (Gislind Nabakowski): Ja, das war der Ausgangspunkt, und deshalb haben sie Geld bekommen. Aber zum Schluss war es pervers. Schon in den achtziger Jahren.

Draxler: Das wurde in keiner der ursprünglichen Erklärungen erwähnt.

Fraser: Es gibt einiges zu diesem Punkt, das hier nicht vorkommt. Ich meine, allein aus den Vereinigten Staaten müsste man Künstler*innenorganisationen einbeziehen, die Arbeit von Gordon Matta-Clark, Ausstellungen wie *Rooms* im P.S. 1 [Ort für zeitgenössische Kunst in New York], ich meine, es gibt alle möglichen Dinge, die hier überhaupt nicht behandelt werden.

Draxler: Das sind viele offene Fragen!

Fraser: Wirklich viele offene Fragen. Ich denke, wir machen hier einen Punkt.

Draxler: Ich glaube aber, aus diesem Material hier geht sehr klar hervor, dass es diese frühe aktivistische Phase der Selbstrepräsentation gab, dann ging es um das Verhältnis zum Museumspersonal der Institutionen, und gibt es einige Beispiele wie diese sehr spezifischen individuellen künstlerischen Praktiken, die sich später mit Institutionskritik beschäftigt haben. Deshalb gibt es in diesem Zusammenhang Proteste, dann Verträge, höhnische Perspektiven auf das Vorgehen von Seth Siegelaub und Hans Haackes „Besucher Umfrage"-Arbeit [*MoMA Poll*, 1970]. Wir haben einfach versucht, all das zu integrieren und zu zeigen, dass diese Praktiken in direktem Bezug zu diesen Anfängen stehen – aber es gibt natürlich immer Lücken – und all dies zieht sich bis in die achtziger Jahre.

Barry: Ich wollte nur zwei Punkte hinzufügen. Es ist wichtig, über die Interdisziplinarität minimalistischer Kunst zu sprechen. Ich denke, dass sie mehr als jede andere Kunstform tatsächlich Ideen von außerhalb der Kunstarena auf sehr offensichtliche Weise in ihre Praxis integriert hat. Dies ist insbesondere in der Arbeit von Robert Smithson ziemlich gut dokumentiert, sogar Rosalind Krauss hat darüber geschrieben. Wenn man noch ein wenig weiter zurückgeht, in die dreißiger und vierziger Jahre, wenn man sich den Rückgang der Bewegung des sozialen Realismus in den USA und den Marshall Plan anschaut, Serge Guilbauts Buch

schreibt darüber im Detail. Und Barnett Newmans Schriften über diese Zeit sind ebenfalls sehr interessant.

Draxler: Der Rockefeller-Fall, den wir hier erläutert haben, geht in eine ähnliche Richtung. Er ist eine Art Vorgeschichte der Institutionskritik.

Barry: Die WPA-Bewegung [Works Progress Administration's Federal Art Project] in den USA ist in diesem Zusammenhang auch interessant. Obwohl sie nicht offenkundig über diese Themen gesprochen hat, war die Art und Weise, wie Künstler*innen bestimmte gesellschaftliche Fragen behandelt haben, oft auf implizite Art institutionskritisch. Soweit ich weiß, wurde dazu leider nicht geforscht. Vielleicht weiß jemand hier mehr darüber. Aber aus der Korrespondenz zwischen den Mitgliedern geht hervor, dass in dieser Zeit viele Arbeiten entstanden sind, die durch das Mittel der Repräsentation auf bestimmte Themen aufmerksam gemacht haben.

Draxler: Also von der Art Workers' Coalition gibt es ein paar historische Texte dazu. Ich kann mich jetzt nicht mehr erinnern, wer genau diesen Punkt über die Fortsetzung einiger dieser Arbeiten aus den dreißiger und vierziger Jahren hervorhebt, diese sehr speziellen Gewerkschaftsbildungsprozesse der Künstler*innen und verschiedener Künstler*innengruppen.

Fraser: Das ist nicht so klar, aber das Verhältnis zwischen Künstler*innen und Institutionen, vor allem im Zusammenhang mit der Entwicklung, dass Künstler*innen institutionelle Rollen einnehmen, und durch diese sich wandelnden Sympathien, kuratorische Funktionen innerhalb ihrer

Arbeit und auch Kurator*innen, die ein Interesse an der Zusammenarbeit mit Künstler*innen entwickeln, anstatt die Arbeiten nur auszuleihen – dies war im Grunde, was wir versucht haben, aus einer sehr breiten Reihe von Auseinandersetzungen herauszuarbeiten, aus einer sehr komplexen Reihe von Auseinandersetzungen. Die anderen Dinge, die zu der Zeit bezüglich künstlerischer Praxis passierten, von denen wir keine Dokumentation haben, sind zum Beispiel Christian Boltanskis Ausstellungen, bei denen er museale Installationen aus Dingen produziert hat, die er in Privathaushalten gefunden hat, und Claes Oldenburgs *The Store* [1961], was wiederum ein völlig anderer Ansatz ist. Von Daniel Buren haben wir kein Material. Mit John Knight hatte ich eine etwas schwierige Situation als es darum ging, einen Weg zu finden, Material zu präsentieren, das die Art wie er seine Richtlinien entwickelt hat dokumentiert – bestimmte Honorarstrukturen, und bestimmte vertragliche Verhältnisse, mit denen er arbeitet. Und bei Michael Asher ist es ebenfalls kompliziert. Und Daniel Buren. Das sind drei Personen, die für ihre Arbeit in den frühen siebziger Jahren Honorarstrukturen entwickelt haben. Im Zusammenhang mit dem Begriff der Dienstleistung, den wir uns anschauen wollten. Was kuratorische Aktivitäten und solche Dinge angeht, fangen wir hier mit Group Material an, die 1980 aus Organisationen wie Artists Meeting for Cultural Change entsprangen, die sich in der zweiten Hälfte der siebziger Jahre bildeten. Dies waren Organisationen von Künstler*innen, die sich um nicht-künstlerische Ideen formierten. Group Material entsprang mehr daraus als einige der institutionskritischen Ansätze.

Dadurch hatten sie eine Art alternative Galerist*innen-Position – sie organisierten Ausstellungen, luden Menschen aus der Nachbarschaft ein, Arbeiten vorbeizubringen, inszenierten Ausstellungen in der U-Bahn und solche Dinge. Das schauen wir uns also hier an. Wir haben uns hauptsächlich auf Group Material und Louise Lawler konzentriert, die in den späten siebziger Jahren anfing, mit Werbematerial zu arbeiten, das Galerien rausschickten, mit Einladungskarten, Pressemitteilungen; sie hatte verschiedene Positionen in Institutionen und nutzte ihre Funktionen in Galerien als Teil ihrer Arbeit. Das hier ist der erste mir bekannte Fall, bei dem ein*e Künstler*in eine Installation aus einer Museumssammlung gemacht hat, und zwar war das Louise Lawlers Ausstellung *Home/Museum* im Wadsworth Atheneum [Kunstmuseum in Hartford, Connecticut] 1984. Damit fangen wir also in den achtziger Jahren an, um uns einige der damals aktuellen Praktiken und der Zusammenarbeit zwischen Künstler*innen und Institutionen anzuschauen. Obwohl es viele andere Beispiele und Ansätze gibt, die man sich ansehen könnte. Aber das ist, was wir haben.

Fred Wilson: Ich wollte nur noch ein anderes Beispiel aus den späten sechziger Jahren und frühen siebziger Jahren erwähnen, zeitgleich zur Art Workers' Coalition gab es die Spiral Group. Das war eine Schwarze Kunstgruppe in New York, die bestimmt auch an der Art Workers' Coalition beteiligt war, aber sie haben sich hauptsächlich über Fragen der Ausgrenzung zusammengefunden. Und was Aufmerksamkeit auf sie zog, war die Ausstellung *Harlem on My Mind* im Metropolitan Museum [in New York], die aus

Thomas Hovings [Direktor des Met] Bemühungen resultierte, Harlem ins Met zu bringen, aber fast zu einer ethnographischen Bemühung wurde und keine afroamerikanischen Künstler*innen zeigte. Es gab also einen riesigen Streik, und Treffen, die von der Spiral Group zu der Ausstellung organisiert wurden. Weißt du wann *Harlem on My Mind* war? Ich glaube es war 1969.

Bauer: Die Lücke für Deutschland ist enorm. Ich glaube ihr wisst, dass hier viel mehr aus Deutschland hätte gezeigt werden können.

Fraser: Ja. Wie ich vorhin sagte, wir haben nicht versucht, etwas Allumfassendes zu zeigen. Es wäre sicher möglich.

Publikum (Gislind Nabakowski): Werden Sie dann im Verlauf des Projekts europäische Zusammenhänge weiter erforschen?

Fraser: Ich habe mir zuerst den amerikanischen Kontext angesehen, also ich bin raus, ich habe…

(Gelächter)

Draxler: Europa ist so viel dezentralisierter, es gibt ganz viele verschiedene Entwicklungen und sehr unterschiedliche Orte. Es ist nicht so, als gäbe es ein [einziges] Museum für moderne Kunst. Die Situation ist also eine ganz andere. Ich meine, dieses Problem besteht überall. Es gibt einige europäische Institutionen, die die amerikanische Kunstszene sehr stark unterstützen, öffentliche Institutionen. Auch Universitäten. Christian kann euch erzählen, wie schwierig es ist, eine Stelle bei der Cooper Union [in New York] zu bekommen, und wie

leicht es für eine*n amerikanische*n Künstler*in ist, hier eine Stelle als Hochschullehrer*in zu bekommen.

Müller: In den USA ist es ungewöhnlich, dass jemand, der unterrichtet, nicht Amerikaner*in ist. Und Hans Haacke hat mir erzählt, dass man sich quasi nackt machen muss. Dafür muss man Anwälte teuer bezahlen…

Draxler: Es ist einfach zu vereinfachend, die europäische Entwicklung als defizitär zu beschreiben. Die Situation ist sehr komplex. Aber man hat eben nicht diesen Mainstream-Diskurs.

Guttmann: Wenigstens ist in Frankreich die Kritik an Museen sehr stark ausgeprägt. In dem Fall hat diese Kritik die Künstler*innen natürlich nicht in Richtung Dienstleistung geführt; im Gegenteil, sie hat sie eher dahin gelenkt, mehr Geld zu fordern. Meiner Meinung nach sollte diese Diskussion, wenn es um Frankreich geht, in den späten fünfziger Jahren beginnen. Was in gewisser Weise den Unterschied ausmacht, ist, dass '69 kam, nachdem Amerika sich ein ganzes Jahrzehnt der Welt in Form von Kunst präsentiert hatte. Und deswegen war '69, zum Höhepunkt des Vietnamkriegs, mit sehr viel politischem Aktivismus, ein Moment, bei dem Künstler*innen sich in New York der Kunst gegenüber positionieren konnten und das Gefühl hatten, etwas Sinnvolles zu tun. Das ist etwas schwer zu verstehen, denn hier ist das eine der ereignisreichsten Phasen der jüngeren Geschichte und alles, was diese Künstler*innen tun, ist, das Museum of Modern Art zu kritisieren – und die Bedeutung ihrer Aktivitäten ist offensichtlich. Aber gleichzeitig denke ich, dass

Kunst so eine zentrale Rolle in der Selbstdarstellung der Vereinigten Staaten gegenüber der Welt hatte, dass Leute, die Kunstpolitik machten, tatsächlich das Gefühl hatten, etwas extrem Wichtiges zu tun.

Fraser: Ja, aber es ging auch darum, aufzuräumen. Es geht nicht nur darum, was zu einer bestimmten Zeit „das Wichtigste auf der Welt ist.". Ich glaube, die wenigsten von uns leben ihr Leben so.

Guttmann: Das ist zu einfach. Ich denke, das ist zu einfach.

Fraser: Ein Teil davon ist strategisch, und das ist das Hans Haacke-Beispiel: Herrn Rockefeller dahin zu bringen, wo er so gut wie möglich aussehen will.

Guttmann: Ja, aber gleichzeitig fanden 1968 und '69 die Aufstände an der Columbia [University in New York] statt, man kann sich also vorstellen, es ist dieselbe Stadt, kulturell sehr ähnlich. Die Studierenden haben versucht aufzuräumen, und haben es tatsächlich geschafft, die ganze Bevölkerung zu mobilisieren. Sie haben die Aktivist*innen aus der Harlem Gemeinschaft dazu gebracht – ihr wisst schon, sie haben wirklich…

Fraser: Aber es gab auch Menschen in der Kunstszene, die in Gemeinschaften gearbeitet haben, die Teil der Bewegung waren, nochmals, die sich in der Antikriegsbewegung engagiert haben.

Wilson: Ja. Es ist alles das Gleiche, es ist alles das Gleiche.

Draxler: Es gab Paris, und es gab Düsseldorf, und es gab viele andere Orte. Dieselbe Protestbewegung, mehr oder weniger, hat auch hier [in Deutschland] eine Menge radikales Zeug produziert. Aber es ist unmöglich, diese Geschichten zu rekonstruieren. Man kommt immer wieder nur zu Figuren wie Jörg Immendorff oder Beuys. Beuys ist das am stärksten ausgeprägte Symptom dafür, wie diese Geschichte hier in Deutschland historisiert wurde. Wie konstruieren wir also Geschichten wie diese? Ist das überhaupt möglich?

Fraser: Ob es möglich ist – und es gibt so viele verschiedene Geschichten, über die man sprechen könnte – aber die Frage ist für mich, wo stehen wir und was ist unsere Geschichte?

Guttmann: Ich glaube nicht, dass sie nichts Interessantes gemacht haben, nur weil sie sich nicht an Aufständen beteiligt haben. Im Gegenteil, sie haben etwas Wichtiges getan, und wussten, dass sie etwas Wichtiges taten. Und das ist für mich der wirkliche Unterschied zwischen der europäischen und der amerikanischen Situation, nämlich dass Kunst in den sechziger Jahren in den Vereinigten Staaten sehr wichtig war und in Europa einfach nicht den gleichen Stellenwert hatte. Weil die ganze amerikanische Nachkriegskultur nach Europa verkauft wurde, in großen Ausstellungen wie der Biennale von Venedig und der documenta, so hat Amerika sich präsentiert.

Fraser: Das würde sich mehr auf Aktivitäten in Europa beziehen als in den Vereinigten Staaten. Ich weiß nicht, wie viele von diesen Künstler*innen wirklich viel in Europa gearbeitet haben. Als es

Demonstrationen in Venedig gab, ging es definitiv um amerikanischen Imperialismus und sein Verhältnis zur Ausbeutung der Kultur, und das Museum of Modern Art steht dahinter, aber man findet es nirgendwo in diesen Dokumenten [die für die Arbeitsgruppe gesammelt wurden]. Es geht dabei nicht um den internationalen Rat, es geht nicht um Programme in Lateinamerika, oder um die Programme in Europa, darum geht es nicht. Es geht dabei um etwas anderes.

Guttmann: Ja, aber das war eine Tatsache.

Fraser: War es das?

Guttmann: Ich denke schon, ja. Ich meine, es gibt Massaker in Vietnam, und man zerschneidet ein paar Blöcke und legt sie auf den Boden, wie Carl Andre.

Fraser: Viele Leute würden die gleiche Frage in Bezug darauf stellen, was man 1988 in New York macht, wo hunderttausende Menschen an AIDS sterben. Es ist also eine Frage dessen, wo man ist und was für eine Vergangenheit die eigene Vergangenheit ist, oder mit welcher man sich identifiziert. Für mich geht es darum, wo wir in unserer Praxis sind, in welche Art von Beziehungen wir involviert sind und zu fragen, was die gesellschaftlichen und politischen Möglichkeiten dieser Situationen und Beziehungen sind. Einige von uns arbeiten in Institutionen und einige von uns arbeiten auf unterschiedliche Art in Gemeinschaften. Und es gibt verschiedene Praktiken, die hier in diesem Raum gezeigt werden. Aber ich finde es sehr problematisch, eine Hierarchie zu konstruieren und sie als Grundlage

für eine Diskussion darüber zu nutzen, was wir hier gerade machen.

Bauer: Es gab eine sehr starke Bewegung in Europa und es gibt einige sehr herausragende Momente der Freundschaft. Ich meine, es kann nicht alles repräsentiert werden, das ist klar. Man kann keinen Vergleich zwischen amerikanischer und europäischer Geschichte machen, denn wie du gesagt hast [Helmut], es ist dezentralisiert. Aber es gab viele Bewegungen, viele Projekte.

Fraser: Nun ja, ich betrachte das als eine Fallstudie von New York und den dortigen Geschehnissen. Es entspricht nicht dem, was ich gern hätte, aber es ist, was es ist.

Publikum (Gislind Nabakowski): Sammeln Sie also weiterhin Material? Was suchen Sie im Moment?

Fraser: Nun, ich war daran interessiert, mehr Material über die konkreten Beziehungen der Kunstarbeiter*innen zu sammeln, in ihren Arbeiten und hinter den Arbeiten. Ich habe viel Zeit damit verbracht, Kontakt mit verschiedenen Künstler*innen aufzunehmen, um darüber zu sprechen: Material nicht teilen zu wollen oder nicht teilen zu können.

Bischoff: Ich glaube nicht, dass wir versuchen sollten, die gesamte Geschichte zusammenzubekommen – es ist gut, einige Aspekte zu haben, um die Diskussion weiterzuführen und wenn bestimmte Aspekte falsch sind, dann hören wir auf. Aber wir sollten nicht versuchen, ihr gerecht zu werden, weil es zu viel ist.

Fraser: Ich wurde hierher eingeladen, aber als Amerikanerin finde ich es nicht angemessen, deutsche

Kulturproduktion und politische Aktivität der letzten fünfundzwanzig Jahre auf mich zu nehmen. Das kann ich nicht machen. Ich möchte darüber wirklich mehr wissen, aber so etwas könnte auch als eine Art Aneignung funktionieren.

Bauer: Dann glaube ich, muss der Kontext für diese Materialauswahl einfach klar sein. Das Land dieser Forschung.

Green: Aber wenn es ein fortlaufendes Projekt ist, dann könnten wir schauen, was die Studierenden tun wollen.

Fraser: Ja, denn wenn das hier [das *Services* Projekt] weiter reist, ist es meiner Meinung nach nicht für Institutionen mit allgemeinem Publikum geeignet, sondern eher für solche Institutionen, die sich auf die eine oder andere Art mit Bildungsprogrammen beschäftigen. Und dass dies [die Kunstraum-Ausgabe] der Anfang ist und dass Menschen es mit ihrer eigenen Forschung erweitern. Ich hoffe, dass dies ein Katalysator ist.

(Die Arbeitsgruppe beendet ihre Diskussion des an der Pinnwand angebrachten Forschungsmaterials und geht für weitere Gespräche zurück zum Tisch.)

Guttmann: Die Frage ist also: Wie kamen sie dazu zu glauben, dass es wichtig war? Haben Personen, die zu der Zeit Kunst gemacht haben, geglaubt, dass was sie machten wirklich wichtig war? Die Antwort ist nicht so eindeutig, einige glaubten es und einige nicht. Aber die Art Workers' Coalition hat es geglaubt und zwar aus gutem Grund. Die Frage ist –

Fraser: Was ist der Grund?

Guttmann: Ja und ich würde sagen, dass es etwas damit zu tun hatte, dass sie die Kunst dazu benutzt haben, die Herausforderungen der Welt darzustellen.

Fraser: Was ich sagen wollte, ist, dass es mit einer kontinuierlichen Untersuchung der Künstler*innen zu tun hatte, ihrer eigenen Bedingungen und den Verbindungen ihrer Praktiken, und darauf konzentriere ich mich. Und die Erweiterung hiervon, von formellen und institutionellen Bedingungen, führt die Diskussion in einem viel weiteren Sinne ins Politische.

Cahan: Was ist deiner Ansicht nach die Verbindung zwischen den Sachen aus den sechziger und siebziger Jahren, die du präsentiert hast, und dem was jetzt gerade passiert?

Fraser: Was ich am stärksten herausarbeiten wollte, waren die kollaborativen Beziehungen zwischen Künstler*innen und Museumsfachleuten, die in diesem Moment des Aufruhrs entstanden sind, und zwar darüber, was zu einem gewissen Grad professionelle Interessen waren, die allerdings durch die Identifikation einer Reihe von sozialen Konflikten, Klassenkonflikten bedingt waren. Die Interessen der Künstler*innen und Museumsfachleute standen in Konflikt mit den Interessen des Vorstands. Die Funktion und Geschichte dieser Institutionen wurden durch diese Interessen definiert. Ich denke, das bezieht sich absolut auf das, worum es hier geht: Es geht um neu entstehende Formen der Zusammenarbeit und des Konflikts zwischen Künstler*innen und Kurator*innen und

Künstler*innen und Institutionen, aber vor allem Museumsfachleuten.

Draxler: Wir sollten mit den Vorträgen anfangen.

Fraser: Seid ihr alle schon erschöpft? Judith, Renée und Fred wollten heute Vorträge zum Thema „Den Institutionen Dienen" halten und ihr drei könnt euch denke ich selbst die Reihenfolge aussuchen, in der ihr sprechen möchtet.

Barry: Wer möchte zuerst?

Green: Du hast mehr begleitendes Bildmaterial [Fred].

Wilson: Ja, das wird ziemlich schnell gehen, also können wir es auch gleich hinter uns bringen. Ich dachte, ich würde ganz kurz drei Projekte vorstellen und einfach über die Probleme sprechen, die bei diesen Projekten aufgetreten sind, ganz offen. Wie ich vorhin erwähnte, habe ich in Museen [in New York] gearbeitet – dem American Museum of Natural History, dem Metropolitan und dem American Craft Museum, in all ihren Vermittlungsabteilungen gleichzeitig, Mitte der siebziger Jahre. Diese Erfahrung hat mich wirklich nicht nur das Verhältnis von Künstler*innen zu Museen in Frage stellen lassen, sondern auch wie Museen Materialien und Informationen aus verschiedenen Kulturen präsentieren und wie unterschiedlich sie in den jeweiligen Kontexten sind, in denen sie diese präsentieren. Obwohl sie im Grunde alle kulturelle Produktion verschiedener Gruppen sind, werden sie auf unterschiedliche Weise präsentiert. Nach dieser Erfahrung fing ich also an, in Galerien zu arbeiten und führte Projekte für Künstler*innen durch, und leitete letztendlich eine Galerie [Longwood Art Gallery] in der South Bronx für Künstler*innen und hatte dort Besucher*innen aus der lokalen Gemeinschaft und aus der Kunstgemeinschaft, die sich in die South Bronx wagte. Eine der ersten Ausstellungen, die ich [in der Longwood] gemacht habe hieß: *Rooms with a View: The Struggle Between Culture, Content, and the Context of Art*. Das war nicht die erste Ausstellung, sondern vielleicht die dritte oder vierte. Und das war 1987. Das ist die erste Reihe von Bildern, diese hier, und im Grunde war das in einer ehemaligen öffentlichen Schule in der South Bronx, und es gab noch andere Räume in dem Gebäude, ein Alphabetisierungsprogramm für Erwachsene, ein Wohn-Reha-Programm – [der Künstler und Aktivist] Tim Rollins und K.O.S. waren im Gebäude – und eine städtische Agentur für Wohnungswesen. Im Grunde genommen war es wie P.S. 1, aber es war viel stärker in die Gemeinschaft eingebunden; viele Leute aus der Gemeinschaft kamen auch aus anderen Gründen, außerhalb des Kunstprogramms, durch das Gebäude. Die ganze zweite Etage des Gebäudes, in dem sich Atelierräume befanden, war ein weiterer wichtiger Aspekt des Galerieprogramms, da ständig Künstler*innen dort waren, die sich auf verschiedenen Ebenen mit der lokalen Gemeinschaft zusammengetan haben, indem sie sie engagiert haben, Dinge für sie zu erledigen, oder indem sie selbst für Leute aus der Gemeinschaft gearbeitet haben. Es gab eine ständige Interaktion, die über das hinausging, was ich in der Galerie gemacht habe, und die auch der Galerie selbst geholfen hat. Die Ausstellung, die ich gemacht habe, umfasste drei verschiedene Räume, die umgestaltet wurden.

Ein Raum sah aus wie ein Salon der Jahrhundertwende, ungefähr; ein Raum sah ungefähr aus wie ein ethnographisches Museum; und ein Raum war ganz und gar „White Cube". Dreißig Künstler*innen haben daran teilgenommen, und ich sagte ihnen, dass ich mit ihren Arbeiten experimentieren würde, dass es keine reguläre Ausstellung sein würde. Jede*r Künstler*in hatte zwei Arbeiten in der Ausstellung, eine im „White Cube" und eine in einem der anderen Räume. Die ursprüngliche Idee war, die Ausstellung in drei verschiedenen Museen zu veranstalten: dem Natural History Museum, dem Met und der Frick [Collection in New York]. Natürlich wurde das nichts, also habe ich sie nur an diesem einen Ort organisiert. Die Arbeiten veränderten in diesen Räumen wirklich ihre Bedeutung. Im ethnographischen Raum zum Beispiel, wo auf den Beschriftungen so etwas stand wie „Keramikobjekte, gefunden im Raum Williamsburg, Brooklyn, spätes 20. Jahrhundert", aber sonst weder die Namen der Künstler*innen, noch irgendetwas anderes im Raum waren. Wobei die Namen aller Künstler*innen im „White Cube"-Raum standen, und daher hat allein das Umfeld die Bedeutung dieser Arbeiten verändert, und das hat wirklich mein Interesse daran geweckt, das Umfeld, in dem Kunst gezeigt wird, neu zu beurteilen.

Danach habe ich ein paar Ausstellungen mit meinen eigenen Objekten gemacht, und dann wurde ich von verschiedenen Museen eingeladen, das zu tun. Die nächsten Fotos [in meiner Präsentation] stammen aus der Maryland Historical Society, einem sehr öden Museum in Baltimore, Maryland, alles ur-amerikanische Geschichtsobjekte,

Silber und Stühle und solche Sachen, ältere Gemälde und Objekte aus dem 19. Jahrhundert. Im Grunde genommen habe ich aus dieser Sammlung Dinge ausgesucht und den dritten Stock mit ihren eigenen Objekten umgestaltet – mit vielen Dingen, die sie in ihrem Archiv hatten, von denen sie gar nicht wussten, dass sie sie haben oder nie geplant hatten, zu zeigen. Ich habe sie herausgeholt und ausgestellt. Wie ihr hier sehen könnt, habe ich neben dem klassischen Silber dort Fußketten von Sklaven mit der Beschriftung „Metallarbeit 1700–1870" platziert, die in der Sammlung waren, aber nie ausgestellt wurden. Die ganze Ausstellung zeigte also nicht nur Dinge aus ihrer Sammlung, die noch nie gezeigt worden waren, sie ergab auch eine Geschichte des Museums und der Gemeinschaft, über die sie nicht sprechen wollten, und möglicherweise die Geschichte der afroamerikanischen Menschen in diesem Teil der Vereinigten Staaten, die Ausgrenzung oder Missbrauch erlebt haben, sowie den Standpunkt des Museums dazu. Das war im Wesentlichen das, was ich mir angeschaut habe – wie das Museum sich selbst durch seine Sammlungsmuster sah, seit Beginn der Sammlung 1840. Sodass es wirklich zeigte, wo sie stehen, durch das, was sie sammelten und was nicht. Ich könnte immer weiter darüber sprechen, aber das werde ich nicht.

Um diese Ausstellung machen zu können, da ich nicht aus Baltimore stamme, habe ich im Grunde das ganze Personal der Institution interviewt – vom Geschäftsführer bis hin zu der Frau, die das Silber gereinigt hat, zum Aufsichtspersonal und dem Technik- und Reinigungspersonal. Nur um ein Gefühl dafür zu bekommen, wie sie zum Museum standen, wie sie ihre Stadt und ihre Arbeit empfanden, und um ein wenig mehr über die Institution und ihre Hierarchien und Verhältnisse zu lernen. Was am Ende auch passiert ist – etwas, das ich jetzt ausnutze, aber zu der Zeit war es nur per Zufall – dass ich durch meine Anwesenheit – weil ich kein Kurator bin und ich nicht innerhalb der etablierten Museumsstruktur fungiere – auf verschiedenen Ebenen Informationen vom Personal erfragen konnte. Informationen, die sie niemandem erzählen konnten, weil sie außerhalb der Institution mit niemandem sprechen können, weil sie nicht wollen, dass Kolleg*innen aus anderen Häusern wissen, dass es innerhalb der Institution Probleme gibt. Und dann sprechen sie nicht miteinander, weil sie generell nicht miteinander sprechen – was eine weitere Sache ist, mit der ich mich gerne beschäftige, wenn ich mit Museen arbeite. Und so wurde ich Resonanzkörper für viele ihrer Probleme und im Grunde Bestandteil der Institution. Dabei stellte ich auch fest, dass ich kooperieren musste, um das zu tun, was ich wollte, und dafür auch manches aufgeben musste, was bedeutet, dass ich nicht umhergehe und alles herumerzähle, was ich über die Institution erfahren habe, weil die nächste Institution mir wahrscheinlich nicht erlauben würde, das zu tun, was ich vorhabe. Ich tue also immer noch, was ich tun will, plappere aber nicht darüber, nachdem ich die Institution verlassen habe. Das erlaubt mir in anderen Institutionen eine gewisse Autonomie.

Was in dieser Situation [an der Maryland Historical Society] außerdem passierte war, dadurch, dass ich verschiedene Personalebenen in das Projekt einbezog, hat sich das Verhältnis zwischen einigen Personen verändert. Manche Personen aus dem unteren Personal waren sogar physisch an dem Projekt beteiligt. Ich habe manche Mitarbeiter*innen auf Video aufgenommen, so wurden sie Teil der Bildsprache der Ausstellung, da ich Videos und Ton usw. verwendet habe. So wusste das Technik- und Reinigungspersonal mehr darüber, worum es in der Arbeit ging, als die kuratorischen Mitarbeiter*innen. Wenn jemand kam, um die Ausstellung zu sehen, egal mit wem sie sprachen, wusste derjenige sehr viel über das Projekt. Und die Kolleg*innen wussten das. Da es um afroamerikanische Geschichte ging, konnte das Technik- und Reinigungspersonal viel besser erklären, worum es ging, als die kuratorischen Mitarbeiter*innen, die nicht Afroamerikaner*innen waren und außer, dass sie mit dem Technik- und Reinigungspersonal zu tun hatten, ansonsten überhaupt keinen Kontakt zu Afroamerikaner*innen hatten. Auf gewisse Weise hat sich also ihre Beziehung während meiner Ausstellung verändert.

Ein weiterer Aspekt, der seit dieser Ausstellung einen großen Unterschied macht, ist, dass das Projekt großen Anklang in der Museumsgemeinschaft und in der Baltimore Gemeinschaft fand. Weil Fragen über ethnische Herkunft [im Englischen benutzt der Sprecher das Wort „race"] in Baltimore nie diskutiert wurden. Sie waren immer nur unter der Oberfläche. Keiner wollte darüber sprechen, weil alle Angst davor hatten, was passieren würde, sobald man es erwähnte, und weil ich es angesprochen habe, war die Erleichterung darüber groß, dass sie es nicht zur Sprache bringen mussten. So konnte ein Dialog zwischen den verschiedenen Gemeinschaften entstehen. Denn um dieses Projekt zu machen, habe ich nicht nur mit der Museumsgemeinschaft gesprochen, sondern auch mit anderen Gemeinschaften in der Gegend von Baltimore. Ich bin zu Schwarzen Historiker*innen und Personen vor Ort gegangen, die einfach viel über die Geschichte ihrer Familien wussten. Dadurch [durch diese Zusammenarbeit] kamen sie ins Museum, und so entstanden neue Wege der Zusammenarbeit, die es vor meinem Projekt nicht gab. Jetzt ist es ein Jahr her, bei dieser Institution, und sie haben mich wieder eingeladen, um eine permanente Ausstellung genau dieser Arbeit zu machen, weil sie so gut ankam. Und weil sie so gut ankam, konnten sie sich ohne Angst hinter die Themen stellen, die ich mit der Arbeit angesprochen habe. Was Museen nicht immer anerkennen wollen, ist die implizite Kritik solcher Arbeiten. Da dieses Projekt sich mit ethnischer Herkunft [im Englischen benutzt der Sprecher das Wort „race"] auseinandersetzte, konnten sie für sich selbst die Kritik an ihrer Institution verbergen. Sie betrachteten es als gute Tat in der Auseinandersetzung mit ethnischer Herkunft und „Rasse". Aber tatsächlich war es eine Kritik an ihrer Institution. Das war für jeden völlig verständlich, der es sich anschaute, aber für das Museum selbst war das der Aspekt, den sie in Vorträgen über diese Ausstellung nicht einmal erwähnten. Aber was es verursacht, wenn Menschen kommen, um die Ausstellung zu sehen, ist, dass sie diese Fragen stellen, während sie in der Institution herumlaufen, wo andere Dinge sind, und sie fragen, warum bestimmte Dinge nicht da sind.

Jetzt, da [das Museum] mit dieser Frage konfrontiert wurde,

sind weitere kulturelle Fragen in Bezug auf seine Ausstellungspraxis im Zusammenhang mit anderen Gemeinschaften als der Afroamerikanischen aufgeworfen worden. Das ist eine Institution, die im Grunde privat war, die sich mit niemandem auseinandersetzen musste, weil sie viel Geld erhalten hatte, um diesen Ort zu finanzieren. Und meine Ausstellung wurde tatsächlich von einem der Vorstandsmitglieder mit „Oh, diese Farbige Installation" beschrieben. Sie waren also wirklich weit entfernt sogar davon, womit sich ihre Museumskolleg*innen beschäftigten. Ich denke, meine Praxis ermöglicht den Personen innerhalb von Institutionen, die mehr Visionen haben als manch andere, es befähigt sie, etwas mit ihrer Vision zu tun, denn was ich getan habe, zerstört nicht ihre…Sie sehen, dass es nicht das Gebäude einstürzen lässt. Also befähigt es sie, etwas auszuprobieren, was sie vorher nicht ausprobiert hätten. Ich betrachte es, je nach Institution, danach, wie viel sie verbessern werden, wie viel sie verändern werden. In dieser Institution in Maryland machen sie sehr kleine Schritte, aber ich betrachte es trotzdem als kleine Schritte [in die richtige Richtung], da die Gemeinschaften vor Ort nun die Institution fragen: „So, warum tun Sie jetzt nicht das?" Eines der Dinge, die mir an diesen Projekten gefällt, ist, dass sie Gemeinschaften darin bestärken, Institutionen zu fragen: „Warum machen Sie das nicht? Warum machen Sie nicht so eine Ausstellung?" Allein das Beispiel macht ihnen etwas Feuer unter dem Hintern, und zwar aus dem Grund, weil ich mit den Gemeinschaften spreche, was Museen generell nicht tun.

Ich glaube, diese Ausstellung [an der Maryland Historical Society] hat hauptsächlich historische Museen beeinflusst, weniger Kurator*innen, aufgrund der Art, wie ich das Material eingesetzt habe. Selbstverständlich haben schon viele Personen Installationen in historischen Museen gemacht, aber historische Museen in den USA sind nicht so sehr mit [dieser Art von Projekt] vertraut. Es war direkt an sie und die Art und Weise gerichtet, wie sie mit ihrem Material umgehen und wie sie das Publikum ansprechen. Im vergangenen Jahr haben mich viele Personen gefragt, ob ich in ihre Museen kommen würde, um [in ihrem Haus] dasselbe zu tun. Ich mache nicht genau dasselbe, wenn ich dort bin, aber es hat sich daraus eine Möglichkeit entwickelt, in ein paar Museen hereinzukommen. Wegen ihrer naiven Vorstellung davon, was sie glauben, dass ich tun werde: sie denken, durch mich kommen alle Afroamerikaner*innen der Gegend ins Museum. Was nie meine Intention ist. Aber es ist, auf ihre naive oder rassistische Art, ein Grund, mich einzuladen. Und dann nutze ich das einfach aus und bringe es in die Richtung, in die es dann eben geht, wenn ich in der jeweiligen Institution bin.

Eine weitere Situation, die ich erlebe, ist, dass wenn Leute mich einladen, sie feststellen, dass ich dieser Außenseiter in ihrer Institution bin, dass ich dann zu einem Museumstherapeuten werde. Die Mitarbeiter*innen wollen mir einfach von all ihren Problemen erzählen, die sie mit den verschiedenen Personen in ihrem Museum haben. Das ist etwas unangenehm, weil es nicht das ist, was ich vorhabe, wenn ich in eine Institution gehe, aber es scheint etwas zu sein, das immer häufiger passiert, weil Institutionen wissen, dass sie sich verändern müssen, aber keine Ahnung haben, was sie tun sollen.

Die dritte Installation [in meinem Vortrag] ist am Seattle Art Museum, ein übergreifendes Kunstmuseum, und die Installation war überall im Museum zu finden. Ich habe mir im Grunde ihre Sammlung angeschaut und Dinge an falschen Orten platziert – die mir als die richtigen Orte erschienen. Aber für das Museum habe ich sie an den falschen Orten platziert, was die verschiedenen Kurator*innen dazu zwang, miteinander zu sprechen, was sie in der Regel in Museen nicht tun – Kurator*innen für dekorative Künste sprechen nie mit den Kurator*innen für indigene Kunst, Kurator*innen für indigene Kunst sprechen nie mit den Kurator*innen für zeitgenössische Kunst und so weiter und so fort. Wobei natürlich alle Objekte miteinander zu tun haben. Also habe ich sie im Grunde dazu gezwungen, miteinander und auch mit Mitarbeiter*innen zu sprechen, die mehr mit dem Publikum zu tun haben, ob mit Café-Mitarbeiter*innen oder dem Aufsichtspersonal. Um Feedback dazu zu bekommen, wie das Pulikum auf ihre und auf meine Ausstellungen reagiert hat. Der neuste Nebeneffekt, der mir aufgefallen ist, ist der Katalog, den sie zusammenstellen. Ich war daran nicht wirklich beteiligt, aber es sieht so aus, als hätten ganz im Sinne meiner Ausstellung alle Mitarbeiter*innen ihre Meinung dazu abgegeben, was der Katalog sein und wie er aussehen sollte. Der Kurator, der mich für die Ausstellung eingeladen hat, liefert also keine Meistererzählung des Projektes ab. Einige Kurator*innen und Mitarbeiter*innen haben dem Chefkurator des Projektes gesagt, dass ein Ausstellungsüberblick von ihm [allein] für dieses Projekt nicht angemessen sei. Also haben alle besprochen, wie der Prozess ablief.

Ich weiß nicht, ob dieses Durchbrechen von Hierarchien auch über
meine Anwesenheit hinaus bestehen
bleibt, aber in diesem Moment ist es
mir jedenfalls aufgefallen. Ich denke,
dabei belasse ich es und komme
später nochmal darauf zurück.

Fraser: Vielen Dank, Fred. Judith?

Barry: Also, soll ich Dias zeigen?
Ich kann es nicht in zehn Minuten
machen, wenn ich Dias zeige.

Draxler: Ich finde es ist absolut notwendig, sie zu sehen.

Fraser: Kannst du ein paar von ihnen
zeigen?

Barry: Ja, ich kann ein Projekt
zeigen.

Fraser: Richtig, das hatte ich so
gedacht, weil du vier Projekte hast.
Also kannst du dich vielleicht auf
eines konzentrieren.

Barry: Nun, ich kann über die anderen sprechen, aber nur Dias von
einem zeigen. Und noch eine Frage
ist, wo?

Fraser: Auf dem Projektor hinter dir.

Barry: Und soll ich ein Videoprojekt
zeigen?

Fraser: Welches Videoprojekt wolltest du zeigen? Wir wollten die Projekte als eine Art Sprungbrett nutzen,
um über die Themen zu sprechen,
die aufkamen, als du die Projekte
gemacht hast. Statt die Projekte im
Ganzen vorzustellen. In der Ausstellung [der *Services* Ausstellung] soll
es möglich sein, die Projekte richtig
anzusehen, aber wir haben jetzt nicht
die Zeit, alles durchzugehen.

(Stille)

Fraser: Renée, könntest du stattdessen vortragen?

Green: Ja, ich glaube, zehn Minuten
kann ich schaffen.

Fraser: Renée wird also als nächstes
präsentieren.

Green: Ich möchte mich auf ein
Projekt konzentrieren, an dem ich im
Moment arbeite, also es ist eigentlich eine fortlaufende Sache. Und
ich möchte auch ein paar Hinter-
grundinformation dazu geben, weil
ich vorher nicht wirklich viel gesagt
habe. Einen historischen Zusammenhang zu meiner Arbeisweise
zu geben, sollte ein wenig dabei
helfen. Mit einigen der Personen hier
habe ich tatsächlich zusammengearbeitet und sie haben etwas mit
der Entstehung einer Praxis zu tun.
Fred ist beispielsweise einer davon,
weil ich in den achtziger Jahren viel
in alternativen Räumen gearbeitet
habe, und ich habe an einem Ort
in Tribeca gearbeitet, den er im
Grunde genommen leitete, der Just
Above Midtown oder JAM hieß. Und
an diesen verschiedenen Orten zu
arbeiten, hat mir irgendwie erlaubt,
andere Möglichkeiten zu sehen
oder zumindest andere Praktiken,
die sich von den kommerziellen
Galerien abgehoben haben. Und wie
man Ausstellungen extrem kosten-
günstig hinbekommt, sowie diverse
improvisierte Arbeitsmethoden in
verschiedenen Gemeinschaften. Es
war eine spannende Zeit. Die Dinge,
die in diesen Räumen passierten,
waren im weiteren Sinne nicht
bekannt, aber sie waren es schon
innerhalb einer bestimmten Gemeinschaft von Menschen, die an
diesen Orten gearbeitet haben. Aber

was die kommerzielle Kunstszene betrifft, wurden diese Sachen nicht anerkannt, man wusste noch nicht mal von ihnen. Die Räume waren in der Bronx und in Tribeca, und das machte sie interessant. Aus dem Grund, weil sie kleine Nischenaktivitäten waren, die sich ebenfalls auf verschiedene Gemeinden auswirkten, wie zum Beispiel der Longwood Raum, den Fred früher geleitet hat.

Ich habe ebenfalls mit Susan Cahan am New Museum zusammengearbeitet, als ich dort als Künstlerin in der Vermittlungsabteilung arbeitete. Ich habe an einem Highschool-Kunstkritik-Projekt gearbeitet, das dazu diente, Kritik unter den Schüler*innen in öffentlichen Highschools zu verbreiten. Wir haben mit Lehrer*innen in den Schulen gearbeitet, die entweder im Fachbereich Englisch oder Geschichte tätig waren, und eine Art Lehrplan mit ihnen entwickelt, der meist auf einem Thema basierte, das wir, die Künstler*innen, vorgeschlagen haben, um zu sehen, ob die Lehrer*innen damit einverstanden waren. Während dieser Zeit habe ich auf verschiedene Weise mit anderen Organisationen gearbeitet, zum Beispiel an einer Art Medienkritik mit diesen Highschool-Schüler*innen und ebenfalls mit obdachlosen Schüler*innen in einer ganz anderen Situation, sowie mit zwölf- oder dreizehnjährigen Kindern am Bank Street College, das mit den Universitäten Columbia und Barnard zusammenhängt. Susan hat ein Beispielvideo von einem der Projekte, das wir am New Museum mit ihnen gemacht haben.

Wie auch immer, dies führt alles darauf hinaus, dass ich als Kuratorin am Drawing Center [in Manhattan] gearbeitet habe, und das Projekt, über das ich sprechen möchte, ist ein Projekt, zu dem mich das

Drawing Center [in Manhattan] als Künstlerin eingeladen hatte, nachdem meine Arbeit für sie beendet war. Sie wollten Förderung von der Lila Wallace Foundation beantragen, die Lila Wallace Reader's Digest Foundation, und das Stipendium hieß Arts International. Mit diesem Stipendium werden Künstler*innen ausgewählt, um mit verschiedenen Institutionen zu arbeiten, und die Künstler*innen reisen normalerweise in ein bestimmtes Land. Einige Länder werden vorgeschlagen, weil zu ihnen bereits Verbindungen bestehen. In gewisser Weise ist es wie eine Art Vereinte Nationen-Projekt, um freundschaftliche Beziehungen zwischen verschiedenen Ländern aufzubauen. In dem Jahr, in dem ich zur Teilnahme ausgewählt wurde, gab es ein paar Veränderungen – die Mitglieder des Auswahlkomitees und Vorstands wollten weg von den üblicherweise ausgewhälten Personen, deren Arbeit sich mehr mit Handwerk beschäftigte. Also wurde ich ausgewählt; Mark Dion ebenfalls.

Was ich hier an Dokumentation habe, ist unvollständig – es beinhaltet nicht alle Teile der Korrespondenz; es ist Material, das vor ungefähr zwei Jahren angefangen hat. Ende 1991 wurde ich eingeladen, und das Projekt steht noch aus. Nachdem ich eingeladen wurde, sollte ich ein Konzept darüber schreiben, was ich machen will und welches Land ich aussuchen würde. Ich entschloss mich, mich auf Portugal zu konzentrieren, wegen früherer Arbeiten über das Meer und den Sklavenhandel, die ich gemacht hatte. Ich suchte nach einem Ort, an dem die Spuren der afrikanischen Diaspora in der aktuellen Zeit sichtbar waren. Lissabon war ein Ort, an dem man sich das anschauen und auch historische Verbindungen mit

Afrika über das Meer nachverfolgen konnte. Das war eins der Dinge, die ich vorgeschlagen habe und die ich dann auch gemacht habe.

Ich wollte Material präsentieren, das diesen Prozess des Hin und Her beschreibt, der entsteht, wenn ein*e Künstler*in eingeladen wird, mit einer Institution zu arbeiten und die Einladung annimmt, mit der Institution zu arbeiten. Und den Versuch, eine Art Balance zu finden zwischen dem, was Künstler*innen versuchen zu tun, und dem, was die Institution versucht zu tun. Das Projekt war meiner Meinung nach ein Künstler*innenprojekt, aber das war natürlich nicht vollständig möglich, weil es alle möglichen erschwerenden Umstände gab. Zum Beispiel die Agenda des Drawing Centers, und der Vorstand muss besänftigt werden und verschiedene Dinge, die vielen institutionellen Strukturen gemein sind. Und der Schriftwechsel zeichnet den Konzeptionsprozess nach – wie es organisiert wurde und wie mein Konzept an die institutionelle Sprache angepasst wurde, damit es der Art und Weise entsprach, wie das Drawing Center es präsentieren wollte. Wie ich in ihre Agenda gepackt wurde, damit wir die Förderung zusammenbekamen. Die Korrespondenz zwischen uns, während ich weg war, die verschiedenen Rollen, die ich innehatte, während ich dort war.

Mein erster Vorschlag in diesem Anfangsstadium war, eine Ausstellung mit dem Drawing Center zu machen, die ich aus Landkarten aus einer Sammlung in Lissabon kuratieren würde. Dies veränderte sich im Laufe der Zeit und wurde zu dem, was es jetzt ist, nämlich ein Symposium – es wird keine Ausstellung geben – die im Moment *Negotiations in the Contact Zone* [„Verhandlungen in der Kontaktzone"] heißt. Der Begriff „Kontaktzone" ist aus einem Text adaptiert, den Mary Louise Pratt geschrieben hat, eine Professorin für vergleichende Literaturwissenschaft, die darüber als sprachwissenschaftlichen Begriff spricht, der aber auch in einem weiteren Sinne interpretiert werden könnte und zwar, um Interaktionen zu bezeichnen, die zwischen Menschen und Orten, die aus unterschiedlichen Orten kommen, stattfinden, die aber am gleichen Ort enden und die Bedingungen darüber, wie sie leben werden, aushandeln müssen. Das Projekt hat sich kontinuierlich verändert und verlagert, und ich habe die Einladungen dokumentiert, die ich an verschiedene Personen, die ich dort haben wollte, verschickt habe. Der Fokus war bisher eine Kombination aus Wissenschaftler*innen, Kulturproduzent*innen, Schriftsteller*innen, bildenden Künstler*innen. Einer der Schwerpunkte hat mit einer Neubeurteilung verschiedener theoretischer Ideen zu tun, die Mitte der achtziger Jahre wichtig waren. Und ich habe dabei an Bücher wie *Art after Modernism* gedacht und andere Publikationen, Dia Art Foundation-Publikationen. Ich wollte Personen einladen, die an deren Veranstaltungen teilgenommen hatten, sowie bestimmte Künstler*innen, denen die Themen bekannt waren und ihre Ideen und Praktiken um diese Neubeurteilung herum gestalteten. Ich denke, dieses Treffen hier hat auch etwas mit dieser Neubeurteilung zu tun. Das ist das Material, das ich mitgebracht habe, und vielleicht können wir über einige der Probleme sprechen, die bei dieser Art von Interaktion aufgetreten sind.

Barry: Ich habe verschiedene Arten von Arbeiten mitgebracht, mit denen ich mich beschäftige, manchmal zusammen mit dem Architekten Ken Saylor, das ist dann im Rahmen von Ausstellungsdesign. Und dann habe ich auch einige installative Arbeiten mitgebracht, die ich als Künstlerin mache, sowie kommerzielle Projekte, die Ken Saylor und ich beide machen. Also vier verschiedene Dokumente, die wir besprechen könnten. Es gibt zwei Fragen, die mir in Bezug auf die Idee ortspezifischer Praxis und institutionelle Rahmung sofort einfallen. Eine Perspektive darauf wäre, es als eine Art philosophischen Ansatz zu beschreiben, was meinem Ansatz entspricht. Das beinhaltet, den tatsächlichen Inhalt zu hinterfragen, den die Institution ins Zentrum ihrer Projekte rückt, im Gegensatz zu einigen sehr praktischen Fragen wie zum Beispiel: Wer ist das Publikum? Wie wird man bezahlt? Und so weiter. Denn was mir in der heutigen Diskussion auffällt, ist, dass vielfach über das Problem der Bezahlung oder sehr praktische Dinge gesprochen wird. Und wie ihr anhand meiner Dokumentation sehen könnt, tendiere ich in der Kunstwelt zum Beispiel dazu, sehr genaue Verträge zu schreiben, die tatsächlich viel detaillierter sind als die, die ich für meine kommerzielle Praxis schreibe. Der Grund dafür ist, dass die Geschäftsmethoden in der Kunstwelt so vage und lose sind, dass man die Dinge auf eine viel direktere Art ausformulieren muss, als man es oft bei einem kommerziellen Projekt muss. Ich denke, das hat viel damit zu tun, wie sich die Kunstwelt über die Jahre entwickelt hat, das könnt ihr in den Dokumenten, die wir mitgebracht haben, sehen.

Ein weiteres Thema, das ich daneben ansprechen möchte, ist die ganze Frage nach politischer Wirkung, also die Frage danach, wie Kultur Politik produziert. Ich zeige euch ein Ausstellungsdesign. Für mich und Ken beginnt es axiomatisch mit der Vorstellung, dass jeder Raum ideologisch ist, das ist innerhalb der Ausstellungsdesigns, die wir entworfen haben, eine Art gegebene Tatsache, und wir erwarten, dass wir alle mit den Konventionen aus unserer Geschichte relativ vertraut sind, daher bringen wir diesen Aspekt normalerweise nicht offen zur Sprache. Was wir stattdessen tun, ist, die kuratorische Praxis zu isolieren und unsere eigene Methode zu verwenden. Um also ein Beispiel zu nennen, werde ich dieses eine Projekt zeigen, das ich mit Brian Wallis 1987 im Clocktower [in New York] gemacht habe [das This Is Tomorrow Today hieß, hergeleitet von der Ausstellung This Is Tomorrow im Jahr 1956 in der Whitechapel Art Gallery, London]. Dabei ging es um die Arbeit der Independent Group, eine kollaborative Gruppe von Künstler*innen, Architekt*innen, Schriftsteller*innen und Designer*innen, die auf die Produktion einzelner Objekte verzichtete und stattdessen Ausstellungsdesigns für neue Formen von Kunsträumen produzierte. 1990 gab es eine Wanderausstellung über die Independent Group; sie begann in London und reiste zum MoCA [the Museum of Contemporary Art, Los Angeles]. 1987, vor dieser Wanderausstellung, entschieden Brian und ich, zwei Arbeiten aus der Gruppe im Clocktower zu zeigen. Es waren Richard Hamiltons Gruppe und Alison und Peter Smithsons Gruppe. Ich versuche, anhand dieses Beispiels zu zeigen, wie Ken und ich als Ausstellungsdesigner*innen versuchen, kuratorische Praxis zu erweitern, indem wir Ideen in den tatsächlichen Arbeiten ausformulieren. Einer der interessantesten Aspekte in den

Arbeiten der Independent Group ist, dass es einer der erste Momente in der jüngeren Kunstgeschichte war, in dem Fragen über Massenkultur in die Kunstwelt eingeführt wurden. Wir waren besonders daran interessiert, Richard Hamiltons Arbeiten gemeisam mit John Voelcker and John McHale zu reproduzieren. Er hat uns die Pläne gegeben und wir haben versucht, die Arbeit zu reinszenieren, eine Struktur, durch die man hindurchgehen konnte, und in der Struktur gab es ganz viele Dinge zum Anfassen. Im Raum selbst gab es auch Musik.

Dieses Bild ist von 1956 aus der Whitechapel Gallery in London. Wir haben Clipart [herausgetrennte Magazinseiten] gezeigt, die alle Mitglieder der Independent Group sammelten. Wenn Studierende zu Besuch kamen, konnten sie erzählen, dass jemand diese Magazinseiten in den achtziger Jahren arrangiert hatte, nicht in den fünfziger Jahren. Den Studierenden fiel dieser subtile ideologische Aspekt nicht auf. Dieses Material wurde von der Independent Group gesammelt, weil Konsumkultur nach dem Zweiten Weltkrieg in Großbritannien nicht verfügbar war, also gingen sie in die USA, und kehrten mit Koffern voller Zeitschriften, Platten und anderen Konsumgütern zurück. In der oberen Etage haben wir die Arbeiten von Alison and Peter Smithson präsentiert, die mit Eduardo Paolozzi und Nigel Henderson zusammenarbeiteten, und sie bauten Patio und Pavillon, die Britische Vorstellung davon, was das Minimum zum Überleben in einer Stadt war, und das waren ein Garten und ein Schuppen.

Worüber ich darüber hinaus auch sprechen wollte, ist meine Herangehensweise an Installationskunst. Meine Methode ist forschungsbasiert. Ich habe das Konzept eines aktuellen Projekts auf Korsika mitgebracht. Ihr werdet sehen, dass der dazugehörige Vertrag detaillierter ist als andere Verträge aus meiner Dokumentation. Das Projekt besteht aus mehr konkreten Leistungen als alle anderen Verträge hier, und der Grund ist, nochmal – neben der Idee, eine Arbeitsmethode deutlich zu machen – auch der Wunsch, einen Raum zu gestalten, in dem die Institution und die Künstler*innen sich gemeinsam einigen können, wie Renée sagte, auf bestimmte Fragen. Ich denke, dass sich in der Ausstellungsdesign-Arbeit die ich mache, sowie in meiner eigenen Kunstpraxis ein spezifisches Verhältnis zwischen Künstler*innen und Kurator*innen entwickelt. Ich denke, wenn ich an Projekten arbeite, mache ich sie sowohl in Bezug auf den institutionellen Rahmen, als auch in Bezug auf den kuratorischen Rahmen, den wir im Laufe der Zeit entwickeln. Diese Verhältnisse sind meiner Meinung nach sehr schwer zu beschreiben und mehrdeutig. Aber nichtsdestotrotz sind sie die Basis meiner individuellen Praktiken. Ich weiß nicht, wie andere darüber denken, aber für mich persönlich ist das eine sehr wichtige Frage. Ich glaube, das ist alles, was ich sagen wollte.

Wilson: Ich habe eine Frage. Findest du, dass es einen Unterschied in der Art und Weise gibt, wie die Institution dich behandelt, wenn du als Künstlerin eine Installation machst, oder wenn du als Künstlerin einen Installationsentwurf für die Arbeit von jemand anderem entwickelst?

Barry: Nicht im ersten Moment. Eines der Projekte, die ich nicht gezeigt habe, war ein Projekt, das ich als Ausstellungsdesignerin für *Damaged Goods* [am New Museum in New York, 1986] gemacht habe. Das Projekte habe ich als in der Ausstellung ausstellende Künstlerin gemacht, und ich sollte beiläufig dazu sagen, dass ich nicht wirklich einen Unterschied zwischen meinen verschiedenen Praktiken mache. Wohingegen Ken, der Architekt, mit dem ich zusammenarbeite, auf Basis abrechenbarer Stunden arbeitet, ein Konzept, das es in der Kunstwelt einfach nicht gibt. Wenn man sich seine Verträge also genau anschaut, sieht man, dass alles stundenweise abgerechnet wird, wie es in vielen dienstleistenden Berufsfeldern üblich ist. Die Arbeit von Künstler*innen wird nicht stundenweise abgerechnet; das ist also ein riesiger Unterschied. Was im Laufe der Zeit geschieht, kommt üblicherweise auf die jeweilige Institution an, und man stellt fest, dass man verschiedene Arbeitsweisen für verschiedene Institutionen benötigt.

Bischoff: Darf ich eine Frage stellen? Hast du an einer Ausstellung teilgenommen, die 1988 in Los Angeles am Temporary Contemporary [the Museum of Contemporary Art, Los Angeles] stattfand?

Barry: Ja.

Bischoff: Wir haben vorhin über diese Ausstellung diskutiert und darüber nachgedacht, wie man den kuratorischen Rahmen festlegt. Was ist für dich der erste Schritt, um den kuratorischen Rahmen zu entwickeln?

Barry: Wir verwenden eine traditionelle Methode aus der Architektur, die ich sehr praktikabel finde, die auch die Identifikation

des Programms umfasst. Wenn Ken und ich mit einer*m Kurator*in zusammenarbeiten, versuchen wir, das ganze Material zu lesen, das der- oder diejenige vorbereitet hat, um die Hauptausstellungsziele herauszuarbeiten. Was dann oft passiert, ist, dass wir am Ende eine Erstrecherche und -analyse durchführen, damit wir diese Ziele besser angehen können. Eine der Herausforderungen des Projekts, das ich gerade gezeigt habe – und das ist anders als in herkömmlichen Ausstellungen – ist, dass wir als Ausstellungsdesigner*innen die Arbeiten in der Ausstellung sowohl reproduzieren, installieren, als auch zeigen. In der Independent Group Ausstellung haben wir alle Arbeiten produziert. In einem Museum ist es normalerweise so, dass ein*e Künstler*in mit einer Arbeit kommt und man installiert sie. Bei zwei der anderen Ausstellungen, die wir für das New Museum gemacht haben, mussten wir die Arbeiten ebenfalls anfertigen, was wiederum viele der Arbeitsproblematiken verändert. Es ist also für jede Ausstellung spezifisch, und wir verwenden einen konventionellen Ansatz aus der Architektur, um das Programm zu identifizieren, und von da aus gehen wir durch die verschiedenen Designphasen.

Bischoff: Sollen wir das jetzt besprechen, oder später?

Draxler: Es wäre sehr schön, die *Damaged Goods* Dias anzusehen, weil man dort auch – als Künstler*in und als Designer*in – dieses kuratorische Engagement, bis zu einem gewissen Grad, für die Künstler*innen in der Ausstellung sieht. Ich denke, das ist eine sehr wichtige Arbeit, die wir nicht verpassen sollten.

Fraser: Ich denke, wir können über diese Themen sprechen. Ich denke, es gibt schon viele Fragen.

Müller: Eine Frage, die ich habe ist: wenn ihr diese Arbeiten für die Ausstellungen baut, wem gehören diese Arbeiten dann, wenn die Ausstellung abgebaut wird?

Barry: Da wir beauftragt werden, üblicherweise nicht uns. Üblicherweise gehören sie dem Museum.

Müller: Aber New Museum oder Clocktower, die haben doch keine Sammlungen.

Barry: Wir haben einen Teil der Clocktower Ausstellung an das ICA [Institute of Contemporary Arts] in London verkauft. Wir persönlich haben kein Geld dafür bekommen, aber die Ausstellungsproduktion war teuer für das Clocktower, insofern war das gut…

Müller: Ihr habt kein zusätzliches Honorar bekommen.

Barry: Nein. Für diese Ausstellung habe ich $1000 bekommen.

Fraser: Du sagtest, dass eure Herangehensweise an Ausstellungsdesign auf der Idee basiert, dass jeder Raum ideologisch ist, und ich würde dann annehmen, dass ihr euer Installationsdesign in gewisser Weise als Ideologiekritik betrachtet.

Barry: Nicht unbedingt Kritik, aber wir gehen davon aus, dass es eine oder mehrere ideologische Positionen gibt, die man gegenüber der Arbeit im Raum aufgreifen kann.

Fraser: Weil du das Wort „erweitern" benutzt hast und „den kuratorischen Ansatz erweitern" und den kuratorischen Rahmen „identifizieren" oder „festlegen" und das Arbeiten mit Kurator*innen.

Barry: Das ist der psychologische Aspekt, von dem Fred sprach. Man versucht, sich mit ihnen hinzusetzen und herauszufinden, was sie tun möchten und was Betrachter*innen sehen sollen, weil das nicht neutral ist. Design ist eine bestimmte Art, etwas zu rahmen.

Fraser: Aber meine Frage ist: wird das kuratorische Konzept selbst jemals zum Gegenstand ideologischer Kritik? Du sagst, dass es nicht Ideologiekritik ist, aber was wäre der Gegenstand und wie wäre dieser Gegenstand gelagert? Wäre es das kuratorische Konzept, wäre es die Institution? Du sagtest, dass es in den Gesprächen Inhalte gibt, die die Institution zur Geltung bringt, aber wenn es Inhalte gibt, die „die Institution" zur Geltung bringt, woher genau kommt dann der Inhalt aus dem Inneren der Institution?

Barry: Ich glaube, es ist kollaborativer. Ich kann es nicht auf eine Antwort runterbrechen. Beispielsweise, die Fernseh-Ausstellung [*From Receiver to Remote Control: The TV Set*, New Museum, 1990] war eine vom Künstler Matthew Geller kuratierte Ausstellung. Er hatte viele Fernsehgeräte, aber er hatte keine wirkliche Vorstellung davon, was sie bedeuteten, also war unsere Aufgabe, die sozialen Räume, die das Fernsehen produziert, zu definieren. Diese Ausstellung war schwierig, da wir das Fernsehprogramm nicht vollständig kontrollieren konnten, was uns mehr Detailarbeit erlaubt hätte. So blieben einige dieser sozialen Räume unter-ausformuliert.

Fraser: Ich wollte Verbindungen zwischen dir und Fred und den verschiedenen Positionen, die ihr gegenüber Kurator*innen einzunehmen scheint, und den Arten von Einladungen, die ihr bekommt, herstellen. Judith, du sprichst davon, mit Kurator*innen zusammenzuarbeiten, um einen kuratorischen Rahmen zu konkretisieren, und Fred, du sprichst von einer ganz anderen Art der Beziehung, scheint mir.

Green: Ich möchte etwas einwerfen. Ich habe auch über die Art der Beziehung nachgedacht, die ich versucht habe, mit dem Drawing Center im Rahmen des Projekts aufzubauen, das ich ursprünglich mit ihnen machen wollte, das auch das Ausstellungsdesign umfasste. Ich habe versucht, die Anforderungen des Drawing Centers an die Zeichnungen portugiesischer Künstler*innen zu hinterfragen. Ich habe versucht, diese Position, gleichzeitig Künstler*in zu sein und Kritik an der Situation zu üben, zu verhandeln. Aber gleichzeitig innerhalb der Situation zu bleiben, damit Kritik möglich ist. Das war eines der Dinge, die mich wirklich umgetrieben haben. Genauso wie Fred dich [Judith] nach dem Unterschied zwischen deiner Wahrnehmung als Designerin und als Künstlerin gefragt hat, ist mir aufgefallen, dass es einen Unterschied gab, wenn ein Kunstprojekt vorgeschlagen wurde, das Design beinhaltete – das dies irgendwie verloren ging. Wohingegen ich denke, dass wenn man als Designberater*in oder als Designexpert*in dort ist, dass dies eventuell eine andere Art von Autorität hinzufügt. Am Drawing Center wollte ich an allen Aspekten des Designs beteiligt sein, die mit dem Projekt zu tun hatten – der Gestaltung des Raumes, der Gestaltung des Plakats – aber was normalerweise passierte, war, dass ich erst im Nachgang gefragt wurde, dass sie ihre*n eigene*n Designer*in einsetzen wollten. Ich hatte bestimmte Vorstellungen darüber, was die Schrift sein und wie alles präsentiert werden sollte und was in der Pressemitteilung stehen sollte. Und ich habe Erfahrung damit, da ich im Verlagswesen gearbeitet habe. Aber etwas an dem Begriff „Künstler*in"…die Vorstellung davon, welche Fähigkeiten man besitzt – ob man die Fähigkeit hat, beispielsweise, zu schreiben, etwas zu theoretisieren – scheint in Frage gestellt zu werden. Das ist es, womit ich in Berührung gekommen bin. Mich würde interessieren, ob das auch anderen passiert ist.

Wilson: Wenn ich für eine Ausstellung in eine Institution gehe, ist es eher im Sinne der Herstellung einer Installation, statt als Designer, weil ich nicht mit Kurator*innen arbeite, um ihre Ideen zu realisieren. Oft versuche ich, ihre Vorstellung über eine bestimmte Kultur, ein Kunstwerk oder ihren Blick auf die Welt, der aus der Struktur stammt, die sie bereits haben, aus ihrem Ausstellungskonzept herauszuarbeiten. Und oft stellt sich dann heraus, dass es eine sehr eng gefasste Ideologie ist, von der sie so tun, als wären sie sich ihrer nicht bewusst. Und je tiefer ich gehe, desto klarer wird, dass sie sich dessen sehr wohl bewusst sind und ich stoße dann sozusagen vor eine Wand, in Bezug darauf, wer sie sind. Das ist das, was ich wirklich zu durchbrechen versuche, auch für die Öffentlichkeit: dass ihre angeblich offene und objektive Sicht im Grunde sehr eng und sehr spezifisch ist.

Guttmann: Ich denke, dass der Gebrauch des Begriffs „Ideologie" irreführend sein kann. Es gibt einen Unterschied dazwischen, ob man mit einer Person arbeitet, die eine Idee hat, und sie zu konkretisieren und daran zu arbeiten, oder ob man versucht, institutionelle Grundlagen herauszuarbeiten. Ich denke, das ist ein wichtiger Unterschied.

Barry: Das ist ein großer Unterschied.

Wilson: Judith sagt – du sagst, dass du beides machst.

Barry: Ich übe meine Institutionskritik nicht zwangsläufig offen aus. Manchmal tue ich das, aber nicht immer, und der Grund ist, dass es mich einfach nicht so interessiert, wenn es so offensichtlich ist. Ich bin viel mehr an den tieferen psychoanalytischen, sozialen oder politischen Verbindungen interessiert, die man in der ersten, investigativen Forschungsphase in jedem Projekt aufdecken kann. Deswegen interviewe ich Kurator*innen gerne und finde heraus, woran sie am meisten interessiert sind.

Guttmann: Würdest du mit jedem*r Kurator*in arbeiten?

Barry: Wenn die Themen interessant sind, interessiert es mich auch. Ich bin persönlich sehr an dem Verhältnis zwischen „hoher Kunst" und „Massenkultur" interessiert. Und wie wir als Künstler*innen die großen paradigmatischen Veränderungen, die wir erleben, aushandeln werden. Wie zum Beispiel die Veränderungen, die Informationstechnologien hervorrufen. Ich fand Renées Punkt darüber, wie einige Künstler*innen und Konzepte aus der Mitte der achtziger Jahre von der jüngeren

Vergangenheit überdeckt wurden, interessant. Sie sprach davon, einige Ideen von *Art after Modernism* und einige der Dia-Unterhaltungen erneut zu untersuchen, da dieser Moment in der Geschichte einen viel komplexeren Blick darauf wirft, wie dies alles zusammenpasst, anstatt alles in kurzen Soundschnipseln zusammenzuschmeißen. Und das ist sehr verstörend, wenn man diese Zeit so durchlebt hat, wie ich. Aber was die Frage betrifft, mit welchen Kurator*innen ich arbeiten würde oder nicht, habe ich keine vorgefertigte Vorstellung. Es geht viel mehr um die Person, die Kurator*innen, und ihre Ideen.

Guttmann: Aber kümmerst du dich um ihre Politik?

Barry: Klar kümmere ich mich um ihre Politik, aber es ist sehr schwierig zu wissen, was die politische Position einer Person wirklich ist, es sei denn man lernt sie sehr gut kennen. Ich würde nicht mit bekennenden Faschist*innen arbeiten wollen. Ich wurde noch nie eingeladen, mit dem KKK [Ku-Klux-Klan] zu arbeiten, noch würde ich das tun.

Wilson: Das ist eine spannende Frage, denn wenn man mit Kurator*innen arbeitet, die man nicht wirklich kennt oder Kurator*innen, die es nicht wirklich verstehen, oder die nicht einmal eine ähnliche ideologische Perspektive haben oder nicht verstehen, in welche Richtung deine Arbeit geht…Ich habe diese Erfahrung gemacht und es ist schwierig, weil man auf Dinge reagieren will, die man wichtig findet und Dinge, die wichtig für die Gemeinschaft sind, aber dann ist die Person, mit der man arbeitet, hundert Jahre hinterher. Aber sie wollen dich da haben, weil sie dich als etwas betrachten, das modisch ist. Es stellt sich also die Frage: Ignoriert man diese Person und tut etwas, dass wirklich etwas damit zu tun hat, was diese Gemeinschaft braucht und was man selbst braucht? Oder ist das nicht hilfreich, wenn die Institution oder eine Person, die diese Institution repräsentiert, davon in Kenntnis gesetzt werden muss, dass es große Verständnislücken gibt? Kann man das tun, oder wird man von der Situation ausgenutzt, wenn man sich nicht direkt mit der Person auseinandersetzt, die einen dorthin eingeladen hat?

Barry: Ich habe als junge Designerin Ausstellungsdesigns für Unternehmer*innen gemacht. Beispielsweise habe ich mit Coca-Cola gearbeitet, was natürlich nicht das fürsorglichste Unternehmen ist. Ich habe versucht, ihre Werbung zu kritisieren. Nichts, was dies auf eine offensichtliche Weise tat, wurde jemals abgenommen, weil sie nicht dumm sind, aber Humor hat manchmal funktioniert. Die Kunstwelt ist eine wohlwollende, rassistische, homophobe Kulturinstitution, in der man auf eine Art als schlechtes Gewissen agieren kann, die Unternehmen niemals zulassen würden. Man kann nicht ihr schlechtes Gewissen sein, weil man keine Macht hat.

Beatrice von Bismarck: Ich habe eine Frage. Demnach zu urteilen, was ihr erzählt, hört es sich so an, als ob Kurator*innen dazu neigen, besonders dumm zu sein. Weil sie besonders lang zu brauchen scheinen, um zu realisieren, was ihr dort genau macht. Und laut dem, was du gesagt hast, Fred, kann ich mir vorstellen, dass das auch der Fall ist. Aber es muss doch eine Reaktion

von den Kurator*innen geben, nachdem sie realisiert haben, dass etwas passiert ist.

Wilson: Währenddessen und danach. Drei der Museen, mit denen ich gearbeitet habe, haben ihre Geschäftsführer entweder gerade, bevor ich dort ankam oder gleich nachdem ich mein Projekt beendet hatte, verloren. Ich würde gern behaupten, dass ich etwas damit zu tun hatte, aber das stimmt nicht wirklich. Mir ist aufgefallen, dass sie selbst eine umstrittene Situation so drehen können, dass sie gut aussehen, weil es eine vorübergehende Situation ist. Im Allgemeinen realisieren sie irgendwann, was man tatsächlich macht und sie versuchen einen aufzuhalten.

Von Bismarck: Aber wozu führt das? Führt es zu der Idee, dass Kurator*innen zum Thema einer Diskussion werden? Wie verändert dies das ganze Verhältnis zwischen Kurator*innen und Künstler*innen?

Fraser: Darum geht es ja in der ganzen Diskussion hier.

Barry: Ich wollte damit nicht andeuten, dass Kurator*innen dumm sind, weil sie Ausstellungsdesigner*innen beauftragen – denn das stimmt nicht. Ich denke, dass Design oft nicht genannt wird in Bezug auf die Art und Weise, wie das Publikum Informationen aufnimmt. Ein gutes Ausstellungsdesign kann bestimmte Themen glasklar darstellen, wohingegen ein schlechtes Ausstellungsdesign alles verschleiern kann. Es ist nicht so, dass Kurator*innen dumm wären oder ihre Arbeit nicht gut machen, Designer*innen haben eine andere Art, Material zu organisieren und in einem Rahmen zu präsentieren, der dem Publikum Wege eröffnet, die Ausstellung zu verstehen. Das ist anders als Grundlagen- oder akademische Forschung. Denn wenn man ein akademisches Journal liest, ist es normalerweise voller Fachsprache, die man nicht versteht, wenn man nicht auf diesem Gebiet promoviert hat.

Wilson: Der Unterschied, den ich sehe, besteht darin, dass Kurator*innen so tun, als sei das System, das sie für das Ausstellungsdesign verwenden, schlimmstenfalls ein wenig elitär oder unkommunikativ, aber je tiefer ich grabe, scheint es, als hätten sie einen sehr persönlichen Grund dafür, Informationen auf die Art und Weise zu kontrollieren, wie sie es tun. In einem Museum, in dem ich gearbeitet habe, hat ein weißer Kurator für indigene Kunst mir erlaubt, etwas in seiner Galerie zu machen, es war eine neue Galerie, die bei den Museumsmitarbeiter*innen sehr beliebt war, weil das Design sehr aufwendig war. Er hat mir nicht viel Input gegeben, aber es war in Ordnung, dass er mit mir gearbeitet hat.

Ich gab jungen indigenen Künstler*innen aus der Region Videokameras und bat sie, Videos über irgendetwas zu produzieren, was sie wollten. Kurze Videos, die ich in der Ausstellung zeigen würde. Ich hatte den Kurator gefragt, ob er mich mit indigenen Künstler*innen aus der Gemeinschaft in Kontakt setzen könnte, um mit ihnen zu arbeiten, was er letzlich nicht hinbekommen hat, also bin ich losgegangen und habe indigene Künstler*innen gesucht. Ich habe diese Videos auf zehn Monitoren im Raum installiert und es liefen die eigenen Arbeiten der Künstler*innen und Arbeiten anderer Künstler*innen, eine Rockband mit indigenen Musiker*innen, Lyriklesungen. Der Kurator dachte, dass es nur einen Monitor im Ausstellungsraum geben würde. Dadurch, dass zehn Monitore übereinander gestapelt waren, wie in einem Geschäft, in dem Fernseher verkauft werden – das stand wirklich in starkem Kontrast zum Raumdesign. Der Ausstellungsraum war in diesem „tote Indianer*innen" Modus eingerichtet, mit theatralischem Licht und Artefakten, die auf dramatische Weise platziert waren und somit leugnete, dass es lebende nord-amerikanische indigene Kulturen gibt. Also, nochmal, meine Installation konkurrierte mit seinem Design und das Problem war nicht so sehr die Information oder der Inhalt, sondern der Effekt davon, wie mein Design mit seinem Design konkurrierte. Es waren nicht so sehr die Informationen, die wir präsentiert haben: es war der Effekt von konkurrierenden Designs, von dem er wusste, dass er die Besucher*innen viel stärker beeinflussen würde als die Informationen, die in einer Ecke des Raumes präsentiert wurden. An diesem Punkt wollte er die ganze Ausstellung schließen. Die Strategie des Chefkurators war nicht, zu sagen, dass es ihm nicht gefiel. Stattdessen sagte er: „meinen indigenen Berater*innen würde es nicht gefallen." – Berater*innen, von denen er mir nie erzählt hatte, dass es sie gab. Diese Berater*innen waren traditionelle indigene Künstler*innen, die seine Perspektive üblicherweise nicht in Frage stellten. Viele ethnographische Museen in den USA, die indigene Kunst zeigen, stellen solche Berater*innen nur dann ein, wenn die Kurator*innen sie brauchen, um ihre Vision voranzutreiben. Die

Künstler*innen, mit denen ich arbeitete, standen nicht in so einem Dialog mit ihm; sie standen mit einem Fuß in der Tradition und dem anderen in der Gegenwart. Und er sah, dass die Künstler*innen aus den Videos bekannt waren, wichtige Mitglieder der regionalen indigenen Gemeinschaft. Er machte also einen Rückzieher. Völlig verrückt. Sie [meine Kollaborateur*innen] waren kurz davor das Haus zu bestreiken, und ich war dazu bereit, es so weit kommen zu lassen, auch weil es eine wirkliche Zusammenarbeit war. Aber so weit kam es nie.

Fraser: Ich wollte in diese Diskussion die Unterscheidung einbringen, die das Programm [der Arbeitsgruppe] zwischen Institutionen dienen und dem Publikum dienen macht. Ich glaube, diese Unterscheidung könnte hilfreich sein, wenn es in dieser Diskussion darum geht, was die Grundlage der Beziehung zwischen Künstler*innen und Kurator*innen in den jeweiligen Fällen ist, und ob die Künstler*innen sich in der Rolle sehen, dass sie den Kurator*innen dienen, der Institution oder dem Publikum. Und wenn sie dem Publikum dienen, ob sie dem Publikum dann gemeinsam mit der Institution dienen, oder indem sie Kritik an der Institution üben. Worüber du sprichst, Fred, dabei geht es glaube ich darum, dem Publikum zu dienen, indem man Institutionskritik übt, obwohl man genauso sagen könnte, dass dies zu einem gewissen Grad auch der Institution dient, weil die Institution vermeintlich im öffentlichen Interesse gegründet wurde. Und Judith, du kommst vielleicht aus einer etwas anderen Richtung: aus der Arbeit mit Kurator*innen, die du dabei unterstützt, dem Publikum zu dienen, indem du ihnen hilfst, ihr

kuratorisches Programm überzeugender zu formulieren.

Barry: Und auch dadurch, dass man bestimmte Fragen beleuchtet, die ansonsten möglicherweise unbemerkt oder ungefragt bleiben würden, aber nicht auf eine so offene Weise. Einige dieser Themen, wie zum Beispiel ethnische Herkunft und Rassismus, stehen momentan so stark im Vordergrund, und Fred wird eingeladen, diese Themen offen anzusprechen, und du [Andrea] wirst eingeladen, um offen Institutionskritik zu üben.

Fraser: Eine Frage, die ich Fred stellen möchte ist: Wenn du versuchst, dem Publikum mithilfe von Institutionskritik zu dienen, inwiefern ist der Erfolg deiner Projekte von der Zusammenarbeit mit der Institution und der Einbindung verschiedener Vertreter*innen der Institution in diese Projekte gemäß ihrer eigenen Interessen und entsprechend der institutionellen Mission abhängig? Das ist für mich auch eine ethische Frage, weil ich an verschiedenen Orten vieles offengelegt habe, was für einige sehr unangenehm war, und auch für mich auch nicht angenehm war, weil ich ja mit ihnen arbeiten möchte und sie nach dem Ende meiner Projekte ja [noch] da sind, wisst ihr? Wenn ich also irgendwo hinkomme, nur um Konflikt oder Blamage zu produzieren, ist es, wenn ich gehe, schlimmer als vorher.

Wilson: Ja, ich stimme dir zu. Die Situation mit dem Kurator für indigene Kunst war sehr speziell, da er seine echten Gefühle darüber versteckt hat, dass er eine sehr bestimmte Art hatte, wie er indigene Kultur präsentieren wollte und nicht wollte, dass irgendjemand das durcheinanderbringt, einschließlich indigener Menschen selbst. Weil er das bis zur Ausstellungseröffnung unter den Tisch gekehrt hat, konnte ich mich während des Projekts nicht damit auseinandersetzen.

Green: Eine Sache, die ich in die Diskussion einbringen wollte, ist die Frage nach Gemeinschaften und danach, was eine Gemeinschaft sein könnte und was das bedeutet. Ich glaube nicht, dass wir über eine einheitliche Gemeinschaft sprechen können, die wir klar definieren können. Es gibt bestimmte Aspekte einer Gemeinschaft, die man nicht zuordnen kann. Ich denke, allein die Vorstellung von Gemeinschaft ist gespalten. Ich denke dabei auch daran, was du [Andrea] in Bezug auf das Publikum gesagt hast. Was passiert, wenn man sich nicht sicher ist, mit was für einer Art Gemeinschaft man es zu tun hat?

Ein Projekt in diesem Zusammenhang, das ich mit einem Museum in Massachusetts gemacht habe, in Worcester [das Worcester Art Museum, 1991], hieß *Bequest*. In dem Projekt ging es auch um die Arbeit mit Museen, mit Kurator*innen und mit der Idee vom Publikum. Herauszufinden, wer das war, war einer der Aspekte des Projektes. Ich musste daran denken, als Fred darüber sprach, als eine Art Spannungsventil für dieses Museum in Baltimore zu fungieren, oder über die Funktion, Schuld oder Verantwortung zu lindern – diese therapeutische Funktion. Ich habe darüber nachgedacht und mich gefragt, was passiert, wenn die Rezeption keine positive Rezeption ist. Durch die Medienrezeption und die unterschiedlichen Informationen, die das Publikum aus diesen Medien bezieht. Im *Bequest*-Projekt wollte ich wirklich

hinterfragen, wer das Publikum ist, wer es an verschiedenen Orten werden kann, und wie es auf bestimmte Informationen reagiert.

Fraser: Ich denke Publikum als ein dynamisches Modell. Das Publikum wird auf eine Art aus dem Diskurs der Institution produziert. Man hat die urbane Bevölkerung, dann hat man bestimmte Interessengemeinschaften, wie zum Beispiel die Interessengemeinschaft, die das Museum als öffentliche Institution repräsentiert. Und somit ist das Publikum eine Bevölkerungsgruppe, die zu einer Interessengemeinschaft wird. Das ist mein Verständnis von Publikum. Man kann also ein Publikum nur anhand der Unterschiede zwischen dem, für wen sich das Museum selbst präsentiert, und dem, was es repräsentiert, verstehen.

Green: Was ich versucht habe aufzudecken, war eine Situation, in der das Publikum mit sich selbst darum kämpft, ein Publikum zu sein. Das Publikum im Fall des *Bequest*-Projekts umfasste das Aufsichtspersonal, die Museumskurator*innen – alle brachten sich ein und stritten miteinander, wie man diese Arbeit betrachten sollte.

Guttmann: Kannst du das beschreiben?

Green: Ich werde kurz versuchen, es zu beschreiben. Es war eine von diesen Einladungen eines Museums, eine Arbeit zu schaffen, ohne dass sie definierten, was für eine Arbeit das sein sollte. Das Museum hat in den letzten zehn Jahren nur ein zeitgenössisches Kunstwerk präsentiert, aber sie versuchten, es zu einem lebendigen zeitgenössischen Ort zu machen. Es liegt in einer wirtschaftlich schwachen Region in Worcester, Massachusetts, in der Nähe von Boston. Sie haben versucht, Personen zum Museumsbesuch zu bewegen, waren sich aber nicht sicher, wer außer den Vorstandsmitgliedern, Förder*innen und Unterstützer*innen des Gartenkomitees oder was auch immer hingehen würde. Das war die Ausgangslage.

Ich wollte mich mit meiner eigenen Vergangenheit zu New England auseinandersetzen. Aber nicht auf eine Art und Weise, die als „Schwarze Perspektive" bezeichnet werden würde, oder auf eine Art, die sie als solche identifizieren würden. Ich wollte mich mehr mit psychologischen Aspekten und Puritanismus auseinandersetzen, mit der Vorstellung des „Unheimeligen" in der Gegend und mit der Geschichte des Museums selbst. Das Projekt hieß *Bequest,* weil es sich mit all den Objekten auseinandersetzte, die der Gründer dem Museum geschenkt hatte. Ich wollte die Genealogie des Museums zurückverfolgen. Es gab große Textarbeiten an den Außenwänden des Gebäudes, die ich als Teil der Ausstellung machte, mit Texten von W. E. B. Dubois, Edgar Allen Poe und verschiedenen Personen, die sich auf Konzpete des Schwarz- und Weißseins fokussierten. Und es gab wirklich ein breites Spektrum an Reaktionen, die in einem Buch festgehalten wurden, das Teil des Ausstellungsprojekts war, die das Publikum enorm gespalten wirken ließ.

Wilson: Das ist eine sehr typische Situation, in der die Institution versucht, eine Art radikale Veränderung zu machen, aber weil sie es nicht persönlich tun wollen, laden sie dich dazu ein. Das ist etwas, das wir alle nachvollziehen können: es muss nichts mit ethnischer Herkunft zu tun haben, es kann um alles Mögliche gehen. Tatsächlich geht es um ihre jeweilige Verleugnung ihres Dilemmas, den Platz innerhalb ihrer eigenen Gemeinschaft und den Versuch, ein Pflaster darüber zu kleben. Was immer man also tut, wenn es nicht ihre Art, ein Publikum zu erreichen neu definiert, wird es in gewisser Weise eine ähnliche Reaktion von diesem Publikum hervorrufen, da sie nicht deine Arbeit sehen – sie sehen die Institution, die sie seit X Jahren kennen. Und das strahlt auf dich ab, nur das du es nicht wirklich bist. Man findet also das heraus, wie viel sie [die Institutionen] verändern wollen, indem du sie dazu bringst, ihr Modell zu verändern, ihren Modus Operandi.

Fraser: Das wirft so viele Fragen auf. Wir könnten allein über diesen Punkt drei Tage lang diskutieren.

Michael Clegg: Sie betrachten es nur als vorübergehende Veränderung. Sie setzen es nicht strukturell um, nachdem der Ausstellungsraum an jemand anderen übergeht.

Wilson: Sie wollen es nicht als fundamentale Veränderung betrachten, die sie vornehmen müssen. Sie wollen es als einen Moment betrachten, und dann können sie zu dem zurückkehren, womit sie sich wohl fühlen.

Fraser: Ich hatte ein Erlebnis mit dem Wadsworth Atheneum in Hartford, Connecticut, was eine extrem problematische Stadt ist. Ich würde sagen, dass sie stärker segregiert ist, als die meisten Teile des Südens. Das aktivste Kapitel des Ku-Klux-Klan im Norden spielt dort, und der Grand Wizard des Ku-Klux-Klan stammt aus Connecticut. Aber das Wadsworth Atheneum Museum ist auf eine Art eine der progressivsten Institutionen des Landes, mit einem äußerst liberalen Programm und einer der progressivsten Kuratorinnen für zeitgenössische Kunst des Landes [Andrea Miller-Keller], die Louise Lawlers erste Museumsausstellung organisiert hat und die vieler anderer Personen.

Was ich dort versucht habe, war, diese beiden Dinge zu bearbeiten und herauszufinden, was meine Funktion innerhalb dieser Ökonomie war. Basierend auf der Annahme, dass es eine Ökonomie zwischen der Institution, ihrem progressiven kuratorischen Programm und der extremen Rassentrennung in der Region gab. Es war sehr schwierig – wahrscheinlich eines der schwierigsten Projekte, das ich je gemacht habe – denn es bedeutete, jemanden zu kritisieren, den ich zutiefst respektierte als eine sehr progressive Kuratorin mit beeindruckenden Erfolgen. Meine These war, dass man hier in dieser Stadt 300 Jahre alten Liberalismus vorfindet, der auf kolonialer „Yankee"-Identität beruht, und dessen Funktion es ist, sich selbst mit der fiktiven Autonomie einer vorindustriellen Gemeinschaft zu erhalten. Und die liberale Tradition ist die Instanz, die die Rassentrennung in gewisser Weise durchsetzt. Sie unterstützt die Fiktion, dass es keine Interessenkonflikte gibt. Der andere Kommentar, den ich habe, ist, dass ich in Bezug auf verschiedene Publika immer angenommen habe, dass es einen Konflikt gibt. Und dass Institutionen gegründet wurden, um sich mit gesellschaftlichen Konflikten auseinanderzusetzen. Um eine soziale Alterität anzuerkennen. Wenn Institutionen zum Beispiel für Bildungszwecke da sind,

beinhaltet das Weiterbilden schon eine Anerkennung dessen, dass es jemand anderen dort draußen gibt, der die Kultur der Institution noch nicht teilt. Aber das Wadsworth Atheneum hat nicht anerkannt, dass es dort draußen jemand anderen gab. Ich habe noch nie eine unmittelbare Ablösung vom Publikum erlebt, außer bei diesem Projekt. Und ich weiß, warum…

Clegg: Wie hat sich das offenbart?

Fraser: Die Ablösung des Publikums?

Clegg: Ja.

Fraser: Nun, ich wurde zu einer Performance beim jährlichen Abendessen der Lehrenden-Versammlung eingeladen. Ich sagte ihnen, dass es möglicherweise keine gute Idee sei, aber sie haben darauf bestanden, sie wollten mich unbedingt dabei haben. Und dann hat nach der Performance niemand auch nur ein Wort zu mir gesagt. Nicht ein Wort. Ihre Reaktion war zu sagen, dass sie „Hartford lieben", ohne die Kritik auch nur anzuerkennen oder sich zur Performance zu äußern. Es war pure Verdrängung. Es war genau das, was sich in jeder kulturellen Institution der Stadt abspielte. Das war das, was mir gespiegelt wurde, und es war eine entsetzliche Erfahrung.

Wilson: Ich bin mittlerweile schon so weit, dass ich nicht mehr mit Vermittlungsabteilungen in Museen arbeiten möchte, weil ich wirklich merke, dass die Vermittlungsabteilungen – natürlich nicht deine Vermittlungsabteilung am New Museum, Susan (Gelächter in der Gruppe) – so eingerichtet sind, dass das Museum nicht das tun muss, was es eigentlich tun sollte. Daher ist es egal, wie gut die Vermittlungsabteilung ist oder wie fortschrittlich die Personen in der Vermittlungsabteilung sind. Die Vermittlungsabteilung gibt es, weil das Museum nicht das tun will, was es tatsächlich tun sollte, um die Aufmerksamkeit des Publikums zu wecken. Also diese vorgeschriebene Bemühung –

Cahan: Ich nenne es das Alibi des Kunstmuseums.

Wilson: Richtig, das Alibi. Ich möchte also über Institutionen sprechen, statt über das Publikum, da ich mich mit der Institution auseinandersetze, und wenn sie das tun würde, was sie tun sollte, wäre das Publikum nicht so ein Thema. Ich wende mich nicht an das Publikum. Das Museum tut dies, indem es sagt: „Wir wollen sie, sie sind dort draußen. Wir wollen, dass sie hier reinkommen". Wenn man aber wirklich anspricht, wer man ist und worum es eigentlich geht, wenn man das wirklich anspricht, dann wird die Reaktion des Publikums ein Gleiches tun.

Barry: Ich denke, dass man auf sehr direkte Weise mit Gemeinschaften arbeiten kann. Einer der Verträge, die ich mitgebracht habe, stammt von einem fortlaufenden Oral-History-Projekt. Als weiße Frau kommt für mich manchmal die Frage auf, warum ich auf verschiedene, häufig ungleiche kulturelle Bedingungen in unterrepräsentierten Gemeinschaften aufmerksam mache. Eine Art, wie ich damit umgehe, ist sicherzustellen, dass das Projekt auch wirklich die Gemeinschaft widerspiegelt, mit der ich arbeite, indem ich direkt mit dieser Gemeinschaft, die ich zu „repräsentieren" versuche, zusammenarbeite. Das erste Mal, dass ich so gearbeitet

habe, war 1987 für das Projekt *First and Third* am Whitney Museum [in New York]. Es war ein Oral-History-Projekt. Während ich zwar das Einverständnis der Personen hatte, deren Geschichten ich verwendete, habe ich sie sehr spontan gesammelt. Als ich dieses Vorgehen später reflektiert habe, habe ich mich für eine viel kollaborativere Methode entschieden. Im nächsten Oral-History-Projekt in den Riverside Studios in London [1990] habe ich mit Gruppen aus fünf verschiedenen Gemeinschaften gearbeitet, die verlorene oder vergessene Geschichten sammelten, die sie wichtig fanden und erzählt wissen wollten. Ich war vielmehr Vermittlerin als Künstlerin. Das Projekt richtete sich an Gemeinschaften, und die Namen der Gruppen waren auf der ganzen Literatur abgedruckt, sodass der kollaborative Ansatz des Projekts sichtbar und damit auch herausgestellt wurde, dass die Gemeinschaften gleichberechtigte Teilnehmer*innen im Projekt waren. So wurde klar, dass ich nicht für sie sprach.

In einem anderen Projekt, an dem ich in Brüssel arbeitete, ging es um das kolonialistische Verhältnis zwischen Belgisch-Kongo und Belgien und um die Entwicklung des Jugendstils als Stilrichtung [*The Work of the Forest*, Fondation pour l'Architecture, 1992]. Bei diesem Projekt habe ich mit mehreren unterschiedlichen Gruppen gearbeitet, die konkurrierende ideologische Positionen vertraten. Es gab die Position des Museums, welches ein anthropologisches Museum war, das Abertausende überwiegend gestohlener Artefakte besaß, die [König] Leopold II gesammelt hatte. Daher hatte das Museum seine eigene Version der Geschichte. Dann gab es noch die kunsthistorische Gemeinschaft, die ihre eigene Version dieser Geschichte hatte, und Künstler*innen- und Architekturgemeinschaften. Ich habe all ihre Perspektiven in einem Panorama versammelt, um so viel Reibung wie möglich zu erzeugen. In der Presse wurde das kontrovers diskutiert und brachte Themen hervor, die in Brüssel lange nicht diskutiert worden waren. Für mich ist es weniger interessant, Einheit in Form einer klassischen Erzählung herzustellen, als solche versteckten Geschichten aufzudecken.

Fraser: Was machst du, wenn der Konflikt so unterdrückt ist? Wenn man irgendwie nicht an ihn rankommt.

Wilson: Zumindest bei dem Baltimore-Projekt [*Mining the Museum*, 1994] ging es mir so, dass man herausfindet, wer die verschiedenen Interessensgemeinschaften sind und dann arbeitet man mit ihnen auf der Ebene, die für sie am besten funktioniert. Das variiert. Bei Dozent*innen haben Vorlesungen besser funktioniert. Bei bestimmten Schwarzen Gemeinschaften in Baltimore machte es mehr Sinn, sie Zuhause zu besuchen. Und bei einer anderen Schwarzen Gemeinschaft war ein sehr formeller Rahmen sinnvoller. Es hing auch von den jeweiligen wirtschaftlichen Strukturen der unterschiedlichen Schwarzen Gemeinschaften in Baltimore ab. Ich spreche ein Publikum nicht direkt an, aber ein Publikum ist definitiv implizit Bestandteil dieses Prozesses. Denn die Museumsgemeinschaft wird einem nicht erzählen, was die Probleme sind.

Guttmann: Es sollte nicht als axiomatisch betrachtet werden, dass Kunstinstitutionen ein Publikum haben. Sie haben Besucher*innen. Besucher*innen sind kein Publikum, und schon gar keine Öffentlichkeit. Und noch weniger eine Gemeinschaft. Diese Definitionen sind wichtig. Aber Museen müssen auch keine Eintrittskarten verkaufen, um zu überleben. Viele von ihnen müssen das zumindest nicht, wobei jedes Museum ein spezifischer Fall für sich ist. Viele Kunstinstitutionen brauchen wirklich keine rigorose Definition ihres Publikums zur Erzeugung ihrer Selbstidentität. Das ist ein zentraler Punkt, den man nicht vergessen darf. Sie haben Besucher*innen, aber Besucher*innen sind kein Publikum.

Bischoff: Ich habe eine Frage an alle anwesenden Künstler*innen: Was würdet ihr sagen, wenn Personen aus dem Kunstmuseum euch zum Hauptpublikum machen würde, oder zu Besucher*innen? Sodass wir nach euch suchen würden. Denn die Institution, von der ich komme, ist ein Behälter voller Kunstwerke und Materialien aus Gemeinschaften und der Gesellschaft. Und wir sind froh, wenn jemand mit diesem Material arbeitet. Die einzigen Personen, die wirklich mit diesem Material arbeiten, sind Künstler*innen. Für einige Personen, die im Museum arbeiten, ist das die einzige Chance, mit Künstler*innen zu arbeiten.

Fraser: Bevor wir darauf antworten – Susan, du wolltest etwas sagen?

Cahan: Wenn man sich die Rhetorik in den Vereinigten Staaten anschaut, ist der Auftrag von Museen „dem Publikum" zu dienen. Was absichtlich undefiniert bleibt, sodass Museen sich als demokratische Institutionen positionieren können. Und wenn man sich tatsächliche demographische Daten und Statistiken über das Publikum anschaut, sieht man, dass das Publikum in amerikanischen Museen sehr spezifisch und sehr eindeutig ist – es ist überwiegend weiß, überwiegend mittleren Alters, etwas mehr Frauen als Männer, das Einkommen der Museumsbesucher*innen ist höher als der nationale Durchschnitt und ihre Hochschulbildung liegt etwa im Mittel. Ich glaube, der Grund, warum Museen nicht klar formulieren, wer ihr Publikum ist, liegt daran, dass sie befürchten, dass es Institutionen ein Armutszeugnis ausstellen würde. Es wird angenommen, dass Museen die breite Bevölkerung repräsentieren, und indem man diesen Punkt verschleiert, kann man diese Vorstellung aufrechterhalten.

Guttmann: Als ich sagte, dass Besucher*innen kein Publikum sind, es mag zwar einige statistische Regelmäßigkeiten geben, die diese Besucher*innengruppen vom Rest der Bevölkerung unterscheiden, aber sie bilden trotzdem kein Publikum, da es nicht sehr viele Kunstinstitutionen gibt, die eine Atmosphäre schaffen, in der Menschen das Gefühl haben, Kunst als Publikum zu erleben. Wenn jemand beispielsweise zu einem Rockkonzert geht, ist ein Teil der Erfahrung die Interaktion mit dem Publikum selbst. Bei manchen Konzerten werden Musiker*innen zu Vermittler*innen und versuchen, ein Gemeinschaftsgefühl zu schaffen, oder zumindest scheint das in diesem Kontext ein Auftrag zu sein. Das ist also ein Unterschied. Es unterscheidet sich sehr von einem Kunstmuseum, wo ein paar einzelne Personen ein- und ausgehen.

Fraser: Sehr wenig von der Kunst, die von Institutionen gesammelt wurde, wurde für eine kollektive Erfahrung gemacht. Deshalb würde ich deinen Vergleich hinterfragen. Aber das andere, was ich noch einmal sagen wollte, ist, dass ich einen Unterschied zwischen einem Publikum und einer Interessensgemeinschaft machen würde. Was du ein Publikum nennst, Martin, würde ich eine Interessensgemeinschaft nennen. Ich will nicht sagen, dass es unbedingt partizipatorisch ist, aber es gibt gewisse gemeinsame Interessen. Und was du „Besucher*innen" nennst, würde ich „Publikum" nennen – und ich würde sagen, dass durch Türen rein- und rausgehen, wie du es nennst, tatsächlich ziemlich kompliziert ist. Es ist nicht so einfach. Das Betreten und Verlassen des Museums hat eine eigene Geschichte und folgt einer Reihe von Mechanismen und Regeln.

Guttmann: Der Salon in Frankreich, zum Beispiel, war ein sehr wichtiger Ort für die Entwicklung einer demokratischen Atmosphäre. Die Personen, die im Salon zusammenstanden, kamen aus verschiedenen Klassen, und es war das erste Mal, dass sie aufeinandertrafen, und sie konnten sich über das Medium der Kunstkritik miteinander unterhalten.

Fraser: Ich würde aber sagen, dass die Geschichte in den Vereinigten Staaten ganz anders ist. Die Institutionen in den Vereinigten Staaten wurden erbaut, um bestimmte Personen davon abzuhalten, hereinzukommen. Das Philadelphia Museum [of Art] ist schwer zu erreichen, es ist eine große Verkehrsinsel ohne Stoppschilder. Es gibt viele Museen, die schwer zu erreichen sind, und zwar nicht nur aus städtebaulicher Planungs- und architektonischer Perspektive.

Draxler: Wir sind [zeitlich] bereits in unserer dritten Session, und ich würde vorschlagen, dass wir jetzt eine Pause machen und in zwanzig Minuten zurückkommen und versuchen, hiermit weiterzumachen. Mit ein paar anderen Teilnehmer*innen. Und Fritz und ich haben kurz gesprochen und [finden], dass wir versuchen sollten, eine stärker europäisch ausgerichtete Diskussion über diese Themen zu führen.

Arbeitsgruppe
Sitzung Drei

Dem Publikum dienen
Samstag, 22. Januar 1994

Vorträge: Susan Cahan
Iwona Blazwick
Andrea Fraser

*Da die meisten Kulturinstitutionen im Interesse der Öffentlichkeit gegründet werden, schlagen viele Projektkünstler*innen vor, nicht der Institution zu dienen, sondern eher ihrem Publikum.*

*Kurator*innen und andere Museumsfachleute haben zunehmend ein Interesse daran, Künstler*innen einzuladen, um mit ihnen zusammenzuarbeiten und den öffentlichen Auftrag zu erfüllen, den sie oder die Institutionen festlegen.*

*Was passiert, wenn die Interessen der Künstler*innen, der Institution und des Publikums miteinander in Konflikt stehen? Kann dieses Modell einem anderen Zweck dienen, außer der institutionellen Reform?*

Susan Cahan: Ich möchte ein paar Punkte ansprechen, die Fragen aufwerfen. Da ich ein kurzes Video habe, werde ich fünfzehn Minuten lang präsentieren. Ich werde meinen Vortrag so kurz wie möglich halten. Das Video ist ungefähr fünf Minuten lang und wird in der Mitte meines Vortrags abgespielt. Ich möchte mich auf die Stellung des Publikums in Museen konzentrieren und worüber ich sprechen werde, wird wahrscheinlich mehr für Museen in den Vereinigten Staaten gelten, als in europäischen. Ich möchte mit meiner einfachen Analyse der historischen Position, die die Vermittlung in Museen bisher eingenommen hat, beginnen, und das ist folgende: dass Kurator*innen diejenigen sind, die Wissen entwickeln und Pädagog*innen diejenigen, die dieses Wissen vermitteln sollen. In der Regel in vereinfachter Form, an eine möglichst umfangreiche Personengruppe. Historisch betrachtet, hatte diese Formulierung eine Unterteilung zur Folge, die von vielen als „das Interesse der Kurator*innen an der Kunst" und „das Interesse der Pädagog*innen an den Menschen" bezeichnet wurde. Dies ist eine Dichotomie, die in ihrer beliebtesten Form von denjenigen zum Ausdruck gebracht wurde, die in den siebziger Jahren über die Museumspraxis geschrieben haben. Was im Grunde ziemlich interessant ist, da in den siebziger Jahren viele Künstler*innen Dinge gemacht haben, die speziell diesem Gegensatz widersprachen. Stattdessen haben sie das Museum als einen Ort genutzt, an dem soziale Beziehungen zwischen unterschiedlichen Interessengemeinschaften und Beteiligten völlig voneinander abhängig waren. An dem man diese einfache Unterteilung zwischen Kunst und Menschen nicht machen konnte. Ich begann damit, neue Ideen für Vermittlung in Museen zu entwickeln, die sich auf Literaturkritik bezogen, speziell auf Rezeptionsästhetik und Rezeptionstheorie. Mich interessierte das sich wandelnde Verhältnis zwischen Kulturproduktion und Kulturrezeption, im Speziellen die Auseinandersetzung mit Rezeption als eine Form der Kulturproduktion. In der Literatur wurde dies ziemlich häufig thematisiert, aber seltsamerweise nicht so sehr in der bildenden Kunst. Das war Mitte bis Ende der achtziger Jahre, und in dieser Zeit beeinflusste mich die Arbeit von Group

Material sehr. Ein Teil ihrer Arbeiten ist auch hier in der Ausstellung [*Services* im Kunstraum der Universität Lüneburg]. Darüber hinaus beeinflusste mich eine Demonstration, die ACT UP 1988 am MoMA [das Museum of Modern Art in New York] veranstaltete, und die sich auf eine Ausstellung von Fotografien von Nicholas Nixon über Menschen mit AIDS bezog. Außerdem schaute ich mir Programme an, die für Angestellte der First Bank in Minneapolis entwickelt wurden. In jedem dieser Fälle ging es um Rezeption als eine Form der Kulturkritik. Oder Rezeptionstheorie und Kulturkritik, die im Verhältnis zueinander zum Tragen kamen. Die Arbeit, mit der ich also am New Museum [am New Museum of Contemporary Art, New York] begann, bestand darin, den Vorgang der Rezeption zu konkretisieren. Der Versuch, eine sichtbare Form dafür zu schaffen, was geschieht, wenn Menschen sich Kunst ansehen. Das, was allgemein unsichtbar ist, sichtbar zu machen, und das in Zusammenarbeit mit Künstler*innen zu tun. Desweiteren machte ich es mir zur Aufgabe, kritische Rezeption zu fördern.

Das erste Projekt, das ich [am New Museum for Contemporary Art] machte, war 1989. Es war eine Videoarbeit in einer Retrospektive von Nancy Spero [*Nancy Spero: Works since 1950*], in der einer meiner Kollegen und ich Besucher*innen dazu interviewt haben, welche Arbeiten sie am wirkungsvollsten fanden und warum. In der Tat fingen die Besucher*innen an, kurze Vorträge im Museum zu halten, und wir dokumentierten das Ganze auf Video. Das alles hat in der ersten Woche stattgefunden, in der die Ausstellung eröffnet wurde. Wir nahmen ungefähr fünfunddreißig

Stunden Video auf und schnitten sie auf ein zehnminütiges Orientierungsband zusammen, das am Eingang der Ausstellung präsentiert und während ihrer gesamten Dauer gezeigt wurde.

Das nächste Projekt machte ich 1990 in Zusammenarbeit mit einer Künstlerin namens Branda Miller, und es wurde in einer Ausstellung, die *From Receiver to Remote Control: The TV Set* hieß, realisiert, die Judith vorhin [in der vorherigen Sitzung] erwähnte. Sie wurde von Matthew Geller konzipiert und organisiert, und von Judith Barry und Ken Saylor entworfen. In der Ausstellung ging es um die Rolle, die das Fernsehen in amerikanischen Haushalten und für die amerikanische Familie gespielt hat. Judith und Ken hatten die Installation so entworfen, dass jeder Ausstellungsraum einen Raum eines Hauses nachbildete, zu einer jeweils anderen Zeit seit der Erfindung des Fernsehers, so dass die Zeitspanne von den späten zwanziger Jahren bis in die späten achtziger Jahre reichte. Das Projekt, an dem ich beteiligt war, ermöglichte Besucher*innen, innerhalb der Ausstellung ihre eigenen Videoaufnahmen zu ihren persönlichen Erfahrungen mit dem Fernsehen zu machen. Oder sie konnten Aufnahmen machen, die die Ausstellung kritisierten. Die fertigen Videoaufnahmen sind in einem Archiv gesammelt worden, das kontinuierlich in die Ausstellung integriert wurde und somit die Themen der Ausstellung erweiterte. Und Branda war jedes Wochenende vor Ort, um den Schnitt mit denjenigen zu machen, die mehr an ihrem Filmmaterial arbeiten wollten. Jede*r erhielt eine Kopie des von ihm oder ihr erstellten Videos. Die Besucher*innen konnten nochmals zurück in die Ausstellung kommen, um ihre

Aufnahmen zu schneiden. Ungefähr zweitausend Personen nahmen über einen Zeitraum von zehn Wochen an diesem Projekt teil. Es war ein riesiges Projekt. Das Videoband, das ich euch zeigen werde, stammt aus diesem Projekt.

Ein weiteres Beispiel, das ich nur beiläufig erwähnen möchte – und wenn ihr mehr über dieses Projekt erfahren wollt, die Informationen stehen hier oben an der Wand – ist ein Gemeinschaftsprojekt, das ich mit Julie Ault entwickelt habe.

Andrea Fraser: Julie Ault ist auch ein Mitglied von Group Material.

Cahan: Die Ausstellung, in deren Rahmen dies stattfand, hieß *Rhetorical Image* und sie wurde von Milena Kalinovska organisiert [1990-91]. Das Thema der Ausstellung bezog sich darauf, wie verschiedene Kommunikationsmethoden Machtverhältnisse verkörpern und wie Künstler*innen in die Repräsentation von Machtverhältnissen im öffentlichen Raum oder in der Architektur eingegriffen haben. Ein Großteil der Arbeiten war konzeptionell. Julie und ich wollten ein Vermittlungsprojekt entwickeln, das als Intervention in das Museum funktionieren und Besucher*innen mehr auf die Verkörperung von Machtverhältnissen im Museum aufmerksam machen würde. Besucher*innen wurden also gebeten, eine Reihe von Fragen zu beantworten und dazu eingeladen, auf einer Postkarte auf diese Fragen zu reagieren und sie dann an die Wand zu heften. Diese kleine Broschüre beinhaltet zirka fünfzig Reaktionen.

Über die Ausstellungsdauer wurde der ganze Raum mit diesen Antworten tapeziert, was ihr auf den Fotografien sehen werdet. Wir hatten überhaupt nicht mit so einer großen Anzahl an Reaktionen gerechnet, die wir bekamen, und tatsächlich nahmen die Stimmen der Besucher*innen den Raum für sich in Anspruch. Aber es war wirklich eine sehr schöne Metapher für das Ziel, das wir versuchten zu verwirklichen, und zwar, den Raum Menschen zu überlassen, die ihre eigenen Stimmen normalerweise nicht in konkreter Form in Museumsräumen artikulieren können. Ich möchte noch erwähnen, dass die einzigen, die ein Problem mit diesem Projekt hatten, Kunstkritiker*innen waren, und ich denke, dass es sehr interessant ist und Hinweise darauf gibt, wie es möglicherweise in das Gebiet eingegriffen hat, das Kunstkritiker*innen normalerweise beanspruchen.

Das letzte Projekt in diesem Vortrag ist von Laurie Parsons, und hier hat sie die ganze Beschilderung einer Gruppenausstellung, die *The Spatial Drive* (1991-92) hieß und von Laura Trippi organisiert wurde, entfernt. Statt herkömmliche Vermittlungstexte zu nutzen, hat Parsons Schulungen für unser ganzes Sicherheits- und Einlasspersonal organisiert, damit diese alle Künstler*innen der Ausstellung kennenlernen und sich über ihre Arbeiten informieren konnten. Somit wurden alle sachlichen und interpretatorischen Informationen zu der Ausstellung durch informelle Gespräche zwischen den Besucher*innen und dem Museumspersonal ausgetauscht. Das hatte einen sehr normalisierenden Effekt auf den Museumsraum: man konnte hineingehen und alles anfassen und mit allen sprechen, und es gab nicht das übliche formelle Protokoll und den Abstand, den man gewöhnlich in einem Museum erlebt.

Diese Projekte haben gewisse Ähnlichkeiten, Lauries ist jedoch etwas anders, da es sich nicht ausschließlich auf das Publikum konzentriert hat.

Ich möchte auch ein Video zeigen, das im Home Made TV Projekt gedreht wurde und dann mit euch über die Frage sprechen, auf die wir uns Andreas Bitte nach fokussieren sollten. Die Frage danach, was geschieht, wenn Konflikte zwischen Künstler*innen, Institutionen und dem Publikum entstehen.

Das war eine der herausforderndsten Videoaufnahmen, die im Verlauf der Ausstellung gemacht wurde – herausfordernd auf die unmittelbarste und eindeutigste Art.

(Video läuft)

(Art Jones, Sprecher auf dem Video: „…es ist voll gepackt mit so viel Zeug, aber gleichzeitig ist es sehr beschränkt. Ich gehe durch diese Räume und es ist alles so wie in einer Autowerbung, etwas, das man im Fernsehen sehen würde. Aber in meinem Haus sieht es nicht so aus, hat es noch nie. Das sind die Häuser von Weißen. Ich habe noch nie etwas in meiner Gegend gesehen, das so aussieht. Geht es hier um die Auswirkung, die Video auf Amerika hat…?

Wem gehört dieses Amerika? Also frage ich mich, ob ihr, die Museumsbesucher*innen, das Gefühl der Entfremdung wahrnehmen könnt, die von dieser Ausstellung ausgeht. Ich meine, was ihr macht, ist interessant. Aber ich weiß nicht, es ist schwierig nachzuempfinden. Das ist also weniger eine Kritik, als vielmehr ein Hinweis darauf, was meiner Meinung nach jeder intelligente Mensch über die Einschränkungen des Museums in seinem Kontext und Konzept weiß, wenn es darum geht, etwas anderes als die Perspektive der weißen Mittelschicht auszudrücken. Die ganze Idee eines Museums ist für jemanden wie mich naturgemäß entfremdend, da ich das Gefühl habe, schon die Bedingungen neu definieren zu müssen, die einen Ort wie diesen möglich machen und attraktiv oder interessant für die Menschen, die ihn zusammengestellt haben. Und überhaupt, diese Idee des Multikulturalismus: ‚Oh ja, wir wollen alle Menschen miteinbeziehen.‘ Fakt ist, dass es Kulturen zusätzlich zu derjenigen gibt, die in dieser Ausstellung repräsentiert wird. Und zwar existieren sie seit Jahren und die Idee, dass ihr plötzlich etwas miteinbeziehen werdet, ist irgendwie sau-rückwärtsgewandt. Das hättet ihr schon vor Hunderten von Jahren realisieren müssen. Es ist ein bisschen spät, Leute. Vielleicht versucht ihr, diese Ausstellung Uptown ins Studio Museum [in Harlem] zu bringen und seht, was die Leute sagen. Vielleicht verändert das eure Perspektive.“)

Cahan: Das nächste Video ist von einem Kurs, den Renée Green unterrichtet hat, als sie am Bank Street College [in New York] war.

(Nächstes Video läuft)

(Titel des Videos: „Tape #593 von Renée Greens Junior High School Klasse, Bank Street College“)

(Zwei nicht zu identifizierende Sprecher, beide im Junior High School Alter, führen ein Video-Interview durch. Interviewer: „Wie heißt du?“ Befragter: „Ich heiße Alonzo Lewis.“ Interviewer: „Wie findest du dieses Museum?“ Befragter: „Nun, ich kann nicht viel dazu sagen, weil ich mich nicht umgesehen habe, aber

es sieht in Ordnung aus.“ Interviewer: „Bist du verargert, weil du dich nicht umsehen kannst?“ Befragter: „Ja, ich hatte gehofft, dass ich eine Gelegenheit haben würde, die Dinge zu erkunden, aber ich verstehe die Situation.“ Interviewer: „Was ist das Problem im Museum?“ Befragter: „Na ja, es gibt ein Leck und sie lassen niemanden dort hinten hin, wie du weißt.“)

Cahan: Ich muss das erklären: Es gab an diesem Tag ein Wasserleck im New Museum, also mussten wir herausfinden, wie man das Leck beheben konnte, bevor die Schulgruppe dort ankam. Renée brachte ihre Klasse mit und die Kinder mussten sehr lange in der Lobby warten – das waren Dreizehnjährige. Also gaben wir ihnen einfach die Kamera und ließen sie spielen und sich selbst filmen, während sie warteten. Was an diesem Abschnitt auffällig ist, ist, dass er sich diesen genialen Weg ausgedacht hat, wie er sich selbst und die anderen Schüler*innen in die Ausstellungsräume bringen kann, indem er so tut, als ginge er zur Toilette, und dann liefert er dieses Nachrichtenformat: „Exklusivinterviews zum Leck“. Aber sie hängen auch einfach in der Lobby herum und interviewen sich gegenseitig. Und an einer Stelle fokussieren sie auf die Tafel in der Lobby, auf der die Vorstandsmitglieder des New Museum aufgelistet sind.

(Cahan zeigt einen Ausschnitt, in dem einer der Schüler die Namen der Vorstandsmitglieder vorliest. Green, die im Video spricht, sagt, dass ein anderer Schüler darüber diskutierte, dies seien nicht die Namen der Personen, die am Museum arbeiten, sondern die Namen der sehr Reichen.)

Cahan: Ich wollte diese Ausschnitte bloß zeigen, weil sie auf einige Dinge hinweisen, die Museumsangestellte als selbstverständlich empfinden und von Museumsbesucher*innen nicht als selbstverständlich empfunden werden. Die Idee hinter diesen Projekten ist, den Vermittlungsprozess in einen Wechselseitigen zu verändern und die Art und Weise, wie Wissen im Museum gestaltet wird, neu zu definieren. Das Museum in einen Ort zu verwandeln, an dem Wissen nicht nur übermittelt, sondern auch produziert wird. Um dies voranzutreiben, muss man der Praxis der Wissensproduktion eine Art physische, erkennbare, konkrete Form geben, und sich auf die Idee der Abweichung konzentrieren und den hohen Stellenwert, der die Themen betrifft, die wir behandeln sollen, und der damit zu tun hat, was passiert, wenn Konflikte auftreten. Offen gesagt, eines der wichtigsten Ziele dieser Projekte war es, anzuerkennen, dass diese Konflikte existieren, und wenn man sie diskutieren kann, dann ist das ein produktiver Vorgang. Ein Problem, auf das ich gestoßen bin, ist die Art, wie die Methoden und die Informationen in diesen Projekten entstanden sind. Ich meine, man sieht es in dem ersten Video von dem jungen Mann Art Jones: seine Kritik war ziemlich konfrontativ. Ich war erstaunt darüber, wie weit das Museum in der Lage war, diese Informationen zu absorbieren, und zwar das zu absorbieren, was durch diese Methodik erzeugt wurde. Ich hatte gedacht, dass es eventuell institutionelle Veränderung anspornen würde. Aber stattdessen fand das Museum das Vorgehen spannend und sagte: „Na ja, wir sollten das eben bei jeder Ausstellung machen." „Nun, wenn man das bei jeder Ausstellung machen würde, dann müssten wir die jeweilige Kritik, die in Projekten ausgedrückt wird, nicht unbedingt anbringen". Und das wurde für mich zu einer Frustrationsquelle, und deshalb mache ich solche Projekte nicht mehr. Ich befasse mich jetzt mit einer anderen Praxis. An solch einem Projekt habe ich seit 1992 nicht mehr teilgenommen.

Mich beunruhigt, inwieweit die Partizipation des Publikums von Museen in den USA als eine Art demokratischer Akt verstanden wird. Das wird in der steigenden Anzahl an Büchern über „Publikumsresonanz" erkennbar, die meiner Meinung nach sehr wenig mit realen Fragen der kulturellen Demokratie und kultureller Teilhabe zu tun haben. Meine derzeitige Arbeit ist also mehr auf Zusammenarbeit mit denjenigen ausgerichtet, die sowohl innerhalb als auch außerhalb von Institutionen stehen. Ich arbeite nun an einem Projekt, das ein Konsortium von Künstler*innen, Aktivist*innen und Graduierten der Kulturwissenschaften an der City University of New York [CUNY] beinhaltet. Wir haben versucht, neue Strukturen für die Zusammenarbeit mit Personen zu entwickeln, damit sie mit unserem Museum arbeiten können, hoffentlich ohne völlig von ihm vereinnahmt zu werden, und gegenseitige Interessen erfüllt werden können.

Iwona Blazwick: Ich möchte über ein Projekt sprechen, an dem einige von euch letztes Jahr beteiligt waren. Es war eine Einladung, die ich und zwei andere Kuratorinnen bekommen haben, Eva Patita und Carolyn Christov-Bakargiev, um ein Projekt für ein Festival zu organisieren, das anstrebte, die europäische Einheit zu feiern. Es fand in Antwerpen statt, das 1993 europäische Kulturhauptstadt war und natürliches einiges an Parado-xien mit sich brachte. Auf eine Art waren wir Gastarbeiterinnen, da wir wie mit einem Fallschirm in dieser speziellen Situation im Museum für zeitgenössische Kunst in Antwerpen landeten. Dort wurden wir mit einer Reihe spannender, aber schwieriger Probleme konfrontiert. Im Grunde schafften wir eine Schnittstelle zwischen verschiedenen Gruppen und Absichten. Die eine war die EK [Europäische Kommission] selbst, hinter deren Bestreben, die euro-päische Einheit mit Hilfe von Kultur zu fördern, eindeutig ein wirtschaft-licher Imperativ steckt. Die andere war die Stadt Antwerpen selbst und die flämische Gemeinde innerhalb der Stadt, die eine sehr spezielle Identität und ihre eigene Sprache hat, die völlig getrennt von der fran-zösischen Gemeinde in Belgien ist.

Der andere Teil dieses Pakets war das Wissen darüber, dass der Stadt-rat dieser Stadt, die für ihre liberalen Werte bekannt ist und zum Beispiel eine Geschichte des Verlagswesens und der freien Verbreitung von Ideen besitzt, derzeit zu 25 Prozent vom Vlaams Belang belegt ist, der in vielerlei Hinsicht eine protofa-schistische Organisation ist. Er ist im Grunde rassistisch, und das war die Situation, in der wir gearbeitet haben. Ein weiterer Teil des Pakets war, dass von den Organisatoren der Antwerp 93 niemand aus Antwer-pen stammte und alle verschiedene Kulturproduzenten und Intellektuelle aus unterschiedlichen Disziplinen waren. Sie alle waren männlich, und alle Assistentinnen waren weiblich. Keine dieser verschiedenen kulturel-len und intellektuellen „Abteilungen" umfasste Vertreter*innen aus den Gemeinden in Antwerpen selbst,

weder aus der flämischen Gemein-de, noch seitens der vielen anderen Bewohner*innen, die in Antwerpen, einer der größten Hafenstädte Europas, leben. Es gibt zum Beispiel einen großen marokkanischen Be-völkerungsanteil, einen türkischen, griechischen sowie spanischen. All diese unterschiedlichen Bevölke-rungsgruppen haben ihre eigene Ge-schichte und ihre Gründe da zu sein, aber keine von ihnen wurde dazu eingeladen, auf irgendeine Weise an dem Entscheidungsprozess rund um dieses Festival teilzunehmen. Als wir die Organisatoren dazu befragten, antworteten sie, dass diese Gruppen nicht professionell genug seien, um zu verstehen, wie man sich an einer solchen Veranstaltung beteiligen könnte. Das war also die spezielle Situation, in der wir uns befanden.

Andererseits waren wir in einem Museum, das an sich eine andere Agenda vorschlug. Es war so etwas wie eine Karikatur des White Cubes. Jemand nannte es „wunderbar miss-verstanden", da es ein umgebautes Depot war, in der großen Tradition der umgebauten Industriegebäude, in der sechziger Jahre-Tradition des Kunstraums als Labor. Aber durch seinen Umbau verdrängte es eine gesamte Gemeinde, die zuvor in der Gegend gearbeitet hatte, in der das Museum entwickelt wurde. Das Museum selbst kam eigentlich auf eine nebensächliche Weise durch die Arbeiten von Gordon Matta-Clark zustande – seine vorletzte Arbeit enstand in Antwerpen. In dem Bemühen, diese Arbeit von Matta-Clark zu retten, stifteten mehrere Künstler*innen Kunstwerke. Und obwohl dies nicht Matta-Clarks Ge-bäude rettete, wurde es zur Grund-lage des Museums, und ironischer-weise wurde das Museum dann zum Antrieb für die Gentrifizierung einer

Gegend in Antwerpen, die bisher eine industrielle Hafengegend gewesen war.

Wir bekamen also eine Reihe von Koordinaten, mit denen wir arbeiten sollten, und dazu luden wir dann einige Künstler*innen ein, von denen einige hier sind. Ich wollte mich allerdings auf einen anderen Aspekt des Projekts konzentrieren, der mit dessen Publikum zu tun hat. Dabei haben wir versucht, ein Gefühl dafür zu bekommen, wie man das Geschehen im Museum an verschiedene Publikumsgruppen wiedergeben könnte. Eine war ganz klar eine Kunstwelt – eine Kunstwelt, die dazu tendiert, von einem körperlosen Raum in den anderen zu wandern, und die mehr oder weniger nicht wahrnimmt, ob sie in Venedig ist oder in Kassel oder in New York. Aber was im Grunde geschieht ist, dass sie sich von einem weißen Raum in den anderen bewegen, miteinander sprechen und eine Reihe von Erfahrungen teilen. Wir haben also versucht, dies möglichst aufzubrechen, indem wir sie dazu brachten, eine andere Verbindung zu dem Kontext herzustellen, in dem sie die Arbeiten erlebten. Und das war also ein Publikum. Wir versuchten das [umzusetzen], indem wir ihnen zuallererst eine örtliche Geschichte erzählten, nämlich die Geschichte von Antwerpen und seiner Beziehung zur Avantgarde. Zu einem Zeitpunkt zwischen 1958 und 1969, als verschiedene künstlerische Gemeinschaften Kontakt miteinander hatten und was daraus entstand. Diese Art von lokal-internationaler Tätigkeit geschieht überall zu jeder Zeit, und die Idee dahinter ist, dass es keine Mitte oder eine Begrenzung gibt, sondern ständige Punkte der Interaktion. Das war also ein Versuch. Der Zweite war, die zahlreichen

Gemeinschaften in Antwerpen wirklich wiederzuspiegeln und zu versuchen, sie im Museum zu repräsentieren, aber gleichzeitig in unsere Arbeit einzubinden. Wir entschieden uns, dass es am sinnvollsten wäre, über die Gemeinschaftsvorstände und die sogenannten öffentlichen Netzwerke auf sie zuzugehen. Wir haben drei verschiedene Gremien eingeladen. Eines war die Universität, und sie waren in ein Projekt involviert, das sich die Beziehung zwischen städtischer Erneuerung und städtischem Verfall anschaute, zwischen Gentrifizierung und all den verschiedenen Gesichtspunkten der Stadtentwicklung und das soziale Gefüge der Stadt. Wir besuchten auch eine Gruppe aus der Nachbarschaft, die versuchte, sich mit städtischem Verfall zu befassen und der Art, wie verschiedene Gemeinschaften kulturelle Identitäten bilden. Drittens haben wir mit einem Piraten-Radiosender gearbeitet. Wir haben alles mit avantgardistischen Karten dargestellt, die in der Ausstellung gezeigt wurden, und wir hatten einige ziemlich außergewöhnliche Ausstellungen, finde ich, die von zwei ortsansässigen Gemeinschaften zusammengestellt wurden. Unser Ziel war tatsächlich, uns die Form der Ausstellung anzusehen und zu berücksichtigen, welche Kraft oder Bedeutung sie für Publikumsgruppen haben könnte. Eine der Ausstellungen, die wir organisierten, war etwas kitschig, und unser Argument dabei war einerseits, dass man diese Megabudgets, diese enormen Räume, diese Art der Ausstellung eigentlich nicht benötigt. In der Tat gibt es eine andere Form, die ausdrucksstark ist, wenn nicht sogar noch ausdrucksstärker, und der Zweckmäßigkeit halber entwickelt wurde, jedoch unglaublich effektiv ist. Diese Ausstellungen hatten ausklappbare Pappstände, die eine Gemeinschaft aus der Nachbarschaft zusammengestellt hatte, und sie hatten sie angefertigt, weil die Präsenz des Museums, in dem wir arbeiteten, die Gruppe der Gemeinschaft insofern beeinflusste, als dass die Wohnungskosten in der Gegend um das Museum herum alle angestiegen waren. Es war also das übliche Muster der Gentrifizierung, in der Menschen sich die Miete nicht leisten können, wegen der Galerien und Boutiquen, die sich dort niederlassen. Zweihundert Menschen, die in zwei Wohnblöcken wohnten, die der Stadt gehörten, sollten vertrieben und diese Gebäude an Bauunternehmer*innen verkauft werden. Als Reaktion darauf dokumentierten die Bewohner*innen all die Probleme der Wohnsituation, aber darüber hinaus gaben sie dem Ganzen eine visuelle Form, die sehr anspruchsvoll und sehr zugänglich war, und wir integrierten das mit in die Ausstellung.

Wir fragten auch die Lokalzeitung, die umsonst ausgegeben wurde, ob sie jemanden aus der Gemeinschaft, zum Beispiel Kinder, Reporter*innen sein lassen würden, um die Abläufe an diesem Ort zu untersuchen.

Schließlich haben wir Radio Central eingeladen – für mich einer der wichtigsten Aspekte des ganzen Projekts, was wirklich mit meiner anderen Erfahrung mit dem Publikum am Institute of Contemporary Arts [ICA] in London zusammenhängt. Anscheinend war eines der wichtigsten Dinge, die diesen Raum bedeutend für mich und bedeutend für London machten, das «Talks» Vortragsprogramm. Das ist eine Plattform mit einer regelmäßigen Diskussionsreihe. Anstatt also solch eine fragmentierte individuelle

Erfahrung zu erleben und in Ausstellungen zu gehen, gab es eine Anhängerschaft, die sich anhand eines bestimmten Diskurses entwickelte, eine Anhängerschaft, die immer wieder zurückkam und miteinander reden konnte. Es gab ein Literaturforum, in dem südafrikanische Schriftsteller*innen aus Townships auf eine Weise zusammenkamen, die in Südafrika gar nicht möglich war, und gleichzeitig konnten sie dadurch ein breiteres Publikum in London ansprechen. Und auf ähnliche Weise gibt es ein Forum für Psychoanalytiker*innen, das sich dort immer wieder trifft, ein Forum für Philosoph*innen, das sich immer wieder trifft, und verschiedene Gruppen, die das ICA als Treffpunkt nutzen. Das schien mir also ein brauchbares institutionelles Modell zu sein, eine Plattform zu schaffen, zu der die Teilnehmer*innen etwas beitragen können. Die Buchhandlung hatte meiner Meinung nach eine ähnliche Funktion, beispielsweise verschiedene Publikationen von Fanzines bis Broschüren einzuführen. Der Versuch, das in Antwerpen umzusetzen, war sehr schwierig, da sich in London eine Diskussionskultur entwickelt hatte und man diejenigen kannte, die daran teilnahmen. Aber als wir in Antwerpen landeten, wussten wir gar nicht, wer was machte, wo die Schriftsteller*innen waren, wo die Aktivist*innen waren. Das war also ein Problem.

Eine Form, die wir gefunden haben, war dieser Radiosender, der eine fantastische Organisation war. Er bekommt keinerlei öffentliche Gelder und keine private Förderung und er agiert im Grunde aus einem besetzten Haus. Von dort haben sie ein Programm aufgesetzt, für jeden Tag, und jede Stunde wird das Programm von unterschiedichen

Personen zusammengestellt, und jedes hat einen Titel. Beispielsweise läuft montags um 18 Uhr „The African Bureau". Keiner der DJs wird bezahlt, sie arbeiten alle freiwillig. Und in den zehn Jahren, in denen sie bisher gesendet haben, sind alle immer dagewesen. Nie ist ein Programm ausgefallen, was ziemlich großartig ist. Es funktioniert so, dass montags um 18 Uhr etwa drei DJs Platten mitbringen. An dem Abend, an dem ich dort war, spielte eine Band aus Kinshasa [in der DR Kongo] irgendwo in Holland. Sie wussten von dem Sendeplatz, also kamen sie dorthin. Es gab einen DJ, der aus Zaire zu Besuch war, und er kam vorbei. Es ist also eine flexible Struktur, in der die Namen nicht an besondere Sendeplätze gebunden sind. Der Sendeplatz existiert einfach und man kann vorbeikommen und teilnehmen.

Eines Tages ging ich dorthin und es gab einen Berber Sendeplatz und drei marokkanische Jugendliche strahlten eine Sendung aus – sie waren sensationell. Die Struktur existierte bereits und wir haben sie ins Museum eingeladen. Nachdem es sich einmal herumgesprochen hatte, dass man einfach ausstrahlen konnte, fanden wir – obwohl es durchaus ein Spektakel hätte werden können, dass es funktionierte. Und zwar weil sich der Sender ebenfalls bewegt und aus unterschiedlichen Situationen ausstrahlt, je nach der Gruppe, die gerade sendet. Und es machte ihnen Spaß, dort [im Museum] zu sein, teilweise, weil sie sehr viel Raum hatten – sie konnten an die Leute herantreten, die zur Ausstellung kamen und sie interviewen. Das wurde zu einer Art Forum: aus dem Museum heraus verschiedene Programme zu senden. Beispielsweise neue hybride Formen der

lokalen Technomusik, Belgien ist für Techno bekannt, also konnte man das hören. Aber gleichzeitig gab es eine Sendung, die „Women Trading" hieß, und die sich mit Prostitution in Antwerpen beschäftigte, wohin viele Frauen aus Entwicklungsländern gebracht werden. Man nimmt ihnen ihre Pässe ab und sie sind dort gefangen. Während der Ausstellungslaufzeit gab es einen Sendeplatz, zu dem diese Frauen eingeladen und ihre Geschichten anonym ausgestrahlt wurden. Für mich stellte dies eine Art virtuelle Architektur dar, bei der wir durch die Institution ein Publikum anziehen konnten, das nicht nur kam, um am Geschehen teilzunehmen, sondern dort auch senden konnte.

Das ist also mein Vortrag zu einer Arbeitsweise, die ich als erfolgreich empfunden habe. Der Nachteil daran war – und darüber haben wir auch gesprochen, dass das Museum sich gestört fühlte, und es versuchte, sehr viel Arbeit in einem kondensierten Zeitraum zu erledigen. Ich meine, Renée, als du deinen Vorschlag für die Ausstellung eingereicht hast, da mussten wir wirklich noch einmal nachdenken. Und zwar aus dem Grund, da du tatsächlich sagtest: „Einige kulturelle Formen haben Handlungsmacht und damit meine ich die Fähigkeit, Menschen dazu zu befähigen, zu handeln…Handlungsmacht für wen, und wo findet man diese Handlungsmacht?" Also mussten wir noch einmal überlegen, wie wir dieses Projekt angehen. Es gab dort eine Buchhandlung und ich versuchte, ihr Interesse dafür zu wecken, dass sie beispielweise Publikationen wie *Third Text* aufnehmen, was ein äußerst weit entwickeltes Magazin ist, was das Schaffen eines Diskussionsforums betrifft. Ich versuchte, die Buchhandlung dazu zu überzeugen, all diese Publikationen und Bücher und Fanzines aufzunehmen. Aber es war aussichtslos, wir bestellten alles und sie haben die Kartons nie geöffnet. Es war so ein Problem, bei dem man selbst täglich vor Ort sein muss, um dranzubleiben. Wir waren also sozusagen wie Außenseiter*innen und beide in dieser Situation, in der wir viel Freiheit hatten, aber gleichzeitig war es sehr schwierig, irgendetwas aufrechtzuerhalten. Und eigentlich ist es auch nicht genug, einfach nur in einer Situation zu landen: man muss wirklich ein langfristiges Arbeitsverhältnis haben, um einen Dialog und überhaupt Vertrauen in ein Projekt zu entwickeln.

Helmut Draxler: Worum geht es bei deinem Material?

Blazwick: Dieses Material ist eine Demografie von Antwerpen. Ein Text von Gordon Matta-Clark, darüber, wie man Strukturen als Methoden der Kommunikation nutzt und die verschiedenen öffentlichen Netzwerke, die Nachbarschafts-Ausstellungen und die Radiosendung.

Andrea Fraser: Was ich dazu zu sagen habe, hätte eventuell in der letzten Sitzung besser gepasst. Es hat einen anderen Ton als das, was bisher diskutiert wurde. Trotzdem werde ich ein paar Minuten lang etwas abspielen. Nicht mehr als fünf Minuten von einem Band. Die Einleitung erklärt, was es ist, aber ihr werdet wahrscheinlich nicht wirklich einen Eindruck davon bekommen, was danach daraus entsteht.

(Fraser spielt eine Audioaufnahme ihres Beitrags zur Whitney Biennale 1993 in New York ab.)

Fraser: „Hallo, willkommen bei einer Biennale 1993 Ausstellung des Whitney Museum of American Art. Ich heiße Andrea Fraser, ich bin eine der teilnehmenden Künstler*innen in der diesjährigen Biennale Ausstellung."

David Ross, Direktor: „Ich heiße David Ross und ich bin der Direktor des Whitney Museum of American Art. Wie hört sich das an?"

Elisabeth Sussman: „Ich heiße Elisabeth Sussman, ich bin Kuratorin des Whitney Museums. Und ja, ich bin die Person, die die ernannte Leiterin der Whitney Biennale 1993 ist."

Thelma Golden: „Ich heiße Thelma Golden, ich bin stellvertretende Kuratorin am Whitney und eine der vier Kurator*innen der Whitney Biennale 1993 am Whitney Museum of American Art."

Fraser: „Für meinen Beitrag zur Ausstellung habe ich die Kurator*innen der Biennale 1993 interviewt, sowie die Vermittlungskuratorin und den Direktor des Museums. Und ich habe das Material zusammengestellt, um den Audioguide zu produzieren, den Sie nun hören werden."

John Hanhardt: „Ich heiße John Hanhardt, ich bin Film- und Video-Kurator und Leiter der Film- und Videoabteilung, und ich war einer der Co-Kurator*innen der Whitney Biennale 1993."

Connie Wolf: „Ich heiße Connie Wolf, ich bin Kuratorin für Vermittlung am Whitney Museum."

Lisa Phillips: „Ich heiße Lisa Phillips, ein Mitglied des Biennale 1993 Teams."

Ross: „Willkommen im Whitney Museum, ich hoffe Ihr Besuch gefällt Ihnen. Willkommen im Whitney Museum, freue mich auf Ihre Reaktionen. Ich würde die Aufgabe der Biennale definieren, eine Kunstausstellung zu sein, die uns die Gelegenheit gibt, den Zeitgeist zu

verstehen oder zumindest zu präsentieren. Und um erneut die institutionelle Unterstützung für amerikanische Künstler*innen, die Dinge
voranbringen, zu demonstrieren. Sie
hat einen besonderen Platz in der
amerikanischen Kultur, die Biennale.
Sie bewertet zwei Jahre der Aktivität
aus dieser außergewöhnlich großen
und komplizierten Nation."

Wolf: „Wir müssen diese Kom-
plexität vermitteln und unserem
Publikum erlauben, diese Komplexi-
tät zu verstehen."

Ross: „Um über zeitgenös-
sische amerikanische Kunst
nachzudenken."

Wolf: „Um zu sehen, was in den
letzten zwei Jahren der 1990er entstanden ist."

Ross: „Ich bin sehr stolz auf die Biennale. Und ich bin besonders stolz
auf die amerikanische Kunstwelt.
Daher ist es eine Chance für diejenigen, die sich nicht so sehr damit
beschäftigten, die Ausstellung mit
dem Gedanken zu verlassen: ‚Mein
Gott, so etwas Außerordentliches
geschieht hier.' Männer und Frauen
mit großartigen Visionen, großem
Engagement, großer Leidenschaft
und einer Art, wie sie diese Ideen
und diese Vision und diese Bilder an
uns kommunizieren, auf Wegen, die
ich zuvor nie in Betracht gezogen
habe. Es ist ein Projekt, es ist eine
Ausstellung, es ist ein Programm,
von dem ich im Laufe der Jahre als
treuer Teilnehmer sehr viel gelernt
habe. Das ist für mich ebenfalls eine
elementare Quelle der Aufgabe."

Fraser: „Nun lassen Sie uns gemeinsam die Ausstellung ansehen.
Bitte nehmen Sie den Aufzug
oder die Treppen hoch bis in die
vierte Etage. Wenn Sie in der vierten
Etage ankommen, gehen Sie auf
den Wandtext zu Ihrer Rechten zu,
nachdem Sie den Aufzug verlassen

haben. Schalten Sie Ihren Audioguide ab, wenn Sie den Piepton hören. Stellen Sie ihn wieder an, wenn
Sie den Wandtext in der vierten
Etage erreichen."

Ross: „Schnallen Sie sich an, es
wird eine holprige Fahrt."

(Fraser schaltet Audioaufnahme ab)

(Gelächter)

Fraser: Oh Gott, das habe ich mir zuletzt vor einem Jahr angehört.

Renée Green: Ich habe das überhaupt noch nie gehört.

Cahan: Ich schon. Wisst ihr, was
der Typ am Empfang gesagt hat? Er
sagte: „Wisst ihr, es ist nicht wirklich
ein Audioguide."

Fraser: …Ich bin ein bisschen
schockiert davon und von meiner
Reaktion. Ich weiß nicht, ob es an
der Erfahrung liegt, es zu produzieren, oder ob es eine andere Form
von Stress ist. Es war eine extrem
schwierige Erfahrung, dieses
Audioband zu produzieren. Und ich
betrachte es als das katastrophalste
Projekt, das ich je gemacht habe. Es
war katastrophal wegen der Konflikte, die es auslöste, Konflikte, die ich
nicht vorhergesehen hatte. Und ich
habe meine eigene Ambivalenz nicht
erkannt und die Art und Weise, wie
meine eigene Ambivalenz zu diesen
Konflikten beigetragen hat. Was ich
nun also machen will, ist, die Umstände der Arbeit zu erklären und
den Verlauf, und vielleicht ist etwas
davon für die Diskussion relevant.

Ich wollte hier darüber sprechen,
weil ich von Elisabeth Sussman
und Connie Wolf zu einem frühen
Zeitpunkt der Zusammenstellung
der Liste für die Biennale eingeladen

wurde. Und ich wurde zu diesem frühen Zeitpunkt hauptsächlich aufgrund einer Ausstellung im Kunstmuseum der Berkeley Universität [Berkeley Art Museum and Pacific Film Archive] eingeladen, bei der es sich um eine Installation der ständigen Sammlung handelte. Ich setzte mich dort mit einem Nachlass auseinander, um mir die Probleme anzuschauen, die sich um diesen Nachlass herum abspielten – ich glaube nicht, dass sie es so gesehen haben. Aber jedenfalls, diese Personen und der Direktor des Museums, der neu war, brachte die Chefkuratorin der Biennale, Elisabeth Sussman mit, und Connie Wolf kam noch ein wenig später dazu. Sie vertraten die neue Verwaltung des Museums, und dies war ihre erste Biennale Ausstellung, eine Ausstellung, die während eines Großteils ihres Bestehens unter viel Beschuss gekommen ist, aber vor allen Dingen in den letzten zehn Jahren. Sie wurde jedes Jahr angegriffen. Daher waren sie anfangs ziemlich besorgt wegen der Ausstellung, aber sie waren auch daran interessiert, mit der Ausstellung ein Statement über die neue Verwaltung am Museum zu machen, und wie das Museum sich veränderte. Und ich glaube, sie waren auch daran interessiert, nicht bloß ein Statement über das neue Whitney zu machen, sondern auch eines über das alte Whitney. Mein Eindruck war, dass es das war, was sie von mir wollten. Sie wollten, dass ich etwas mit der ständigen Sammlung mache oder etwas über die Geschichte des Museums und eventuell mit der ständigen Sammlung.

Mein Gefühl war, dass das für eine Ausstellung, die das ganze Museum in Anspruch nehmen würde und bei der die ständige Sammlung eingelagert würde, nicht geeignet war,

während einer Ausstellung, die sich gänzlich zeitgenössischer Kunst der letzten zwei Jahre widmete und sie ausstellte.

Also machte ich eine Reihe von Vorschlägen, von denen die ersten drei abgelehnt wurden, ohne viel Erklärung. Ihr erster Vorschlag war, dass ich die Lobby im Erdgeschoss nutze, um eine Art Orientierungsraum zu gestalten. Diese Idee gefiel mir, aber als ich anfing, Möglichkeiten vorzuschlagen, merkte ich, dass diese Option aus irgendeinem Grund vom Tisch war – wieder ohne Erklärung. Ich schlug vor, dort eine Performance ohne Installation mit Objekten zu machen, und dies wurde als unangemessene Nutzung von erstklassigen Immobilien oder erstklassigen Ausstellungsflächen betrachtet. Da die Live-Performance nicht durchgehend zu sehen sein würde, meinten sie, der Raum würde nicht sinnvoll genug genutzt werden. Ich wollte selbst keine Führung machen, weil ich keine Kommentare zu den Arbeiten der anderen Künstler*innen in der Ausstellung produzieren wollte, und ich wollte außerdem nicht für die ganze Dauer der Ausstellung anwesend sein. Der nächste Vorschlag war, die Wandtexte zu produzieren, die man liest, wenn man in die Ausstellungsräume kommt, und die meisten Whitney Biennalen installieren lange kuratorische Statements auf jeder der Etagen. Ich habe also ein paar Wochen mit Recherche dazu verbracht und diskutierte es mit den Kurator*innen, aber dann wurde mir gesagt, dass es keine gute Idee sei, da die Kurator*innen in dieser Biennale Verantwortung für ihre Entscheidungen und für den Entscheidungsprozess übernehmen wollten, und diese Wandtexte seien einer der Hauptorte, an denen sie ihr Publikum ansprechen könnten. Und sie hätten die Verantwortung, dieses Publikum anzusprechen und Rechenschaft über Entscheidungen abzulegen und die kuratorischen Entscheidungen, die gemacht wurden. Das war ein sehr starkes Argument, das auch vom Direktor des Museums vertreten wurde: Anstatt wie üblich vom Komitee kuratiert zu werden, würde es eine Person geben, die die Hauptverantwortung trägt.

Dann habe ich letztendlich diesen Vorschlag gemacht: ich habe vorgeschlagen, die Kurator*innen, den Direktor und die Direktorin der Vermittlungsabteilung zu interviewen und ihre Stimmen zusammenzuschneiden, um einen Audioguide zu produzieren. Es war sogar eine meiner ersten Ideen, aber ich dachte, sie würden sie niemals annehmen. Sie wurde jedoch akzeptiert und vielleicht zum Teil aus dem Grund, weil meine früheren Vorschläge abgelehnt wurden und es etwas angespannt wurde. Ich weiß es nicht genau. Als ich dann weitermachte, um die Interviews zu führen, wurde deutlich, dass es große Sorge gab. Mir war klar, dass es von Anfang an große Sorge um die Ausstellung gab, aber irgendwie habe ich nicht erwartet, dass das solch eine Einschränkung in ihren Diskussionen mit mir sein würde, und im Verlauf dieses Projekts verstärkte sich diese Sorge noch. Obwohl es etwas Spannung gab, die durch die Ablehnung meiner ersten Vorschläge entstand, lag mein Interesse darin, mit den Kurator*innen zusammenzuarbeiten – das wollte ich. Zuvor habe ich sogar der Vermittlungsabteilung einen Besuch abgestattet, habe eine Präsentation für die Dozent*innen dort gegeben und eine Reihe von Diskussionen mit der Vermittlungsdirektorin gehabt. Ich hatte einige

Besprechungen mit der Kuratorin für Vermittlung, ich unterstützte ihre Bemühungen, die Richtung des Museums zu verändern, und obwohl ich vielleicht einige Fragen hatte, habe ich im Grunde die Richtung, in die sie gehen wollten, unterstützt. Ich wollte mit ihnen zusammenarbeiten, um das Publikum anzusprechen, und ich spürte, dass die Prämisse war, dass sie wollten, dass ich mit ihnen zusammenarbeite. Auch, dass es eine Art Zusammenarbeit sein würde. Aber der Vorgang der Arbeit als ein Prozess der Zusammenarbeit zerfiel völlig in angedrohte Verschiebungen und die Forderung, dass ich die Arbeit überarbeiten sollte. Ich war in diesem Projekt sehr hin- und hergerissen. Denn einerseits habe ich mich als teilnehmende Künstlerin an der Ausstellung beteiligt, und als Künstlerin bin ich es gewohnt, eine gewisse Autonomie und Kontrolle zu haben. Es besteht die Annahme, dass jede Form des direkten Eingriffs eine Zensur darstellt. Aber andererseits hinterfragt die Prämisse der Zusammenarbeit vielleicht einige dieser Dinge und wenn ich mit ihnen zusammenarbeite und sie bitte, mit mir zu sprechen und die Prämisse ist, ihre Stimmen direkt einzusetzen, dann kann ich möglicherweise nicht an all diesen Rechten festhalten, ohne das Vertrauen zu gefährden, das mit dieser Beteiligung impliziert wird. Es war unklar, und mir ist es immer noch nicht klar.

Obwohl ich damit arbeiten musste, was sie sagten und was ich tatsächlich mit der Aufnahme tun konnte, versuchte ich dennoch, verschiedene Dinge mit der Aufnahme zu tun. Erstens bat ich sie, mit mir zu sprechen, um zu beschreiben, wer ihrer Meinung nach ihr Publikum war. Die Fragen, die ich stellte, waren: Wer ist Ihr Publikum? Was denken Sie, das eine bestimmte Arbeit diesem Publikum bieten kann? Was denken Sie, muss dieses Publikum wissen, um Zugang zu dieser Arbeit zu bekommen? Und was wollen Sie, dass Ihr Publikum aus der Erfahrung mit einer bestimmten Arbeit herausholt? Also was man auf dem Band hört, wenn man [als Besucher*in] zuhört, man hört die Kurator*innen, wie sie über einen selbst in der dritten Person sprechen. Da ich verschiedene Stimmen zusammenschneide, hört man die Widersprüche in der Vorstellung, die einzelnen Kurator*innen von einem selbst haben. Was sie von einem halten, darüber, was man selbst aus einer bestimmten Arbeit herausholt, was man selbst denkt, und was das Museum für einen tut. Und das wollte ich machen, aber in Zusammenarbeit mit ihnen [dem Museumspersonal], ich wollte die Themen, auf die sie in der Biennale eingehen und in Bezug auf ihre eigenen Interaktionen und Konflikte im Museum ansprechen wollten, versuchen zu repräsentieren und ihre eigenen unterschiedlichen Auffassungen des Publikums. Und dadurch, wie es sich im Verlauf des Bands abspielte, direkt zu kommunizieren. Obwohl ich irgendwie wusste, dass es nicht genauso war, wie sie es haben wollten, hatte ich trotzdem das Gefühl, dass ich es in gutem Glauben getan habe. Was so unangenehm daran war, sich das Band anzuhören – vor allem für diejenigen von uns, die vielleicht an der Biennale beteiligt waren und diese Leute kennen – ist, dass es diese starke Reaktion und viel Gelächter gab. Die Art, wie diese Arbeit von denen, die sie gut fanden, wahrgenommen wurde und auch von denen, die sie nicht gut fanden, war eine ziemlich gemeine Darstellung dieser Personen. Möglicherweise fanden sie sie deswegen nicht gut, und vielleicht gerade aus dem Grund, aber das war nie meine Absicht. Das ist war überhaupt nicht mein Ziel, und ich weiß nicht, wie es letztendlich dazu kam, dass es so wahrgenommen wurde. Ich werde hier aufhören.

Green: Meine Reaktion auf das Band war teilweise sehr gemischt. Es ist etwas schwierig auszumachen, wo die Reaktion herkommt, da ich diese Erfahrung auch als eine sehr traumatische empfunden habe. In gewisser Weise war es eine der traumatischsten Ausstellungserfahrungen, die ich je in meinem Leben gemacht habe. Also könnte es das hysterische Gelächter des Wiedererlebens und die Erinnerung an den Schmerz sein. Aber es brachte mich auch zum Lachen, denn es erinnerte mich an die Werbekampagne für die Olympiade. Irgendwie hatte es einen ähnlichen Pathos wie die „Berlin 2000" Plakate, die noch immer überall hängen, nachdem Australien die Bewerbung für die Olympischen Spiele 2000 gewonnen hat. Es löst Gefühle von Verlust, Hoffnung und Ambitionen, aber auch von kompletter Fehlbarkeit. Es ist schon irgendwie deprimierend. Aber für mich ist es keine bösartige Sache. Die sich überschneidenden Stimmen sind eigentlich ganz interessant.

Fraser: Ich habe die Wahrnehmung zum Teil so interpretiert – und das wollte ich auch erreichen – dass man normalerweise niemanden, der eine Institution repräsentiert, auf diese unvorbereitete Art sprechen hört. Man hört sie nicht unbedingt vollständige Sätze sprechen, nicht unbedingt auf minutiöse intellektuelle Art und Weise. Sie sprechen ganz natürlich. Aber auch das, was man hört, hängt mit den Umständen des Interviews zusammen, und weil es von Anfang an klar war, dass dieses Material veröffentlicht werden würde, kann man hören, wie sie versuchen, sich zu präsentieren. Man hört das Bemühen um Selbstdarstellung heraus und die Unsicherheit, die dahintersteckt. Das war mir bewusst, und ich dachte, dass es für das Publikum befreiend wirken könnte – zu hören, wie sogar die Vertreter*innen einer Institution sich nicht vollkommen mit der Institution identifizieren können. Aber natürlich verspürt man Unsicherheit nie auf solche Art.

Judith Barry: Ich habe mich nur gefragt, was sie so gestört hat. War es die Tatsache, dass du Dinge aus dem Kontext genommen hast? Mich würde interessieren, welche Begründung sie hatten, dich es noch einmal bearbeiten zu lassen.

Fraser: Zu dem Zeitpunkt, als sie mich darum baten, hatte ich schon aufgehört, mit ihnen zu sprechen, ich hatte die Diskussionen beendet. Hätte es einen richtigen kollaborativen Prozess gegeben und richtige Unterstützung und einen richtigen Dialog, wäre ich einer Neubearbeitung gegenüber nicht so abgeneigt gewesen. Da das aber vollkommen gescheitert war, fand ich es so unfassbar. Ich habe sie also nie wirklich darauf angesprochen.

Barry: Hast du mit ihnen oder jemand anderem seitdem darüber gesprochen?

Fraser: Nein.

Michael Clegg: Aber sie haben nicht versucht, es zu unterbinden.

Cahan: Auf subtile Art und Weise schon. Ich wusste von Andreas Projekt, und als ich ins Whitney Museum ging, um die Biennale anzuschauen, wollte ich mir auf alle Fälle den Audioguide anhören. Allein deswegen, weil mich die Person, die die Audioguides austeilte, darüber informierte, „dass es kein richtiger Audioguide sei", sondern ein „Kunstprojekt", und ob ich denn trotzdem einen haben wolle –

Fraser: Er hat dich gefragt, ob du ihn trotzdem haben willst?

Cahan: Ja. Erstens hat er dadurch die Verteilung eingeschränkt, und zweitens hat er die subversive Komponente [des Projektes] untergraben und den Überraschungseffekt.

Fraser: Ich habe in der Einleitung und mit der Beschilderung genau erklärt, worum es geht – dass ich eine an der Ausstellung beteiligte Künstlerin bin und dass diese Arbeit mein Beitrag war, und dass sie die Stimmen von diesem und jenem beinhaltete…Ich meine, ich habe es ja nicht manipuliert…Ich habe es erarbeitet.

(Gelächter)

Martin Guttmann: Willst du wirklich sagen, dass du es nicht lustig fandest, als du es dir zum ersten Mal nach der Bearbeitung angehört hast?

Fraser: Du hast keine Ahnung, in was für einem Zustand ich war, als ich damit fertig wurde.

Guttmann: Manche denken, dass wenn etwas komisch ist und Personen daran beteiligt sind, es auch gemein sein muss. Ich weiß nicht, aber es ist wirklich komisch.

Ulrich Bischoff: Ich glaube, dass wenn ich in dieser Institution arbeiten würde, ich sofort die Gefahr dieser Arbeit verstehen würde – da sie sehr authentisch ist. Wenn eine Institution wie das Whitney Museum tatsächlich in Gefahr ist und man das offenbart, dann hätten sie davor Angst. Aber das liegt daran, dass die Arbeit sehr authentisch ist.

Clegg: Etwas an dieser Aufnahme ist real, das sich von der Arbeit in München unterscheidet.

Fraser: In München waren es nicht die tatsächlichen Interviewaufnahmen – die befragten Personen waren nochmal in einem Studio und lasen das, was sie gesagt hatten, direkt aus den Interviews.

Bischoff: Aber in München waren einige Leute auch verärgert.

Fraser: München war dagegen ein Traum. München hat gut funktioniert.

Bischoff: Das liegt daran, dass die Vorstandsmitglieder in München nicht in so einer Kunstwelt-Gesellschaft leben. Aber die Leute am Whitney müssen sich wirklich vollkommen mit dem Whitney identifizieren. In München halten sie lieber ein wenig Abstand.

Helmut Draxler: In München war es ein Vorstand und sie sind Geschäfts-führer*innen. Es war also nicht so leicht.

Guttmann: Ich glaube, eine Sache die passierte, war, dass sie wahr-scheinlich eine grundlegende Ambivalenz gegenüber jeglicher Hervorhebung hatten, da sie einer-seits wollten, dass das Whitney

einen anderen Weg einschlägt, aber andererseits ihre Kandidatur aus den falschen Gründen befördert wurde. Sie wurden wirklich aus den falschen Gründen gewählt, aus politischen Gründen. Sie waren also leichte Beute. Sie wussten, dass es ihnen gegenüber viel Widerstand gab.

Fraser: Ich möchte darüber spre-chen, inwiefern dies vielleicht eine Möglichkeit darstellt, ein Publikum anzusprechen. Es gibt hier eine Prämisse, „dass ich ein Recht habe, so etwas zu tun", und dass dies Vertreter*innen einer öffentlichen Institution sind, was sie zu einer gewissen Transparenz verpflich-tet. Aber gleichzeitig sind sie auch Individuen, die das gleiche Recht auf Privatsphäre haben, wie jede*r andere auch. So gesehen ist es eine ethische Frage, und für mich ist das in Bezug auf diese Arbeit die größte Frage. Der Grund, wieso ich es hier vorstellen wollte, war, Folgendes zu diskutieren: Wenn eine Institution mich dazu einlädt, sich gemeinsam an ihr Publikum zu richten, und die Art und Weise, wie ich das umsetze, macht öffentlich auf ihren wider-sprüchlichen Diskurs aufmerksam, ist das dann ein möglicher oder empfehlenswerter Ansatz?

Ute Meta Bauer: Ich wollte Renée fragen, warum die Whitney Biennale für sie die schwierigste Ausstel-lungserfahrung war. Wieso?

Green: Aus verschiedenen Gründen. Zum Teil wegen meiner eigenen Zweifel daran, wie sie bereits vorab situiert wurde. Und wie sie inter-pretiert wurde. Sie wurde beispiels-weise die „multikulturelle Biennale" genannt. Und ich habe mir gedacht: Wieso würde ich Teil von so etwas sein wollen, wenn ich diesen Begriff

„Multikulturalismus" schon seit geraumer Zeit lautstark kritisiere? Ich habe einen ziemlich simplen Ansatz erwartet. Wenn sie schon so definiert wurde, bevor überhaupt etwas präsentiert wurde, war mir klar, dass es Probleme geben würde.

Dann auch noch die Sorge, die ich bei den Kurator*innen wahrnahm, die sich ebenfalls als problematisch erwies. Da ich der Meinung war, dass sie wegen dieser Sorge nicht richtig in der Lage sein würden, ihren Standpunkt überzeugend zu kommunizieren, ihre Entscheidungen und die Gründe zu rechtfertigen, weshalb sie bestimmte Personen ausgewählt haben. Ich glaube nicht, dass sie das je getan haben, und das empfand ich als den traurigsten Aspekt der ganzen Sache. Sie haben sich so dargestellt, als würden sie sich aus dem Fenster lehnen, was deswegen schon ein Problem war, weil dadurch die Arbeiten marginalisiert werden und somit auch die Menschen, die diese Arbeiten schaffen. Und dann war da noch ihre Verhaltensweise gegenüber der Öffentlichkeit, die mich extrem gestört hat. Als wir beispielsweise die obere Etage installierten, waren die unteren Etagen bereits eröffnet worden und David Ross erzählte uns, dass eine Frau, nichtwissend, dass er der Museumsdirektor war, sehr kritisch über die Ausstellung sprach und ihm dann sagte, dass er mit seiner Tochter, die gerade neben ihm stand, ins Metropolitan Museum of Art gehen solle, damit sie „eine Dosis richtiger Kultur" bekäme, oder so etwas ähnliches. Er hat sich aber keineswegs auf besonders starke Weise gerechtfertigt, als er diese Begegnung mir und einer*m anderen Künstler*in dort schilderte. Die Reaktionen der Kurator*innen auf die Ausstellung,

die ich mitbekam, fand ich auch unglaublich verstörend. Zum Beispiel war da dieses Ausweichen, ich meine ein buchstäbliches Ausweichen gegenüber der Künstler*innen von Seiten der Kurator*innen, eine Vermeidung der Kurator*innen, sich den Künstler*innen zu stellen. Das war zumindest meine Erfahrung. Ich meine, Fred war auch da. Ich war in der Zeit nach dem Ausstellungbeginn selten in New York. Aber es war eine seltsame Situation. Zum einen wurde die Arbeit für die Ausstellung nicht zu meiner Zufriedenheit angefertigt. Die Details waren nicht so, wie ich sie haben wollte und ich habe es immer wieder mit ihnen diskutiert, aber es wurde letztendlich nie richtig gemacht, also war ich darüber enttäuscht. Während des Empfangs war ich nur kurze Zeit anwesend, aber ich habe alles aus der Ferne mitbekommen und das machte es umso schlimmer. Ich konnte mich nicht mit anderen über den Empfang austauschen, daher habe ich einen verzerrten Eindruck, denke ich.

Fred Wilson: Ich bin geteilter Meinung. Ich denke, dass diese Ausstellung nicht für Installationen gemacht ist, dass aber die meisten Teilnehmer*innen welche konzipiert haben – sie wollten etwas besonderes für ihre Ausstellung machen – und sie haben das ohne Zeit und ohne Geld gemacht. Ich glaube, dass viele aus dem Grund sehr enttäuscht waren.

Fraser: Meiner Meinung nach sollten wir morgen auf diesen Punkt zurückkommen. Vielleicht in der letzten Sitzung.

Draxler: Um auf das Publikum zurückzukommen, nehmen wir einfach mal, was du zuletzt gemacht hast, Andrea, und betrachten die symbolisch-künstlerische Verwendung einer Dienstleistung innerhalb einer Institution – eine Praxis, die wie eine kuratische Tätigkeit aus einer Institution selbst entsteht. Können wir versuchen, die Unterschiede in den Ergebnissen zu analysieren und was die Möglichkeiten sind?

Fraser: Das interessiert mich, da die Art von Vermittlungsstrategien, von denen Susan gesprochen hat, alle auf gewisse Weise von außen kommen. Es ging darum, die Widersprüche im Inneren einer Institution zu erklären – wie sprechen wir die Widersprüche, die einer Institution innewohnen, selbst an. Ich glaube, dass es mittlerweile viele Vermittlungsprojekte gibt – und wir können darüber auch in Bezug auf dein Projekt in Antwerpen sprechen, Iwona – es werden Themen behandelt, die entweder eher als äußere Widersprüche betrachtet werden oder versuchen, die Widersprüche einer Institution zu bewältigen, indem man sie öffnet oder die Anhängerschaft verändert.

Cahan: Was ich zum Schluss meines Vortrags angesprochen habe und mich sehr herausgefordert hat, ist: Wie realisiert man diese Projekte, über die ich gesprochen habe, ohne sie in symbolische Gesten zu verwandeln, ohne dass sie zu symbolischen Repräsentationen werden? Natürlich handelt es sich um Repräsentationen, aber sie stellen keine Form des Diskurses dar, die analog zu dem sind, was du tust, Andrea, wenn du mit Montage arbeitest oder aufgenommenes Material neu schneidest. Ich denke, dass das zu

der Leichtigkeit beiträgt, mit der die Institution, mit der ich zusammenarbeite, sehr konfrontierende Aussagen in ihr laufendes Programm absorbiert, ohne dass es wirklich eine störende Wirkung erzeugt.

Fraser: Auf gewisse Weise, falls meine Aufnahme auch nur irgendetwas offenbart hat, dann war es die gute Absicht der Kurator*innen und die gute Absicht, die hinter dieser Art von Absorption steht.

Wilson: Ich glaube, dass es eine andere Reaktion gegeben hätte, wenn sich die Personen wirklich wohl gefühlt hätten und wenn es nicht die Whitney Biennale gewesen wäre, und wenn sie sich nicht so sehr über diese eine Ausstellung Gedanken gemacht hätten. Repräsentation ist das eigentliche Problem. Ich kenne das ja von mir, wenn ich interviewt werde, neige ich dazu, mir mehr oder auch weniger Sorgen zu machen, je nach Vertrieb und Publikum. Ich glaube also, dass es eben genau darum geht. In meiner Ausstellung [in Maryland] *Mining the Museum* hätten sie auch einfach die Etage absperren können, wenn es ihnen nicht gefallen hätte, und so gab es Momente, in denen ich es nicht wusste [ob sie dies tun würden]. Man bringt sie also an ihre Grenzen, aber letztendlich haben sie die Macht über ihre eigene Stimme.

Guttmann: Wenn ich an die Aufnahme denke, und warum du, Susan, der Meinung warst, sie sei so leicht absorbiert worden: meine eigene Reaktion darauf ist – und ich sage dies sehr vorsichtig, weil es eine interessante und komplexe Frage ist, auf die man nicht so schnell antworten sollte – dass mein Gefühl mir sagt, was uns vielleicht damit vermittelt werden soll, ist, dass etwas mit der Logik der Störung nicht stimmt. Man fungiert nicht als Künstler*in, aber nehmen wir an, dass es eine Form der Kunst ist…

Cahan: Nun, die Kunst hat ja jemandem gehört. Alle Projekte, die ich angesprochen habe, sind insofern irgendwie seltsam, weil sie sich schon existierenden Kategorien nicht zuordnen lassen. Und obwohl sie tatsächlich zu den aufregendsten Projekten gehören, mit denen ich während der vielen Jahre meiner Museumsarbeit jemals in Berührung gekommen bin, haben keine davon Förderungen erhalten. Denn wenn wir uns in einzelnen künstlerischen Kategorien bewerben, wird uns gesagt: „Das sind keine Kunstprojekte, das sind Vermittlungsprojekte." Und wenn wir uns auf Vermittlungsförderung für Museen bewerben, wird uns gesagt: „Das sind keine Vermittlungsprojekte, sondern Kunstprojekte." Sie sind alle entweder in Zusammenarbeit mit Künstler*innen entstanden, oder im Falle des Videoprojekts wurde die Idee durch Matthew Geller ins Leben gerufen, der Künstler ist, und das Projekt wurde von Branda Miller konzipiert, die es mitbetreute. Aber meine Rolle ist irgendwie seltsam – meine Rolle ist, innerhalb der Institution zu arbeiten und es ist meine Aufgabe dafür zu sorgen, dass das Projekt realisiert wird und hoffentlich mit Integrität und so, wie die Künstler*innen es vorgesehen haben. Ergibt das Sinn?

Guttmann: Ja, das ergibt Sinn, aber über diese Debatte der „Qualifikation" hinaus, ist meine Überlegung, dass uns dies eigentlich sagt, dass etwas mit der Logik der Störung nicht stimmt. Mit anderen Worten: ein Projekt umzusetzen, bei dem das

Hauptanliegen darin besteht, Diskontinuität in einer nahtlosen Struktur zu schaffen, ist an sich schon problematisch. Erstens, weil die Dinge nicht so nahtlos sind wie sie aussehen und zweitens, weil es eine sehr temporäre Geste ist, die über einen längeren Zeitraum einfach nicht funktioniert. Wenn man die Erwartungshaltung hat, dass Kunst über einen etwas längeren Zeitraum hinweg wirkt, dann können solche Dinge vielleicht auch funktionieren – vielleicht gab es fünf Minuten lang eine Störung, aber dann passieren andere Dinge, die das ursprüngliche Ereignis auf den Kopf stellen. Mein Gedanke dazu ist, dass einige dergleichen Ideen umformuliert und in Anliegen überführt werden können, die eher counter-hegemoniale Verfahren erzeugen, bei denen es gezielt darum geht, ungewollte Wut hinter sich zu lassen und andere Dinge in Gang zu setzen. Anstatt darauf zu beharren, die fehlerhaften Dinge, die man verändern will, hervorzuheben.

Cahan: Das ist genau die Art der Umgestaltung, die ich in meiner eigenen Praxis erlebt habe.

Blazwick: Ich würde mich dem gerne anschließen, weil ich das ganze Konzept der „Subversion" für unmöglich halte. Es ist naiv und nichts, was möglich ist. Ich bin noch nicht mal der Meinung, dass es als Strategie lohnenswert ist, weil man sich mit einer gesamten Gesellschaft auseinandersetzt – dem gesamten 20. Jahrhundert. Ich bin deiner Meinung: man arbeitet entweder innerhalb eines Rahmens und versucht, ihn bloßzustellen – wobei ich mich dabei unwohl fühle, weil die Bloßstellung ja eine Selbstverständlichkeit ist – oder ich glaube, dass man eine parallele Praxis entwickelt. Man arbeitet innerhalb eines Rahmens, oder man nutzt ihn auf irgendeine Art und Weise aus, und das ist die einzige Möglichkeit. Aber mit dem Konzept der Subversion schießt man sich in gewisser Weise ins Knie.

Fraser: Was sind die Optionen? Eine parallele Praxis, innerhalb von etwas arbeiten, oder…

Blazwick: Etwas außerhalb zu entwickeln, oder nebenher, oder bereits existierende innere Strukturen zu verwenden. Aber zu denken, dass man langfristig eine Unterbrechung oder eine Art Bruch schaffen kann…ich will nicht sagen, dass es hoffnungslos ist, aber man muss mit einer bestimmten Anzahl von Gegebenheiten rechnen und dass man unter diesen Gegebenheiten arbeiten muss.

Cahan: Ich habe meine eigene Arbeit nie vorwiegend als „subversiv" betrachtet. An erster Stelle sah ich sie als Möglichkeit für eine Vielzahl von Erzählungen.

Wilson: Mir ist es ziemlich klar, warum das New Museum diese Aufnahmen [der Meinungen der Museumsbesucher*innen] absorbieren konnte: es liegt an der Autorität derjenigen auf den Aufnahmen. Die Befugten geben den Personen auf den Aufnahmen keinerlei Autorität, sie verspüren den Machtdruck nicht, der ihnen sagt, was sie zu tun haben. Wenn es Vera List wäre oder Charles Luce oder einer der Spender*innen, die exakt das Gleiche sagen – ich meine, das wäre ziemlich komisch – jedenfalls, wenn sie exakt das Gleiche sagen würden, hätte es tatsächlich eine Auswirkung auf die Leute im Museum.

Barry: In der Ausstellung war auch das Konzept des Fernsehens als Repräsentation der weißen US-amerikanischen Mittelschicht implizit. Wenn man sich die Ausstellung anschaut, dann vermischen sich US-amerikanische Politik und Fernsehen nie. Es gibt nur einen kurzen Moment zwischen 1968 und 1970, in dem es ein wenig politisches Fernsehen gab. Aber die Ausstellung hat die weiße Mittelschicht Amerikas sehr klar und auf eine sehr offene Art und Weise dargestellt. Das ist ein Grund, warum seine [Museumsbesucher Art Jones] Kritik Teil der Ausstellung war, und er hat es verstanden.

Wilson: Ich fand seine Kritik äußerst überzeugend, aber es entstand aus einem Ausdruck der Machtlosigkeit, dass er eine Stimme bekam. Daher reicht diese Stimme nicht noch weiter, weil sie verstanden wurde.

Guttmann: Aber sie war ziemlich bedrohlich, sehr konkret. Er sagte, „das ist nicht mehr die Postmoderne, es sind jetzt die Neunziger." Er meinte das völlig ernst.

Wilson: *Inwiefern* meinte er es ernst, das ist die Frage, die ich versuche zu stellen.

Green: Das war Art Jones, er ist selbst Videoproduzent. Ein Filmemacher und Multimedia-Künstler. Er hat mit der Videogruppe gearbeitet, sehr interessant.

Wilson: Man kann nicht erwarten, dass dies die Machtstrukturen beeinflusst, da es natürlich seit geraumer Zeit schon solche Stimmen gibt, die sich direkt an die Museumsstruktur richten. Es liegt daran, dass sie von Leuten kommen, die keinen Einfluss auf die Machtstrukturen nehmen können – es ist ja kein Vorstandsmitglied, es wird keine grundsätzliche Veränderung hervorbringen. Es kann absorbiert werden, weil er nicht mit einem Stock in der Hand über jemandem steht, was eine Bedrohung wäre. Versteht ihr?

Fraser: Ich möchte dem, was Susan und Iwona über unterschiedliche Strategien gesagt haben, etwas entgegensetzen. Susan hat gesagt, dass Leute im Museum, die diese Dinge sahen, gesagt haben: „Oh, lasst uns das immer so machen", damit, das war deine [Susan] Interpretation, „wir nichts verändern müssen". Damit wir ein dauerhaftes selbstreflexives, pseudokritisches Zusatzprogramm anbieten können, was immer weiterläuft und selbst wenn es eine erkennbare Partizipation gibt, ist es keine richtige Partizipation. Ich dachte, es ist keine „richtige" Partizipation, da das Subjekt immer das Museum ist und das lässt nicht zu…Und dann dachte ich an das, was du, Iwona, in Antwerpen gemacht hast, wo das Subjekt nicht das Museum war, und ich habe überlegt, ob dies einer der Unterschiede zwischen einer partizipatorischen Arbeitsweise oder einem demokratischen Prozess ist, und einem verwalteten, bei dem man eine Plattform schafft. Aber was sind dann die Anliegen, die formuliert werden können?

Blazwick: Es gibt auch ein interessantes Modell, was in Großbritannien entwickelt wurde und Anefa heißt, bei dem über den Arts Council [of Great Britain] öffentliche Gelder dazu verwendet werden, ein loses Netzwerk rund um Ausstellungs- und Publikationsaktivitäten aufzubauen. Beispielsweise wurde einem Verlagsprogramm Geld gegeben, zu dem *Third Text*, aber auch andere Verlagsinitiativen gehörten. Zum Beispiel haben sie gerade alle Texte von Jimmie Durham publiziert. Aber der Punkt ist, dass sie den Druck und den Vertrieb finanziert haben, und das finde ich essentiell. Es geht um Kommunikation. Dann haben sie auch Gelder für Ausstellungen vergeben. Der Künstler Sunil Gupta hat daran gearbeitet, Ausstellungen aufzubauen, die dann verschiedenen Einrichtungen angeboten werden. Und Gupta, als [süd]asiatischer Fotograf, der auch zufällig schwul ist, schaut sich Anhängerschaften an, die in Managementstrukturen nicht repräsentiert wurden. Man baut sich seine eigene Struktur auf, und dann schafft man einen eigenen Ansatz, um sie zu kommunizieren und zu vertreiben, anstatt ständig den Kopf gegen diese Granitwand zu schlagen. Schrittweise verändern sich natürlich zunehmend auch Dinge: die Tatsache, dass es Frauen in diesen Strukturen gibt, dass es verschiedene Anhängerschaften gibt, die langsam und schrittweise ihren Weg durch diese Strukturen finden. Aber ich denke, dass es auch andere Wege gibt, dies zu erreichen.

Bauer: Aber glaubst du nicht, dass ein großer Unterscheid zwischen Anefa und beispielsweise dem Whitney ist, dass die Künstler*innen selbst diese Situation schaffen? Wir wissen selbst, was wir brauchen. Ich glaube, es hat viel damit zu tun, dem Publikum zu dienen. Wenn das Whitney Museum sagt, dass sie eine multikulturelle Biennale machen, wollen sie das ja nicht für sich machen. Sie wollen die politischen Probleme verstecken, die sie nicht lösen können, und das tun sie, indem sie es in einen Kunstkontext setzen.

Green: Das wollte ich deutlich machen. Viele der Projekte, die in diese Ausstellung einbezogen wurden, waren in anderen Situationen viel wirkungsvoller. Und Leute wie Art Jones haben ihre Arbeiten selbst verbreitet, nutzten Technologien für ihre Interventionen, und haben ständig das Thema der Absorption angesprochen. Dies sind Menschen, die sich immer der Gefahr bewusst sind, von hegemonialen Strukturen absorbiert zu werden.

Bauer: Wenn man gerade eine große Ausstellung macht, wird einem immer gesagt, dass sie multikulturell und gesellschaftlich sein muss, weil sie diese Themen in der Kunst für das Publikum aktuell fördern wollen, aber darüber hinaus verändern sie nichts. Die Kunstwelt ist so klein. Man kann sehr offen und sehr sozial sein, aber das Publikum ist begrenzt. Es ist ein spezielles Feld, in dem man gesellschaftlich nichts verändern kann. Es ist wie eine große Falle.

Guttmann: Repressive Toleranz.

Fraser: Aber glaubt ihr nicht, dass es eine wesentliche Dimension gesellschaftlicher Erfahrung gibt, die man eigentlich kulturell nennt? Und das einiges davon in Museen stattfindet? Ich habe mich schon vor einiger Zeit, zumindest bewusst, von dem subversiven Modell abgewandt, aber ich möchte nicht darauf verzichten, weiterhin etwas in Museen zu machen. Und ich möchte auch keinen parallelen Ansatz, da Museen Orte sind, an denen eine ganz bestimmte soziale Erfahrung stattfindet, mit all den Dynamiken und Geschichten des Ortes, die sich für eine Auseinandersetzung lohnen. Ich bin der Meinung, dass es sich lohnt, die Erfahrungen, die Menschen in Museen machen, anzusprechen.

Draxler: Aber hast du eine Idee, wie man das Publikum ansprechen soll? Denn so, wie du von der Whitney Arbeit gesprochen hast, klang es, als wäre es zufällig passiert, dass du auf dieses konfrontative Modell gestoßen bist. Was du wolltest, war eine Zusammenarbeit. Hätte diese Zusammenarbeit also funktioniert, was für eine Ansprache wäre es gewesen?

Fraser: Ich glaube, es wäre dieselbe gewesen. Ich wollte nur nicht, dass es für die anderen Teilnehmer*innen so ein Problem darstellt. Ich wollte sie repräsentieren. Ich wollte sie nicht verletzen. Ich wollte sie nicht falsch darstellen, aber ich wollte Dinge darstellen, die nicht unbedingt mit der Erhaltung einer verbindlich legitimen Repräsentation dieser Art von Institution einhergehen. Ich war der Meinung, dass dies mit ihren eigenen Absichten übereinstimmte: sich mit einer Kritik der Institution und ihrer Geschichte zu befassen, eine Kritik, die von der Legitimität der Kultur, die diese Institution traditionsgemäß repräsentiert, handelt. Ich hatte angenommen, dass das mit ihrer Vorstellung übereinstimmte.

Wilson: Auf einer theoretischen Ebene tat es das auch. Aber es ging vor allem um ihr Bedürfnis, in diesem bestimmten Fall von heroischen Bildern getragen zu werden.

Fraser: Oder, dass dieser ganze gesellschaftliche Widerspruch einfach ein bisschen zu viel für eine Einzelperson ist, um sie persönlich vor einem Publikum von Tausenden von Menschen zu verkörpern.

Clegg: Was ich spannend finde ist, dass das Whitney als Institution so viel stärker ist als seine Kurator*innen. Die Veränderungen seiner Politik waren aufgrund all der Einschränkungen, die die Kurator*innen haben und den Künstler*innen aufzwingen, bisher so gering. Die Probleme, von denen du in Bezug auf die Biennale von 1993 sprichst, sind andere Versionen von dem, was wir vier Jahre vorher erlebt hatten. Da brachte man uns im Grunde genommen dazu, uns glücklich zu schätzen, überhaupt Teil der Ausstellung sein zu dürfen. Sie haben sich die Arbeit sehr genau angeschaut, und sie hatten ihre eigene Idee und ihre persönliche Auswahl. Eine Sache, die wir zu dem Zeitpunkt gemacht haben, waren Porträts der Kurator*innen, die sie natürlich nicht in der Ausstellung haben wollten. Und es war noch nicht mal so klar warum, außer dass sie diese Art der Selbstdarstellung nicht in der Show haben wollten. Es geht also bei diesen Whitney Biennalen immer um Veränderung. Aber ohne jegliche konkrete repräsentative Veränderung der Biennale selbst, was ortsspezifische Projekte nicht wirklich zulässt.

Barry: Ich möchte etwas über den Katalog sagen, den Andrea [auf der Leinwand] zeigt, *The Desire of the Museum*, was ein Projekt von Whitney-Studierenden aus dem Kurator*innen-Programm war. Ich habe ihnen 1989 bei der Konzeptualisierung und dem Design der Ausstellung *The Desire of the Museum* geholfen. Bei dem Projekt wollten die Studierenden, hauptsächlich Postgraduates des Whitney Independent Study Program, das Whitney und seine Geschichte aus psychoanalytischer Perspektive

untersuchen und ausstellen. Und das Whitney hat alles völlig zensiert. Wir durften keine Dokumente zeigen, wir durften noch nicht mal eine Chronologie des Whitneys als Museum zeigen. Statt also einer Ausstellung über das Verlangen der Studierenden nach einem anderen institutionellen Rahmen zu sein, wurde sie stattdessen zu einer Ausstellung über das Verlangen von Künstler*innen nach einer anderen Form der institutionellen Repräsentation. Das Whitney zensierte sich selbst und entzog sich selbst seines eigenen Kontextes. Und das ist kein ungewöhnliches Whitney-Verhalten – vielmehr ist es in dieser Institution, genauso wie in vielen anderen Museen, systemisch.

Renate Lorenz: Ich wollte sagen, dass ich deine Meinung nicht teile [Ute], dass es nicht wichtig ist, was sich im Kunstbereich abspielt. Ich glaube, dass es für die Gesellschaft sehr wichtig ist, wie Entscheidungen im Kunstbereich getroffen werden. Da sich viele dafür interessieren, finde ich, dass es zu einfach wäre, zu sagen: „Oh, es ist nicht wichtig, weil die gesamte Gesellschaft viel größer ist." In einer Ausstellung wie der am Whitney ändern sie die Strukturen nicht, weil sie diegleichen Entscheidungsstrukturen und Probleme haben, die in der Gesellschaft auch vorhanden sind. Und auch wenn es viele Künstler*innen gibt, die vorher nicht wahrgenommen wurden, dann ist das nur eine repräsentative Veränderung.

Green: Genau, und ich wollte noch einmal etwas ansprechen, was du vorhin gesagt hast, Ute. Da ich strikt dagegen bin, was am Whitney passiert ist. Aber es kommt noch ein weiterer Punkt hinzu. Trotz der

Schwierigkeit, sich aus dem bestehenden Rahmen des Museums zu befreien, ist da noch die Tatsache, dass das Publikum dieser Biennale größer war als das vorherige, und das hat bei vielen für Gesprächsstoff gesorgt. Ich war von den Reaktionen des Publikums überrascht – nicht der Kritiker*innen, weil das ja etwas ganz anderes ist. Aber trotz der Einschränkungen dieser Strukturen auf die Arbeiten entstand doch etwas anderes, und ich glaube, dass es da ein paar positive Aspekte gab.

Bauer: Ich bin nicht der Meinung, dass das, was im Kunstbereich passiert, nicht wichtig ist. Ich würde nicht so viel von meiner Energie in ihn investieren, wenn ich das glauben würde, oder wenn es nur darum ginge, Spaß zu haben. Beispielsweise kann die Stadt Stuttgart einerseits nicht die Probleme asylsuchender Menschen lösen, während sie andererseits Institutionen wie unsere dazu auffordert, mehr sozial-kulturelle Arbeit zu leisten. Das ist eine Falle. Sie versuchen, politische Probleme kulturell zu lösen, indem sie sagen, dass wir eine multikulturelle Gesellschaft sind, und auch wenn es wichtig ist, dass man das erkennt, kann es das allein nicht sein – sie müssen auch ihre Politik ändern.

Lorenz: Ich denke, dass man mit diesen großen Ausstellungen die Strukturen nicht verändern kann. Man muss seine Energie in einen anderen Bereich stecken, in dem man die Positionen und Richtungen des gesamten sozialen Bereiches besser steuern kann.

Jochen Becker: Die Whitney Biennale war eine Zentralisierung dezentralisierter Projekte in sehr verschiedenen Gegenden. Aber diese Projekte waren in Midtown [Manhattan]. Das Whitney zentralisierte sie also dort, und damit schadeten sie der Institutionskritik und anderen Arbeitsweisen.

Guttmann: Das stimmt, in großem Maße. Keiner hätte mehr Schaden an dieser Art von Arbeit anrichten können, als das Whitney. Die Arbeiten wurden auch so schlecht ausgestellt, dass man keine Gedanken oder Ideen dazu entwickeln konnte. Es war alles schlechte Form. Es wurde alles zusammengeworfen.

Wilson: Es ist für Amerikaner*innen sehr typisch, sich um 180 Grad zu drehen, um etwas zu bewältigen und sich dann wieder völlig umzuentscheiden.

Becker: Die Frage ist: Warum passierte es so? Wenn man dabei Bauchschmerzen hatte oder von Anfang an so große Bedenken und wusste, dass es offensichtlich ein Problem für eher gemeinschaftsbezogene Projekte sein würde… Ich meine, die Whitney Biennale wird hier in Deutschland jetzt als die große Ausstellung bezeichnet, und als Wendepunkt, und so weiter.

Draxler: Das ist wichtig zu erwähnen, dass die kritische Wahrnehmung der Ausstellung in Deutschland wirklich unglaublich war. Auf eine sehr einfache Weise wurde sie wie neuer Kunstklatsch präsentiert und in Zeitschriften aus einer sehr konservativen Perspektive diskutiert, sogar in Publikationen wie *Der Spiegel*. Peter Weibels Ausstellung über die Entwicklung der Institutionskritik, *Kontext Kunst* [Neue Galerie Graz am Landesmuseum, 1993], war haargenau gleich, nur dass sie nicht in Manhattan war.

Becker: Gab es nach der Ausstellung in Hinsicht auf das Interesse für gemeinschaftsbezogene Projekte irgendwelche Veränderungen?

Green: Ich möchte etwas über „Bauchschmerzen" sagen. Ich fühlte mich sehr entfremdet. Wenn ein*e Kurator*in eine Arbeit auswählt, kann man entweder sagen: „ich will an der Ausstellung nicht teilnehmen" oder „ich will teilnehmen, aber nur, wenn es auf diese Weise gemacht wird". Und dann sagen sie entweder ja oder nein dazu.

Fraser: Ich würde die Arbeiten, die Teil der Whitney Biennale waren, nicht als gemeinschaftsbezogen betrachten. Ein großer Teil der Arbeiten wurde in Gegenden außerhalb SoHos ausgestellt, aber das bedeutet nicht, dass sie eine partizipatorische Beziehung zu den Gemeinschaften hatten, in denen sie zum ersten Mal gezeigt wurden. Das meiste davon war nur Atelierarbeit. Es waren einfach Künstler*innen, die Ateliers außerhalb Lower Manhattans hatten.

Cahan: Ein Problem war, dass es sich auf Dinge bezog, die auf thematische Weise politisch waren. Es hatte also so eine merkwürdige thematische Überlagerung.

Fraser: Nancy Spero war Teil dieser Whitney Biennale, und sie war vorher noch nie Teil einer Biennale.

Cahan: Oh, verstehe, also war es eine Wiedergutmachung dieses Versäumnisses.

Clegg: Es war sehr seltsam. Dadurch zeigten sie, dass New York mit dem Rest der USA politisch nicht synchron ist. Denn all diese Fragen bezüglich der Installation und der Darstellung – sie erklären nicht, warum die Ausstellung so eine Gegenreaktion bekam. Mir hat es bewiesen, dass New York wirklich in den achtziger Jahren verankert ist.

Wilson: Die Ausstellung hatte mehr Besucher*innen als jede andere Biennale zuvor. Die Presse war eigentlich eine reaktionäre Presse, eine reflexartige Presse. Sind die Probleme der Whitney Biennale und allen Whitney Biennalen nicht die gleichen Probleme der Venedig Biennale und der documenta? Diese großen Ausstellungen, die versuchen, einen Höhepunkt und einen bestimmten Zeitraum zusammenzufassen, oder die Kulturen bestimmter Orte zu repräsentieren. Die Organisator*innen investieren in diese riesige symbolische Geste, die individuell gestaltet wird…und dann hat man auch noch ein Problem mit den Kurator*innen, weil sie so daran hängen, die Ausstellung sei eine Verwirklichung ihrer Idee.

Fraser: Die Whitney Biennale wurde schon immer schlechtgemacht. Ich habe mir zehn Jahre Presse durchgelesen und sie wurde wirklich schon immer schlechtgemacht. Die New Yorker Presse neigt dazu, internationale Ausstellungen wie diese schlechtzumachen. Ich bin überrascht darüber, dass die documenta in der Presse gefeiert wurde.

Blazwick: Das Whitney sollte nicht so im Vordergrund stehen. Es ist nur eine kleine Institution.

(Gelächter)

Blazwick: Nein wirklich – wir unterhalten uns nie über diese anderen Veranstaltungen und Ausstellungen. Das ist leider der Imperialismus.

Fraser: Genau, ich möchte auch nicht über Venedig und die documenta sprechen.

Blazwick: Havanna, Istanbul – es gibt andere wirklich wichtige Veranstaltungen und Ausstellungen, über die man sprechen kann.

Draxler: Ich glaube, es wäre gut, ein paar dieser anderen spezifischen Kontexte zu besprechen und die strukturellen Bedingungen zu diskutieren. Oder wie Arbeitsweisen dort übernommen wurden. Oder der Kulturbürgermeister von Stuttgart – ich weiß nicht, ob irgendeine andere Stadt einen hat, aber die Stadt Stuttgart hat einen. Und das ist eine sehr einflussreiche Position, die viel mit dem Publikum und dem Ansprechen von Publikum zu tun hat.

Ich wollte übrigens noch sagen, dass ich Sympathie für das Subversive habe. Was der Typ im [New Museum] Video, Art Jones, gemacht hat, war gewissermaßen sehr subversiv. Aber was du, Susan, gemacht hast, war es nicht.

Cahan: Was meinst du? Ich würde dir nicht unbedingt widersprechen, aber ich möchte wissen, was du damit meinst, Helmut.

Draxler: Was du machst, würde ich eher als das Schaffen einer Ansprache an ein Publikum beschreiben.

Cahan: Nun, ich weiß nicht, ob es das ist, was du sagen wolltest, aber was ich inzwischen unterscheide, ist das Verändern gewisser institutioneller Praktiken und anderer Aktivitäten, die ich als politisch betrachte. Da ich nicht glaube, dass das Verändern institutioneller Praktiken oder Beziehungen unbedingt politisch ist. Es kommt auf die Politik derjenigen an,

die involviert sind. Künstler*innen mehr Freiheit oder mehr Autonomie in Museen zu geben, ist politisch nicht unbedingt sehr progressiv. Es kommt auf den oder die Künstler*in an. Wenn es Helen Frankenthaler ist, ist es nicht unbedingt progressiv. Renée, du hattest mich vorhin gefragt, woran ich momentan arbeite. Nun, ich arbeite momentan an einer Langzeitkollaboration mit Künstler*innen-Aktivist*innen und erwachsenen Studierenden in drei überwiegend lateinamerikanischen Wohngegenden in New York, um eine Installation zu entwickeln, die sich mit der jüngsten Geschichte der Einwanderung von Lateinamerikaner*innen nach New York anhand von individuellen Lebensgeschichten und persönlichen Zeugnissen befasst. Sie wurde gerade im New Museum gezeigt und geht jetzt weiter an Orte in diesen Wohngegenden. Aus pädagogischer Sicht war es bisher sehr interessant, da sie Aspekte der Geschichte New Yorks beinhaltet, die in Schulbüchern nicht vorkommen, sodass viele Schulgruppen zu uns gekommen sind, um etwas über diese Geschichte zu lernen. Es ist eher eine produktive als eine dekonstruktive Verfahrensweise, was die Beziehungen zwischen Kunst und Institutionen betrifft. In diesem Konsortium von fünfzehn Personen einigten wir uns darauf, alle Verwaltungsentscheidungen für das Projekt in Bezug auf die Förderung, die Finanzierung und wie es der Presse präsentiert wird, kollektiv zu treffen. Zum jetzigen Zeitpunkt ist es ein funktionierendes Experiment. Es gibt bei dieser Form der Gruppenarbeit immer Konflikte, aber da so viele Leute im Konsortium aus der Aktivist*innenszene kommen, wissen sie wirklich, wie man mit solchen kollaborativen Situationen umgeht.

Blazwick: Ich möchte wissen, welche Erfahrungen in Arnheim während Sonsbeek 93 gemacht wurden. Mich interessiert die Frage in Bezug auf das Publikum in einer solchen Situation, wenn man sich außerhalb einer Institution und in dieser Stadt befindet. Ich frage mich, was für mögliche Beziehungen daraus entstanden sind.

Draxler: Stephan, du warst doch da.

Stephan Dillemuth: Ich war da. Es war ein Tagesausflug nach Arnheim und man musste Ostereier suchen. Das war's. Manchen macht das Spaß.

Blazwick: Anscheinend war es sehr angespannt. Ich habe von den Organisator*innen gehört, dass viel Aggression gegen die Kunst gerichtet wurde und Arbeiten zerstört wurden.

Dillemuth: Das könnte stimmen, aber das war mir nicht bewusst. Ich habe einen Film über die Ausstellung gemacht, und dann bin ich verschwunden. Ich habe gehört, dass es viele Beschwerden wegen Schäden gab, aber wenn man so eine Ausstellung macht, muss man damit rechnen. Der Schaden verrät etwas, das meiner Meinung nach vielleicht gar nicht so schlimm ist. Vielleicht war die Art und Weise, wie sie mit den Schäden umgegangen sind, aber problematisch. Beispielsweise weiß ich, dass Andreas Siekmann den Organisator*innen sagte, sie sollten es bitte beschädigt lassen, so wie es ist, da es etwas zeige. Dann fingen sie aber an, aufzuräumen und die gesprühten Slogans zu überstreichen und es wieder so aufzubauen, wie es vorher war. Sie haben das ein paar Mal

gemacht und dann Siekmann gebeten, eine öffentliche Diskussion zu moderieren und das Ventil auf diese Weise zu öffnen. Ich finde es gut, dass Kunst Druck auf ein bestimmtes Publikum ausübt, das normalerweise anonym bleibt, und wenn Kunst das bewirken kann, dann ist das vielleicht positiv.

Blazwick: Im letzten Jahr gab es in Newcastle ein Projekt, das so viel Wut und Beschwerde auslöste, dass es meiner Meinung nach für jeden Beteiligten ein Schock war. Die Arbeiten wurden nicht nur vandalisiert, sondern einige Personen haben sogar ihre Stelle verloren. Es war eine wirklich gewaltsame Reaktion. Wieder einmal war der Kurator in der Position, dass er dort landete und scheiterte, ich glaube, um die Lokalpolitiker*innen und das Museumspersonal, die das Gefühl hatten, sie werden aus ihrer Rolle gedrängt, zu kooptieren. Und deshalb übernahmen sie die Kontrolle über das Projekt und die Ausgaben jedes einzelnen Kunstprojekts und bestanden darauf, dass der Leiter des Museums jeden Antrag persönlich absegnet. Also man muss sich vorstellen: wenn man Schrauben brauchte, musste der Leiter dieser riesigen bürokratischen Pyramide diesen Zettel unterschreiben. Schließlich unterbrach er das Projekt, und das war ganz eindeutig die Absicht. Eine*r der Kurator*innen für Vermittlung am Museum unterschrieb die Anträge, damit die Künstler*innen mit ihrer Arbeit fortfahren und ihre Spesen erhalten konnten. Und die Person hat ihre Stelle verloren und wurde der Unterschlagung beschuldigt. Es ist wirklich ernst, und einige Zahlen gelangten auch an die Öffentlichkeit, was die Kosten des Projekts betraf. Unvermeidbar war dann auch ein gewisser Rückschlag aufgrund all dieser Probleme, die mit Unterkunft und städtischem Verfall zu tun hatten. Das gesamte Ausstellungsprojekt diente dann als Auslöser für diese verschiedenen Probleme. Ich habe mich gefragt, was die Leute davon hielten, dass Künstler*innen in diese unterschiedlichen Situationen gebracht werden, in denen man mit einer fremden Gemeinschaft umgehen muss, die sehr komplex ist.

Bischoff: Es tut mir leid, dass ich wieder auf das Whitney zurückkomme, aber das erinnert mich an die Zeit, als sie Warhols Gemälde *Before and After* (1961) über den Mitgliedstresen hängten. Und der neue Direktor nahm es dann sofort wieder herunter. Es ist also nicht möglich, Kunstpolitik zu machen. Eine große Institution muss Dinge wie Produktmanagement regeln.

Die Sonsbeek Ausstellung war '69 sehr gut, danach nicht so gut, und dieses Mal wollen sie, dass die neue Kunst nicht nach künstlerischen Vorstellungen, sondern durch Kunstpolitik gestaltet wird. Das ist für große Ausstellungen typisch. Es war durchaus erstaunlich, dass es in den Niederlanden diese Gewalt gab.

Dillemuth: Vielleicht haben die Leute in den Niederlanden aber genug von Kunst im öffentlichen Raum, weil sie so viel davon haben.

Clegg: Oft liegt das Problem bei der Arbeit selbst, bei der Kulturpolitik, die in der Kunst von oben kommt. Wie an vielen Orten in Frankreich, wo man sich fragen muss, ob diese Museen erforderlich sind, die offenbar kein Publikum haben und sich auch nicht wirklich darum bemühen, eins zu bekommen, Kunst aber als

etwas präsentieren, das einfach gut für die Gesellschaft ist. Dass die Kunst sie beflügelt. Daher finde ich es interessant, über das Scheitern einer bestimmten Art der Arbeit von Künstler*innen nachzudenken und wie sie mit den Orten, an denen sie ihre Arbeit ausstellen, interagieren.

Barry: Die Frage, wie Menschen mit Kunst im öffentlichen Raum umgehen und wie sich der Diskurs über Kunst entwickelt – Künstler*innen und Kurator*innen versuchen, das zu steuern, aus unterschiedlichen Perspektiven. Aber sie versuchen nicht, das zu steuern, was dem Publikum direkt über die Presse vermittelt wird, weil sie das nicht können. In den USA hatten wir die Zensur vom NEA [National Endowment for the Arts] und den Verlust von Förderung was Fragen von Kunst und Meinungsfreiheit anging, und das Abzielen der Rechten auf das Thema Sexualität und die Darstellung von Homosexualität. Das wurde deutlich. Kunst war ein leichtes Opfer.

Guttmann: Aber es gibt hier einen wichtigen Punkt, denn wenn man in einer Stadt ist, in der die Menschen wirklich arm sind, in der es chronische Probleme gibt, dann müssen Künstler*innen den Vorgang der Rechtfertigung tatsächlich ernst nehmen. Es ist ja nicht nur, dass die Rechte sich ein leichtes Opfer ausgesucht hat. Die Art und Weise, wie die Neue Rechte auf Kunst abzielt, ist ein billiger Trick, aber wir sprechen hier von etwas, mit dem glaube ich jede Person, die mit Kunst zu tun haben will, umgehen muss.

Barry: Hier geht es aber um das Publikum und darum, einen Diskurs aufzubauen, der mit diesem Niveau der Kulturkritik umgehen kann,

wenn es letztendlich die Boulevard-
presse erreicht.

Guttmann: Ich glaube, dass sich die
Leute in den meisten Fällen nicht
einmal ansatzweise darum bemühen, diejenigen, die in unmittelbarer
Nähe der Kunst leben, anzusprechen. Sie versuchen ja noch nicht
mal herauszufinden, wer dort lebt,
was sie vielleicht wollen, wie sie
diese Orte genutzt haben. Solche
Fragen sind das A und O im Umgang
mit einer Situation. Es gibt so viele
Kunstprojekte, die bereits auf dieser
elementaren Stufe scheitern, sodass
alles, was darüber hinausgeht,
reine Spekulation ist, da es einen
echten Mangel an Bewusstsein
für die grundlegendsten Aspekte
einer Arbeitsethik im öffentlichen
Raum gibt.

Fraser: Ich muss etwas sehr Wichtiges ansprechen, nämlich das es,
wenn wir nicht in den nächsten fünf
Minuten aufhören, nichts zu essen
gibt.

Cahan: Ich möchte mich zu dem,
was Judith gesagt hat, äußern.
Ich glaube, dass das, worüber du
sprichst, das wirklich sehr unterent-
wickelte Verständnis von Rezeption
widerspiegelt. Worauf sich meine
Arbeit konzentriert hat. Es spiegelt
auch die traditionelle Vorstellung
von Kunst als Objekt wider an Stelle
der Vorstellung von Kunst und ihrer
Rezeption als Prozess.

Barry: Worüber Martin gesprochen
hat, hat mit anderen Themen zu tun.

Guttmann: Ich habe die Probleme
in Newcastle so verstanden, dass es
eine sehr problematische Gegend
ist. Und die Leute sind ausgeflippt,
ja, aber ich finde, dass sie das Recht

haben, auszuflippen. Es sollte ein
neues Maß an Verantwortung dafür
geben, wie Geld in der Kunst ausgegeben wird. Ich glaube das wirklich.
Es gibt einfach keinen Platz für un-
seriöse Abenteuer. Es macht keinen
Sinn mehr, falls es überhaupt jemals
Sinn gemacht hat.

Fraser: Renée könnte von Abenteu-
ern mit Agenturen für öffentliche
Kunst in New York erzählen, und
dem Versuch, etwas außer Kacheln
an den Wänden von Schulgebäu-
den zu befestigen. Man hat keine
Chance. Wenn man versucht, etwas
Gemeinschaftsbezogenes aufzu-
ziehen oder mit Schulkindern ein
Schulprojekt machen möchte, führt
das zu nichts. Es ist ein Unterschied
wie Tag und Nacht. Die Dinge, die
wir uns von öffentlicher Kunst erhoffen, stoßen auf allen möglichen
Widerstand, der nicht unbedingt nur
Widerstand von Künstler*innen ist.

Wilson: In der South Bronx, die ja für
Vandalismus und Graffiti bekannt
ist, gibt es viel öffentliche Kunst, die
immer in makellosem Zustand ist
und sehr gepflegt und respektiert
wird. Die Menschen leben einfach
damit. Arbeiten von John Ahearn
und Rigoberto Torres werden nie an-
gerührt – sie sind Teil des Viertels.

Blazwick: Können Künstler*innen
erstens diese enorme Verantwortung auf sich nehmen, die Komplexitäten der lokalen Umstände
zu bewältigen. Ich glaube, dass es
unglaublich schwierig ist und es unglaublich viel Zeit und Energie und
Ressourcen in Anspruch nimmt, mit
diesen Komplexitäten auf eine be-
friedigende Art und Weise umzugehen. Zweitens war es [in Newcastle]
ein Lehrbeispiel dafür, wie man
etwas nicht organisiert. Es gab eine

Art patrizische Missachtung der bestehenden Mächte. Ich glaube, dass man wirklich sehr vorsichtig mit ihnen arbeiten muss, denn sobald man sich in einer Situation befindet, in der man sie „idiotische Politiker*innen" oder „bescheuerte Hierarchien" nennt oder dass „wir uns nicht mit ihnen befassen wollen" – dann ist die Arbeit grundsätzlich nicht mehr möglich.

Guttmann: Aber das ist albern. Das ist ja der springende Punkt. Man will von A nach B kommen und C steht im Weg. Man sagt also „Lass uns einfach so tun, als würde C nicht existieren."

Blazwick: Ich glaube, dass die Künstler*innen sich wirklich bemüht haben, und dass sie sich in der hierarchischen Struktur verfangen haben.

Bischoff: Ich denke, dass diese Frage, bis wohin die Verantwortung von Künstler*innen und Kurator*innen reicht, morgen besprochen werden sollte.

Draxler: Danke, Uli!

(Gelächter)

Green: Lasst uns zu Abend essen.

Arbeitsgruppe
Sitzung Vier

Den Gemeinschaften dienen
Sonntag, 23. Januar 1994

Vorträge:
Stephan Dillemuth
BüroBert
Clegg & Guttmann

Kritik über Kunstinstitutionen und den Kunstmarkt *haben einige Künstler*innen dazu bewogen, alternative Kunstorganisationen zu gründen* und /oder *Projekte in Gemeinschaften zu erarbeiten, denen Künstler*innen herkömmlicherweise nicht dienen.*

*Ist die anarchistische und radikale demokratische Basis vieler alternativer Organisationen mit der Professionalisierung, die in Expert*innen/ Klient*innen-Modellen angedeutet wird, vereinbar?*

*Können Kunstinstitutionen nicht-künstlerischen Gemeinschaften dienen? Was passiert, wenn die Interessen der Künstler*innen und der nicht-künstlerischen Gemeinschaften, denen sie dienen wollen, in Konflikt geraten?*

Helmut Draxler: Guten Morgen. Es gab einige Beschwerden, dass die gestrigen Vorträge nicht eindeutig genug waren, was die Bedingungen anging. Daher wollte ich das ansprechen, und hoffentlich können wir im Laufe unserer heutigen Diskussionen zu diesem Punkt zurückkehren.

Andrea Fraser: Diejenigen, die heute vortragen, sollten vielleicht darüber nachdenken. Die Kommentare bezogen sich auf das Verhältnis zwischen der Schilderung des Projekts und einer Einleitung in die

Themen, die das Projekt aufwarf. Wir möchten uns auf den letzten Teil ein wenig mehr konzentrieren, als wir es gestern konnten.

Draxler: Stephan, ist es in Ordnung, wenn du anfängst?

Stephan Dillemuth: Erstens, um mit einem Scherz zu beginnen: ich habe mein Manuskript im Zug verloren, also musste ich es noch einmal neu schreiben. Ihr kennt die Geschichte.

(Gelächter)

Dillemuth: In Ordnung. Erster Teil: Praxis.

A: Friesenwall 120, fing 1990 an, einen Atelierraum zu suchen, fand diesen Ort in Köln, in dem sich die Galerien befinden. Gruppenarbeit, mit Josef Strau, Nils Norman, Merlin Carpenter und Kiron Khosla. Experimente für eine andere Definition von Ausstellungen, alle Ausstellungen hinterfragen, was eine Ausstellung sein kann.

B: Raum als Teil einer Künstler*innengemeinschaft, ein Aufenthaltsort, ein Video-/Informationsaustausch und Lieferung der Archiv-Ausweitung.

C: Akzeptanz davon. Und als „alternativer Raum" bezeichnet zu werden, der auch die Funktion einer Galerie erfüllt und manchmal Künstler*innen zeigt.

D: Einladungen an andere Orte, beispielsweise Pat Hearn [Galerie in New York] und Forum Stadtpark [in Graz], das Problem, eine aktuelle Situation in andere zu übersetzen. Meine Teilnahme an Sonsbeek 93, 5.000 DM Honorar, Firminy [für

Projekt Unité, 1993], kein Honorar. Ich habe versucht, einen Film über diese beiden Ausstellungen zu machen, um die ganze Ausstellung versuchsweise von außen zu betrachten.

E: Andere, die den Vertrieb selbst in die Hand nehmen. Das passierte bei der Unfair [in Köln, 1992].

Zweiter Teil: Theorie. Ich beschäftige mich eigentlich kaum damit, aber als ich meinem Freund Kiron Khosla von der hier statt findenden Diskussion erzählte, gab er mir einen Artikel über Gilles Deleuze, der „Postskriptum über die Kontrollgesellschaften" heißt. Das bezieht sich auch darauf, was wir gestern so viel diskutiert haben. Und zwar die Frage, was eine Institution ist, die allgemein kritisiert wird. Um also einen kurzen Überblick zu schaffen, Michel Foucault stellt die Anerkennung disziplinärer Gesellschaften im 18. und 19. Jahrhundert vor, die aus der Organisation von Räumen der Einschließung bestehen – dass man im Leben aus der Organisation der Familie, in die Schule, in die Baracken, in die Fabriken, ins Krankenhaus, ins Gefängnis und ich füge jetzt hinzu: in das Museum übertritt. Das ist eine Struktur des Kapitalismus nach der alten Definition. Die Krise kam um die Jahrhundertwende. Die Reform dieser Organisationen bedeutete, dass neue Kräfte und neue Technologien entstanden.

So entwickelte sich das mehr und mehr zu Kontrollgesellschaften, in denen Räume der Einschließung sich öffnen und andere Strategien der Autorität und Macht einbeziehen, um die alte Kraft erneut aufzubauen. Das Unternehmen ersetzte die Fabrik. Das System der Prämien wird durch Herausforderungen,

Wettbewerbe, Gruppensitzungen und eigene Kritik realisiert. Sogar Gewerkschaften erfüllen eine gesunde Form der Integration. Ständige Weiterbildung ersetzt die Schulausbildung. Codes und nicht Wörter markieren den Zugang zu Informationen oder lehnen ihn ab. Surfen ersetzt Sport. Maschinen entwickelten sich aus Hebeln und Uhren zu Computern. Der Kapitalismus veränderte sich aus der Konzentration der Produktion, der Spezialisierung und der Kolonialisierung in den Verkauf von Dienstleistungen und den Kauf von Aktien. Und sogar die Kunst hat Räume der Einschließung verlassen, um offene Kreisläufe zu betreten. Der Mensch ist nicht länger der eingeschlossene Mensch, sondern der verschuldete Mensch.

Das stammt alles aus diesem Artikel, nicht von mir.

Kontrolle ist nicht nur die Erosion von Brüchen, sie ersetzt zugleich die Räume der Einschließung. Museen, Kunstvereine, andere Elendsviertel oder Ghettos – je nachdem, was für eine Krise proklamiert wird. Austausch statt Sanktionen, ständige Weiterbildung statt Forschung, neue Arten, mit Geldern und Gewinnen umzugehen. Die Krise der Institutionen wird auch die Unfähigkeit der Gewerkschaften betreffen, die mit ihrer Geschichte des Kampfes gegen Disziplin verbunden ist.

Es endet also alles mit meiner Frage: Was sind die neuen Formen des Widerstands gegen Kontrollgesellschaften? Wenn wir das darauf übertragen, was hier geschieht, glaube ich nicht, dass wir jemals über Kunstinstitutionen als Machtpositionen im differenzierten Komplex der Kontrollgesellschaft gesprochen haben. Kunstwerke auszusuchen und sie auszustellen, wirkt wie eine Einschluss-Gesellschaft.

Und obwohl das auch eine Dienstleistung ist – eine Dienstleistung für wen? Für Künstler*innen, um sie in kuratorische oder kritische Funktionen einzubinden. Um Publikumspartizipation und Kritik einzubinden. Marginalisierte Positionen, wie beispielsweise Fragen ethnischer Herkunft, Piraten-Radiosender und Diskos einzubinden, ist immer noch eine Strategie der bereits erwähnten Unternehmenspraxis innerhalb der Kontrollgesellschaft. Ich glaube, dass diese Strategien eine gute Dienstleistung bedeuten können – aber noch einmal: für wen? Es ist eine Frage der Authentizität.

Für die Institutionen der Kunst scheint es eine neue Strategie zu geben, um die Machtstruktur am Leben zu halten – um die Arbeitnehmer*innen einzubeziehen, um Kritik eine Chance zu geben, sich um Spielräume zu kümmern und mit den Gewerkschaften zusammenzuarbeiten. Aber das nannte Martin gestern „repressive Toleranz“. Andererseits, Susan sagte gestern, dass Publikumsbeteiligung aufzubauen gleichzeitig heißt, zu hinterfragen, ob Bildung nicht auch dazu dient, das System zu stabilisieren. Oder wie Iwona, glaube ich, gesagt hat, der Piraten-Radiosender auf dem Museumsdach entzieht den Menschen, die ihn nutzen, noch mehr Macht und bringt letztendlich das Unternehmen in eine stärkere Position. Außerdem ist es kein Wunder, dass die Kurator*innen der Whitney Biennale Andreas drittes Proposal bewilligt haben – die Schuld ihrer eigenen Autorität und ihr Wunsch nach Transparenz waren in diesem Fall eine pseudotransparente Selbstdarstellung und eigene Legitimation. Das wurde allerdings durch das Schneiden der Aufnahme verkompliziert.

Nun ein kurzes Fazit. Aus meiner Perspektive gibt es nur wenige Möglichkeiten, wie man aus diesem Teufelskreis herauskommen könnte. Meine Kommentare über den Zeitplan dieser Veranstaltung: Es gab viele Einführungen, aber wir befinden uns mitten im Thema. Institutionen zu dienen bedeutet eigentlich, sie zu zerlegen. Meiner Meinung nach ist es für Künstler*innen am Besten, Institutionen so vollständig wie möglich zu nutzen. Wir haben noch nicht speziell über finanzielle Probleme gesprochen, Gebühren, Honorare, und so weiter. Seid euch dessen bewusst, dass sie euch benutzen, also benutzt ihr sie auch. Für Kurator*innen und Pädagog*innen würde ich sagen, nehmt die Institution, mit der ihr arbeitet, auseinander oder baut Brüche ein. Oder falls das nicht möglich ist, zeigt Kunst als Kunst und dient dem Mainstream, nutzt die Institution als eine bürgerliche Hülle… Was hatte ich da geschrieben…

(Gelächter)

Dillemuth: Oh ja, dem Mainstream dienen, aber zugleich eine gespaltene Persönlichkeit haben und dabei eine weitere Persönlichkeit aufbauen, die wirklich auf knallharter Politik, sexuellen Extremen, Terrorismus und Suizid basiert.

Dem Publikum dienen – das bedeutet für mich, je mehr wir es mögen, desto härter kommt es. Den Gemeinschaften dienen – eigentlich dienen sie euch, das sollte man nie vergessen. Kunst und Künstler*innen dienen: es ist wie eine gute Beziehung oder eine Ehe, etwas, das man selbst arrangiert, etwas, bei dem man sich streitet und sich gegenseitig liebt. Und ich freue mich auf die abschließende Diskussion.

Als Nachwort zu meinem Material – nun ja, es ist nicht wirklich allein meines – es liegt auf dem Tisch. Es gibt ein Dokument über Friesenwall 120, einige Dias, und einen neuen Katalog, den wir gerade herausgebracht haben. Es gibt eine Kopie des Deleuze Textes, den Kiron Khosla mir gegeben hat. Und es gibt Material über alternative Räume in den USA von *Paper Tiger*. Und ihr könnt Informationen über die Sonsbeek und Firminy Ausstellungen finden. Vielen Dank.

Draxler: Vielen Dank für deinen Vortrag.

Renate Lorenz: Ich habe einige Notizen über die Diskussionen gestern und möglicherweise für die abschließenden Diskussionen. Bezüglich des Programmtextes glaube ich nicht, dass das „Expert*innen/Klient*innen-Modell" für Projekte geeignet ist, die mich interessieren. Ich fühle mich nicht als Expertin und daher versuche ich, Koalitionen zu realisieren, um Wissen, Kritik, Erfahrungen und Ideen zu sammeln. In meinem nächsten Projekt, das technologiekritisch ist, greife ich beispielsweise sogar Expert*innen wie Gentechnolog*innen an. Die selbsternannten Expert*innen verwandeln andere in Nicht-Expert*innen. Für mich scheint es wichtig, beispielsweise das Modell des menschlichen Körpers aus verschiedenen Perspektiven zu beschreiben, Textanalyse oder feministische Kritik oder Naturwissenschaft zu verwenden. Ich möchte mich auf einen Text von Pierre Bourdieu aus *Die Tageszeitung* (*taz*) beziehen, in dem er versucht hat, ein Modell für die Verbindung von Kunst, Wissenschaft, Politik und Philosophie vorzuschlagen. Das ist etwas, dass wir meiner Meinung nach diskutieren könnten, denn er sagt, dass die Aufteilung dieser Bereiche sehr unpolitisch ist. Auf dieselbe Weise will ich mich auch nicht Künstlerin nennen, denn ich bin und tue auch andere Dinge, die nicht gut mit dieser Kategorie beschrieben werden können oder mit Kategorien wie Frau, Schriftstellerin und so weiter. Da ich mich nicht als Expertin identifiziere, gefiel mir die Situation gestern nicht, in der die Studierenden hinter den Monitoren versteckt waren. Ich hätte es besser gefunden, wenn die Studierenden, die an der Veranstaltung und der Ausstellung gearbeitet haben, hier gewesen wären, nicht als Publikum, sondern als Teilnehmer*innen. Es ist auch ihr Geld, das für diese Veranstaltung verwendet wird. Ich glaube persönlich nicht daran, dass eine größere Anzahl an Teilnehmer*innen die Situation verändert hätte, jedenfalls nicht mehr als die Kameras und Mikrofone, die vielleicht Einfluss darauf haben, was besprochen wird und wie.

Wie der Begriff „Kunst" entsteht, was er bedeutet – wir alle müssen uns damit auseinandersetzen. Kunst ist nicht unabhängig von akademischer Arbeit, von Ausstellungen wie dieser und von Studierenden, die an Themen arbeiten. Beispielsweise hat die Art Workers' Coalition möglicherweise etwas daran verändert, wie wir Kunst definieren. Mein zweiter Punkt ist der, dass ich gestern realisiert habe, dass es nicht die beste Idee ist, wenn jeder Vortragende über sein Projekt spricht, denn einige von uns haben die Projekte gesehen, während andere sie nicht gesehen haben. Und deshalb muss die Diskussion auf einem sehr allgemeinen Niveau bleiben. Als ich urspünglich an Copyshop gearbeitet

habe [*Copyshop…Kunstpraxis und politische Öffentlichkeit*, 1993], musste ich einen umfassenden Text über alle Projekte verfassen, die in der Publikation beschrieben wurden, beispielsweise darüber, dass sie nicht-institutionell oder selbstorganisiert sind, und so weiter. Aber dann wurde mir klar, dass alle Projekte so unterschiedlich hinsichtlich ihrer Umsetzung sind, dass es sie zu sehr vereinfacht, wenn man sie auf diese Art behandelt. Meiner Meinung nach ist „Institution" ein sehr unklarer Begriff. Was macht eine Situation zu etwas, das wir Institution nennen? Die Frage, was eine Institution ist, hat mit ganz konkreten Dingen zu tun: mit Menschen, Raum, wieviel Geld zur Verfügung steht, und wo es herkommt. Ich bin der Meinung, dass die Entscheidung, mit einem Raum oder mit Menschen zu arbeiten, eine Frage dessen ist, ob man eine Koalition eingehen kann, die die geplanten Themen und Projekte unterstützt. Um konkreter zu werden, schlage ich vor, dass wir hier über diese Ausstellung sprechen, die morgen eröffnet. Lasst uns darüber diskutieren, wie Besucher*innen dieser Ausstellung Zugang zu dem hier präsentierten Material bekommen können, über die Art Workers' Coalition, Organisationen und weitere Informationen dazu. Wie können wir mit dem Sprach- und Übersetzungsproblem umgehen, das wir sogar hier haben? Ist es möglich, ein spezielles Publikum anzusprechen, das nicht nur ein Kunstpublikum ist? Wie können wir hier an Theorie anknüpfen? Wie kann sie auf akademischer Ebene genutzt werden und wie können Studierende mit ihr arbeiten? Nur, um ein paar Fragen zu stellen.

Michael Clegg: Wir rasen hier heute wirklich auf das Mittagessen zu. Wir [Martin Guttmann und ich] wollen mit einer sehr kurzen Beschreibung eines Projekts beginnen. Allerdings glaube ich, dass es notwendig ist, über dieses eine Projekt zu sprechen, das wir im Kopf haben und die Diskussion in etwas Konkretem zu verankern. Vielleicht hat es damit zu tun, was du gerade vorgeschlagen hast, Renate. Ich werde es sehr kurz beschreiben.

Das Forschungsmaterial, das wir präsentieren, bezieht sich auf die Gliederung der Gesellschaftsschichten in Hamburg, die uns geholfen hat, zu entscheiden, wo wir die einzelnen Bibliotheken, die das Projekt umfasste, positionieren sollten. Das Material haben wir von der Stadt bekommen. Aber die Ratschläge dazu, was wir mit diesen Informationen machen sollten, haben wir von Ulf und dem Kurs, den er unterrichtete. Wir haben drei kleine Leihbibliotheken in drei Teilen der Stadt Hamburg eingerichtet – Süd, Mitte, Nord. Das sind sehr diverse Stadtteile, auf wirtschaftlicher und sozialer Ebene. Wir sammelten Bücher in diesen verschiedenen Wohngegenden, nach einer aufwendigen Prozedur, das Projekt lokal anzukündigen, dem Sammeln von Feedback der lokalen Anwohner*innen und Interviews, die vor Einrichtung der Bibliotheken geführt wurden. Danach waren die Bibliotheken drei Monate lang geöffnet. Man ermutigte die Anwohner*innen, Bücher mitzubringen.

Martin Guttmann: Die Bücher wurden in diese unverschlossenen Bücherschränke gestellt. Ohne Aufsichten oder Bibliothekar*innen. Wir haben die Bücherschränke aus wiederverwerteten Stromkästen der Stadtwerke hergestellt [wetterfeste Kästen, in denen elektrische Schalter untergebracht sind]. Stromkästen, die wir zur Nutzung als offene Bibliotheken recycelt haben.

Clegg: Diese Stromkästen sind sehr gängige Gegenstände. Wenn es jemanden interessiert, können wir später darüber sprechen, was die verschiedenen Ergbnisse und die Unterschiede zwischen den Wohngegenden waren. Ich glaube aber, in Bezug auf die Diskussion heute ist es wichtig, die anderen Elemente dieses Projekts zu betonen. Und zwar, dass wir auch eine Installation im Kunstverein in Hamburg gezeigt haben. Sie war Teil einer Ausstellung mit Stephan Schmidt-Wulffen, die *Backstage* [1993] hieß. Dieser Bereich unserer Installation fungierte als ein Dokumentationszentrum, in das Studierende, die für das Projekt recherchiert haben, Material über die derzeitige Lage der Leihbibliotheken einbrachten. Dort wurden die Fragebögen ausgestellt. Es gab auch einen Fragebogen, der den Besucher*innen des Kunstvereins präsentiert wurde, um eine Beziehung zwischen dem Institut hier an der Universität [Lüneburg] und den Gemeinschaften herzustellen. Das ist eine sehr grobe Beschreibung des Projekts, um die Themen aufzuzeigen.

Guttmann: Was wir auf einer eher theoretischen Ebene vorschlagen wollen, ist, das Modell der Porträtkunst zu erweitern und die Idee, eine Gemeinschaft zu porträtieren. Um über dieses Projekt als Porträts einer Gemeinschaft nachzudenken. Und diese Idee ist heuristisch – sie löst etwas aus seinem eigentlichen Kontext und erweitert ihn, aber sie erlaubt auch, dass man einige Richtlinien festlegt, vor allem ethische Richtlinien, die aus dem Bereich der Porträtkunst übertragen werden, um mit einer Gemeinschaft zu arbeiten. Das Modell kann natürlich kritisiert werden, aber es war – zumindest für uns – ein sehr wichtiges. Erstens, weil unsere vorherige Arbeit sehr viel mit Porträtkunst zu tun hatte, also was das etwas, das wir kannten und weiterverfolgen konnten. Außerdem ist es aber hoffentlich etwas, das einen eigenständigen Wert hat. Auf eine sehr abstrakte Art können Porträts als ein Instrument definiert werden, um Reaktionen hervorzurufen. Das Instrument wird an einem bestimmten Ort platziert, Reaktionen werden hervorgerufen, aufgenommen und der Gruppe, die reagiert hat, zur Verfügung gestellt. Der letzte Aspekt ist optional, da nicht jedes Porträt tatsächlich zurückgegeben oder als Einzel- oder Gruppenporträt ausgestellt wird. Gleichzeitg ist die Idee der Porträtkunst aber, dass man über die Repräsentation etwas anbietet, das einen kognitiven Wert hat. Denn ein Porträt kann zum Mittelpunkt dafür werden, Gedanken über Identität zu organisieren. Das ist im Grunde die Idee: dass man durch den Fokus auf materielle Repräsentation Gedanken über Subjektivität organisieren kann. Und das ist besonders für Körper wichtig, die solche Repräsentationen nicht haben, weil sie marginalisiert sind oder sich nicht als Einheiten präsentieren. Der ganze Mechanismus des Darstellens kann also tatsächlich von den Dargestellten profitieren.

Natürlich müssen wir über gute und schlechte Porträts sprechen. Nur gute Porträts sind wertvoll, schlechte Porträts geben den Personen, die porträtiert werden, einfach nicht genug zurück. Wir sagen also nicht, dass ein Porträt an sich einen Wert hat. Die Idee ist, ein gutes Porträt abzugeben, sodass es etwas sein kann, was tatsächlich verwendet wird.

Der andere Aspekt der Porträtkunst ist, dass Künstler*innen sich nicht als Sozialarbeiter*innen präsentieren oder als jemand, der Experten*innenwissen über das Porträt hat. Die Künstler*innen präsentieren ein Instrument und das ist ihre Dienstleistung. Das Instrument ist das Kunstwerk, aber nur so, wie es von der Person, die im Porträt repräsentiert wird, vollendet wurde. Es gibt also ein Element der Symbiose zwischen dem oder der Künstler*in, die porträtiert, und dem Porträt. Die Frage ist nicht, ob man jemandem einen Gefallen tut, sondern vielmehr, ob man wirklich die Symbiose zwischen der Person, die in dem Kontext arbeitet und dem Kontext selbst versteht. Vor allem Personen, die aus der Tradition der Konzeptkunst kommen, sollten die Tatsache zu schätzen wissen, dass der Nachdruck, in bestimmten Kontexten zu arbeiten, kein Luxus, sondern eine Notwendigkeit für Kunst ist, die nicht eskapistisch ist. Das ist ein Punkt, den es zu betonen gilt. Und die Selbstdarstellung der Künstler*innen als Helfer*innen der Gemeinschaft hat viel mit falschem Bewusstsein zu tun. Es sollte völlig klar sein, dass die Künstler*innen davon profitieren, es ist nicht nur für die Gemeinschaften da.

Clegg: Um denselben Vergleich des Porträts zu verwenden: die Gemeinschaft hat die Möglichkeit, Porträtkunst abzulehnen, in dem Sinne, dass sie den Vorgang abbrechen kann. Sie muss bei der Nutzung der Bibliotheken nicht kooperieren. An einem bestimmten Ort war es so, dass alle Bücher schon am ersten Tag nicht mehr da waren. Ein wichtiger Teil des Projekts ist also, von Anfang an eine Beschreibung dessen zu liefern, was geschehen könnte, und wie Menschen darauf reagieren würden. Es gibt eine Pressekonferenz, in der man einfach erscheinen kann und sagen: „Wir wollen dieses Projekt nicht in unserer Gemeinschaft." Ein sehr wichtiges Merkmal ist meiner Meinung nach die Aussage, dass wir einen Eingriff in die Gemeinschaft vornehmen, und es gibt verschiedene Interessen, die davon ausgehen. Es gibt außerdem verschiedene Verwendungszwecke für diese Intervention. Wir haben eine bestimmte Beteiligung, wir bekommen bestimmte Dinge, die Gemeinschaft kann es auf eine bestimmte Weise nutzen, es kann zu einem Fokus werden. Die Gemeinschaften sprechen die Frage an, wie man diesen Fremdkörper, die Bibliotheken, behandeln kann, die drei Monate lang dort sind. Außerdem wurde das Projekt in diesem bestimmten Fall als Forschungsarbeit der Universität konzipiert, deshalb gibt es verschiedene Aspekte in diesem Zusammenhang. Wir freuen uns, dass sehr unterschiedliche Interessen beteiligt sind, das Projekt vielschichtig ist und dass man es auf verschiedene Art nutzen kann.

Guttmann: Etwas anderes, das unsere Arbeit betrifft und biografischer ist, aber möglicherweise für die Diskussion hier von Nutzen sein könnte, wäre, dass es eine Transformation in unserer eigenen Arbeit von galerie- oder museumsbezogenen Arbeiten zu galerie-/museumsabseitigen Arbeiten gegeben hat. Oder zumindest Arbeiten, die sich nicht allein darauf verlassen, in Institutionen wie Galerien oder Museen

auszustellen. Dieser Punkt könnte meiner Meinung nach vielleicht eine gewisse Relevanz für die allgemeine Diskussion haben.

An einem bestimmten Punkt sollten wir uns alle wirklich eine simple Frage zur Struktur der Kunstinstitution stellen: Nehmen wir an, die Rezession hält noch zehn Jahre an und es steht viel weniger Geld zur Vefügung. Die meiste Unterstützung von Unternehmen würde aufhören und das Budget der staatlichen Förderung für die Künste wäre extrem niedrig – bedeutet das, dass Kunst eingestellt würde? Es ist eine einfache, aber ziemlich grundsätzliche Frage. Viele, die wirklich in den sauren Apfel beißen müssten, würden sagen: „Ja, Kunst ist im Grunde eine Dienstleistung für das Bürgertum – wir können nicht über Kunst ohne das Bürgertum sprechen, da Kunst die Art ist, wie das Bürgertum sich selbst gegenüber sich selbst artikuliert." Was also könnte eine Kunstform sein, die nicht unter das Paradigma des Bürgertums subsumiert würde, dieses Paradigma ihrer Selbstdarstellung? Eine Antwort auf diese Frage ist die Suche nach Alternativen, wie man Kunst zeigen kann, indem man analysiert, was einen Kunstkontext oder eine Kunstinstitution ausmacht. Mit anderen Worten, es geht wirklich darum, einige Aspekte der Kunstpräsentation, die wirklich notwendig sind, reflexiv zu identifizieren. Und zu versuchen, zwischen ihnen und denen der Epi-Phänomene der Kunst für und über das Bürgertum zu unterscheiden. Unser Projekt greift da zu kurz. Es ist einfach eine sehr breite theoretische Ebene, auf der wir gerade arbeiten. Ich glaube aber, dass etwas in dieser Richtung tatsächlich als eine der grundlegendsten Fragen dargestellt werden sollte, über das Verhältnis zu Institutionen. Da wir die Existenz solcher Institutionen nicht weiterhin als selbstverständlich verstehen können, und das sollten wir auch nicht. Eine der Fragen sollte also sein: Wie kann man die Praktiken, die aus der Institutionskritik kommen, in eine Welt übersetzen, in der das Bestehen von Institutionen nicht selbstverständlich ist?

Fraser: Ich möchte nur sagen, dass euer Standpunkt, dass Kunst dem Bürgertum dient und man andere Möglichkeiten ausarbeiten muss, sehr wohl zur Kenntnis genommen wird. Aber darum geht es bei allen Kategorien dieser Veranstaltung: Institutionen, Publikum, Gemeinschaften und Künstler*innen. Es geht darum, sich hier auf entstandende Strategien zu konzentrieren und auf Arbeitsweisen, die versucht haben, sich von diesem Modell abzuwenden. Und zwar auf eine Weise, die ihnen eventuell größere Wirkmöglichkeiten bieten könnte. In diesen drei Vorträgen gab es einige wichtige Punkte, auf die man sich konzentrieren sollte. Deine Aussage über die Gemeinschaft hier, Renate, wie wir uns diese Veranstaltung anschauen und erkennen, wie effektiv oder auf welche Art sie einer Gemeinschaft dient und welcher Gemeinschaft sie gedenkt, zu dienen. Und dann stellt man eine Verbindung zwischen eurem Projekt, Clegg & Guttmann, her, bei dem ihr zwischen dem Universitäts-Institut und der Gemeinschaft unterscheidet. Warum sagen wir allerdings nicht, dass es im Grunde zwei Gemeinschaften gibt: die Gemeinschaften in Hamburg, in der die Bibliotheken eingerichtet wurden, und die Gemeinschaft hier. Und ihr dient beiden und das auf verschiedene Weise. Ich wollte dies auf den Tisch bringen, als etwas,

worauf man sich in der Diskussion konzentrieren könnte.

Lorenz: Ulf, vielleicht kannst du uns einige Informationen zu diesem Ausstellungsprojekt geben. Ich wäre sehr daran interessiert zu wissen, wie dieses Projekt von deiner Seite aus unterstützt wird und wie die Pläne aussehen, um damit weiter voranzukommen. Was sind die Verbindungen, die in diesem besonderen Fall zwischen der Universität Lüneburg und dem Ausstellungsraum geplant sind?

Ulf Wuggenig: Unser allgemeines Konzept ist dieses Projekt – diese Diskussionen – stark in den Unterricht zu integrieren. Es gab anfänglich ein Problem wegen des Zeitmangels. Dann haben wir aber Seminare um das Projekt organisiert und wir werden uns an dem orientieren, was wir hier sehen, an dem, was hier geschieht. Wir wussten auch nicht genau, was in diesen Diskussionen geschehen oder worum es dabei gehen würde. Wier werden uns das sehr genau ansehen, uns mit Studierenden treffen und mit ihnen arbeiten, um zu verstehen, worum es in der Ausstellung geht. Wir haben natürlich auch die Möglichkeit, es in einen eher theoretischen Rahmen zu stellen, beispielsweise das Problem der Dienstleistungen ist da relevant. An der Universität haben wir eine Wirtschaftsfakultät, die sich auch mit Dienstleistungswirtschaft befasst oder der Wirtschaft gemeinnütziger Organisationen und so weiter. Das wäre also eine Möglichkeit. Eine andere Möglichkeit wäre, diese Diskussionen in einem gedanklichen Rahmen der Austauschtheorien zu sammeln, die eine lange Tradition in der Soziologie vom 19. Jahrhundert bis heute haben. Denn worüber wir diskutieren, ist Folgendes: Was ist Gerechtigkeit des Austauschs zwischen Künstler*innen und Institutionen? Meiner Meinung nach gibt es viele verschiedene Theorien, die geeignet sind, um sich mit diesen Fragen und Problemen auseinanderzusetzen.

Draxler: Ich muss sagen, als wir dieser Veranstaltung hier zugesagt haben, habe ich noch mehr Dienstleistung für die Studierendenschaft angeboten, was aber aus verschiedenen Gründen nicht passiert ist. Dieser Kunstraum wird hauptsächlich von der Stiftung Niedersachsen und nicht der Universität gefördert, und daher hat er eine bestimmte Eigenständigkeit. Denn dieses Projekt wird auch in anderen Räumen stattfinden, damit es mit unterschiedlichen Gemeinschaften und verschiedenen Diskussionen vernetzt werden kann. Ich sehe das Ganze auch als eine interessante Gelegenheit, um einerseits die teilweise eher theoretische Frage der Dienstleistungserbringung weiterhin zu diskutieren und andererseits zu überlegen, worum es bei diesem Projekt geht.

Meiner Meinung nach ist es eine sehr wichtige Frage, wie man die Gemeinschaft hier anspricht, wir haben das ausführlich diskutiert. Gleichzeitig glaube ich allerdings auch nicht, dass es eine umfassende Identität für alles, was hier im Kunstraum und den Universitätsseminaren geschieht, gibt. Dieser Unterschied zwischen den Studiengängen ist auf eine gewisse Art auch, was diese Veranstaltung ausmacht. Das schließt nicht aus, dass der Kunstraum diese anderen Projekte, wie das von Clegg & Guttmann beispielsweise in einer sehr direkten Beziehung zu der Studierendenschaft hier nutzt. Und das war auch unsere Empfehlung: dass der Kunstraum für diese verschiedenen Möglichkeiten genutzt werden sollte.

Fraser: Für mich stellt sich auch die Frage, die ich tatsächlich an die Gruppe richten möchte: Wie und wem kann es [das Projekt] dienen? Und wie meinen wir, sollte es beispielsweise von einer Universitätsgemeinschaft genutzt werden. Ich glaube, dass ich das Ganze bei der Organisation dieser Arbeitsgruppe hauptsächlich als Veranstaltung verstanden habe, die einer praktizierenden Gemeinschaft dienen würde und einer Gemeinschaft, die sich mit praktischer Arbeit beschäftigt. Und nicht um einem allgemeinen Publikum in dem Sinne zu dienen, wie viele Organisationen, die Kunst präsentieren, beabsichtigen. Und darüber hinaus auch nicht als Material für eine theoretische Studie zu dienen, sondern viel direkter im Zusammenhang mit gegenwärtiger und zukünftiger Arbeit zu stehen. Das war für mich die Voraussetzung. Meiner Meinung nach würde es sich sehr lohnen, diesen Punkt zu diskutieren, denn wenn das Projekt weiterzieht, wird es sich auf einige Organisationen, die künstlerische und studierende Anhängerschaften haben, verlagern.

Susan Cahan: Ich möchte mich zu der Frage aus Martins Vortrag äußern. Ich glaube, dass es wichtig ist, darüber nachzudenken, wie dieses Material verwendet wird, aber ich habe das Gefühl, dass es ein Meta-Diskurs ist, den wir während der abschließenden Sitzung diskutieren könnten. Meiner Meinung nach ist es eine sehr interessante Frage: Was würden wir tun, wenn es keine Museen oder gemeinnützigen Kunstorganisationen gäbe? Ich glaube, dass es ganz klar viele Formen der kulturellen Produktion gibt, die außerhalb von Museeen und Kunstorganisationen existieren, die entweder als Praktiken der bildenden Kunst identifiziert werden können oder auch nicht. Wir können alle darüber diskutieren, was „es" ist, aber es scheint mir, dass einige Museen tun, was andere Einrichtungen nicht tun, sie sammeln und bewahren und erhalten es. Und ich glaube, dass die Arbeit, über die wir hier sprechen, sich am meisten dazu eignet, außerhalb des Kontexts von traditionellen Sammler*innenmuseen entwickelt und gepflegt zu werden. Und wie es hier existieren kann, in schulischen Kontexten und anderen Unternehmen. Verlagswesen ist ein Anlaufpunkt, Video – ich meine, die Möglichkeiten sind tatsächlich ziemlich umfangreich. Und was mich ziemlich interessiert, ist, ob das Konzept des Sammelns neu durchdacht werden muss und wie. Museen in den USA bemühen sich, mit anderen Organisationen mitzuhalten, die mehr dienstleistungsorientierte Kunst machen und wirklich in Frage stellen, ob der Fokus noch immer auf ihren ständigen Sammlungen liegen sollte.

Guttmann: Ich glaube, das Dokumentieren, Pflegen, Aufbewahren der Rückstände ist ganz klar etwas, dass notwendig ist. Es stellt sich aber eher die Frage, was einen Rahmen oder ein Podest oder etwas anderes ausmacht, das eine Handlung zu Kunst macht. Und diese Frage entstammt tatsächlich einer grundlegenden Tradition der Avantgarde des 20. Jahrhunderts. Was bedeutet es, einen Gegenstand auf ein Podest zu stellen und

ihn „Kunst" zu nennen. Wenn es ein Gegenstand ist, ist es etwas einfacher; wenn es eine Handlung ist, etwas schwieriger. Aber diese theoretische Frage wurde schon vor langer Zeit gestellt. Dahinter steht die Frage, ob es schon immer einen starken Sinn für Sicherheit gab, was die grundlegenden Räumlichkeiten der Kunstinstitutionen angeht. Diese Gebäude, in denen die Kunstwerke untergebracht, gesammelt und geschützt werden. Und die Idee, dass es zu einem radikalen Wechsel der objektiven Bedingungen kommen kann, erfordert auch, dass wir die Frage unter anderen Vorzeichen stellen. Nicht als ein abstraktes philosophisches Thema, sondern als eine sehr konkrete Frage darüber, was mit dem Geist der Avantgarde passieren wird, unter Bedingungen, in denen institutionelle Förderung nicht selbstverständlich ist.

Fraser: Ich wollte nur einbringen, dass es mir so vorkommt, als wäre dies das Thema der nächsten Sitzung: der Kunst und Künstler*innen zu dienen und wie Institutionen gegründet wurden, und wie ihre Sammlungen zustande kamen. Ich wollte sehen, ob wir auf irgendeine Weise zu den Gemeinschaften zurückkehren könnten.

Dillemuth: Was diese Gemeinschaft angeht, glaube ich, dass die Studierenden vielleicht etwas dazu sagen möchten, wie sie es wahrnehmen. Es wäre gut, von dieser Gemeinschaft zu hören. Vielleicht sollten die Studierenden also dabei sein und wir hören es direkt von ihnen.

Fraser: Das ist meiner Meinung nach ein guter Vorschlag. Uli, gab es noch etwas, dass du sagen wolltest?

Ulrich Bischoff: Ja. Ich werde versuchen, es kurz zu machen, denn es könnte in die nächste Sitzung gehören.

Dillemuth: Jetzt sind wir also wieder bei dieser Sache – ich weiß nicht, ob das eine gute Strategie für eine Diskussion ist…

Fraser: Ich habe Uli unterbrochen, ich hätte das klarer ausdrücken sollen.

Bischoff: Die Frage betrifft die Rahmung und ich denke, ein Argument für die Teilnahme an dieser Diskussion ist, dass Künstler*innen einen Rahmen für Kunst schaffen, die außerhalb des Museums agiert, und einen Rahmen für die Kunst, die mit Museen zusammenarbeitet. Das wollte ich bloß dazu sagen.

Guttmann: Ich glaube nicht, dass wir solch eine strenge Unterscheidung zwischen den Kategorien machen sollten. Unser Vortrag hatte mit der Tatsache zu tun, dass unsere Arbeit mit Gemeinschaften eine gezielte Reaktion auf eine Veränderung der äußeren Umstände ist. Unserer Meinung nach gibt es einen echten Zusammenhang zwischen den beiden Themen, und es ist möglich, sie zu trennen, so lange die Verbindung sichtbar ist. Die Idee, mit einer Gemeinschaft zu arbeiten, ist kein separates Thema, sondern eine Frage dessen, wie man den Rahmen der Kunst des 20. Jahrhunderts auf andere Bereiche erweitern kann und nicht in erster Linie eine Frage der Auseinandersetzung mit der Gemeinschaft. Denn wir sind Künstler*innen, wir sind keine Sozialarbeiter*innen.

Fraser: Das ist eine Frage, und ich denke, sie sollte als solche gestellt werden.

Guttmann: Ich glaube einfach nicht, dass wir jetzt über „Gemeinschaftsarbeit" und dann erst über „Museumsarbeit" sprechen…

Fraser: Ich finde es angemessen, dass du das Thema der Gemeinschaft mit diesem Thema verbindest, aber ich glaube, Christian wollte etwas sagen.

Christian Philipp Müller: Wer könnte die Verbindung zwischen den Gemeinschaften und den Künstler*innen sein, wenn es nicht die Institution ist? Wer beauftragt dich überhaupt mit einer Arbeit? Wer repräsentiert die Gemeinschaft?

Clegg: Es gibt mehrere Lösungen. Es gibt einige, die nicht mit Museen arbeiten, sondern mit lokalen Organisationen.

Müller: Wer ist die Verbindung zwischen den Gemeinschaften und uns?

Lorenz: Ich stehe aber nicht außerhalb der Gemeinschaft. Wie ich schon sagte, ich sehe mich selbst nicht nur als Künstlerin – ich bin auch Teil verschiedener Gemeinschaften, und die Frage ist, ob es Möglichkeiten und Verbindungen zwischen ihnen gibt.

Fred Wilson: Ich habe das Gefühl, dass ich völlig außerhalb dieses Gesprächs stehe, denn den größten Teil meines Lebens, den ich mit Kunstschaffen verbracht habe, stand ich außerhalb der Kunstszene. Die meisten Afroamerikaner*innen standen außerhalb der Kunstszene und zwar nicht absichtlich. Unsere

Kunstpraxis hatte also von Natur aus nichts mit der Kunstgemeinschaft zu tun, sondern immer mit den lokalen Gemeinschaften. Und erst vor Kurzem wurde die Kunstgemeinschaft in den Vereinigten Staaten dazu gezwungen, die Kunst von anderen zu akzeptieren. Meiner Meinung nach ist also die Grundlage, um Gemeinschaften zu verbinden, den hierarchischen Markt und das Star-System, das in der Kunstgemeinschaft so heimtückisch ist, zu verdächtigen oder sich ihm zu widersetzen. Es hat viele Künstler*innen gegeben, die aus anderen Gemeinschaften in die Kunstwelt kamen.

Renée Green: Ich glaube, das ist ein hilfreicher Punkt. Ich möchte hier die Verwendung verschiedener Begriffe ansprechen. Beispielsweise die Vorstellung von „Künstler*innen". Wir alle haben verschiedene Hintergründe und ich denke nicht, dass wir uns mit der Idee von „Künstler*innen" anfreunden sollten als etwas, das unbedingt von anderen Aktivitäten isoliert ist. Man könnte auch „Kulturproduzent*in" sagen, obwohl dieser Ausdruck so überstrapaziert ist. Begriffe an sich sind problematisch: es ist ein Problem der Sprache – wie wir Sprache und Übersetzung nutzen. Künstler*innen waren schon immer mit verschiedenen Hintergründen und Studienbereichen verbunden. Das ist allerdings etwas, was uns meiner Meinung nach in dieser Diskussion bewusst sein sollte, damit wir nicht stecken bleiben. Was Fred erwähnte, ist wirklich wichtig bezüglich der Kontexte, in denen gearbeitet wird oder aus denen man stammt, und für das Nachdenken darüber, wie man es praktisch angeht. Die Idee einer Institution als „Zwischen"-Raum ist interessant. Ich glaube, wenn wir uns andere Modelle anschauen, sehen wir andere Wege, wie Menschen in Bezug auf Kommunikation fungieren. Die Geschichte der kulturellen Produktion von Afroamerikaner*innen ist gänzlich eine, in der sie Situationen untergraben mussten, weil sie ausgeschlossen wurden. Es war also notwendig, andere Kanäle zu schaffen oder mit anderen Institutionen zusammenzuarbeiten, die in anderen Gemeinschaften existierten und die aus sozialen Strukturen hervorgingen. Es gibt so viele verschiedene Möglichkeiten, wie Menschen miteinander kommunizieren, es hängt davon ab, was man für Ziele hat, es hängt davon ab, welche Agenden man hat und wie man vertreten werden möchte und ob man versucht, Teil eines hierarchischen Modells zu sein. Das ist eine Art zu denken. Die Möglichkeiten sind allerdings sehr umfangreich, wenn man über all die verschieden Wege nachdenkt, wie Menschen kulturelle Konzepte übermittelt haben.

Lorenz: Ich möchte noch einmal sagen, dass ich nicht nur Künstlerin bin. Man muss den Begriff „Künstler*in" viel differenzierter betrachten. Wie in feministischen Gruppen möchte ich nicht mehr davon sprechen, dass wir nur „Frauen" sind – wir sind auch Frauen, die Mütter sind, Frauen, die es nicht sind. Das Problem ist Identifikation. Man will sich selbst nicht nur mit einer Gemeinschaft identifizieren, einem Label und so weiter.

Fraser: Ich glaube, das machen Institutionen mit einem. Ich glaube, das war Teil von Christians Argument.

Müller: Richtig, zum Beispiel bin ich schwul und ich habe keine Stimme in der Schwulengemeinschaft.

Ich weiß zum Beispiel nicht, wie ich meine Stimme in der New Yorker Schwulen-Community erheben soll. Als Künstler steht meine Praxis völlig außerhalb dieser Gemeinschaften.

Draxler: Ich habe dich so verstanden, Fred, dass es für eine bestimmte Gemeinschaft interessant sein könnte, „Künstler*in" zu sein, da sie traditionellerweise aus einem bestimmten Kunstkontext ausgeschlossen ist. Es ist eine äußerst spezifische Situation, in der man sagen kann: „Oh, ich möchte nicht *nur* als Künstler*in identifiziert werden." Während es aus einem anderen Blickwinkel interessant sein könnte, als Künstler*in in Institutionen zu sein, aus denen man die letzten dreihundert Jahre ausgeschlossen wurde.

Green: Ich möchte mich von einer gewissen Unbeweglichkeit und der Isolierung verschiedener Praktiken, mit denen gearbeitet wird, distanzieren und das wirklich in Frage stellen. Ich glaube, das ist viel fließender. Zumindest das Verlangen ist es; ob die Ergebnisse auf diesem Wege sichtbar sind oder nicht, ist vielleicht eine andere Frage.

Publikum (Vera Kockot, Studentin): Es ist sehr interessant zu sehen, wie beide Seiten, die Institutionen und die Gemeinschaften, angesprochen werden können. Vielleicht hat die Institution eine besondere Rolle und man wird von ihr definiert, aber andererseits ist man frei, um verschiedene Gemeinschaften anzusprechen oder eben nicht. Und bei diesem Projekt hier versuche ich jetzt beispielsweise, die Studierendenschaft zu vertreten. Das Projekt von Clegg & Guttmann war sehr interessant, da es verschiedene Werte entwickelte. Es gab einen Gegenwert und

es war ein Kunstwerk, also wurden verschiedene Werte berücksichtigt und unterschiedliche Gemeinschaften konnten es auf verschiedenen Ebenen nutzen. Einige haben in den Gemeinschaften Bücher getauscht, während andere es nur im Kunstverein als Kunstwerk betrachtet haben. Ich glaube, das ist eine interessante Überschreitung der Grenzen von Institutionen – wenn man wirklich Gemeinschaften berücksichtigen kann, die üblicherweise überhaupt keinen Kontakt mit Kunstinstitutionen hätten. Das Projekt war auch mit dieser Universität verbunden. Es war interessant, dass Sozialforschung und -wissenschaft einen solch wesentlichen Teil dieses Projekts ausmachten. Ich kann behaupten, dass es für uns Studierende ein sehr ergiebiger Austausch war; es hat echte Möglichkeiten aufgezeigt.

Draxler: Interessen der Universität und der Kunstgemeinschaft sind in einem sehr weiten Sinne nicht unbedingt diegleichen. Diese Arbeitsgruppe definiert sich dadurch, dass man sich gegenseitig als Teilnehmer*in der Gruppe anspricht, und das bedeutet nicht, dass wir uns ausschließlich gegenseitig als Künstler*innen oder Kurator*innen ansprechen, sondern als Teilnehmer*innen, die in bestimmten Situationen mit bestimmten Zielen arbeiten. Und dieser Ansatz der Arbeitsgruppe könnte auf andere Modelle oder andere Formen der Aktivität übertragen werden. Natürlich sollten wir darüber sprechen, welche Möglichkeiten existieren, um die Interessen der Universität mit den hier diskutierten Themen zu verbinden. Aber meiner Meinung nach ist das keines der Hauptthemen.

Ute Meta Bauer: Es ist ein Unterschied, ob man Gemeinschaften dient, wenn dabei eine Institution – ob Museum oder Universität – die Künstler*innen bittet, ein Projekt für eine Gemeinschaft zu machen. Wie veranlasst die Institution das? In deinem Fall, Fred, hast du dich dieser Gemeinschaften selbst angenommen, die Institution hat das nicht veranlasst. Ich glaube, es ist etwas ganz anderes, wenn Künstler*innen ein eigenes Interesse daran haben, Gemeinschaften zu motivieren und mit ihnen auf einer langfristigen Basis zu arbeiten, über die institutionelle Einladung hinaus. Das ist ein Unterschied. Und man muss sich fragen, wie eine Institution gedenkt, für diese Dienstleistung zu zahlen, welchen Status sie Kulturarbeit beimisst und wie sie mit solchen Dingen umgeht. Es wäre für Künstler*innen ein anderer Arbeitsbereich, wenn sie nicht diese Vorstellung von „Künstler*innen" hätten, die ein ernsthaftes Kunstwerk erarbeiten. Wenn sie sich selbst als Kulturarbeiter*innen verstehen könnten, hätten wir ein anderes Verständnis von ihrem Beruf.

Bischoff: Ich glaube, es gibt einen Unterschied zwischen Sozialarbeiter*innen und Künstler*innen, denn als Künstler*in arbeitet man zunächst für sich selbst.

Bauer: Hmmmm…ich weiß nicht.

Bischoff: Nun, das ist meine Meinung.

Bauer: Sozialarbeiter*innen arbeiten aber auch für sich selbst.

Wilson: Ja, das ist so eine Sache. Ich habe mit vielen Sozialarbeiter*innen gearbeitet und… Nun, wir können darüber reden.

Fraser: Das ist für mich der springende Punkt, und das war tatsächlich der Auslöser hierfür – wenn ich für mich selbst arbeiten würde, hätte ich wahrscheinlich nicht so viele Fragen über die Gerechtigkeit dieses Austauschs. Die Tatsache aber, dass ich fast ausschließlich auf Einladung von Institutionen und Organisationen und in einer Weise arbeite, die meine Tätigkeit von diesem Kontext abhängig macht, ergibt eine völlig andere Geschichte.

Wilson: Sozialarbeiter*innen und Künstler*innen und überhaupt alle tun das, was sie tun, um einen Teil ihrer eigenen Bedürfnisse zu erfüllen.

Fraser: Das heißt, wenn wir uns nicht alle völlig auf entfremdete Arbeit beschränkt haben.

Wilson: Ich glaube allerdings, dass dieser Aspekt in Berufen, die den Anschein erwecken, etwas für andere zu tun, manchmal verloren gehen kann.

Bischoff: Wenn man für eine Arbeit an einem Haus angefragt wird, gibt es spezifische Konditionen. Man sagt also entweder „Ich mache es" zu diesen Konditionen oder man macht es nicht. Es bleibt die Frage, was einen selbst interessiert.

Fraser: Das ist im Wesentlichen die Situation des freien Berufs: man muss Bedingungen aushandeln, aber man ist nicht völlig frei. Es handelt sich um relative Autonomie. Eine relative Unabhängigkeit.

Jochen Becker: Ich habe mich an den Begriff „Projekt" gewöhnt, aber ich würde lieber den Begriff „Initiative" verwenden. Was du am

Münchner Kunstverein [*Eine Gesellschaft des Geschmacks*, 1993] gemacht hast, Andrea, war natürlich ein Projekt, aber diesen Ausdruck würde ich nicht dafür verwenden, was Stephan mit Friesenwall 120 macht.

Vielleicht können wir zwischen einem „Projekt", einer „Initiative" und einer „institutionellen Einladung" unterscheiden. Es ist möglich, Geld oder Infrastruktur aus verschiedenen Quellen zu bekommen, wenn man sehr hart arbeitet, aber es ist sehr schwierig. Man kann entscheiden, wo man die Arbeit platzieren möchte, wen man ganz gezielt ansprechen möchte, vielleicht ist das in einem Museum nicht möglich. Wenn man als Initiative arbeitet, ist die Verbindung mit Initiativen im sozialen Umfeld vielleicht einfacher.

Guttmann: Ich möchte darauf antworten, was du [Jochen] gesagt hast und mich auch darauf beziehen, was Renate gesagt hat. Und versuchen, zwischen dem gleichzeitigen Dazugehören zu verschiedenen Kontexten und der Idee, die Grenzen verschiedener Kontexte aufzulösen, zu unterscheiden. Ich glaube, es ist eine wichtige und interessante Frage, ob wir das Modell des Grenzen auflösens und unserer Selbstbezeichnung als „Kulturproduzent*innen" bevorzugen, oder ob wir sagen sollten, dass wir Verschiedenes parallel tun. Und weil wir keine vereinten Individuen sind und Widersprüche verkörpern, kommen in verschiedenen Momenten verschiedene Aspekte von uns selbst zum Ausdruck. Um diese Unterscheidung vielleicht weniger philosophisch und dafür praktischer zu gestalten: was mir wirklich auffiel, als Fred über den Kontext in der South Bronx sprach, und lange Zeit eine Galerie zu leiten…

Wilson: Ich habe gerade eben über meine Erfahrung gesprochen, bevor ich eine Galerie leitete, nämlich als ich sieben Jahre in einer Agentur für Sozialdienstleistungen gearbeitet habe.

Guttmann: Ich verstehe. Jedenfalls scheint es einen Bedarf zu geben zwischen einer Situation zu unterscheiden, in der jemand in einem bestimmten Kontext arbeitet, der viele verschiedene Funktionen erfordert und man möglicherweise ein starkes Identitätsgefühl hat, aber nicht viel Kontrolle darüber, was man macht, im Gegensatz zu einer anderen Situation, in der man aufgrund seiner Umstände von einem Ort der Welt zum anderen reisen muss. Man verliert nicht sein Gefühl für den Kontext, stattdessen nimmt man tatsächlich viel mehr wahr, dass man jeden Kontext unter seinen eigenen Bedingungen betrachten muss. Und natürlich schafft es ein ganz anderes Gefühl, mit dem Kontext zu arbeiten.

Wir kommen ursprünglich aus Israel, sind in die USA gegangen und arbeiten jetzt in Deutschland. Diese Tatsache an und für sich erzeugt einen Rahmen für die Tätigkeit, mit der wir uns beschäftigen. Wir beziehen das Material für die Arbeit aus dem konkreten Ort, an dem wir arbeiten. Man bildet einen anderen Kontrast zwischen der Vorstellung von nomadischen Künstler*innen, die ständig ihren Kontext wechseln und mehr Mittel, aber weniger Identität haben, und einem weiteren Modell, bei dem man vielleicht mehr Identität, aber dafür weniger Mittel hat. Manche haben beides, andere weder noch.

Wilson: Ich war dabei, auf deine Frage zu antworten: „Was wäre, wenn es keine Förderung mehr für die Kunstproduktion gäbe?" Und ich sagte gerade, dass es eine ganze Reihe von Gemeinschaften gibt, in denen dieses Problem seit Jahren ein Thema ist und die sich damit auseinandersetzen. Das sind also möglicherweise Modelle, die wir uns anschauen könnten.

Guttmann: Absolut. Es ist äußerst vorteilhaft, sich diese Modelle des Arbeitens, die nicht viel institutionelle Unterstützung haben, anzuschauen, keine Frage.

Fraser: Ich dachte darüber nach, worüber du, Iwona, gestern gesprochen hast, die Situation in Antwerpen mit nomadischen Künstler*innen [für das Europäische Kulturhauptstadt Projekt, an dem Iwona Blazwick beteiligt war]. Und diese Situation scheint ein Problem darzustellen, das mit dem Bedienen von Gemeinschaften zu tun hat, und wie das geschieht, wenn nicht durch Institutionen... Hier, scheint mir, dienen wir unseren eigenen Gemeinschaften und den Gemeinschaften, die aus dieser institutionalisierten Repräsentationsstruktur ausgeschlossen wurden, und anderen Gemeinschaften dienen wir durch Institutionen. Das scheinen die Optionen zu sein, die hier vorgestellt wurden.

Bauer: Ich finde es sehr interessant, was Fritz in Berlin mit Büro Berlin gemacht hat, denn in Berlin gab es zu der Zeit noch nicht diese institutionelle Struktur. Und es ist eine so große Stadt mit so vielen Künstler*innen. Für die Künstler*innengruppe, an der ich beteiligt war, war dieses Projekt Büro Berlin immer ein Vorbild, das uns sehr inspiriert hat. Da sie ihre eigene Struktur geschaffen haben, waren sie ihre eigene

auftraggebende Organisation. Daher ist es schade, dass es gestern nicht besprochen wurde. Und zwar, weil sie immer ihre Arbeit gemacht haben – sie haben nicht auf jemanden gewartet, der sie anfragt. Sie haben es einfach gemacht. Sie haben es finanziert. Sie haben Wege gefunden, die Erwartung zurückzuweisen, dass Künstler*innen nicht wissen, wie man Projekte organisiert und Gelder aufbringt. Es wäre für mich interessant, mehr über ihr Projekt zu erfahren.

Fritz Rahmann: Ich kann jetzt versuchen, zu beschreiben, was wir gemacht haben, aber das werde ich sowieso in wenigen Augenblicken tun, in der nächsten Sitzung.

Dillemuth: Ich glaube, wir sollten bei diesem Thema den Gemeinschaften zu dienen auch einen Unterschied machen – ich glaube, es gibt keine Dienstleistung für Gemeinschaften. Ich glaube, dass eine Gemeinschaft bis zu einem bestimmten Grad etwas gemeinsam schaffen kann, aus sich selbst heraus. Ich habe nicht das Gefühl, dass ich der Gemeinschaft diene, sondern, dass sie teilnimmt. Wenn wir dieses Modell auf ein höheres Niveau bringen, dann wird es institutionalisiert. Vielleicht kommt es einmal vor, dass ich Geld benötige, dann benötige ich es jedes Jahr, dann benötige ich noch mehr und schließlich bekomme ich vielleicht sogar das Geld und dann wird es so etwas wie ein Kunstverein. Dann stellt sich die Frage, ob diese Institution die Mission hat, jedem etwas zurückzugeben. Wenn sie diese Mission hat, etwas zurückzugeben, dann müssen die Künstler*innen dieses Bedürfnis oder diese Mission der Institution erfüllen, in der Schuld einer Funktion der Dienstleistungsbranche zu stehen.

Draxler: Mit Friesenwall 120 hast du allerdings der Kölner Kunstwelt eine Menge Dienstleistungen angeboten – ihnen ein Archiv mit ganz bestimmten Videobändern zu stellen, ist eine Dienstleistung. Sie haben davon Gebrauch gemacht. Das ist mehr oder weniger, was Auftragnehmer*innen von Institutionen tun. Ich glaube, in deinem Fall war es eindeutig, wie das von Friesenwall aufgebaut wurde, im Zusammenhang mit den Galerien am Friesenplatz.

Dillemuth: Wir haben etwas ausprobiert. Und dann hat die Gemeinschaft eine Chance ergriffen, etwas beizutragen, sich auszutauschen.

Lorenz: So würde ich unsere Arbeit auch beschreiben, wie Copyshop [in Cologne], das nicht das gleiche Projekt geworden wäre, wenn viele Personen daran gearbeitet und teilgenommen hätten. Ich kann nicht sagen, dass ich ihnen gedient habe. Ich habe den Raum und die Finanzierung gesucht, aber es wäre nicht das gleiche Projekt gewesen, und ich glaube, dass es mit Friesenwall 120 genauso ist. Ich mag dieses Konzept der „Dienstleistung" auch nicht.

Iwona Blazwick: Bist du aber der Meinung, dass auf die Gründung jeglicher Initiative Institutionalisierungsprozesse folgen? Man eignet sich Expertise an, indem man einen Ort aushandelt, die Miete zahlt, die Rechnungen zahlt, eine Plattform oder Programme entwickelt und Kommunikationsformen darüber, was an diesem Ort passiert. Richtet man dann nicht die gesamte Infrastruktur einer Institution mit eine*r Expert*in ein?

Lorenz: Ich weiß nicht, ob es einen so großen Unterschied zwischen Institution und Nichtinstitution gibt. Wenn man kein Geld hat, hat man trotzdem noch dieses Verhältnis zu Geld, weil man sonst bestimmte Projekte nicht durchführen kann. Die Frage ist: Was sind die Strukturen? Wie werden Entscheidungen getroffen? Wer entscheidet? Und so weiter.

Becker: Der Unterschied zwischen Friesenwall 120 und einem Kunstverein ist, dass Friesenwall jetzt schließt. Ein Kunstverein würde nicht von alleine schließen, sie würden nicht sagen: „In Ordnung, wir schließen morgen."

Guttmann: Eine Institution existiert über die Individuen, die sie leiten, hinaus.

Fraser: Reneé versucht schon seit einiger Zeit, etwas zu sagen.

Green: Ich wollte sagen, dass das etwas mit der Idee der Gemeinschaften zu tun hat. Was Stephan über Friesenwall 120 gesagt hat und wie es zustande kam, hat mich an die Idee einer Gemeinschaft als etwas erinnert, das man in Anführungszeichen setzen muss. Es ist nicht unbedingt etwas, das wir hinterfragen müssen. Eine Gemeinschaft wird geschaffen – sie ist nicht unbedingt etwas, das bereits existiert. Und ich glaube, dass Expertise und Dienstleistung in dieser Frage inbegriffen sind, zusammen mit der Vorstellung, was die Rolle von Künstler*innen ist. Wenn beispielsweise jemand eine Idee hat und sie vorstellt und dann herausfindet, wie man sie verbreitet, dann ist es wie Flaschenpost. Und ich glaube, das ist oft das, was Künstler*innen tun, und danach sehen sie, wer darauf reagiert. Es ist nicht unbedingt klar, wer reagiert, aber es ist die Reaktion darauf, was herauskommt. Friesenwall war nicht definitiv, sondern flexibel. Ich erinnere mich, als ich zum Friesenwall kam, fand ich, es war eine andere Art, mit der Idee des Raums umzugehen.

Ich möchte die Frage untersuchen, wie Gemeinschaften aufgrund der Art, wie etwas begonnen wird, gebildet werden, und nicht unbedingt ausgehend von einer festen Institution.

Fraser: Ich möchte das einfach mit dem vergleichen, wöruber Martin und Michael während ihres Vortrags darüber, Gemeinschaften zu vertreten, gesprochen haben. Ich habe überlegt, dass das in der Tat ein anderes Modell ist. Ihr habt von einem Ort gesprochen, an dem eine Gemeinschaft sich durch ihr eigenes kollektives Handeln bilden könnte, und andererseits von der Idee einer Gemeinschaft zu dienen, die bereits existiert. Das scheint mir einer der Unterschiede hier zu sein.

Guttmann: Es ist eine interessante Unterscheidung, aber in unserem Fall haben wir einen Ort ausgesucht, an den wir als Porträtkünstler und nicht als Auftragnehmer kamen. Das ganze Projekt war wie eine große Kamera und etwas entsteht daraus. Wenn man sie richtig einstellt, gibt sie etwas zurück. Das hat was von einer Dienstleistung. Denn die Vorstellung des „Künstlers als Porträtkünstler" entspringt der Idee, die Fähigkeit zu besitzen, Selbstdarstellung beizusteuern. Es scheint mir, dass manche das besser können als andere, selbst wenn sie die Gemeinschaft nicht wirklich gut kennen. Solange Menschen nicht in einem festen Kontext arbeiten, stellt sich

tatsächlich die große Frage, was wir an einem bestimmten Ort tun. Wir befinden uns immer an Orten, in denen wir die Sprache nicht sprechen – Was machen wir hier, was wollen wir hier, wie können wir eine solche Tätigkeit rechtfertigen? Und die Antwort hat nicht so sehr mit der Frage der Expertise in dem Sinne zu tun, dass es eine neue Technologie gibt, die vorher noch nicht existierte, sondern eher damit, dass man etwas aufgebaut hat, das genutzt werden konnte und zu seinen eigenen Konditionen Bestand hatte. Solange wir die richtige Resonanz bekommen haben – und das gehört zur Verantwortung des Arbeitens in einer solchen Situation dazu – denn nur sehr wenige können behaupten, wirklich die Gemeinschaften zu verstehen, mit denen sie arbeiten. Das sollte hervorgehoben werden, da die meisten Künstler*innen nicht in Situationen arbeiten, in denen sie die Gemeinschaft wirklich verstehen.

Wilson: Diese Idee, ein Problem mit Expertise zu haben, ist merkwürdig. In den Gemeinschaften, in denen ich gearbeitet habe, ist die Idee von Expert*innen oder jemandem mit anderer Erfahrung, wenn sie diese in die Gemeinschaft einbringen, haben sie tatsächlich etwas zu bieten, und das wird respektiert. Das wird zu einem wichtigen Aspekt für die Einbindung in eine bestimmte Gemeinschaft, weil man etwas hat, oder eine besondere Perspektive auf die Welt hat, die in der Gemeinschaft als neu oder wertvoll geschätzt wird. Oder es wird durch das eigene Engagement mit der Gemeinschaft zu etwas Wertvollem. Ich sehe also nicht, was das Problem mit Expertise ist, es sei denn, man stellt sich als größere*r Expert*in dar, als man eigentlich ist.

Clegg: Es geht darum, dass sie [die Institutionen] sehr oft von uns verlangen, dass wir dort etwas ganz Bestimmtes schaffen. Und ich glaube, eine Situation ist problematisch, wenn man von jemandem eingeladen wird und sie sagen: „Nun, ich weiß, Sie machen eine bestimmte Art von Arbeit, und das wollen wir." Es ist schwierig, über Expertise zu sprechen, wenn die erbrachte Dienstleistung keine konkrete ist. Wir können Verschiedenes tun, aber für uns bleibt immer eine Frage: Wie bestimmen wir, was dort tatsächlich gebraucht wird und inwieweit denken wir darüber als hauptsächlich motivierende Bedingung nach?

Cahan: Ich glaube, es ist wichtig zu erkennen, dass es mehrere Formen von Expertise gibt. Nicht nur die, die Künstler*innen an einen geographischen Ort mitbringen, mit dem sie vielleicht nicht vertraut sein mögen, sondern auch die Art von Expertise, die auf gelebter Erfahrung und der Verhandlung dieser Vielfältigkeit beruhen.

Fraser: Meiner Meinung nach hat das Problem der Expertise mit Arbeits- und Wissensteilung innerhalb der Hierarchien zu tun, die von Organisationen und professionellen Strukturen etabliert werden. Dieses Problem ist spezifisch und hat weniger mit Erfahrung zu tun.

Wilson: Oder dem Individuum. Es geht um die Struktur, die um das Individuum platziert wird. Ich war beeindruckt von dem, was du über Porträtkünstler*innen in einer bestimmten Gemeinschaft gesagt hast. Allein anhand meiner Erfahrungen mit Künstler*innen in verschiedenen Gemeinschaften kann ich festmachen, wie Künstler*innen in der Gemeinschaft Werte beigemessen werden, auch wenn sie nicht so sehr mit der Form dessen vertraut sind, was die Gemeinschaft tut. Manchmal reicht die Beteiligung und Interaktion der Künstler*innen aus, um die Perspektive der Gemeinschaft auf die Welt oder den Standpunkt des*r Einzelnen zu erweitern. Und das allein kann wertvoll für diese Gemeinschaft sein. Dann wird das, was auch immer man produziert, wichtiger, weil sich diese Beziehung entwickelt hat.

Guttmann: An einem der Orte, an dem eine Bibliothek eingerichtet wurde, hat man tatsächllich eine Petition gestartet und Unterschriften gesammelt, um sie zu erhalten. Sie haben Plakate drucken lassen, auf denen deutlich wurde, dass sie die Bibliothek übernehmen wollten. Sie wurde Teil von etwas, das ihre Identität als Gemeinschaft definierte. In dem Moment, als es akzeptiert wurde, war es sehr eindeutig: die Gemeinschaft wollte sie haben – und lehnte uns ab.

Clegg: Und es ist ein Moment der Veränderung, denn dann wurde es zu etwas anderem: nur die Bibliothek dort, und die Verbindung zu uns wurde unterbrochen.

Wilson: Ich empfinde das oft bei einigen meiner Projekte – und die Organisation wird dann zu so etwas wie meiner Gemeinschaft – wenn sie eine Arbeit für sich beansprucht, als wäre sie ihre eigene und mich sozusagen aus dem Weg drängt. Wenn sie dann beschließen, dass es ihnen gehört, weil es irgendetwas für sie verändert, dann funktioniert das aus meiner Sicht. Selbst wenn es merkwürdig ist. Es wirkt, obwohl, erwähnen wir einfach nicht, dass ich daran beteiligt war.

Fraser: Einerseits gibt es dieses Problem, Expertise aus einem institutionellen Kontext herauszunehmen und sie innerhalb einer Gemeinschaft anzuwenden, die möglicherweise existiert oder auch nicht, und die man möglicherweise selbst konstruiert oder auch nicht.

Blazwick: Könnten wir das Wort „Fähigkeiten" [statt „Expertise"] verwenden?

Fraser: Nun, das könnten wir, allerdings wollte ich einen Unterschied zwischen dem und dem Versuch machen, eine partizipatorische oder demokratische Situation innerhalb einer Institution zu entwickeln. Einerseits gibt es also eine Kritik über den Status der Expertise oder Fähigkeiten, spezialisierter Fähigkeiten innerhalb nicht-spezialisierter Gemeinschaften. Und andererseits gibt es die Frage: Ob man eine partizipatorische, demokratische Struktur für Gemeinschaften entwickeln kann, die selbst nicht den Unterteilungen unterliegen, die Expertise impliziert? Ich glaube, das ist die Ansicht, die Stephan und Renate in ihren Vorträgen vertreten haben und vielleicht auch das, was Iwona in Antwerpen [mit dem Europäische Kulturhauptstadt Projekt] versucht hat.

Judith Barry: Das wird alles durcheinanderbringen, aber ich wollte über bestimmte aktivistische Kunst in den USA sprechen. Insbesondere über Künstler*innen, die ehrenamtlich mit anderen Non-Profit-Organisationen zusammenarbeiten. Bei der Women's Action Coalition [WAC, in New York], meldeten sich beispielsweise eine ganze Reihe von Künstler*innen freiwillig, um Medien zu produzieren, unter anderem eine große Plakat- und Diakampagne zu

[Bill] Clintons Wahl im letzten Jahr und der Democratic Convention. Innerhalb großer Teile von Clintons Wählerschaft gab es ein enormes Misstrauen gegenüber der Verwendung visueller Hilfsmittel, um bestimmte Positionen zu markieren. Wir arbeiteten freiwillig, verlangten für unsere Dienste kein Geld, und man misstraute uns völlig, weil wir ein Spektakel anfachten und anspruchsvolle bildliche Hilfsmittel verwendeten, um breite Aufmerksamkeit innerhalb der Wählerschaft in Texas zu erwirken. Denn wenn man sich das Modell der Künstler*innen anschaut, die an ACT UP beteiligt waren, sieht man, wie effektiv ihre Bild-Kampagne gewesen ist. Sie hat eine Identität geschaffen und hat unter anderem dem Aufuf zur AIDS-Forschung in den USA wirklich einen Platz und eine Stimme gegeben.

Fraser: Ich glaube nicht, dass das irgendetwas durcheinander bringt. Es wird ein dritter Begriff der künstlerischen Fähigkeiten eingeführt, die zum Einsatz kommen, um demokratisch organisierte Gruppen oder Gemeinschaftsgruppen zu beeinflussen oder ihnen zu dienen.

Barry: Vielleicht ist es eine andere Vorstellung von Institutionen.

Fraser: Nun, ich finde nicht, dass es sich so sehr von der Art der Interaktionen unterscheidet, die du mit Copyshop hattest, Renate. Das sind auch politische, zielorientierte Organisationen.

Cahan: Haben sich Fragen des Spektakels auf feministische Anliegen bezogen?

Barry: Das Spektakel spielt sowohl für feministische Anliegen als auch für die Art, auf die es einen selbst positioniert und subsumiert, eine Rolle. Ich glaube, in vielen gemeinschaftlichen Gruppen – und ich habe über die Jahre mit vielen zusammengearbeitet – gibt es ein inhärentes Misstrauen gegenüber Visuellem. Es sitzt tief und ist systemisch. Es kommt daher, dass Gemeinschaften nicht die Ressourcen und keinen Mainstream-Effekt haben, sodass sie sich weder vorstellen noch damit identifizieren können, auf diese Weise repräsentiert zu werden. Ich habe versucht, mit Frauengruppen zu arbeiten, die auf einen sehr simplen grafischen Ansatz bestehen, was das Visuelle angeht, und visuell Komplexeres oder Anspruchsvolleres ablehnen.

Lorenz: Ich weiß, dass das WAC Kapitel in Berlin nur wenige Künstlerinnen hat, und sie dachten immer, dass die gesamte WAC Gruppe organisierter sei und interessantere Künstlerinnen habe, die diesen asketischen Zugang zu Bildmaterial verfolgen.

(Gelächter)

Barry: Einige der WAC-Kampagnen waren für die gesamte WAC-Organisation akzeptabler als andere. Und im Allgemeinen war es simpleres Bildmaterial.

Fraser: Diese Fragen der Spezialisierung, Arbeitsteilung, sind für radikale Frauengruppen so zentral gewesen. Es gibt einige Argumente, die besagen, dass es diese Art von Auseinandersetzungen waren, die die radikalen feministischen Gruppen der späten sechziger und frühen siebziger Jahre zerstört haben. Sie haben mit dem Argument auf radikal egalitäre Gruppenstrukturen

gezielt und lehnten beispielsweise Sprecherinnen ab, verweigerten denjenigen, die eine Neigung zu oder Erfahrung mit öffentlichen Reden hatten, die Gruppe zu vertreten, um gleichwertige Beteiligung in der Gruppe zu fördern und zu verwalten. Folglich gab es aber viele Probleme. Das passiert vermutlich, wenn man jegliche Art der Fähigkeiten ablehnt.

Guttmann: Was mir bei ACT UP aufgefallen ist, ist, dass ihre Grafik zu dominant war. Man dachte an dieses sehr flotte Bildmaterial und diese Slogans, anstatt an Menschen. Ich glaube, die organisierte Grafik entmenschlichte die Gruppe ein wenig.

Fraser: Bei den meisten öffentlichen Kunstprojekten, die ich mir anschaue, die beispielsweise Plakatwände benutzen, stellt sich die Frage nach den Ressourcen. Wenn Kunst Plakatwerbung auf subversive Weise nutzt, aber jede*r weiß, wie viel es kostet – Plakatwerbung soll ja eine demokratische Form sein, aber sie ist natürlich sehr teuer, und wer hat schon Zugriff darauf? Man weiß also, wenn jemand Zugriff darauf hat, heißt das, der- oder diejenige bekommt eine gewisse Unterstützung von Institutionen, von Unternehmen, von Individuen.

Guttmann: Es ist auch nicht unbedingt sinnvoll angelegtes Geld. Wenn man weiß, wie viel diese Plakatwerbung kostet und das Beste, was man daraus machen kann, ist ein wenig Subversion…

(Gelächter)

Clegg: Nein, sie [ACT UPs Plakatwerbung] war am Anfang extrem erfolgreich. Jetzt verändert sie sich.

Barry: Ich möchte etwas zu ACT UPs visueller Strategie sagen. Nach einer gewissen Zeit war das rosa Dreieck etwas abgenutzt. Seine ikonische Kraft löste sich auf. Genauso wie wenn man als Künstler*in mit einer bestimmten Art der Produktion in Verbindung gebracht wird und sich die Kraft der Arbeit auflöst.

Bauer: Ich wollte dich in Bezug auf Plakatwerbungskosten nur fragen – was kosten Veranstaltungen wie diese?

Guttmann: In den frühen achtziger Jahren sprachen viele davon, die Botschaft zu untergraben. Brüche in der nahtlosen Textur des Lebens zu schaffen. So etwas als Hauptstrategie. Es gibt nur eine Gefahr, wenn man das tut, man schaut dann wirklich auf das Publikum herab. Und diese Haltung hat einen sehr paternalistischen Beigeschmack. So etwa wie: Wir sind die Klugen, wir haben die richtige Politik, und alle anderen im Land sind dumme Hinterwäldler. Alles, was wir brauchen, sind ein paar nette Grafiken, um sie aufzurütteln, und sobald wir sie aufgerüttelt haben, werden sie zur Erkenntnis kommen.

Cahan: Ich glaube, das Thema, das Judith unterstreicht, ist, ob Künstler*innen ihre Grafik- oder Designfähigkeiten teilen, aber auf eine Art auch andere Fähigkeiten, die damit zu tun haben, die Zusammenhänge zwischen verschiedenen kulturellen Bereichen auszuhandeln. Und Zugriff auf verschiedene öffentliche Kulturräume auszuhandeln. Ich glaube also, wenn wir über Plakatwände sprechen, müssen wir darüber auf dieser Ebene sprechen und nicht nur in Hinsicht auf Künstler*innen, die Werbestrategien anwenden.

Fraser: Denn ein Massenpublikum ist keine Gemeinschaft.

Barry: Ich glaube nicht, dass Künstler*innen im Allgemeinen die naive Vorstellung haben, dass sie soziale Lösungen bieten, nur weil sie etwas popularisieren. Beispielsweise hat Barbara Kruger gerade ein großes Projekt über misshandelte Frauen gemacht, das von [dem Modehaus] Liz Claiborne finanziert wurde, und ein Teil des Projekts waren Plakatwände. Gleichzeitig gab es auch Gelder, die an Unterkünfte für misshandelte Frauen gespendet wurden und es wurde soziales Engagement in den Städten geleistet, in denen das Projekt stattfand.

Lorenz: Um noch einmal auf diesen Punkt der Expertise zurückzukommen: Ich würde nicht sagen, Andrea, dass es keine qualifizierten Grafiker*innen oder andere qualifizierte Arbeitskräfte geben sollte. Was allerdings Sprecher*innen angeht, beispielsweise in der Studentenbewegung 1968 – dort waren es die Medien und das Fernsehen, die Sprecher*innen suchten und sie haben sie in die Schulen gebracht, und das ist einer der Gründe, warum die Bewegung endete.

Fraser: Nun, ja. In den Vereinigten Staaten entstand die Frauenbewegung aus der Neuen Linken heraus, vor allem weil es sehr gut definierte Hierarchien von Sprechern innerhalb der SDS [Students for a Democratic Society] gab, die Frauen nicht zuhörten und Frauen nicht erlaubten, zu sprechen.

Cahan: Group Material hat ein Projekt gemacht, das „Your Message Here" [1990] hieß, und sie wurden von der Randolph Street Gallery als

Berater*innen hinzugezogen, um ein Projekt zu entwerfen und umzusetzen, bei dem jede*r einen Entwurf für ein Plakatprojekt einreichen konnte. Ich glaube, es wurden insgesamt achtzehn Plakatwände produziert. Die Künstler*innen halfen also bei der Umsetzung dieses spezifischen Projekts. Es war nicht so, dass ihre eigenen Stimmen öffentlich übertragen wurden – sie halfen stattdessen dabei, die Präsentation anderer Stimmen zu realisieren, vor allem Stimmen in den Gemeinschaften, in denen die Plakatwände sich befanden. Die Idee von Künstler*innen, die eine Dienstleistung erbringen, ist also sehr weit.

Draxler: Es gibt diese Fragen über die Bedeutung des Begriffs „Dienstleistung", wir können ihn aber auch verwenden, um das Verhältnis zu verstehen.

Lorenz: Man kann die Dienstleistung immer von der anderen Seite aus betrachten.

Cahan: Ich kann nicht für Group Material sprechen, aber wenn man anhand ihrer früheren Arbeiten urteilt, lag ihr Interesse möglicherweise bei Fragen des kulturellen Zugangs: Wer erzeugt Kultur und für wen wird diese Kultur erzeugt?

Lorenz: Aber das ist ein politisches Ziel, dass Menschen Zugang zu Kultur haben sollten. Und ich bin einfach gegen diese Idee der Dienstleistung, bei der es eine Institution gibt, die einem Geld gibt, 20.000 Mark, und dann erbringt man eine Dienstleistung und man hat keine Ziele und keine Idee davon, wie man sie umsetzen kann.

Jochen Becker: ACT UP hat die Infrastruktur genutzt. Die Infrastruktur der Werbeagenturen, von Medienunternehmen, der Presse, der Galerien und so weiter. Das sind auch Institutionen. Möglicherweise können wir aber auch das Infrastruktur nennen.

Blazwick: Das ist es, was ich gestern versucht habe, zu sagen. Dass man die Verbindung zwischen verschiedenen Kommunikationsmitteln findet. Für mich war die größte Dienstleistung oder Funktion, die eine Institution hatte, als ich studiert habe und zum ICA [Institute of Contemporary Arts] in London ging, diese Sache zu entdecken, die Feminismus hieß. Und dort andere Frauen zu treffen, sie sprechen zu hören, ihre Kunst und ihre Filme anzuschauen. Das war für mich eine radikale, zentrale Erfahrung in meinem Leben. Dieser Punkt des Austauschs war etwas sehr Wertvolles. Es war diese regelmäßige Plattform, zu der man jede Woche gehen konnte und wo jemand einen Beitrag leistete.

Guttmann: Ich glaube, die Vorstellung Kollektivität zu bilden, um das Gefühl zu verlieren, dass man allein ist und ein atomisierter Einzelner ist, und dann Strukturen zu organisieren, die diese Kollektivität fördern – das ist ein etwas anderes Projekt als das des „Ansprechens". Folglich ist eine Dienstleistung, die Künstler*innen erbringen können, einen Raum für Kollektivität zu schaffen. In den achtziger Jahren gab es so viele Künstler*innen, die Aussagen an undifferenzierten Orten präsentiert haben, ob es nun Keith Haring oder Jenny Holzer waren.

Green: Ich möchte auf etwas zurückkommen, was Judith über

Fähigkeiten und Misstrauen gesagt hat. Ich habe über die Unterschiede zwischen WAC und ACT UP hinsichtlich der Art und Weise nachgedacht, wie sie sich zusammengeschlossen und entwickelt haben. WAC war von Anfang an in bestimmte Personengruppen und Gemeinschaften unterteilt, die an spezifischen Projekten arbeiteten, zu denen juristische Fälle gehörten. Und ganz am Anfang – ich war nur ganz am Anfang dort –, wollten sie ein Medienevent schaffen, um Aufmerksamkeit auf die spezifische Situation zu lenken, aber es war nur ein liberaler Wunsch, „Gutes zu tun". Es gab eine Trennung zwischen denjenigen, die schon dort waren und die juristische Arbeit machten, bevor die Aufmerksamkeit aufkam. Daher ist diese Aufmerksamkeit ein Problem. Und ich habe mich nach dieser Dienstleistung gefragt – was ist, wenn sie nicht vertrauenswürdig ist?

Barry: Nun, wisst ihr, WAC hatte eine sehr spezielle Vorgeschichte, denn sie begann in der Kunstwelt und war somit schon zu Beginn problembehaftet – die Mehrheit war weiß und sie gehörte ausschließlich zur oberen Mittelschicht. Es gab also von Anfang an unglaubliche Spaltungen. Und da einige sehr berühmte Künstler*innen darunter waren, führte das zu weiteren Spaltungen. Dennoch ist das größere Problem des Misstrauens in Bezug auf Bildmaterial innerhalb öffentlicher Dienstleistungsgruppen systemisch.

Green: Richtig – ich versuche, darauf einzugehen, was du „systemisches Misstrauen" nennst. Es ist eine Spaltung, die sich mehrmals innerhalb politisch aktiver Gruppen wiederholt hat. Und in Berlin habe ich mit Beatrice darüber gesprochen, dass

einige Studierende verschiedene kunstbezogene Zeitschriften zu einer Diskussion eingeladen haben. Und die Diskussion entwickelte sich dann darüber, dass es einige Konflikte mit einer der Zeitschriften gab, die anspruchsvoller zu sein schien – und zwar, dass die Produktion teurer, sie aber inhaltlich dann vielleicht nicht echt oder authentisch war.

Fraser: Ob man über eine Vorlesungsreihe am ICA spricht oder grafische Arbeiten oder was auch immer – geht es dabei um Diskurs oder kulturelle Produktion, oder legt es einen bestimmten Standard des Diskurses oder kultureller Produktion fest, der an bestimmte materielle Bedingungen der Individuen und Gruppen und Gemeinschaften gebunden ist? Für mich ist das ein Problem, weil ich Jahre gebraucht habe, um mich von diesen Diskursstandards zu befreien, die die Foren in New York in den frühen achtziger Jahren auferlegt haben.

Cahan: Nicht, dass ich auf WAC herumreiten will, aber es gab eine Spaltung in der Gruppe zwischen denjenigen, die eher einen expressionistischen Ansatz zum politischen Engagement vertraten, und denen, die einen eher neo-konzeptionellen Ansatz vertraten. Und diese Unterteilung bezieht sich auf Definitionen davon, was es bedeutet, Künstler*in zu sein, und welche Definitionen oder Sprachen oder Praktiken für eine*n Künstler*in angemessen sind, um sich zu engagieren.

Fraser: Diskurs ist spezialisiert und muss sich einer internen Struktur und Vorgaben fügen, die durch Konkurrenz definiert werden.

Guttmann: Ich lebe seit ein paar Jahren in San Francisco, und es gibt einen großen Unterschied zwischen der Politik New Yorks und der Politik Nordkaliforniens. Sehr viel davon hat mit dieser Problematik zu tun.

(Bauer stellt in deutscher Sprache eine Frage, die teilweise nicht hörbar ist und mit dem Wohlfahrtsausschuss zu tun hat.)

Becker: Ute, du hast also auf Deutsch eine Frage über den Wohlfahrtsausschuss gestellt. Hierzu gibt es einige Vorgeschichten. Ich werde eine erzählen, meine eigene Vorgeschichte dazu: Er wurde nach dem Attentat in Hamburg gegründet, dem Mord an türkischen Menschen und dem Niederbrennen von Häusern, in denen Migrant*innen in Rostock wohnten [1992]. Es gab die Idee, eine Koalition von Menschen aus besetzten Häusern zu bilden, die in Hamburg im politischen Fokus stehen. Kritiker*innen, Musiker*innen, Clubleute. Und es gab verschiedene Gruppen in Düsseldorf, Köln und München mit unterschiedlichen Hintergründen. Ein loser Zusammenschluss. Ich war erstaunt, die Beschreibung der Art Workers' Coalition zu lesen, dass es der gleiche lose Verbund sehr unterschiedlicher Personen war. Und eine Organisation zu finden, die nicht nur ein Thema vertrat. Das ist eine Idee des Wohlfahrtsausschusses. Sie organisierten Aktionen gegen eine Ausstellung in Düsseldorf, die *Deutsch Sein* hieß, die kurz vor der Entscheidung stattfand, die Einwanderungsgesetze in Deutschland zu widerrufen – ein deutsches Grundgesetz, das nach dem Zweiten Weltkrieg geschaffen wurde, um Einwander*innen und Migrant*innen zu schützen. Zu dieser Zeit beseitigten, hoben sie

[die Regierung] also genau dieses Grundgesetz auf. Es gab daraufhin Demonstrationen rund um diese Ausstellung.

Dillemuth: Ich finde diese losen Konfigurierungen aus dem Nichts interessant, und es gab sie in jeder Großstadt. Diese Wohlfahrtsausschüsse wurden von verschiedenen Menschen organisiert. Und man hat versucht, sie zu definieren, aber es war schwierig – ist es eine Partei, ist es ein Club, was ist es? Man wollte zusammenkommen und miteinander sprechen. Und das waren Menschen aus ganz verschiedenen Fraktionen.

Draxler: Ja, es gab viele Konflikte zwischen diesen Gruppen.

Dillemuth: Genau, und es scheint, dass es dafür ein Bedürfnis gibt! Und in diesem Forum hier scheint es auch ein Bedürfnis dafür zu geben, mit unseren sehr unterschiedlichen Positionen.

Lorenz: Es gibt einen Unterscheid zwischen praktischer Arbeit oder sehr spezifischen Diskussionen wie diesen hier und einer breiteren, allgemeineren Diskussion. Und ich kenne jetzt mehr Personen, die ich anrufen könnte, wenn irgendetwas passiert. Das ist wichtig.

Publikum (Vera Kockot, Studentin): Diese Gemeinschaft hat sich aus einem bereits bestehenden Netzwerk zusammengesetzt, und daraus sind bestimmte Gruppen entstanden. Es ist aber wichtig zu erwähnen, dass es schon etablierte Netzwerke gab, beispielsweise aus Köln und aus Hamburg. Das waren soziale Netzwerke, die dann eine Infrastruktur aufgebaut haben, um politische Arbeit zu leisten. Und Renate weist auf ein wichtiges Argument hin, dass das hier die gleiche Situation ist, in der es ein bereits bestehendes Netzwerk gibt, das sich aus selbstständiger Arbeit mit Gemeinschaften entwickeln kann. Aus dieser Gruppe, und in Korrelation zu diesem Modell hier.

Fraser: Ja, ich danke dir. Ich sollte erwähnen, dass jetzt schon zwei Stunden um sind. Beatrice findet tatsächlich gerade heraus, ob man Pizza bestellen kann. Hört sich das nach einer guten Idee an? Da kommt sie, vielleicht kann sie es uns sagen.

Guttmann: Pizza vom amerikanischen Pizza-Zentrum?

(Gelächter)

Fraser: Oder wir könnten für eine Stunde hinausgehen – es scheint gerade mal nicht zu regnen.

Arbeitsgruppe
Sitzung Fünf

Im Dienste der Kunst
und der Künstler*innen
Sonntag, 23. Januar 1994

Vorträge:
Fritz Rahmann
Ulrich Bischoff
Ute Meta Bauer
Christian Philipp Müller
Helmut Draxler

*Viele Kunstinstitutionen wurden gegründet, erstens, um Kunst und Künstler*innen und zweitens, um der Öffentlichkeit zu dienen. Viele Museumsfachleute befinden sich im Zwiespalt zwischen diesen beiden Interessengemeinschaften.*

*Kurator*innen fühlen sich oft von den Institutionen oder den Künstler*innen selbst eingeschränkt, sodass sie sich in Rollen der Dienstleistung, Betreuung und Produktion für Künstler*innen und deren Galerist*innen wiederfinden.*

*Gleichzeitig empfinden viele Projektkünstler*innen, dass sie nicht die Unterstützung bekommen, die sie benötigen. Wie können diese Konflikte angesprochen werden?*

Helmut Draxler: Wir hatten uns in einer der vorherigen Sitzungen darauf geeinigt, morgen speziell den Studierenden das Material zu präsentieren. Selbstverständlich lade ich jede*n ein, die*der dann noch hier ist, sich uns anzuschließen, gegen 12:30 Uhr oder 13:00 Uhr. Und später sollten wir auch ein wenig darüber diskutieren, wie wir den öffentlichen Vortrag organisieren. In Ordnung, Fritz, also würdest du bitte anfangen?

Fritz Rahmann: In Bezug auf den Begriff „Dienstleistung" habe ich die ganze Zeit schon Zweifel. Die Möglichkeit, darüber zu sprechen, bot sich gestern, als du, Andrea, gefragt wurdest, ob deine Arbeit bei der Whitney Biennale je nach Antwort der Vorstandsmitglieder – ob sie sie akzeptiert hätten oder nicht – anders ausgesehen hätte. Für mich schien es ganz normal, dass du gesagt hast, es wäre dieselbe Arbeit gewesen, die igendwie der Institution gedient hätte. Dass es aber praktisch nicht auf die Reaktion dieser Personen ankam, ist ein Beweis dafür, dass sie autonom ist. Das ist das Argument, das ich unterstreichen möchte.

Wir sprechen immer über diese schwierigen historischen Konzepte, die gleichzeitig auch die des Kunstdiskurses sind. Es gibt immer eine historische Dimension. Es gibt eine zeitliche Position, die beachtet werden muss, auch wenn wir von „Kunst" sprechen und wir hier über „Dienstleistung" reden und historische Beispiele zitieren, wie die aus den späten sechziger Jahren. So viel ist passiert und darum ist es sehr wichtig, sich auf die Position eines Konzepts in einem bestimmten Kontext zu konzentrieren. Ich wollte erwähnen, dass wir diesem Punkt meiner Meinung nach nicht genug Aufmerksamkeit schenken. Deshalb ist es wichtig, den Zweck, den ihr diesen Sitzungen gegeben habt, im Kopf zu behalten – dauerhaft tragbare Konzepte für die professionelle Praxis zu etablieren. Das kann aber nicht gelingen. Das steht im Gegensatz zu all den Erfahrungen, die ich in meiner Praxis gemacht habe. Das ist ein allgemeiner Einwand.

Was ich über Büro Berlin sagen kann, ist, dass es um Zeit geht, und deswegen mache ich diese allgemeine Bemerkung. Das Hauptargument der Praxis war, Orte zu entwerfen – die eigentlichen materiellen Arbeiten waren die Orte. Es war nicht die Kunst; es war der Ort. Die ersten Erfahrungen zeigten uns, dass es einen sehr starken Einfluss auf das Design der Projekte und Arbeiten hatte, dies als Absicht jedes Projekts zu haben. Ich erinnere mich, dass diese Absicht sehr stark war: interessante Arbeiten Orte werden zu lassen. Ideologisches Erbe war zu dem Zeitpunkt durch. Ich kam aus Holland und hatte mich in gewisser Hinsicht diesen allgemeinen moralischen Diskussionen über Kunst in der Gesellschaft hingegeben, und als ich nach Berlin kam, war das absolut out. Es ging nur darum, interessante Arbeit zu machen. Und jede Diskussion, wie die, die wir hier führen, wäre als pedantisch betrachtet worden. Das war die Situation. Aus dieser Situation entstand dieses Bewusstsein, eine kleine Gelegenheit – dass der Ort selbst einem das geben würde, was man brauchte, um eine Arbeit zu machen. Und über diese Praxis werde ich hier versuchen, kurz zu sprechen.

Es war mir damals nicht klar, aber jetzt weiß ich, dass der Immobilienwert, der soziale Wert von Immobilien, als konsequenter Teil des Projekts eingesetzt wurde. Und das ist eine sehr politische Angelegenheit. Es war uns aber damals nicht bewusst. Das ist auch eine sehr starke Arbeitsbedingung. Man kann es also nur als vorübergehend betrachten. Nicht als dauerhaft. Sonst ist man einfach diese*r monumentale Künstler*in, die oder der diese großen Denkmäler hinstellt. Einige Bereiche des Ortes als beständige Teile der Arbeit zu nutzen, war nur vorübergehend möglich. Ich glaube, wir haben beobachtet, dass ein Ort nur für einen kurzen Zeitraum diese Kraft besaß – manchmal nur ein paar Tage. Man konnte diese Orte nicht einfangen. Und das wollten wir auch nicht. Es gab also eine Tendenz zur Performance. Obwohl alle Teilnehmer*innen aus der bildenden Kunst stammten, arbeiteten sie mit Theater und Performance. Bei der Bedeutung dieser Arbeiten, dieser Orte, ging es um Kunst in der Gesellschaft. Allerdings war die Hauptaussage des Projekts, dass es auf kurze Zeiträume begrenzt war.

Ich habe immer Projekte mit dem Bewusstsein über den Zeitaspekt in der Aufführung der Arbeit gemacht. Ich arbeite gerade mit dem Platz neben der Alten Pinakothek in München. Ich glaube, es gibt eine Verbindung zwischen diesem Projekt und dem, was ich mit der Büro Berlin Praxis versucht habe zu beschreiben, weil das Gebäude in München und seine Umgebung historisch sind. Wir sprechen über dieses historische Konzept der Kunst, das dort zur Architektur geworden ist und ich glaube, ich bin sehr an dieser Aufgabe interessiert, weil ich das Bewusstsein der Geltung eines Bauwerks aus einer bestimmten Zeit praktizieren kann. Ein Gebäude, das entworfen wurde, um das Konzept der Kunst zu etablieren, so wie wir es hier in Europa noch haben und es nach Amerika exportiert wurde. Klassische Arbeiten in einer bestimmten Zeit. Jemand wie König Ludwig [der II. von Bayern] kaufte sie in Italien oder in Paris, um bewusst die Macht des Landes durch das Sammeln von Kunst zu etablieren. Und genau das war die Idee des Museums. Vielleicht aller Museen. Man kann diese sehr eindeutige Geschichte des Museums in den Dokumenten lesen, als Ludwig das Gebäude

1810 und 1815 geplant hat. Meine Arbeit lag darin, die Geschichte des Gebäudes zu untersuchen. Die Bedeutung des Gebäudes und das Konzept der Kunst waren miteinander identisch – wie die Architektur auch, sollten sie dauerhaft präsent sein. Dieses historische Konzept des Gebäudes und seiner Kunst, ein ewiges Bauwerk zu sein, war also für mich die Angelegenheit selbst. Auf gewisse Weise war es das, was die katastrophale Geschichte des Gebäudes verursacht hat. Es wurde Teil der nationalsozialistischen Planung in München, als repräsentatives NS-Bauwerk. Das Gebäude wurde als Kulisse für die Ideologie der Nazi-Macht benutzt. Alliierte bombardierten dann später das Gebäude. Dann kam ein modernistischer Architekt, um das Gebäude zu rekonstruieren. Der Gegensatz zwischen der Moderne und dieser klassischen Idee der ewigen Kunst. Dann gab es die Münchner Gesellschaft, und ein Komitee wurde gegründet, um die Wiederaufbauarbeiten am Gebäude einzuschränken. Etwas Arbeit wurde durchgeführt und einiges wurde verändert, während anderes unverändert blieb. Man betritt das Gebäude jetzt durch den Hintereingang. Es ist so eine verrückte Situation. Sie haben Skulpturen aufgestellt, um es irgendwie attraktiver zu machen. Seht ihr, diese Skulpturen – diese Kunst – fungiert, um einem zerstörten Ort und einer Idee ein besseres Aussehen zu geben. Das ist also das Thema der Arbeit, die ich dort mache.

Draxler: Was sind deine Vorschläge?

Rahmann: Nein, es gibt keine Vorschläge, ich habe es die ganze Zeit versucht…

Ulrich Bischoff: Vielen Dank für die Einladung, hierher zu kommen und hier zu sprechen. Warum ich hierher eingeladen wurde, weiß ich wirklich nicht. Vielleicht, weil ich die Person war, die Fritz in die Alte Pinakothek in München eingeladen hat, als ich in diesem Museum gearbeitet habe. Nun arbeite ich aber in einem anderen Museum. Das ganze Thema der „Dienstleistungen" ist für mich eine Chance, mir anzuschauen, was die Künstler*innen, mit denen ich in dieser Situation gearbeitet habe, getan haben. Und um zu sehen, was ich gemacht habe und was ich jetzt tue. Mir selbst vorzustellen, wie Dienstleistungen die Rahmenbedingungen verändern können.

Mir fällt eine Arbeit von Chris Burden ein: *Exposing the Foundation of the Museum*, die er vorübergehend in der Temporary Contemporary [Museum of Contemporary Art, Los Angeles, 1986] gemacht hat. Und falls ihr es nicht wisst, Burden hat eine Ausgrabung der ursprünglichen architektonischen Fundamente gemacht. Aber die [metaphorische] Fundierung des Museums zu enthüllen, ist natürlich eines der wichtigsten fundamentalen Dinge, an denen wir arbeiten sollten.

Die Situation hier ist eine, die für mich jenseitig ist. Ich fühle mich hier in einer anderen Welt, ganz anders als in meiner alltäglichen. In meiner normalen Welt hatte ich besipielsweise am Freitagabend ein Treffen im Museum in Dresden, in dem ich arbeite [Gemäldegalerie Neue Meister, Staatliche Kunstsammlungen Dresden]. Die Museen in Dresden sind einer der wichtigsten Orte, die Tourist*innen besuchen, um dieser alten Stadt ein neues Leben zu geben. Es gibt einen Freundeskreis, der auf Latein Muse Saxony e Usui heißt, und der 180 Personen aus ganz Deutschland eingeladen hat, die den Mussen Geld spenden. Und sie hatten dort eine Sitzung – wir hatten das Treffen im Zwinger, wo heute die wichtigsten Sammlungen von Gemälden aus dem 17. und 18. Jahrhundert in Deutschland untergebracht sind. Dann zogen wir mit Fackeln an einen anderen Ort in der Stadt, der Albertinum heißt. Diese 180 Personen konnten zum ersten Mal die [Wilhelm] Lehmbruck-Skulptur [*Kniende*, 1911] sehen, die von den Nazis aus dem Museum entfernt und dann in New York gekauft und zurück nach Dresden gebracht wurde. Das ist für mich nun eine ganz normale Situation. Aber andererseits gibt es eine Situation, in der ich in einem Museum in Ostdeutschland [Gemäldegalerie Neue Meister, Staatliche Kunstsammlungen Dresden] arbeite, in der die normalen Rahmenbedingungen zerbrochen sind, und die Strukturen der Erhaltung und der Vermittlungsinitiativen zerbrochen sind, und die Hälfte der Mitarbeiter*innen entlassen wurde. Wir haben nun sehr wenige Mitarbeiter*innen. Und wir müssen die Strukturen wieder aufbauen. Ich bin also hier, um Hilfestellung von Künstler*innen zu bekommen, um bessere Strukturen für dieses Museum zu schaffen.

Als ich noch in München war – wisst ihr, es gibt in den Museen in München eine sehr starke Struktur. Bayerische Staatsgalerien sind extrem gut etabliert. Und meine Arbeit bestand darin, bloß diese Kunstwerke auf dem Rasen hinter der Pinakothek in München neu zu arrangieren. Das ist ungefähr das, was der Museumsdirektor normalerweise zuhause macht, wenn er in seinem eigenen Garten Objekte arrangiert: „Da in die Mitte kommt das hin, und da ist das, und ein wenig hiervon."

Einfach auf eine simple, ästhetische Art zu arbeiten und diese Dinge zu tun, ohne die sozialen Strukturen oder die Funktion des Gebäudes oder der Institution zu sehen. Ich war allerdings nicht in der Lage, das zu tun. Ich kannte Fritz schon sehr lange, und so hatte ich hohe Erwartungen daran, dass er etwas sehen würde, was ich nicht sah. Ich weiß es nicht – wir werden sehen, und wir werden nächstes Jahr eine Publikation herausgeben und wir nehmen einige Umstrukturierungen vor. Das ist also meine Situation im Museum.

Ich denke, in der sehr kurzen Zeit, die wir haben, sollten wir darüber diskutieren, was unternommen werden kann. Denn zuallererst benötigt das Museum Unterstützung. Und das ist eine Dienstleistung, um die ich die Künstler*innen bitte. Meine Frage lautet: Warum seid ihr daran interessiert, diese Art von Arbeit zu leisten? Es geht um die Frage, was diese Institution für euch bedeutet. Ist es Kunst? Wie kann diese Kunst bezahlt werden, gekauft werden? Ich denke, wir beide, Kurator*innen und Künstler*innen, müssen über diese Art von Kunst diskutieren. Ich denke, dass diese Kunst das ist, was Fritz produziert, wenn er eine Beschreibung der Pinakothek macht.

Ich hatte vor zwei Jahren die Möglichkeit, eine Ausstellung mit John Cage in der Neuen Pinakothek zu organisieren, die im Juli 1991 eröffnet wurde. Er machte den Museum Circle. Er arrangierte das Museum neu. Die Idee des Museum Circle war auch, dass er Angst vor dem Museum hatte – dass es nicht das beste Format für eine Präsentation war. Er bat mich also als Kurator, mit all meinen Kolleg*innen in den anderen Museen in München zu sprechen – vom historischen Museum,

vom Paläontologischen Museum, vom ethnologischen Museum – von allen Museen, die mit der Pinakothek assoziiert waren und aus den verschiedenen Stadtmuseen. Cage bat mich, diese Kolleg*innen um Leihgaben zu bitten. Er bat also um Leihgaben, aber er sagte nicht, was für welche. Die Idee war, dass ich meine Museumskolleg*innen bitten würde, uns zehn oder zwölf Leihobjekte aus ihren Sammlungen zu geben, aber Cage hatte keine Liste mit *welchen*. Er sagte mir: „Du fragst sie einfach nach einer Liste von Objekten und dann mache ich es per Zufallsprinzip und werde willkürlich aus diesen Listen auswählen." Meine Kolleg*innen dachten, das wäre Unsinn, aber die Pinakothek ist eine wichtige Institution, also arbeiteten sie mit uns zusammen. Cage benutzte das Zufallsprinzip auch, um zu entscheiden, wo die Leihgaben in der Pinakothek ausgestellt würden. Es gab also plötzlich eine ganz neue Struktur im Museum, und das war sehr erfrischend. Das Publikum und die Menschen waren sehr zufrieden damit. Es war sehr schön, denn ein Porträt von [Otto von] Bismarck stand neben einem sehr alten zwanzigtausend-jährigen Bären.

Das war aber nur eine Erfahrung mit John Cage. Es war ein einfaches Beispiel dafür, wie Künstler*innen echte Veränderungen an Strukturen vornehmen können. Ich habe noch vier weitere Seiten Vortrag, aber ich denke, ich werde jetzt aufhören.

Draxler: Christian?

Christian Philipp Müller: Ich möchte mit euch über ein Projekt sprechen, das ich 1987–88 gemacht habe, weil ich denke, dass es in die Kategorie Kunst und Künstler*innen zu dienen passen könnte. Ich wurde 1987 von einem Verein aus Amsterdam, der Arti et Amicitiae oder „Kunst und Freundschaft" heißt, eingeladen, dort eine Ausstellung zu kuratieren. Es war aber völlig unklar, was ihre Vorstellung davon war, was meine spezielle Aufgabe für die Arbeit dort sein sollte. Ich verstand es als eine Gelegenheit zur Reflexion und Forschung über diese Institution. Ich habe über vierzig Interviews mit neuen Mitgliedern der Organisation geführt. Diese Organisation ist, soweit ich weiß, einer der ältesten Kunstvereine. Er wurde 1839 von Künstlern gegründet, in gewisser Weise in Anlehnung an die Struktur des deutschen Kunstvereins. Der Unterschied besteht darin, dass die Gründer keinerlei bürgerliche Personen waren. Er wurde tatsächlich nur von Künstlern gegründet, weil diese Künstler frustriert über ihre Konditionen in Amsterdam waren und es zu dieser Zeit keine Museen für sie gab. Im 19. Jahrhundert war ein berühmtes Gemälde von Rembrandt, *Die Nachtwache* [1642], nur tagsüber für ein paar Stunden im Sommer in einem Treppenaufgang zu sehen. Deshalb wollten sie mehr Kontrolle darüber haben, wie Kunst gezeigt wurde.

Sie wollten ihren sozialen Status als Künstler steigern. Die einzige Möglichkeit, die sie hatten, ihre Arbeiten auf normale Weise zu zeigen, war an überfüllten Wänden im jährlichen Salon. Sie waren also mit den Konditionen unzufrieden. Für mich war das sehr interessant, weil sie ihre Konditionen wirklich steuern wollten. Sie legten also Geld zusammen und kauften einen Teil eines Hauses und dann ein wenig später das ganze Haus. Und sie verwandelten es in ihre Vision davon, was ein Museum sein sollte. Ein Raum, in dem ihre Arbeiten entsprechend

gezeigt werden konnten. Einer der Punkte, über den wir sprechen, ist Kontrolle und wie viel Kontrolle wir als Künstler*innen bekommen können. Diese Personen haben wirklich versucht, 100 Prozent Kontrolle zu bekommen, indem sie ihren eigenen Raum entwarfen. Sie entwarfen eine Kombination aus Ausstellungsräumen auf den oberen Etagen, und im Erdgeschoss hatten sie einen Ort, wo sie Leute treffen und einladen konnten. Und auch potenzielle Käufer treffen konnten.

Sie entwarfen ebenfalls ein Format, sodass sie den König der Niederlande dort empfangen konnten. Im Laufe von 150 Jahren haben diese Personen, diese Künstler, die Kontrolle verloren. Sie haben ihre Richtung verloren. Ich habe mich also ein Jahr lang mit Forschung beschäftigt und ging jeden Monat in ihr Archiv. Ich habe versucht herauszufinden, was am Anfang das Ziel dieser Künstler war und ich fand heraus, dass es nicht nur um die Kontrolle ihres eigenen architektonischen und sozialen Raumes ging – sie entwickelten auch ihre eigene Publikation und ihre eigene Kunstkritik. Sie haben versucht, ihre eigene kritische Rezeption zu kontrollieren; oft haben die Künstler sogar Kritiken über ihre eigenen Arbeiten geschrieben. Das ganze Modell funktionierte nur für diese Künstler-Generation. Für die nächste Generation, die Impressionisten, war diese historische Zunft nicht mehr von Nutzen.

Meine Frage war also, wie eine historische Struktur einer zeitgenössischen Kunstgemeinschaft dienen könnte. Die neuen Vereinsmitglieder waren mit der Organisation unzufrieden und wählten einen künstlerischen Leiter, der Änderungen vornehmen würde. Ich machte mehr als vierzig Besuche in den Ateliers der neuen Mitglieder und ich fragte sie, was sie an der Organisation verändern würden. Ich habe die Hauptausstellungsräume leer gelassen; ich habe nur eine Tapete mit dem Symbol des heiligen Lukas entworfen, welches das Symbol des Vereins ist. Ich habe das erste Symbol von 1839 benutzt und dann auch das Symbol des Vereins aus den achtziger Jahren, das eine abstrakte Form hat. Ich habe das wiederholt als Tapetenmuster benutzt, um den häuslichen Charakter der Institution zu unterstreichen, weil es für die Mitglieder wie ein Zuhause ist. Das Buch, das ich entworfen habe, ist wie ein Reisebericht geschrieben – ich, der eingeladene Künstler, der nach Amsterdam kommt und in das Haus eintritt und Leute im Treppenhaus kennenlernt und all die verschiedenen Räume besucht und beginnt, mit anderen zu sprechen. Eine Fiktion, die aus Interviews geschrieben wurde, die ich wirklich mit den Mitgliedern geführt habe. Die Ausstellung, die ich gemacht habe, rief heftige Reaktionen hervor – sie haben sofort den künstlerischen Leiter entlassen und gingen dahin zurück, Kompromiss-Ausstellungen zu machen, die voll und ganz damit verbunden waren, einen Sponsor zu finden. Beispielsweise kam die holländische Eisenbahngesellschaft auf sie zu und sagte: „Okay, wir haben $100.000, können sie eine Ausstellung über Bahnhöfe machen?" Ich meine, vielleicht sollte ich einfach etwas daraus vorlesen, was der künstlerische Leiter in der Einleitung für das Buch geschrieben hat. Denn ich fand es merkwürdig, wie aggressiv ihre Reaktion war und die Ablehnung gegenüber dieser Ausstellung. Ich sah mich selbst nur als einen Spiegel, der ihnen zeigte,

was sie besaßen – und zwar die unglaubliche Struktur und die Möglichkeiten, die sie hatten. Ich wollte bloß mit den neuen Mitgliedern sprechen, aber in gewisser Hinsicht konnten sie das nicht ertragen.

Der künstlerische Leiter schreibt in der Einleitung: „Arti et Amicitiae stellt seine neuen Mitglieder vor, indem er ihre Arbeiten ausstellt. Ich habe den Schweizer Künstler Christian Philipp Müller gebeten, dazu einige neue Ideen zu entwickeln." Ich wurde als Künstler eingeladen, aber sie erwarteten von mir die Dienstleistung eines Kurators als jemand, der nur die Kunst von vierzig neuen Mitgliedern arrangiert. Ich entschloss mich, nicht die Arbeiten von vierzig Künstler*innen zu zeigen, sondern die Möglichkeiten, die sie hatten.

Um nur noch einmal aus den Interviews vorzulesen, ein Mitglied sagte: „Ich weiß zu schätzen, dass Arti et Amicitiae keine Galerie ist und das Potenzial darin sieht, hier ein lebendiges Forum zu schaffen. Ich liebe die sorgfältig erhaltene Oase inmitten der hektischen modernen Stadt, trotzdem sehe ich ihren Tod durch Ersticken aufgrund der selbst auferlegten Isolation." Und ein anderes Mitglied: „In der Kunstgeschichte kamen die guten Ideen immer von Individuen. Jeder muss seine eigene Arbeit vorantreiben. Um Kunst zu machen, muss man sich in sich selbst zurückziehen." Ein anderes Mitglied erklärte: „Kunst sollte dem Publikum von Amsterdam die neuesten Entwicklungen in der Kunst präsentieren. Ein Vorteil von Arti et Amicitiae ist, dass es weder Museum noch Galerie ist – kommerzielle Konditionen sollten nicht das Ausstellungsprogramm bestimmen. Dadurch, dass zum richtigen Zeitpunkt gut gelegene

Immobilien erworben wurden, konnte eine gesunde finanzielle Basis geschaffen werden." Ich versuchte herauszufinden, was die Mitglieder selbst unter dem Unterschied zwischen einem kleinen Museum oder Kunstverein und Arti et Amicitiae als eine Institution verstanden. Mein Verständnis war, dass bei Arti et Amicitiae die Kontrolle immer noch völlig in den Händen der Künstler*innen lag. Warum brauchten sie also einen Ausstellungsorganisator, der Ideen liefert? Einige Mitglieder waren allerdings der Meinung, dass der künstlerische Leiter dadurch, dass er vom Verein angestellt war, viel öfter in diesem Haus anwesend war als sonst jemand und dadurch Kontinuität garantierte – er kannte verschiedene Leute und konnte dadurch Arti-Künstler*innen die Arbeit anderer Künstler*innen vorstellen, die sie noch nicht kannten.

Auf jeden Fall wurde ich im Zusammenhang mit diesem Projekt noch einmal eingeladen, mit einer Künstler*innenorganisation in Frankreich zu arbeiten. Mitten während dieses Projekts fand ich heraus, dass ich nur angestellt wurde, um das Sprachrohr des Kurators zu sein, der dort arbeitete, um eine Kritik zu liefern, die er selbst nicht liefern konnte. Oder er wollte es einfach nicht. Und somit spielte ich die Rolle, André Malraux [französischer Schriftsteller und Kunstkritiker des frühen 20. Jahrhunderts] zu kritisieren. Gleichzeitig stellt sich aber die Frage, wie man eigentlich zeitgenössische Kunst in einem modernistischen sechziger Jahre-Gebäude zeigt, in dem der Kunstraum sich befand. Wie wichtig ist der Kontext oder der Rahmen, in dem man Kunst betrachtet und sie anschaut? Es war immer ein Kampf, diese Leute davon zu überzeugen, dass man einen Künstler, der ein halbes Jahr lang Forschung betreibt, bezahlen sollte. Sie dazu zu bringen, ein Künstlerhonorar zu zahlen, war unmöglich. Wisst ihr, am Ende bin ich nicht mit einem Produkt dort herausgekommen. Bei Arti et Amicitiae sagten sie, ich hätte die Räume leer gelassen. Sie sagten, ich hätte sie nicht benutzt! Das ist das gleiche Argument, dass sie mit Andrea wegen des Eingangsraums im Whitney Museum hatten – man darf sie nicht leer lassen. Aber natürlich waren sie nicht leer. Ich habe dort auch eine Drag-Performance gemacht, in der ich mich wie der niederländische König gekleidet habe. Und ich habe eines der Gemälde gezeigt, das die Vereinskünstler im 19. Jahrhundert gemalt hatten, um dem König zu imponieren.

Draxler: Ute?

Ute Meta Bauer: Ich kann an der gleichen Stelle beginnen, an der Christian gerade aufgehört hat, denn das Künstlerhaus Stuttgart, deren künstlerische Leiterin ich bin, ist auch ein von Künstler*innen gegründeter Raum. Und es gibt eine Vielzahl solcher Räume, nicht nur in Deutschland, sie sind Mitte bis Ende der siebziger Jahre entstanden, als Künstler*innen ihre eigenen Räume und ihre eigenen Strukturen forderten. Die Situation in Stuttgart am Künstlerhaus ist allerdings so, dass sie eine*n Direktor*in haben, die oder der in der Programmgestaltung unabhängig ist. Mein Vorgänger war Sozialarbeiter, und davor war es ein Künstler. Der Unterschied zu anderen Institutionen besteht darin, dass das Künstlerhaus Künstler*innen bittet, für einige Jahre Programmdirektor*in zu sein. Es ist klar, dass die Personen, mit denen ich mich

auseinandersetzen muss, Künstler*innen sind und ein spezialisiertes
Publikum. Das Künstlerhaus hat
nicht mit einem allgemeinen Publikum zu tun. Die Programmstruktur
muss also anders sein.

Was aber von Anfang an ein
Kampf war, ist, dass ich nicht die
Arbeiten von unseren Mitgliedern
zeigen wollte. Es gibt ungefähr
fünfhundert Mitglieder unseres
Vereins, und die meisten von ihnen
sind Künstler*innen. Der Raum wird
mit Geldern der Stadt finanziert, aus
dem Kulturetat, und somit betrachten die Mitglieder es als ihr eigenes
Geld. Die Frage war, was kann ich
dort tun, außer lediglich die Arbeiten
der Mitglieder zu zeigen…was ich
albern fand. Ich dachte also, dass es
das Richtige wäre, an der Struktur zu
arbeiten. Einerseits Ausstellungen
zu zeigen, die mit den Möglichkeiten der künstlerischen Praxis
zusammenhängen – verschiedene
Praktiken, mit denen Künstler*innen arbeiten – um den Mitgliedern
unterschiedliche Arten von Arbeiten
vorzustellen. Andererseits habe
ich Künstler*innen eingeladen und
bat sie, mit dem Raum und seiner
Topografie zu arbeiten. Maria Eichhorn hat zum Beispiel mit unserer
Kinderwerkstatt gearbeitet, die sie
in den Ausstellungsraum übertragen hat. Oder Serge Kliaving – er
wollte nicht anderen Künstler*innen
seine Kunst zeigen, er war mehr am
öffentlichen Raum interessiert. Wir
halfen ihm also, eine Arbeit draußen
im öffentlichen Raum zu präsentieren. Wir versuchen, den Künstler*innen, die wir einladen, eine Art
Struktur und Arbeitsausstattung zu
bieten. Gleichzeitig versuchen wir
auch, lokalen Künstler*innen diese
Ausstattung anzubieten – es gibt
dort Werkstätten und Ateliers, wie
beispielsweise Druck-Werkstätten

und Videoproduktions-Ateliers.
Künstler*Innen können auch den
Büroraum, das Faxgerät und das
Telefon nutzen. Was meiner Meinung nach am wichtigsten ist, ist
jüngeren Künstler*innen zu zeigen,
dass sie nicht darauf warten sollen,
von jemandem für eine Ausstellung
angefragt zu werden, sondern zu
lernen, dass sie es selbst können,
es erzwingen und den Rahmen des
Möglichen erweitern können.

Ich habe auch erkannt, dass man
in solch einer Situation enorme
Macht hat. Selbst wenn wir nicht viel
Geld haben. Plötzlich wähle ich aus,
wen ich einladen möchte – wenn
ich an einer Künstler*in interessiert
bin, kann ich sie oder ihn anrufen
und sagen: „Komm, wir zahlen
deinen Flug" und so weiter. Es ist
eine luxuriöse Position. Man hat viel
Macht in solchen Positionen. Wir
sagen immer, dass Künstler*innen
und Kurator*innen für sich selbst
arbeiten, aber eigentlich laden sie
beide Personen ein, mit denen sie
arbeiten wollen. Es ist also immer
ein Dienst, in beide Richtungen. Die
Frage ist, wie man mit den Personen
arbeitet, die man einlädt. Und wie
kommt man wieder zu diesem
Punkt, der Kunst und Künstler*innen mit Honoraren zu dienen. Wie
bezahlt man die Künstler*innen für
das, was sie tun? Beispielsweise
für das Magazin, das ich mache,
habe ich eine*n Künstler*in für das
Layout. Und wieder ein*e andere*r
Künstler*in hält einen Vortrag. Und
es ist klar, dass sie dafür bezahlt
werden sollten, aber Künstler*innen
werden nicht immer für diese Arbeit
bezahlt. Das sind Dinge, die wir verändern können.

Mit dem Künstlerhaus Stuttgart
werde ich auch Teil der Struktur
der Stadt. Wir sind ein Teil einer
lokalen Kunstgemeinschaft. Auch

darauf bin ich angewiesen. Ich bin ihr Publikum, und sie sind unser Publikum. Man ist also auch sehr mit der örtlichen Struktur verbunden. Darüberhinaus ist es wichtig, eine Art Verbindung zu haben, wenn man Außenstehende hinzuzieht. Man kann diese Verbindung aber nicht institutionalisieren – das geschieht nur durch Solidarität oder wenn es ein gemeinsames Interesse gibt. Das Letzte ist, dass ich nicht nur dort Programmdirektorin bin, sondern auch Mitglied der IG Medien, einer Art Gewerkschaft für Künstler*innen, und das zeige ich dort oben an der Wand [im Kunstraum]. Sie setzen sich dafür ein, dass Künstler*innen bezahlt werden und organisieren Honorare für ihre Arbeit. Aber eine Sache in der Herangehensweise der IG Medien, mit der ich unzufrieden bin ist, dass sie verlangen, dass Künstler*innen für ihre einzelnen Arbeiten bezahlt werden, was eine Vorstellung der Arbeit als individuelles Objekt ist, anstatt…

Jochen Becker: Ja, ein Bild – sie beschreiben ein Kunstwerk als „ein Bild". Das ist eine sehr traditionelle Perspektive.

Bauer: In gewisser Weise denke ich, dass die IG Medien eine gute Idee ist, weil sie sagen, dass Künstler*in zu sein ein Beruf ist wie andere auch, und sie brauchen Gewerkschaften, und wenn sie alt werden, brauchen sie eine Versicherung. Wir sind immer noch Menschen. Künstler*innen werden alt, sie sind nichts Außergewöhnliches oder irgendwie unverwundbar. Es ist also eine gute Idee, die die IG Medien initiiert hat. Ihre Vorstellung von Kunst und Künstler*innen ist aber äußerst traditionell, und sie identifiziert sich nicht mit dem, was eigentlich

vor sich geht. Das ist ihr Problem. Ich denke aber, Diskussionen wie diese können ihnen helfen. Sie wollen das Thema tatsächlich forcieren und sind wirklich in die politische Struktur involviert. Über diese Qualitäten hinaus müssen wir meiner Meinung nach eine Art Teamarbeit lernen. Teamarbeit, bei der es auch um die Bedingungen geht. Wenn Kurator*innen Künstler*innen um kuratorische Arbeit bitten, dann sollten sie das Geld, das sie erhalten, teilen. Ich habe das noch nie getan – aber das sind Dinge, über die wir sprechen können. Wir müssen über Geld sprechen. Auf einer abstrakten Ebene, aber wir müssen damit auch beginnen, indem wir über diese konkreten praktischen Punkte sprechen. Das war's.

Draxler: Es gibt mehr Material [das der Arbeitsgruppe zur Verfügung steht] zu diesen Fragen über Gewerkschaften und deutsche Künstler*innen-Organisationen, zur Versicherung und so weiter. Und du hast Recht, dass sie auf einer sehr traditionellen Vorstellung von Kunst beruhen. Das spiegelt einen besonderen historischen Vorgang hier in Deutschland wieder. Als der BBK, der Berufsverband Bildender Künstlerinnen und Künstler, 1971 gegründet wurde, waren in ihm bereits bestimmte konservativ-bürokratische Elemente angelegt. Das bedeutet nicht, dass sie in bestimmten Situationen in den siebziger Jahren keine gute Arbeit geleistet hätten, aber sie etablierten eine Tradition, die nicht offen genug war. Sie hatten eine gute Idee, etwas Ausgefeiltes, aber gleichzeitig ist ihr Versuch, etwas zu vermitteln, völlig bürokratisch und völlig konservativ. Und deshalb glaube ich, dass es hier viele Probleme gibt, die diskutiert werden sollten.

Der Kunstverein München, in dem ich arbeite, ist ein ganz anderes Modell als ein Künstlerhaus. Es ist wichtig für die amerikanischen Teilnehmer*innen hier, diese Unterschiede zu verstehen. Wir haben Institutionen, die auf Mitgliedschaft von Künstler*innen beruhen, wie ein Künstlerhaus, und dann gibt es die Institution, in der ich arbeite, diese Kunstvereine, die hauptsächlich von kleinbürgerlichen Kunstliebhaber*innen unterstützt werden. Sie wurden im 19. Jahrhundert in Deutschland konstituiert, als Gegenpol zu den Museen, die vom König gegründet wurden. Und im Gegensatz zu dem, was in Frankreich und England geschah. Die nationalen Museen dort wurden nämlich vom bürgerlichen Staat gegründet. Das geschah in Deutschland nicht. Das Kleinbürgertum gründete also seine Kunstvereine. Sie verbündeten sich und machten, auf einer niedrigeren sozialen Ebene, ihre eigene Politik. Und es gab einige sehr wichtige Momente in ihrer Geschichte. Beispielsweise wurde die Edvard Munch-Ausstellung Ende des letzten Jahrhunderts von der Staatsverwaltung in Berlin durch direkten Eingriff des Kaisers abgesagt. Dann schritten aber die Kunstvereine ein und übernahmen die Ausstellung. Dadurch konnten sie diese Arbeit zeigen, sie konnte durch Deutschland reisen und hatte enormen Einfluss darauf, die Moderne hierzulande zu etablieren. Natürlich gab es nach dem Krieg viele Veränderungen. Von den frühen sechziger Jahren an bekamen Kunstvereine erstmals öffentliche Gelder. Durch den Erhalt öffentlicher Gelder konnten sie nicht mehr nur ihre eigenen Mitglieder ansprechen und sich nicht nur auf Jurymodelle verlassen oder auf den Entscheidungsprozess, der von Ärzt*innen und Anwält*innen aus einer bestimmten Stadt dominiert wurde und so weiter.

Es gibt mehr als hundert Kunstvereine in Deutschland, jeder mit einer sehr komplexen Geschichte. In München übernahmen beispielsweise Anfang der siebziger Jahre Mitglieder der Deutschen Kommunistischen Partei den Kunstverein München und veranstalteten dort ausdrücklich linke Programme, aber sie wurden hinausgeworfen, da die Gelder vom Staat Bayern sofort gestrichen wurden. In den siebziger Jahren übernahmen dann die Sozialdemokraten den Kunstverein und implementierten ein Finanzierungssystem über die Stadt München selbst – nicht über die Landesregierung Bayern. 1985 gab es dort sozusagen eine späte konservative Revolution, obwohl die Gruppe, die das verursachte, nicht unbedingt konservativ war. Es waren auch Sozialdemokrat*innen dabei – daher war es eine komplexe Situation. Und sie wandten sich von der siebziger Jahre Idee der Teilhabe und der beliebten kulturhistorischen Programmgestaltung ab, die auch dazu da war, Menschen aus den Vorstädten anzuziehen und sie im Kunstverein in Ausstellungen über politische Themen wie Apartheid in Südafrika und Ausstellungen mit weiblichen Künstlerinnen zusammenzubringen. Stattdessen wurde also eine Art Kunstwelt-Modell umgesetzt. Sie wollten die Figur eines Kurators als „starker Mann, der in der Lage ist, starke männliche Entscheidungen zu treffen", im Gegensatz zu einem sehr starken Vorstand – das wurde in sehr konservativer Sprache ausgedrückt, insbesondere die Definition der Funktionen. Und ich glaube, dieses Modell des „starken Kurator-Mannes" ist im Allgemeinen seit den späten sechziger Jahren präsent. Wir kennen sie – Harald Szeemann und Leute wie ihn.

Von dieser Konkurrenzsituation zwischen Institutionen und freien Ausstellungsorten aus ist es spannend, dem Weg zu folgen, den Szeemann von der Arbeit in einer Institution, der Kunsthalle Bern, bis zum Verlassen dieser Institution gegangen ist. Sein Leben repräsentiert im Grunde diesen komplexen historischen Prozess, mit dem diese soziale Funktion des Kurators etabliert wurde. Was daher daraus entstand, und was wir bei jemandem wie Jan Hoet sehen können, ist dieser völlig verrückte Kurator, in dieser absoluten Machtposition, die nicht von seinem besonderen künstlerischen Wissen bestimmt wird, sondern nur von der Geschichte, die er hinter sich hat. Und wegen dieser Art der Korruption ist er in der Lage, eine Position im Dienste bestimmter touristischer Branchen einzunehmen – dies gilt insbesondere für Kassel. Ich glaube allerdings, dass es immer auch eine andere Vorstellung des sehr engagierten Kurators gab, der diese Arbeitsweise in bestimmten Strukturen öffnen würde und der versuchte, Arbeit zu ermöglichen, die auch ein kritisches Verhältnis innerhalb der Institution etablieren würde. Edward Fry hatte beispielsweise nicht wirklich viele Anhänger*innen, und Szeemann, Hoet und Rudi Fuchs waren viel erfolgreicher. Und dann gab es in den frühen achtziger Jahren Kasper König, der dieses Modell des Kurators als totalen Pragmatiker schuf – und was das für die Diskussion hier bedeutet, ist der Anfang von Kurator*innen, die Künstler*innen einfach völlig dienen. Künstler*innen dienen als höchste kuratorische Dienstleistung. Diese Art von Kurator*innen, die

künstlerische Arbeit ermöglichen und Künstler*innen unterstützen, und der Glaube, dass das das einzige Ziel der kuratorischen Tätigkeit sein sollte.

Als ich diese Stelle in München [am Kunstverein München] übernahm, war mir klar, dass das nur eine extrem ambivalente Position sein konnte, eine Position, auf die schon vorab viel projiziert wurde. Denn der Vorstand, der mich bat, die Position anzunehmen, war der gleiche Vorstand, der 1985 dieses starke männliche Modell eingeführt hatte. Und ich wusste ganz genau, was sie von mir erwarteten. Und das war mehr oder weniger die vorgegebene Situation, in der ich versuchte, meine Arbeit zu beginnen. Und was ich im Grunde versucht habe, hat auf verschiedenen Ebenen funktioniert. Künstler*innen zu dienen konnte ich mir nicht als ausreichende Basis für kuratorische Arbeit vorstellen. Ich denke, es gibt einige Aspekte, die man beachten muss, um diese Art von Arbeit zu beschreiben, und für mich war einer davon wichtig: einen Diskurs über die soziale Bedeutung dieser Institution zu entwickeln – wie sie aufgebaut ist und wie sie in einem historischen und spezifisch gesellschaftlichen Sinn funktioniert. Möglicherweise hat dieser historische Aspekt eine Bedeutung, da der Standort des Kunstvereins dort ist, wo die Ausstellung *Entartete Kunst* [1937] stattfand. Und er hat auch eine ganz spezifische Bedeutung im Zusammenhang mit Münchner Institutionen wie beispielsweise dem Haus der Kunst und der Pinakothek, die Fritz vorhin beschrieben hat. Daher ist das Problem für Kurator*innen, das enorme Problem, bestimmte Funktionen zu übernehmen und Vertreter*innen einer Institution zu sein – und wie macht man das, wenn man gleichzeitig versucht, innerhalb der Entwicklung von Institutionskritik mit bestimmten Personen zu arbeiten. Ich denke, dass die Ergebnisse von der Frage abhängen, inwieweit Institutionen überhaupt verändert werden können. Bis zu einem bestimmten Grad akzeptiert der Vorstand, was ich dort mit Hilfe von Künstler*innen mache, was immer mehr in die Richtung der projektorientierten Arbeit geht. Der Vorstand akzeptiert das bis zu einem gewissen Grad, aber er ist nicht mehr wirklich involviert. Ich habe einen Vier-Jahres-Vertrag, und nach vier Jahren werden sie eventuell wieder versuchen, jemanden zu finden, der mehr arbeitet und ihre Erwartungen auf noch konkretere Weise erfüllt.

Bauer: Ich möchte erwähnen, dass es genau zur gleichen Zeit an diesem Wochenende eine Podiumsdiskussion am Reina Sofía Museum [Museo Nacional Centro de Arte Reina Sofía in Madrid] über die ideale Ausstellung gibt. Und das ist sehr interessant, weil Achille Bonito Oliva, Kasper König und Dan Cameron dort [auf dem Panel] sind. Es gibt also keine Künstler*innen, sie [diese Kunsthistoriker und Kuratoren] entscheiden, was die ideale Ausstellung ist und was in den Institutionen stattfinden wird.

Müller: Es gibt im Moment in Bonn noch ein weiteres Symposium über die Funktion des Museums, und unter anderem ist Hans Haacke auf dem Panel.

Fraser: Und deswegen konnte er heute nicht hier bei uns sein.

Wilson: In den Vereinigten Staaten passiert momentan überhaupt nichts.

(Gelächter)

Draxler: Worauf ich hinaus wollte, waren die praktischen Dinge, aber ich habe mich am historischen Material aufgehalten. Ich glaube – und das ist ebenfalls ein Thema dieser Arbeitsgruppe – dass es einerseits das Verhältnis gibt, das Kurator*innen zu Künstler*innen haben, und sie involvieren sie in ihren eigenen Diskurs, und versuchen, durch kuratorische Arbeit auf verschiedenen Ebenen eine bestimmte Institution zu etablieren. Die Konflikte innerhalb der Institution auf der Ebene des Vorstands anzusprechen. Es geht nicht darum, ob unterschiedliches Publikum an einem allgemeinen Diskurs interessiert ist, sondern darum, wirklich zu versuchen, diesen praktischen Aspekt einzuführen – wie kann institutionelle Veränderung tatsächlich stattfinden? Die Erfahrung hier ist für mich eine sehr komplexe. Und es bedeutet, dass ich dahin tendiere, weniger mit einzelnen Künstler*innen und direkter mit bestimmten Gruppen zu arbeiten, wie beispielsweise mit Studierenden der Akademie, oder durch Programme, die keine Ausstellungen sind. Weil der Prozess, Künstler*innen in kuratorische Situationen zu bringen, in vielerlei Hinsicht so schwierig ist, und das letzte Jahr fast ausschließlich voll war von ungesteuerten, absolut unproduktiven Prozessen. Weil die Konditionen, die wir für Künstler*innen ansetzen können, einfach so unklar waren. Darin lagen die Konflikte.

Ein Künstler forderte beispielsweise einfach vollständige Unterstützung, er forderte diesen Typ Kurator, der seine Vision unterstützen würde. Er wollte aber auch einen Kurator, der eine bestimmte Art von Diskurs schafft. Und ich glaube, diese beiden Dinge sind ziemlich verschieden. Ich denke, das ist der Grund, warum es ein echtes Bedürfnis für diese Diskussion gibt, weil so viel Zeit und Energie mit der Erwartung daran, was ein*e Kurator*in tut, verschwendet wird, auf dieser sehr grundlegenden Ebene des Verständnisses darüber, was ein*e Kurator*in tut. Und genau dort findet sich kuratorische Arbeit sehr oft wieder, und das löste für mich eine sehr ernste Krise aus.

Fraser: Meiner Erfahrung nach, und ich weiß nicht, ob Fred diese Erfahrung auch gemacht hat – aber während der Whitney Biennale war der Grund der angedrohten Unterbindung oder „Verzögerung" meiner Arbeit die Sorge der Kurator*innen darüber, wie meine Arbeit sich auf die Arbeiten der anderen Künstler*innen in der Ausstellung auswirken würde. Diese vermeintliche Zusammenarbeit hörte also an dem Punkt auf, an dem sie sich gezwungen fühlten, den anderen Künstler*innen in der Ausstellung zu dienen. Und indem ich diese Arbeit machte, hatte ich in gewisser Weise die Position der Künstlerin verlassen.

Bischoff: Ich möchte zu Stephans gestriger Äußerung zurückkehren, als er sagte: „Sie benutzen euch, also benutzt sie auch." Ich möchte wissen, was du genau meinst, wenn du sagst: „Nutzt die Institution." Denn mein Interesse liegt natürlich an der Institution. Es gibt dort ein Archiv und es gibt einen regulären Weg, mit dem Museumsarchiv umzugehen, aber das ist nicht immer der beste Weg, das Archiv zu handhaben. Daher lautet meine Frage: Was meinen Künstler*innen, wenn sie sagen, „wir wollen es nutzen", so etwas wie das institutionelle Archiv?

Gibt es einen anderen Weg, mit dem Material umzugehen? Auf welche Art würdest du das Museum lieber nutzen?

Stephan Dillemuth: Als ich das gesagt habe, meinte ich, dass man sich der Tatsache bewusst sein sollte, dass man daran gewöhnt ist, die Machtstruktur der Institution wiederherzustellen. Ein Bewusstsein dafür also, was sich hinter dieser Machtstruktur verbirgt, und das Wissen darüber, kann einem mehr Selbstbewusstsein geben. Normalerweise ist man froh, wenn man die Möglichkeit bekommt, eine Ausstellung in einem Museum zu machen – man denkt: „Jetzt habe ich es, jetzt habe ich es endlich geschafft, jetzt bin ich dort, wo ich schon immer sein wollte." Aber sich dessen auch bewusst zu sein, dass man diese Machtposition nutzt, dass dieser ganze Apparat noch größer ist, als man ihn sich je vorgestellt hatte. Wenn man an die Kapazität dieser Institutionen denkt, Gelder aufzubringen, diesen Zugang zu bekommen – das ist enorm.

Bischoff: Unserer Vorstellung nach ist das die übliche Art, wie Künstler*innen das Museum nutzen.

Dillemuth: Das Museum mit seinem Archiv und dem Lager ist tatsächlich ein super Spielplatz. Andererseits will ich aber auch nicht das, was während Sonsbeek 93 passiert ist, denn dort schien es eine enorme Summe an Geldern zu geben. Ich hatte das Gefühl, dass viele Künstler*innen dachten: „Jetzt ist meine Zeit gekommen und jetzt kann ich wirklich meine Träume verwirklichen." Die Künstlerin Ann Hamilton hat drei Monate lang einen riesigen Frachtkahn mit einem Fahrer und einem Haufen von siebzehntausend Tulpenzwiebeln auf dem Kahn gemietet und mit einem Jongleur, der angeheuert wurde, um auf den Tulpen zu sitzen. Ich meine, Entschuldigung, aber…

Ich kann euch ein Beispiel dafür geben, was mir passiert ist, als ich in ein Museum eingeladen wurde und ich diese Kunst-Fanzine Leute gebeten habe, dort mit mir zu arbeiten, und wir Zugang zu dem gesamten Lager des Museums hatten, was natürlich ein interessanter Aspekt der Museumsarbeit ist. Das Museum zeigt, was es zeigen will, aber dann gibt es unten im Lager diese Arbeiten. Wir konnten das also alles aus dem Lager herausholen und zeigen. Und wir wollten es alles mit den alten Kunstwerken zusammen präsentieren und es als Material für ein Layout verwenden. Wir hatten die Idee, die Wände nicht als Gelegenheit zu nutzen, um dort Arbeiten aufzuhängen, sondern stattdessen mit all diesen Dingen so etwas wie ein Layout oder eine Collage zu gestalten. Wir hatten viele Probleme mit der Restaurierungsabteilung – sie wollten nicht, dass wir die Drucke auf den Boden legen, obwohl sie verpackt waren. Dann kam der Direktor und sagte: „Bitte, wir müssen einen Schlussstrich ziehen." Es gibt bestimmte Einschränkungen.

Fraser: Das war zum Teil das, wovon ich gesprochen hatte. Ich möchte das an Susan richten, weil es besonders mit Museumsvermittlung zu tun hat, aber auch in kuratorischer Interpretation vorhanden ist. Wenn man davon spricht, lebenden Künstler*innen zu dienen, aber auch verstorbenen Künstler*innen, dann bedeutet das am Ende oft, der künstlerischen Intention zu dienen

– diese Verpflichtung gegenüber der Idee der künstlerischen Intention, die eingeschränkt wird, wenn man einem Publikum dient, eine Einschränkung der Interpretationsmöglichkeiten, die Kurator*innen und Pädagog*innen haben.

Wilson: Man muss ein wenig die Berufe innerhalb der Museumsstruktur verstehen – womit sie sich selbst beschränken und was die Grundlage dafür ist – und dann kann man selbst entscheiden, inwieweit man sich damit beschäftigen möchte. Oder wie man sie darauf aufmerksam macht, wie wenig Grundlage diese Einschränkungen in der Realität haben – es sind einfach Dinge, die sie entwickelt haben, wie beispielsweise die Tatsache, dass Künstler*innen erst seit kurzem ihre Gemälde betiteln und vorher die Titel von den Sammler*innen oder Galerist*innen oder Kurator*innen erfunden wurden. Es scheint also absurd, den Titel eines Gemäldes zu ändern, aber dieser Titel war vielleicht überhaupt nicht die Entscheidung der Künstler*innen. Und so kann es auch mit der Platzierung der Objekte sein, beispielsweise auf den Kopf gestellt oder richtig herum. Kurator*innen fällen ständig diese Werturteile über die Platzierung der Objekte und ihrer Bedeutung, und manchmal wollen sie nicht zugeben, dass sie eingreifen. Sie schieben die Verantwortung auf die Künstler*innen – sie versetzen einen in eine Lage, die destruktiv für die Arbeit ist, wobei man lediglich ihre Ansicht über den oder die Künstler*in verletzt. Man muss also unter die Oberfläche gehen und herausfinden, was real ist und was im Laufe der Zeit entstanden ist.

Fraser: In vielen der Einladungen von Kurator*innen oder Museen, von älteren Museen zumindest, geht es darum, wie du sagst, Uli, dass Museen Hilfestellung von Künstler*innen benötigen. Das hat viel damit zu tun, dass man in dieser Rolle, den Künstler*innen zu dienen, festgefahren ist. Man bittet also Künstler*innen, einem zu helfen, weil man selbst in der Rolle, diesen historischen Vorstellungen zu dienen, feststeckt. Und wir haben in dieser Hinsicht nicht unbedingt eine Verpflichtung, und daher haben wir eine gewisse Freiheit.

Bauer: Manchmal hört es bei sehr pragmatischen und unsinnigen Dingen auf. Wir sprechen auf einer theoretischen Ebene, aber Katharina Fritsch hat beispielsweise bei der Bi-Nationalen Biennale [1988-89] in der Kunsthalle Düsseldorf lediglich um drei ruhige Tage gebeten, um ihre Arbeit zu installieren. Und sie haben sie ihr nicht gegeben. Also hat sie am letzten Tag abgesagt. Und als Antwort darauf sagten sie: „Oh, sie ist eine sehr schwierige Künstlerin." Und das hatte eine sehr negative Auswirkung auf die Einladungen, die sie danach bekommen hat. Sie hat nur um drei Tage gebeten, und die Arbeit braucht das. Oder mit *Metropolis* [*Internationale Kunstausstellung*, Martin-Gropius-Bau, Berlin, 1991], die Künstler*innen wurden noch nicht einmal dafür bezahlt, um zur Eröffnung zu kommen.

Was ich verlange, ist, dass die Künstler*innen Stellung nehmen und sagen: „Nein, ich werde daran nicht mehr teilnehmen." Und Kurator*innen sollten ehrlicher sein. Wenn ein*e Künstler*in sie um etwas bittet, sollten Kurator*innen nicht sagen: „Nein, das kann ich nicht tun" oder „Das ergibt keinen Sinn", und sich deutlich ausdrücken. Meistens wird alles auf eine sehr vage Art und Weise gehandhabt. Sagt einfach, ob wir es tun können oder nicht.

Wilson: Oft verschleiert das System eines Museums die persönlichen Bedürfnisse oder Vorlieben der Kurator*innen. Sie sagen, das Museum könne etwas nicht tun, obwohl es in Wahrheit lediglich ihr fehlendes eigenes Interesse ist.

Fraser: Für mich ist es auch eine Frage der Prioritäten. Vor allem in den Vereinigten Staaten, wo Institutionen für jede Ausstellung Gelder aufbringen müssen.

Draxler: Hier ist es genauso.

Fraser: Dann sollten sie aber sagen: „Wir können das einfach nicht." Aber es ist eine Frage der Prioritäten, und es ist eine Frage der institutionellen Politik, wie und wem Gelder zuge-teilt werden.

Susan Cahan: Ich denke, dass sich Projekte oft aus praktischen und finanziellen Gründen in Richtung Bewahrung der Institution be-wegen. Dem Verständnis folgend, dass Institutionen existieren, um ein Programm zu präsentieren. Ich wollte mich aber zu deiner [Andrea] vorherigen Frage äußern, bezüglich der Projekte, die ich durchgeführt habe, die möglicherweise nicht die Intentionen der Künstler*innen in den Vordergrund stellen. Ich denke, dass es absolut erforderlich ist, Vertrauen und Beziehungen aufzu-bauen. Für Individuen – selbst wenn sie Vertreter*innen von Institutionen sind, die mit anderen Individuen zu-sammenarbeiten – ist ein wichtiger Punkt, den ich wahrgenommen habe, damit man tatsächlich viel erreicht und dort dieses Vertrauen haben kann, mir wirklich Klarheit über die Ziele zu verschaffen, die ich zu erreichen versuche. Menschen sind im Allgemeinen vernunftig, wenn man eindeutig erklärt, was man tun will. Es ist möglich, einen Konsens herzustellen. Für mich war es wichtig, mich auf Methoden aus anderen Bereichen zu berufen. Ideen aus anderen Disziplinen haben dazu beigetragen, im institutionellen Rahmen der Kunst Sinn herzustellen, was sonst vielleicht nicht möglich gewesen wäre. Wenn es in den späten achtziger Jahren keinen Konsens über die Infragestellung von Ideen der künstlerischen Intentionalität gegeben hätte, hätte ich diese Projekte niemals machen können.

Fraser: Es ist für mich ein Widerspruch in meiner eigenen Erfahrung, denn ich habe Ausstellungen gemacht, in denen ich die Arbeiten anderer Künstler*innen so präsentiert habe, dass sie nichts mit den üblichen Maßstäben musealer Praxis zu tun hatten oder mühelos so hätten interpretiert werden können, dass sie gegen die Intention der Künstler*innen gerichtet waren. Mit Leuten wie John Knight beispielsweise oder Daniel Buren, die sehr genaue Richtlinien haben, finde ich aber absolut, dass diese Richtlinien respektiert werden sollten. Das ist ein Widerspruch, bei dem ich mir nicht sicher bin, wie ich ihn lösen soll.

Wilson: Es hat mit grundsätzlichem Respekt zu tun. Kurator*innen nehmen hier auch wirklich die ganze Bandbreite in Anspruch: entweder sie respektieren, was ihrer Meinung nach die Intention der Künstler*innen ist, oder überhaupt nicht. Aber als Künstler*in hat man die Verantwortung, ein bestimmtes Maß an Respekt zu zeigen, so wie es eben sinnvoll ist. Das kann eine Einschränkung sein, aber es ist eine Einschränkung, mit der man arbeiten kann.

Draxler: Am Kunstverein München haben wir bisher nur eine Gruppenausstellung gemacht – die eine eher thematische Intention hatte – und das war das einzige Mal, dass wir eine Künstler*innenliste verwendet haben. Denn die Künstler*innenliste selbst gilt als ein sehr zweifelhaftes Objekt, das üblicherweise sehr oft aus Prestigegründen in einem kuratorischen Prozess verwendet wird. Daher haben wir versucht, die Liste sehr lang und in sehr kleiner Schrift zu gestalten und nur die Vornamen zu verwenden, und uns überhaupt nicht darum zu kümmern, wer tatsächlich dabei war und wer nicht. Eine völlig absurde Künstler*innenliste zu erstellen. Und das war der Grund für den Fehler bei diesem Gruppenprojekt und die Einladung von John Knight. Der einzige Weg, dies zu umgehen, ist letztendlich, überhaupt keine Liste zu machen. Einerseits gibt es einen absoluten Respekt für diese Art von Politik, andererseits gibt es diese völlig absurde Künstler*innenliste. So wie Kasper König immer eine Liste Künstler*innen in seinem Notizbuch hat und diese Liste einfach von einer Ausstellung zur nächsten umordnet.

Becker: Ich habe eine Frage an Uli: Was können Künstler*innen, was du nicht kannst? Wenn du also eine*n Künstler*in einladen willst, um dir zu helfen [die Infrastruktur der Institution zu verändern], warum machst du nicht das, was deiner Meinung nach Künstler*innen machen können?

Bischoff: Erstens, meine Arbeit besteht zu 80 Prozent darin, mich um Konservierungsprobleme zu kümmern, und die sind enorm. In Dresden gibt es in dem Gebäude ein großes Lager, das aus dem 16. Jahrhundert stammt. Und ich muss mich um das Personal und um andere Dinge kümmern. Andererseits – und das ist ein Problem – ist es einfacher, deine Frage durch das Arrangieren der Skulpturen draußen vor der Pinakothek in München zu beantworten. Ich möchte nicht jemand sein, der ein schönes Wohnzimmer auf ästhetische Weise gestaltet, ich benutze nicht gern meinen persönlichen Geschmack, um bloß eine Anordnung von Kunstwerken zu machen. Denn wenn man sieht, wie diese Außenskulpturen platziert sind – es ist furchtbar und ich möchte das nicht einfach auf eine andere furchtbare Weise verändern. Das kann ich nicht.

Becker: Aber wo liegt der Unterschied? Warum kann man sie nicht wegwerfen, wegräumen oder so arrangieren, wie Fritz es vielleicht tun würde?

Bischoff: Ich habe keine Möglichkeit, Nachforschungen anzustellen, wie Fritz sie als Künstler macht, da meine Arbeit in München darin bestand, Ansprechpartner für alle Künstler*innen in Bayern zu sein. Ich war der Landesbeauftragte, der sich die Arbeit von jedem anschauen musste, der mich einlud. Ich musste herumreisen, in all die großen Städte und so weiter, und ich musste die Vorbereitungen in der Galerie Neue Meister treffen, und das ist ein großer Unterschied zu den Vereinigten Staaten. Es gibt nur zwei Museen in Deutschland, ich glaube jetzt sind es drei, die einen Registrar haben. Und in den USA hat jedes große Museum eine ganze Abteilung mit

drei oder vier, zehn, zwölf, sechzehn Registrar*innen. So ist die interne Situation ganz anders. Ich kenne viele Kolleg*innen, die sehr schnell Vorkehrungen treffen. Wisst ihr, man hat vierzig Kunstwerke, und „dies kann dorthin und das ist nett und das kann dahin", und in einem Nachmittag ist es fertig. So geht man nicht mit Kunst um.

Ich habe die Erfahrung gemacht, dass Künstler*innen jahrelang in ein Museum gehen, um sich ein oder zwei Kunstwerke anzuschauen, und sie kennen die Werke besser als die oder der Kurator*in. Künstler*innen sind Menschen, die sich für Kunst interessieren, nicht nur für ihre eigene, sondern auch für andere Kunst. Und das ist es, was ich mich gefragt habe. Das Museum ist ein Kasten mit Kunstwerken, und diese Werke sind vor allem für die Künstler*innen von Interesse. Das ist meine Erfahrung, und ich möchte die Künstler*innen einladen, mit den Werken zu arbeiten, die für sie von Interesse sind. Tourist*innen kommen in eine Stadt, um die Stadt und die wichtigsten Kunstwerke zu sehen. In Dresden ist es Raffaels *Sixtinische Madonna* [1521], dort wird sie betrachtet, und dann geht man wieder. Das ist nicht die richtige Art, mit Kunst umzugehen, aber es ist die übliche Praxis. Und deshalb arbeite ich gerne eng mit Künstler*innen zusammen. In München habe ich drei Jahre lang Künstler*innen eingeladen, sich in etwa für einen halben Tag ein Gemälde anzuschauen, und dann lud ich andere Leute ein, und wir saßen da und schauten einfach zusammen. Das ist eine Art, der Kunst im Museum näher zu kommen.

Ulf Wuggenig: Ein Problem könnte sein, dass es viele verschiedene

Arten von Künstler*innen gibt, mit vielen verschiedenen Interessen. Daher ist es keine wirkliche Lösung für das Problem des Geschmacks von Kunsthistoriker*innen oder Kurator*innen, es an die Künstler*innen abzugeben.

Bischoff: Ich verändere mich, Kurator*innen verändern sich, die Museen verändern sich, wir verändern uns. Aber wir müssen diese Vorstellung der „Veränderung" mit der Qualität betrachten, die von der künstlerischen Sicht auf die Kunst ausgeht, und nicht von der kunsthistorischen Sicht auf die Kunst.

Cahan: Einige Kurator*innen nutzen tatsächlich ungewöhnliche Ausstellungsstrategien, und dann werden sie oft auf eine Weise kritisiert, wie es bei Künstler*innen nicht der Fall ist. Sie werden dafür kritisiert, dass sie ihre Ideen auf die Kunstwerke übertragen. Ich bin neugierig, warum das so ist und warum du glaubst, dass Kurator*innen so etwas nicht tun.

Beatrice von Bismarck: Du hast das Wort „Vertrauen" verwendet, und ich habe heute ein paar Mal gehört, wie das Wort „Ausbeutung" von beiden Seiten verwendet wurde – Kurator*innen, die Künstler*innen ausbeuten, Künstler*innen, die Kurator*innen ausbeuten. Mich interessiert, ob man das auf eine positive Weise formulieren könnte. Und was die Erwartungen beider Seiten daran wären. Denn bis jetzt haben wir tatsächlich nur über die Konflikte gesprochen, die aufkommen könnten. Können wir noch über etwas anderes sprechen? Es scheint mir, Helmut, dass jegliche Zusammenarbeit in dieser Hinsicht nicht in deinem Interesse wäre.

Dillemuth: In meinem letzten Beitrag habe ich gesagt, das ist wie eine Ehe, das ist eine Beziehung. Manchmal muss man den anderen hassen, und dann liebt man ihn wieder.

Michael Clegg: Ich verstehe nicht, warum du [Helmut] solch eine Betonung auf Künstler*innen als Publikum legst. Ich denke, wir sprechen über Künstler*innen, die für andere arbeiten.

Draxler: Ich glaube, es gibt einen historischen Grund, ich bin Kunsthistoriker. Akademiker aus dem späten 19. Jahrhundert haben diese Funktion von Künstler*innen als Verwalter*innen von Museen übernommen. Und nun geben wir die Stelle zurück. Ich verstehe es also eher als eine Krise der Kunstgeschichte als akademische Disziplin.

Cahan: Jetzt sind Künstler*innen auch Akademiker*innen.

Fraser: Das schafft meiner Meinung nach eine Krise.

Wilson: Ich wollte auf die Frage zurückkommen, warum Kurator*innen sich an Künstler*innen wenden, um Ausstellungen zu machen. Ich denke, es hat damit zu tun, dass Kurator*innen und ihre Kolleg*innen den Druck verspüren, dass ihre Arbeit eventuell als unwissenschaftlich angesehen werden könnte oder an Grenzen stößt und sie dem Blick ihrer Kolleg*innen ausgesetzt sind. Sie laden also Künstler*innen ein, die möglicherweise nicht diesen Druck haben, historische Positionen neu zu schaffen. Aber ich finde auch, dass Künstler*innen oft die Funktion haben, etwas zu entfachen, das die Kurator*innen vorantreibt, sodass sie wenn sie [die Kurator*innen] zu dem Punkt zurückkehren, zwar nicht das tun, was ein*e Künstler*in tun würde, ihre Praxis aber durch die Erfahrung der künstlerischen Arbeitsweise erweitert wurde.

Fraser: Ich habe die Erfahrung gemacht, dass Künstler*innen, die bestimmte institutionelle Formen oder Praktiken von Kurator*innen übernommen haben, die Möglichkeiten der Kurator*innen nicht erweitern, sondern sie sogar einschränken. Denn diese Formen und Praktiken werden dann mit bestimmten Künstler*innen identifiziert, und Kurator*innen können sie nicht weiter einsetzen. Ich hatte eine Erfahrung mit der *Desire of the Museum* Ausstellung [am Whitney Museum of American Art, New York, 1990], bei der die Studierenden Labels anbringen wollten, die nicht direkt mit den Arbeiten zu tun hatten, und die verantwortliche Person sagte: „Das können Sie nicht machen – glauben Sie, Sie sind Andrea Fraser?" Es war pervers. Und es gibt diese Arbeitssteilung. Und Kurator*innen werden für Interventionen kritisiert.

Bischoff: Außerdem denke ich, dass Kurator*innen viel mehr an der Bedeutungshierarchie der Kunstgeschichte interessiert sind. Beispielsweise in der National Gallery in London gab es glaube ich in den letzten fünf Jahren Ausstellungen, bei denen Künstler*innen eingeladen wurden, Gemälde auszusuchen, an denen sie interessiert waren, um sie auf neue Art und Weise zu zeigen. Es ist enorm wichtig, sich von dieser traditionellen kunsthistorischen Bedeutung freizumachen. Künstler*innen – und das ist eine Antwort auf deine Frage [Jochen], wie ich Künstler*innen sehe – sie haben das Privileg, sich mehr mit

Kunst zu beschäftigen als Kunsthistoriker*innen. Weil die Kunsthistoriker*innen, die an Universitäten oder Museen arbeiten, so sehr mit Aktivitäten beschäftigt sind, die überhaupt nichts mit Kunst zu tun haben. Es ist also eine Chance, zur Kunst zurückzukehren. Ich verstehe auch, warum einige Künstler*innen Kurator*innen oder Kunsthistoriker*innen immer wieder fragen, was sie dort in diesen Bereichen des Museums oder des Archivs die ganze Zeit tun. In Wirklichkeit geschieht es sehr selten, dass ein*e Künstler*in sich Zeit nehmen kann, um im Lager oder dem Archiv des Museums zu arbeiten.

Becker: Ich möchte nur zwei Beispiele nennen. Erstens, das Osthaus Museum [in Hagen], in dem Michael Fehr, der Kunsthistoriker ist, arbeitet. Er hat das Museum so organisiert, dass er mit dem arbeiten kann, was er dort hat, und er ermöglicht kulturelle Projekte. Er hat eine Ausstellung über Stromlinienführung gemacht, in der er einen Zeppelin und Bomben in Kombination mit Kunstwerken und kulturellen Artefakten, die keine Kunst waren, in einer sehr einzigartigen Ausstellung verbunden hat. Das andere Beispiel ist, dass ich überlege, eine Arbeit mit dem Landesmuseum für Volk und Wirtschaft in Düsseldorf zu machen. Sehr interessant. Ich bin mehr daran interessiert, in diesem Museum zu arbeiten, als in einem Kunstmuseum.

Martin Guttmann: Ich glaube, es geht um das Thema der Demokratisierung der Museen. Ich denke, es ist ein sehr ernstes Thema. Unterschiedliche Museen haben unterschiedliche Satzungen, aber wenn Museen ein Mandat haben, ihren

Interessengemeinschaften Kunst zu präsentieren, dann gibt es eine gewisse Verpflichtung und Verantwortung, es richtig zu tun. Bei dem Mandat geht es darum, einen Input von den Interessengemeinschaften zu erhalten. Und in verschiedenen Kontexten gibt es unter Museumsfachleuten das Gefühl, dass es ein wirkliches Bedürfnis ist, Input zu erhalten, und möglicherweise könnten Künstler*innen als die erste Phase eines Demokratisierungsprozesses nützlich sein. Es sollte als erste Phase betrachtet werden, nicht als Frage des Austauschs eines Geschmacks gegen einen anderen, sondern Input von einer Interessengemeinschaft zu erhalten, die normalerweise keine Stimme hat. Wenn Künstler*innen zwischen einer Interessengemeinschaft und einer bürokratischen Struktur verhandeln können, dann könnte das eine gute Position für die Kunst sein. Wenn das funktioniert…

Bischoff: Das funktioniert nur, wenn die Künstler*innen ein Interesse am Kunstmuseum haben. Cage zeigte großes Interesse an der geologischen Abteilung in München und anderen Abteilungen im Museum. Ich möchte erwähnen, dass viele Kunstwerke, die in Museen gezeigt werden müssen, entsprechend der Vertragsbedingungen derjenigen Personen gezeigt werden, die Kunst an das Museum gespendet haben. Vor allem in den Vereinigten Staaten gibt es viele Regeln, beispielsweise dass man alles zusammen und für eine bestimmte Zeit ausstellen muss, man darf es nicht einlagern, usw. In einigen Museen unterliegen 60 Prozent oder 40 Prozent der Arbeiten, die die ganze Zeit über gezeigt werden müssen, diesen Vertragsvereinbarungen. Wenn man

also mit Künstler*innen arbeitet, ist es auch einfacher, diese Regel zu brechen, als wenn man Kurator*in ist. Auf diese Weise kann man die Institution demokratisieren. Vor allem im Osten Deutschlands will man wirklich neue Strukturen haben. Das Kultusministerium ist meiner Meinung nach die demokratischste Struktur in einem Museum.

Fraser: Dein Beispiel dafür, was in Museen in Amerika und hier geschieht, ist ein Beispiel dafür, was Kurator*innen dazu motiviert, häufig Künstler*innen einzuladen. Und das heißt, einen Konflikt mit dem Vorstand aufzuarbeiten, den Vorstandsmitgliedern oder dem Kultusministerium. Ähnlich wie Christians Erfahrung am MCC [Maison de la Culture et la Communication] in Frankreich, wohin du eingeladen wurdest, um die Kritik des Kurators am Kulturministerium auszudrücken – ich denke, dass so etwas häufig passiert. Die andere Sache, die noch nicht besprochen wurde, ist beispielsweise, was am Museum für angewandte Kunst in Wien passiert ist, wo sie alle Räume neu eingerichtet und die Künstler*innen die Installationen gemacht haben. Und ich denke, diese Art Phänomen – es ist wie bei Jan Hoet, der in Kassel [für die documenta IX, 1992] den *David* installiert hat – es geht um Spektakel und darum, dass Museen im Wettbewerb mit anderen…

Bischoff: Aber das ist so wie Michael Asher, als er die Statue von George Washington in Chicago [am Art Institute of Chicago für die 73. Amerikanische Ausstellung, 1979] neu installiert hat.

Fraser: Das ist aber ganz anders.

Renée Green: Das ist es, was an dem Projekt so komisch ist.

Fraser: Genau darum geht es aber hier: darum, wie die Arbeitsweisen dieser Personen – Michael Asher und Hans Haacke und Daniel Buren und John Knight und Louise Lawler – immer geläufiger werden und sich ihre Bedeutung völlig ändert.

Bauer: Ich möchte von den Künstler*innen hören, wie sie die Museen abschaffen möchten, denn so oft stören die Museen die Arbeit einfach. Wenn man an die Retrospektive von Marcel Broodthaers im Jeu de Paume [in Paris, 1991-92] denkt, finde ich, dass sie Broodthaers Werk tatsächlich zerstört hat. Oder wenn man die Neuinstallationen von Joseph Beuys Arbeit sieht, sie haben tatsächlich das Werk des Künstlers zerstört. Wie können Künstler*innen sich davor retten, dass sie von den Museen vereinnahmt werden? Und Museen schaffen Kunstgeschichte, aber Kunst, die kein Objekt ist – wie die Situationisten oder aktivistische Kunst – die nicht in Museen ist, wird aus der Kunstgeschichte ausgelassen. Wenn wir also darüber sprechen, der Kunst und den Künstler*innen zu dienen, was können wir dann tun?

Draxler: Dabei geht es um die Bedeutung solcher Orte und welche soziale Bedeutung sie ausdrücken. Vielerorts, vor allem in deutschen Museen, versuchen sie stets ohne Unterbrechung diese durchgehende Linie aus den dreißiger Jahren zu ziehen. Von [Emil] Nolde bis [Georg] Baselitz [in den sechziger Jahren], und das ist ein völlig revisionistisches Ideal dieses Landes. Da geht es darum, sehr strikte kunsthistorische Kategorien zu bestimmen.

Natürlich bleibt alles andere dann einfach außen vor. Da muss noch viel getan werden, aber so lange die gesellschaftliche Reproduktion der Museumsfachleute auf diesem unglaublich akademischen Modell beruht, wird sich daran nichts ändern. In bestimmten Situationen wie der in Dresden glaube ich, dass es absolut notwendig ist, diese Arbeit zu leisten, weil die Situation dort offener ist. Beim Museum für angewandte Kunst in Wien gibt es einfach enorme Gelder, die verteilt werden, und es geht dabei nicht um die Bedeutung des Museums. Ich glaube, es ist eine Frage dessen, wie man diese Dinge unterscheidet, und sehr präzise Wege zu definieren, genau das zu tun.

Judith Barry: Das wirft die Frage nach den verschiedenen Arten des Sammelns auf. Beispielsweise, wie Künstler*innen, die vor allem ephemere Arbeiten machen, ihre Praktiken erhalten können. Gleichzeitig wirft es Fragen auf, wie Arbeit gesammelt wird wenn sie kein Objekt ist. Ich war schon bei mehreren Museumspanels, von denen ich dachte, das würde dort angesprochen, aber wurde es nicht. Niemand scheint über die Erhaltung ephemerer Werke zu sprechen. Werden einige Kunstformen für zukünftige Generationen verloren gehen? Ich unterrichte Geschichte der Performance-Kunst, und man kann einer Klasse von Neunzehnjährigen in den USA keine Fotografie von drei Typen in einem Café zeigen und meinen, dass sie für die Geschichte des Dada steht. Oft ist das aber das Einzige, womit man arbeiten kann.

Fraser: Das bezieht sich auf das temporäre Modell, von dem Fritz sprach. Man sollte das aber nicht als Problem der Institutionalisierung von Institutionen betrachten, sondern als eine Kritik an Institutionen und daran, wie Institutionen aktiv institutionalisiert werden. Anstatt dass Kurator*innen Geschichtsmodelle in Installationen objektivieren müssen, könnten temporäre Interventionen, die in einer Dauerausstellung nicht untergebracht werden können, Dinge öffnen.

Cahan: Im Diskussionskonzept für diese Sitzung wurde „eine Überidentifikation zwischen Kurator*innen und Künstler*innen, die die Museumsfachleute gegen ihre Gremien aufbringen kann", erwähnt. Nun, was du gerade gesagt hast, Judith, erinnerte mich an die andere Identifikation in einigen Fällen von Institutionen mit Künstler*innen. Und ich denke, dass Museen in den USA sich selbst so wahrnehmen, dass sie eine Veränderung von primären Sammlungs- und Präsentationsorganisationen, in stärker dienstleistungsorientierte Organisationen vollziehen. Das ist möglicherweise analog zu den Veränderungen, die in der künstlerischen Praxis stattfinden. Und ich denke, was du angesprochen hast, ist ein sehr wichtiges Thema, denn es ist eine weitere Möglichkeit, wie Museen ihre Rolle als Sammlungsinstitutionen neu konzipieren können.

Iwona Blazwick: Ich wollte eine begriffliche Klärung zwischen „temporärem zeitgenössischem Ausstellungsraum" und „Museumssammlung" anbieten, denn sie werden ständig vermischt. Aber ich denke, dass sie in Bezug auf das, was sie bewirken können und was nicht, ziemlich verschieden sind. In Bezug darauf, einen Sinn für das Erbe zu entwickeln oder den Aufbau eines Archivs oder den Schutz von Kunstwerken oder Geschichten zu entwickeln – das ist eine sehr spezifische Funktion. Und das andere ist mehr ein vorübergehender Einwand. Ich denke, die Frage ist, wie das Modell der temporären Kunsthalle – wenn es existiert und eine Plattform bietet – welche Bedeutung hat es, wenn es temporär ist?

Auf einer sehr praktischen Ebene, beruhte ein Projekt, in das ich mit einigen der Künstler*innen hier involviert war, auf dieser Art von Modell – es gab weder Fähigkeiten noch Expertise, sich um die Dinge zu kümmern. Daher gab es keinerlei Instandhaltungsarbeit bei der Betreuung der Kunstwerke. Nachdem das Event, die Eröffnung stattgefunden hatte, gingen alle Überlegungen zum nächsten Thema über. Soweit es sie betraf, war es vorbei. Diese Arbeiten verkümmerten also alle in dem Raum. Sie wurden nicht eingeschaltet, sie wurden nicht instand gehalten, keiner der Leute in dem Raum hatte eine Möglichkeit zu besprechen, worum es bei der ganzen Sache ging. Und trotzdem standen sie an vorderster Front. Sie waren so entfremdet von den Dingen, zwischen denen sie sich befanden, und so losgelöst davon. Es war eine Katastrophe. Nach dem Tag der Eröffnung lag das Projekt brach.

Guttmann: Als provisorischen Vorschlag zu der Frage, wie man ephemere Kunst erhalten kann, könnte ethnographische Forschung einige Antworten bieten. Die ethnographischen Standards sind schrecklich, und vielleicht kann dieses Problem eine Chance sein, um diese Standards zu überdenken – die Probleme damit, wie wir andere Kulturen „erhalten", würden einwärts gerichtet werden.

Green: Kannst du das näher erläutern? Was meinst du mit den Aspekten der Ethnographie, die etwas ermöglichen?

Guttmann: Die Art Tanz, Musik, Rituale aufzuzeichnen. Es gab alle möglichen Techniken, die von Ethnograph*innen entwickelt wurden… Diese schlechten Methoden könnten hervorgehoben werden und hilfreich für eine Neubetrachtung sein…

Green: Ich habe darüber nachgedacht, was Ute erwähnt hat, die Frage, die sie stellte und die Kommentare, die darauf folgten. Ich meine, es muss so etwas wie einen Ort geben, etwas das den Menschen erlaubt, eine Art Zugang zu dem zu bekommen, was geschehen ist. Wenn nicht ein Museum, dann etwas anderes für Dinge, die vergänglich sind. Ich spreche von Dingen, an denen ich selbst gearbeitet habe – bei denen dieser Prozess, der in ethnographischen Methoden verwendet wird, Informationen und Ereignisse aufzuzeichnen, eingebunden wurde. Um eine andere Art von Archiv zu schaffen und die Art, wie ein Archiv funktionieren kann, zu überdenken. Und es in ein Computerzeitalter zu überführen, oder sich bewusst zu sein, dass der Platz begrenzt ist und man Tresore nicht behalten kann. Aber sich andere Wege zu überlegen, wie Arbeiten dargestellt werden können. Und dann, was Iwona über den Unterschied zwischen einem Raum gesagt hat, der für temporäre Werke bestimmt ist, und einem Raum, der sich um die Pflege der Werke kümmern soll und die Intention der Künstler*innen weiterverfolgt. Ich vermute, es erfordert einfach eine Neubewertung der Methoden, Fachpersonal auszubilden und die Informationen zwischen den

Künstler*innen und den Personen auszutauschen, die mit dem Material arbeiten, sodass es möglich ist, eine Art Bezug zu ephemeren Werken herzustellen, selbst wenn man weiß, dass es eine veränderte Form ist.

Fraser: Ich möchte nur sagen, dass ich zutiefst ambivalent bin. Und ich denke, viele Künstler*innen, die ephemere Arbeit machen, sind zutiefst ambivalent darüber, was mit ihnen passieren soll. Denn wenn ich eine Performance mache oder wenn ich ephemere Arbeiten mache, dann tue ich das aus einem bestimmten Grund. Aber gleichzeitig möchte ich nicht, dass sie verschwinden. Michael Asher sorgt dafür, dass alles zerstört wird, wenn er geht, wenn die Ausstellung vorüber ist. Andere Künstler*innen haben auch andere Bedingungen.

Green: Aber man sieht Darstellungen der Michael Asher Arbeiten.

Fraser: Ja, aber diese Darstellungen werden nicht in Institutionen präsentiert, sondern in Büchern. Und vielleicht sind die Bücher in Bibliotheken, aber sie sind völlig marginalisiert.

Green: Bücher sind aber Teil dieses Prozesses, Informationen über die Zeit hinaus zu übermitteln, in der etwas passiert. Wir sprechen über zwei verschiedene Dinge.

Fraser: Ja, wir sprechen über zwei verschiedene Dinge. Ich will damit sagen, dass es andere Formen der Dokumentation gibt, welche die Intentionen von Künstler*innen, die ephemere Arbeiten machen, befriedigen können. Aber sie werden innerhalb von Kunst präsentierenden Strukturen, wie diese zum jetzigen

Zeitpunkt definiert sind, marginal bleiben.

Clegg: Ich glaube, dass man sich bei diesen Fragen vorstellen kann, wer der Hüter der Flamme sein sollte. Die Last liegt in vielerlei Hinsicht auf den Künstler*innen, sich vorzustellen und daran zu erinnern, dass man das Leben einer Arbeit einfach nicht steuern kann. Es gibt nur eine begrenzte Anzahl an Arten, eine Arbeit zu dekontextualisieren, und sicherlich, wenn man objektbasierte Kunst produziert, reist sie um die Welt, von Hand zu Hand und ändert ihre Bedeutung.

Ich fand es immer interessant, sich diese Eventualitäten vorzustellen und eine Art Schutzmaßnahme einzubauen, die einfach all die Dinge, die mit der Arbeit passieren könnten, berücksichtigt. Meiner Meinung nach ist es nicht angemessen, von einer Institution einzufordern, neue Wege zu finden, diese Arbeiten, die produziert werden, zu schützen, weil sie vergänglich oder schwierig zu dokumentieren sind. Denn das hat tatsächlich viel mit den eigenen Absichten zu tun.

Draxler: Es gibt sogar eine Historie künstlerischer Strategien, die das erkunden.

Bauer: Auch Museen sind sehr geschichtsträchtig. Es gibt diese Aufnahme von [der Tänzerin und Choreografin] Simone Forti, die von ihrer Geschichte handelt und davon, wie die meisten Künstler*innen, die mit Malerei und Bildhauerei arbeiten, Kunstgeschichte schreiben und dass Künstlerinnen in anderen Bereichen arbeiten, sodass Frauen in der Geschichte nicht vertreten sind.

Bischoff: Ich glaube, wir haben das gleiche Problem wie vor fünfzehn bis zwanzig Jahren, denn Künstler*innen sind mehr an Situationen und Strukturen interessiert und nicht so sehr an ihren eigenen Produkten, die sich verkaufen lassen. Und der Kunstmarkt reagiert nicht darauf. Wisst ihr, 1982, nach der *Zeitgeist* Ausstellung [im Martin-Gropius-Bau, Berlin], sagte der Markt: „Wir ziehen Gemälde vor, bitte." Und hier wiederholt sich die gleiche Situation. Es geschah schon zu Anfang der sechziger Jahre, als Künstler wie Stanley Brouwn in Amsterdam sagten, wir sollten über Museen nachdenken, wir sollten über die Möglichkeit nachdenken, unsere Archive zu verändern. Ein Museum ist ein Archiv und Freds Arbeit, zum Beispiel – das ist die einzige Form der Dokumentation hier an der Wand [des Kunstraums], Fred, von deiner Arbeit.

Wilson: Ja, leider. Nun, das stimmt nicht ganz, ich habe mittlerweile schon einige permanente Installationen. Worüber wir hier anscheinend sprechen… Es ist interessant, wie wir von ephemeren Arbeiten zu ethnographischem Material übergegangen sind, bis hin zu dem, was verschwinden soll. Aber worüber wir sprechen, ist nicht, die eigentliche Arbeit zu retten, sondern einen Teil, von dem Künstler*innen denken, dass es sie selbst oder die Arbeit repräsentiert. Die gesamte Museumsstruktur, insbesondere in den USA, von dem was ausgestellt wird und was nicht, beruht auf dem finanziellen Wert der Dinge. Wenn wir uns also mit ephemeren Arbeiten und Reproduktionen beschäftigen, geht der Wert tatsächlich verloren. Aber da Museen immer mehr zu dienstleistungsorientierten Bildungsstätten werden – oder das ist zumindest die Rhetorik – sprechen wir über Strukturen und Räume für Archive, die ebenfalls einfachen Zugang zu Informationen bieten können, sei es Video oder Computer. In vielen Museen gibt es jetzt Resource Areas, die im Grunde Bildungszwecken dienen. Aber worüber wir hier sprechen, ist keine Umgebung, die einfach angefügt wird, sondern eine „Hauptveranstaltungs"-Umgebung, die der Darstellung früherer Ereignisse und ephemerer Kunstwerke einen gewissen Wert hinzufügt. Und der neben dem Dialog von dem, was an den Wänden dieser Ausstellungsräume hängt, steht.

Meine Erfahrung war aber bisher, dass jedes Museum seine Ausstellungen dokumentiert. Meine Erfahrungen haben gezeigt, dass sie einfach nicht damit vertraut sind oder es ihnen nicht bewusst ist, dass es einen Bedarf für groß angelegte Dokumentation von Installationen oder ephemeren Werken mit ein wenig mehr Genauigkeit gibt. Wenn man einen Katalog produziert, kommt man dieser Genauigkeit etwas näher. Ich habe begonnen, die Museen zu bitten, architektonische Grundrisse zu erstellen, sobald die Arbeit getan ist, damit es ein tatsächliches Dokument darüber gibt, wo sich die Dinge befanden. Alle Medien, die in die Dokumentation einfließen, müssen stärker formalisiert werden, und möglicherweise könnte sich eine Gruppe wie diese konkrete Vorschläge für ein Museum einfallen lassen.

Fraser: Wenn ich eine Performance mache, fordere ich vonseiten des Museums Videodokumentation ein.

Wilson: Richtig, und wenn sie mit Bewegung arbeitet, dann benötigt man eventuell mehr als eine Videoaufnahme.

Wuggenig: Ich möchte auf diese Diskussion über Konservierung und das Museum zurückkommen, denn ich glaube, sie hat viel mit dem theoretischen Begriff der „Dienstleistung" zu tun, der bisher nicht wirklich als alltäglicher Begriff der Dienstleistungen diskutiert wurde. Ein Begriff der Dienstleistungen, der hier an der Universität sehr oft verwendet wird. Ich glaube, dass es in der Wirtschaft zwei Arten gibt, diesen Begriff zu verstehen. Eine ist die Klassische. In der klassischen politischen Ökonomie sagt zum Beispiel Jean-Baptiste Say, dieser französische Ökonom [aus dem 18. Jahrhundert], dass es Produkte gibt, deren Konsum im Moment der Erzeugung stattfindet. Und das Gleiche findet sich in der Arbeit von Karl Marx – das ist meine Übersetzung: „Der nützliche Effekt ist ausschließlich während des Produktionsprozesses konsumierbar." Dienstleistungen sind daher sozusagen Dinge, die auf frischer Tat konsumiert werden – sie können einen Tauschwert, aber danach keinen Nutzwert haben. Ich glaube, das könnte ebenfalls ein interessanter Rahmen dafür sein, um über dieses Problem der ephemeren Arbeit und der Konservierung nachzudenken.

Fraser: Aber sie haben einen Nutzwert für eine professionelle Gemeinschaft.

Wilson: Es ist ein Ideenwert und ein historischer Wert. Das ist etwas, das in dem Moment umgesetzt werden muss, in dem man anfängt, mit einem Museum darüber zu sprechen, ein Projekt zu machen.

Fraser: Apropos diese Definition der „Dienstleistung".

Wuggenig: Das ist nur eine Definition der „Dienstleistung". Es gibt viele.

Fraser: Richtig. Es gibt Honorare und Entschädigung – und darüber nachzudenken, war eines der Motive dafür, diese Gruppe hier zu organisieren. Michael Asher legte eine Honorarstruktur fest und hatte starke Meinungen zu Produktionshonoraren für Künstler*innen. Dass Produktionshonorare nicht integer sind und eine Zweckentfremdung dessen sind, was ein Honorar sein sollte. Dass ein Honorar außerhalb der Marktstrukturen von Warenproduktion liegt. Dafür ist ein Honorar da. Ein doppeltes Spiel zu spielen, ist inkonsistent. Das geschah bei Firminy [für Projekt Unité, 1993], wo es hieß: „Nun, Sie werden das Ding verkaufen, also warum soll ich Ihnen auch noch ein Honorar geben?" Ich möchte also nur sagen, dass ich wirklich eine Richtlinie entwickeln möchte, die Künstler*innen und Kurator*innen schützt.

Barry: Ich möchte bloß darauf zurückkommen, was Fritz und Christian über die Umnutzung von Räumen angesprochen haben. In Hinblick darauf, was Fred über ephemere Gegenstände gesagt hat, die einen Wert haben, selbst wenn dieser nicht monetisiert wird. Ich glaube der Punkt, den du angesprochen hast, dass ephemere Sammlungen keinen Wert haben, wie Ashers – persönlich bin ich darüber verärgert, dass er nicht in einem Museum vertreten sein kann, aber er kann es nicht. Es ist eine wichtige Frage über Räume und wie der Raum für temporäre Arbeiten überdacht werden könnte, einschließlich der Installationen und wenn Künstler*innen ihr Einverständnis geben.

Wilson: Worüber wir sprechen, sind die verschiedenen Arten von Museen und wie sie Dinge ausstellen. Es gibt Museen, die nicht dieselbe Wertehierarchie haben, wie die, die Kunstmuseen haben, um ihre Sammlungen zu bewerten.

Bischoff: Die beste Idee im größten Raum, was?

Draxler: Ich denke, es ist eine Frage der politischen Strategien, die entwickelt werden. Wenn Michael Asher diese Strategie der Honorarstruktur in den frühen siebziger Jahren entwickelt hat, dann hat er vielleicht Gründe dafür gehabt. Seine Strategie war sehr erfolgreich, um ihn als eine Autorität im ethischen Umgang mit Kunstfragen zu etablieren. Warum also, vielleicht, sollten wir uns darum kümmern, was in Museen vor sich geht? Was die Art Workers' Coalition gemacht hat, war kollektive Partizipation, nicht Reform. Ich denke also, wir müssen uns mit dieser sehr spezifischen Art von Arbeit befassen, sehr spezifische Strategien entwickeln.

Cahan: Ich versuche, den Unterschied zwischen „Partizipation" und „Reform" zu verstehen. Wenn ich über die Entstehung von Partizipationsstrategien nachdenke, oder ihre Wurzeln, denke ich an bestimmte kulturelle Ideen, die aus Kuba kommen, revolutionäre Kontexte der sechziger Jahre oder postrevolutionäre Kontexte, aber ich sehe das nicht in den Vereinigten Staaten. Vielleicht gab es dort in den späten sechziger Jahren ein quasi-revolutionäres Klima… Jedenfalls sehe ich dort keinen Unterschied zwischen dem und dem, was man als „reformistisch" bezeichnen könnte.

Draxler: Ich würde dort auch keinen großen Unterschied sehen, aber ich habe gerade nur auf Aussagen der Art Workers' Coalition hingewiesen, die gegen reformistische Ansätze waren. Ich meine, heutzutage sind wir so weit von solchen Forderungen entfernt, die für Künstler*innen entwickelt wurden, damit sie in Museumsvorständen sitzen können. In den letzten zwanzig Jahren haben wir so viel verloren; noch viel mehr, was wir bewältigen müssen.

Guttmann: Susan, glaubst du nicht, dass Künstler*innen ein Problem damit haben, sich in kollektiven Aktionen zu organisieren?

Cahan: Nein, das sage ich überhaupt nicht. Ich habe nur an den Unterschied der Begriffe gedacht, der im Material über die Art Workers' Coalition gemacht wurde, „Partizipation" und „reformistisch". Und meine Frage ist: Was hätte zu diesem Zeitpunkt in der Geschichte etwas anderes als eine reformistische Position darstellen sollen?

Guttmann: Aber es gibt sicherlich einen Weg, zwischen themenbezogenen Forderungen zu unterscheiden, die man als reformistisch beschreiben kann, und Partizipation, bei der es eher um Aktivitäten geht, die nicht von Themen hergeleitet werden.

Cahan: Aber ich glaube ich habe gerade Künstler*innen hier an diesem Tisch bei der Diskussion darüber zugehört, deren Arbeit so anfällig dafür ist, bestehenden institutionellen Zwecken zu dienen. Man kann also nicht davon ausgehen, dass Partizipation zu revolutionären Zwecken führt.

Publikum (Gislind Nabakowski): Ich wollte nur auf die Arbeit aufmerksam machen, die die Studierenden für diese Veranstaltung geleistet haben: Installation, Kaffee servieren, gestern den Raum reinigen. Es war ihnen nicht möglich, hier ein Publikum zu sein. Ich will niemandem die Schuld geben, aber nur damit Sie es wissen, einige der Studierenden hier fühlen sich in gewisser Weise ausgenutzt. Ich habe auch eine praktische Frage zu dieser Ausstellung und wie sie reisen wird. Werden die Ergebnisse dieser Forschung Teil der zukünftigen Forschung sein – wie in Stuttgart zum Beispiel?

Fraser: Es hat einige Diskussionen über die Punkte gegeben, die Sie erwähnen. Und wir sollten das ins Fazit [in der nächsten Sitzung] aufnehmen. Wir müssen jetzt eine Pause machen. Und diese Diskussionen wurden vorher nicht erwähnt, was mit den Bedingungen dieses Raums, des Kunstraums, zu tun hat. Und mit der Tatsache, dass es keine Struktur dafür gibt. Es entsteht also erst jetzt. Diese Veranstaltung war von Anfang an als geschlossene Arbeitsgruppe gedacht, nicht als Seminar, nicht als öffentliche Veranstaltung. Und der Fachbereich hier hat Helmut oder mir nie eine Frage dazu gestellt…erst letzten Dienstag. Dann musste auf unzufriedenstellende Art damit umgegangen werden. Das liegt daran, dass man sich bis zu diesem Zeitpunkt nicht damit auseinandergesetzt hatte. Dies ist der Ort, an dem diese Videos produziert werden. Und es konnte nur ein Ort für die Art von Arbeit sein, die wir produzieren wollten, wenn es ein Arbeitstreffen zwischen Praktiker*innen wäre, die bestimmte Erfahrungen teilen. Damit wir diese Erfahrungen diskutieren konnten, ohne sie auf eine Weise anzusprechen, wie es öffentliche Panels oder

Symposien erfordern. Denn wir sind mit den Problemen dieser öffentlichen Panels oder Symposien gut vertraut.

Dies war also eine Bemühung, eine Struktur zu schaffen, die diese Probleme umgehen konnte. Möglicherweise war es nicht notwendig… Wissen Sie, ich hatte nicht erwartet, dass die Diskussion so einfach sein würde. Denn die Geschichte dieser Gruppe, oder Teile dieser Gruppe, in den letzten ein oder zwei Jahren waren wir in viele komplizierte Interaktionen, Konkurrenz und Konflikte involviert. Angesichts dieser Vorgeschichte bin ich davon ausgegangen, dass es auch hier Komplikationen geben würde. Ich denke, Helmut und ich können also eine gewisse Verantwortung übernehmen, aber diese Diskussion, die Sie angeregt haben, hätte schon viel früher stattfinden sollen, als das Konzept eingeführt wurde. Und dann zum zweiten Punkt [darüber, dass die Ausstellung weiterreist]: Ich habe das [die Ausstellung und Veranstaltung im Kunstraum der Universität Lüneburg] immer als Ausgangspunkt betrachtet. Um an das, was hier geschehen ist, anzuschließen und damit weiterzuarbeiten. Dass, wenn es nach Genf weiterreist, wo es einen kuratorischen Studiengang gibt, es ein Gespräch zwischen den Studierenden dort und den Studierenden hier geben könnte. Das ist also meine Antwort.

Barry: Haben die Studierenden eine Meinung dazu, was sie sich von unserer Interaktion erhoffen? Neue Modelle, die sich die Studierenden für solche Situationen anschauen?

Publikum (Bettina von Dziembowski, Studentin): Die Studierenden hatten nur auf die Möglichkeit gehofft, zuhören zu können. Nicht, daran teilzunehmen.

Publikum (Vera Kockot, Studentin): Vielleicht können wir Sie erneut einladen, ein Seminar zu geben, um darüber nachzudenken, was hier passiert ist.

Fraser: Ich möchte nur noch einen weiteren Punkt über die Arbeit der Studierenden an dieser Veranstaltung ansprechen – Bildung mit der eigenen Verarmung zu subventionieren. Ich weiß nicht, wie die Situation hier genau aussieht, aber in den USA ist es üblich, Studierende im Hauptstudium dazu zu zwingen, Studierende im Grundstudium quasi umsonst zu unterrichten. Möglicherweise wird die Situation hier ähnlich gehandhabt. Kaffeekochen und Aufräumen sind keine lehrreichen Tätigkeiten, aber es wird von ihnen als Bezahlung für die Teilnahme verlangt. Und gleichzeitig wird von uns die Dienstleistung einer pädagogischen Arbeit verlangt, die nicht Teil der Bedingungen unseres Engagements ist. Daher ist das also ein echtes Problem, und es hängt mit dem zusammen, was wir hier diskutieren, wenn wir über Institutionen sprechen. Wie können die Bedingungen des Austauschs definiert werden? Und ich finde, die Studierenden müssen dies sowohl von der Schule und dem Kunstraum als auch von den Teilnehmer*innen verlangen.

Bischoff: Das ist nicht so schön.

Fraser: Es ist nicht so schön, aber es ist notwendig. Es ist ein harter Job – das ist ernst. Aber können wir jetzt eine Pause machen? Und wir brauchen Stühle für die öffentlichen Vorträge. Wir können alle Stühle besorgen. Ich werde mich auf den Boden setzen!

Arbeitsgruppe
Sitzung Sechs

Abschließende Diskussion
Sonntag, 23. Januar 1994

Helmut Draxler: Wir haben also eine etwas komplizierte Situation im Moment. Es wurde das sehr komplexe Problem angeschnitten, wie diese Gruppe hier im Raum funktioniert, wie dieser Raum konzipiert wurde und wie er aus der Perspektive der Studierenden aussieht. Ich würde sagen, dass es wirklich ein wichtiges Thema ist, das wirklich diskutiert werden sollte. Andererseits hat die letzte Sitzung mit einigen Punkten geendet, die interessant zu sein schienen. Und ich denke, es ist auch absolut wichtig, dies jetzt zu beenden und diese abschließende Diskussion zu führen. Was ich also vorschlagen würde, ist, dass wir jetzt mit dieser Diskussion fortfahren und morgen dann das Treffen, das wir [für die Studierenden] angeboten haben, dafür nutzen, die spezifische Frage der Verankerung dieser Veranstaltung im Kunstraum zu diskutieren. Ich würde sagen, wir sollten in etwa um 13 Uhr anfangen, wenn das in Ordnung ist. Und wer dann hier ist, nimmt teil, und wir sollten versuchen, uns sehr explizit auf dieses Problem zu konzentrieren. Denn ich glaube, dass es sehr wichtig ist, wie der Kunstraum [der Universität Lüneburg] diese Arbeit weiterführen wird und welche Problemstellungen – das Verhältnis zwischen einer akademischen und einer künstlerischen Gemeinschaft – definiert werden. Sie sollten auf sehr offene Art und Weise angesprochen werden, damit wir versuchen können, einen Weg aus dieser etwas schwierigen Situation zu finden.

Andrea Fraser: Wir sollten auch den Teilnehmer*innen Bescheid geben, denke ich, weil sie nicht wissen, dass morgen diese Sitzung stattfindet. Wir hatten mit den Studierenden vereinbart, morgen um 13 Uhr über die Ausstellung und die Gruppe zu sprechen. Das ist also, was Helmut damit meint, und ich weiß, dass einige von euch morgen abreisen, aber es wäre sehr schön, wenn diejenigen, die nicht abreisen, auch dazukommen und an der Diskussion teilnehmen könnten. Ja? Ist das –

Draxler: Nein?

Fraser: Oder –

Susan Cahan: Ich möchte eine Sache sagen, und zwar dass die Themen, bei denen es um die Studierenden und das Verhältnis dieses Projekts zum Studiengang dieser Universität und des Kunstraums geht, eines der Dinge sind, die mich persönlich am meisten interessieren und dass ich das für sehr wichtig halte, um Anschluss zur Zukunft herzustellen. Wenn es also in diesem Raum Zuspruch dazu gibt, heute Abend kurz darüber zu sprechen, dann möchte ich das als eine Möglichkeit vorschlagen, vor allem weil ich morgen nicht hier sein werde, da Fred und ich tagsüber abreisen müssen.

Fraser: Nun, vielleicht – ja?

Martin Guttmann: Ich stimme dem Vorschlag zu und denke, dass eine Möglichkeit, daraus ein interessanteres Thema zu machen – obwohl es interessant genug ist (Lacht) – wäre, über ein etwas größeres Thema nachzudenken, das in keiner der Sitzungen wirklich zutage kam, aber eigentlich hätte erwähnt werden können. Und das ist die Möglichkeit, Projekte in Zusammenarbeit mit akademischen Kontexten durchzuführen, was ein sehr breites Thema zu sein scheint. Gleichzeitig haben wir viel über das Verhältnis von Kunst, Publikum und Museum gesprochen. Und den Kontext zu berücksichtigen, wisst ihr, das könnte auch in einer direkteren Form passieren. Es scheint, dass es tatsächlich großes Potential für weitere äußerst produktive Zusammenarbeit mit akademischen Institutionen gibt. Deswegen könnte es tatsächlich ein interessantes Thema für sich sein.

Fraser: Möchtest du auf Susans Bemerkung antworten?

Fred Wilson: Ich meine, ein Gedanke ist, vielleicht auch ein Modell für ein Symposium dieser Art entwickeln oder schaffen zu können, bei der eine Kerngruppe über etwas spricht, das sie sehr persönlich betrifft, und es dann eine größere Gruppe gibt, die das Thema auch nachvollziehen kann. Und da sollte es eben einen Weg geben, wie eine Interaktion stattfinden könnte. Ich meine, das ist nicht das erste Symposium, an dem ich teilgenommen habe, bei dem sich solche Situationen ergeben haben. Es könnte also auf diese Art und Weise von Nutzen sein.

Fraser: Nun, ich denke, dass ich auch die Gruppe fragen möchte, die an diesem Wochenende an den Sitzungen teilgenommen hat, welche anderen Themen sie für wichtig halten, um sie abschließend zu diskutieren, über die Frage der Beziehung zwischen der Arbeitsgruppe, dem Projekt und den Hochschulen hinaus.

Iwona Blazwick: Ich denke, zuallererst muss der geografische Rahmen weiter sein, denn der ist äußerst begrenzt. Es ist vollkommen auf Amerika fokussiert und auf einen Teil von Europa und dieser Achse. Es scheint mir, dass einige sehr interessante Modelle entwickelt werden und funktionieren – das meine ich ernst –, die hier überhaupt nicht vertreten sind. Und unsere Terminologie ist auch ein wenig vage, beispielsweise diese ganze Sache über „Museen" gegenüber „temporären Räumen". Es scheint mir, dass es einfach so ein breites Spektrum an Institutionen gibt, von denen keines ein Gebäude besitzt, über Publikationen bis hin zur Technologie. Es gibt ein riesiges Sortiment an möglichen Begriffen für den Vertrieb und Kommunikation und so weiter. Sodass wir eventuell genauer sein müssen, wenn es darum geht, diese Modelle zu identifizieren. Das wären meine beiden Kommentare.

Fraser: Du möchtest also mehr darüber in der abschließenden Sitzung sprechen oder ist das eine – ?

Blazwick: Oh. Das ist nur eine allgemeine Beobachtung.

Fraser: In Ordnung.

Cahan: Nun, werdet ihr in Zukunft noch mehr solcher Arbeitsgruppen veranstalten?

Fraser: Nun…

Cahan: Weil eine Sache, die –

(Gelächter)

Wilson: Sie ist müde.

Cahan: Nun, falls es nämlich in Zukunft möglicherweise weitere Diskussion gibt, könnten einige der

Punkte aus diesen Diskussionen auch in diesen Foren aufgegriffen werden.

Fraser: Ja, sicher.

Cahan: Es wäre aber vielleicht interessant zu hören, was diese anderen Themen sind.

Fraser: Nun, wenn niemand einen Einwand hat, dann denke ich, könnten wir die Diskussion in Bezug auf die Frage des Kunstraums und dessen Verhältnis zu den Studierenden öffnen, wenn das von Interesse ist. Ich meine…

Cahan: Was habt ihr geplant?

Fraser: Nun, ich denke, dass es oft notwendig ist. Es ist eine Art symbolischer Abschluss des Prozesses, der zwischen verschiedenen Personen stattgefunden hat. Das kann nützlich sein, kann eine vorteilhafte psychologische und noch weitere Auswirkung haben. Insbesondere möchte ich aber auf die Frage zurückkommen, die am Ende der letzten Diskussion darüber aufkam, ob dies eine Reform ist oder nicht, was eine Reform ist, was Institutionen reformiert und was nicht. Und ob diese ganze Diskussion hier auf der Annahme beruht, dass es bestimmte gegebene Begriffe in zeitgenössischen Strukturen gibt – ob die Strukturpositionen akzeptiert werden oder nicht, so würde ich es ausdrücken. Das scheint mir eine sehr wichtige Diskussion zu sein, aber ich denke auch, dass es keine Diskussion ist, bei der wir zu irgendeinem bestimmten Schluss kommen werden. Das ist also das Eine, das ich vorschlagen würde, aber wenn ich nicht, wisst ihr… In Ordnung, nun, lasst uns…

Draxler: Es wäre gut, einige Meinungen zu hören.

(Stimmen, die durcheinander sprechen)

Guttmann: Wie lautet die Frage?

Fraser: Die Frage, die ich vorhin gestellt habe? Oder die jetzige Frage?

Guttmann: „Es wäre schön, ein paar Meinungen zu hören" in Bezug worauf?

Fraser: Bezüglich der Frage, was wir abschließend diskutieren sollen.

(Gelächter)

Renée Green: Möglicherweise brauchen wir eine Tafel oder so etwas. (Lacht) Damit wir alles durchgehen und auf den Tisch legen können. Beispielsweise bestimmte Punkte, um sie sozusagen hervorzuheben und dann wären sie sichtbar, damit wir sie nicht vergessen und uns darauf beziehen könnten.

Fraser: Es gab hier irgendwo eine Tafel.

Green: Oder eben in diese Richtung denken. Darüber nachzudenken – einfach eine Art Struktur. Es wäre vielleicht zu diesem Zeitpunkt eine gute Idee, wenn die verschiedenen Personen, die Anmerkungen darüber machen möchten, wie sie weiter vorgehen wollen mit dem was besprochen wurde und was nicht, und worauf sie nicht eingegangen sind oder so etwas. Dann könnte es vielleicht aufgelistet werden, damit wir eine Übersicht behalten und diese Dinge besprechen können. Das war's.

Fraser: Es scheint mir, dass das eigentlich ziemlich sinnlos wäre, denn in der Tat… Ich meine, ich denke, durch die Anwesenheit von euch allen und der Art, wie die letzte Sitzung abgeschlossen wurde, ist es eigentlich gar nicht möglich, sich eine abschließende Diskussion vorzustellen, die diese Veränderung nicht anerkennt. Ich denke also, wir sollten als Nächstes einfach die Fragen ansprechen, die am Ende der letzten Sitzung über den Status dieser Veranstaltung im Verhältnis zu einer Studierenden- und einer Berufsgemeinschaft aufkamen. Ich möchte also die Diskussion an diesem Punkt eröffnen. Und ich möchte natürlich auch die Studierenden einladen, sich einzubringen.

Ulrich Bischoff: Die Form der Darstellung dieses Punktes war zu elegant, glaube ich, ich habe es nicht verstanden. Die Frage der Gemeinschaft?

Fraser: Die Frage, die vorhin aufkam, betraf nämlich – ich glaube, Uli, du hast es zuerst erwähnt – wie diese Veranstaltung funktioniert, um einer Studierendengemeinschaft, einer akademischen Gemeinschaft zu dienen oder nicht und auch einer professionellen Gemeinschaft aus Künstler*innen und Kurator*innen. Wie ich oder wie wir gesagt hatten, wurde sie vermutlich am direktesten und in erster Linie konzipiert, um ein Forum zu bieten und um tatsächlich einen Zweck zu erfüllen. Oder ihr Gebrauchswert – ihr anfänglicher oder primärer Gebrauchswert – hat sich an einer Gemeinschaft von Fachleuten im Verhältnis zu deren Praxis orientiert. Um eine praktische Diskussion für Fachleute zugänglich zu machen und eine zweite Funktion zu haben, deren Ausmaß

ich außerhalb eines geschlossenen Forums nicht für möglich gehalten habe, was aber dann über Videoaufnahme für eine Gemeinschaft funktionieren könnte, die – aus geographischen und anderen Gründen – nicht an dieser Diskussion teilnehmen würde, dann aber in Richtung Kulturmanagement und viel praktische Arbeit in Institutionen und kulturellen Einrichtungen gehen würde.

Die Frage ist also, ob die Tatsache, dass die Diskussionen nicht die Möglichkeit der direkten Teilnahme geboten haben, ein Verstoß gegen unsere eventuelle Verpflichtung ist, einer Studierendengemeinschaft zu dienen. Oder gegen die Verpflichtung des Raumes. Oder, ich meine, es könnte auf verschiedene Art und Weise formuliert werden, ich weiß es nicht. Jemand anderes – jemand anderes soll bitte übernehmen.

Green: Nun, hat sich jemand während der Pause mit den Studentierenden unterhalten? Ich habe das gemacht. Mir fiel auf, dass einige andere Leute sich auch unterhalten haben. Vielleicht könnten wir einige der Dinge besprechen, die wir mit ihnen besprochen haben.

Fraser: Ja, ich möchte, dass jemand anderes außer mir spricht.

Green: Jedenfalls, um direkt darauf einzugehen, was du gerade gesagt hast, und was Fred über die Struktur einer Art der Veranstaltung wie dieser gesagt hat, bei der es diese Idee einer Arbeitsgruppe gibt, die tatsächlich versucht, bestimmte Probleme anzusprechen, die dafür relevant sind, was sie tut, und die versucht, etwas herauszufinden: Ich sehe eigentlich kein Problem darin, das so zu machen und dies auch eine Art Diskussion untereinander sein zu lassen, die irgendwann…

Ich habe mit einer*m der Studierenden besprochen, dass einige Studierende vielleicht an der Diskussion teilnehmen wollten und wieder andere der Diskussion nur zusehen und zuhören wollten, um zu sehen, was daraus werden würde. Daher glaube ich, ist dies möglicherweise ein Weg, eine Diskussion über bestimmte Situationen zu führen, die wir ansprechen müssen, oder so etwas, und dann den anderen zu einem anderen Zeitpunkt zu ermöglichen, darüber zu sprechen. Ich glaube, in diesem spezifischen Fall hatte ich den Grund für unser Treffen sozusagen so verstanden, dass wir Dinge klären und eine Art des Arbeitens konzipieren wollten. Wenn das [*Services* Projekt] aber in irgendeiner Form weitergeführt werden soll, dann können wir einige dieser Punkte für zukünftige Situationen [zukünftige Ausstellungen und Arbeitsgruppen im Zusammenhang mit dem Projekt] berücksichtigen.

Bischoff: Vielleicht kann ich einen Vorschlag machen. Wenn ich morgen wieder in Dresden bin, wird meine Situation so sein, dass sie mich fragen werden: „Was haben Sie da in Lüneburg gemacht?" Und ich werde antworten: „Es wurden ein paar Dinge diskutiert." Meine Erfahrung ist, dass Künstler*innen für sich sprechen und ein Interesse daran haben, die Kunstwelt zu verändern und die Institutionen zu besuchen. Es gibt eine [historische] Bewegung [die wir untersucht haben], vor ungefähr dreißig Jahren begann sie mit Künstler*innen – aber sie [die Situation der Künstler*innen in Bezug auf die Institutionen] ändert sich ständig. Im Moment bin ich daran interessiert, hier zu sein, um

zu hören, welche Arten der Bewegungen diskutiert werden, um sie [Künstler*innen] in die Institution zu bringen und sie zu verändern… Welche Art des Machens… Entschuldigung, ich kann mich nicht auf diese besondere Weise ausdrücken. Ich meine: auf welche Weise sie sich gerne einbringen würden und welches Interesse sie haben.

Dein [Fred] Beispiel dafür, wie du in Museen arbeitest, war für mich ein gutes. Und es gibt sehr unterschiedliche Formen, wie Künstler*innen in Institutionen gehen. Dann blicke ich wieder auf meine eigene Institution zurück, in der ich arbeiten muss, und ich sehe: „Oh, es gibt eine Menge Künstler*innen, die das machen wollen." Insofern ist es also eine gute Idee. Ich könnte sie einladen, nach Dresden [Gemäldegalerie Alte Meister, Staatliche Kunstsammlungen Dresden] zu kommen. Das wäre beispielsweise eine Antwort, die ich geben könnte, wenn sie [meine Kolleg*innen] mich fragen: „Was haben Sie hier gemacht?"

Und es ist wirklich sehr interessant, dass die gleiche Frage aufkam, als ich in einer anderen Gruppe war, die eine Ausstellung vorbereitete, die sich mit den Landproblemen in Polen und in der Türkei beschäftigte – ein Projekt, das fünf Jahre dauerte, indem sie sich anschauten, was dort mit ökologischen Problemen gemacht wurde. Der Unterschied liegt darin, dass wir nicht in einer Situation sein sollten, in der wir die Künstler*innen fragen müssen: „Wollt ihr euch an diesen Fragen beteiligen?" Stattdessen müssen wir uns aber die Künstler*innen ansehen, die auf diese Weise arbeiten. Wisst ihr, was ich meine? Den Unterschied. Und ich glaube, das ist nicht sehr häufig der Fall. Und andererseits, im Gegensatz zu dieser Situation: Künstler*innen arbeiten auf ihre eigene Art und Weise – sie haben verschiedene Methoden, ihre Projekte und Lösungen zu entwickeln, um mit der Situation zu arbeiten. Sie kommen also aus unterschiedlichen Richtungen, und dieser spezifische Aspekt ist, glaube ich, sehr hilfreich, um das klar auszudrücken.

Publikum (Bettina von Dziembowski, Studentin): Darf ich Sie etwas fragen? Glauben Sie, dass Sie genug Informationen bekommen haben, um zu verstehen, was Sie in dieser Institution verändern möchten?

Fraser: In welcher Institution?

Publikum (Bettina von Dziembowski, Studentin): Dieser, der Universität.

Fraser: Ich habe nicht das Gefühl, dass es meine Aufgabe ist, eine Empfehlung zu geben. Ich meine, als Helmut und ich ursprünglich im Sommer hier herkamen, haben wir tatsächlich eine Reihe von Empfehlungen geschrieben. Das wurde nicht von uns erwartet, wir haben einfach beschlossen, eine Reihe von Empfehlungen über das Konzept des Raumes zu formulieren. Aber ich meine, ich denke nicht, dass außer auf die Einladung zu reagieren – da ich nicht Teil dieser Institution bin oder hier arbeite, gibt es bestimmte Grenzen in Hinblick darauf, was ich tun kann, und auch darauf, was ich denke, was für jeden von Vorteil wäre, bei dem das ich tue. Denn ich kann Empfehlungen geben bis zum Gehtnichtmehr, und sie mögen völlig falsch oder völlig nutzlos sein. Und ich denke, es ist sowieso nicht unbedingt eine Frage des Inhalts der Empfehlung, sondern eine Frage der Art der Partizipation innerhalb eines Systems, in dem es bestimmte Verantwortlichkeiten und bestimmte Arten von Austausch gibt.

Publikum (Bettina von Dziembowski, Studentin): Sie wollen hier also etwas produzieren.

Fraser: Sie meinen mit dieser Veranstaltung? Bis zu diesem Zeitpunkt habe ich schon ziemlich viel Material produziert.

Ulf Wuggenig: Wenn wir über dieses Video sprechen, das ihr [Andrea und Helmut] morgen zeigen werdet, da es eine Form der Kommunikation mit einem größerem Publikum ist: Was meint ihr, wie ihr dabei vorgehen werdet?

Draxler: Ja, ich meine, das ist eine Frage, die wir besprechen müssen: wie man den öffentlichen Vortrag organisiert. Der Sinn der Diskussion ist allerdings mehr oder weniger, wie der Kunstraum seine Rolle zwischen einer eher künstlerischen und einer akademischen Gemeinschaft definieren will. Ich denke, das ist der Punkt, an dem die meisten Probleme entstehen. Ich denke, es geht auch viel darum, wie du [Ulf, als Direktor des Kunstraums] dich dazu entschließt, wie diese [Institution] funktionieren könnte. Ich meine, das Problem ist: Ist der Raum nur dann legitim, wenn er eine Art Seminarraum ist? Oder ist es der Prozess, den du auch beschrieben hast: dass dieser Raum mehr oder weniger die Funktion eines Seminarraums hat, sich aber von dieser Beschreibung entfernen und zu einer Art Kunstraum werden konnte. Ich sage nicht, dass ich so wahnsinnig an diesen Unterschieden interessiert bin. Überhaupt nicht. Aber ich denke, es ist sehr wichtig für euch – ihr müsst die Entscheidungen treffen und den

Personen, die ihr einladet, sehr klar die Information darüber kommunizieren, worum es geht, und auch die Studierenden auf genau die gleiche Art [informieren]. Denn meiner Erfahrung nach fehlte es etwas an Kommunikation.

Wuggenig: Ja, du hast Recht. Aber ihr müsst es so sehen, dass wir gesagt haben, dass ihr zuerst kommen solltet, um ein Seminar zu gestalten. Ihr beide oder einer von euch. Und wenn das passiert wäre, hätten wir viele dieser Probleme nicht gehabt. Das ist ein Problem, weil es aus Zeitmangel nicht möglich war. Ich denke also, man sollte die Probleme nicht größer machen, als sie sind. Sie sind meiner Meinung nach sehr einfach. Wäre das Seminar im Dezember [letzten Monat] gewesen, hätten wir die Teilnahme und all diese Dinge besprechen können. Das sehe ich als einziges Problem. Wir haben einen Kompromiss gefunden. Ich glaube nicht, dass es noch so notwendig ist, darüber in diesem Umfang zu diskutieren, weil wir es in den letzten Tagen schon so ausgiebig besprochen haben. Denke ich…

Fraser: Es scheint mir nicht geklärt zu sein. Sonst wäre es nicht schon vor einer halben Stunde eine Frage gewesen. Tut mir Leid.

Publikum (Vera Kockot, Studentin): Ich habe eine Frage… Viele unterschiedliche Personen hier erleben unterschiedliche Institutionen und für unseren Studiengang, der Kulturwissenschaft heißt, versuchen wir, die Berührungspunkte zwischen verschiedenen Kulturarbeiter*innen zu finden. Es gab viele Fragen, die an diesem Tisch aufkamen, aber ich habe bisher keine Antworten gehört. Und wir suchen nach Antworten,

forschen nach ihnen. Wie können Künstler*innen und Institutionen zusammenarbeiten? Wie weit können sie gehen? Und was sind die Unterschiede und Gemeinsamkeiten dieser institutionellen Organisationen und die Freiheit der künstlerischen Arbeit? Das sind die Themen, die uns interessieren.

Cahan: In Ordnung, ich habe das Gefühl, dass es eben eine sehr interessante Verschiebung gegeben habt. Als ihr beide [Ulf, Bettina, die Studentin] euch ausgetauscht habt, sind diejenigen von uns, die zur Arbeitsgruppe eingeladen waren, auf einmal zu Zuschauer*innen dieser Interaktion zwischen denen geworden, die mit der Universität assoziiert sind. Was eine Art Transformation dessen ist, von dem wir ursprünglich dachten, was passieren würde, nämlich dass die Studierenden die Zuschauer*innen sein würden. Aber gut – nun, ich lasse das mal so stehen.

(Gelächter)

Fraser: Ich möchte nur etwas klarstellen. Meine Annahme war, dass fünf Studierende direkt an diesem Kunstraum-Projekt arbeiten und Teilnehmer*innen sein würden. Nicht, dass dies Teil eines Seminars sein würde, an dem die Studierenden teilnehmen würden und wir die Seminarleiter*innen wären. Das war von Anfang an meine Annahme. Und das wurde an alle Teilnehmer*innen kommuniziert. Für mich wäre es sicherlich möglich gewesen, darüber nachzudenken, die Struktur zu ändern, um alle von Ihnen [den Studierenden] dabei zu haben. Ich habe gesagt, wenn das der Fall ist, dann müssen sie alle Teilnehmer*innen kontaktieren und sie darüber informieren, dass die Struktur sich geändert hat. Denn ich bin bestimmte Verpflichtungen eingegangen, für die ich mich unter Prämissen, die ich für sehr deutlich gehalten hatte, verantwortlich gefühlt habe. Das wollte ich nur klarstellen.

Cahan: Jetzt tut es mir Leid, dass ich das gesagt habe, denn es wurde dann irgendwie zu einem Brennpunkt für die Fortsetzung dieser Diskussion, was überhaupt nicht meine Intention war. Meine Intention war es, einen Weg vorzuschlagen, der das Thema der Kulturwissenschaften und Kunstinstitutionen von einem anderen Standpunkt aus beleuchten würde, der eventuell produktiv sein könnte.

Worüber wir in den letzten paar Tagen viel gehört haben, ist, wie einige der Personen an diesem Tisch ihre Praxis betrachten, wenn es um die Vielfalt der kulturellen Bereiche geht. Judith hat erwähnt, wie ihre Arbeit sich mit Fragen der Massenkultur auseinandersetzt. Fred und Renée haben darüber gesprochen, wie sich ihre Arbeit mit Methoden oder Kritik an den Methoden aus der Ethnographie beschäftigt. Ich sehe meine Arbeit im Zusammenhang mit verschiedenen Arten, die Idee der Populärkultur zu begreifen, und damit, wie Populärkultur im Sinne einer „Volkskultur" in die Kunstinstitutionen integriert werden könnte, die im Allgemeinen mit Hochkukltur in Verbindung gebracht werden und nicht mit der Kulturproduktion der Menschen. Und um die Zeit produktiv zu nutzen, wäre es vielleicht interessant zu hören, was einige der Personen an diesem Tisch darüber zu sagen haben, wie ihre Arbeit mit dem Bereich der Kulturwissenschaften zusammenhängt. Darüber, wie die Verbindung zwischen Kulturwissenschaften und Kunstinstitutionen aussieht. Und darüber, wie Personen das in ihrer Praxis behandelt haben. Und noch einmal, es ist nur ein Vorschlag, da ich denke, dass wir die Zeit, die wir zusammen haben, nutzen sollten.

Beatrice von Bismarck: Ich habe einen weiteren Vorschlag. Und das wäre der Versuch, vielleicht zwei Interessen zu kombinieren. Ich habe das Gefühl, dass es wirklich sinnvoll für diese Sitzung wäre, vielleicht nicht als abschließende Diskussion, aber um zu zeigen, was alles offen geblieben ist. Was du gesagt hast, ist entscheidend, weil du [Andrea] dies ja fortsetzen möchtest und wahrscheinlich eine weitere Arbeitsgruppe gründen willst.

Es wäre interessant zu hören, was alle meinen, was wir nicht besprochen haben und was vielleicht für die Arbeit, die jede*r macht, interessant gewesen wäre. Und ich persönlich denke, dass wir viele Themen umkreist haben. Und heute ist es präziser geworden als gestern. Dennoch hat jede*r seine oder ihre eigenen Interessen, und vielleicht haben wir Fragen, die überhaupt nicht angesprochen wurden.

Eine der Fragen, die mich beschäftigt – und das hat vielleicht einiges mit den Fragen zu tun, die wir hier besprochen haben – ist genau diese Weise, auf die verschiedene Gemeinschaften, sogar die Mitglieder dieser Gemeinschaften sich tatsächlich zwischeneinander hin- und herbewegen, und wie diese Gemeinschaft funktionieren kann. Ich denke, die wissenschaftliche Gemeinschaft oder die Universitätsgemeinschaft ist eine weitere Teilnehmerin oder könnte eine weitere Teilnehmerin für diese Art des Austauschs sein. Deshalb habe ich das Gefühl, dass wenn wir weiter darüber sprechen, was nicht beantwortet wurde, wir zwangsläufig mehr Fragen über den Kunstraum berücksichtigen, denn das ist zumindest ein Teil meines Interesses.

Wilson: Darüber hinaus meine ich, dass manche vielleicht Dinge haben, die sie speziell aus dieser Diskussion gelernt haben, die im Gegensatz zu vorher jetzt einen besonderen Sinn ergeben. Wenn ich Dinge aufschreibe, fallen mir Sachen ein, die nicht unbedingt weitreichend und umfassend sind, die sozusagen eine abschließende Vorstellung davon sind, worum es zwangsläufig bei dieser Konferenz geht. Dennoch sind mir drei Dinge eingefallen, mit denen ich nicht hierherkam – drei verschiedene Ideen, die am Ende der letzten Sitzung entstanden sind, von denen ich meine, dass sie greifbar sind und die auf andere Weise weiterentwickelt werden können. Im Gespräch mit anderen Arbeitsgruppen oder mit Studierenden oder mit wem auch immer.

Diese drei Dinge sind: Diese ganze Vorstellung, dass wir ein Modell für dieses Galerie-Archiv der ephemeren Materialen entwickeln könnten. Das Modell sollte aber, glaube ich, zentraler in der Museumsstruktur sein und verschiebt sozusagen die Art und Weise, wie Museen ephemeres Material betrachten und es in die Struktur des Museums einordnen. Ich habe gesehen, dass verschiedene Museen versucht haben, das ein wenig zu tun, aber es war einfach nicht genug durchdacht. Und jetzt haben wir wirklich sehr viel Material in dieser Richtung, daher macht es Sinn, darüber irgendwie ein wenig tiefer nachzudenken. Das nächste – was definitiv dazu passen würde – war, die Dokumentation sehr ernst

zu nehmen. Das wurde auch über Ethnographie gesagt, aber Ethnographie ist ein sehr schwieriges Modell. Aber zumindest wirklich die Entwicklung, die Dokumentation der verschiedenen Formen der ephemeren Kunstproduktion anzuschauen. Wenn also dieses Modell für die Galerie – ein Archivmodell oder so etwas – entsteht, dass es etwas gibt, das für ein Publikum wirklich aktivierend ist, das einen Dialog zwischen dieser Art von Material und anderen Formen der künstlerischen Praxis entstehen lässt. Drittens haben wir natürlich das Modell für ein Symposium diskutiert, was meiner Meinung nach auch ein wichtiger Aspekt für ein Museum wäre.

Guttmann: Ich muss sagen, dass ich die Diskussion zeitweise als sehr interessant empfunden habe und es viele interessante Punkte gab, aber ich zögere etwas, das Seminar zusammenzufassen. Ich meine, die letzten paar Tage der Konferenz verliefen zu schnell, ich denke, es sollte wirklich – oder zumindest stelle ich es mir so vor – als ein sehr vorläufiges Gespräch zwischen Leuten aus verschiedenen Disziplinen und mit verschiedenen Standpunkten betrachtet werden. Wir teilen eine gewisse Unzufriedenheit mit dem jetzigen Verhältnis zwischen Künstler*innen und Institutionen; möglicherweise kann es in einem interessanten Austausch von Anmerkungen erweitert werden, indem man sich über die gegenhegemonialen Praktiken der jeweils anderen Seite austauscht. Und ich denke, dass dies für mich gut genug ist, insofern, dass wenn man das Gefühl hat, dass diese Unzufriedenheit nicht bloß etwas ist, das uns als Einzelne betrifft, sondern dass es einige strukturelle Gründe dafür gibt, warum verschiedene Unzufriedenheiten miteinander verknüpft werden können. Ich denke, dass dies an und für sich ein ziemlich wichtiger Schritt ist. Es ist für mich sehr eindeutig, dass diese Unzufriedenheit aus verschiedenen Richtungen kommt. Meiner Meinung nach ist es ziemlich eindeutig, dass verschiedene Teilnehmer*innen daran interessiert sind, die Diskussion auch in andere Richtungen zu bewegen. Vor allem die Idee, die Diskussion auf die Frage zu reduzieren „Was können Künstler*innen für das Museum tun?" – das ist nicht gerade der erste Punkt auf meiner Prioritätenliste. Und ich möchte die ganze Angelegenheit nicht wirklich auf Fragen der Dokumentation reduzieren.

Ich glaube aber, dass ich mich wirklich mit einer fundamentalen Idee der „Dienstleistung" identifizieren kann, weil ich denke, dass es eine bessere Formulierung für eine bestimmte Aktivität ist, die nicht so sehr objektorientiert ist. Meiner Meinung nach war es daher eine gute Idee, um sie [die Arbeitsgruppe] zu definieren. Wenn man dies aber berücksichtigt, denke ich, dass die Art der Aktivitäten, mit denen ich selbst Erfahrungen gemacht habe und die Dinge, die ich von anderen höre, wirklich sehr weit von konstruktiven Fragen entfernt sind, die mit einer bestimmten Sache zu tun haben oder damit, was man mit einer Sache anfangen soll. Ich denke, dass viele Anwesende hier ein Interesse an viel stärker politisierten Aktivitäten und an der Arbeit mit echten Konfrontationssituationen haben. Und meiner Meinung nach ist es wichtig, einfach im Hinterkopf zu behalten, dass wir von verschiedenen Gesichtspunkten aus denken und dass man wirklich nicht aus der Diskussion

herauskommen und annehmen sollte, dass wir von jetzt an alle die gleiche Art von Projekt machen werden.

Ich glaube, wenn man das im Kopf behält und man einen Schritt weitergeht und das Anliegen kommuniziert oder an die Frage der Beteiligung der Studierenden anschließt – dass es dann viel mehr sein wird… Ich meine, die Bedingung für eine Erweiterung der Diskussion sollte sein, dass die Personen nicht nur anwesend sind, um zuzuhören, sondern ihre eigene Unzufriedenheit artikulieren, und wenn sie mehr Erfahrungen mit der Universität gemacht haben, sie ihre eigenen Vorstellungen darüber entwickeln sollten, wie man die Universität reformieren kann. Das scheint mir im Allgemeinen ein besseres Modell für weiterführende Diskussionen zu sein. Anders ausgedrückt, die Leute würden eher ein Problem ansprechen, als sich selbst in die Lage der Zuhörer*innen zu versetzen, weil es nicht wirklich etwas zu hören gibt, außer Notizen über verschiedene Arbeitsweisen zu vergleichen. Das ist mein Gefühl.

Draxler: Ja, ich glaube, die Idee, eine Arbeitsgruppe einzuladen – und eine Arbeitsgruppe innerhalb eines extrem engen Zeitrahmens einzuladen – war mehr oder weniger auch, dass die Chance dagewesen wäre zu sagen: „Lasst uns alles viel mehr ausarbeiten. Lasst uns alles viel später machen." Dann hätten wir vielleicht nicht diese Pausen gehabt und die Liste der Materialien [wäre vollständiger gewesen] und solche Dinge. Ich denke wir hatten das Gefühl, dass die Probleme vor allem im letzten Jahr, in zunehmend konkurrierenden Situationen um sehr viele große Ausstellungen und ähnlichem zu sein – also sehr öffentliche, äußerst schlechte Erfahrungen in unterschiedlichen künstlerischen Gruppen – diese Situation auf eine kollektivere Ebene zu bringen und diese kollektive Ebene auf der Basis dieses Materials, auf der Grundlage dieser Geschichte zu initiieren. Der Versuch, einen Diskurs zu entwickeln – nicht als unseren oder Andreas Diskurs, nicht als Andreas Kunst oder so etwas, oder als meinen kuratorischen Diskurs über irgendetwas – sondern tatsächlich etwas darüber hinauszugehen.

Ich glaube wirklich, dass der Begriff „Dienstleistungen" insofern interessant war, für mich zumindest, weil er die Möglichkeit zur Integration bietet. Ich meine damit nicht, dass es keine Unterschiede zwischen den verschiedenen Bereichen gibt – sagen wir, zwischen einem alternativen Raum oder alternativen Interessen oder geopolitischen Interessen einer Initiative bis hin zu den Interessen eines Direktors der Neuen Galerie in Dresden – sondern dass die Dienstleistungsorientierung auf schematischer Basis von ihnen allen geteilt wird. Somit ist es ein Versuch – ich meine, überhaupt nicht, um einen Kompromiss zu finden –, aber um ein Gespräch zu ermöglichen, das über die nicht so positive Situation, die in den letzten Jahren zu spüren war, hinausgeht. Und ich denke, darum geht es. Ich würde sagen, wir sollten wahrscheinlich versuchen, ein wenig auf diese Ebene zurückzukommen, auf der wir in gewisser Weise angefangen haben. Ich meine, es gibt hier natürlich noch viele andere Gründe, die mit der Entwicklung von verschiedenen Geschichten und Verläufen zu tun haben, aber das ist es…ich meine, das war's.

Judith Barry: Meiner Meinung nach kamen Martins Punkt und dein Punkt [Helmut] sehr gut an, weil es in den Vorträgen faszinierend war, die individuellen Erfahrungen von allen Beteiligten zu hören. Allerdings denke ich, dass es möglicherweise gut wäre, die letzten Momente damit zu verbringen, die Dinge miteinander zu verknüpfen, um bestimmte Fragen oder Vorstellungen zu unterstreichen. Meine Frage an einige der Kurator*innen, diejenigen unter euch, die ortspezifische Ausstellungen gemacht haben: Was denkt ihr über die letzten zwei Jahre bezüglich dessen, was ihr produziert habt und der Organisation dieser ortspezifischen Ausstellungen und der Rückstände, die sie hinterlassen haben? Und Künstler*innen stelle ich ähnliche Fragen. Es scheint mir – und das wurde nicht wirklich erwähnt –, dass Künstler*innen und Kurator*innen in ortspezifischen Ausstellungen mehr Zeit damit verbringen zusammenzuarbeiten, als in konventionelleren Ausstellungen. Und dass es in diesen Momenten der Zusammenarbeit ist, dass diese neuen institutionellen Rahmen ein wenig verbogen werden, verwandelt oder sogar verändert. Proaktiv gedacht frage ich mich einfach – wenn man bedenkt, dass diese Modelle so entwickelt und geschmiedet werden könnten, dass die Diskussion nicht immer so zwiespältig ist: Künstler*innen auf einer Seite und Kurator*innen und/oder Institutionen auf der anderen, was bei diesen großen Ausstellungen oft der Fall ist.

Vielleicht würde das zu einer Annäherung führen. Das war für mich in der letzten Sitzung besonders interessant.

Bischoff: Ich möchte eine Frage stellen, die wir nicht speziell an die

Künstler*innen gerichtet haben. Macht es für euch einen großen Unterschied, ob ihr eine Ausstellung mit Fragen von Institutionen und anderen in einem alternativen Raum, einem normalen Museum oder in einer privaten Galerie macht? Ich glaube, wir haben nicht über Privatgalerien gesprochen und ich weiß beispielsweise, dass du [Andrea] dich tatsächlich an mich aus einer Galerie in Köln erinnert hast. Es gibt Privatgalerie-Kontexte, und macht das für die Künstler*innen einen großen Unterschied?

Fraser: Nun, wir haben eine Frage an die Künstler*innen und eine Frage an die Kurator*innen. Wer von euch möchte beginnen?

Ute Meta Bauer: Zu deiner Frage, bevor ich anfing in Stuttgart [als künstlerische Leiterin] zu arbeiten, habe ich an einem Projekt in Hamburg gearbeitet, das Hamburg Project hieß. Es ging um Kunst im öffentlichen Raum. Und ich habe beispielsweise mit Michael Asher gearbeitet, der alle Personen erwähnt hat, die an der Ausstellungsbroschüre, die für sein Projekt produziert wurde, gearbeitet haben. Dann gab es andere Künstler*innen. Wir haben wochenlang wirklich hart gearbeitet, und die Leute [Assistent*innen und andere Personen, die Vorarbeiten für die Künstler*innen erledigten] haben wirklich gearbeitet. Und es wurde ihnen wenig bezahlt… Es gab Künstler*innen, die waren so schrecklich zu ihnen. Und teilweise war es am Ende so, dass es zwar ihre Arbeit [der Künstler*innen] war, aber sie nur eine Skizze geschickt hatten. Nach diesem Projekt war ich sehr glücklich, nach Stuttgart zu gehen und mit Künstler*innen zu arbeiten, die ich selbst aussuchen konnte. Manchmal ist es wirklich… Was sie [Künstler*innen] von einem erwarten und wie sie die Menschen behandeln… Ich meine, man hat es wirklich satt. Vor allem, wenn man an ortspezifischen Projekten arbeitet, an denen viele Personen beteiligt sind. Mit anderen Künstler*innen, die immer deine Arbeit [als Kurator*in] respektieren, wie wir erwähnt haben, Dan Graham oder Michael Asher oder Lawrence Weiner zum Beispiel – man arbeitet gern mit ihnen. Und es ist ehrlich… Ja, ich denke es gibt noch viel mehr, als das, was wir hier besprochen haben. Was die Künstler*innen von einem erwarten und wie man sich manchmal fühlt…wie eine wirkliche „Dienstleisterin", die den ganzen Scheiß für sie erledigen muss. Und am Ende steht schließlich ihr Name auf der Einladungskarte, und es ist ihre Vernissage und die Leute, die hart gearbeitet haben [die Personen, die Vorarbeit leisten und Assistent*innen] – ich meine, sie werden nicht einmal zu den Essen eingeladen. Und ich finde, Künstler*innen, die auf diese Art arbeiten, haben auch Verantwortung. Wenn man beispielsweise einen Film dreht, dann wird der oder die Regisseur*in erwähnt, aber all die anderen Personen auch. Ich denke, diese Künstler*innen sollten auch über Autor*innenschaft nachdenken und darüber, welche Rolle sie in dieser Arbeit haben, und sie sollten das ein wenig mehr teilen und etwas transparenter sein.

(Wilson und Müller fangen gleichzeitig an zu sprechen)

Wilson: Es tut mir leid, aber ich glaube, es funktioniert in beide Richtungen.

Christian Philipp Müller: Nein…

Wilson: Denn manchmal war ich in Situationen, in denen die Kurator*innen nicht wollten, dass man all diese Leute mitbringt, die so hart gearbeitet haben und sie wollen nicht, dass man sie auflistet, weil sie dieses veränderte Modell nicht kennen. Es ist eine großartige Situation, wenn die Kurator*innen gleicher Meinung sind, aber manchmal habe ich es gegenteilig empfunden: dass die Kurator*innen das alte System von Kurator*in und Künstler*in mögen und sich irgendwie ausmalen, dass sonst niemand an dem Projekt beteiligt war.

Fraser: Es muss meiner Meinung nach aber als Assistenz anerkannt werden. Ich meine einfach… In Ordnung, du zuerst [Christian].

Müller: Ich wollte bloß Ute danken. Denn diese Idee, den Abspann eines Films nachzumachen, ist wirklich gut, und das sollten wir versuchen auszuarbeiten. Nicht nur für die Assistent*innen der Künstler*innen, sondern auch für die Assistent*innen der Kurator*innen. Ich meine, so viele große Ausstellungen werden tatsächlich von den Assistent*innen produziert, die überhaupt nicht bezahlt werden. Und die Nennungen in den Credits sollten sehr viel länger und breiter sein und…

Fraser: In Bezug auf den Punkt, den ich allerdings ansprechen wollte – und ich schätze, es ist derselbe Punkt wie vorher [zu den Personen, die Vorarbeit leisten und Assistent*innen], aber es ist ein System, bei dem…es tut mir leid, fahr du fort [Christian].

Müller: Ich wollte nur sagen, dass auf beiden Seiten einfach mehr Personen beteiligt sind als nur die Star-Kurator*innen und die Star-Künstler*innen. Und diese Leute sollten irgendwie erwähnt werden. Ich meine…

Fraser: Es geht aber nicht nur darum, dass sie bloß erwähnt werden, sondern sie sollten…

Müller: Sie sollten mit einbezogen werden!

Fraser: Es sollte ein klares System geben, in dem die Arbeitsweise und die Ressourcen, die erforderlich sind, um diese Art Projekt durchzuführen, die Künstler*innen und Institutionen wollen, die öffentliche Kunstagenturen wollen, die Kulturministerien wollen, die Vorstandsmitglieder wollen, dass die notwendigen Konditionen und Ressourcen und die Arbeit klar benannt werden sollten, und ein gerechtes Verteilungssystem für diese Dinge ausformuliert wird. Denn ansonsten haben wir dieses System, in dem man, naja, wenn man in einer bestimmten Situation ganz oben ist, kann man alle anderen ausbeuten. Und sonst ist man ganz unten. Und diese Positionen verschieben sich, ob es die *Metropolis* Ausstellung [*Metropolis. Internationale Kunstausstellung*, Martin-Gropius-Bau, Berlin 1991] ist, bei der die Künstler*innen nicht zur Vernissage eingeladen werden, oder ob es das Hamburg Project ist, bei dem die Mitarbeiter*innen, die an der Ausstellung gearbeitet haben, nicht zur Vernissage eingeladen werden. Diese Positionen kursieren, weil es nicht – Iwona oder Susan? Iwona?

Blazwick: Ich möchte mich noch einmal zu dieser Erfahrung äußern, in einer Art Vermittlerinnenposition zu arbeiten, in der man weder zur Institution gehört noch Künstler*in ist, sondern in gewissem Sinne wie ein sekundärer Agent fungiert. Ich denke, dass diese Rolle ein wenig Filmproduzent*innen ähnelt, da man viele verschiedene Agenden und unterschiedliche Interessengemeinschaften navigieren muss. Und meiner Meinung nach war einer der Gründe, warum das Projekt [Antwerp 93] scheiterte, genau dieses Thema, dass sowohl die Einführung in die ganze Angelegenheit es schaffen sollte, gewissermaßen alle Personen, die teilgenommen haben, mitzunehmen und Informationen zu vermitteln. Und dann ist es ein sehr langer und komplexer Prozess, überhaupt einen Diskurs zu teilen und eine Basis für ein Verständnis dafür zu schaffen, was geschehen wird. Und es daraufhin fast schon in das Projekt einzubauen, das man macht. Weil es im Grunde dieses Syndrom ist – und ich glaube, das ist in Sonsbeek 93 passiert und ich weiß nicht, ob es in Chicago [für die Ausstellung *Culture in Action*, 1993] zutrifft? Nun, wenn entweder ein*e Künstler*in oder ein*e Kurator*in oder die Person, die an dem Projekt beteiligt ist, es nicht einfach nur eröffnet und dann wieder verlässt, sondern tatsächlich während des gesamten Projektverlaufs in gewisser Weise wesentlich an seiner Lebensdauer beteiligt ist. Es gibt alle möglichen banalen Aspekte der Instandhaltung, die absolut wichtig dafür sind, wie die Arbeit ankommt und wie viele Informationen man darüber zur Verfügung stellen kann und was für einen Zugang sie erfährt und was für eine Bedeutung sie hat. Und meine Enttäuschung darüber – am Tag nach der Eröffnung, zack, das war's. Es gab keine Möglichkeit für uns [die Teilnehmer*innen] zu

bleiben, es gab kein Geld, es gab kein Protokoll. Das erzeugte große Probleme für alle Beteiligten.

Fraser: Ich glaube, Susan war als nächstes dran.

Cahan: Danke, aber falls du willst…

Müller: Ich wollte bloß einen ganz kleinen Kommentar über Chicago machen. (Lacht) Es gab zwei zentrale Unterschiede oder Wege, das zu tun. Extreme Personen wie Mark Dion, der die ganze Zeit dort bleibt und ständig seine Studierenden unterrichtet. Das ist völlige Selbstausbeutung. Und wieder andere schicken dann einfach einen Vorschlag in dieselbe Ausstellung, in der es nur acht Künstler*innen gibt. Das war's. Ich denke, beide Wege sind extrem – man sollte sich irgendwo in der Mitte treffen.

Cahan: Nun, ich bin weder Künstlerin noch Kuratorin. Als Pädagogin hatte ich aber die Möglichkeit, mit Künstler*innen in einer pädagogischen Funktion und mit ihnen an ihren Ausstellungsbeiträgen zu arbeiten. Was ich bemerkt habe ist, dass Künstler*innen, die mit mir an Vermittlungsprojekten arbeiten, in gewisser Hinsicht viel weniger persönliches Engagement zeigen – oder ihr persönliches Engagement völlig anders ist als die Arbeit mit mir am New Museum [in New York], im Gegensatz zu ihrem künstlerischen Beitrag für eine Ausstellung. Und ich habe festgestellt, dass wenn ich mit Künstler*innen arbeite, deren projektbezogene Arbeit ihr Beitrag zur Ausstellung ist – ihr Kunstwerk – dass es dazu führt, dass auf einmal die Rahmenbedingungen oder Grenzen dieser Projekte plötzlich… nun ja, sie verschwinden. Bestimmte

Grenzen und bestimmte Arten…

Ich habe die Erfahrung gemacht, dass es viel schwieriger wird, die Projekte zu verwalten, dass die Künstler*innen bestimmte Dinge, die ich normalerweise voraussetze, nicht unbedingt voraussetzen. Jeder Punkt muss also auf eine Art neu verhandelt oder überhaupt verhandelt werden. Viele der Projekte, von denen wir in den letzten zwei Tagen gehört haben – und woran ich insbesondere denke, ist Laurie Parsons Projekt [*The Spatial Drive: Security and Admissions Project*, 1991-92], an dem ich im New Museum beteiligt war, bei dem ihre Intention wirklich darin bestand, den normalen Ablauf des Museums durcheinanderzubringen, indem sie das Aufsichtspersonal zu Pädagog*innen umfunktioniert. Das bedeutete für meine Rolle als Vermittlungsdirektorin, dass ich ihr als Künstlerin ein großes Maß an Autorität übergeben musste. Die Rolle des Aufsichtspersonals hat sich völlig verändert. Ich meine, das ganze Museum wurde überholt. Die Kuratorin wurde dann sozusagen die Vermittlungskoordinatorin. Es war extrem kompliziert. Und wir haben alle mitgemacht. Fakt war allerdings, dass es dann sehr schwierig wurde zu wissen, was wir überhaupt machen sollten, um unsere Arbeit durchzuführen. Ich denke, das hat eine Menge Herausforderungen und Probleme geschaffen. Es hat ebenfalls viele Möglichkeiten und viel Spannung erzeugt. Ein Ergebnis dieses Projekts war, dass unser Aufsichtspersonal nun weiterhin an Seminaren mit Künstler*innen, die am New Museum ausstellen, teilnehmen, und sie fungieren immer noch informell als Vermittler*innen in den Ausstellungsräumen.

Es scheint mir allerdings, dass es bei vielen der Projekte, die wir hier diskutieren, etwas wesentlich Störendes gibt, und so schafft es neue Faktoren und neue Variablen, auf die es zu diesem Zeitpunkt nicht unbedingt kodifizierte Antworten gibt und auf die es im Wesentlichen keine kodifizierten Antworten geben wird.

Fraser: Renée?

Green: Ich wollte dem einfach folgen oder unterstreichen, was Susan gesagt hat, nur bezüglich der Arbeitserfahrungen mit Museen, und ich dachte über diese Idee der Störung nach. Auf diese Weise, die aber eigentlich ziemlich interessant ist und die Art und Weise beeinflussen kann, wie die verschiedenen Menschen, die im Museum arbeiten, fungieren. Meiner Erfahrung nach hatte es etwas damit zu tun – eigentlich aus der Perspektive meiner Arbeit in der Vermittlungsabteilung am New Museum –, andere Wege der Kommunikation mit dem Publikum zu entwickeln und dann irgendwie auf die verschiedenen Personen, die im Museum arbeiten, sensibel zu reagieren. Das hat sich aus bestimmten Problemen entwickelt, die ich wahrgenommen habe, als ich am New Museum war, weil wir viele Gespräche geführt haben, an denen alle beteiligt sein sollten und wir versucht haben, die Idee der Hierarchie im Museum und all diese Dinge zu hinterfragen.

Bezüglich eines konkreten Beispiels habe ich allerdings daran gedacht, wie ich mit dem MOCA [Museum of Contemporary Art] in L.A. gearbeitet habe. Als ich damals dort für längere Zeit an einem Projekt tätig war, meiner Ausstellung, kam ich mehrfach zu Besuch und traf mich mit Personen aus allen Bereichen. In dieser Zeit wurden die Personen also von Anfang an über das Projekt informiert. Ich glaube, die ersten Personen, mit denen ich mich getroffen habe, war das Produktionsteam, um zu versuchen, ein Verhältnis mit ihnen aufzubauen, anstatt sie nur als die Personen zu betrachten, die die Sache ausführen, ohne ein Verständnis davon zu haben, worum es bei der Arbeit geht. Zu versuchen, sich wirklich mit all den verschiedenen Gruppen zu treffen. Und das wurde am Anfang auch [vom MOCA] unterstützt. Das wollte die Kuratorin – zumindest offiziell. Und das versuchte ich zu tun. Was glaube ich geschah, war, dass ich sehr damit beschäftigt war, meine eigenen Verbindungen mit den Personen aus allen Bereichen aufzubauen. Ich war also direkt mit der Produktionsabteilung in Kontakt, und ich habe mit der Vermittlungsabteilung gearbeitet, ich war direkt mit der Publikationsabteilung in Kontakt – mit all den verschiedenen Abteilungen des Museums, die an der Ausstellung beteiligt waren. Es lag mir sehr daran, eine Art Zugang zu ihnen zu haben. Was im Verlauf der Ausstellung passierte, war, was du [Susan] erwähnt hast, und zwar diese Art der Störung, sodass die Kuratorin verwirrt darüber war, was ihre Rolle im Verhältnis zu mir war. Es war, als wäre ich eine Art Regisseurin von allem geworden, und es gab deshalb tatsächlich verschiedene Konfrontationen. Ich meine, sie hatte das Gefühl, als wäre sie eine Sozialarbeiterin. Es war so, als sei sie die Vermittlungszuständige, und das war sehr interessant in Bezug darauf, wie die Rolle wahrgenommen wurde. Deshalb glaube ich, dass es nützlich wäre, öfter so zu arbeiten, um die Institutionen auf die Art zu öffnen, in der wir denke ich über sie sprechen. Und das war sehr intensiv.

Bischoff: Das ist ein privater Raum, oder? Ich frage nach eurer Erfahrung: Gibt es einen Unterschied, wo ihr lieber Ausstellungen machen würdet, denn beispielsweise weiß ich, dass einige der Künstler*innen hier mit einer [privaten] Galerie in Köln zusammengearbeitet haben.

Fraser: Ich denke zum größten Teil…

Guttmann: Die Mehrheit der Künstler*innen…

(Gelächter)

Green: Auf welche Weise kontextualisieren sie das Arbeiten in der Galerie selbst, meinst du?

Fraser: So wie ich es verstehe, ist es eine völlig andere Sache. Ich meine, es gibt viele Probleme, von denen ich denke, dass die Künstler*innen hier – soweit ich aus meinen Diskussionen mit euch feststellen kann – sich auch sehr gerne damit beschäftigen und auseinandersetzen würden. Ich glaube aber, das ist ein Thema für ein anderes Forum.

Guttmann: Es ist wahrscheinlich in Ordnung zu behaupten, dass viele Personen, die hier anwesend sind, ein gewisses Problem damit haben, ausschließlich mit Galerien zu arbeiten.

Bischoff: Es ist aber eine andere Art von Institution. Es ist also möglich, dies gemeinsam mit…zu diskutieren…

(Stimmen, die durcheinander sprechen)

Michael Clegg: …Wir sprechen eher von Museen, weil es in der privaten Sphäre bestimmte Probleme mit

Galerien gibt. Es gibt einen Grund dafür. Ich meine, wir können das definitiv vertiefen und darüber sprechen, aber es gibt eine ganze Reihe anderer Probleme. Strukturell gibt es allerdings einen Grund dafür, dass es noch nicht wirklich erwähnt wurde, da es eine Art Wandel der Möglichkeiten gegeben hat –

Draxler: Projekte und Dienstleistungen sind aber dazu bestimmt, organisatorische Probleme zu erzeugen, die wir hier diskutieren wollten, und was wir eigentlich nicht getan haben. Und das findet im Moment außerhalb der Galerie, der Sammler*in und der Museumssysteme statt. Die Frage war also auch an das Museum gerichtet: Wie arbeitet das Museum mit bestimmten Arten von Praktiken?

Cahan: Wenn Künstler*innen in Institutionen gehen, um einige der Dinge zu tun, über die wir gesprochen haben, tun sie das oft unter – ich meine, ich weiß nicht, ob sie es oft so machen. Ich weiß aber beispielsweise von dir, Fred, als du nach Baltimore gegangen bist, hast du bestimmte Konditionen gehabt und die Freiheiten, die du dir selbst nimmst, sind eigentlich viel größer als die Freiheiten, die viele Museumsfachleute in ihrer eigenen Arbeit haben. Die Beziehungen mit Verantwortung sind für Künstler*innen sehr, sehr unterschiedlich. Worüber du gesprochen hast, Renée. Ich meine, das ist für mich als Museumsmitarbeiterin eine der größten Herausforderungen, die man in der Zusammenarbeit mit Künstler*innen in dieser Funktion hat.

Wilson: Ich meine, deren Einschränkungen [der Museumsmitarbeiter*innen] sind selbst auferlegt.

Sie werden durch den Begriff der „reinen Wissenschaft" bestimmt. Ich meine, mehr ist es wirklich nicht.

Cahan: Es ist ebenfalls sehr logistisch.

Wilson: Was meinst du?

Cahan: Nun ja.

Wilson: Ich glaube nicht daran, etwas zu tun, was einer Arbeit schaden würde oder gegen die Konservator*innen etwas einzuwenden hätten oder so etwas. Woran ich allerings arbeite, ist der Bereich, der eine konstruierte Realität ist, die nicht wirklich existiert – aber im Laufe der Geschichte der Museen wurde diese Museumstruktur entwickelt, und es gibt eigentlich überhaupt keinen Grund dafür. Deswegen haben Kurator*innen, die in dieser Struktur arbeiten, Angst aus ihr auszubrechen, aus einer Art Erwartungsdruck.

Guttmann: Ich glaube, es gibt noch einen weiteren Punkt für die Fortsetzung, zumindest meiner Meinung nach, und zwar die Diskussion über das Verhältnis zwischen Kunst als Institution. Ich denke, das sollte verallgemeinert werden, tatsächlich über die Frage hinaus, wie Künstler*innen mit Museen zusammenarbeiten. Und ich denke, dass viele von uns diesen Punkt in verschiedenen einzelnen Vorträgen formuliert haben, aber irgendwie wieder dort hineingezogen werden, und ich denke, es ist sehr wichtig, diesen Punkt noch einmal zu betonen.

Ich denke, dass wenn ich etwas in diese Idee der „Dienstleistungen" hineininterpretieren würde, wäre es, dass wir Museen als besondere Atmosphären betrachten sollten, mit denen Künstler*innen arbeiten können, und nicht als etwas, das ihre künstlerischen Aktivitäten definiert. Mit anderen Worten ist es ein Weg, wie man die Frage der Museen normalisieren und sagen kann, dass diese Einrichtungen eine bestimmte Art von Atmosphäre sind, vielleicht sogar Gemeinschaften, die ihre eigenen Probleme haben. Vor allem bei Fred – als ich hörte, wie du über deine Erfahrung gesprochen hast, wurde es wirklich sehr deutlich, wie es auf einmal dazu kam, dass du auf der Liste des Museums [von begehrenswerten Künstler*innen, mit denen man arbeiten will] standest, dass dies wirklich spezielle Umgebungen sind, die spezielle Probleme haben. Möglicherweise sind es Gemeinschaften; vielleicht ist ein Teil der Absicht der „Dienstleistungen", die Institution als Gemeinschaft zu betrachten, als Umgebung. Die Voraussetzung dafür ist aber, dass die Diskussion auf einer abstrakteren Ebene geführt wird. Mit anderen Worten, im Grunde nicht über Museen zu sprechen, sondern eher über die Frage des „Aktivismus", der zwischen Künstler*innen stattfindet, die mehr oder weniger privat agieren, außer sie organisieren sich als Gruppe, und „Institutionen", deren Existenz dauerhafter ist…sie haben ihr eigenes Budget und identifizieren eigene Problematiken. Über Aktivitäten nachzudenken, die das Thema der Kunst innerhalb institutioneller Umfelder verhandeln und zwar auf eine Art, bei der das ganze Problem der „Museen" wirklich zweitrangig wird. Mit anderen Worten, dass analoge Themen angewandt werden können.

Beispielsweise, wenn ein*e Künstler*in – dies ist nur ein Beispiel – von einer Arbeiter*innengewerkschaft konfrontiert wird oder von einer Universität oder von anderen Arten von Institutionen, die sagen: „Nun, hier ist ein Umfeld. Hier ist eine Gemeinschaft, Sie haben Erfahrung damit, in Umfeldern und Gemeinschaften zu arbeiten. Glauben Sie, dass ein Teil Ihrer Aktivitäten in diese Art von Institution eingebunden werden kann?" Meine Meinung ist, dass viele Probleme, die wirklich die Verhältnisse zu Museen definieren, im Grunde überschaubar sind. Wisst ihr, ich glaube aber, es ist einfach so, dass vieles, das speziell mit dem Museum zusammenhängt, ziemlich schnell, sehr banal werden kann. Ich meine, es ist nur eine Struktur, nur eine Institution. Das ist wichtig, aber es ist wirklich nicht das einzige Thema, das besprochen werden sollte.

Bauer: Trotzdem, vom Standpunkt der Künstler*innen aus… Ich meine, wie betrachtest du deine Arbeit, und was definierst du als deine Arbeit, und wie übernimmst du die Kontrolle über diese Arbeit?

Guttmann: Es ist kompliziert.

Bauer: Es ist kompliziert. Ich meine, aus diesem Grund sind wir hier.

Guttmann: Das Leben ist keine Versicherungsgesellschaft.

Bauer: Ich wundere mich manchmal, mit welcher Leichtigkeit Künstler*innen ihre Arbeiten verkaufen. Und das lässt sich auf jeden Kontext übertragen – ich meine, glaubst du, es ist so, dass man den Arm abschneiden kann und dann gehört er nicht mehr zu einem? Als Beispiel: ich meine, wenn du diesen Vertrag siehst, den du haben willst, ob sie [eine Arbeit] verkauft oder wiederverkauft wird, dann möchte man wissen, wo sie hingeht… Vielen

Künstler*innen ist es egal, wo sie hingeht. Ich meine, die Arbeit besteht für sie darin, sie anzufertigen, und wenn sie dann weg ist, ist es wie etwas, das nichts mehr mit ihnen zu tun hat.

Guttmann: Über welchen Vertrag sprichst du?

Fraser: Den Wiederverkaufsvertrag.

Guttmann: Ach so, den Wiederverkaufsvertrag.

Bauer: Wie handhabt man das mit Worten, die dann zum Beispiel nicht länger ein Gemälde, oder etwas anderes darstellen? Wie wird man mit so etwas fertig?

Guttmann: Das scheint mir die eigentliche Idee der „Dienstleistungen" zu sein, nicht wahr? Vielleicht ist das nur meine eigene Interpretation. Ich denke allerdings, hinter der Idee der Dienstleistungen steht der Versuch, künstlerische Tätigkeit jenseits der Einschränkungen für bestehende Ideen zu verallgemeinern. Und die Idee der Dienstleistungen kann man auf das Museum anwenden, aber es kann sich auch auf andere Institutionen beziehen, und die Idee der Dienstleistungen hat eine integrierte Fähigkeit, den Kunstbegriff zu erweitern. Zumindest sehe ich es so –

Fraser: Ja, nach dem, was du gerade gesagt hast – ich habe das Ende nicht gehört, aber ich finde es bedauerlich, dass Mark Dion nicht hier sein konnte, weil er Erfahrungen mit Konservierungsinstitutionen und Organisationen hat, wie beispielsweise Zoos und Umweltaktivist*innenorganisationen. Und er kann euch Geschichten darüber erzählen, wie

schwierig es ist, dort einen Fuß in die Tür zu bekommen und wie völlig desinteressiert sie daran sind, mit Künstler*innen zusammenzuarbeiten, also…es ist nur ein Kommentar. Es ist nicht wirklich eine Antwort. Ja, Vera?

Publikum (Vera Kockot, Studentin): Zu diesem Punkt möchte ich noch einmal erwähnen, dass es hier meiner Meinung nach die Möglichkeit gibt, dass die Universität helfen könnte, Definitionen zu finden, die schon in anderen Theorien existieren, und es einen Austausch geben könnte. So dass ein Modell der Dienstleistung präsentiert und diskutiert werden könnte und man könnte sehen, ob es Überschneidungen im System gibt oder nicht. Man könnte also die verschiedenen anderen Systeme miteinander vergleichen, und möglicherweise könnte es einen Austausch verschiedener Theorien geben, um zu erklären, was im Kunstsystem geschieht. Sie haben von dieser speziellen Erfahrung mit Kunstsystemen gesprochen, aber ich glaube, es gibt auch viele Gemeinsamkeiten mit anderen Systemen. Wie Sie erwähnt haben, Andrea, dass Dion Erfahrungen mit anderen Systemen hatte, und wie in einem anderen Kontext bereits gesagt wurde, sind wir alle Teil anderer Gemeinschaften und haben Erfahrungen mit eventuell ähnlichen Strukturen. Ich denke also, das könnte ein guter Austausch zwischen den beiden Bereichen sein: dem akademischen und dem Kunstbereich. Vielleicht könnte das etwas sein – wenn dieses Forum weitergeführt würde – wo jede Seite der anderen Informationen liefern könnte. Und ich denke, andererseits, für die Universität ist es auch sehr interessant, wie sie mit bedeutungslosen

Dingen umgeht. Denn in der Hochschulwelt gibt es ebenfalls Vorträge, und sie hängen damit zusammen, wie berühmt eine Person ist, und in welcher Universität man etwas präsentiert, und so weiter. Es gibt also Gemeinsamkeiten zwischen diesen beiden Systemen. Vielleicht ist das also einfach ein kleiner Kommentar zu dem, was Martin gerade gesagt hat, zur Idee der Dienstleistungen.

Green: Ich denke, das ist wirklich ein hilfreicher Punkt. Ich denke, das ist ein interessanter Punkt und ich denke, es hat damit zu tun, was Susan vorhin gesagt hat, das Thema der Kulturwissenschaften hervorzuheben und wie die Praktiken verschiedener Personen sich mit dem Bereich der Kulturwissenschaften überschneiden. Ich dachte tatsächlich, dass einige der Diskussionen, die wir hier führen, irgendwann verdeutlicht werden, oder wir könnten einige Ideen aus anderen Bereichen verwenden – zum Beispiel aus der Wirtschaft oder verschiedenen Bereichen der Sozialwissenschaften –, um einiges, was wir hier tun, zu analysieren. Nicht unbedingt abschließend, aber einfach, um sie besser zu veranschaulichen. Ich meine, Susan, du hattest das vorhin erwähnt: verschiedene Methoden anzuwenden und dass bestimmte Methoden hilfreich sein könnten. Du hattest Literaturkritik als ein nützliches Modell erwähnt, um sich auf eine Art an einen visuellen Bereich anzugleichen. Das schien etwas Konkretes zu sein, das tatsächlich möglich wäre.

Fraser: Ein Teil des Ansporns für mich, diese Veranstaltung [diese Arbeitsgruppe] zu organisieren, ist mein Gefühl, dass während es einen Nutzen für Mitglieder der künstlerischen Gemeinschaft innerhalb der akademischen Diskurse hatte, es bisher keinen Austausch gegeben hat. Weil es eine Hierarchie zwischen theoretischem und praktischem Wissen gibt, kann es meiner Meinung nach keinen wahren Austausch geben, bis dies gelöst wird. Mein Interesse war, ein Forum für diese Art von praktischem Wissen zu entwickeln. Und dann ist die zweite Frage als Antwort auf Ihren Kommentar [Vera], es ist eine Frage über die Nutzung und wofür es genutzt wird. Und was sind die Konditionen des Nutzens und was… Ich meine, das könnte uns zu der Frage der Dienstleistung zurückführen, zu einer anderen Bedeutung von Dienstleistung.

Clegg: Eine Hoffnung, die wir für diese Zusammenkunft haben und über die wir in unserer ersten Kommentarrunde gesprochen haben, war ein plötzliches Interesse daran zu sehen, ob sich hier ein Diskurs entwickeln könnte, der zu einem Gemeinschaftsgefühl wird. Uns in der Lage zu befinden, dass wir unsere Praktiken in einem Modus besprechen können, der etwas anders ist. Ich habe das auch während der letzten Pause mit einigen Personen besprochen und ich glaube, es gab eine Art Konsens, dass wir alle dachten, dass dieser Anlass etwas Besonderes ist, weil wir tatsächlich mit sehr unterschiedlichen Formen vertraut sind, einander öffentlich anzusprechen. Natürlich ist es damit verbunden, warum es sinnvoll ist, dass dies eine Arbeitsgruppe ist – wir hatten das Gefühl, dass es eine Möglichkeit gab, einander zuzuhören, nicht die Impulse zu haben, die man oft in diesen Diskussionen findet, Unterschiede zu erkunden und einander anzugreifen, indem man seine eigene Praxis markiert. Ich möchte also nur sagen, dass es ein weiterer Punkt ist, der sich ergeben hat. Es bietet uns eine Möglichkeit für etwas, dass mit der Weiterführung dieses Projekts verbunden werden kann. Es wäre interessant, ein wenig mehr darüber zu hören, wie ihr [Andrea und Helmut] genau gedenkt, das zu tun. Was ich aber durchaus für nützlich halte, ist, solch eine Möglichkeit vor Augen zu haben. Für mich war dies eine sehr wertvolle Erfahrung. Ich möchte aber einfach fragen, was ihr technisch gesehen denkt, wie…

Draxler: Ich denke, wenn wir das [*Services* Projekt] weiterführen wollen, sollten wir jetzt dazu in der Lage sein, einige Gründe dafür zu nennen. Ich meine, das hier war eine Art Umriss. Wir sollten jetzt aber nicht sagen: „Okay, lasst es uns noch einmal machen", denn ihr wisst, wenn es nie passiert, dann ist es klar. Es sollte allerdings eine Art…

Ich glaube, wir haben einige der Diskussionen zu einem sehr interessanten Punkt gebracht, weil wir zu diesen leidenschaftlichen politischen Strategien und so gekommen sind. Beispielsweise wie man Institutionen anspricht, was sehr kompliziert ist, und wie man innerhalb von Institutionen arbeitet, und mit Künstler*innen arbeitet, oder mit wem auch immer. Und dieses Interesse zu haben. Ich glaube, dass wir alle in einer nicht so klar definierten Situation wie dieser leben. Es gibt einige andere Modelle hier, die sehr eindeutig sind – was wir eher im politischen Sinne tun – aber ich glaube, dass die meisten von uns nicht so leben; die meisten von uns leben in sehr widersprüchlichen Situationen, und wir versuchen Klarheit zu finden. Und

ich glaube, dass dies auch ein sehr wichtiger Punkt ist. Ich meine, wir sind nicht einmal zu einer praktischen Diskussion gekommen, und das ist natürlich sehr wichtig, und ich bin sicher, es gibt Gründe dafür. Ich denke aber, diese praktischen Diskussionen sollten stattfinden, in einem bestimmten Bezug zu diesen politischen Diskussionspunkten über den Sinn dessen, was wir tun. Mit dem Begriff „Dienstleistungen" wurde versucht, genau das miteinander zu kombinieren. Es wäre notwendig gewesen, diesen Begriff auf eine eher historische Weise zu verdeutlichen, zu sagen: „Was bedeutet er vor allem im Verhältnis zu Produktion im klassischen Sinne?" Und was ist, mehr oder weniger, aus dem produktivistischen Ideal der künstlerischen Produktion geworden? Und wie diese Dinge mit dem Begriff „Dienstleistungen" verknüpft werden können. Oder, wenn man zu dem Ergebnis kommt, dass es nicht möglich ist, es auf diese Weise zu tun, dann sollten wir den Begriff wahrscheinlich vergessen: „Es geht nicht um den Begriff ‚Dienstleistungen'. Ja, darum geht es nicht." Er sollte nur hilfreich sein, um ein paar Punkte zu verdeutlichen, weil wir diese Punkte verdeutlichen müssen. Ansonsten, würde ich sagen, ist es absolut nutzlos, es [diese Services Arbeitsgruppe] zu wiederholen.

Fraser: Welcher Punkt ist klar?

(Gelächter)

Guttmann: Nein, aber ernsthaft: Wie hattest du gedacht, es weiterzuführen? Du hattest etwas im Kopf, richtig?

Fraser: Oh, ich hatte einen großen Plan! Ja, ich dachte daran, es nicht unbedingt mit den gleichen Teilnehmer*innen weiterzuführen, sondern mit ein paar anderen. Die Idee, es weiterzuführen, stammte aus einer Diskussion, die ich per Zufall mit einer Frau aus Genf geführt habe. Zum gleichen Zeitpunkt als Helmut und ich dieses Proposal formulierten, und es schien mir ein sehr passender Kontext zu sein – ein Kontext, der vielleicht diesem etwas ähnelt, soweit ich es verstehe. Ich habe ihr also das Projekt beschrieben, und sie hat Interesse bekundet, und dann haben andere Interesse bekundet. Es geschah also auf Basis des Interesses, das bestand, bevor die Idee der Fortsetzung [der *Services* Arbeitsgruppe] in die Tat umgesetzt wurde. Obwohl ich auch dachte, dass es nicht nur um diese verschiedenen Institutionen geht, die daran interessiert sind, so etwas zu sponsern, sondern auch um die Idee, eine Publikation zu produzieren. Etwas zu produzieren, das weiter existieren könnte – eine Publikation, die als öffentliches Forum für Diskussionen existieren könnte, von dem ich nicht glaube, dass es im Moment ein Forum dafür gibt. Wisst ihr, bei vielem, was wir besprochen haben, glaube ich nicht, dass es dafür ein Forum gibt. Ich glaube es immer noch nicht. Ich meine, es ist eine andere Frage, ob es wichtige Themen sind, über die man sprechen sollte.

Green: Zum Teil geht es hier aber darum.

Fraser: Ja. So ist die Idee der Weiterführung also entstanden und die Idee, ein weiteres Projekt mit diesem Material zu schaffen. Ich meine, die Art Workers' Coalition Angelenheit, das ist irgendwie ein separater Deal,

weil dieses Zeug verschwunden ist und jemand es herausbringen sollte. Ich glaube also, das ist eine Sache für sich. Und zwar ein Buch zu entwickeln, das die verschiedenen Arten dokumentiert, wie Künstler*innen – zumindest würde ich es so beschreiben – die konkreten Verhältnisse ihrer Arbeit formalisiert haben. Ob diese Dinge in einer Institution sind oder auf einem Markt oder was sonst noch. Denn ich denke, dass das ein so zentraler Aspekt dessen ist, was Künstler*innen in den letzten fünfundzwanzig Jahren getan haben, und es ist etwas, worüber nicht geschrieben wird. Das war also meine Vision.

Bauer: Würdest du sagen, die Ausstellung sollte mit dem Material reisen?

Draxler: Ja, sicher.

Bauer: Das heißt, die Leute, die es mitnehmen [die mit der *Services* Ausstellung in die verschiedenen Institutionen reisen], bekommen einen Karton mit Fotokopien und Videoaufnahmen? Oder bekommen sie irgendwelche Instruktionen, was sie damit machen sollen oder…?

Fraser: Ich meine, das ist eine Frage, weil ich nicht möchte, dass dies *unsere* Ausstellung wird, weißt du. Es ist eine Ressource.

Bauer: Ja.

Fraser: Ich würde also dokumentieren, wie es präsentiert wurde. Und wenn du es genauso aufbauen willst, dann mache es genauso. Wenn du andere Sachen aufhängen möchtest, hänge andere auf. Falls du meinst, dass dieses Material sich beispielsweise zu sehr an einer bestimmten New Yorker Erfahrung orientiert, dann hänge einen Teil dieses Materials auf und füge noch anderes dazu.

Ich hoffe, dass die gesamte Installation vermitteln würde, das es etwas ist, das genutzt werden kann. Das ist eine genauso wichtige Voraussetzung, wie jede andere auch. Worum es hier [mit dieser Arbeitsgruppe] ging, war, ein Ausstellungsmodell zu entwickeln, das nach den Bedingungen des Gebrauchswerts definiert wird, im Gegensatz zu einer Art „Prestigewert" für Künstler*innen, für Kurator*innen oder für Institutionen. Und das dann für wen genutzt wird? Nun, für eine professionelle Gemeinschaft, für eine akademische Gemeinschaft. Hoffentlich für beide, wisst ihr. Ich denke aber, um genutzt zu werden, muss es eine offene Struktur sein, ansonsten wird es einfach übertragen, oder angeeignet, oder missbraucht.

(Langes Schweigen)

Draxler: Wir sollten also immer noch darüber nachdenken, wie wir morgen so etwas wie einen öffentlichen Vortrag halten können.

Blazwick: Wie wäre es mit einer Person für die Übersetzung? Oder ist das zu…

Fraser: Übersetzung?

Blazwick: Nun, das meiste von diesem Material ist auf Englisch, es sollte in anderen Sprachen erhältlich sein.

Draxler: Sollte es.

Fraser: Wenn man Förderung bekommt. Ja.

Draxler: Ich meine, die Universität Lüneburg hat viele Übersetzungen zu verschiedenen Themen [in der *Services* Ausstellung] gemacht. Es ist ein sehr grundlegendes Problem, mit dem wir uns viel in unserer Arbeit beschäftigen müssen. Ich glaube aber, es besteht nicht nur aus dem, was an der Wand hängt. Ich meine, das Problem liegt viel mehr in Situationen wie diesen, die auch für die Teilnehmer*innen und so weiter da sind, die in dieser Art von Struktur [nicht-Englisch-Sprecher*innen] von Anfang an völlig auschließen. Ich glaube allerdings auch, dass es absolut notwendig ist, weiterzumachen. Wir können nicht sagen, wie wir es in Wien nach verschiedenen Veranstaltungen getan haben, die ganz klar amerikanische Kunst in bestimmte Strukturen importiert haben, bei denen die Studierenden zu uns kamen und sagten: „Oh, nein, wir möchten selber." Aber es ist auch sehr typisch, dass es diesen Druck von außen gibt, in den verschiedenen gegebenen Möglichkeiten. Und daher verläuft das [die Notwendigkeit, Dinge übersetzen zu lassen] von innen nur als eine Art absolute Konkurrenz um diese wenigen Orte, die eine institutionelle Situation ausmachen. Und auf eine Weise ist die Reaktion natürlich völlig falsch. Sie ist aber sehr typisch. Wir hatten das schon mal, als Ute vor zwei Jahren ihr Symposium gemacht hat. Das war das erste, woran ich mich erinnern kann. Vom Konzept an war es bereits absolut klar, dass dieses Symposium auf Englisch stattfinden würde. Es gab verschiedene Versuche, das zu ändern und mit anderen Modellen zu arbeiten. Aber all die verschiedenen Übersetzungen, die ich bisher gehört habe, sind einfach schrecklich.

Cahan: Ich denke, dass die Frage der Übersetzung… Es sagt mir, was der Großteil dieses Materials wert ist. Mein persönlicher Wunsch ist zu erleben, wie es für Menschen zugänglicher wird. Ich hoffe, dass ihr die Arbeit an diesem Projekt fortsetzen werdet. Und in der Tat denke ich, dass ein Buch, das das historische Material und weitere Forschung einschließt, die vielleicht von den Studierenden dieses Programms generiert wird oder von Einzelnen an anderen Orten, die eventuell bestimmte Fachkenntnisse haben, eine absolut außergewöhnliche Sache wäre. Ich würde es sehr begrüßen, wenn das [*Services*] Projekt eine weiter ausgearbeitete Form annehmen würde, die dann mit einem breiteren Publikum geteilt werden könnte.

Fraser: Ich möchte eigentlich auf die Frage der Fortsetzung der Arbeitsgruppe zurückkommen, denn Material kann auf eine bestimmte Art gesammelt werden. Das ist eine separate Angelegenheit, glaube ich. Wir könnten alle Material sammeln und an einen zentralen Ort schicken. Ich meine aber, dass ich glaube, dass deine Frage…

Cahan: Es geht nicht nur darum, wieviel Material es ist. Der Rahmen des Themas ist: Wozu führt das Material?

Fraser: Nein, richtig – ich versuche das auch nicht zu reduzieren. Ich wollte eigentlich nur zu diesem anderen Punkt zurückkehren, weil es eine Frage dessen ist… Wenn ihr alle darüber sprechen könntet… Wenn das noch einmal stattfinden würde, wie würde es ablaufen, oder was wäre euer Interesse daran?

Draxler: Ja, ich meine, ich denke, das ist die Frage. Wir hätten wahrscheinlich eine Tafel verwenden sollen, auf die unternehmerische Art, um diese Punkte aufzuschreiben.

Fraser: Ich glaube, es gibt irgendwo eine Tafel, die hier hinten gelagert wird, ich kann sie hochhalten [simuliert das Hochhalten einer Tafel].

(Gelächter)

Barry: Ich denke, eine Vorgehensweise könnte sein, die Aufnahmen anzuhören [die Videoaufnahmen der Arbeitsgruppen-Sitzungen] und sie nicht unbedingt sehen zu müssen. Es kommt mir in den Sinn, wie du [Andrea] und Michael vorhin gesagt habt, dass die Universität ein sehr nützliches Hilfsmittel sein könnte, um dieses Material zu analysieren und einige Ergebnisse zu formulieren: „In Ordnung, hier gibt es Übereinstimmung, und hier gibt es Unstimmigkeit." „Es gibt einige grundlegende philosophische Fragen, die vielleicht in diesem Abschnitt zur Geltung gebracht werden könnten", und so weiter. Wir alle könnten das auch auf eine bestimmte Art tun. Ich wäre einfach interessiert daran, was wir gesagt haben, weil ich keine ausgiebigen Notizen gemacht habe. Ich denke, auf der Ebene der Analyse könnte etwas weiteres aus der Verwendung dieses Materials entstehen. Ich glaube nicht, dass es heute entstehen kann.

Green: Ich denke, dass es sehr hilfreich war, zu dem Begriff „Gebrauch" zurückzukehren. In Bezug darauf, woran ich interessiert war.

Fraser: Das ist nicht die Frage, die ich stellen möchte. Die Frage, die ich stellen möchte, ist: „Würdest du es noch einmal tun? Und wenn ja, wie würdest du – ?"

Green: Deshalb möchte ich sagen, warum ich es noch einmal machen würde. Ich meine, was die Gründe dafür wären, was die ursprüngliche Sache angeregt hat. Und dann, seit wir uns getroffen haben, und wie ich es jetzt sehe. Ich denke, es hängt damit zusammen, warum ich es wieder tun würde – wie beispielsweise sein Nutzwert ist, um bestimmte Wege zu finden, über Dinge zu sprechen. Ich glaube, die Erfahrungen der Teilnehmer*innen sind durchaus wichtig – ihre jeweiligen Erfahrungen – weil ich glaube, dass sie nicht…

Ich habe vorhin mit Christian darüber gesprochen: es scheint nicht wirklich viele Personen zu geben, die diese Ideen entwickeln. Ich meine, wie du [Andrea] gesagt hast, es scheint kein Forum für sie zu geben. Und es mag verschiedene Punkte geben, an denen manche Personen etwas darauf eingehen, aber nicht auf eine ausführliche oder eine andere, tiefergehende Art. Und ich denke, dass es in diesem Kontext möglich ist, etwas zu tun, das gründlicher ist als vorher – und ich denke, es existiert momentan ein echtes Vakuum in Bezug darauf, was vorhanden ist. Ich meine, ich spüre es ganz sicher. Und das ist zum Teil das, was mich angeregt hat, mein Fördergeld dahin zu steuern, das Symposium für das Drawing Center zu machen [*Negotiations in the Contact Zone*, das 1994 stattfand]. Das war für mich nützlich, um darüber nachdenken zu können, wie das hier weitergehen kann, und auch was andere hier zu sagen haben, was sich mit manchen meiner Ideen überschneidet, die ich in einer Art Isolation formuliert und dargelegt

habe. Und zu sehen, was die Reaktionen sind, und die Reaktionen dann neu zu bewerten und vor- und zurückzugehen.

Ich denke, es ist sogar möglich, in dieser Situation mit einer Universität zu arbeiten – diese Informationen zu sammeln auf eine Art, die anders ist, als beispielsweise einige der Dia [Art Foundation] Symposien [in New York], die ich sehr anregend fand, als ich diese Mitte bis Ende der achtziger Jahre besuchte. Und was mich veranlasste, andere Fragen in Bezug auf die jetzige Situation zu stellen. Ich weiß also nicht, in welcher Form es weitergehen soll. Ich glaube aber wirklich, dass es in gewisser Hinsicht den Bedarf für eine Fortsetzung gibt.

Guttmann: Ich denke, dass einer der Erfolge dieses Forums die Tatsache ist, dass es wirklich einige Sphären heraussucht und sie sich überschneiden. Und schließlich sitzen wir in einer Universität, nicht in einem Museum. Ich finde das sehr interessant. Ich denke, dass einige der logistischen Probleme – seien wir ehrlich – einige der logistischen Probleme kommen daher, dass es nicht genügend Personen gibt, die in die Idee investiert haben, die Dinge innerhalb der Institution zu verändern. Also haben die wenigen, die das tun, am Ende Probleme. Ich denke, es ist wirklich wichtig, sich das vor Augen zu halten. Wisst ihr, der gemeinsame Ort ist immer viel einfacher. Und ich glaube tatsächlich, dass wenn man die Dinge verändert, alle möglichen Probleme entstehen.

Ich denke also, dass dies eine ziemlich interessante und positive Erfahrung war, auch wenn einige Probleme entstehen, weil mir die Probleme wie die unvermeidliche

Konsequenz davon erscheinen, auf nicht traditionellen Wegen zu arbeiten. Ich denke, dass diese Komponente etwas ist, dass ich gerne weitergeführt sehen würde, anstatt die Dinge in einem, wisst ihr, in einem voll und ganz durchdefinierten Kunstkontext zu machen. Denn ich denke, das ist ziemlich wichtig. Und was du [Andrea] darüber gesagt hast, die Art von Ausstellungen zu machen, die einen größeren Gebrauchswert haben als – mir fällt das Zitat nicht mehr ein…

Fraser: Als Prestigewert.

Guttmann: Richtig, mehr Gebrauchswert als Prestigewert. Ich denke, dass sie [diese Arbeitsgruppe] tatsächlich auf so etwas Ähnlichem beruht, weil ein Teil der Fähigkeit, sich Problematiken anzuschauen und zu versuchen, sie zu erkunden, genau auf dieser Möglichkeit beruht, sie nicht aus der Perspektive des Prestigewerts zu betrachten, was wiederum einen gewissen institutionellen Wandel erfordert. Das ist meiner Meinung nach etwas, das weitergeführt werden sollte, einschließlich der Probleme, die aufkommen, und es gibt wirklich keine Möglichkeit, sie zu umgehen, denn das liegt tatsächlich in der Natur der Bestie.

Fraser: Was du sagst [Martin], stimmt ziemlich mit dem überein, was du vorhin gesagt hast, Iwona? Dass es darum geht, sich andere Kontexte und Möglichkeiten anzuschauen, dass du die Diskussion mehr öffnen wollen und nicht so sehr auf Institutionen fixieren würdest. Aber an welche Dinge hast du da genau gedacht, als du das gesagt hast?

Blazwick: Nun, es ist etwas anders. Ich habe da beispielsweise an die Havanna Biennale auf Kuba gedacht und ein paar Personen, die daran beteiligt waren. Und ich habe an ein paar sehr interessante Methoden, die dort entwickelt wurden, gedacht. Allerdings auch an andere Dinge… Denn ich denke momentan sehr viel über Verlagswesen und Vertrieb und Computerprogramme nach. Das ist einfach etwas, mit dem ich mich in den letzten sechs Monaten sehr viel befasst habe, mir diese verschiedenen Formen anzusehen. Das Gebäude, die Institution als Form der Kommunikation, die nicht unbedingt ein Museum oder ein Kunstraum ist.

Fraser: Du würdest also sagen, dass die Funktion der Versuch wäre, die Entwicklung dieser Art von…

Blazwick: Vermutlich befinden sich Menschen im Laufe der Zeit in verschiedenen Arbeitssituationen, entweder, um etwas daraus zu gewinnen – was ich sicherlich tue – und um es wieder in das, was wir hier tun, einfließen zu lassen. Und im Grunde die Gelegenheit, von diesem Prozess zu berichten. Ich denke, es wäre sehr wertvoll, sich anzuschauen, was in einem Jahr oder später geschehen wird. Hat sich etwas verändert? Was hat sich daraus etwas entwickelt?

Bischoff: Ich würde vorschlagen, wenn wir oder andere solche Treffen noch einmal veranstalten, dass es meiner Meinung nach gut wäre, wenn es dort praktische Erfahrung gäbe. Ich denke, dieses Mal gab es viele Beispiele, und die sind sehr wichtig. Sodass man nicht allein Strukturen bespricht, sondern Beispiele hat. Wenn die eingeladenen Personen an diesen Beispielen beteiligt sind, dann könnten sie vielleicht sogar ein wenig konkreter sein. Sodass es ein, zwei oder drei Projekte gibt, die diskutiert werden, und die die Diskussion anregen. Ich glaube, das wäre gut. Das ist meine Meinung.

Wilson: Vielleicht muss die nächste Arbeitsgruppe sich die Videoaufnahme anschauen und sich dazu äußern. Ich weiß nicht, wen man dazu bewegen könnte, zu kommen und das zu tun.

(Gelächter)

Fraser: Wir könnten das Video vorspulen.

(Gelächter)

Fraser: Mir wurde mitgeteilt, dass wir um 21:15 Uhr im Restaurant sein sollten, um zu essen, und es ist jetzt 20:56 Uhr. Ich würde also sagen, das gibt uns ungefähr vier Minuten, um das hier abzuschließen. Brauchen wir die? Die Frage des Vortrags morgen: Ich denke, wir machen weiter und treffen uns morgen um 13 Uhr wieder mit den Studierenden aus dem Seminar. Und dann hoffe ich auch, dass diejenigen von euch, die planen, um 17 Uhr hier zu sein, an einer Art Vortrag teilnehmen. Ich habe keine Ahnung, was es für ein Vortrag sein soll, aber hoffentlich können wir morgen um 13 Uhr ebenfalls darüber sprechen.

Draxler: Ich meine, hoffentlich gibt es dann eine Idee.

Fraser: Ja, es wird definitiv eine Idee geben.

Green: Frage: Um wie viel Uhr macht der Raum morgen auf?

Von Bismarck: Dieser Raum?

Green: Ja.

Von Bismarck: Wann ihr wollt.

Green: In Ordnung.

Fraser: Die Diaprojektoren und die Videos müssen aufgebaut werden, und ich weiß, Christian, du brauchst einen Teil der Wand.

Draxler: Ja, ja, das haben wir schon besprochen.

Fraser: In Ordnung, gut.

Draxler: Ich meine, was meiner Meinung nach für eine Wiederholung von Veranstaltungen wie dieser berücksichtigt werden könnte, ist Folgendes… Was mit einigen Künstler*innen begann, die ein wenig über die gleiche Situation nachdachten – Gewerkschaften oder deren Entwicklung. Eine Idee für diese Veranstaltung war, dass sie ausschließlich mit Künstler*innen durchgeführt werden sollte, die speziell über dieses Thema diskutieren und danach mit vereinten Kräften an die Öffentlichkeit gehen. Was wir am Ende entschieden haben, ist, diese Situation ebenfalls mit Kurator*innen und Kritiker*innen zu veranstalten oder Personen, deren Arbeitsdefinition nicht so eindeutig ist, und sie zusammenzubringen. Und ich glaube, das ist wichtig. Ich meine, lasst uns einfach über Nacht etwas darüber nachdenken und es dann morgen ansprechen, falls das Sinn ergibt. Und vor dem Hintergrund dieser Vorgeschichte [zeigt auf die Pinnwand der ausgestellten historischen Dokumente als Teil der *Services* Ausstellung], falls es sinnvoll ist, die Diskussion auf dieser

Ebene zu belassen. Oder ob es nicht viel besser wäre, wenn Künstler*innen und Kurator*innen oder was auch immer sich in ihre Ecken zurückziehen. Ich habe auch ein wenig das Gefühl, dass ich meine eigenen Interessen nicht wirklich artikulieren konnte. Möglicherweise empfinden andere das genauso, und das könnte auch bloß an dieser Struktur liegen. Es ging hierbei [bei dieser Arbeitsgruppe] so sehr um die Art der Beziehungen, aber vielleicht nicht wirklich um Interessen irgendwie.

In Ordnung, gehen wir essen, oder?

Fraser: Wir können auch beim Essen weiterreden. Wir müssen nicht schweigend zu Abend essen!

(Gelächter)

Postscript

Galerie Nagel Draxler, Berlin
May 5, 2019

Helmut Draxler: All right.

Andrea Fraser: We're starting.

Draxler: Let's go.

Fraser: It's recording.

Draxler: OK. So, Eric, the editor of this book, sent us six complex questions. He is situating this conversation at the very end of the publication, so we don't have to present the project. The challenge is for us to bring our own histories into this: personal, artistic…

Fraser: And intellectual and professional.

Draxler: Professional?

Fraser: In terms of employment histories. Or unemployment histories.

Draxler: Of the last twenty-five years.

Fraser: It *has* been twenty-five years. Let's not dwell on that too much.

Draxler: No, let's not. I think Eric put it nicely, asking us about "the contemporary relevance of the *Services* project."

Fraser: One point of entry into that is our trajectories after *Services*. We each went a different way. You went into activist work in Munich. I went on to pursue services in my *Prospectuses* (1993) work on the model of consulting and to explore a kind of critical professionalization. That lasted for about five years. Then I decided that model was not what I wanted to be doing. I ran up against some of the contradictions that were already present in the *Services* Working Group discussions.

Draxler: I think the crucial thing is to locate the project historically. How was it even possible at that moment, in the early 1990s? What were its conditions of possibility, in historical terms? The overlap of artistic and institutional interests, of academic interests, which created that moment was, I think, very specific. Our trajectories after *Services* were different ways out of that situation. My trajectory was, in the beginning, to reject *Services* in many ways. But now, when I look at the art world, I think it really needs something like *Services* (laughs). And I appreciate the work we were doing, because the situation has changed so dramatically.

I think the different paths we took had to do with our different contexts, the US and Germany. In Germany, in the context of so-called reunification, there was a lot of political pressure. We had thousands of neo-Nazis on the streets. Thinking about wages for artistic labour didn't seem so relevant or urgent. Nowadays, it sometimes seems that Germany is the last stronghold of liberal culture—but that was not the case in the 1990s. It was one of the forerunners of neoconservative culture. In the US, on the other hand, it was the beginning of an era of hope after the Ronald Reagan and George H. W. Bush years.

Fraser: With Bill Clinton. That hope didn't last long. When was Gerhard Schröder elected?

Draxler: 1997.

Fraser: So, in 1993 and '94 the Christian Democratic Union and Christian Social Union were still in power.

Draxler: Yes, it was still the Helmut Kohl years.

Fraser: What is your sense of what the context was in 1993 that enabled *Services* to take place?

Draxler: I think that has two sides. On the one hand, it was a very specific moment with the Cologne scene, and with people starting to leave New York for Cologne and bring their knowledge of the history of alternative mobilizations in New York since the 1960s. I was at the Kunstverein München, where there was already a very open question about what it means to work for an institution. For me, one of the more personal reasons for becoming more distant from the *Services* project was that I simply stopped working as a curator.

Fraser: When did you leave the Kunstverein?

Draxler: At the end of 1995.

Fraser: That was just one year after *Services* toured. And then you basically left the art field for, what—five years?

Draxler: Yeah. Around 2000, I started to write for art publications again.

Fraser: That was about the same time that I finally abandoned the "services model." The last projects that I did with the *Prospectuses* was for the Sprengel Museum in Hanover in 1998, but, for me, the end of that period in my life was when I started more actively working with commercial galleries again, around 2000, with three gallery shows in 2001.

Draxler: Right. *Official Welcome* (2001–03) was a real reboot.

Fraser: And *Kunst muss hängen (Art Must Hang)* (2001). So that marks the end, for me, of that post-"services" period. But it is easier for me to think about that in terms of the development of the art field rather than in terms of the political and social economic context more broadly. I was teaching a survey of the art field some years ago, and I was preparing a lecture on museums. I created a timeline of when various museums were established, and I realized that the field of museums—at least of modern and contemporary art museums—hardly existed at the time institutional critique began to emerge in the late 1960s. I received institutional critique as a practice that developed to engage an established institutional field. What I realized was that, in fact, there wasn't really much of an institutional field until the 1980s. Institutional critique was less a response to an established institutional field than a practice that emerged alongside that field. I think it wasn't until the late 1970s and '80s that one could really speak of a field of modern and contemporary art institutions. At that point, it just started to explode. I was surprised to realize that my own development was in the context of the establishment of that field, rather than what it felt like at the time: that I was reacting to a field that was already established.

In retrospect, it is much easier to see what historical developments gave rise to the conditions that we were starting to address with *Services*. If you go forward from the early 1990s to the 2000s, you see the continuation of those developments into globalization and the professionalization of curating and programming, with the biennial boom and the emergence of curatorial studies. What was experienced over these decades was the establishment, not just of a field of institutions, but of a whole economy of exhibitions that did not exist before—which was subsequently largely overtaken and overwhelmed by the much greater expansion and financialization of the art market.

Draxler: Right. But an important part of the context of *Services* was the art market crisis of the early 1990s, which confronted many artists with the question of how to survive. Speculative money went into new technologies, and the seemingly inflated auction prices of the late 1980s seemed to warrant correction. It was when Hauser & Wirth started with its first Zurich location, and Friedrich Christian Flick began to amass his collection. Prices were low. They were the profiteers from the crisis, and I still see them as major symptoms of the subsequent developments. The strange thing, however, is that it is not so bad, what Hauser & Wirth is doing. The gallery is showing a lot of Black artists and the old avant-garde, and it takes up critical discourse. For me, this is one of the really disturbing things: in the 1980s, you could identify the conservatives and you could position yourself against them. Now, the territory is much more complex.

Fraser: Hauser & Wirth created what is basically a private, for-profit *Kunsthalle* in Los Angeles. It feels like a public museum space with community services like a bookstore and a café and spaces to have events. But, of course, it's for-profit. That's the most disturbing aspect of that development, for me: not so much what Hauser & Wirth represents in the context of the gallery world but what it represents in the context of the space of public exhibitions.

Draxler: It's not bad, but it should be confronted more, because these models destroy the possibility of avant-garde galleries. On the other hand, we all were a little bit naive in the 1990s. The discourse about museums was that museums will die, that we are standing on the museum's ruins and we will burn it down. At the same moment, the whole thing exploded.

Fraser: We learned that the avant-garde's failure was, in fact, its incredible success.

Draxler: Right—*unbelievable* success, which was at the same time as destructive for the avant-garde as a regulative idea of artistic practice.

Fraser: The avant-garde failed and was successful beyond its wildest dreams. This is why we need psychoanalysis. Negation is never a negation of its manifest object, but of the relation to that object, which is usually the desire for that object. It's always an inversion of the wish that the negation aims to realize. But I think we need to focus a bit more.

Draxler: But I think it's good to have some context, because what happened really was foreseeable. For example, when Pat Hearn opened her gallery in Chelsea in 1995.

Fraser: And Colin de Land and Hearn started the Gramercy International Art Fair in 1994, which became the Armory Show.

Draxler: There was still the model of the avant-garde gallery. In the early 1990s, that was an important context. It's hard to imagine any gallery today doing shows like de Land and Hearn and Christian Nagel did then.

Fraser: When I reflect on the past decades, I always have to stop myself and wonder what's ontogeny and what's phylogeny. What's a matter of historical development and what's a matter of social aging? We exist with our own generational blindness to the positions that are developing.

Draxler: While we accuse people from the 1970s of being completely blind (laughs).

Fraser: Was there ever really any question of whether the market would triumph? By 2000, the financialization of the art market solidified, with the explosion of art fairs, and this happened alongside the explosion of exhibitions, including biennials, most of which were *publicly* funded. So there was a dual expansion of both the for-profit and the public or nonprofit sectors of the art field, and they became increasingly synchronized.

Draxler: I would say that in Europe the market is not that strong, but the institutional dimension was always more differentiated with *Kunstvereins*, *Kunsthallen*, *Fracs*, and so on dedicated exclusively to contemporary art. And then the biennial culture emerged. The strange thing is, however, that the rhetoric of biennials and other big exhibition formats has gotten increasingly anti-market. The critique of a market-driven art world has become one of the basic rationales of the publicly funded exhibition spectacles, even while there is now very little space between the market and the institutions.

Fraser: This is part of your point about the disappearance of the avant-garde gallery.

Draxler: Yes, it got lost in between the market boom and the exhibition boom. You have all these institutional exhibitions like biennials becoming educational, just on the level of content. And you see the new candidates for documenta using all the same rhetoric, especially that of radical democracy and education. On the other hand, you have the market that is identified with the Gagosian model of the supranational corporation gallery. But the small market that supported avant-garde galleries, which made a certain living possible and provided artists with certain structures, has disappeared. Now curators don't even really need artists anymore. They just do their own job. If you look at most of the biennials, the only figure you remember is the curator. By the 1990s, it already was a problematic role for me. I couldn't imagine continuing as a curator, much less becoming a kind of mega-curator. It would have been completely ridiculous.

Fraser: Frankfurt School critique has been peripheral to my approach to institutional critique, but I do see how the exhibition field broadly, including the field of museums and public exhibitions, really has become a culture industry. That's still the most efficient way to think about that shift in the early 1990s: it didn't quite yet feel like an industry, but that is what we were facing. That development can be identified in the emergence of certain kinds of relations and positions like the project manager, in the professionalization of the curatorial role, and in the development of economic relations of contracting. Those developments, which we were trying to understand with *Services*, are all elements of the transformation of the field of exhibitions into a culture industry. And in an industry, negation is no longer possible. The reproduction of the industry, its institutions and positions and economy, became its primary aim. Negation becomes just a discourse, a product, at best an experience. In the early 1990s, the loss of autonomy and the potential of negation was still at stake. But even then, some people were questioning whether the "services model" was itself part of the erosion of autonomy.

Draxler: Maybe there was a double naïveté in our attempt to overcome, or resolve, the paradox of autonomy by providing services. On the one hand, that kind of overcoming was part of the development of the culture industry in general anyhow, and on the other hand, we took autonomy for granted and could afford to question it, meaning that it represents the precondition for any attempt to question it. Nowadays I would rather address that paradox. But we did not understand the term "services" so literally even then. I always felt a slight sense of irony using it.

Fraser: OK. Enough with the context.

Draxler: Eric's first question, about how *Services* is relevant today, also mentions the exploitative conditions of artistic production. But already in the late 1990s we had a discussion in Munich about how you have to be pretty privileged in order to be exploited. You have to be in the field. Today, I see younger artists who are desperate to be exploited, who strive to be exploited.

Fraser: The alternative to exploitation is just marginalization, which is what we see today in this tremendous reservoir of surplus labour of aspiring artists. The expansion of art degree programs have played a big role in that. It is also a consequence of what I hate to call the "culture of narcissism" that makes this field so attractive to so many people.

Draxler: If one reads "services" as a kind of tactical term, then it has a literal meaning with regard to a moving away from the production of goods. But it always also implied providing a service for someone as a benefit to society in a positive or, even more so, in a negative way. The one who provides a service is a servant. What I still like about the term is this ambivalence. It's not one-dimensional. Saying "I provide services" as an artist or even as a curator made a significant point about the relation between a critique of institutions and the reflexivity of one's role within them. That aspect was also in the *Services* project and very present in the Working Group discussions.

Fraser: Serving audiences, serving institutions, serving communities…

Draxler: Or *not* serving audiences. Serving ourselves (laughs).

Fraser: (Laughs) Yeah, that should've been one of the sessions! There were social scientists who were writing about the "self-service economy" and the "self-service society," and that was even before the selfie! I wasn't willing to be that cynical. Today, you have the whole "Bartleby" discourse, about *not* serving. But, certainly, the problem of artists being functionalized and instrumentalized by museums to satisfy the demands of both public and foundation funders for community outreach and more quantifiable social impact was a central point.

Draxler: Services also could be criticized in terms of the transition from the production of goods to promotional material, in the widest sense, which Alexander Alberro has written about in the context of conceptual art in the 1960s and '70s. The *Services* project was clearly part of that. *Services* was situated at the intersection of neoliberal self-economies and a strong belief in institutions, which were supposed to provide resources for artistic practice and personal survival. There is a specific kind of symbolic subjectivity involved, which I guess we weren't really aware of then. We wanted to participate in certain avant-garde traditions that did not refer to the artist-genius model anymore—getting rid of ourselves, trying to become mere service providers. In a similar way, there was a far-reaching neglect of the differences between artistic, cultural, or even theoretical and critical work; everything was considered to be "cultural production." Curators still promote that discourse because it serves their interests so well. On the other hand, however, the *Services* project promoted all our careers precisely in that artistic or authorial way. Today, I would insist much more on the differences and the relations between those different roles, and what these relations imply in terms of subjectivity and in terms of artistic, political, and theoretical practice. The *Services* project does not simply represent changing economic conditions; it enacted intersubjective relations within art institutions and economies.

Fraser: That was certainly central to my interests as well. The interpersonal dimension of social relations and relations of exchange are more prominent in thinking about

services than in thinking about goods production. But for
me, it also had to do with the influence of psychoanalysis
on my interest in services, and on my attempts to formulate
a radical professional model. I looked to psychoanalysis for
an example of a professional model that was critical of the
conditions of professional authority and expertise while at
the same time maintaining a remarkable level of autonomy.

Draxler: That relates to the challenges I faced at the
Kunstverein München of performing the role of the curator and the representative of the institution without identifying completely with it—of being inside and outside of
the institution at the same time. That is still a crucial question now, in my academic world, which is even less open
to that discussion. The academy is a "greedy institution"
that wants to swallow you up. People think that you can
be so critical inside academic institutions, but not about
those institutions themselves. My experience of the academic world is that there is very little institutional critique.
Even when it comes to Pierre Bourdieu.

Fraser: That's not true! *Homo Academicus! The State Nobil-
ity!* I have to defend Bourdieu.

Draxler: Yeah, sure, but even he is not really self-critical.
It's always about the *other* academics. And that is what
these others are saying themselves: we are critical! It's not
self-critique.

Fraser: Let's go back to the contemporary conditions of
exploitation. I think the *Services* project has been relevant
to recent efforts to address those conditions. For example,
W.A.G.E. (Working Artists and the Greater Economy) in
the US, which I've been involved with: when W.A.G.E.

developed its certification program for institutions and its schedule for artist fees, there was a conversation about a "royalty" or "intellectual property" model, versus a "fee for services" model. We looked at CARFAC (Canadian Artists' Representation/Le Front des artistes canadiens), which oversees artist fees in Canada and was created through lobbying efforts and legislation to guarantee artists a royalty when their work is exhibited in noncommercial venues. I don't know why we didn't mention CARFAC in the *Services* material. We must have known about it.

W.A.G.E. ultimately developed on the "fee for services" model, and I think that *Services* had some influence on that. But W.A.G.E. does not represent, from my perspective, the realization of the goals of *Services*, or at least my goals in the early 1990s, because its model doesn't distinguish between the services provided by artists showing art objects and those involved in projects that do not include goods production. It is not about developing an alternative to the goods production model, which was my focus with *Services*. I wanted to develop an economic basis for an artistic practice that would not depend on the commercial market. I wanted to see the field of exhibitions that was emerging as an alternative that could provide artists with sustainable conditions of practice. It was important to me that there would be a distinction between artists who were making things that could be sold in the market, who I did not necessarily think should get fees, and those who were not. The argument of W.A.G.E., with which I also agree, is that, even when you're showing something previously made, a lot of labour goes into participating in an exhibition. The implicit—and sometimes explicit—response that artists are compensated with publicity, which supports sales, is really offensive.

Draxler: I think the services model didn't work as an alternative because of increasing precarity and exclusion, which, in political terms, turned the discussion toward a universal basic income, which would not be for goods or for services.

Fraser: That is the more radical position.

Draxler: But that also implies that capitalism is still in place.

Fraser: But we don't live under capitalism anymore. It's just wealth management.

Draxler: For the past ten years in Germany, there have been discussions of returning to industrial production from too much services. We have our skills in industry, but we have to digitize them, and these are the future markets. After 2008, the immaterial became synonymous with speculation, which reduced its symbolic value. It created a very different constellation. W.A.G.E. took up an early twentieth-century model of a labour organization and understanding of artistic production in terms of wages. But I would say that a universal basic income is the only solution we have, not just for artists and for unemployed curators and critics, but for everyone.

Fraser: The conditions of exploitation have intensified for curators and for other people working in the field of exhibitions. For a number of years, my most optimistic vision for the art world was that it would fragment into increasingly autonomous subfields: the market subfield, the academic subfield, the activist and community-based DIY subfield, and the exhibition subfield. *Services* included a discussion of community-based practices, but was focused primarily on the exhibition subfield, which now has become much more fully institutionalized. I think it's more generative to envision the separation of these subfields than to criticize their intersection—for example, of exhibitions and the market. There are artists who have developed sustainable practices within the exhibition field. The number of artists who are successful in one subfield and have no existence in the other subfields is strong evidence of this fragmentation.

Draxler: That's where we're at today.

Fraser: What the market field produces is *value*, whether you call it artistic or economic value. I think what the exhibition field produces is *experience*, mostly in the form of spectacle. Producing an experience for others is a service.

Draxler: But the exhibition field also has a content-related side, because there is a lot of project-based and research-based production, which is also interesting.

Fraser: Research and the production of *knowledge* are what define the academic subfield, not the exhibition subfield. There are a lot of claims for knowledge production in the exhibition field, but I think they rarely hold up. But education is also a service. In the US context, all art nonprofits are defined as educational institutions.

Draxler: For me, "educational" is a crucially difficult term. It opens the door for curators to claim that they don't need the artists anymore because they can serve audiences better with educational work. They don't have to mess around with difficult subjectivities or misbehavior.

Fraser: I don't think we're seeing that in the United States. I have heard senior and chief curators in major institutions say that curating is dying out, that curators have become project managers and fundraisers, that it's not possible to curate anymore because artists are so intent on controlling every aspect of their work and its interpretation and presentation. More and more of the job of curators in US museums is to serve as art consultants to institutional patrons, while artists and their gallerists put the shows together. Serving the audience is the job of the education department or the public programs department. It's not central to the role of the curator anymore.

Draxler: That's precisely why it's important that the positions of the artist and the curator remain distinct. When artists themselves define their work as a service—for example, Mierle Laderman Ukeles, who wrote the "Manifesto for Maintenance Art 1969!": I saw her show at the Queens Museum in New York in 2016–17. It was great, but how the show became the rationale of the whole institution was very problematic. It takes away the tension between serving audiences, serving institutions, and serving ourselves. They probably shouldn't go together.

Fraser: It takes away the *not*-serving aspect. People involved with community-based practice, relational aesthetics, and social practice used to come to me and say, "Oh, I heard you did a project about service." They thought it was about social service, community service, etc. I had to explain that it wasn't actually about that at all.

Draxler: We still have to discuss the term "project-oriented work," which was also central to *Services*. The project culture that we identified then is still with us today and has become very successful, with a lot of funding. It also offers itself as a solution for critical production beyond those tensions.

Fraser: It also has become a standard part of corporate culture, where project teams are supposed to create a more dynamic and motivated workforce. Outside the corporate context, project work has become part of the precarification of labour in the gig economy.

Draxler: Sure. You have two or three projects, and then they're over, and you still have twenty years until you get your pension.

Fraser: By the early 1990s, people had been talking about services as part of a major socioeconomic shift for decades, but I don't remember much reflection on "projects."

Draxler: That became a reality afterward.

Fraser: So we were prescient!

Draxler: Yeah, absolutely! (Laughs)

Fraser: We were ahead of our time!

Draxler: We have some responsibility for that shift.

Fraser: We can't be blamed for it, but there is the question of whether it is critique or simply emulation when artists appropriate such socioeconomic structures. It often does seem like the critical projects and formulations of artists and intellectuals are just symptoms of social and economic developments, if not harbingers of their uncritical embrace.

Draxler: You can always interpret any attempt at critique as serving different purposes.

Fraser: We can take this back to the question of your trajectory versus my trajectory after *Services*. You got involved in radical politics, while I pursued a course that I think many saw as a kind of liberal reform, at best. But I think my position then, as now, is that radical positions are not always in the end actually all that radical, particularly if they have no potentially effective vision of institutional change—which is true of almost all anti-institutional politics. But I was feeling trapped in the services model by the end of the 1990s.

Draxler: I think every model has its time. The conditions were changing, and also for me personally, as I became interested in more radical models. But my experience was that radical models were even less self-reflexive than cultural institutions, which were open to precisely that. Radicality has become an institutional and especially academic success model since then.

Fraser: That openness to self-reflexivity is the extraordinary thing about cultural institutions.

Draxler: Yeah, you try to storm the doors, but the doors are already wide open and you're welcome. So, retrospectively, I value the *Services* experience. There is what Fred Wilson was doing, what you were doing, and all the others: artistic practices that were not just performing their own radicality, which you can't really distinguish from the rationales of the institution themselves in serving audiences. It's precisely that difference that counts. Because institutions can always do things "radically" better than we can, and if we serve these institutions by providing them with seemingly critical content, we are avoiding artistic, political, and philosophical contradictions and conflicts. "There is," however, as Theodor W. Adorno said, "no right life in the wrong one." And that's why I think that, in the brief moment in time in which *Services* was possible, it had its historical importance. But there were also good reasons why that model stopped working for you and for me. The context shifted and different assumptions were necessary, especially for me with the growing curatorial craze. You know, when Hans Ulrich Obrist was doing *Utopia Station* for the 50th Venice Biennale, in 2003, I said I'd rather just kill myself than do something like that (laughs). I didn't want to continue as a curator. But the emerging "project" culture obviously also had its interesting aspects. It just needs more reflection.

Fraser: There's certainly an enormous amount of room for a more equitable distribution of resources within art institutions—particularly larger art institutions in the United States that have very high salaries at the top and very low salaries at the bottom and huge amounts of money spent on image costs and so on. One of the things that I struggle with now in my advocacy for W.A.G.E. and for artists' fees is that the high fees paid to some artists, just like the high salaries of some curators, are part of the increased costs overall for art institutions. What that means in the US is that museums just become more and more dependent on very, very wealthy people to cover those rising costs. I don't think that I thought about that in the early 1990s with the services model. I thought of the exhibition field as an alternative to the speculative art market. But at this point, at least in the US, art institutions and the art market are supported by the same highly concentrated wealth. In some respects, I would now even say that this is worse in museums, because it renders them fundamentally plutocratic in their governance structure. Artist fees become just another component of a US economy of cultural institutions that is completely dependent on a plutocratic donor class, which is the same class that controls the political process. The focus really needs to be on equity.

Draxler: It's really very different in Europe. Still, becoming entirely overreliant on wealthy patrons was one of the reasons theorists and artists started defending institutions and their autonomy, which Bourdieu did, for example, over the course of the 1990s, and insisting that institutions shouldn't define themselves vis-à-vis the market.

Fraser: In the US, that's a battle we don't even know how to start.

Draxler: I just received an invitation from Museum Ludwig in Cologne to give a talk about a show with work loaned by a private gallery—works that will be part of how this museum will historicize the 1990s. I accepted the invitation because I think that is precisely the point I would like to talk about: How does this museum see itself in this context, and what kind of history from the 1990s is being narrated?

Fraser: But, in some sense, the history of art in the Rhineland is a history of avant-garde private galleries.

Draxler: Absolutely. The ads that Paul Maenz did for *Avalanche* were amazing. Really unbelievable.

Fraser: Remember the booklet that we had in *Services* called *What do you want?* It was produced by an art dealer asking his artists—Joseph Kosuth, Daniel Buren, I think

Douglas Huebler and others—"What do you want from me?"

Draxler: Amazing, yeah (laughs). The logic of the big galleries that came after, like Hauser & Wirth, is really how to transform the avant-garde into big commodities. It's like the collector who opened the Brandhorst Museum in Munich. You have photos of what Cy Twombly did in the 1950s alongside Merce Cunningham and John Cage, but the focus is on the huge paintings that they turned into a few years later. It's a very specific logic, and I think in that context it still makes sense to insist that projects like *Services*, even if they fail, are important.

Fraser: From my perspective, the ideal result of the fragmentation I was talking about earlier is that the art market would become its own completely autonomous field, and the exhibition and academic subfields would just ignore it completely. That's a fantasy, but to the extent that anything like the autonomy of the historical or even the neo-avant-gardes can exist today, it could only be as a tiny field, like "tiny mutual admiration societies," as Bourdieu once described the most autonomous fields. It would be tiny and poor and probably pathetic and marginal, and it would not have anything to do with the market or the exhibition culture industry. As much as we might long for that autonomy, we're so embedded in the fields that have developed that it's hard even to imagine what it would be like to exist in that kind of microfield.

Draxler: Autonomy is surely a fantasy, but a necessary one. Even if it keeps us economically and socially deprived.

Fraser: We would be like poets: no money, no audience, no institutions. That kind of autonomy is a social reality under certain conditions, which doesn't mean that it is not also a fantasy.

Draxler: Autonomy is a kind of rearguard action in times of pressure, a position from which one can at least infiltrate certain social spheres and tactically pursue critical ideas and practices. The small-scale approach worked at least for a while for avant-garde galleries like Galerie Paul Maenz in Cologne and several galleries in New York in the 1970s. It worked as a promise and as a symbolic horizon. It even worked as an economic model for a while. We can't just criticize the market and wait for goodwill institutional support. Instead, we should go between the different registers of economics, politics, and culture. None are fundamentally good or fundamentally bad. If we ended up in only one field or subfield, it would be really depressing.

Fraser: (Laughs) Well, here we are sitting in a gallery right now! But I did pretty much get out of the art market, again, in the early 2010s.

Draxler: Galleries are great if they do their job.

Fraser: In that respect, you've become the liberal reformist while I maintain a certain degree of radicality! (Laughs) I did abandon the services model, and I did start making works that circulate as commodities, but I finally resolved at least some of my conflicted relationship to the market by deciding to not sell my work to individuals. So I try to define my market and limit it to institutions and exhibitions. That's my compromise.

Draxler: Yeah, well, mine is just the institutional market.

Fraser: An academic job, yes. I did that too. I got the last secure job in America outside the postal service: a tenured professorship.

Draxler: We still have to talk about the model of the information exhibition and the working group exhibition.

Fraser: The information model was being practiced by Ute Meta Bauer at the Künstlerhaus Stuttgart, BüroBert with Copyshop in 1993, and Stephan Dillemuth with Friesenwall 120 in Cologne—all of whom participated in *Services*. So their work was one inspiration.

Draxler: But their shows were always a bit different. They were more punk. It wasn't just information. There was stuff, like videos, but also an idea of collectivity in terms of both production and reception. For example, Dillemuth invited the Grey Panthers do to something.

Fraser: For me, the exhibition model of *Services* was partly rooted in a distinction I made in my *Prospectuses* at that time, between what I called "cultural constituency organizations" and "general audience institutions"—basically institutions for insiders versus those for outsiders. I tried to make a clear distinction between the works that I did for those different kinds of institutions. My argument was: let's recognize that we're talking to each other here, and have a conversation about what we're doing. With regard to political work in particular, what is generated for insider spaces must be critically self-reflexive, otherwise it's just an exercise in self-affirmation.

Draxler: Right, but another important aspect I was thinking about was how the exhibition could be more than pure information or spectacle. I was interested in turning the exhibition itself into a discursive format, into something like a discursive exhibition. For example, I did not work as an institutional curator after *Services*, but I did two shows in 2007 and 2013. Judith Barry's work with exhibition design, and the experience of working with you and people like Louise Lawler, Christopher Williams, and Christian Philipp Müller, became important for thinking about how the exhibition could be more than just spectacle and could be a means to manifest a particular discourse in an exhibition format.

Fraser: My ambition with *Services* wasn't just to manifest a critical discourse but also to develop a new set of relations that would transform the existing conditions. At least that's what I remember. I hoped that, as the project toured, it would develop into a larger and larger conversation that could then develop into standards and protocols and contracts and fee schedules—things that would change material and social relations within the field. For me, *Services* was not an end in itself, and its aim was not to produce critical discourses. I didn't have the capacity to really develop that, though. I didn't have the social skills (laughs). I have learned since then that I'm really not a community-based person, even though I worked collaboratively before and since, with the V-Girls, then Parasite, and then Orchard. Also, you and I stopped collaborating, in different ways, after Lüneburg. I think it was too important for me to have authorial credit, to claim the project as an individual artist at that time.

Draxler: I can understand that critique, but I would also turn it around nowadays and say that this authorial component was the strong side of it. If there is a possibility to reflect on that, it's great, but in my experience with collectives, it's that collectives—

Fraser: Have fucked-up group dynamics?

Draxler: So fucked up! Collectives can be cruel and fascist. I think we all have to negotiate our individual and our collective desires in one way or another. If I used my collective work to promote only myself, then I would agree and say, "Fuck me." But if there's something else at stake, a reverberation across the group, I think it's great. This is still for me a current issue, because I'm more or less making only my own stuff at this point.

Fraser: And I've become a serial board member and a Group Relations groupie! I'm on three boards and two advisory councils, and I'm a certified Group Relations consultant. I have more experience now. Some people may see that administrative involvement as a contradictory element of my position as an artist, but I have never been anti-institutional. For me, institutional critique is about building critical institutions.

Draxler: That's like the trajectory of the documentary filmmaker Frederick Wiseman: from being extremely critical of institutions to celebrating institutions—like the public library. And for good reason!

Fraser: Social, psychological, or emotional aging may play a role, but it's not just that. *Services* was already about institution building, and I was only in my late twenties then. It may have to do with being part of a generation that went from a society of public administration in the postwar era to a deinstitutionalized society of private administration in the 1990s. But I do see institution building as the basis for the success of W.A.G.E. The founders of W.A.G.E. managed to create a nonprofit arts organization to carry out that work. But it still faces all the challenges of institutional life, like how to create organizational structures that don't replicate the fucked-up structures of the art institutions that we're trying to change.

Research for my book *2016 in Museums, Money, and Politics* has led me to think a lot more about institutional governance and the relations between institutions and their stakeholders. I think models of radical politics, like the kind you lived through, tend to be totally fight-flight, to use the formulations of the psychoanalyst Wilfred Bion, while the models of art institutions are deeply dependent. The plutocratic-philanthropic model fosters much more direct dependency on donors than the social-democratic model of public funding, which invites and even requires— at least in theory—active engagement, and not just in fundraising. This isn't a problem of just art institutions. The professionalization of advocacy and civic organizations in the US has turned what used to be members, communities, constituencies, and stakeholders into clients, or even just consumers of advocacy products. That process has significantly undermined democracy as well as the potential for political mobilization.

Draxler: Radical politics are definitely fight-flight in terms of their group dynamics. The problem is that reformist models are not any better at negotiating the differences between individual and collective ambitions. They just tend to homogenize the differences and thus erase their political dimension. That is why the historicity of projects like *Services* is so important to me. Historicity, both in terms of conditions and of outcomes, is highly contingent. But something happened. And what happened, and is still happening in reflecting on this project, has to respect these contingencies. They force us to think through the contradictory and dysfunctional moments of a system. That's what I'm more and more interested in. When things become functional and get administrated, that's very scary for me.

Fraser: What, you're saying that the only hope is in the dysfunction?

Draxler: Yes, in the dysfunction. Sure, there is a culture that has fantasies about art and there is an industry growing around them. But you can also use those fantasies, you can work through them, and you can produce something that at least for a moment feels right and cool, as long as it doesn't get too dominant. These moments are valuable and important. As we were talking about Friesenwall 120 earlier: it's not just what it seems to be, a sort of alternative art space that sooner or later collapses into the system; it also has a social logic that gives dysfunctionality a certain symbolic framework. I like that. Stephan Dillemuth also is having shows now and works in different academic, institutional, and market worlds. He has an ongoing website. But Friesenwall 120 is definitely history. The problem, then, is how to historicize without that becoming another triumphant narrative. And maybe this is also true of *Services*: it's good because it was dysfunctional, it did not work out, and we did not become administrators of a so-called great moment in history. *Services* rather responded to certain specific needs and ambitions, and this specificity should be addressed now from a historical perspective.

Fraser: I still think that artists need a professional guild. I still believe that.

Draxler: Yeah, that's what I'm currently writing about in my Flemish painting project.

Fraser: Great! The standard narrative of social art history has been the "liberation" of the artist from the guild.

Draxler: That is obviously wrong.

Fraser: Its high time to revise that narrative and rethink the guild. In the early 1990s, even the traditional professions were moving away from the guild model. Doctors in corporatized hospitals and lawyers in corporate firms have been proletarianized to such an extent that the guild model doesn't make sense anymore. They need unions. But, at the same time, I wonder about the political fantasies and projections that draw artists to the model of the industrial union, when in fact the guild is the historical model for artists and still suits our status as self-employed professionals.

Draxler: I think that traditional social art history underestimates what the guild made possible. It's just seen as a constraint, especially within the liberation model of modern art history and its deeply liberal narrative of artists as exemplary subjects in getting rid of all the traditional fetters. That is Adam Smith, and that's obviously completely ridiculous in relation to historical realities. The guild had a productive as well as a protective function, and it was not the only organizing structure in early modern times. Between the monasteries and other ecclesiastical structures in the medieval era and the court, the guilds emerged with the city. They are essentially an urban form of social organization. That implied a certain dynamism as well as controlling and repetitive structures. Modern art emerges not in rejecting these structures but in exploring the interstices of court, guild, and church. Maybe the academy represented something like a transitional model, in and through which the exhibitionary complex could emerge.

Fraser: So the dynamism was not in autonomous structures but rather in the tensions between the different heteronomous structures. That makes a lot of sense.

Draxler: The claim made in art history of the 1970s is that the court artist is the model of the modern artist, because the court artist distanced himself from the city and from the guild, and had the privilege to look at society from above. But that's not really true. It was precisely being in between the court and the guild, or their modern equivalents of markets and institutions, that created the possibility of an artist in the modern sense. That is the most interesting symbolic space, and it's still there, for example, in the fact that you can do something like your *2016* book. We have been living more or less in the same social structures for the past six hundred years. Not everything was invented in the middle of the nineteenth century. It's not about individual freedom, but about social relations, and these social relations have to be reflected, historically, theoretically, and practically. From this perspective, reconsidering a dimension in artistic practice that has been overlooked in the discourse of modern art and looking at the guild as a model of organizing contemporary artistic practice could be very interesting and useful.

Fraser: I have a friend, Jeff Preiss, who's a member of the Directors Guild of America. If you direct films with any major studio, you have to be a member. It was created in the 1930s. It works because every member director has to give a percentage of their income from every movie to the guild. Since the income itself goes through the guild, there's no hiding it. It's the same if you're making a blockbuster or a low-budget film. So that guild is incredibly wealthy. It offers health insurance and pensions. Film, sports, classical musicians, many types of writers, dancers—they all have guilds. Only visual artists don't, I think in part because of this ridiculous narrative and the artistic habitus it produced. We have to talk about that artistic habitus. That's really the problem, ultimately. We can talk about institutional structures and funding structures and so on, but it's all rooted in the artistic and the intellectual habitus and the individualism, atomization, and competition they foster, which is what makes organizing artists like herding cats.

Draxler: Why is it so difficult to have that type of organization in the visual art field? Why is art so symbolized in a different model for subjectivities, with the high-low split, and the split between autonomous and applied art, and so on? There are whole areas of art—design, filmmaking, and so on—that do not have substantial problems in organizing. But you have those problems in visual art, and I think it is important to reflect on that and how it creates its own habitus. But it is starting to change. More and more artists and other workers in the art field are employed in the large studios of the most successful artists, including some artists working primarily in the exhibition field. These super successful artists have studio managers, fabricators, and other contractors, and lots of assistants. But clearly this workshop scenario hasn't developed in the same direction as it has in film, where every single participant in a production is recognized and named and—in Hollywood, anyways—is a member of a union or guild. I think that may slowly start to change.

Fraser: I think we're going to see a revolt of the studio assistant. W.A.G.E. recently launched a program called WAGENCY, which directly helps artists negotiate fees. But being a WAGENT also requires you to follow guidelines for the payment of assistants. Immediately, there was pushback from some successful artists. Now is a very different moment in this respect from the early 1990s. I knew only a few artists back then who had assistants, and they were more often a kind of social decor, like an entourage for hire.

Draxler: Now the artist–art assistant relationship is a different business, but it poses this art worker question in a new way. The symbolic system produces its own structures. In a certain way, it's still based on the subjectivity model, on fetishizing genius or whatever, but, at the same time, it undermines it, because with this kind of subjectivity, if you need ten or twenty or more assistants, then the idea of "genius" becomes something difficult to maintain.

Fraser: There has been litigation over copyright ownership of images appropriated by artists since the 1990s, but more recently there have been a few instances of litigation by assistants claiming authorship of works that, in some cases, the named artists had almost nothing to do with creating. What's most likely to happen is that this situation will just increase artists' use of lawyers to create bulletproof contracts—but maybe it will also contribute to the organization of assistants.

Draxler: The whole criterion of authorship needs to be more clearly defined, because, in these cases, it's getting very blurred. Martin Kippenberger's assistants even made an artwork *out of* this blurring of authorship.

Fraser: From my perspective, this is one of the big contradictions of the art field: it is really one of the worst fields from the standpoint of equity, even compared to other cultural fields. I've focused more on the plutocratic nature of its institutions, and the labour relations with and within institutions, but artists themselves are now practicing the worst form of exploitative entrepreneurial capitalism.

Draxler: Absolutely. They were the forerunners in this developing situation.

Fraser: And, yet, the art field's radical self-representation still persists. It is radical only as an extreme form of capitalism with an extraordinary and completely unregulated capacity to exploit and extract surplus value.

Draxler: But, still, there is a possibility to work through that from within.

Judith Barry is an artist and writer based in Cambridge, Massachusetts. Since 2017, she has served as Acting Director and Professor at the MIT Program in Art, Culture and Technology. She has exhibited extensively internationally, including at the Venice Biennale (2000); Sharjah Biennial (2011); and dOCUMENTA (13), Kassel, Germany (2012). Barry's work is included in the collections of the Museum of Modern Art, New York; Whitney Museum, New York; and Centre Pompidou, Paris, among others. Recent solo exhibitions include *imagination, dead imagine* (2017) and *…cairo stories* (2018), both at Mary Boone Gallery, New York, and *untitled: (Global Displacement)*, at Isabella Stewart Gardner Museum, Boston (2018). Her publications include *Public Fantasy* (ICA London, 1991) and *Projections: Mise en abyme* (Presentation House Gallery, 1997), as well as catalogues for *Study for the Mirror and Garden* (Centro José Guerrero, 2003) and *Body without Limits* (DA2 Domus Atrium, 2009).

Ute Meta Bauer is Founding Director of the NTU Centre for Contemporary Art Singapore and Professor at the School of Art, Design and Media, Nanyang Technological University, Singapore. Previously, she was Dean of Fine Art at the Royal College of Art, London, and Associate Professor and Founding Director of the Program in Art, Culture, and Technology at the MIT School of Architecture and Planning, Cambridge, MA. Additionally, Bauer was Founding Director of the Office for Contemporary Art, Oslo, and served as Artistic Director of the 3rd Berlin Biennale. She was a co-curator of documenta11 (2002) and of the US Pavilion at the 6th Venice Biennale (2015, with Paul C. Ha), featuring the artist Joan Jonas.

Jochen Becker is a Berlin-based author, lecturer, and curator. He is a founding member of metroZones— Center for Urban Affairs. Becker has edited and co-edited several books, including *Bignes?* (b_books, 2001), *Kabul/Teheran 1979ff* (b_books, 2006), *Faith Is the Place* (b_books, 2012), and *Global Prayers* (Lars Müller Publishers, 2014). He has curated and co-curated exhibitions such as *Urban Cultures of Global Prayers*, held at nGbK, Berlin, and Camera Austria, Graz (2011–12), and *Self Made Urbanism Rome*, held at nGbK and Metropoliz and Maxxi, both in Rome (2013–15).

Ulrich Bischoff is an art historian and writer. From 1994 to 2013, he was Director of the Gemäldegalerie Neue Meister at the Staatliche Kunstsammlungen Dresden. He has published extensively in the areas of classical modernity and contemporary art. His recent books include *Munch* (Taschen, 2016); *The Power of the Avant-Garde: Now and Then*, co-edited with Katarina Lozo (Lannoo Publishers, 2016); *Constable, Delacroix, Friedrich, Goya. Die Erschütterung der Sinne* (Sandstein Verlag, 2013); *Jeff Wall in München: Werke aus drei Jahrzehnten in privaten und öffentlichen Sammlungen* (Pinakothek der Moderne, 2013); and *Jeff Wall: Transit*, co-edited with Mathias Wagner (Staatliche Kunstsammlungen Dresden, 2010).

Beatrice von Bismarck teaches art history, visual culture, and cultures of the curatorial at the Academy of Fine Arts Leipzig, where she founded the MA in Cultures of the Curatorial in 2009. She was previously Curator of Twentieth-Century Art at the Städel Museum, Frankfurt (1989–93) and cofounded and directed the

Kunstraum at the University of Lüneburg (1993–99). Von Bismarck is also cofounder of the project-space /D/O/C/K-Projektbereich, Leipzig. She co-edited the book series Cultures of the Curatorial for Sternberg Press, and her book *The Curatorial Condition* is forthcoming from Sternberg.

Iwona Blazwick is Director of Whitechapel Gallery, London, and is a curator, critic, and lecturer. She has formerly held positions at Tate Modern and the Institute for Contemporary Art, both London. Recent exhibitions she has organized at Whitechapel include *Adventures of the Black Square* (2015); *Thomas Ruff Photographs, 1979–2017* (2017); and *Mark Dion: Theatre of the Natural World* (2018). Blazwick is editor of the Documents of Contemporary Art series, co-published by Whitechapel Gallery and MIT Press. She is the author of monographs on Gary Hume (Other Criteria, 2012) and Cornelia Parker (Thames and Hudson, 2013) and has contributed to publications such as *Elmgreen and Dragset: This Is How We Bite Our Tongue* (Whitechapel, 2018); *Finding, Transmitting, Receiving: Hannah Collins* (Black Dog Press, 2007); and *Fischli and Weiss: Flowers and Questions: A Retrospective* (Tate Publishing, 2007).

Susan Cahan is Dean and Professor of Art History at the Tyler School of Art and Architecture at Temple University, Philadelphia. She has held positions at the New Museum of Contemporary Art, Museum of Modern Art, and Metropolitan Museum of Art, all in New York. From 1996 to 2001, she was Senior Curator for the private collection of Eileen and Peter Norton and Director of Arts Programs for the Peter Norton Family Foundation. Her publications include *Mounting Frustration: The Art Museum in the Age of Black Power* (Duke University Press, 2016); *I Remember Heaven: Jim Hodges and Andy Warhol* (Contemporary Art Museum St. Louis, 2007); and, with Zoya Kocur, *Contemporary Art and Multicultural Education* (Psychology Press, 1996).

The artist duo Clegg & Guttmann (Michael Clegg and Martin Guttmann) live and work between Berlin, Vienna, and New York. Clegg is Professor of Artistic Photography at the State University for Design in Karlsruhe, Germany. Guttmann is Professor in the Institute for Fine Arts at the Academy of Fine Arts, Vienna. They have produced major public artworks including *Die offene Bibliothek in Graz* (1991), *Breaking Down the Boundaries between Art and Life*, at the New School for Social Research, New York (1995), *Die sieben Brücken von Königsberg*, in Duisburg, Germany (1999), *A Monument for Historical Change*, at Rosa-Luxemburg-Platz e.V., Berlin (2004), and *Die Sieben Künste von Pritzwalk*, Potsdam, Germany (2014). Clegg & Guttmann's works have been shown in numerous exhibitions, most recently at Kunsthaus Graz (2011); BAWAG Contemporary, Vienna (2012); and Kunstverein Brandenburg, Potsdam (2015).

Stephan Dillemuth is an artist based in Bad Wiessee and Munich, Germany. From 1989 to 1994, he ran the influential project space Friesenwall 120 in Cologne with Josef Strau, Merlin Carpenter, Kiron Khosla, and Nils Norman. His numerous exhibitions include *Bilder vom Künstler*, Frankfurter Kunstverein

(2009–10); *Stephan Dillemuth: Regulär 10 Euro. Ermäßigt 5*, Lenbachhaus, Munich (2018); *Diskodekorationen: From Another Century*, Les Bourgeois, London (2019); and Busan Biennale 2020, South Korea.

Helmut Draxler is an art historian, critic, theorist, and curator who lives and works in Berlin and Vienna. He is currently Department Head and Professor in the Art Theory department at the University of Applied Arts Vienna. Previously, from 1999 to 2012, he was Professor of Aesthetic Theory at the Merz Akademie, University of Applied Art, Design and Media, in Stuttgart. He was Director of the Kunstverein München from 1992 to 1995. In 2004, he co-organized, with Sabeth Buchmann and Stephan Geene, the research project *Avant-Garde, Film, and Biopolitics* at the Jan van Eyck Academie, Maastricht, and in 2007, he curated the exhibition *Shandyismus. Autorschaft Als Genre*, Secession, Vienna. In addition to serving on the editorial board of *Texte zur Kunst*, Draxler writes extensively on contemporary art and theory for a variety of international magazines and artists' catalogues.

Andrea Fraser is an artist and Department Chair and Professor of Interdisciplinary Studio in the Department of Art at the University of California, Los Angeles. She is a founding member of the feminist performance group the V Girls (1986–96), the project-based artist initiative Parasite (1997–98), and the cooperative art gallery Orchard, New York (2005–08). Major works include projects for the Venice Biennale (1993), Tate Modern, London (2007), and Whitney Museum of American Art, New York (2016), among

performances and exhibitions at many other venues. Her essays and performance texts have appeared in, among others, *Artforum*, *October*, and *Texte zur Kunst*. Her books include *A Society of Taste* (Kunstverein München, 1993); *Report* (EA-Generali Foundation, 1995); *Andrea Fraser: Works, 1984–2003* (Dumont, 2003); *Museum Highlights: The Writings of Andrea Fraser* (MIT Press, 2005); *Texts, Scripts, Transcripts* (Museum Ludwig, 2013); *Andrea Fraser* (Hatje Cantz, 2015); *Andrea Fraser: de la crítica institutional a la institutión de la crítica* (Siglo Veintiuno Editores, 2016); *2016 in Museums, Money, and Politics* (MIT Press, 2018); and *Andrea Fraser Collected Interviews, 1990–2018* (A.R.T. Press and Koenig Books, 2019).

Renée Green is an artist, filmmaker, and writer and Professor at the Massachusetts Institute of Technology, Cambridge, MA. Her work has been exhibited widely in museums, biennials, and festivals and at venues such as the Whitney Museum of American Art, New York (2016–17); Walker Art Center, Minneapolis (2016 and 2017); MAK Center for Art and Architecture, Los Angeles (2015); New Museum of Contemporary Art, New York (2013); the Museum of Modern Art, New York, (2013); and Whitney Biennial, New York (1993). Her essays and fiction have been published widely, including in *Transition*, *October*, *Frieze*, *Texte zur Kunst*, *Spex*, and *Multitudes*. Her books include *Other Planes of There: Selected Writings* (Duke University Press, 2014); *Endless Dreams and Time-Based Streams* (Yerba Buena Centre for the Arts, 2010); *Ongoing Becomings* (JRP | Ringier, 2009); and *Negotiations in the Contact Zone* (Assírio & Alvim, 2003).

Renate Lorenz is a Berlin-based artist and cultural scientist. She has collaborated with Pauline Boudry since 2007, producing installations and films. Lorenz has exhibited at the Venice Biennale (2011); Paris Triennial (2012); Tate Modern, London (2013); Kunstverein Karlsruhe (2013); Modern Mondays at the Museum of Modern Art, New York (2014); Kunsthalle Wien (2015); and Kunsthalle Zürich (2015), among others. Lorenz is the co-editor of *Copyshop—Kunstpraxis und politische Öffentlichkeit* (Edition ID-Archiv, 1993), a foundational publication about art and politics in German-speaking Europe. Her recent publications include *Temporal Drag* (Hatje Cantz, 2011); *Aftershow* (Sternberg Press, 2014); and *Not Now! Now! Chronopolitics, Art & Research* (Sternberg Press, 2014).

Christian Philipp Müller is a Berlin-based artist. From 2011 to 2015, he was Professor of Visual Art at Kunsthochschule Kassel, Germany, where he was appointed Rector in 2011. Müller participated in the 45th Venice Biennale (1993); documenta X, Kassel, Germany (1997); and dOCUMENTA (13), Kassel, Germany (2012). In 2007, the Kunstmuseum Basel staged a retrospective of his work. He is included in the collections of, among others, the Museum of Contemporary Art, Los Angeles; Museum Ludwig, Cologne; mumok – Museum moderner Kunst Stiftung Ludwig, Vienna; Kunstmuseum Basel; and Migros Museum, Zurich. Müller's publications include *Christian Philipp Müller* (Hatje Cantz, 2007); *Portrait of the Museum as a Chair* (Revolver, 2006); and *The New World: A Sort of Locus Amoenus* (Walther König Verlag, 2008). In 2016, he was awarded the Prix Meret Oppenheim.

Fritz Rahmann (1936–2006) was a German artist whose practice encompassed public art installation, painting, drawing, and objects. He worked together with Raimond Summer and Hermann Pitz as the artist group Büro Berlin, which aimed to develop a social practice that situated art in public space outside commercial or gallery contexts and to redefine the social role of artists and artistic work. From 1993 to 2001, Rahmann was Professor in the Faculty of Design at the University of Architecture and Building, Bauhaus-Universität, Weimar. His work has been exhibited in numerous international exhibitions, including documenta 8, Kassel, Germany (1987); Sydney Biennial (1990); and Haus am Lützowplatz, Berlin (2003, solo exhibition). His publications include *Fritz Rahmann, unter anderem zwei Rösser, Skulptur im Bereich der Pinakotheken* (Hatje Cantz, 1994); *Fritz Rahmann, mehrere Arbeiten, 1970–2002* (Haus am Lützowplatz, 2003); and *Büro Berlin: ein Produktionsbegriff* (Künstlerhaus Bethanien, 1986).

Fred Wilson is a New York–based artist. He has exhibited widely at, and his work is included in the collections of, museums around the world. His seminal exhibitions include *Mining the Museum*, Maryland Historical Society, Baltimore (1992), and *Insight: In Site: In Sight: Incite*, Southeastern Center for Contemporary Art, Winston-Salem, North Carolina (1994). In 2001, Wilson was the subject of a retrospective organized at the Center for Art and Visual Culture, University of Maryland, Baltimore County. He has represented the United States at the Venice Biennale (2003) and Cairo Biennale (1992). Wilson was elected

to the American Academy of Arts &
Sciences (2020), received the Larry
Aldrich Foundation Award (2003)
and MacArthur Fellowship (1999),
and serves on the board of trustees
of the Whitney Museum of American
Art, New York.

Ulf Wuggenig is Professor of
Sociology of Art and Dean of the
Faculty of Humanities and Social
Sciences at Leuphana University of
Lüneburg, Germany. With Susanne
Leeb, he is Codirector of the Kunst-
raum of the Leuphana University of
Lüneburg, where he has overseen
seminal exhibitions including
Services, initiated by Andrea Fraser
and Helmut Draxler (1994); Clegg &
Guttmann, *The Open Public Library*
(1993–94); and Renée Green, *Import/
Export Funk Office* (1996–97). His
recent publications include *Art in the
Periphery of the Center* (Sternberg
Press, 2015); *The Artfield: A Study of
Actors and Institutions of Contempo-
rary Art* (Migros Museum, 2012); and
"Valuation Beyond the Market," in
Art Production beyond the Art Market
(Sternberg Press, 2013).

Fillip

Artistic Director
Jeff Khonsary

Editorial Supervisor
Kate Woolf

Editorial Board
Jaclyn Arndt, Jeff Khonsary, Jaleh Mansoor,
Sohrab Mohebbi, Jenifer Papararo, Antonia Pinter,
Eric Golo Stone

Board of Directors
Weiyi Chang, Jeff Derksen, Victoria Lum, Emma
Novotny, Cason Sharpe, Courtenay Webber

Fillip gratefully acknowledges the ongoing support of the
Canada Council for the Arts, the City of Vancouver, and
the British Columbia Arts Council. Additional assistance provided by the Andy Warhol Foundation for the
Visual Arts.

Colophon

Fillip Folio Series: F
Services Working Group
Published by Fillip
ISBN 978-1-927354-38-4

Editor: Eric Golo Stone
Editing: Jaclyn Arndt
Transcription: Robert Dayton, Nevin Kallepalli,
  and Romy Range
Translation: Fiona Bryson and Johanna Schindler
English Copyediting: Jaclyn Arndt
German Copyediting: Johanna Schindler
English Proofreading: Jaclyn Arndt and Kate Woolf
German Proofreading: Fiona Bryson and Johanna
  Schindler
Printed in Belgium by die Keure

Translation support for this publication was provided
by Künstlerhaus Stuttgart and the Kunstraum of the
Leuphana University of Lüneburg.

Fillip
305 Cambie Street
Vancouver, BC
Canada V6B 2N4
www.fillip.ca